MAY 13 '96

Psychophysical Explorations of Mental Structures

Gustav Theodor Fechner
(1801–1887)

Psychophysical Explorations of Mental Structures

Edited by

Hans-Georg Geissler, Leipzig

in collaboration with Martin H. Müller and Wolfgang Prinz, Bielefeld

Hogrefe & Huber Publishers
Toronto • Lewiston, NY • Bern • Göttingen • Stuttgart

BF
237
P87
1990

Library of Congress Cataloging-in-Publication Data

Psychophysical explorations of mental structures / H. G. Geissler, M. G. Müller,
W. Prinz (editors)
  p. cm.
  Includes bibliographical references.
  1. Psychophysics. I. Geissler, Hans-Georg. II. Müller, M. H., 1960– . III. Prinz,
Wolfgang.
  [DNLM: 1. Mental Processes—physiology. 2. Nervous System—physiology.
3. Psychophysiology. WL 102 P97446]
  BF237.P87   1990   153.7—dc20   90-4265 CIP

Canadian Cataloguing in Publication Data

Main entry under title:
Psychophysical explorations of mental structures

Papers presented at the symposium Gustav Theodor Fechner: Experimental
Psychology, its Historical and Contemporary Developments, held July 6–10, 1987,
in Leipzig, GDR.
Includes bibliographical references
  1. Psychophysics—Congresses. 2. Fechner, Gustav Theodor,
1801–1887—Congresses. I. Geissler, Hans-Georg. II. Müller, M.H. (Martin
Helmut), 1960– . III. Prinz, Wolfgang.

  BF237.P89   1990   152.1   C90-093705-X

P. O. Box 51
Lewiston, NY 14092

12–14 Bruce Park Ave.
Toronto, Ontario M4P 2S3

ISBN 3-8017-0365-7
ISBN 0-88937-031-1
Hogrefe & Huber Publishers • Toronto • Lewiston, NY • Bern • Göttingen • Stuttgart

Printed in Germany on acid-free paper

Preface

On the occasion of the centenary of the death of Gustav Theodor Fechner a symposium was held in Leipzig from July 6 to 10, 1987, in commemoration of his work. While similar events around the world focused on the subject of Fechner as the father of psychophysics, this large-scale conference was devoted to a broader appreciation of Fechner as a cofounder of Experimental Psychology and, in the light of present-day scientific knowledge, discussed basic problems of psychological theory as first formulated by Fechner.

The contributions assembled in the present volume have been selected with a view to Fechner's central and recurring theme. But in concentrating on problems relating to the formation of social judgment and perception as well as their psychophysiological correlates, a broad range of specific aspects could be covered at the same time, involving fundamental problems of sensory functioning and the measurement of sensation, the formation of social judgment, the structural-temporal frame of perceptual processes, the physiological mechanisms of attention, memory, and activation, as well as problems of motor programming and action organization.

Two contributions set the scene, so to speak, for the other chapters of the book, but can claim a certain significance of their own: the Prologue discusses the central ideas and impact of the Fechnerian concept of psychophysics as an "exact science of mind-body relations" from a modern viewpoint, i.e., in light of current research problems. This will have the added advantage of acquainting English-speaking readers with the particular meaning of the term psychophysics in this sense as opposed to a narrower definition of it. The Epilogue, on the other hand, focuses on approaches to perception that Fechner did not address and that view perception as being an integral part of action control. The bridge between Prologue and Epilogue is provided by the systemic aspects of perception as a process — a problem that is going to pose a major challenge for future research.

The present volume is the result of a sustained and prolonged effort, and it is therefore all the more encouraging that through an efficient cooperation all matters relating to publication could be resolved.

Scientific contacts and exchange of information in connection with visits undertaken by one of the editors to a number of western countries as well as the Soviet Union helped prepare the ground for the scientific structure of the book to which we hope readers of all persuasions will be able to relate and, at the same time, be stimulated into reading about some of the recent developments described in it.

Having reached our goal of publishing this book, we naturally extend our thanks to all those who, in many ways, contributed to its realization. Three names stand for many others who made the symposium a success: Hans Fuchs who looked after organizational matters, Harry Schroeder, head of the psychology section in Leipzig, whose commitment and determination ultimately made this conference possible, as well as Herr Meyer who, in his capacity as translator and interpreter, provided an indispensable service during the symposium and also assisted with the English versions of some of the contributions. The scientific organization of the psychophysiological session lay in the hands of Lothar Pickenhain, Leipzig. Peter Schönemann, of Purdue University, chaired the session on Multidimensional Psychophysics. The preparatory work was undertaken in Leipzig by Birgit Ackermann and Klaus–Dieter Schmidt, and Eva Böcker, Cordula Eckert, Heike Hartwig, Markus Neumann, and Barbara Vavra, Bielefeld, contributed to its finalization.

It is planned to publish a further volume with contributions, inter alia, on aspects of Experimental Aesthetics and Fechner's place in the history of psychology.

The publication of 'Psychophysical Explorations of Mental Structures' comes at a time that is full of hope, and we would like to think that it will mark the beginning of a new era of cooperation which would naturally include a cooperation in all areas of science.

Leipzig, December 1989
Hans–Georg Geissler

CONTENTS

Prologue

Hans-Georg Geissler
Convergent Theorizing and General Psychophysics: A Personal View 1

I. Foundations of Judgment and Decision

Stephen Link
The Psychological Design of Psychological Experiments 15

László Mérö
A Uniform Mathematical Framework for Both Fechner's and Stevens'
Psychophysical Theory 36

Michael H. Birnbaum
Scale Convergence and Psychophysical Laws 49

Marc Brysbaert and Géry d'Ydewalle
The Difference between Stimulus and Background: An Explanation of the
Psychophysical Function Based on Partition Scales? 58

Norman H. Anderson
Integration Psychophysics 72

Allen Parducci and Douglas H. Wedell
The Context for Evaluative Judgments: Psychophysics and Beyond 94

Gert Haubensak
Primacy Effects in Absolute Judgments 104

Barbara Mellers
A Psychophysical View of Equity Theory 114

Andreas Hinz and Hans-Georg Geissler
The Influence of Class Membership of Stimuli on Judgment 124

Joseph C. Stevens
The Chemical Senses and Aging: Applications of the Method of
Magnitude Matching 130

Peter Petzold
The Influence of Anchor Stimuli on Judgments of Attributes 138

II. Multidimensional Psychophysics

Peter H. Schönemann
Psychophysical Maps for Rectangles 149

Hannes Eisler and Ralf Lindman
Representations of Dimensional Models of Similarity 165

Tarow Indow
On Geometrical Analysis of Global Structure of Visual Space 172

Ch. A. Izmailov and E.N. Sokolov
Multidimensional Scaling of Line and Angle Discrimination 181

III. Psychophysical Aspects of Time and Structure

Hans-Georg Geissler
Foundations of Quantized Processing 193

Gerald S. Wasserman, Lolin T. Wang-Bennett and Richard T. Miyamoto
Temporal Dispersion in Natural Receptors and Pattern Discrimination
Mediated by Artificial Receptors (Cochlear Implants) 211

Ervin R. Hafter
Binaural Adaptation and the Limitations on Localization of
High–Frequency Sounds 228

Hannes Eisler
Breaks in the Psychophysical Function for Duration 242

Robert B. Wilberg and Richard D. Frey
Prior Entry: Information Processing Requirements and the Judgment of
Temporal Order 253

Alfred B. Kristofferson
Timing Mechanisms and the Threshold for Duration 268

Klaus-Dieter Schmidt and Birgit Ackermann
The Structure of Internal Representations and Reaction–Time Related
Matching Task Phenomena 278

Martina Puffe
Quantized Speed–Capacity Relations in Short–Term Memory 290

Arthur N. Lebedev
Cyclic Neural Codes of Human Memory and Some Quantitative
Regularities in Experimental Psychology 303

Stephan Haake
Task–Dependent Structuring of Motor Programs 311

IV. Towards Inner Psychophysics

Brigitte Rockstroh and Thomas Elbert
On the Regulation of Excitability in Cerebral Cortex — A Bridge between
EEG and Attention? 323

Jirina Radilova
Toward a State–Dependent Psychophysiology of Visual Perception and
Cognition 333

Tomas Radil, Zdenek Bohdanecky and Miroslav Indra
Toward State–Dependent Psychophysics 340

Bernd Schönebeck
Psychophysiological Identification of Working–Memory Subsystems 348

Norbert Roth and Günther Roscher
A Psychophysiological Study of Perception and Retrieval after Repeated
"Subliminal" Stimulation 357

Peter Bartsch
Some Aspects of Interpreting ERP's as Space Functions of the Brain 368

Gabriele Freude and Peter Ullsperger
Changes of Bereitschaftspotential Due to Different Workload by Muscular
and Mental Activities 378

Lothar Beyer, Thomas Weiß and Ellen Hansen
The Dynamics of Vegetative Parameters During Mental Training 387

Klaus Eckoldt and Volker Lange
Heart Rate and Heart Rate Variability — Occurrence and Diagnostic
Significance 396

V. Explorations of Complex Perception

Wolfgang Prinz
On Dynamic Pertinence Models 411

George Mandler, Carmen Overson and Yoshio Nakamura
Specific and Nonspecific Effects of Activation 422

Emanuel Leeuwenberg and Johan Wagemans
Just Noticeable Impossible Patterns: An Exploration of the Capacities and
Shortcomings of Perception 431

Odmar Neumann and Jochen Müsseler
"Judgment" vs. "Response": A General Problem and some Experimental
Illustrations 445

Uwe Kämpf and Joachim Hoffmann
The Latency Course of Feature Encoding Interfaced with Algorithm
Based Figure Classification 456

James T. Townsend and Trisha Van Zandt
New Theoretical Results on Testing Self-Terminating vs. Exhaustive
Processing in Rapid Search Experiments 469

Epilogue

Wolfgang Prinz
Beyond Fechner 491

Author Index 499
Subject Index 504

Psychophysical Explorations of Mental Structures
Edited by H.-G. Geissler
in collaboration with M.H. Müller and W. Prinz
© 1990 by Hogrefe & Huber Publishers

Prologue

Convergent Theorizing and General Psychophysics: A Personal View

Hans-Georg Geissler
Karl-Marx-Universität Leipzig
Leipzig, G.D.R.

In experimental psychology perception had long been given preference as a paradigmatic field. But it is only recently that it has become again a focus of theoretical interest, involving psychology as a whole as well as neighboring disciplines.

This development must be seen against the background of enormous progress in empirical research which has emphasized the need for a general conceptual framework capable of integrating myriads of facts into one unique picture.

While this description of the situation is broadly accepted there is still no unanimous answer to the question of what such a framework should look like. In fact there is a deeply rooted tendency of each of the disciplines involved to claim a key position for its own approach. Psychologists, for example, tend to argue that mental activity as an integral whole provides the ultimate basis for an appreciation of the contributions of partial mechanisms. On the other hand, physiologists might point out that mental activity is constrained *a priori* by properties of the underlying mechanisms in the substrate. Representatives of mathematical physics − to name a final and more recent candidate − might suggest that more developed versions of formal neural networks can account for virtually all perceptual functioning.

There is, however, quite a different, non-reductionist possibility of envisaging an integrative theoretical framework which the chapters in this volume share, whether explicitly or implicitly. It implies that out of a host of complementary aspects each of the competing disciplines is concerned with one specific aspect.

From this position it follows that the construction of such a framework ought be the task of a superordinate branch of science which, with regard to its empirical basis, refers to the evidence accumulated by the various disciplines as to its empirical basis, and which must thus be interdisciplinary *par excellence*.

This notion coincides with the most fundamental claim of psychophysics, defined as the "exact science of mind-body relations" advanced by Gustav Theodor Fechner in his famous *Elemente der Psychophysik* (Elements of Psychophysics) 130 years ago.

The concept of psychophysics in this broad sense was mainly developed in the second volume of Fechner's book which was never translated into English. In our opinion this might have been a major reason for the restricted scope of topics that psychophysics as a science is commonly assumed to deal with. We will use the term "general psychophysics" in order to contrast the metadiscipline that we have in mind with its narrower namesake which, against the background of Fechner's complete work, is no more than a special discipline.

Note that there is nothing mysterious about the superordinate nature of general psychophysics as it might have seemed to some of Fechner's contemporaries. From a great number of recent advances in neurosciences and systems theory we know that perception embraces specifically constrained processes of self-organization within a complex multi-layered system. Therefore, it goes without saying that overall performance cannot be reduced to special components acting on specific levels, e.g. to synaptic transducer mechanisms.

A major unsolved problem with this perspective is how each of the disciplines involved can establish its own subject matter and strategy on firm ground and at the same time systematically contribute to an integrated theory of mental activity. In other words, what are the prerequisites for convergent development in experimental research and theorizing?

In this brief introduction we will highlight two aspects that can be directly illustrated by examples taken from this volume. First, it will be suggested that psychology, in its progress toward a more deductive formulation of theories of perception, produces fragments of the psychophysical framework under consideration. Second, it will be claimed that a small number of parameters of temporal dynamics are decisive for bridging the gap between descriptions in terms of psychological and psychophysiological variables.

Psychophysical versus Psychological Laws

A focal issue of Fechner's (general) psychophysics to which he himself made various methodological and experimental contributions is that of the "psychophysical law." In its now classical version it amounts to this question: Given a stimulus variable x and its mental counterpart y, by which function

$y = f(x)$ are both related? It will be shown that this most elementary problem provides a suitable background for discussing the first claim made above.

Fechner's original answer is based on the idea that the quantity of sensation can be measured by using smallest step–like increments of it as units of measurement. Using Weber's law he derived, from this assumption, his logarithmic approximation of the psychophysical law $f(x)$.

There have been several alternative proposals, and Fechner himself later admitted that this might not be the only possible analytic form of $f(x)$. Within the present context it is particularly important to spell out the distinction between two classes of approaches: in modern psychophysics a mode of stating the problem, called "Fechnerian scaling", became prominent. This approach takes as its starting point laws of discrimination and looks for scales consistent with these laws. From the way it looks at the issue this conception may be termed the outside–in view. In terms of this classification Fechner's original proposal should accordingly be termed the inside–out view. What matters here is the methodological non–equivalence of both these views with respect to generalization: Fechnerian scaling centers around relaxation of empirical constraints, i.e., it aims to construct scales for broader generalizations of Weber's law. Hence, generalization will be largely based on formal criteria which, from a theoretical point of view, may not relate to significant structures of mental activity. Also, this procedure corresponds to a local strategy which confines itself to a neighborhood of empirical relations which originally were selected by a theoretically motivated choice, namely Fechner's idea on just noticeable differences. In contrast to this position, within the frame of Fechner's general scheme, generalization must be based on criteria of consistency and on theoretical plausibility and should be an organic part of theoretical development as a whole.

The far–reaching implications of a general turn to an inside–out perspective already become obvious within the empirical confines of Fechnerian scaling: Mérö (this volume) refers to just noticeable differences as theoretically relevant units of sensation which he considers merely to be the simplest possible option. Given his supposition and Weber's law, it follows from purely mathematical argument that there are two chief alternatives of the analytic form of the law, a logarithmic function and the class of power functions.

There are indications that this result represents more than a speculative construction. One comes from Birnbaum's investigations as summarized in his chapter by the intimately related fact that subjects under changes of instruction obviously can switch between a difference mode and a ratio mode of judgment.

Birnbaum's conclusions rely on the rationale of scale convergence. This methodology, though important, represents a special case of validation techniques and criteria emerging necessarily in the course of developing comprehensive theories from more restricted, local ones. One possibility this affords is that problems originally posed within a narrow context can be given a proper solution on a more complex level, thereby binding together paradigms and results which traditionally have been considered unrelated.

With regard to the psychophysical law issue, the paper by Brysbaert and d'Ydewalle is a case in point. In customary terms their experiments investigate the effect of physical intensity contrast upon the difference limen of (apparent) lightness. However, their formal analysis bears directly on the issue because of the invariants extracted from the complicated patterns of interaction observed. These are, first, a psychophysical power law including an exponent which proves to be constant across experimental conditions and, second, an inner, psychological constraint, known as Ekman's law.

This example shows that the problem of the psychophysical law is nested within a broader field of inquiry deriving from the more general question of how mental states and structures, on the one hand, and outside, physical ones, on the other, are interrelated. This problem represents the subject matter of a province of general psychophysics that Fechner christened "outer psychophysics."

As a programmatic concept outer psychophysics differs in various respects sharply from thinking habits of modern psychophysics as a special discipline: Not only that the argument of the relations considered can themselves become complexly structured. There is also no direct causal relationship implied which would transform physical inputs into mental outputs. Rather, mental representations are considered relatively autonomous entities which play an active part in perception. The following discussion might help to demonstrate that outer psychophysics represents a frame concept suitable for structuring accumulated evidence, marking out lines of progress, and posing new questions.

The Brysbaert and d'Ydewalle paper suggests close relationships between inner, "psychological" laws and "the" "psychophysical" law. But what exactly is the nature of these relationships, and what is the exact status of the psychophysical law, in particular?

A satisfactory answer to these questions requires a deeper understanding of the notion of a psychological law.

Within the present context there is one class of psychological laws of particular importance, the laws of information integration. Anderson's paper summarizes and condenses the contribution of many experimental studies which have shaped the concept of information integration. A preliminary record of achievements from a formal point of view reads as follows: (1) Laws of information integration involve a small number of operations and their inversions, namely addition, multiplication, and weighted arithmetic averaging; (2) there is a small number of specific ways in which psychological variables combine with these operations to form integration laws or 'cognitive algebras'; (3) information integration is hierarchically organized; as a rule, lower level arguments are left unchanged by changes at higher levels of integration; (4) formally similar rules hold for constituents which correspond either to conscious or preconscious psychological entities.

Of primary relevance to the psychophysical law issue is the fact that, if certain requirements are met, the values of the variables undergoing integration can be estimated without making reference to physical stimulus values. The relevant procedures are called "functional measurement" and yield measures on an interval or even ratio scale level.

In a functional measurement perspective the psychophysical law thus seems to be a derivative, secondary relation which can always be constructed when physical stimulus measures are available. In a sense, the whole issue seems to be fruitless since the form of the function might well differ from case to case and, at least within the framework of information integration theory, there is no theoretical argument available to distinguish one analytic form as "the" psychophysical law.

Is this the end of the psychophysical law story? I do not think so.

On the contrary, it will be claimed that the problem and, in addition, generalizations of it, will inevitably reappear within a more complete, deductively stated theory. The reason, roughly speaking, is that mental structures model structures of outside reality, and that this entails further constraints restricting the possible relations between both realms.

The principal argument in favor of this view will be illustrated within the confines of classical psychophysics, i.e., by reference to univariate functions. The argument is part of the "indirect calibration (validation)" approach as summarized in Geissler (1981). With reference to loudness perception, for example, it may be formulated as follows: Let q, d, and e be the energy emitted by a source of sound, its distance from the observer, and the energy received by the ears, respectively. The physical relation between these variables can be written in the form:

$$e \sim q \times d^{-2} . \tag{1}$$

Assume now that the mental algebra models this relation isomorphically. Let E, Q, and D be the inner equivalents of e, q, and d. This then reads:

$$E \sim Q \times D^{-2} . \tag{2}$$

The only requirement with regard to the inner equivalent E of the "proximal" stimulus value e is in a unique relation to e which may be described by the strictly increasing function $E = f_1(e)$. Combination with (1) and (2) yields:

$$Q \times D^{-2} \sim f_1(q \times d^{-2}) . \tag{3}$$

To arrive at specifying statements about psychophysical laws for loudness and distance denoted by $f_2(q)$ and $f_3(d)$, respectively, further constraints are needed.

Most fundamental constraints follow from requirements of perceptual stability. A paradigmatic case is ideal perceptual constancy which in the present example implies that perceived loudness Q remains constant if there is a change in distance from the source. If this holds it can be concluded on purely mathematical grounds that the hitherto unspecified functions f_1, f_2, and f_3 must be power functions.

The basic rationale can be used to derive fully specific solutions under more realistic conditions. In the given example there is reason to assume that a simpler rule, $E \sim Q \times D^{-1}$, holds instead of (2). Together with the assumption that distance is represented veridically, a square root law

$$Q \sim \sqrt{q} \tag{4}$$

obtains for loudness, for which Warren found considerable experimental support. Indirect calibration for these conditions collapses into a special case, axiomatizing Warren's so-called Physical Correlate Theory.

To sum up, specific psychophysical laws seem to be a consequence of psychological laws which model laws of outside reality and of invariance conditions which warrant stability of perception. Generalizations of this notion as suggested by the principle of indirect validation involve expansions of the concepts of modeling and/or stability.

One such expansion is very straightforward: perception normally refers to entities which are embedded in sections or domains of reality containing more entities of the same or a similar status. This implies the possibility of multivariate generalizations of psychophysical laws. Descriptions of this type were first developed by Helson and are known as quantitive theories of "frames of reference."

The term frame of reference is used for a broad variety of phenomena in the literature. From the present considerations it seems advisable to make a fundamental distinction between "sensory" and "judgmental" frames of reference which correspond to qualitatively different mental structures under consideration. The first category refers to attributes of coherent percepts, an example being the perceived color of complexly structured object surfaces. The second category signifies valuations referring primarily to representations in memory. An example is absolute judgment of size which is restricted to classes of objects.

The papers in this volume reflect the remarkable progress that has been made in the area of judgmental frames of reference. Link joins Fechner directly in developing a new method of scaling which avoids the positional bias involved in paired comparison. Another focus is Parducci's range–frequency approach. In fact, his finding that category judgments represent a compromise between range and frequency values proved to be a very robust one. Parducci maintains the view that this regularity reflects not just a special kind of output transformation but a rather fundamental mode of valuation. Barbara Mellers' study seems to support this by showing that equity can be understood in a way similar to cross–modal matching, but on a range–frequency basis. The majority of contributions related to this issue stress that the crucial task is now to uncover the inner mechanisms behind the range–frequency law and to illuminate the psychological nature of its constituents. Specific questions that the chapters deal with include the following: Which laws govern the formation of ranges? How is the impact of frequency mediated? How do stimuli outside a given range become integrated? Finally, how do the established frames of reference differentiate between different classes of objects?

At this point we should touch at least briefly on two other basic problems involved in multivariate expansions of the psychophysical law issue.

The first problem concerns the relevant definition of subjective attributes. Most studies in information integration presuppose that the attributes involved are known in advance and used by different subjects in accord with the instructions. There is not only reason to doubt these assumptions, but also a need, generally, for procedures permitting exact specification of subjective attributes. Powerful procedures which meet these requirements under certain conditions have been developed in multidimensional scaling. The heading "multidimensional psychophysics" proposed by Schönemann for one part of this volume is, therefore, valid, at least as a programmatic direction. Despite the sophistication of the work presented it should be kept in mind that only some first steps have been made toward merging the concepts of frames of reference and multidimensional analysis.

The second issue to be mentioned is the structural co-determination of psychophysical laws. The fact has first been stressed by the Gestaltists and can most easily be demonstrated by changes of apparent lightness of surfaces as a function of structural interpretation in ambiguous figures. As a basis of explanation a direct correspondence between hierarchical levels of object representation, on the one hand, and levels of information integration, on the other hand, has been suggested in Geissler (1976). This idea might help us to arrive at a more deductive reformulation of surprising results obtained by Anderson's techniques.

Without going into detail a general implication of this idea will be briefly discussed here.

Hierarchies of information integration have often been conceived as hierarchies of stages in sequential information processing. The flexible dependence on structural stimulus interpretation makes such a notion very implausible. One alternative is the assumption of a complete coordination between structural representations and mental algebras which suggests that hierarchical levels of information integration represent separable parts of holistic meta-stable outcomes of fast, massively parallel processing. In agreement with modern theories of self-organization in neural networks, the relation between such sub-units are adequately described by such concepts as self-consistency, multiple constraint satisfaction and resonance rather than sequential transformation and causality.

Processing of Structure, Structure of Processing: Steps toward Complex Perception

The latter consideration does not imply that the meta-stable structures portrayed by laws of information integration are of no significance for processing research. On the contrary, from an analytic point of view these ordered states provide the cue information for exploring their temporal genesis.

This claim extends to psychological models of processing as derived from observable temporal characteristics. Although these characteristics represent a simplified projection of dynamic properties of underlying substrate processes, they nevertheless constitute the background lattice against which those properties must be viewed in order to be deciphered.

Despite this analogy it makes sense to ask whether the concept of general psychophysics introduced within the context of scaling and judgment can be applied profitably to paradigms of complex processing which this volume deals with.

A good vantage point from which this may be answered in the affirmative is provided by Sternberg's item recognition paradigm to which many papers refer in one way or another.

To give a brief summary: in this task subjects are asked to judge whether a presented test item is a member of a memorized set of items or not. Under Sternberg's standard conditions a typical outcome is that mean RTs plotted against memory set size approximate straight lines which are parallel for positive and negative instances. This result led Sternberg to suggest a serial exhaustive search model for the ongoing information processing.

One of the problems with this model is that outside the standard conditions a number of different trends have been established. From a plain "outside-in" view this may be taken, and has often been taken, as evidence militating against the model.

Inside-out approaches naturally are more careful in preserving the gist of the serial model since any alternative proposal must be at least equally plausible in terms of generalizable principles of processing.

In order to ensure final convergence, naturally, a variety of complementary strategic routes have to be pursued. One major line, as represented by Townsend's article, relies on formal specification of general purpose rules. From the systems point of view mentioned above, such rules may be interpreted as descriptions of global laws specifying the behavior of a large system which under certain conditions closely mimics that of a very simple serial processor.

The following remarks concentrate on a different aspect. In the psychophysical law discussion above an attempt was made to demonstrate that a deeper theoretical analysis must involve the content of perception and judgment on a broader scale, i.e., their function in reflecting outside reality. In a similar vein, the examples that follow will be used to illustrate the claim that temporal patterns of processing are largely determined by task-specific representations of sets of objects to which they refer.

With reference to item recognition *sensu* Sternberg, this claim is based on ample evidence showing that processing in detail depends strongly on specific properties of the memory set which obviously have something to do with the format of its internal representation. To cite some well-known instances: Item complexity has been demonstrated to alter speed of processing; multiplicity of memory codes may result either in hierarchical processing — categories first, exemplars second — or in a horse race between rivaling processes; structural relations among memory items can effectively affect the units of processing within a given case. Elimination of Sternberg's set-size effect due to sequential structuring of the target set, suggesting a one-step decision, and logarithmic item-plots pointing to a tree-like hierarchization, are examples of the latter type.

From such findings three things become apparent. First and foremost, the processes involved should be controlled in a top-down manner, guided by the memory representations of the target set. Comparison, therefore, is to be understood as matching the memories of targets against representations of test items rather than the other way round.

Second, seriality may become approximated as a consequence of at least two different types of conditions: It may become logically enforced or it may result from requirements of uniqueness of decision in a top-down procedure.

An example of the first type is the temporal sequentiality of category and exemplar checks. The second one is exemplified by the ordinary case of item–recognition in which, in order to arrive at a unique decision, each of the targets must be processed separately while the sequence of sequential operations is arbitrary.

These interpretations reflect a line of thinking that in a sophisticated form represents the principle of "guided inference" and has worked surprisingly well in a number of reactive tasks in predicting reaction times (cf. Geissler & Puffe, 1983; Buffart & Geissler, 1984; Geissler & Buffart, 1984; Geissler, 1987). Roughly, the principle assumes, in contrast to traditional thinking, that perception does not operate on the basis of detailed action plans. Rather, it supposes that weakly constrained command structures become specified and driven by flexible, task–dependent representations of stimulus structures.

An approach of this type requires several steps of specification. A first, basic step concerns the exact meaning of "task–dependent" representations and a clear understanding of their guiding role in shaping procedures of information processing. A first approximation of a suitable rationale is the "double minimum principle" stated within the confines of the Structural Information Theory (SIT). Its basic idea is that in a stationary state of operation there is a minimal structural representation of the response categories in terms of syntactic rules for stimulus representation. The operative procedure under these conditions is proposed to be the shortest admissible sequence of operations acting upon these representations (in terms of number of operations or time).

The foregoing remarks on guided inference as a general principle make obvious the close correspondence of the rationale to the above reinterpretation of the psychophysical law issue: Just as the form of the relation which maps physical states onto mental ones has been looked upon as a consequence of inner modeling, its specific constraints and invariances, so the temporal course of perception is now being conceived as fully (or largely) determined by laws of inner modeling of stimuli and tasks and their invariances.

Within the present context our primary aim is to illustrate the claim that this type of reinterpretation is not only in sharp contrast to traditional views even with regard to most elementary problems of perception, but that it also seems to provide powerful tools of investigation.

To illustrate the point take everyday tasks of scanning a set of objects for some target object. Our intuition reveals two things about the way we cope with such tasks, namely, that the target is serially compared with the objects in that set, and that as an operation comparison involves direct matching of internal representations of the objects.

Prinz, working with visual search paradigms, shows in his chapter that the first part of this intuition is untenable: The effect of list organization on speed of search leads to the conclusion that termination of search is controlled by a mismatch with non–targets rather than by a match with targets.

This seemingly is in keeping with the guided inference view since in the task under consideration, in contrast to item recognition, the overwhelming majority of input elements are non–targets. The global strategy in accord with the (double) minimum principle is, therefore, expected to depend solely on non-target based processing, and it is only after interrupting this mode of processing that stored target information becomes accessed.

The findings of Schmidt and Ackermann suggest that the second part of the above intuitive account may, under some circumstances, also be invalid. Their paper is concerned with a paradigm for which the direct matching idea appears most convincing, viz. the paired comparison of structured visual stimuli for their identity. Using figures first introduced by Garner, the authors have been able to demonstrate for physical identical stimuli in a categorical same-different task that the size of the 'inferred set' (Garner) represents a very stable predictor of RTs even on the level of individuals.

One conclusion from this finding may seem surprising to many readers: the result strongly suggests that even in the case of physical identity the idea of a direct matching process should be replaced by a more indirect procedure which first locates a given stimulus within a representation of a set of expected stimuli and then decides on the basis of this kind of task-specific encoding.

So far we have confined ourselves to structural characteristics, thereby disregarding stable metrical properties of temporal behaviour. These, however, are of great importance on two counts: First, they constitute necessary complements of structural descriptions and their invariance across task and stimulus variation is an integral part of model validation. Second, invariant parameters of temporal dynamics are most likely to be directly associated with temporal characteristics of the underlying processes within the nervous tissue.

With reference to our illustrative example, item recognition, an elementary fact to be mentioned here is a slope of 37 ms repeatedly found for digits. Even though reaction time distributions make it seem doubtful whether this period can be directly interpreted as the time necessary for one comparison operation, its relatedness to basic features of neural dynamics is quite clear. A major argument in favor is provided by the robustness of the numerical finding which remains unchanged under substantial variations of conditions, significantly affecting the absolute values of reaction times, such as time pressure, prolonged practice, and even effects of drugs, or psychotic diseases.

The attempt to establish some kind of quantal approach to mental operation time must be seen against the background of converging evidence from various sources. Results based upon models predicting reaction times, e.g., those reported in the Schmidt-Ackermann study, are part of these sources. A serious objection to this kind of evidence relates to the fact that the number of operations assumed is strongly model-dependent.

This problem may be solved by an analysis of temporal fine-grain patterns of response behavior. There are, however, higher-order characteristics of processing to which the objection does not apply. Of considerable interest in this respect is a well-known finding of Cavanagh (1973). When assembling evidence on search rates and short-term memory spans he found a linear increasing relation between scan times per item and reciprocal spans. In other words, the time needed for scanning a full short-term memory seems to be a constant independent of the type of items concerned.

Later investigations have shown that this statement needs to be qualified. A particular aspect of qualification is treated in the paper of Martina Puffe. In her diagram, traditional span measures are replaced by functional measures which can be defined within the task itself. These span measures use the break within bilinear characteristics obtained for larger item sets as an indicator of the upper bound of normal short-term memory performance. Instead of one line Puffe obtained a regular fan structure exhibiting a double quantization: average performance under the condition of a given set of tasks seems to be associated not only with a small number of upper time limits but also, consistent with other research, with the smallest quantal period of some 9 ms.

The Way toward "Inner Psychophysics": A Final Remark

The sketchy discussion above is of course far from having exhausted the themes by which psychological process research is called upon to contribute to psychophysical theory. Even within the confines of this book a more complete account would have to consider processes of different types. An account of the kinds of processes of activation treated by Mandler and coauthors, for example, is indispensable. Recent developments of network theory, in particular a model for structural learning developed by Buffart, has lent independent support to the earlier fundamental work by Mandler.

This short final paragraph should direct attention to a central problem of general psychophysics which in spite of considerable empirical progress remains unsolved even to the extent of its logical foundations. In Fechner's terms this problem concerns the subject matter of "inner psychophysics", the province of general psychophysics that deals with the correlative interface between mental phenomena and their underlying basis in the brain, which is necessary and sufficient for them to occur.

Fechner anticipated that general psychophysics would not have to wait until scientific development permitted the identification of direct relationships between rows of psychological observations and series of, for instance, physiological observations. His rationale for this, the "functional principle", is based upon the assumption that models of mental structure can be constructed by just relying on inner, psychological relations, such as similarity, and on the inner consistency of admissible models. Some of the modern achievements reflected in this book, such as information integration theory and multidimensional scaling, are obvious triumphs of the functional principle. The paper by Izmailov and Sokolov may even be an encouraging step beyond this because its constructs are fully interpreted in physiological terms.

It would be unfair not to mention promising signs of converging developments which bring psychological and psychophysiological research closer together. They are evident in most of the psychophysiological contributions to the volume. Such developments are particularly obvious in research directed toward uncovering basic mechanisms underlying conscious representation: its attentional basis, componential processes of short-term memory and the hitherto mysterious subconscious accumulation of information and its sudden conscious display.

It should, however, be emphasized that the growing body of interrelated findings is a challenge calling for more conceptual efforts to create a truly integrating theoretical framework. A few comments here are fairly personal in character and may, therefore, be somewhat biased. First, I would claim that temporal characteristics of mental activity will become nuclei of conceptual crystallization and that in translating his ideas into modern terms Fechner was right when he assumed undulating carrier processes to be the ultimate basis of the "psychophysical process." Second, I believe it is a prerequisite of success that no level of empirical research and theorizing be left out, e.g., that the major, possible logical variants of basic integrating theories have to be designed without waiting for them to emerge from the contact maintained by the various disciplines in the course of empirical research or from the merging of local models.

This volume includes two chapters that attempt to meet these claims (Lebedev; Geissler). Compared to reports on special topics they may appear rather speculative. During the Fechner symposium an eminent scholar said: "You are trying to design a kind of periodic system, aren't you?" Indeed, perhaps these attempts approach periodic systems rather than theories. It would not be bad if it were so.

It is a long way to the framework we are looking for and, to be sure, the path will be thorny and full of pitfalls. But there is no alternative.

References

Buffart, H., & Geissler, H.-G. (1984). Task–dependent classification of categories and memory–guided inference during classification. In E. Degreef & J. van Buggenhaut (Eds.), *Trends in mathematical psychology* (pp. 33−58). Amsterdam, New York, Oxford: North–Holland.

Cavanagh, J.P. (1972). Relation between immediate memory span and the memory search rate. *Psychological Review, 79*, 525−530.

Geissler, H.-G. (1976). Internal representation of external states: Aspects of an indirect validation approach to psychophysics. In H.-G. Geissler & Yu.M. Zabrodin (Eds.), *Advances in psychophysics*. Berlin: VEB Deutscher Verlag der Wissenschaften.

Geissler, H.-G. (1983). Physical correlate theory versus the indirect calibration approach. *The Behavioral and Brain Sciences, 2*, 316−317.

Geissler, H.-G. (1985). Task–dependency and quantized processing in classification. In G. d'Ydewalle (Ed.), *Cognitive information processing and motivation* (Selected/revised papers of the 23rd International Congress of Psychology, Vol. 3, pp. 277−294). Amsterdam, New York, Oxford: North–Holland.

Geissler, H.-G. (1987). Guided inference: Components of task–dependence in human information processing. In J. Hoffmann & E. van der Meer (Eds.), *Knowledge aided information processing* (pp. 221−240). Amsterdam, New York, Oxford: North-Holland.

Geissler, H.-G., & Puffe, M. (1983). The inferential basis of classification: From perceptual to memory codes. In H.-G. Geissler et al. (Eds.), *Modern issues in perception*. Berlin: VEB Deutscher Verlag der Wissenschaften. Amsterdam, New York, Oxford: North-Holland.

I. Foundations of Judgment and Decision

Psychophysical Explorations of Mental Structures
Edited by H.-G. Geissler
in collaboration with M.H. Müller and W. Prinz
© 1990 by Hogrefe & Huber Publishers

Chapter 1

The Psychological Design of Psychological Experiments

Stephen Link
*Department of Psychology, McMaster University
Hamilton, Canada*

The title of this paper suggests that the psychological problem under investigation should determine the design of psychological experiments. While this uncontentious idea receives broad support, even a casual study of today's psychological journals reveals a wide gap between the idea and its application. Many analyses of psychological experiments assume that the mathematical models developed by statisticians for agriculture and industry are directly applicable to psychological research. However, like other mathematical models, these statistical models require laboratory confirmation before the measures derived from the models are accepted as measures of the psychological phenomenon under investigation.

The failure to provide laboratory confirmation of such mathematical models leaves wide gaps between the mathematics assumed to model the psychological phenomenon, the experimental design selected to expose the effect of experimental variables on the phenomenon, and the resulting measurement of the phenomenon itself. In Psychology the gap is particularly large in the case of linear statistical models, such as those leading to t-tests, the analysis of variance, and correlational analysis. To narrow these gaps this paper shows how psychophysical theorizing leads to mathematical/statistical modeling which in turn leads to a suitable choice of experimental design and data analysis.

The Method of Right and Wrong Cases

The gap between theory and data analysis was not always so wide. Indeed, Psychology started well. Gustav Fechner's justly famous theory of discrimination provided Psychology with the first example of how a theory and its associated mathematical/statistical representation produces a close correspondence between the mathematical model and the experiment used to investigate it.

The theory proposed that the sensory system was a measuring device and, like any physical device, prone to error. Measuring the size of this error depended upon first establishing a theory of the relationship between the physical stimulus and its error-prone mental representation.

According to the theory advanced by Fechner, a feeling of heaviness, for example, derived from two sources. First, a measurement process transduced the weight of a lifted object into heaviness. Second, the transduction introduced error, with the consequence that some of the feeling of heaviness depended upon the error contributed by the measurement process.

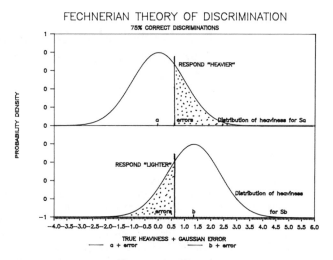

Figure 1. Fechner's Gaussian model for sensory discrimination.

The model for discriminating the weight of two objects proposed that the average heaviness of the objects was a threshold (criterion) to decide which of the two objects weighted more. As shown in Figure 1, lifting an object generates a heaviness value that is distributed as a Gaussian random variable. For two objects there are two Gaussian distributions separated by a difference equal to the mean difference in heaviness between the two objects. When lifting two objects in succession, for example, the heaviness of the second object is compared against the average heaviness of both objects. The weight attributed to the second object is judged to be greater, or lesser, than the first depending upon whether the heaviness of the second exceeds, or fails to exceed, the average heaviness. [In recent times a similar theory, Ideal Observer Theory (Green and Swets, 1966), gained much prominence.]

By counting how often the lighter object felt heavier than the more weighty object, and *vice versa*, Fechner estimated the probability that the sensory system produced an erroneous measure of which object weighed more. That is, the subject's personal verbal reports provided relative frequency estimates of the probability of an error of classification. This probability equals the stippled area within the Gaussian distribution and beyond the decision criterion (threshold).

Notice that the theory postulates that the error is identical for both objects. Therefore, the variances for both distributions are equal and the stippled area to the right of the decision criterion equals the corresponding unstippled area to the left of the decision criterion. Thus, comparing either object's heaviness to the average heaviness generates the same probability of an error.

Using an experimentally determined estimate of this error probability permitted Fechner to calculate from his famous tables of *hD* the number of standard deviation[1] units between the decision criterion and the mean of one distribution. Notice that a measure of the difference between the two distributions equals twice the distance to the decision criterion from either mean.

In Fechner's experiments weight gave rise to the sensation of heaviness, but the subjects' personal accounts of heaviness determined the value of the error probability used to measure the size of the error in sensory system. The theory launched psychology on its course as a natural mental science. The measurement found two important applications.

First, the method found application to the measure of a psychological difference in heaviness, and thus the study of difference thresholds. According to Weber's Law, multiplication of the physical values of the weights of two objects by a constant should not lead to a change in the perceived difference between the objects. Applied in this probabilistic context, Fechner's interpretation of Weber's Law predicted that multiplying two weights by a constant should not change the probability of an error — a prediction easily derived from the mathematical/statistical theory proposed by Fechner.

The argument follows: If physical multiplication of weight is transduced as multiplication of heaviness, then multiplication by a constant makes no difference in the relative distance of the decision criterion from the means of the two distributions of heaviness. Thus, the probability of an error remains constant. To see this most clearly, define "relative" to be a standardized random variable (RV). Let Z_X be the standardization of a Gaussian RV, X, having mean μ_X, variance σ_X^2, and associated decision criterion X_C. Then the standardized value of the decision criterion is,

$$Z_{XC} = (X_C - \mu_X)/\sigma_X .$$

---

[1] In Physics, common practice dictated the use of the Error Function rather than the more modern standardized Normal Distribution. Thus Fechner's measurements differ from standard deviation units by a factor of the square root of 2.

Multiplication of the RV X by a constant K yields a new RV,

$$Y = KX$$

which has mean $\mu_Y = K\mu_X$ and variance $\sigma_Y^2 = (K\sigma_X)^2$. If X is Gaussian, then so is Y.

Examining the standardized value for $Y_C = KX_C$ shows that Z_{YC} equals Z_{XC}. That is,

$$Z_{YC} = (Y_C - \mu_Y)/\sigma_Y$$
$$Z_{YC} = (KX_C - K\mu_X)/K\sigma_X$$
$$= Z_{XC}\,.$$

Therefore, if the sensory system passes multiplication through the heaviness measurement process unchanged, then the relative distance of the decision criterion X_C from μ_X is the same as the relative distance of the decision criterion Y_C from μ_Y. Consequently, the probability of an error of classification, the stippled area from X_C or Y_C to infinity remains constant.

To examine this mathematical model Fechner adopted the well known Method of Right and Wrong Cases. The method blended theory and experimental rigor to produce a measure of the unknown probability of error. Whatever the values of the initial pair of weights, the experimenter simply multiplied the standard and comparison weights by a constant in order to create a pair of new stimuli that should be judged with the same probability of error as the previous set.

Table 1. Error proportions and decision criteria.[a]

| Value of the Standard, P | Value of Comparisons, D | | | |
| | D = .04P | | D = .08P | |
	Error proportion	Z_{XC}	Error proportion	Z_{YC}
300	.340	.41	.274	.60
500	.339	.42	.236	.72
1000	.298	.53	.216	.79
1500	.285	.57	.176	.93
2000	.276	.59	.187	.89
3000	.287	.56	.157	1.0

[a] from Fechner (1860/1966, p. 155)

Fechner obtained the error proportions shown in Table 1. For each standard, P, the subject judged either of two comparison stimuli against the standard. The smaller comparison stimulus equaled P plus four percent additional weight while the larger comparison equaled P plus an additional eight percent. The first column of Table 1 gives the various values of the standards ranging from 300 to 3000 grams. The second and third columns give the measured error proportion and the value of Z_{XC}, the decision criterion, for the comparison stimulus weighing $P + .04P$ grams. For the larger comparison stimulus the fourth column gives the error proportion and column five gives the value of the decision criterion, Z_{YC}. In each case the error proportions are based on 1024 judgments.

While there appears to be some agreement between theory and data in Table 1, the measurements show beyond a shadow of doubt that performance improved, rather than remained constant, as the weights of standard and comparison stimuli jointly increased. For a standard of 300 g a comparison of 312 g yielded an error response proportion of 0.34. This proportion decreased to 0.297 when the standard increased to 3000 g and the comparison equalled 3120 g. When the standard was 300 g and the comparison 324 g the error response proportion was 0.274. This proportion also decreased, to .157, when the standard increased to 3000 g and the comparison to 3240 g. Fechner noted:

Should these experiments prove the law to hold directly and precisely, all (response proportions) for the different standards should be not only approximately but exactly alike, when the same ratio of additional weight to standard holds everywhere. This is not the case. The deviation of the experimental values from those predicted by the Law should, nevertheless, be given no more importance as a true deviation than the one we found at the lower limits in the field of photoreception, but rather should be regarded in the same way as an analogous consequence of the Law. Just as we had to take into account in the case of light sensations the inner sensation which exists, even if no external light is admitted, we have to consider the weight of the arm and possible covering pieces of clothing (in my experiments only shirt sleeves) which are present without the external weight P and are lifted when it is lifted. (Fechner, 1860/1966, p.155).

The second application of the model laid the foundation for the Method of Constant Stimuli. Fechner sought to determine whether the Gaussian error distribution remained constant when the size of the comparison stimulus varied. Thus, when using a standard weight of 300 g Fechner used two comparisons, both a 312 g and a 324 g comparison stimulus. After results for one case were determined, the other should be predictable on the basis of a single Gaussian distribution of error.

When a single distribution of error applies to a particular size of a standard, it is simple enough to determine whether increasing the difference in the comparison weight by a factor of two results in a factor of two increase in the corresponding decision criterion. The values of the decision criteria for each standard are shown in columns three and five of Table 1.

Fechner's interpretation of the influence of arm weight on judgments gains some support from the fact that as the weight of the standard increased the results more closely appoximated the prediction that Z_{YC} equals $2Z_{XC}$, as can be seen by comparing these values in columns three and five of Table 1. Encouraged by these results, Fechner suggested that the measurements revealed a flaw in the experimental procedure, not a flaw in the logic of the method, and that, in the limit, with very large weights, the arm's weight is insignificant and thus the desired results should be obtained.

Many assumptions went untested here, but the turning point for Psychology was the measurement of the unknown error in the sensory system which depended upon the sensory system's precision or resolving power. The experimental method, the Method of Right and Wrong Cases, derived from the mathematical characterization of the scientific problem under investigation. The important lesson here is that the theory of discrimination and the experimental method complement each other.

In spite of this remarkable achievement, Fechner never reached his most sought-after goal, the measurement of psychological attributes, such as beauty, that lacked any corresponding physical measure. Lacking any further theoretical progress Psychophysics became immersed in minor technical issues.

The next model of the psychophysical decision process waited sixty years to appear until G. H. Thomson (1920), in an elegant eight-page paper entitled "A new point of view in the interpretation of threshold measurements in pschophysics", proposed an urn model for sensory discrimination. This theory is the classic application of the stimulus sampling of mental elements that derives from the Herbartian tradition of the psychophysical theoretician. The theory accounts for the known facts about three-category responding and postulates that decision criteria are under the willful control of the subject. Somehow the advanced nature of the theory's statistical treatment of psychophysical issues doomed it to a few forgotten pages in the *Psychological Review*.

The Method of Paired Comparisons

Measuring more elusive psychological attributes required a new theory. The new theory was nearly an accidental consequence of L. L. Thurstone's desire to brighten-up the teaching of a dull subject by introducing to students in Psychophysics more appealing experimental stimuli. As Thurstone (1952) put it:

When I started to teach psychological measurement in 1924, it was natural that I should encourage the students to learn something about psychophysical methods. The standard reference was, of course, the two big volumes on quantitative psychology by Titchener. The determination of a limen was the basic problem in old-fashioned psychophysics. In order to be scholarly in this field, one was supposed to know about the old debates on how to compute the limen for lifted weights to two decimal places with a standard stimulus of one hundred grams. One could hardly worry about anything more trivial. Who cares for the exact determination of anybody's limen for lifted weights? In teaching this subject I felt that we must do something about this absurdity by introducing more interesting stimuli. Instead of lifted weights we used a list of offenses presented in pairs with the instruction that they should be judged as to their relative seriousness. The subject checked one of each pair of offenses to indicate which he thought was the more serious. Instead of selecting one of the offenses as a standard, we asked the subjects to compare every stimulus with every other stimulus. It was now apparent that the classical method of constant stimuli is a special case of the more complete psycho-physical method of paired comparison. We followed this same procedure with a list of nationalities that were also presented in pairs. For each pair of nationalities the subject was asked to check the one which he would prefer to associate with. I did not realize at the time that it was going to be necessary to rewrite the fundamental theory of psychophysics in order to cope with data of this type. (Thurstone, 1952, pp. 306 – 307).

Figure 2 illustrates the simplest (Case V) version of the theory. In a critical departure from Fechner's theory, Thurstone proposed that a stimulus presentation evoked a psychological value defined on a mathematical continuum. The sampled value characterized the relevant psychological attribute of that stimulus for that subject at that time.[2]

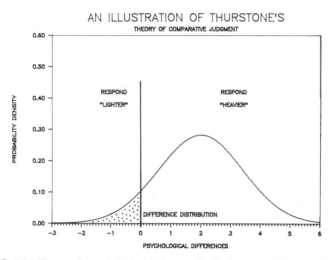

Figure 2. L.L. Thurstone's psychological difference distribution for paired comparisons.

Subjects identified which stimulus produced a greater value of the psychological attribute by determining whether the difference between the two psychological values exceeded zero. Within the probability distribution for such differences, the area to the right of zero equals the probability that a comparison stimulus is judged greater than the standard. Because the mean difference between the two stimuli equals the difference between the means, the distance from zero to the mean of the difference distribution is a measure of the mean psychological difference between the two stimuli. With respect to the form of the difference distribution, subtracting two Gaussian distributed psychological

---

[2]   The idea of the psychological continuum originated with Thurstone (personal communication with Paul Horst).

values produces a Gaussian distributed difference. Therefore, tables of the Gaussian distribution, well known from Fechner's pioneering work, allowed for ready computation of the standardized distance from the unknown mean difference to zero.

In this case, the experimental design yielded data that forced Thurstone to develop a new theory of judgment. Thurstone's achievement advanced psychophysics to the measurement of differences between stimuli that have no physical measurement. The focus of psychophysics shifted to measurement of how much difference existed between stimuli rather than the precision or resolving power of the sensory system.

An apparent theoretical stumbling block to the wide-scale acceptance of Thurstonian methods occurs when there is no easily identifiable measurement error that limits discriminability or the resolving power of the measurement system. Comparisons between stimuli such as those first investigated by Thurstone, the seriousness of crimes or nationality preference, illustrate that stimuli can be unambigously identified by subjects who are quite consistent in their preferences. A subject who prefers coffee to tea may always prefer coffee to tea. Yet, when many subjects are questioned there is seldom unanimity among the responses. In the sense of relative frequency a probability exists that a subject will prefer coffee to tea, but only with probability zero or one will an individual subject's preference be for coffee or tea.

Thus, rather than treat response probabilities as indices of error, Thurstone considered each subject to provide a societal response to a pair of stimuli. Each subject represented an opinion or feeling within the population of feeling about the objects undergoing comparison. The probability represented the proportion of individuals for whom the difference between the standard and comparison psychological values exceeded zero. In other words, there was no assumption of an additive error in Thurstone's theory.

As an application of Thurstone's theory, imagine that each subject is to compare each one of the ten Rorschach inkblots against another and decide which inkblot evokes more thoughts about "Mother." The experimental design matrix, shown in Table 2, contains N^2 cells, with the N main diagonal cells empty because the same stimulus is never compared against itself. The data in each cell are Thurstonian Case V scale values derived from the estimated probability that, for this sample of individuals, the column stimulus evokes more thoughts of "Mother" than the row stimulus. By replicating the entire experiment, but asking the same subjects which of a pair of inkblots generates more thoughts about "Father," a second set of scale values is obtained.

In the present case, 17 subjects were all undergraduates enrolled in my course on Psychological Measurement. The design matrix in Table 2 gives the normal deviate values for the Case V application of the Law of Comparative Judgment (Thurstone, 1927). Only 16 subjects responded to the "Mother" question while all 17 answered the "Father" question. Means at the bottom of each column are the resulting Thurstone Case V scale values for the inkblots.

By plotting the two scale values for each inkblot against each other we obtain the two dimensional representation shown in Figure 3. Inkblots 1, 6, 9, and 10 are rather neutral on the measures derived from the Father question.

Others, such as 3, 5, and 8, are neutral for Mother. Only two inkblots yield values that are impressively high on one dimension and low on the other. These are inkblots 4 and 7.

Table 2. Rorschach–Thurstonian Paired Comparison Matrix. Entries are scale values of Rorschach inkblots for (F)ather and (M)other.

				Inkblot						
Inkblot	1	2	3	4	5	6	7	8	9	10
1 M	.00	.67	.33	.33	.67	.15	.88	.50	.33	.88
F	.00	.23	.39	.71	−.55	−.75	−.39	−.23	−.08	−.23
2 M	−.50	.00	.15	−.50	−.31	−.16	.00	−.67	−.15	−.50
F	−.08	.00	−.23	.55	−.92	−.08	−.39	−.71	−.39	−.55
3 M	−1.1	−.31	.00	−.67	−.31	−1.1	.15	.50	.33	.33
F	.08	.23	.00	.39	−.39	−.08	−.55	−.39	.08	.08
4 M	−.15	.88	.00	.00	.05	−.67	.15	.88	.88	.67
F	−.55	−.23	−.71	.00	−1.2	−.71	−1.2	−.55	−.71	−.71
5 M	−.67	.50	.15	−.50	.00	−.50	.15	−.15	.33	.15
F	.39	.55	.71	.71	.00	.71	−.23	.08	.39	.55
6 M	.33	1.6	.88	.33	.50	.00	1.2	.50	1.6	1.6
F	−.39	.39	−.08	.55	−.55	.00	−.55	−.39	−.23	−.03
7 M	−.88	.00	−.15	−.15	−.15	−1.1	.00	.00	−.33	−.15
F	.39	.55	.91	1.2	.08	.39	.00	.39	.71	.39
8 M	−.15	1.2	−.50	−.31	.00	−.88	−.15	.00	.15	.50
F	.23	.71	.23	.71	−.08	.39	−.23	.00	.23	.08
9 M	−1.1	.15	.00	−1.1	.15	−1.6	.33	−.31	.00	.15
F	.08	.55	−.03	.71	−.55	.23	−.92	.08	.00	.08
10 M	.33	.33	−.31	−.67	.15	−1.9	.00	−.50	−.15	.00
F	.08	.23	−.23	.71	−.71	.08	−.39	−.39	−.23	.00
Means										
M	−.40	.50	.06	−.33	.12	−.91	.27	.07	.30	.36
F	.02	.32	.10	.62	−.48	.09	−.48	−.21	−.02	−.04

In the majority of previous psychophysical experiments and theories the subjects and their abilities were the focus of attention. In this study it is the stimuli, the inkblots themselves, that are under investigation. Yet, in a very profound way, the Thurstonian Method of Paired Comparisons is always a study of how subjects respond, because the subjects provide the data for analysis and ultimately the measures of differences between the inkblots.

To view how these stimuli reflect a relationship between Mother and Father held in a single subject's mind a different experiment is needed. The new procedure requires direct comparisons between "Mother" and "Father" for a single stimulus. The between-gender stimulus-based comparison; "Does this inkblot evoke more thoughts of 'Mother' or 'Father'?" investigates the within-subject feeling evoked by the stimulus. The Thurstonian paired comparison method falters because the same response is repeatedly obtained from a single subject for a specific inkblot. The Thurstonian theory of choice cannot measure an individual psychological event, because the response proportions, either 0 or 1, are too extreme to provide scale values.

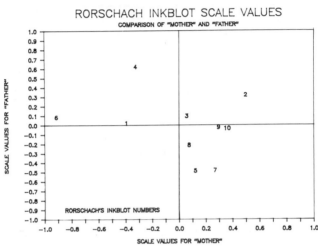

Figure 3. The joint representation of Thurstonian scale values for Rorschach inkblots.

The Method of the Null Hypothesis

While theoreticians like Thurstone sought to measure a subject's psychological experience, statisticians wondered whether there was any experience to measure at all! Sir R. A. Fisher, in his splendid application of the null hypothesis to psychophysical measurement, postulated that the subject experiences nothing at all. In particular, in the often cited "Mathematics of a Lady Tasting Tea" (Fisher, 1956; also Chapter 2 of Fisher, 1951), Sir Ronald investigated whether a lady can, as claimed, discriminate between tests produced by adding first the milk or the tea infusion to a teacup.

For Fisher, the measurement of the effect of a stimulus, such as a liquid applied to the tongue, a fertilizer applied to a field, or its odor applied to the nose, was a matter of assuming, and then rejecting, a suitable null hypothesis. Few ideas did more to divert psychology from its scientific mission. For, rather than creating a model to measure the effect of a stimulus, Fisher developed a model of no effect. When this model was rejected the rejection occurred, claimed Fisher, because there was some effect due to the stimulus. Of course, the rejection can also occur for other reasons, such as the application of an inappropriate model of the null effect!

So compelling became the desire to reject the null hypothesis that experimental designs satisfying the rigors of testing the null hypothesis focused attention on the role chance rather than on the scientific measurement of the phenomenon under investigation. Without measuring the psychological phenomenon brought into existence by the application of experimental stimuli, one can hardly expose to scientific scrutiny the mechanisms of deepest concern to psychology. Yet, by its very nature, the null hypothesis is a model of no effect and provides no model of the effect that is of primary interest.

For the experimental psychologist the important question is whether there is a difference in feeling produced by tasting a drink made by first adding the milk, or the tea infusion, to the tea cup. This is a matter of discrimination and the method of paired comparison seems ideally suited to answering the question. It yields measures of no effect as easily as of some effect.

Using this method, all stimuli are compared against each other in all possible orders in order to estimate the probability of a correct judgment. From the resulting choice proportions, scale values are calculated and then averaged within a column to produce a measure of the psychological difference between the two stimuli. If there is no difference, then the measured difference is zero. But when there is a difference the model produces its measure. Thus, rather than reject a null hypothesis, of dubious value in the first place, the Thurstonian model measures the size of the effect. Then, the scientist decides whether the size of the effect is large enough to merit further attention.

In a cruel twist of fate, Psychophysics created a pantheon of models of psychological processes, but psychologists opened the statistical cookbook in hope of finding an experimental recipe that controlled for chance events. The overwhelming devotion of many psychologists to the peculiar logic of the null hypothesis produced a generation of researchers who chased the null hypothesis like fire in the wind. Yet, while running hard, they hoped to never catch it, because by catching it they failed to reject the null hypothesis. Failing to reject the null hypothesis was the experimental psychologist's *bête noire* — for this failure pushed forward the undesirable possibility that the experimental results were due to chance. Results due to chance were, wisely, unpublishable. Yet, by performing enough experiments, and testing the "Null Hypothesis" at a .95 level of significance, they were assured that even chance phenomena would appear, 5 times out of 100, to yield a "real" psychological effect!

Relative Judgment Theory

All good models lead to their replacement by theories capable of accounting for a broader range of data using fewer or better assumptions. Thurstone's theory of comparative judgment gave rise to rigorous studies of comparative judgment that showed subjects to be capable of substantial response bias (as first theorized by Thomson). For stimuli orderable on a continuum, as Thurstone postulated, the presentation of an extreme stimulus as a standard gives a well-practiced subject a clue about which response is most likely to be correct. Furthermore, each stimulus may be ordered on the psychological continuum, and thus each standard becomes a cue for a certain amount of response bias. In this way, each row of the paired comparison matrix becomes identified with some amount of response bias.

The effect of response bias is particularly clear in paired numerical comparisons. In a typical experiment, the subject sees a two-digit number ranging from 11 to 99. The subject's task is to determine whether a comparison stimulus, unequal to the standard, is larger or smaller than the standard.

To understand how response bias occurs, suppose the subject is presented with a standard equal to 99. A subject who knows the range of the stimuli will have no difficulty in anticipating "Smaller" to be the correct response. In other words, the standard conveys information about the likelihood of a correct response. Only in the mid-range of the standards is little or no information about the correct response conveyed. At the other extreme, when a standard of 11 is presented, the subject can easily determine in advance of the comparison stimulus that "Larger" will be the correct response. Thus, for a full paired comparison design with standards represented on the rows and comparisons as the columns, each standard conveys information about the likelihood that the response "Smaller" or "Larger" is correct. The paired comparison design creates ample opportunity for the effects of response bias to make themselves felt.

And they do, as shown in Figure 4. These mean response times are from four well-trained subjects who made many thousands of numerical comparisons of two-digit numbers using a method of serial paired comparisons (Link, 1989). In this method each stimulus acts as the standard for the next trial. The stimuli were the two-digit numerals ranging from 11 to 99. Each random permutation of a list, which always begins with 55, generates 88 comparisons. After initial training each subject contributed a total of 3168 comparisons for a total across subjects of 12672 trials.[3]

Plotting mean response time as a function of the decade value of the standard stimulus reveals one effect of response bias. The results show relatively fast response times within the 10's decade but substantially slower mean RTs as the standard approaches the 50's decade. Then mean RTs again decrease substantially.

The increase and decrease in response time depends upon a particular response. In the 10's decade the "Smaller" response seldom occurs but its response time is greater than the "Larger" response time, reflecting a bias toward the response "Larger". This relation reverses at the 50's decade and by the 90's decade the "Larger" RT is greater than the "Smaller" RT, again showing the influence of bias. Thurstone's theory of comparative judgment makes no prediction concerning either response bias or response times but Relative Judgment Theory (Link, 1975) does.

---

[3] This experiment was conducted by Miss Karen Rankin as part of her B.Sc. thesis project.

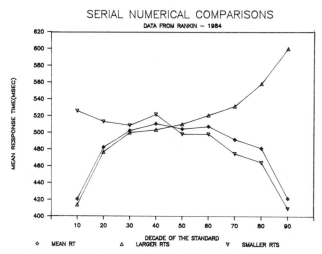

SERIAL NUMERICAL COMPARISONS
DATA FROM RANKIN – 1984

◇ MEAN RT   △ LARGER RTS   ▽ SMALLER RTS
DECADE OF THE STANDARD

Figure 4. Mean response times from a study of differences between two digit numbers.

The model, especially as presented by Link (1975, 1989) and illustrated in Figure 5, shows how the within trial accumulation of differences between the mental values of a standard and comparison stimulus leads, stochastically, to either the "Smaller" or the "Larger" response. The rate at which the stochastic path approaches the thresholds equals the average difference, μ, between the standard and comparison stimuli. This parameter is monotonically related to another parameter θ which, with A and C, determines response probabilities. As the difference between stimuli increase θ and μ increase and generate observable performances that show greater discriminability.

The response thresholds at A and $-A$ determine the *responsiveness* of the subject. When A is small, a response requires little accumulated difference to occur. Responses are quick but the probability of an error is large. When A is large, a longer time is needed to accumulate comparative differences, but responses are more accurate. For the remainder of this discussion the response thresholds will be assumed to be fixed.

When there is no response bias the decision process is characterized by an initial starting position midway between the two response thresholds. Presenting a comparison stimulus larger or smaller than the standard (such as 43 vs 33 or 23 vs 33) should produce equal response times and error rates regardless of which comparison is presented. This is a consequence of equal but opposite rates of accumulated comparative difference.

When there exists an initial bias toward the upper response threshold, the point marked C, the distance to the "Larger" response threshold is reduced. A faster response time occurs when the larger comparison stimulus (say, 43 vs 33) is presented. Also the error rate, the proportion of erroneous "Smaller" responses, decreases. When an equally smaller comparison stimulus is presented (say, 23 vs 33) then the response time is longer than when there was no response bias and the associated error rate also increases.

TWO-THRESHOLD RANDOM WALK MODEL

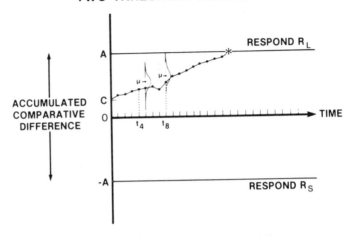

Figure 5. The random walk interpretation of Relative Judgment Theory.

When the response bias is toward the response "Smaller", such as a bias at $-C$, a comparison stimulus smaller than the standard leads to a fast response, but a comparison stimulus larger than the standard will, on the average, lead to a long RT. Again the error rates are also affected by this change in bias. Errors to smaller comparisons are reduced while errors to larger comparisons increase.

The cause of response bias is unknown. The value of the standard may be a cue for bias, but this does not explain how, or how much, response bias comes to be associated with the standard. While the subject is always presented a standard, any information available from the standard about response bias must depend upon previous learning about values of the comparison stimuli that follow the presentation of the standard.

From the viewpoint of a subject who just responded to a particular comparison stimulus, the relation between the most recently presented stimulus, the comparison, and stimulus difference is a salient response bias statistic. Theoretically the subject can associate the just-determined comparative difference with the just presented comparison stimulus. When the value of that comparison stimulus is later presented as a standard, the relation between the comparison stimulus and comparative difference may guide decisions about how to bias responding prior to the presentation of a subsequent comparison stimulus. In this way, after many trials, comparative difference, conditioned on the comparison stimulus, may become a determinant of response bias.

In the method of paired comparisons a large standard is most likely followed by a small comparison. On the average this comparative difference is negative if the standard is subtracted from the comparison. Association of the negative comparative difference with the standard leads to a subject biased toward responding "Smaller" when large standards are presented and a bias toward responding "Larger" when small standards occur.

However, whether the standard is subtracted from the comparison, or the comparison from the standard, is unknown. If, instead, the comparison is subtracted from the standard then for large comparisons the average comparative difference is negative. Thus, if values of comparative difference are associated with values of the comparison stimuli, a natural order for association, and this association governs the subject's bias to future values of standards, the direction of response bias remains the same as in the case where the standard is subtracted from the comparison. The method of paired comparisons does not allow for a definitive test of which kind of association, values of comparative difference with the standard, or values of comparative difference with the comparison, controls response bias.

A second theoretical disadvantage of the Method of Paired Comparisons is that many subtle features of data that Relative Judgment Theory (RJT) is capable of describing in the context of its symmetry relations (Link, 1975; 1989), are difficult to analyze in the context of paired comparisons. To overcome these limitations of MPC, and to remove from the standard any information regarding the likelihood of a particular response being correct, Link (1984) created the Method of Symmetric Differences (MSD).

The Method of Symmetric Differences

The distinguishing features of this method are shown in Figure 6, where, for purposes of analysis, the experimental designs for the Method of Constant Stimuli (MCS) and the Method of Paired Comparisons are also presented. This new experimental design uses symmetric stimulus differences to aid in estimating RJT parameters, and to examine the influence of comparative difference on response bias. The RJT symmetry relations depend upon presenting to the subject stimulus differences equal but opposite in value, as in the case of a standard of 11 and comparisons of either 12 or 10. In the corners of the paired comparison matrix these presentations are not possible. Those cases where symmetric relations do occur are near the center of the paired comparison matrix where response bias, if it exists, is minimal. Thus the paired comparison design obscures the role of response bias by making its estimation most difficult at the extremes where it should be most clear, but providing for estimation where bias plays an insignificant role.

Like MPC, MSD places a uniform distribution over the range of the standard stimuli. Unlike MPC, MSD also places a uniform distribution over the values of stimulus difference in such a way that a standard conveys no information about the likelihood of one or the other response. This is accomplished by requiring that a comparison stimulus be larger or smaller than a standard

Method of Constant Stimuli

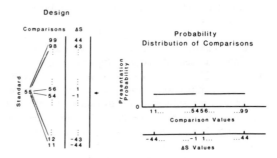

Method of Paired Comparisons

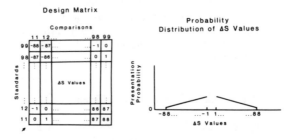

Method of Symmetric Differences

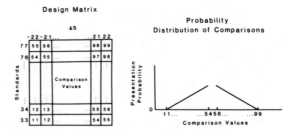

Figure 6. Comparisons of experimental designs showing the Method of Constant Stimuli, Paired Comparisons, and Symmetric Differences.

stimulus with probability one-half. Furthermore, symmetric stimulus differences, on either side of the standard, occur with equal probability. The full design matrix, as shown in Figure 6, places a uniform distribution on the standards and on the values of stimulus difference, thereby forcing a triangular distribution of comparison stimuli.

For this design matrix, the average comparative difference conditioned on the value of the comparison stimulus increases in value as the comparison stimulus increases. For a comparison stimulus equal to 33, the smallest standard, the average comparative difference equals -11.5. As the value of the comparison increases, the value of the average comparative difference increases to a maximum of 11.5 for a comparison of size 77. Were subjects to use the comparison stimulus value as a cue for response bias when the same value occurs as a standard, the subject could expect a smaller comparison stimulus when 33 is presented as a standard, and a larger valued comparison stimulus after 77 is presented as a standard.

This experimental design makes good use of the symmetry relations of RJT when estimating parameter values for differing sizes of stimulus difference. Therefore, the indicators of response bias, θC, and of responsiveness, θA, are computable for each cell of the design matrix. As an example, the values shown in Figure 7 are obtained by application of equations 3 and 4 in Link (1975) or those in Link (1989) to average data for symmetric pairs of stimuli. Specifically, comparison stimuli such as 23 and 43, equally distant from a standard of 33, yield correct and error response probabilities used to estimate the values of θA and θC. For convenience, these estimates are based on decade ranges of the standards.[4]

To further simplify the discussion, without doing any injustice to the theory or its evaluation, the data are also averaged across values of stimulus difference which ranged from plus or minus 1 to 22. The average data yields an average stimulus difference of plus or minus 11.5, slightly more than a numerical decade. This accomplishes the purpose of introducing symmetric values for θ rather than different values for each of the stimulus differences.

The average provides for an assessment of whether the response threshold values at A and $-A$ remain constant across changes in the value of the standard. There is no reason why they should not, but the theory provides a method of determining their value. When stimulus difference is constant, so that θ remains constant, the value of θA, shown in Figure 7, remains quite constant, suggesting that θ and A remain constant across changes in the magnitude of the standard. For A to remain constant, the subject(s) must maintain constant response thresholds regardless of the magnitude of the standard.

When stimulus difference is constant, so that θ remains constant, the value of θC only varies as a function of the amount of response bias, C. For this experimental design response bias, as measured by θC, is negative for small values of the standard, but increases steadily as the standard increases, as

---

[4] This experiment was conducted by Miss Mary Ann Azzarello as part of her B.Sc. thesis project.

shown in Figure 7. Thus, rather than removing response bias, MSD reveals the presence of substantial bias even when the standard contains no information about the likelihood of which response is correct. The bias appears to be strictly linear in the magnitude of the standard. The response bias is, surprisingly, exactly opposite to the bias found when using MPC.

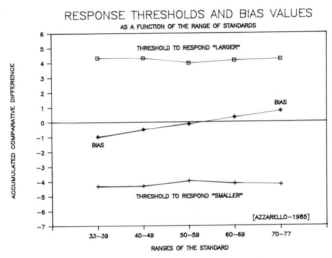

Figure 7. Marginal estimates of response bias and response thresholds as a function of the magnitude of the standard.

The question of whether the standard is subtracted from the comparison or the comparison from the standard can now be examined. For this experimental design the standard contains no information regarding the likelihood of a correct response. The average comparative difference, conditioned on the value of the standard is zero. Thus any response bias must depend upon the joint action of the comparison stimuli and the comparative difference.

For this experimental design, association of comparative difference with the comparison stimulus can occur in two different ways with two different results. If the standard is subtracted from the comparison then positive values of comparative difference are associated with large values of the comparison stimulus. For example, a comparison equal to 99 always has a comparative difference of 22 and a standard equal to 77. Thus, 99 has an associated value of 22. Continuing this argument shows that a comparison of 98 has two possible differences, 22 or 21. The average comparative difference is 21.5, which is again positive. If the relation between the comparison stimulus and comparative difference is applied to a standard then response bias will be toward responding "Large" when the standard is large. This outcome is compatible with the results.

If the comparison is subtracted from the standard a comparison of 99 and a standard of 77 yields a difference of -22. A standard of 98 yields an average difference of -21.5, and so forth. Using this relation to bias responding suggests that a large standard leads to a bias toward responding "Small", a result contradicted by the data.

The rather amazing linearity of θC as a function of the magnitude of the standard, is compatible with the suggestion that response bias depends upon the average comparative difference conditioned on the comparison stimulus. Furthermore, a subtraction of the standard from the comparison generates comparative differences that are large when the comparison is large and small when the comparison is small. When this relation is applied to a standard stimulus in order to determine how to bias responses the subject biases toward "Large" responses when the standard is large and "Small" responses when the standard is small. Yet there is no useful value to the application of this bias because any standard is followed by a comparison that is larger or smaller by equal amounts with probability 0.50.

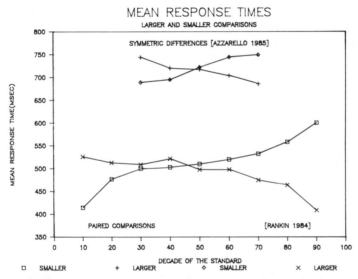

Figure 8. Mean response times for paired numerical comparisons using the Method of Symmetric Differences.

Naturally response bias affects response time. The response times obtained from MSD are shown in Figure 8. As might be expected by the change in direction of response bias from that obtained using MPC, response times show a reversed ordering. When the standard is in the 30's decade, the mean RT for "Smaller" responses is faster than for "Larger" responses. As the decade of the standard increases, the "Smaller" response time increases and the "Larger" response time decreases. These changes are a necessary prediction of the theory because a change in response bias simultaneously affects the distance of the starting position of the random walk from both response thresholds. The subject's response biases are precisely opposite to those obtained from MPC and the response times show a reversed ordering. Consequently, the suggestion that response bias is determined by the subject's assignment of average comparative difference to the value of the comparison stimulus, receives support. Further information concerning this experiment will be found in Link (1989).

Summary

This paper describes four approaches to the analysis of psychological phenomena. As a start, Fechner's model for comparative judgment used the Method of Right and Wrong Cases to examine Weber's Law. Thurstone advanced Fechner's idea to the domain of stimuli having no physical measurements. Fisher and the Method of the Null Hypothesis divert the scientific job of measuring a phenomenon toward the modelling of chance events. The ideas of Fechner and Thurstone are extended by Relative Judgment Theory. Its attendant Method of Symmetric Differences reveals important features of the comparative judgment process that, for many years, went unnoticed. This mathematical theory of discrimination, united with a suitable experimental design, sheds new light on the psychological mechanism governing comparative judgments.

Acknowledgement. This research is supported by the Natural Sciences and Engineering Research Council of Canada.
Correspondence should be addressed to Stephen W. Link, Department of Psychology, McMaster University, 1280 Main Street West, Hamilton, Ontario, L8S 4K1, Canada.

References

Azzarello, M.A. (1986). *Numerical comparisons: An application of relative judgment theory.* Honours B. Sc. thesis. McMaster University, Hamilton, Ontario, Canada.

Fechner, G.T. (1966). *Elements of psychophysics.* (Vol.1; E.G. Boring & D.H. Howes, Eds.; H.E. Adler, Trans.). New York: Holt, Rinehart & Winston. (Original work published 1860.)

Fisher, R.A. (1951). *The design of experiments* (6th ed.). New York: Hafner.

Fisher, R.A. (1956). The mathematics of a lady tasting tea. In J.R. Newman (Ed.), *The world of mathematics* (Vol. 3). New York: Simon and Schuster.

Green, D.M. & Swets, J.A. (1966). *Signal detection theory and psychophysics.* New York: Wiley.

Link, S.W. (1975). The relative judgment theory of two–choice response time. *Journal of Mathematical Psychology, 12,* 114 – 135.

Link, S.W. (1984). How numerical comparisons occur. *Twenty-fourth annual meeting of the Psychonomic Society.* San Diego.

Link, S.W. (1989). Modeling imageless thought: The relative judgment theory of numerical comparison. *Journal of Mathematical Psychology.* In Press.

Rankin, K.E. (1984). *Numerical comparisons using fixed and roving standards: Application of the relative judgment theory.* Honours B.Sc. Thesis. McMaster University, Hamilton, Ontario, Canada.

Thomson, G.H. (1920). A new point of view in the interpretation of threshold measurements in psychophysics. *Psychological Review, 27,* 300–307.

Thurstone, L.L. (1927). A law of comparative judgment. *Psychological Review, 34,* 273–286.

Thurstone, L.L. (1952). Thurstone, L.L. In E.G. Boring, H.S. Langfeld, H. Werner & R.M. Yerkes (Eds.), *A history of psychology in autobiography* (Vol. 4). Worcester, MA: Clark University Press.

Psychophysical Explorations of Mental Structures
Edited by H.-G. Geissler
in collaboration with M.H. Müller and W. Prinz
© 1990 by Hogrefe & Huber Publishers

Chapter 2

A Uniform Mathematical Framework for Both Fechner's and Stevens' Psychophysical Theory

László Mérö
Loránd Eötvös University
Budapest, Hungary

Luce (1959a, pp. 38−39) has pointed out that there is some confusion about the interpretation of Fechner's ideas on psychophysical scaling. As Luce remarks, Fechner's scaling idea comprises two quite distinct parts:

(i) The probabilities of pairwise discriminations, the $P(x,y)$, are so constrained that there exists a real-valued mapping u of the stimuli and a function F of one real variable such that, for $P(x,y) \neq 0$ or 1, $P(x,y) = F(u(x) - u(y))$.

(ii) The function u of part (i) represents "subjective sensation."

This separation of the ideas of difference scaling and subjective sensation has lead to a fertile research direction called "Fechnerian scaling." Since Luce and Galanter (1963) the Generalized Fechner Problem has usually been formulated as follows: find a psychological scale such that equidiscriminable pairs of stimuli are represented by equal scale differences. The reason why the formulation in (i) and (ii) is equivalent to the last sentence will be clarified in more detail in the course of this paper.

Falmagne (1971) gives a general mathematical formulation of this problem, and a complete solution to it can be found in Falmagne (1985, chapter IV). This approach directly generalizes Fechner's scaling idea in the sense that "it is raised for an abstract discrimination index, which in practice can be different from choice probabilities that provided the empirical foundations for classical psychophysics."

The Aim of this Paper

The above discussed approach does not claim at all that the obtained psychological scale is a measure of "sensation." Its goal is to analyse the logical consequences of part (i) of Fechner's original idea, without considering the validity of part (ii). In this paper we shall analyse the reasons why Fechner merged these two parts, and reformulate part (i) in the spirit of Fechner's original train of thought. In other words, we shall pursue the mathematical consequences of a model of sensation in which part (ii) of the above distinction can be reasonably retained and part (i) is substituted by a more general assumption.

Fechner (1966/1860) hypothesized the existence of a general, modality-independent sensory mechanism. This conception led him to his well-known assumption that all just noticeable differences (*jnd*'s) for a sensory dimension are subjectively equal to one another. This assumption implicitly contains both part (i) and part (ii) of the above formulation. The reason for this assumption is that no other general feature has been found that could unequivocally be defined for any sensory continuum in a uniform way, independently of the concrete modality. This consideration has perpetually been valid since the days of Fechner. The *jnd* seems to be the only possible feature that we can imagine being grasped by the hypothesized general sensory mechanism.

In the model discussed in this paper it will be supposed that another part of Fechner's ideas is valid instead of the one supposed in the above mentioned model of Fechnerian scaling. We shall suppose that sensation is, in fact, computed using only the *jnd*'s; however, we shall drop another part of Fechner's ideas, i.e., that sensation is scaled immediately in *jnd*-units.

Extensive work has been done in psychophysics in order to determine the so called "psychophysical function" by using the method of measuring *jnd*'s and cumulating them. This paradigm faithfully follows the originnal ideas of Fechner. Luce and Edwards (1958) have pointed out, that this approach contains a principal error caused by the techniques of unjustified integration of the *jnd*'s, as originally described by Fechner (using the "mathematical auxiliary principle"). Nevertheless, as Luce and Edwards remark, this unjustified technique has not led to severe practical errors. Problems arose only when the methods of "direct" psychophysical measurement have consequently led to results contradicting the predictions of the Fechnerian method. Stevens (1961, 1975) summarizes an impressive amount of results of this type.

However, while *Fechner's Law* has been repealed at least in its original generality, there has never any suitable substitute been proposed for Fechner's arguments on the possible basis of a general modality-independent sensory mechanism. The possibility of the existence of such a mechanism has never been explicitly repealed; it is too appealing an idea to be directly repealed. It has just been swept under the rug.

Stevens (1957, p. 178) refuses the idea of founding psychophysics on the *jnd*'s with the following argumentation: "If something empirically useful is to issue from a model, something empirically known should be put in it. Confusions (failures in discrimination) provide a poor foundation for measuring sensation." On the other hand, if we would like to get some picture about the possible internal mechanisms of sensation we should take some model assumptions into consideration. The importance of the *jnd*'s in founding a model for psychophysics is not just their comforts in measurement but their perpetual unsubstitutability in imagining a way for the working mechnism of sensation. In other words if something theoretically useful is to issue from a model, some theoretically deep conception should be put in it. Except for the *jnd*'s no other mechanism–level coneption has been found so far.

Repealing Fechner's law, at least in its intended generality, is well justified by the results of several kinds of direct psychophysical measurements. Direct measurement methods provide unequivocally more stable foundations for measuring sensation than indirect methods based on confusions, but none of these methods exclude a plausible theory on the working mechanism based on the marginal cases of discriminability. Such a theory may preserve Fechner's most ingenious thoughts in such a way that it could still fit the direct measurement data.

The goal of this paper is to investigate what kind of operations we should suppose to be performed by the sensory mechanism on the *jnd*'s in order to receive some given functions for the sensation. A mathematical formulation of this problem will be given in the next section, and a general solution of this problem supposing that Weber's law is valid will be given in a later section. As a result it will be shown that two very plausible special cases of this approach lead to Fechner's logarithmic law and Stevens' power function law, respectively. This way it will be shown that even the results of the direct measurement methods do not repeal the ingenious core of Fechner's ideas: that the sensation mechanism may be based on the marginal cases of discriminability, i.e., on the *jnd*'s. This means that the possibility of a modality–independent general sensory mechanism has still not been refuted. The chapter closes with further speculation on the possible interpretations of this approach.

Formulation of the Problem

It is usually supposed that function F in (i) is strictly monotonical, so that exists a function G that is the inverse function of F, so that, if $P(x,y)$ is denoted by p, then

$$G(p) = u(x) - u(y)$$

for $p \neq 0$ or 1. This means that

$$u(x) = u(y) + G(p) . \tag{1}$$

In other words, if the discrimination between x and y is not complete, then (i) means that the value of $u(x)$ can be computed according to (1) if the values of $u(y)$ and $G(p)$ are known. The quantity $G(p)$ does not directly depend of x and y, only through the probabilities between them. The fact that the discrimination between x and y is not complete means just that their difference is a *jnd* in a sense to be clarified in more detail below. All this shows that if (ii) is also considered to be valid, then (1) corresponds with Fechner's idea that the value of sensation can be determined by cumulating a constant amount for each of the *jnd*'s.

Now suppose that this last paragraph is discarded while (ii) is still maintained. This means that we do not accept that if the probability of discrimination between x and y is p, then the difference between the subjective sensations of stimuli x and y is a quantity $G(p)$ that depends only on p, but not on the measure of the stimulus. In this case we can still assume that the value of $u(x)$ can be determined if the values of $u(y)$ and $G(p)$ are known, although may be not in such a simple way as described in (1). Let us consider the following generalization of (1):

$$u(x) = M(u(y),p) \qquad (2)$$

where M is an arbitrary function of two arguments. By this way, we shall substitute (i) by the following, more general assumption:

(i') The probabilites of pairwise discriminations, the $P(x,y)$, are so constrained, that there exists a real-valued mapping u of the stimuli and a function M of two real variables such that for $P(x,y)=p\neq0$ or 1 Equation (2) is valid.

Assumption (i') means that we consider Fechner's basic idea still valid: we suppose that the sensory mechanism determines the value of the sensation by using the *jnd*'s in some way. On the other hand, we do not suppose that this mechanism does this by simply cumulating the *jnd*'s; we repeal that part of Fechner's idea that the *jnd*'s act as units of sensation.

Function M in (i') can be interpreted in such a way that this function describes the mental operations performed by the hypothesized general sensory mechanism on the stimuli with small differences. Function M is the general form of "cumulating the *jnd*'s." In Fechner's train of thought we maintain the notion of the existence of a general, modality-independent sensory mechanism and that this mechanism is working on the basis of the *jnd*'s. Thus assumption (i') expresses the most general form of the possible functioning of this mechanism.

In this context it seems reasonable to keep assumption (ii), and a consequent goal is to investigate what kind of function M should belong to a given form of u. So, the question is a reversed one as compared to that of Fechner and his followers. Our question is the following: Supposed that function u is known (e.g., as a result of some kind of "direct" psychophysical measurement), then what kind of mental operation function can account for the given results within the framework of the above described theory. By obvious considerations, we shall suppose that function M is strictly monotonical in both arguments.

Related Work

The reviews of Birnbaum (1978) and Shepard (1981) give thorough overviews on the status of direct psychological measurement methods and scaling based on discriminability. Both papers point out that the following distinction raised by Stevens (1957) has still not been solved in a reassuring way. As Shepard formulates, this distinction is that the fundamental psychophysical relation may be of the general form

$$\psi = f_1(S) \tag{3}$$

where S is the physically measured intensity of a stimulus, ψ is the resulting psychological magnitude and f_1 is the "psychophysical" function that transforms one into the other. However, while the magnitude of S can be observed, the value of internal sensation ψ is unobservable. In order to give any empirical content to it, we must go back to the externally recordable response, R, and introduce another transformation:

$$R = f_2(\psi) . \tag{4}$$

However, as the intervening variable, ψ, is not observable itself, the responses of the subject can at most determine the form of the single, overall relation

$$R = f_3(S) = f_2(f_1(S)) \tag{5}$$

in which ψ does not explicitly appear.

This formulation intimates an interpretation that there may be one single mental representation of the magnitude of stimuli, independent of the way of instructions as to judge differences or ratios, or of the task to be performed. This question will be revisited at the end of this paper.

In order to avoid the effect of the mysterious function f_2 in (3) several techniques of measuring cross-modality matching were elaborated. Much other efforts have also been made in order to give a reasonable base for interpreting the measured data as referring to the result of f_1. The origninal finding of Stevens (1957, p. 162), that "equal stimulus ratios tend to produce equal sensation ratios" is perhaps the first result into this direction, because as Luce (1959b, Theorem 1) points out, this finding on its own entails the power function as the only possible solution to the functional equation emerging from the formalized version of the finding. As Stevens' methods are not based on discriminability tasks, this finding can be considered a direct measurement result, even if the way of obtaining it was not exclusively directly asking the sensed magnitudes. In fact, Stevens' cited finding is the quintessence of several results measured with very diverse techniques.

Another approach to relate empirical data to the model described by (3) − (5) mathematically is to relax the strict assumptions on the numeric mental representation. Krantz, Luce, Suppes and Tversky (1971), Miyamato (1983) and others have elaborated models where instead of the complex numerical representation only ordinal relations are supposed to be used by the sensory mechanism. Krantz (1972) describes several ways of cross–modality matching in these terms.

Our approach is not intended to provide a substitute for any of these efforts. On the contrary, our starting point is, that the sensation function has been determined in some way, and our goal is to interpret a working mechanism that conforms both the core of Fechner's original ideas and matches the results of direct measurement, whatever they are like.

Cross–modality matching intimates some other ways of interpeting working mechanisms as well. Laming (1973, Chapter 3) describes several theories including the possible existence of "internal scales." These theories are quite logical, nevertheless, none of them gives any hint as to how the sensory mechanism could perform the matching of the stimulus continuum to the hypothesized internal scale. As Laming (p. 45) very consequently but somewhat criptically remarks: "As an alternative interpretation, suppose that judgements of sensation are based on the same discriminal properties of the stimulus as threshold discriminations, ultimately because these are the only properties the stimulus has. This means that (subjective) magnitude estimation is a rather perplexing task because all the subject is able to do with the stimuli presented to him is to match differences or jnd–s; there is no quantitative sensation to be estimated..." and "The numbers uttered as estimates are notional physical magnitudes of stimuli of some ideal continuum... which are matched discrimination-wise with the stimuli presented for judgement." Our approach aims at making the notion "discrimination-wise" somewhat more explicit.

Another direction of related research should be mentioned here: theory of meaningfulness. Luce (1959a, p. 44 − 45) showed that if subjective sensation is measurable on a ratio scale, the only possible, dimensionally balanced psychophysical relation is the power law. Falmagne and Narens (1983) developed a theory for generally interpreting the notion of "meaningfulness" for any quantitative law. Roberts (1985) applies this aproach to psychology. In Roberts' terminology, "*In general, we shall say that a statement involving numerical scales is meaningful if its truth value is unchanged when every scale is replaced by another acceptable one.*" Later in his paper Roberts renders this definition more exactly. The function u of (i') complies with the definitions of meaningfulness. However, it may be of more importance, that it also complies with Fechner's notions on the possible working mechanism of the sensory system.

Weber's Law

If two stimuli, x and y, cannot be discriminated for certain (i.e., $P(x,y) = p \neq 0$ or 1), we can say that there is a just noticeable difference between them. The above term "discrimination" can be understood in many ways depending on the concrete experimental technique. It may cover either genuine discrimination or a choice probability as to which of the stimuli is judged as being stronger, or several other notions. However, in order to speak clearly of the *jnd*, the probability p of discrimination must be fixed. In the experiments of Weber underlying the theory of Fechner this probability had been implicitly fixed in a tacit way. However, as Luce (1959a, pp. 43−44) points out, different measurement techniques involved different interpretations of the *p* value.

Weber's law states the measure of the *jnd* is proportional to the measure of the stimulus. The validity of Weber's law is totally independent of the theoretical debates on Fechner's theory: it does not at all claim to have any relation to "sensation". The *jnd* is a clearly measurable quantity that proved very often to obey Weber's law. Luce and Galanter (1963) and Falmagne (1985) recount several results suggesting that it is well justified to generalize Weber's law to any probability value *p*.

The Generalized Weber's Law can be formulated by the following equation: If $P(x,y) = p \neq 0$ or 1 then

$$x - y = c(p)y \tag{6}$$

for every $0 < p < 1$, where $c(p)$ is an arbitrary strictly monotonically increasing function of one variable.

The original formulation of Luce and Galanter (1963) allows in (6) for a possible shift $d(p)$ in the right side, which we shall not take into consideration. In the case of sensory continua that can be scaled by ratio scales, such a shift does not arise. A compromise has been used in generality by Falmagne (1971, part 5), where the shift refers not to the whole right side of (6) but only to *y* in the right side. This generalization could have been adopted in our treatment, too. On the other hand, it is not clear how to adapt the derivation of the next section to the original Luce–Galanter version of the Generalized Weber Law. It is also not clear how this derivation could be set up without supposing Weber's Law.

An implicit meaning of the generalized Weber's law is that there is no distinguished probability in the sensation, or rather, in the errors of discrimination, i.e., in the confusions. Assumptions (i) and (i′), respectively, also embody this belief. This assumption was always implicitly involved in all kinds of the Generalized Fechner Problem, and, in fact, this is one of the core ideas in formulating (i′), where also any values of *p* play the same, symmetrical role. The interpretation of the role of the *p* values at the sensory mechanism level may cause great problems, which will be discussed at the end of the paper. Nevertheless, it seems to be well justified to have the *p*'s play a symmetrical role to each other in the formulation, because the opposite case would involve the existence of distinguished probability levels in our sensory mechanism. This assumption would be highly counterintuitive.

General Solution of (i′), Supposing Weber's Law is Valid

When (6) is substituted into (2), we get

$$u((1 + c(p))y) = M(u(y),p) . \tag{7}$$

Now let us suppose that the sensation function $u(y)$ and the Weber function $c(p)$ is known through some kind of direct measurement, and our goal is to determine "mental function" *M* that satisfies (7) in terms of *u* and *c*.

As $c(p)$ is strictly monotonically increasing, it must have an inverse function, let it call $v(r)$. Substituting the inverse function in (7) yields the following equation:

$$u(ry) = M(u(y), v(r)) . \qquad (8)$$

Let us substitute $y = e^s$, $r = e^t$, $g(s) = u(e^s)$ and $h(t) = v(e^t)$ into (8):

$$g(s+t) = M(g(s), h(t)) . \qquad (9)$$

Let us try to eliminate function g from (9) in order to get a "pure" functional equation for M, in the hope that we can run out to one of the well-known functional equations. Let the notation $g(0) = a$ be used, so

$$g(t) = M(a, h(t)) . \qquad (10)$$

Applying (10) to $s + t$ and (10) into (9) we get

$$M(a, h(s+t)) = g(s+t) = M(M(a, h(s)), h(t)) . \qquad (11)$$

Considering only the two sides of (11), we get an equation, that is very similar to the one treated in Aczél (1966, p. 248). The only difference lays in the inserted function h. However, the solution that is deduced by Aczél, can also straightforwardly be applied to (11). Aczél proves that the unique solution to the equation $F(x, u+v) = F(F(x, u), v)$ is

$$F(x, y) = f(f^{-1}(x) + y)$$

where f is an arbitrary strictly monotonical function. Now we can adapt the derivation of Aczél's theorem to our case. The details will not be given here. They make use of the techniques described in Aczél (1966, pp. 16−18) or Aczél and Saaty (1983), and then going steps (8)−(11) backwards. Finally, we have the following theorem:

Theorem 1. Given any strictly monotonical functions $u(y)$ and $c(p)$, the unique solution of equation (7) for M is:

$$M(x, p) = u((1 + c(p))u^{-1}(x)) . \qquad (12)$$

It is a trivial matter, of course, to ascertain that (12) is really a solution to (7). The importance of the long proof is that it has been proven that (7) does in fact have a solution for all function $u(y)$ and $c(p)$, and that this solution is unique. Now, armed with a general solution and a unicity theorem, we can go to see the consequences of this theorem when some specific assumptions are taken either on the form of M or on the form of u.

Special Cases of the Theory: The Status of the Logarithmic and the Power Law

First, let us investigate which mental functions M can lead to the logarithmic and the power laws, respectively. Knowing Theorem 1, it is enough to guess the solution; the unicity part of the theorem will guarantee that no other solution exists.

For the logarithmic law it is well known that cumulating the *jnd*'s leads to this law. Though the original solution of Fechner was shown by Luce and Edwards (1958) to be deficient, the same authors provide a fully correct solution to it. So we have the following theorem:

Theorem 2. If $u(x)$ has the form $u(x) = a \log x + b$, then the only possible form of function M is $M(x,p) = cx + G(p)$ where c is a constant and $G(p)$ is a uniquely determined function.

The concrete form of $G(p)$ is indifferent now; it is clear, that the solution just describes Fechner's mechanism of cumulating the *jnd*'s. Now we see that Fechner's mechanism is the only possible one that leads to the logarithmic law.

It is a bit more interesting to guess the function M that leads to the power law. The simplest proof of the following theorem follows from the later Theorem 4. Here is the result:

Theorem 3. If $u(x)$ has the form $u(x) = cx^b$, then the only possible form of = function M is $M(x,p) = d(p)x$ where $d(p)$ has also the form $d(p) = sp^t$.

This is a fairly suggestive result in order to make the approach of this paper plausible: why could the sensory mechanism not perform multiplications, instead of adding up constants for every *jnd*? This mechanism would be as simple and imaginable for a simple (neural) hardware as the cumulating mechanism and it would conform the power law. Is it that easy to preserve the spirit of Fechner's idea and accept the power law at the same time? This question will be revisited in the next section.

Let us turn to the other side of the coin: suppose function M has some well defined form. What follows from such assumptions for the form of the sensation function u? We do not have a solvability theorem for M, it is possible that for many kinds of M's there is simply no solution of (7) for u. In fact, we will see that this is the case.

It is fairly counterintuitive that variables x (for stimulus magnitude) and p (for discrimination probability) could be very strongly intertangled in a cognitive mechanism. Following the methodology of E.U. Weber (1984) and Luce and Weber (1986), we shall first investigate an additive and a muliplicative rule for M. (They used this apporach for risk measurement.)

Theorem 4. If $M(x,p)$ has the form $M(x,p) = a(x) + b(p)$ where a and b are arbitrary functions, then the only possible form for $a(x)$ in order to have a solution to (7) is $a(x) = cx + t$, and thus the only solution for u is the logarithmic law.

Theorem 5. If $M(x,p)$ has the form $M(x,p) = a(x)b(p)$ where a and b are arbitrary functions, then the only possible form for $a(x)$ in order to have a solution for (7) is $a(x) = tx$, and then the only solution for u is the power law.

Theorem 6. If $M(x,p)$ has the form $M(x,p) = a(x)^{b(p)}$ where a and b are arbitrary functions, then the only possible form for $a(x)$ in order to have a solution for (7) is $a(x) = x$, and then the only solution for u is c^{x^k} for any c and k constant.

The proofs of theorems 4−6 will not be presented here. They are based on adaptations of the technique of Adams and Messick, cited in Luce (1959a, pp. 41−42).

Theorem 6 has been included just for the sake of logical completeness. It has probably no practical consequences. As Baird and Noma (1978, p. 79) note: "This function has never been seriously considered in the context of direct scaling − and with good reason. There seem few data to support this predicition, although some relevant studies have been reported." On the other hand, the other two theorems may have much more relevance: they show that if the theoretical framework of this paper is accepted, within fairly wide limits the only reasonable functions for M are the linear ones and then the only reasonable functions for u are the two wellknown ones.

It is clear that in general M can take up very many kinds of forms, otherwise no solution could exist for M to every u. Nevertheless, it is interesting that in these special cases there are those very strong limitations for the possible form of M. It is not clear how some more general limitative theorems for the possible form of M could be found. Just one more theorem in this direction:

Theorem 7. If $M(x,p)$ has the form $M(x,p) = a(x)b(p) + c(x) + d(p)$ where a, b, c and d are arbitrary functions, then the only possible form for $a(x)$ and $c(x)$ in order to have a solution for (7) is $a(x) = b(x) = x$, and then the only solution for u is $u(x) = cx^b - 1$.

It is surprising that even this degree of entangling the stimulus and probability parameters is that much restrictive for the possible form of u. It is not clear whether or not this finding has some theoretical or practical importance, nevertheless, this surprisingly strong limitative theorem adumbrates that in spite of the apparent exaggerated generality of (2) the theory outlined in this paper may still have quite a number of implicit constraints in order to describe some mechanisms.

Discussion

There is a permanent controversy on the status of direct psychophysical scaling methods. Probably, the majority of the researchers in this field support the interpretation that there is just one kind of psychological interpretation of the stimuli, and the apparent diversity in the answers in the experimental situations is due to different kinds of mental operations performed in the result of the psychophysical function. As Torgerson (1961, cited in Veit, 1978) puts it: "Judges may perceive only a single relation betwen a pair of stimuli regardless of the instruction to judge differences or ratios." Shepard's formulation of the problem was mentioned above. He writes: "According to the theoretical analysis I have presented, the empirical findings of Stevens imply that the internal representations of sensory magnitude that are compared with each other in any given task are all related to physical magnitude by the same function, g."

Birnbaum and Veit (1974) and Veit (1978) have performed several elegant experiments differing only in their way of instructing the subjects. For weight and greyness they found out, that when a difference or ratio judgement was asked for, the corresponding model had a better fit. Birnbaum and Veit have made their experiments in pursuing the mental operations performed on "the" psychophysical function. They have not at all dealt with the question of how the psychophysical function is acquired or what working mechanisms could underlie it.

In this framework the importance of the present paper is that it proposes a possible working mechanism in the spirit of Fechner's original ideas. The proposed mechanism has been shown to be able to underlie any kind of empirical results on the psychophysical functions. It has been shown that most of the empirically obtained functions can be explained by reasonably simple mechanisms performing only very simple functions on the jnd's.

Theorem 1 provides the general unique connection between the psychophysical function and the jnd's. To describe its logical status, an analogy to the very general equations of physics can be seen. For example, the Maxwell equations describe at a very general level the constraints that electromagnetic field must obey, supposed it has a wave–nature. As an analogy, we could say that equation (12) describes the constraints which the mental function M and the psychophysical function u must obey, supposed the sensory mechanism is of a "Fechner–nature". The Maxwell equations cannot be solved in general and there is no guarantee that in a given application an exact solution can be found. Nevertheless, in many practically important situations the special cases of the Maxwell equations complying to the situation could be solved and had a great practical use. The logical status of Theorems $2-7$ is similar. Luckily, in psychophysics the form of empirical findings are much more similar to each other in form than in the case of electricity.

Theorems $2-7$ also suggest another interpretation of the internal representation. As we have seen, the working mechanism underlying the logarithmic law and the power law are quite similar in complexity (or in simplicity), and both can very easily be implemented in a hardware (or neural) way. This observation propounds the possibility that there may be a dual mechanism for judging differences and ratios, respectively, and the cognitive mechanism accepts the proposal of that mechanism which provides a more satisfactory answer to the given question. At present this interpretation is nothing else but speculation, but the obtained results intimate the possibility of such an interpretation. It seems likely that this conception might provide an alternative explanation of the cited findings without contradicting the empirical results.

Whether the theory described in this paper is considered a deduction of the mathematical constraints of a possible underlying mechanism of the unique internal representation of psychophysical stimuli, or it is considered an argument for the existence of a dual mechanism, or it is considered a basic mechanism to account for any particular kind of psychophysical functions, the problem of interpretation of the probability levels, the p's, remains unsolved in the formulation. As it was already mentioned, the formulation with the symmetrical role of the different p–levels is more or less compulsory. However, the mechanism-level interpretation of the different *p*-levels remains problematic.

At the first approximation it could be said that possibly the *jnd*'s of several *p*-levels are interpolated by the sensory mechanism, but intuition allows only for a finite number of *p*-levels to be interpolated. Fechner did not deal with this problem at all, as he worked with only one *p*-level (this led him to his unjustified integration technique). If we think only in terms of a finite number of *p*-levels, these particular levels should be determined in some way and this would again lead to the problem of the existence of distinguished probability levels. The formulation has succeeded in avoiding this problem, but I do not see how the interpretation could cope with it. I think presently this is the hardest problem with Fechner's ingenious approach to the problem of psychophysical sensation. The present paper attempted to contribute to understanding the mathematical consequences of Fechner's ideas in the light of the results of modern "direct" psychophysical measurement. However, the basic problems are still far form being solved.

Summary

In this chapter a new approach has been proposed to generalize Fechner's original ideas in psychophysics. Fechner was hypothesizing the existence of a general, modality-independent mechanism. This conception had lead him to his well-known assumption that all just noticeable differences for a sensory dimension are subjectively equal to one another. The reason for this assumtion was that no other general feature had been found that could unequivocally be defined for any sensory continuum, independently of the concrete modality. Still nowadays the *jnd* seems to be the only possible feature that could be grasped by the hypothesized general sensory mechanism. However, it is still possible that this part of Fechner's idea proves true in spite of the possible failure of the other part of his idea, i.e., that sensation is scaled in the *jnd*-units. The sensory mechanism can be supposed not only to add up the *jnd*'s in order to determine the sensation, but theoretically it can perform any other function *M* upon them.

In this paper it has been proved that, if Weber's Law is valid, then this generalization of Fechner's ideas leads to a functional equation that has a unique solution for every kind of subjective sensation functions. Specifically, the form of the function *M* has been determined both in the case if the Weber-Fechner Law is valid for the subjective sensation and in the case if Stevens' Power Law is valid for it.

This way the proposed generalization of Fechner's original idea yields a uniform mathematical framework comprising both of the two concurrent psychophysical laws and still maintaining the possibility of the existence of a general, modality-independent sensory mechanism.

Correspondence should be addressed to László Mérö, Institute of Psychology, Loránd Eötvös University, Bp.VI., Izabella u. 46, H−1378 Budapest Pf. 4, Hungary.

References

Aczél, J. (1966). *Lectures on functional equations and their applications.* New York, London: Academic Press.

Aczél, J., & Saaty, T.L. (1983). Procedures for synthesizing ratio judgments. *Journal of Mathematical Psychology, 27,* 93−102.

Baird, J.C., & Noma, E. (1978). *Fundamentals in scaling and psychophysics.* New York: Wiley.

Birnbaum, M.H. (1978). Differences and ratios in psychological measurement. In N.J. Castellan & F.J. Restle (Eds.), *Cognitive theory.* Hillsdale, NJ: Erlbaum.

Birnbaum, M.H., & Veit, C.T. (1974). Scale convergence as a criterion for rescaling: Information integration with difference, ratio and averaging tasks. *Perception & Psychophysics, 16,* 7−15.

Falmagne, J.-C. (1971). The generalized Fechner problem and discrimination. *Journal of Mathematical Psychology, 8,* 22−43.

Falmagne, J.-C. (1985). *Elements of psychophysical theory.* Oxford, New York: Oxford University Press.

Falmagne, J.-C., & Narens, L. (1983). Scales and meaningfulness of quantitative laws. *Synthese, 55,* 287−325.

Fechner, G.T: (1966). *Elements of psychophysics.* (E.G. Boring & D.H. Howes, Eds.; H.E. Adler, Trans.). New York: Holt, Rinehart & Winston. (Original work published 1860).

Krantz, D.H. (1972). A theory of magnitude estimation and cross-modality matching. *Journal of Mathematical Psychology, 9,* 168−199.

Krantz, D.H., Luce, R.D., Suppes, P., & Tversky, A. (1971). *Foundations of measurement.* Vol. 1. New York: Academic Press.

Laming, D. (1973). *Mathematical psychology.* London, New York: Academic Press.

Luce, R.D. (1959a). *Individual choice behavior.* New York: Wiley.

Luce, R.D. (1959b). On the possible psychophysical laws. *Psychological Review, 66,* 81−95.

Luce, R.D., & Edwards, W. (1958). The derivation of subjective scales from just noticeable differences. *Psychological Review, 65,* 222−237.

Luce, R.D., & Galanter, E. (1963). Psychophysical scaling. In R.D. Luce, R.R. Bush & E. Galanter (Eds.), *Handbook of mathematical psychology,* Vol. 1 (pp. 245−307). New York: Wiley.

Luce, R.D., & Weber, E.U. (1984). An axiomatic theory of conjoint expected risk. *Journal of Mathematical Psychology, 30,* 188−205.

Miyamoto, J.M. (1983). An axiomatization of the ratio/difference representation. *Journal of Mathematical Psychology, 27,* 439−455.

Roberts, F.S. (1985). Applications of the theory of meaningfulness to psychology. *Journal of Mathematical Psychology, 29,* 311−332.

Shepard, R.N. (1981). Psychological relations and psychophysical scales: On the status of "direct" psychophysical measurement. *Journal of Mathematical Psychology, 24,* 311−332.

Stevens, S.S. (1957). On the psychophysical law. *Psychological Review, 64,* 153−181.

Stevens, S.S. (1961). To honor Fechner and repeal his law. *Science, 133,* 80−86.

Stevens, S.S. (1975). *Psychophysics.* New York: Wiley.

Veit, C.T. (1978). Ratio and subtractive processes in psychophysical judgment. *Journal of Experimental Psychology: General, 107,* 81−107.

Weber, E.U. (1984). Combine and conquer: A joint application of conjoint and functional approaches to the problem of risk measurement. *Journal of Experimental Psychology: Human Perception and Performance, 10,* 179−194.

Psychophysical Explorations of Mental Structures
Edited by H.-G. Geissler
in collaboration with M.H. Müller and W. Prinz
© 1990 by Hogrefe & Huber Publishers

Chapter 3

Scale Convergence and Psychophysical Laws

Michael H. Birnbaum
Department of Psychology
California State University, Fullerton
Fullerton, U.S.A.

The dream of psychophysics, ever since its creation by Gustav Fechner, has been the possibility of a science of subjective experience. In this dream, we can imagine a mental world with empirical, psychological laws connecting mental measures in a fashion analogous to, but distinct from the physical world with its physical laws connecting physical measures. Fechner saw that Weber's work on stimulus discrimination and Bernoulli's interpretation of decisions among gambles could be understood if subjective magnitude were a logarithmic function of objective measures. With a log function, equal physical ratios produce equal subjective differences, and if discrimination is a function of subjective difference, then stimuli that bear equal physical ratios should be equally discriminable.

However, the nightmare of psychophysics was that different procedures for psychological measurement led to different scales. On the occasion of the 100th anniversary of Fechner's great work, Stevens (1961) argued that we should "honor Fechner" but "repeal his law" in favor of the scale that is obtained by assuming that subjects can "directly" report subjective ratios. Stevens found that magnitude estimations of "ratios" are a power function of physical value. Stevens noted that Plateau and others had realized that if subjective value is a power function of physical value, then stimuli that bear equal physical ratios will have equal subjective ratios. If discrimination were governed by a ratio, then Weber's results are compatible with a power function. Furthermore, Stevens doubted whether stimulus discrimination, as exemplified by the models of Thurstone (1959), should be used to define a scale of magnitude.

Torgerson (1961) theorized that the dispute between Stevens' law and Fechner's was a dispute over theory, not data. Data that would support Fechner's law under the subtractive interpretation would support Stevens' law under the ratio interpretation. Torgerson's argument went further: if subjects only perceive a single relation between stimuli despite variations in the task, then the choice between the subtractive and the ratio theory (and therefore between Fechner and Stevens) would be a decision, not an empirical discovery.

In early psychophysical scaling studies, Torgerson's conjecture could not itself be tested, and the presence of various numerical "biases" and contextual effects in scaling studies led to a confusion of methods, theories, and scales that disturbed the sleep of any theoretician seeking a simple solution. Some argued that different methods contained "biases", and others argued that subjective values themselves might change, depending on the situation. The most troubling fear of this nightmare was the concern that the basic disagreements might not be empirically testable.

In recent years, methods for testing the basic assumptions of the theories have improved, as have the theories and results that allow a better separation of judgmental processes ("response biases") from the basic laws of stimulus comparison (e.g., Krantz, Luce, Suppes & Tversky, 1971; Birnbaum & Veit, 1974). This chapter will give a brief outline of ideas that have emerged from recent research using these newer methods.

The assumption of scale convergence has led to a coherent theory of psychophysical and social relational judgment that uses a single scale of subjective magnitude to interlock a variety of empirical phenomena, including: (1) category ratings and magnitude estimations; (2) "ratio" and "difference" judgments; (3) "reverse" or "inverse" attribute judgments; (4) contextual effects due to variation in stimulus and response distributions; (5) cross–dimensional combinations and comparisons; and (6) comparisons of stimulus relations ("ratios of differences", "differences of differences", etc.).

Definitions and Assumptions

Scale Values (Subjective Scales). The relationship between subjective and the physical scales is termed the psychophysical function:

$$s_i = H(\phi_i) \qquad (1)$$

where s_i is the subjective scale value of stimulus i, which has a physical measurement of ϕ_i, and H is the psychophysical function.

Fechner concluded that H is the log function and Stevens argued that H is a power function. In the present theory, no assumption is made concerning the form of H, but the theory permits estimation of H and allows one to test assumptions about H.

Judgment functions. When subjects are instructed to make judgments of subjective value or relations among subjective values, responses are assumed to be a monotonic function of subjective values. It is important to maintain the distinction between responses and scale values. The judgment function can be written:

$$R_{i,k} = J_k(s_i) \tag{2}$$

where $R_{i,k}$ is the judgment of stimulus i in context k; s_i is the subjective value of stimulus i; and J_k is the judgment function for context k. The word "context" is used to identify the stimulus and response distributions and other experimental conditions affecting J. Note that Equation 2, even assuming that the J_k functions are strictly monotonic, does not permit unambiguous comparisons of responses between subjects or groups of subjects who experience different contexts. For example, if subject A says weight A is "heavy" and subject B says weight B is "light," Equation 2 does *not* imply that the subjective heaviness of A is greater than that of B, because the judgment functions may differ.

Scale convergence. It is explicitly assumed that the scale values, s_i, are the same for the different equations, providing that the stimuli, subjects, and experimental procedures (e.g., stimulus durations, etc.) are the same in the different situations.

Category Ratings and Magnitude Estimations

When subjects are instructed to judge the magnitude of subjective values using category rating or magnitude estimation, the judgment functions are assumed to differ, but the sensations remain constant:

$$M_{i,k} = J_k^*(s_i) \tag{3}$$

$$C_{i,p} = J_p(s_i) \tag{4}$$

where J_k^* and J_p are monotonic functions that depend on the stimulus and response distributions and other factors. Thus, the relationship between category rating and magnitude estimation is the composition of two functions, $M_{i,k} = J_k^*(J_p^{-1}(C_{i,p}))$. There exist contexts k and p for which J_k^* is approximately exponential and J_p is approximately linear. Under these conditions, magnitude estimations are an exponential function of category ratings. However, the relationship between these two can be systematically manipulated.

There is ample evidence that magnitude estimations and category ratings are typically nonlinearly related. Birnbaum (1978) noted conditions under which magnitude estimations are approximately an exponential function of category ratings: space the seven or more stimuli equally in log of physical values; use the middle stimulus (on the log scale) as the standard; present examples for magnitude estimation that are geometrically spaced and symmetric about the "ratio" of 1 (e.g., 1/8, 1/4, 1/2, 1, 2, 4, 8); and use seven to nine categories in the rating scale.

There is also ample evidence that both category ratings and magnitude estimations vary as a function of contextual effects due to factors such as stimulus spacing, relative frequency of presentation, choice of standard, and examples (Poulton, 1979). Therefore, the relationship between ratings and magnitude estimations can also be changed. Mellers and Birnbaum (1982) demonstrated contextual effects in both category rating and magnitude estimation due to stimulus spacing. Magnitude estimations were also found sensitive to the incidental examples used to illustrate the task. When the instructions cited an example of 3, most subjects called the largest physical ratio "3." However, when the instructions also mentioned "if it seems nine times as great, say '9'," then the same physical ration received a modal judgment of "9." Mellers, Davis and Birnbaum (1984) obtained similar results: subjects are strongly affected by the example "ratios," as if the examples are category labels.

"Ratios" and "Differences"

When subjects are instructed to judge either "ratios" or "differences" of stimuli that are inherently interval positions on a subjective scale, it is postulated that subjects use subtraction for either operation. Although continua such as sound pressure and weight have well-defined zero points on the physical continuum, the subjective scales appear to behave as interval scales (it does take effort to "lift" a physical weight of zero). The subtractive, one-operation theory can be written:

$$R_{i,j} = J^*(s_j - t_i) \tag{5}$$

$$D_{i,j} = J(s_j - t_i) \tag{6}$$

where $R_{i,j}$ and $D_{i,j}$ are the judgments of "ratios" and "differences," J^* and J are the judgment functions produced by context and experimental procedures, s_j and t_i are the subjective scale values of the stimuli.

The theory that subjects use only one operation for judging "ratios" and "differences" (Equations 5 and 6) implies that the two judgments will be monotonically related. However, the theory that subjects actually use two operations as instructed on the same scale implies that the two judgments would not be monotonically related, but instead they would show a particular pattern relating the rank orders. Birnbaum (1980) reanalyzed the data from nine studies in which "ratios" and "differences" were obtained for the same stimuli in factorial designs, in order to compare the two theories. These studies were consistent with the theory of one operation. Birnbaum (1982) reviewed five additional studies consistent with the same conclusions, and Mellers, Davis, and Birnbaum (1984) added three more. These studies employed a variety of continua including the loudness of tones, pitch of tones, likeableness of persons described by adjectives, darkness of Munsell gray papers, darkness of dot patterns, easterliness and westerliness of U.S. cities, and heaviness of lifted weights.

In most of these studies, the J^* and J functions are well-approximated by the exponetial function for "ratios" and the linear function for "differences." Under these conditions, data for both tasks appear to fit the model of the instructions, but log "ratio" judgments are approximately a linear function of "differences." Despite the apparent fit of the models when considered individually, the relationship between the two sets of data, together with the assumption of scale convergence, leads to the conclusion that at least one model should be rejected.

"Reverse" or "Inverse" Attributes

When instructions specify either "inverse" or "reverse" attributes, the theory postulates that the judge reverses the direction of the difference. Thus, judgments of "ratios" or "differences" of loudness and softness are compared by Equations 5 and 6, substituting $t_i - s_j$ for $s_j - t_i$. The theory that J^* and J are exponential and linear implies that magnitude estimations of inverse attributes should be reciprocally related and that category ratings of reverse attributes should be linearly related $[\exp(s_j - t_i) = 1/\exp(t_i - s_j)]$.

Birnbaum and Mellers (1978) asked subjects to judge "ratios" and "differences" of easterliness and westerliness of U.S. cities. For example, subjects say that Philadelphia is "eight times as easterly" and "one eighth as westerly" as San Francisco. Birnbaum and Mellers found that "differences" of easterliness and westerliness were linearly related with a negative slope. "Ratios" of easterliness and westerliness were reciprocally related. The ratio model leads to two mental maps that are nonlinearly related to each other. The subtractive model could account for all four matrices of data using a single map that resembled the actual map.

Comparison of Stimulus Relations

Because a difference or a distance has a well-defined zero point when the stimuli are locations on an interval scale, it is theorized that subjects can use two operations for "ratios of differences" (*RD*) and "differences of differences" (*DD*). When instructed to judge either "ratios of ratios" (*RR*) or "differences of ratios" (*DR*) they evaluate differences of differences. These premises can be written as follows:

$$DD_{i,j,k,l} = J_{DD}[(s_j - s_i) - (s_k - s_l)] \qquad (7)$$

$$RD_{i,j,k,l} = J_{RD}[(s_j - s_i)/(s_k - s_l)] \qquad (8)$$

$$DR_{i,j,k,l} = J_{DR}[(s_j - s_i) - (s_k - s_l)] \qquad (9)$$

$$RR_{i,j,k,l} = J_{RR}[(s_j - s_i) - (s_k - s_l)] \qquad (10)$$

where the J functions are strictly monotonic.

Three experiments involving comparisons of stimulus relationships (e.g., ratios of differences) were reviewed by Birnbaum (1978; 1982), all yielding compatible results. Judgments of "ratios of differences" fit the ratio of differences model (Equation 8), showing that subjects do posess the "mental machinery" to compute ratios. Scales derived from this model agree with the subtractive interpretaion of simple "ratios" and "differences." However, when subjects are asked to judge "differences of differences", "differences of ratios" or "ratios of ratios", the difference of differences model describes the data, using the same scale.

A fourth experiment by Birnbaum, C. Anderson and Hynan (in press) illustrates the subtractive theory. Subjects were asked to judge "ratios of distances" and "differences of distances" between pairs of U.S. cities. For example, what is the ratio of the distance from San Francisco to Philadelphia relative to the distance from San Francisco to Salt Lake City? These two judgments were not monotonically related, but they showed instead the proper rank orders dictated by the theory that subjects can compare two distances by either a ratio or a subtractive operation. The scale of city locations derived from these two operations agreed with the subtractive interpretation of "ratios" and "differences" of easterliness and westerliness.

Contextual Effects

There are several possible loci for contextual effects due to variation of the stimulus and response distributions. Evidence so far is consistent with the following:
1. In category rating or magnitude estimation or in judgments of "ratios", "differences", and "total intensities" of stimuli from the same dimension, contextual effects can be attributed to the judgment function.
2. When a subject responds on one dimension to judge subjective value on another, the range–frequency value of the response matches the range–frequency value of the stimulus. Category ratings and magnitude estimations are special cases of cross–dimensional "matching." Judgments and "matching" responses can be treated by extensions of range–frequency theory. A "match" occurs when the range–frequency values are equal for the two dimensions.
3. Range–frequency values are defined, according to Parducci's theory as follows:

$$RF_{i,k} = \frac{a_k(s_i - s_{0k})}{(s_{mk} - s_{0k})} + b_k F_k(s_i) \qquad (11)$$

where $RF_{i,k}$ is the range–frequency value of stimulus i with subjective value s_i in context k; $F_k(s_i)$ is the cumulative density of stimuli less than or equal to s_i in context k; s_{0k} and s_{mk} are the minimal and maximal subjective values in context k; a_k and b_k are linear constants that depend on experimental conditions (e.g., Parducci, 1983).

Mellers and Birnbaum (1982; 1983) have found evidence that contextual effects due to stimulus spacing can be localized in the judgment functions, when the task involves comparison or combination of stimuli from the same dimension. However, cross-dimensional comparisons and combinations appear to involve a contextual transformation prior to comparison or combination.

Additional Phenomena

The study of scale convergence entails the investigation of a variety of empirical relationships involving the same stimuli. There are a number of phenomena that have not yet been linked in the same experiment to "ratio" and "difference" judgments, which (by comparison across different experiments) appear to yield psychological scales that differ from those that arise from the subtractive model. Stimulus discrimination, total magnitude judgments, response variability, and other phenomena are reviewed by Birnbaum (1982), who theorized that it may be possible to revise the theories of these phenomena to yield a consistent representation.

Two phenomena that have been studied in more detail are psychophysical "averaging" and the size–weight illusion (Birnbaum & Veit, 1974a, 1974b), neither of which appears to obey the parallelism-prediction of a class of averaging models. Instead, these phenomena appear to be consistent with a configural-weight averaging model that can be written for two stimuli as follows:

$$A_{i,j} = J_A(as_i + (1-a)t_j + w|s_i - t_j|) \qquad (12)$$

where $A_{i,j}$ is the judged "average"; a is a weight; and w is the configural weight. Luce and Narens (1985) have recently shown that the dual bilinear representation (as in Equation 12) leads to interval scales, and in fact, is the most general representation of its class that does so. Birnbaum and Veit (1974a) found that Equation 12 can account for the nonparallelism of "averaging" judgments and also yields scales that agree with the subtractive representation of "ratios" and "differences" of heaviness.

Fechner's Law and Subtractive Theory

The present theory is based on different foundations, but it has three points of agreement with Fechner's: First, it assumes that for the most continua, stimuli are compared by subtraction. Fechner assumed that discrimination of stimuli was mediated by subjective differences, and the present results favoring a subtractive representation over a ratio representation provide an interesting point of support for Fechner.

Second, the subtractive theory leads to the conclusion that under certain conditions, magnitude estimations are an exponential function of subjective value. If Fechner's law is correct, and if magnitude estimations are an exponential function of subjective value, then magnitude estimations will be a power function of physical value. Therefore, magnitude estimations (obtained under these conditions) that fit the power law can be interpreted as consistent with Fechner's law.

Third, for some continua the subtractive theory leads to psychophysical scales that agree with Fechner's law. It has been found that for pitch (Elmasian & Birnbaum, 1984) and darkness of dot patterns (Birnbaum, 1980, 1982; Mellers & Birnbaum, 1984), Fechner's law provides a reasonable approximation to the psychophysical function that is derived from the subtractive representation of "ratios" and "differences".

However, for loudness (Birnbaum & Elmasian, 1977) and for heaviness of lifted weight (Mellers et al., 1984), it has been found that the subtractive model yields scales that do not agree with Fechner's logarithmic law. The pattern of deviation was the same for both of these continua: as the same physical ratio is moved up the scale, the judged "ratio" and the judged "difference" between the two stimuli becomes more extreme. These same data also show that the ratio model and the power law are incompatible for these two continua. According to the logarithmic law, the subjective difference should be constant as long as the physical ratio is the same; according to the power law, the ratio should have remained constant.

Summary

Subjective magnitudes of dimensions such as loudness or heaviness are theorized to be like positions of cities on a cognitive map. On such an interval scale, differences are meaningful but ratios are not. Thus when the subjects are asked to judge "ratios" of sensation, they are theorized to actually compute differences. These differences are then mapped into numerical responses by the examples used to define the magnitude estimation task. These examples may define an exponential transformation, but the exact nature of the judgmental transformation depends lawfully on the stimulus distribution, the examples used, and other experimental procedures. But on an interval scale, intervals have a meaningful zeropoint, and subjects can judge "ratios of differences" and "differences of differences" using the appropriate operations on the same scale of value. By using the same scales to interlock different phenomena, this approach shows promise of putting old controversies to rest, encouraging us to dream once again Fechner's dream of a coherent science of psychophysics.

Correspondence should be addressed to Michael H. Birnbaum, Department of Psychology, California State University, Fullerton, CA 92634, U.S.A.

References

Birnbaum, M.H. (1978). Ratios and differences in psychological measurement. In N.J. Castellan & F. Restle (Eds.), *Cognitive Theory* (Vol. III). Hillsdale, NJ: Erlbaum.

Birnbaum, M.H. (1980). Comparison of two theories of "ratio" and "difference" judgments. *Journal of Experimental Psychology: General, 109*, 304−319.

Birnbaum, M.H. (1982). Controversies in psychological measurement. In B. Wegener (Ed.), *Social attitudes and psychophysical measurement.* Hillsdale, NJ: Erlbaum.

Birnbaum, M.H., Anderson, C.A., & Hynan, L.G. (in press). Two operations for "ratios" and "differences" of distances on the mental map. *Journal of Experimental Psychology: Human Perception and Performance.*

Birnbaum, M.H., & Elmasian, R. (1977). Loudness "ratios" and "differences" involve the same psychophysical operation. *Perception & Psychophysics, 22*, 383−391.

Birnbaum, M.H., & Mellers, B.A. (1978). Measurement and the mental map. *Perception & Psychophysics, 23*, 403−408.

Birnbaum, M.H., & Veit, C.T. (1974a). Scale convergence as a criterion for rescaling: Information integration with difference, ratio, and averaging tasks. *Perception & Psychophysics, 15*, 7−15.

Birnbaum, M.H., & Veit, C.T. (1974b). Scale-free tests of an additive model for the size-weight illusion. *Perception & Psychophysics, 16*, 276−282.

Elmasian, R., & Birnbaum, M.H. (1984). A harmonious note on pitch: Scales of pitch derived from subtractive model of comparison agree with the musical scale. *Perception & Psychophysics, 36*, 531−537.

Luce, R.D., & Narens, L. (1985). Classification of concatenation measurement structures according to scale type. *Journal of Mathematical Psychology, 29*, 1−72.

Krantz, D.H., Luce, R.D., Suppes, P., & Tversky, A. (1971). *Foundations of measurement.* New York: Academic Press.

Mellers, B.A., & Birnbaum, M.H. (1982). Loci of contextual effects in judgment. *Journal of Experimental Psychology: Human Perception and Performance, 8*, 582−600.

Mellers, B.A., & Birnbaum, M.H. (1983). Contextual effects in social judgment. *Journal of Experimental Social Psychology, 19*, 157−171.

Mellers, B.A., Davis, D., & Birnbaum, M.H. (1984). Weight of evidence supports one operation for "ratios" and "differences" of heaviness. *Journal of Experimental Psychology: Human Perception and Performance, 10*, 216−230.

Parducci, A. (1983). Category ratings and the relational character of judgment. In H.G. Geissler & V. Sarris (Eds.), *Modern issues in perception.* Berlin: VEB Deutscher Verlag der Wissenschaften.

Poulton, E.C. (1979). Models for biases in judging sensory magnitude. *Psychological Bulletin, 86*, 777−803.

Stevens, S.S. (1961). To honor Fechner and repeal his law. *Science, 133*, 80−86.

Thurstone, L.L. (1959). *The measurement of values.* Chicago: University of Chicago Press.

Torgerson, W.S. (1961). Distances and ratios in psychological scaling. *Acta Psychologica, 19*, 201−205.

Psychophysical Explorations of Mental Structures
Edited by H.-G. Geissler
in collaboration with M.H. Müller and W. Prinz
© 1990 by Hogrefe & Huber Publishers

Chapter 4

The Difference between Stimulus and Background: An Explanation of the Psychophysical Function Based on Partition Scales?

Marc Brysbaert and Géry d'Ydewalle
Department of Psychology
University of Leuven/Louvain
Leuven/Louvain, Belgium

One of the oldest problems in experimental psychology is that of relating the magnitude of a sensation to its physical originator. There are two opposing opinions about the relationship: Some state that it has to be a logarithmic relation (they are usually referred to as the Fechnerians); others state that it has to be a power function (the supporters of Stevens).

The adherents of the power funciton in the field of brightness perception are confronted with at least two problems: (a) Stevens has never properly explained why the exponent of the power function is lower when the experimenter uses partition scales than when ratio scales are used; and (b) there is a huge difference between the exponent of the power function for bright targets in the dark and for gray targets viewed against a relatively bright background (Stevens, 1975, p. 15; Stevens & Galanter, 1957, p. 398; Torgerson, 1960, p. 27). This has led Stevens to distinguish between brightness and lightness. Though these problems may be acceptable, they raise serious doubts about the validity of Stevens' approach as a general psychophysical law.

Partition scales are constituted when observers are asked to partition a segment of a continuum into equal intervals (e.g., when they indicate the bisection of two stimuli or when they classify the stimuli into a fixed number of categories). Ratio scales, on the other hand, are obtained when numbers are assigned to the stimuli in such a way that the numbers preserve information about ratios. Stevens holds that partition scales are inferior to ratio scales beause they are susceptible of a systematic error (Stevens & Galanter, 1957). He claims that the sensitivity is unequal over the scale, and, therefore, that a difference between two stimuli that is large and obvious near the low end of the range becomes much less impressive in the upper part of the scale. Although Stevens' objection against partition scales may be appropriate when a person has to classify the stimuli into a considerable number of categories, it is difficult to see why the bias has a substantial influence if a person is asked to make a distinction between only two differences, as is the case in Plateau's (1872) bisection paradigm. Furthermore, the bias does not seem to be applicable for all stimulus continua, which leads Stevens (1975, p. 168–171) to distinguish between prothetic and metathetic continua. Again, this reasoning may be acceptable, but it is another exception to the theory, thereby further diminishing its explanatory power. Helson (1964, p. 173–175), among others, pointed to some other weaknesses in the distinction.

The difference between the exponent of the power function for brightness and lightness is another problem of Stevens' theory. The exponent for brightness has repeatedly been shown to be about .33 (Stevens, 1975, p. 15), whereas the exponent for lightness is about 1.2 (Stevens & Galanter, 1957, p. 398; Torgerson, 1960, p. 27). The difference between the two experimental settings, however, consisted not only of a difference between luminous spots and gray paper, as Stevens and Galanter (1957) claimed, but also of a difference between a dark room and a surface of approximately 18 cd/m^2 against stimuli of at most 32 cd/m^2. The experiments below give evidence that the difference between the two backgrounds probably is the major reason for the different exponents.

A Function Describing the Relation between Difference Limen and Background Luminance

Our greatest doubts about Stevens' explanation of the psychophysical function found by the use of partition scales came about after the discovery that the bisection of two brightnesses changes as a function of the background luminance (Brysbaert & d'Ydewalle, 1984; Graham & Helson, cited in Helson, 1964, p. 178). Even Delboeuf (1873, p. 50) mentioned this possibility in a footnote, but he did not work it out in detail.

Both Graham and Helson (Helson, 1964) and Brysbaert and d'Ydewalle (1984) reported that the bisection of two brightnesses increases as the luminance of the background increases. This shifting of the average due to the background luminace not only indicates that the background does have an influence on the brightness perception of a stimulus, but also that the relation cannot be conceived of as a simple linear transformation because any addition or muliplication by a constant leaves the bisection undisturbed. As the data of both Graham and Helson (Helson, 1964), and Brysbaert and d'Ydewalle (1984) dealt with only one pair of standard brightnesses, it was impossible to get a more precise idea of the relations between the stimuli and the background.

First, we thought to start with a replication of Brysbaert and d'Ydewalle (1984) and to consider a larger number of standard stimuli, but a closer look at the paradigm revealed a difficulty that seriously limited its use in the search for a psychophysical function. The equation $R_b = (R_1 + R_2)/2$ proves to be rather uninformative about the nature of R_b, R_1, and R_2, because every addition or multiplication by a constant is ruled out and, because of the addition in the right half of the formula, arithmetical calculations become quite difficult if R_b, R_1, and R_2 are power functions of several additional components. Although there are iterative procedures (see, e.g., Weiss, 1975) that might be adapted for this problem, they all require an *a priori* concept of the variables. Therefore, we decided to take another starting-point and to keep the bisection procedure as a validation paradigm.

If a black stimulus has a greater influence against a black background than against a white, as can be inferred from the shifting of the bisection value, then one might expect its difference limen (*DL*) to be smaller against a black background than against a white. The opposite should be true for stimuli against a white background. Since Weber (1846) and Fechner (1860), many investigations have concerned the determination of the *DL* because it had become apparent that the ratio *DL/S*, the Weber Fraction, is not constant over the entire stimulus range, as Weber and Fechner originally claimed (see, e.g., Aubert, 1865; Koenig & Brodhun, 1889). It starts from rather high around the absolute threshold, decreases until a minimum is reached at a stimulus intensity of about 20 millilamberts (6 cd/m^2), and then rises again. The high *DL*s at very low intensities will not be considered here, because these intensities are normally not used as standards in a bisection paradigm. The rise of the *DL* at intensities above 20 millilamberts, however, is more relevant, expecially if it is compared with the data of Cobb (1916) and Heinemann (1961), who showed that the Weber fraction is lowest when the intensity of stimulus and background are approximately equal and that it grows for stimuli both above and below this intensity. This is exactly what was to be expected from Brysbaert and d'Ydewalle (1984). Therefore, we decided to study the relation between *DL* and background luminance in order to get a better idea about the relation between stimulus and background intensity.

Method

Subjects and Apparatus. There were two subjects: one male and one female. Both wore glasses for myopia. The equipment consisted of two rotating disks with a diameter of 20 cm before a background of cardboard. The luminance of the disks could be changed by varying the white and black sectors; the luminance of the background was varied by using a white or black cardboard.

The equipment was uniformly illuminated. The brightness of the disks and backgrounds was recorded with a luminance meter (Minolta NT-1). The luminance of the black background was 11.4 cd/m², that of the white background 160 cd/m², and that of the standard disks between 12.4 and 155.6 cd/m².

Procedure. The subjects sat behind a reduction screen (for details, see Brysbaert & d'Ydewalle, 1984), which reduced the visual field to the stimuli and the background. The reduction screen stood 140 cm away from the stimulus screen, which gave the stimuli a diameter of 8.2 degrees. The distance between the stimuli was also 8.2 degrees. The complete visual field had a width of 41 degrees and a height of 20.5 degrees.

The procedure used was the Up-and-Down Transformed Response (UDTR) rule of Wetherill and Levitt (1965), forced choice, with the percentage point estimated .84. The steps were .421 cd/m² (= one degree) or .210 cd/m² if the difference was small. The procedure continued until three peaks and valleys were obtained after the initial minimum. While the experimenter was adjusting the standard and the variable stimulus randomly to the left and the right, a screen of the same luminance as the background was placed between the apparatus and the subject.

The experiment was run in daily sessions of about five hours each. Before each session, the subjects first adapted for ten minutes and then went through a few warming up trials. The subjects exchanged subject and experimenter roles every hour. If the difference was small, the subjects took an average of about one minute before deciding.

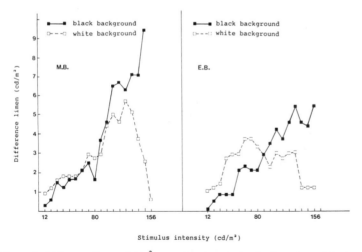

Figure 1. Difference limens (cd/m²) as a function of stimulus intensity and background luminance. Experiment 1.

Results and Discussion

Figure 1 shows the results for each subject. Although there are some differences between the two subjects, the main results are the same: (a) the *DL* for dark stimuli is lower against a black background; (b) the *DL* for the light stimuli is lower against a white background; and (c) the reversal point lies near the middle of the continuum, between 80 and 90 cd/m^2. The average between the luminance of the two backgrounds is about 86 cd/m^2. This clearly illustrates the influence of the background upon the *DL*.

In order to get a more accurate picture of the background influence, multiple regression analyses were calculated. The analyses contained two independent variables, a stimulus– and a background–variable, and one dependent variable, the average *DL* of the two subjects. The background variable (*BV*) was defined as the absolute difference between the intensity of the stimulus (*S*) and the luminance of the background (λ). The stimulus–variable (*SV*) was the stimulus intensity. Three different analyses were performed: (a) Between the *DL* and the *SV*, and the *BV*; (b) between the *DL* and the natural logarithm of the *SV*, and the *BV*; and (c) between the natural logarithm of the *DL* and the natural logarithm of the *SV*, and the *BV*. Because there was a linear relationship between the two independent variables in the first analysis, the analysis had to be carried out with the Weber Ratio as the dependent variable and the absolute difference between the stimulus and the background as the only independent variable. Table 1 shows the results of the analyses and the percentage of variance explained by them.

Table 1. Regression analyses of the difference limen as a function of the stimulus intensity and the difference between stimulus and background. Experiment 1.

Analysis		% variance explained
black background		
1) *DL/S*	$= .03 + .00016(S - λ)$	56%
2) *DL*	$= -14.4 + 5.94 \ln(S) - 1.22 \ln(S - λ)$	88%
3) ln(*DL*)	$= -4.2 + 1.02 \ln(S) + .19 \ln(S - λ)$	96%
white background		
1) *DL/S*	$= .01 + .00038 (λ - S)$	87%
2) *DL*	$= -11.0 + 2.05 \ln(S) + 1.23 \ln(λ - S)$	75%
3) ln(*DL*)	$= -5.8 + .98 \ln(S) + .62 \ln(λ - S)$	89%

Most of the variance is explained when the logarithm of the *DL* is predicted from the logarithm of the stimulus– and the background–variable. This means the *DL* varies according to an power function of the stimulus and the difference between stimulus and background. The exponents 1.02 and .98 do not differ significantly from unity, so that the equations may be written as

$$DL = kS(S - λ)^{.19} \qquad (1)$$

for the black background, and

$$DL = kS(\lambda - S)^{.62} \tag{2}$$

for the white background.

Equations (1) and (2) only differ with respect to the exponent of the background variable. The influence of the background is much larger for the white than for the black background. This agrees with Cobb (1916) and Heinemann (1961). The exponents also resemble Stevens' exponents for brightness and lightness (Stevens, 1975, p. 15), if the latter are corrected for the number scale being related to the sensation continuum by a power function with exponent .40 (Attneave, 1962; Wagenaar, 1975). For Stevens' exponents, we yield .13 for brightness and .48 for lightness.

The basic difference between a black and a white background is that a black background increases the distance between the stimulus and the background as the stimulus becomes brighter, whereas a white background decreases it. Accordingly, Stevens' transformed exponents can be thought of as

$$.13\ln(S) = n_1\ln(S) - n_2(S - \lambda) \tag{3}$$

and

$$.48\ln(S) = n_1(S) + n_2\ln(\lambda - S) \ . \tag{4}$$

Equations (3) and (4) have two unknown variables, n_1 and n_2. In $|S - \lambda|$ can be rewritten as a function of $\ln(S)$. Brightness experiments were always run in a dark room. Thus, the value of the background luminance, λ, in Equation (3) may be taken to be zero, which means that $\ln(S - \lambda)$ can be replaced by $\ln(S)$. The relationship between $\ln(\lambda - S)$ and $\ln(S)$ in Equation (4) was estimated by a regression analysis of Stevens and Galanter (1957). Because there were some difficulties with stimulus intensities around and above background luminance, only intensities below the background luminance were considered. This gave the following result:

$$\ln(\lambda - S) = 3.16 - .54\ln(S) \ . \tag{5}$$

Equations (3) and (4) can then be written as:

$$.13\ln(S) = n_1\ln(S) - n_2\ln(S) \tag{6}$$

and

$$.48\ln(S) = n_1\ln(S) + 1.85n_2\ln(S) \ . \tag{7}$$

From Equations (6) and (7), it follows, that the values of n_1 and n_2 are .253 and .123. Identical analyses of the data of the present experiment gave n_1 and n_2 the value of .261 and .131, respectively. Both estimations lie around $n_1 = .26$, and $n_2 = .13$, which are theoretically more interesting values because they agree with Stevens' transformed exponent and imply that twice as much weight is given to the stimulus than to the difference between the stimulus and the background. Therefore, we use these values to give us the following psychophysical function:

$$R = \frac{S^{.26}}{|S - \lambda|^{.13}} \ . \tag{8}$$

There is an interesting analogy between Figure 1 and the function derived from Equation (8): When the function flattens, the accompanying *DL* in Figure 1 rises. Inversely, when the function becomes steeper, the *DL* decreases. This, of course, immediately recalls Ekman's (1959) statement that the *DL* is not proportional to the physical intensity of the stimulus, as Weber claimed, but to the magnitude of the sensation caused by the stimulus. Stevens (1975, p. 234–235) called this Ekman's Law and Teghtsoonian (1971) demonstrated its applicability over a wide range of sensation continua. Thus, it is quite probable that Ekman's Law gives a better account of the relationship between the *DL* and the stimulus value than the Weber ratio.

In order to see whether the data of Experiment 1 really indicate that *DLs* are just noticeable sensory differences of sensation magnitudes, it is necessary to establish the relationship between the *DLs* and the just noticeable sensory differences. This is done by means of the following equation:

$$\Delta R = \frac{dR}{dS} \Delta S ,\qquad\qquad (9)$$

in which ΔR refers to the just noticeable difference on the sensory continuum, dR and dS to the first derivatives of the sensation and the stimulus intensity, and ΔS to the *DL* that can be measured. Applying Equation (9) to Equation (8), we get:

$$\Delta R = \frac{.26|S-\lambda|^{.13}S^{-.74} \pm .13S^{26}|S-\lambda|^{-.87}}{|S-\lambda|^{.26}} \Delta S .\qquad (10)$$

Figure 2 gives the relationship between the just noticeable difference on the sensory continuum, ΔR, and the magnitude of the sensation caused by the stimulus, *R*.

Three findings are noteworthy. First, the ΔR against the white background increases linearly with the magnitude of *R*, while this was not the case for the *DLs* in Figure 1. Second, the slope of the function against the white background does not differ significantly from the slope of the function against the black background. And, third, both slopes are about .0325, which is not significantly different from Tehgtsoonian's (1971) estimate of $\Delta R/R$ at .03. Both functions account for about 84% of the variance.

There are, however, some serious problems with regard to Figure 2 and Equation (8). First, if the background is not fainter or brighter than all the stimuli but has a value somewhere in-between, two things happen: (a) Equation (8) goes to infinity as the brightness of the stimulus approaches the brightness of the background; and (b) when the stimulus intensity grows above background luminance, Equation (8) gives an initial drop before the normal concave power function is reached. This drop is due to the denominator of Equation (8) initially growing much more rapidly than the numerator when the stimulus intensity exceeds the background intensity. Thus, ΔR and *R* of the stimulus of 12.4 cd/m^2 could not be entered into the regression against the black background (Figure 2a). The value of *R* was 1.92 and that of ΔR −.041, thus quite different from the rest of the data. Additionally, the ΔR of the stimulus of 20.8

cd/m^2 in Figure 2a is too low because of the initial drop. The second major problem with regard to Figure 2 and Equation (8) is, that we should have found a slope of .014 rather than Teghtsoonian's slope of .03 because Teghtsoonian (1971) used the brightness exponent .33, which, as Attneave (1962) has shown, is too high.

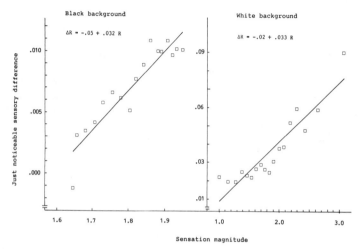

Figure 2. Just noticeable sensory differences as a function of sensation magnitude and background luminance. Experiment 1, Equation (8).

The simplest function which we have found that meets both problems, is:

$$R = \frac{2S^{.26} + \lambda^{.26} - (\lambda - S)^{.26}}{S^{.13} + \lambda^{.13} + (\lambda - S)^{.13}} \quad \text{for } S < \lambda \qquad (11.1)$$

$$R = \frac{2S^{.26} + \lambda^{.26} + (S - \lambda)^{.26}}{S^{.13} + \lambda^{.13} + (S - \lambda)^{.13}} \quad \text{for } S > \lambda . \qquad (11.2)$$

The fit of Equation (11) to the empirical data is given in Figure 3. The slopes of the equations do not differ significantly from the predicted value of .014. Equation (11) explains 72% of the variance against a black background and 65% against a white background.

Because the model is underdetermined, Equation (11) is not the only possible solution. The equation also requires a restriction that does not emerge in this experiment: The variables S and $|S-\lambda|$ must have a lower limit greater than zero, because the transition from zero to one is too abrupt and distorts the continuity of the function.

When the background approaches zero, the equation can be simplified and agrees with Stevens' transformed function of brightness: $R = kS^{.13}$. In addition, when the stimulus intensity equals the background intensity, the function can be simplified and approaches: $R = kS^{13}$. Another interesting characteristic of Equation (11) is that the sensation of stimuli is only slightly influenced by changes in background luminance as long as the stimulus intensities lie above the background intensity. This agrees with experiments on simultaneous contrast (see, e.g., Heinemann, 1955) and brightness constancy (see, e.g., Freeman, 1967).

Application of the Function to Bisection of Two Brightnesses

Experiment 2 concerned the bisection of two brightnesses. As stated at the beginning of the paper, this is one of the main problems in Stevens' theory, because the exponents obtained with its use always prove to be much lower than those obtained with magnitude estimation. Part of the paradox is solved by the number continuum being related to the sensory continuum by a power function with exponent less than one (Attneave, 1962), which implies that the exponents obtained with magnitude estimations are overestimated. However, this does not explain why the bisection varies as a function of the background luminance (Brysbaert & d'Ydewalle, 1984; Helson, 1964). Therefore, we set up a new experiment to see if Equations (8) and (11) give better a fitting of the data.

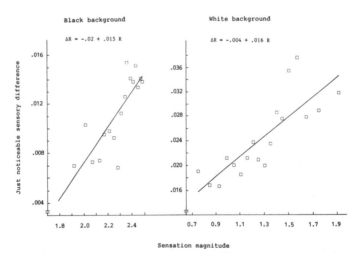

Figure 3. Just noticeable sensory differences as a function of sensation magnitude and background luminance. Experiment 1, Equation (11).

Method

Subjects and Apparatus. The same subjects were used in Experiment 2. The equipment consisted of three rotating disks with a diameter of 20 cm in front of a piece of cardboard. The luminance of the disks could be changed by varying the black and white sectors. The luminance of the background was varied by using either a white or a black cardboard. Because the background was smaller than the one in Experiment 1, the subjects sat at a distance of 90 cm in order to reduce the visual field to the cardboard background. This implied a different illumination that was inferior to the one of Experiment 1. The greatest difficulty was that the right side of the apparatus was more illuminated than the left side. Because it was impossible to eliminate this factor, the experiment was carried out as such. The brightness of disks and backgrounds was recorded with a luminance-meter (Minolta NT-1). The luminance of the black background was 17 cd/m^2 on the left, 18.5 cd/m^2 in the middle, and 22 cd/m^2 on the right. The luminance of the white background was 285 cd/m^2 on the left, 316 cd/m^2 in the middle, and 363 cd/m^2 on the right. The left standard disk varied between a brightness of 23 cd/m^2 and 257 cd/m^2; the right one between 27 cd/m^2 and 323 cd/m^2.

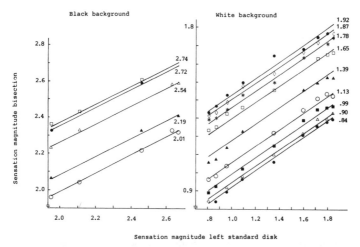

Figure 4. Bisection of two standard brightnesses (left standard: abscissa; right standard: next to predicted values). Experiment 2, Equation (11).

Procedure. The subjects sat behind a reduction screen (for details, see above), that reduced the visual field to the stimuli and the background. The stimuli had a diameter of 12.9 degrees. Between the stimuli, there was a distance of 3.2 degrees. The complete visual field was 51.6×25.8 degrees.

The variable stimulus was the disk in the middle, and the procedure used was the method of limits. There were two ascending and two descending series.

The step size was one degree, or half a degree when the difference between the two standards was small. As in Experiment 1, all trials with the white background were run first and those with the black background afterwards. Because of shortage of time, not all the combinations with the white background were run with the black background. While the experimenter was adjusting the standard and the variable stimuli, a screen of the same luminance as the background was placed between the apparatus and the subject.

The experiment was run in daily sessions of about five hours each. Before each session, the subjects first adapted for ten minutes and then ran a few warming up trials. The subjects interchanged the roles of subject and experimenter each hour. On the average, the subjects looked more than one minute at the stimuli before deciding, especially when the variable stimulus approached the average between the outer two.

Results and Discussion

The values of the ascending and descending series were combined to obtain an estimate of the bisection. The results of both subjects were averaged and modified according to Equations (8) or (11). The brightness of the disks was compared with the brightness of the background in the immediate vicinity. The modified values were entered into a multiple regression analysis with the data of the middle disk as the dependent variable and the data of the outer disks as the independent variables. Table 2 gives the results of these analyses.

Table 2. Regression analyses of the bisection value (S_b) as a function of the left (S_1) and right (S_2) standard disk. Experiment 2.

Analysis	% variance explained
formula (8)	
black: $S_b = -.33 + .56\ S_1 + .59\ S_2$	75%
white: $S_b = \ \ \ .10 + .45\ S_1 + .46\ S_2$	99%
formula (11)	
black: $S_b = -.05 + .50\ S_1 + .52\ S_2$	99%
white: $S_b = \ \ \ .06 + .46\ S_1 + .47\ S_2$	99%

Equation (11) describes the results against a black background more accurately than Equation (8). There is no great difference for the results against a white background. Figure 4 shows the actual data compared to the predicted lines based on Equation (11).

The fit of Equation (11) to the actual data is slightly overestimated because the values of the standard disks lay quite far from each other. At first, we thought that the coefficients of the standard disks against the white background, which are significantly different from 0.50, would give us an indication of how Equation (11) could be improved. However, further analyses suggested that they simply result from the heterogeneous illumination.

Summary and Conclusion

In this paper, a function has been described that takes into account several difficulties of present psychophysics in brightness perception. It is argued that the sensation of a stimulus is determined not only by the intensity of the stimulus itself, as Stevens and Fechner stated, but also by the difference between the stimulus and its surrounding.

The function takes into account: (a) the results obtained both with partition scales and with magnitude estimations; (b) the increase of the bisection value if the background luminance is increased; (c) the difference between Stevens' exponents for brightness and lightness; and (d) the differences in the limens obtained against a white and a black background.

The influence of the background variable has already been introduced into psychophysics (Helson, 1964; Jameson & Hurvich, 1964; Wallach, 1948). The major difference between these approaches and ours, however, is that the background no longer merely causes a linear transformation of the psychophysical function, i.e., a division or subtraction by a constant, but is itself part of a power function. As mentioned before, it is impossible to explain the shift of the bisection value between two brightnesses as a function of the background luminance, if the influence of background luminance is restricted to a linear transformation of the original psychophysical function. It would be interesting to see whether the equation presented here could predict other phenomena in brightness perception as well.

Correspondence should be addressed to Marc Brysbaert, Department of Psychology, University of Leuven, B—3000 Leuven, Belgium.

References

Attneave, F. (1962). Perception and related areas. In S. Koch (Ed.), *Psychology: A study of a science* (Vol. IV, pp. 619—659). New York: McGraw-Hill.

Aubert, H. (1865). *Physiologie der Netzhaut*. Breslau: E. Morgenstern.

Brysbaert, M., & d'Ydewalle, G. (1984). Het subjectieve midden tussen twee helderheden bij een verschillende achtergrondskleur. *Psychologica Belgica, 24*, 115—127.

Cobb, P.W. (1916). The effect on foveal vision of bright surroundings. Part IV. *Journal of Experimental Psychology, 1*, 540—566.

Delboeuf, J.R.L. (1873). *Etude psychologique: Recherches théoriques et expérimentales sur la mésure des sensations et spécialement des sensations de lumière et de fatigue*. Bruxelles: Hayez.

Ekman, G. (1959). Weber's law and related functions. *Journal of Psychology, 47*, 343—352.

Fechner, G.T. (1860). *Elemente der Psychophysik*. Leipzig: Breitkopf und Härtel.

Freeman, R.B. (1967). Contrast interpretation of brightness constancy. *Psychological Bulletin, 67*, 165—187.

Heinemann, E.G. (1955). Simultaneous brightness induction as a function of inducing- and test-field luminances. *Journal of Experimental Psychology, 50*, 89—96.

Heinemann, E.G. (1961). The relation of apparent brightness to the threshold for differences in luminance. *Journal of Experimental Psychology, 61,* 389−399.

Helson, H. (1964). *Adaptation-level theory.* New York: Harper.

Jameson, D., & Hurvich, L.M. (1964). Theory of brightness and color contrast in human vision. *Vision Research, 4,* 310−324.

Koenig, A., & Brodhun, E. (1889). Experimentelle Untersuchungen über die psychophysische Fundamentalformel in Bezug auf den Gesichtssinn. *Zweite Mittheilung, Sitzungsbericht der Akademie der Wissenschaften.* Berlin.

Plateau, J.A.F. (1872). Sur la mesure des sensations physiques et sur la loi qui lie l'intensité de ces sensations à l'intensité de la cause excitante. *Bulletin de l'Académie Royale Belge, 33,* 376−378.

Stevens, S.S. (1975). *Psychophysics.* New York: Wiley.

Stevens, S.S., & Galanter, E.H. (1957). Ratio scales and category scales for a dozen perceptual continua. *Journal of Experimental PSychology, 54,* 377−411.

Teghtsoonian, R. (1971). On the exponents in Stevens' law and the constants in Ekman's law. *Psychological Review, 78,* 71−80.

Torgerson, W.S. (1960). Quantitative judgment scales. In H. Gulliksen & S. Messick (Eds.), *Psychological scaling: Theory and applications* (pp. 21-31). New York: Wiley.

Wagenaar, W.A. (1975). Stevens vs. Fechner: A plea for dismissal of the case. *Acta Psychologica, 39,* 225−235.

Wallach, H. (1948). Brightness constancy and the nature of achromatic colors. *Journal of Experimental Psychology, 38,* 310−324.

Weber, E.H. (1846). Der Tastsinn und das Gemeingefühl. *Wagner's Handwörterbuch, III,* 481−488.

Weiss, D.J. (1975). Quantifying private events: A functional measurement analysis of equisection. *Perception & Psychophysics, 17,* 351−357.

Wetherill, G.B., & Levitt, H. (1965). Sequential estimation of points on a psychometric function. *British Journal of Mathematical and Statistical Psychology, 18,* 1−10.

Psychophysical Explorations of Mental Structures
Edited by H.-G. Geissler
in collaboration with M.H. Müller and W. Prinz
© 1990 by Hogrefe & Huber Publishers

Chapter 5

Integration Pychophysics

Norman H. Anderson
*Department of Psychology, University of California
San Diego, U.S.A*

Integration psychophysics may be dedicated to the pioneering investigations of G.T. Fechner. Scheerer (1987) has given an enlightening discussion of Fechner's inner psychophysics. In cognitive science, Fechner was the first to give central place, empirically and conceptually, to the idea that the mind exhibited exact mathematical law. This idea has fired the imagination of his many successors. The same idea appears in the algebraic models of integration psychophysics.

Integration psychophysics seeks a foundation for psychophysical theory in stimulus integration. For classical psychophysics, the central problem concerned the relation between the physical stimulus and the psychological sensation. For integration psychophysics, the central problem concerns the integration of several psychological sensations into a unified response. Whereas classical psychophysics sought to determine the *psychophysical law*, integration psychophysics seeks to determine the integration function, or *psychological law*.

Theoretical Overview

A brief summary of the main concepts of integration psychophysics is given in this section. This will be followed by a section on empirical applications to a number of areas, including some problems of perception and cognition outside classical psychophysics.

Integration Diagram

The flow of information between physical stimulus and observable response involves three operations, illustrated in the integration diagram of Figure 1. Here and below, uppercase letters, S and R, refer to observable stimuli and response, while the corresponding lowercase letters, s and r, refer to unobservable sensations or perceptions.

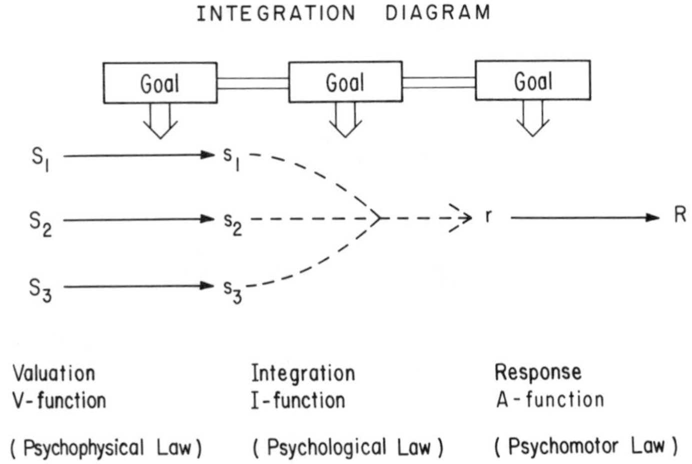

INTEGRATION   DIAGRAM

Valuation	Integration	Response
V-function	I-function	A-function
(Psychophysical Law)	(Psychological Law)	(Psychomotor Law)

Figure 1. Stimulus integration diagram. Sequence of three linked operators, V, I, A, leads from the observable stimulus field, $\{S_i\}$ to observable response R. Valuation operator, V, transforms observable S_i into their subjective representations, s_i. Integration operator, I, integrates subjective stimulus field, $\{s_i\}$, into implicit response r. Action operator, A, transforms implicit response into observable response R. (After Anderson, 1970.)

Valuation. Valuation refers to processes that extract value and meaning from the physical stimuli. Formally, $V(S) = s$. In psychophysical problems, V is the psychophysical law, relating the observable S to the sensation s. Valuation is a more general concept, however, for it may include effects of learning and memory, as illustrated in the later studies of the size–weight illusion, speech perception, and memory psychophysics.

The diagram indicates that valuation depends on the goal. This goal dependence is necessary for general theory, because the immediate goal of the organism affects what aspects of the stimulus field are attended to and what memory storage is utilized. Although often taken for granted, the concept of goal is necessary even in simple psychophysical tasks. Given a tone, for example, subjects may be instructed to judge loudness or pitch. Each instruction defines a different goal and is one determinant of the operative valuation function.

Integration. Integration is the second operation in the diagram. This refers to the integration of the several psychological stimuli into a unitary sensation or perception. Formally, $I(s_1, s_2, ...) = r$. Integration is fundamental because virtually all perception and action have multiple determinants. The central problem of integration psychophysics is to determine the nature of the integration function, or psychological law.

Determining the psychological law depends on psychological measurement. Sensory summation, for example, has been postulated in many different areas. But even the simplest summation rule, $r = s_1 + s_2$, cannot be tested without capability for measuring sensation. Integration psychophysics provides a functional solution to the measurement problem by basing measurement on the psychological law itself.

Action. The last operation in the integration diagram relates to the transformation of the integrated resultant into an observable response. Formally, $A(r) = R$. Although action functions may be indefinitely complex, one very simple case has special importance in psychophysical analysis. This is the linear action function, with R a linear function of r. Such response linearity means that the observable response is a veridical measure of the unobservable sensation, a potentially invaluable property, but one whose realization has been subject to disagreement. Integration psychophysics provides a way to establish response linearity as part of the psychological law.

Functional Perspective. Integration theory embodies a functional perspective, in which thought and action are considered in relations to the goals or purposes of the organism. This is made explicit in the integration diagram, in which the operative goal influences all three operators. This goal dependence has already been illustrated with valuation, and similar dependence holds for the other two operations.

One implication of the functional perspective relates to analysis of action. Most current theories of action begin with the premise that consciousness provides a sufficient basis for theory construction. A corresponding premise may be discerned in classical psychophysics, in which the concept of psychophysical law assumes that conscious sensation has a simple relation to the physical stimulus (Anderson, 1975). Integration psychophysics, in contrast, recognizes the importance of unconscious sensations and provides a way to measure them.

Integration Analysis. Granted that thought and action generally have multiple determinants, it follows that the rules governing the integration of these determinants into a unified perception or behavior have fundamental importance. In fact, problems of integration have been attacked by numerous investigators. Progress has been difficult, however, because it is necessary to allow for three unobservables, as shown in the integration diagram.

The Three Unobservables. Three basic problems underlie the study of multiple determination. These are the three operations of the integration diagram, which, taken together, may be called the problem of the three unobservables. In the symbolic integration equation,

$$r = I(s_1, s_2, ...),$$

all three entities are unobservable, namely, r, I, and the s_j. Solving this equation might seem impossible, for the only constraints available come from the dependence of the observable response on the observable stimuli.

Traditional theory of psychological measurement sought to solve the problem of the three unobservables by a strategy of divide and conquer. Hence the first problem was to solve the problem of stimulus measurement, as epitomized in Thurstonian measurement theory (Anderson, 1981, Section 5.3). The psychophysical law may also be seen as a measurement problem.

Integration psychophysics seeks to solve all three unobservables at once. It does so by looking for structure in the integration function, I. When I has a simple algebraic structure, a solution to all three unobservables can be obtained simply, as illustrated with addition and multiplication in the following theorems.

Parallelism Theorem. Suppose that two stimulus variables are varied in a two-way, row–column matrix. The cells of this matrix then define stimulus pairs, (S_{Ai}, S_{Bj}), where S_{Ai} and S_{Bj} denote the row and column variables. The observable response to each stimulus pair is denoted R_{ij}. Consider the hypothesis that the two stimulus variables are added. This may be tested with the following parallelism theorem.

If an addition rule holds, so that $r = s_{Ai} + s_{Bj}$, and if the action function is linear, so that $R = c_0 + c_1 r$, then (a) the factorial data graph will form a set of parallel curves; and (b) the row (column) means of the data matrix will estimate the psychological values of the row (column) stimuli on linear (equal–interval) scales.

The critical issue is thus the pattern in the factorial graph. Observed parallelism strongly supports both premises of the theorem, which correspond to two of the three unobservables. The second conclusion of the theorem corresponds similarly to the third unobservable, namely, the subjective stimulus value. Proof, extensions, qualifications, and further discussion are given elsewhere (Anderson, 1974, 1976, 1981, 1982).

In this way, observed parallelism supports a joint, simultaneous solution to all three unobservables. Integration psychophysics thus provides one base for experimentation from the psychoregulation point of view advocated by Kovač (1987), for the three unobservables constitute psychological reality.

The two premises of the theorem, it should be emphasized, must be considered jointly. The parallelism theorem provides a strong test, for if one premise is correct, the other incorrect, then the data will be nonparallel. It is possible, of course, that nonadditivity in the integration is just offset and canceled by nonlinearity in the response (see later subsection on Model–Scale Tradeoff). Nevertheless, observed parallelism provides strong support for the two hypotheses taken jointly.

Linear Fan Theorem. A very similar theorem applies to the hypothesis that the integration obeys a multiplication rule. This is the linear fan theorem, which says that the factorial graph of the data should exhibit the pattern of a linear fan.

If a multiplication rule holds, so that $r = s_{Ai} \cdot s_{Bj}$, *and if the action function is linear, so that* $R = c_0 + c_1 r$, *then (a) the appropriate factorial data graph will form a fan of straight lines; and (b) the row (column) means of the data matrix will estimate the psychological values of the row (column) stimuli on linear scales.*

Formally, the two theorems are virtually identical, although the linear fan theorem involves a trick to get the "appropriate" factorial graph. An observed linear fan pattern strongly supports both premises of the theorem, which correspond to two of the three unobservables. The second conclusion of the theorem corresponds similarly to the third unobservable. Further details and discussion are given in the cited references.

Cognitive Algebra. Experimental studies of stimulus integration have demonstrated the operation of a fairly general cognitive algebra. Mathematically, the parallelism and linear fan theorems are elementary, almost trivial. The true foundation of integration psychophysics lies in the empirical investigations – and in the beneficence of nature, which built algebraic rules into the mind.

These algebraic rules, collectively called cognitive algebra, include addition, subtraction, multiplication, division, averaging, and various ratio rules. Such rules have been found in virtually every area of psychology, from psychophysics to psycholinguistics and social cognition. This implies that they reflect a general property of cognition, an interpretation supported by their appearance in young children (Anderson, 1980, 1983b).

Functional Measurement

The measurement theory illustrated in the parallelism and linear fan theorems is called functional measurement, in part because it depends on the integration function, in part because it measures the values that were functional in the task at hand. These are the subjective values of the individual organism, and they refer to the actual functioning in the operative goal and task. A few aspects of this functional measurement methodology require brief comment.

Response Measurement and Stimulus Measurement. Two of the three unobservables refer to measurement. To test an algebraic rule of integration involves measurement both of the psychological stimuli and of the psychological response. Traditionally, stimulus measurement has been primary. Thurstonian scaling theory, for example, consisted of one general method of paired comparisons, intended as a methodological preliminary to substantive inquiry. Response measurement was largely neglected.

Functional measurement methodology inverts the traditional approach by making response measurement primary. Indeed, the parallelism theorem makes no explicit use of stimulus values; the critical test rests on the pattern in the factorial response matrix. Stimulus measurement is implicit in the data, of course, and may be determined in the manner indicated in the second conclusion of each theorem.

Rating and Magnitude Estimation. The rating method and Stevens' (1974) method of magnitude estimation are rather similar. Both ask for numerical judgments and both are easy to use. But, as is well known, they can give radically different results (e.g., Anderson, 1982, Figures 1.1 and 1.3). Not both can be true linear scales of sensation.

Stevens claimed that magnitude extimation was a valid linear scale and that the rating method was biased and nonlinear. But, as various writers pointed out, Stevens provided no validational base to support his claim (see Anderson, 1981, Section 5.4.).

Integration psychophysics provides the validational base that Stevens lacked. The assumption of response linearity is testable as part of the parallelism and linear fan theorems. Neither theorem makes any *a priori* assumption about what empirical method will yield a linear scale. Rating and magnitude estimation have equal opportunity. Not both can succeed, for they are nonlinearly related. Both might well fail.

As it happened, magnitude estimation failed and the rating method succeeded. From the weight lifting study described later, it was concluded (Anderson, 1972, p. 389): *"Since the rating data satisfy both internal and external consistency, they constitute the true measure of sensation. Magnitude estimation, in contrast, must be biased and invalid."* Although considered near-heresy at the time, this conclusion has been vindicated in the subsequent years.

Power Law. In 1961, Stevens published a paper entitled, "To honor Fechner and repeal his law." From his studies with magnitude estimation, Stevens argued that the psychophysical function had the form of a power function, not the logarithmic function claimed by Fechner (1877/1968).

Integration psychophysics has supported Fechner, not Stevens. The psychophysical function may be determined from functional measurement by considering the derived stimulus measures as a function of the physical stimulus dimension (see also Bogartz, 1980). In the main, these studies are consistent with Fechner's assumption that the method of just noticeable differences yields a linear (equal-unit) scale, at least to a fair approximation (see Anderson, 1976, Section 4.4.; Carterette & Anderson, 1979; McBride, 1983).

The bias in magnitude estimation stems from diminishing returns in number usage, so that 110 and 111 are considered less different than 10 and 11. The exponent of the power law is confounded with this response bias and so is artifactually too large. The main outcome of the work instigated by Stevens has been a flood of exponents of power functions for diverse psychophysical dimensions. But these exponents are expressions of response bias, with virtually no scientific value. In this *Jubiläum*, it is fitting to honor Fechner with support from integration psychophysics.

Monotone Analysis. The assumption of response linearity in the parallelism theorem is not necessary. If the addition model holds, it can be used to scale the response. If the observed R is some strictly monotone function of the unobservable r, with $R = M(r)$, then r is inversely a monotone function of R, $r = M^{-1}(R)$. And M^{-1} can be determined, for it is the only transformation that can make the data parallel. With monotone analysis, measurement depends solely on the mathematical structure of the integration rule.

One empirical application of monotone analysis is given in the bisection problem discussed later. Another appears in the study of brain stimulation by Hawkins, Roll, Puerto, and Yeomans (1983). With monotone analysis, as this study illustrates, functional measurement can be used to study algebraic integration using physiological and behavioral measures (see also Farley & Fantino, 1978).

Monotone analysis presents some difficult statistical issues, especially as concerns power and goodness of fit. Practicable solutions have been developed and tested in functional measurement methodology (Anderson, 1982, Chapters 4 and 5), although many uncertainties remain. Investigators intending to use monotone analysis should be aware of these problems beforehand.

Model-Scale Tradeoff. Monotone analysis makes explicit a problem of tradeoff between the algebraic model and the measurement scales. An acute case of the tradeoff problem arose with the finding that young children appeared to judge area of rectangles by adding height and width (see later section). This was hard to believe since they had only to look at the rectangle to see how much was there. It was feared, therefore, that the children might actually perceive area veridically, but use the rating scale logarithmically. The observed data would then appear additive, for $\log H \cdot W = \log H + \log W$. This illustrates that parallelism can result from a nonlinear response that exactly offsets and cancels a nonadditive integration. In general, there is a similar monotone indeterminacy in the psychological law.

Various lines of evidence can be brought to bear on this problem of model-scale tradeoff. Among these are two-operation models, the use of pre-scribed tasks and multiple interlocking tasks to obtain cross-task validity and scale convergence, as well as certain correspondences between psychological and physical realms (see Anderson, 1970, 1972, 1974, 1981, 1982). Indeed, the thought that the line-mark rating method, with a pointing response, suffers serious nonlinearity is hardly consistent with the ability of even young children to maneuver in their spatial environment.

Cogent work on the model-scale tradeoff problem has also been done by Birnbaum, especially with stimulus scale convergence, as summarized in his contribution to this volume. However, his criticism (Birnbaum, 1982) that functional measurement had failed to deal with the model-scale tradeoff problem is gravely incorrect (see also Anderson, 1982, Note 7.1d; Carterette & Anderson, 1987). For example, the first integration study of stimulus scale convergence was the 1972 weight lifting experiment summarized later, which explicitly addressed the tradeoff problem in terms of cross-task validity and scale convergence. The model-scale tradeoff problem has both substantive and formal aspects that have been considered in detail in the references just cited. Although this problem has no easy or final answer, it seems fair to say that the integration studies have built up an interlocking body of evidence that indicates that model-scale tradeoff need not be of concern in most integration studies.

Experimental Studies

Several empirical problems in integration psychophysics are presented in the following sections. These problems have been chosen to illustrate the breadth of possible applications and also to bring out some empirical and theoretical issues in this field (see also Anderson, 1981, 1986, 1989; Petzold, 1984).

Heaviness Sensation

Two interrelated experiments on heaviness sensation are summarized here to illustrate how much information can be gained from a single functional measurement study.

Additivity of Size and Weight. In the left side of Figure 2, subjects lifted a single, visible gray cylinder and judged its apparent heaviness on a numerical scale. There were 25 cylinders, which ranged from 200 to 600 grams in weight and from 3 to 15 centimeters in height. The top curve in the graph shows the heaviness judgments for the five 600-gram cylinders. This curve slopes upwards, showing that smaller cylinders feel heavier, the well-known size-weight illusion.

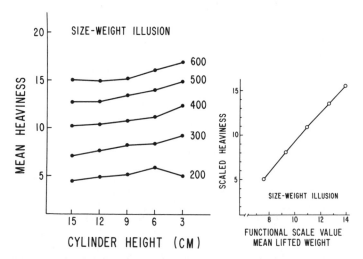

Figure 2. Size — weight illusion. Left panel shows mean judgments of heaviness for 25 weights, varied in height of cylinder (horizontal axis) and gram weight (curve parameter). Parallelism supports addition rule: Heavines = "Size" + "Weight." Right panel plots psychophysical function obtained from this size — weight experiment against psychophysical function obtained from a task of weight averaging. The observed linearity means that both experiments yield the same psychophysical function, which provides cross — task validity, or scale convergence. (After Anderson, 1972.)

The critical feature of Figure 2 is that the five curves are parallel. By virtue of the parallelism theorem, this indicates that the two stimulus variables are integrated by an adding-type rule:

Apparent Heaviness = "Size" + "Weight",

where quotes are used to denote the subjective values of the physical stimuli.

The observed parallelism, it should be noted, jointly supports two theoretical assumptions: additivity of integration and linearity in the response scale. The two hypotheses go together, as already discussed. Cross-task support comes from the companion experiment described below.

Psychophysical Law. The psychophysical law may also be obtained from the data, by virtue of the second conclusion of the parallelism theorem. The graph shows that the curves are closer together near the top: each additional 100 grams adds less heaviness sensation, an illustration of the well-known compressive function of sensory systems. In fact, the psychophysical function is defined by the vertical elevations of curves in the graph. These vertical elevations correspond to the marginal means of the factorial design, which, by the parallelism theorem, constitute a linear scale of the functional stimulus values. If these marginal means are plotted as a function of the gram weight, the resulting curve constitutes the psychophysical function.

Parallelism thus constitutes a base for determining all three unobservables:

The size-weight integration is additive.

The rating response is a linear scale of sensation.

The form fo the psychophysical function is determinable.

Parallelism is not absolute proof, of course, but is does provide a strong validational criterion. This may be buttressed by others, as noted next.

Cross-Task Validity and Scale Convergence. In a companion experiment, subjects lifted two unseen weights, each varied from 200 to 600 grams, and judged their average heaviness. If subjects do average, then the factorial graph should be parallel, as indeed it was. The instructions prescribe additivity, of course, so it is no surprise to find it in the data. But granted an additive integration, parallelism will be obtained only if the response is a true measure of sensation. Parallelism thus has special usefulness in assessing the validity of the rating scale, whereas magnitude estimation would have failed. The prescribed averaging task thus serves an important function, for it supports the validity of the same rating method used in the size-weight task. This may be called cross-task response validity (see Anderson, 1982, Section 3.1).

Similar cross-task support is available on the stimulus side. The psychophysical function was determined from these weight averaging data in the same way as for the size-weight data. The question is whether these two psychophysical functions agree. The answer is *yes*, as shown by the straight line in the right side of Figure 2, which plots one psychophysical function against the other. This straight line relation constitutes stimulus cross-task validation, or scale convergence. Scale convergence for other psychophysical dimensions is given in Anderson (1976, Figures 3 and 4; 1981, Figure 5.3; 1982, Figure

3.6). Further work on this issue has been pursued by Birnbaum (see this volume).

Cognitive Analysis. The two foregoing experiments yield an interesting clue on the role of consciousness in processing psychophysical information. In the size–weight experiment, the sensory effect of the physical weight is pre-conscious. What reaches consciousness is an integrated resultant that includes the effect of the visual cue. Functional measurement fractionates the conscious sensation of heaviness into its preconscious determinants, one of which is preconscious heaviness.

In the weight-averaging task, on the other hand, both weights give a conscious sensation of heaviness. The integration is thus post-conscious, having a locus different from the size–weight integration. Hence there is no necessity for the psychophysical functions to agree in the two experiments. They do agree, however, which suggests a common information source that is available to a range of processing tasks.

Context effects have long been of interest in psychophysics. Often, however, they are considered a nuisance, for the psychophysical law has been conceptualized as a one–variable function, relating the subjective and objective values of the stimulus. Context effects would bias this function. Lifted weights are typically unseen, therefore, to eliminate biasing effects from visual appearance. Integration psychophysics departs from classical method by putting context effects to good use. As the size–weight study illustrates, the integration rule for the context stimulus variable can provide a validational base for mea-surement of the focal stimulus variable – and also of the response measure. Context effects are also studied in the following experiments on optical illusions (see also Anderson, 1975).

Optical Illusions

To the German investigators who founded the science of psychology a century ago, optical illusions were of great interest. Such clear misfunction of perception promised a key to understanding perceptual processes. Although two basic processes were immediately implicated, namely, contrast and assimilation, the promise of this early work never materialized. Illusion theory made little progress and even today is not well grounded. Integration psychophysics has made some theoretical progress on optical illusions, two of which are sum-marized briefly here.

Line–Box Illusion. When a line is flanked by boxes, as in the left of Figure 3, its apparent length changes. It seems as though the large boxes make the line look shorter, whereas the small boxes make the line look longer. Hence this has been considered a typical contrast illusion. Such seeming contrast could be explained in terms of comparative, or relative judgment, in which the line is perceived smaller relative to the large box, larger relative to the small box.

Two theories have attempted to give quantitative form to this concept of comparative judgment. In Helson's (1964) adaptation–level theory, all per-ception is relative; the magnitude of a focal stimulus can only be obtained by comparing it to the prevailing level of adaptation. The basic assumption, accordingly, is that all contextual stimulation is pooled to determine the adaptation level. In the line–box figure, therefore, both boxes would be pooled into this adaptation level, to which the line would be compared by a ratio rule.

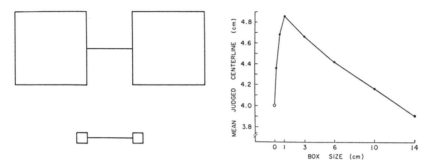

Figure 3. Line–box illusion. Left panel illustrates the line–box illusion. Right panel shows magnitude of illusion as a function of box size. (After Clavadetscher & Anderson, 1977.)

A different conception of comparative judgment comes from integration psychophysics. It allows ratio comparisons of the line to each box separately, with a subsequent addition of these two separate comparisons. Adaptation–level theory cannot allow separate comparisons because the adaptation level is required to be unitary.

A critical test between the two theories can thus be obtained by varying size of left and right boxes independently in factorial design (Clavadetscher & Anderson, 1977). Integration theory expects box–box additivity; adaptation–level theory postulates nonadditivity. The results were clearly additive, infirming adaptation–level theory and supporting a different, more cognitive conception of comparison processes in psychophysics, in agreement with Petzold's contribution to this volume.

An unexpected outcome of the cited experiment was the absence of apparent contrast. This is visible in the right panel of Figure 3, which shows apparent length of a 4 cm line as a function of box size. Even the 10 cm box makes the line look larger, relative to the control line without boxes (open circle at left end of curve). Inspection of the illusory figure in the left panel only seems to be contrast. This apparent contrast is actually a difference between two assimilation effects of different size. This required extension of the integration model, to include both contrast and assimilation processes, which was done by Clavadetscher in the following study.

Two-Process Theory of Illusions. Illusion theories have generally attempted to find pure cases that could be explained in terms of a single process, typically either contrast or assimilation. Such one-process approaches nearly always had promising initial success, but nearly always ran aground on counterexamples. Allowing two processes that acted in opposite directions was unattractive because it carried the double danger of being able to explain almost everything and yet being able to predict almost nothing.

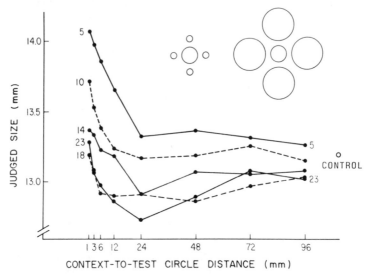

Figure 4. Ebbinghaus circles. Curves show apparent diameter of center circles as a function of size of surrounding context circles (horizontal axis). Control point represents apparent size of center circle with no context circles (After Clavadetscher, 1977, in press.)

A new approach was initiated by Clavadetscher (1977, in press), who applied integration psychophysics to study the Ebbinghaus circles shown in Figure 4. Clavadetscher began with the assumption that contrast and assimilation were both operative and that their effects were averaged to produce apparent size. By virtue of assimilation, both large and small context circles make the center circle look larger. By virtue of contrast, the small context circles also make the center circle larger, but the large context circles make it look smaller. Clavadetscher assumed that contrast, being the result of a process of comparative judgment, operated at much greater distances than assimilation. Hence he was able, by varying both size and distance of the surrounding context circles in an integration design, to verify the joint operation of both contrast and assimilation.

The critical result is the U-shaped curve for the large context circles. These are the 18- and 23-mm curves in the lower part of Figure 4. For these large context circles, contrast and assimilation have opposite effects: contrast makes the center circle look smaller, assimilation makes the center circle look larger. At close distances, both effects have about equal strength but cancel, so the center circle has the same apparent size as the control. As distance increases, assimilation decays rapidly but contrast decays slowly. At the middle distance, therefore, assimilation is negligible but contrast is still strong. Hence the center circle looks smaller. As distance increases still more, the contrast slowly decays, and so the curve slowly rises toward the level of the control. Even at the largest distance, however, the ordering of the curves shows that contrast is still operative. Further evidence and experiments are given in Clavadetscher (1977, in press). A rough calculation by the writer, based on an assumption of exponential decay, yielded decay rates of .10 for assimilation and .01 for contrast. Clavadetscher's model thus provides a foothold on the basic problem of studying joint operation of contrast and assimilation.

Functional Measurement Analysis of Bisection

Functional measurement ultimately depends only on the algebraic structure of the integration function. A linear response scale is convenient, as in the lifted weight experiments, but a monotone (ordinal) scale is all that is necessary. This capability for monotone analysis appears in the classic problem of psychophysical bisection.

Bisection. The bisection task is attractive because the response is non-verbal, on the sensory dimension itself. Moreover, bisection prescribes addi-tivity, as assumed in the standard process interpretation that subjects equate sense distances between the bisector response, R, and the bisectee stimuli, S_1 and S_2. This bisection process, of course, must be written in terms of the subjective values, denoted by lower case letters:

$$w_1(r-s_1) = w_2(s_2-r),$$

where the w_i are weighting factors that generalize the simple bisection model. The response is thus additive in the subjective metric:

$$r = w_1s_1 + w_2s_2.$$

The parallelism theorem could be applied to test the bisection equation –if r were observable. But r is some monotone transformation of the observable $R: r = V(R)$. If the bisection model holds, then this monotone transformation becomes determinate by manipulating S_1 and S_2 in factorial design, for it is the one transformation that will make the data parallel.

To test the bisection model, therefore, vary S_1 and S_2 in a factorial design, measure R, and apply monotone transformation. If the data can be made parallel, that supports the bisection model. It also determines the psychophysical function, which is just the monotone transformation, V. Empirically, bisection has been applied successfully with grayness (see Anderson, 1976, Figure 2, 1981, Section 1.3.8), and loudness (Carterette & Anderson, 1979), but has failed with length (see Anderson, 1982, Figure 4.6).

This bisection analysis depends only on the algebraic structure of the model. No auxiliary assumptions are needed, as noted in the earlier discussion of monotone analysis. As Carterette and Anderson (1979, p. 266) put it: *"All that is at issue is the algebraic form of the bisection model. This algebraic form serves as the base and frame for measurement in a truly scale-free way."*

Cross-Task Validity. Because bisection involves a perceptual rather than a symbolic response, it is interesting to compare psychophysical functions obtained from bisection with those obtained from ratings. This comparison has been made with grayness, comparing bisection with two rating tasks, one that asked for average grayness of two Munsell gray chips, the other that asked for difference in grayness between the two chips. All three tasks yielded the same psychophysical function (see Anderson, 1976, Figures 3 and 4, 1982, Figure 3.1). This scale convergence provides further support for the validity of the rating response.

Axiomatic Measurement Theory. Functional measurement makes measurement an organic component of substantive theory. The theoretical analysis of the bisection task thus begins with consideration of the psychological process involved in bisection, as in the commonsense model of equated sense distances. Because this model has a simple algebraic form, it may — if it is actually correct — be used as the base and frame for measurement. It is this substantive model, involving substantive processes, that constitutes the foundation of measurement.

This empiricist approach contrasts with axiomatic measurement theory, which seeks a set of axioms that will logically guarantee an additive model. These axioms, however, do not refer to psychological process, nor even to the single response, which is the locus of process. Unlike axioms in physics, the measurement axioms do not refer to substantive concepts. Instead, they refer to observable properties of responses across several trials. The sole value of such axioms is to provide a possible base for statistical analysis of observed data, exactly analogous to the methods of monotone analysis used in functional measurement. Such axioms cannot be the foundation of measurement, for they would be useless and empty without an empirical foundation of algebraic integration rules.

This contrast is nicely illustrated with Pfanzagl's (1968) bisymmetry axiom for bisection. Let $B(S_i,S_j)$ be the bisector of the two given stimuli, and consider four given stimuli. Then the bisymmetry axiom reads:

$$B[B(S_1,S_2),\ B(S_3,S_4)]\ =\ B[B(S_1,S_3),\ B(S_2,S_4)].$$

In words, one sequence of three bisections should lead to the same result as another sequence of three bisections. This condition clearly does not refer to the psychological processes involved in any one bisection, as does the foregoing model of equated sense distances. Instead, it refers to a comparison among observable responses across several different bisections. Its only function, therefore, would be for statistical analysis of bisection data.

This same point applies to conjoint measurement (Krantz, Luce, Suppes & Tversky, 1971). The axiom of double cancellation, for example, involves comparisons among responses made on six different trials. These comparisons are made by the investigator, not by the subject. They do not refer to the psychological processes involved in any one response. They are nonsubstantive axioms. In contrast, the model of equated sense distances does refer to processes involved in each single bisection. It is this substantive model, in the functional measurement view, that provides the base for measurement (Anderson, 1981, Section 5.5).

In the functional view, the foundation of measurement lies in the empirical studies that have established algebraic models for stimulus integration. One important outcome of these studies is the validity of the rating method. This depends on certain procedures, especially end anchors and practice to set up a stable frame of reference (Anderson, 1982, Chapter 1). These procedures have been found fairly successful in eliminating various biases to which ratings are subject. Hence ratings may be used more generally, especially in tasks in which no simple algebraic model applies. Functional measurement can thus advance to study stimulus interaction and configural integration, whereas the axiomatic approaches remain limited to simple algebraic models.

Chemical Senses

The need for integration psychophysics is clear in the chemical senses. Taste, which means so much in everyday life, is typically a mixture of sensations that include not only the four basic tastes (sweet, sour, bitter, and salt), but also odor, texture, and others. Classical psychophysics has little to say about mixtures and so has little to contribute to the study of taste. Psychophysical functions for mixtures are not generally well defined, and the psycho-

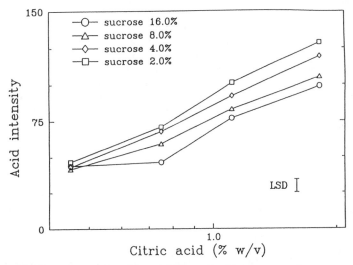

Figure 5. Mixture suppression. Mean judgment of acid component of a sweet—acid mixture as function of sweet and acid concentrations. (After McBride & Johnson, 1987.)

physical functions for the components of a mixture have no necessary or likely relation to properties of the mixture itself (McBride & Anderson, in press).

Some progress has been made in the study of taste integration, with a pioneering study of sweet-bitter integration by Klitzner (1975), a model study of difference judgments by de Graaf, Frijters, and van Trijp (1987), and a systematic program of research by McBride (e.g., 1986; see also survey in McBride & Anderson, in press).

Figure 5 illustrates a study of mixture suppression (McBride & Johnson, 1987). Subjects judged intensity of the acid component in sugar-acid mixtures. The higher the sugar concentration, the lower the perceived acid intensity, an example of mixture suppression.

The pattern in the factorial graph points to a threshold-difference model: perceived acid intensity equals "acid" minus "sugar," but only when this difference lies above a threshold. The difference rule appears in the parallelism of the curves over the right hand portion of the graph. The threshold effect appears in the convergence of the curves at the left hand point. At this point, the acid concentration is lowest and so is masked or suppressed even by the lowest sugar concentration. This interpretation in terms of a threshold-difference model is tentative, for it depends heavily on the assumption that the response is linear. However, it illustrates the analytical power that is available when methods for obtaining linear response measures have been developed.

Pain

How much does it hurt? is an important question that emphasizes a practical need for psychological measurement. Although space limitations prohibit detailed discussion, the pioneering applications by Jones and Gwynn (1984) and Algom, Raphaeli, and Cohen-Raz (1986) illustrate the potential of integration psychophysics in the fascinating but puzzling field of pain. One difficulty is that experimental pain lacks much of the quality of natural or clinical pain. Accordingly, it is desirable to develop integration tasks that embed experimental manipulation within clinical cases (Anderson, 1989).

Categorical Speech Perception

If sound frequency parameters are varied continuously between the phonemes /ba/ and /da/, the listener does not experience continuous variation in the conscious percept. Instead, there is a clear, sudden shift between hearing one phoneme and hearing the other. This feeling of discontinuous perception has led to a theory of categorical perception. Taken at face value, it implies that discrimination within phoneme boundaries is not possible. This is turn implies that perception is top-down in the sense that the learned phoneme category imposes itself on the perceptual process. A number of experiments have supported this categorical interpretation, which has been the predominant view.

A new approach to categorical perception was developed by Massaro (1987), who transformed the issue into an integration paradigm. Massaro argued that speech and general pattern recognition depend on integration of multiple cues. He provided a fuzzy logic model for cue integration, with a simple ratio form, that has done extremely well.

Massaro applied his theory to categorical perception in the integration experiment summarized in Figure 6. One variable is the sound frequency parameters ranging over 9 values from /ba/ to /da/ on the horizontal axis. The other variable was visual, consisting of lip movements characteristic of /ba/ or of /da/ or neutral. The difference among the three curves in Figure 6 shows that the visual cue had substantial effects. The least squares fits for the fuzzy logic model (left panel) and the categorical perception model (right panel) show that the continuous fuzzy logic model does markedly better. This superiority was confirmed in a systematic program of research (Massaro, 1987).

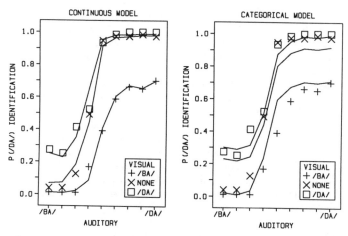

Figure 6. Speech recognition. Identifications of phoneme /da/ as a function of auditory information (horizontal axis) and visual, lip movement information (curve parameter). Same data in each panel. Fuzzy logic model with continuous perception (left panel) fits substantially better than model of categorical perception (right panel). (After Massaro, 1987.)

Massaro's results, taken as a whole, show that the dominant view about categorical perception is wrong. The underlying processes are not categorical but continuous. The conscious perception of discontinuity reflects only a late stage in the information processing. The integration task and design provide strong discriminative tests between the two theories. By focusing on the problem of cue integration, Massaro has developed a new direction in research on pattern recognition.

Commonsense Physics

Integration psychophysics has been concerned with a number of problems that lie at the borders of classical psychophysics. One such border problem appears in commonsense physics, which has been studied extensively in children. One question concerns the relation between physical law and psychological law in the following studies.

The Height + Width Rule. Young children, around 5 years of age, judge area of rectangles by an additive, Height + Width rule (Anderson & Cuneo, 1978; Wilkening, 1980). The empirical evidence came from observed parallelism in the factorial graph. The theoretical interpretation rests on the following assumptions: The children understand that a quantitative judgment is desired; they do not possess adult conceptions of multidimensional quantities; they are sensitive to one-dimensional cues; and they possess a general–purpose adding–type rule. Hence they see that height and width are relevant one–dimensional cues and integrate them with the general–purpose adding rule.

The Height + Width rule is hard to believe. To adult eyes, it clearly disagrees with the physical law of Height × Width. However, it has been extensively corroborated (see Silverman & Paskewitz, 1988), and analogous addition rules have been demonstrated in other tasks of commonsense physics (e.g., Cuneo, 1982; Wilkening, 1982).

An extension to memory psychophysics was made by Wolf and Algom (1987), who used three-dimensional shapes. In an initial training session, children learned to associate circles of different hues with the eight shapes. In the test session, one group of children made volume judgments of the presented shapes. Another group of children was presented only the colored circle and was asked to remember the shape and make a volume judgment. Both groups followed an adding rule: Volume = Height + Width + Depth. This rule may be seen in the three–dimensional parallelism of Figure 7. Here even 10–years–olds follow the adding rule, although they exhibited the normative multiplying rule for two-dimensional rectangles.

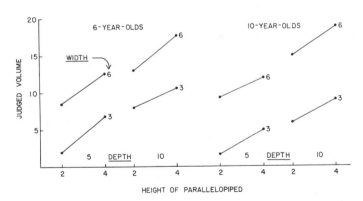

Figure 7. Children judge volume of parallelopipeds by addition rule: Volume = Height + Width + Depth. (After Wolf and Algom, 1988.)

The same integration rule was found by Wolf and Algom in both the perceptual judgments and in the memory-based judgments. This interesting study suggests a new method for studying perceptual memory and imagery.

Time-Speed-Distance. The psychophysics of object motion, so important in everyday life, was studied by Wilkening (1982), with children who made judgments about an animal fleeing from a barking dog. The children's judgments were conceptual, not perceptual, for they did not observe actual motion. In one condition, they were informed about the speed of the animal (turtle, cat, deer, etc.) and how far it had run. They were instructed to judge how long the dog had barked to make the animal run that far. The physical rule is Time = Distance/Speed. The 5-years-olds, however, followed a subtraction rule, Time = "Distance" − "Speed." This outcome is consistent with and buttresses the concept of a general-purpose adding-type rule already mentioned.

With these and other such results, Wilkening completely transformed the developmental conception of time-speed-distance claimed by Piaget. First, the algebraic rule demonstrates that 5-years-olds have conceptual understanding of time and speed, far earlier than recognized by Piaget. Second, their concepts are metric. Whereas Piaget's theory does not allow metric concepts before the stage of formal operations, around 12 − 13 years, Wilkening demonstrated metric concepts in the preoperational stage. Third, the three concepts are inter-locked according to an algebraic rule, which, although different from the physical rule, is ecologically sensible. As these points illustrate, the developmental studies of integration psychophysics have led to a conceptual framework entirely different from that of Piaget (Anderson, 1980, 1983a,b; Hommers & Anderson, 1985, 1989; Wilkening & Anderson, 1982, in press).

Psychological Law and Psychophysical Law

The central concern of integration psychophysics is the psychological law. The difference betwen integration psychophysics and classical psychophysics, accordingly, lies in the several differences between the psychological law and the psychophysical law. Whereas the psychophysical law is concerned with the relation between psychological sensation and physical stimulation, the psychological law deals with relations among sensations. The focus of inquiry thus shifts from the relation between the mind and the external world to relations entirely within the mind itself.

It is still essential to anchor psychological constructs to physical observables. The nature of this anchoring, however, is qualitatively different in the two cases. This difference appears in mathematical structure, for the psychophysical law is a function of a single variable, whereas the psychological law is a function of two or more variables. This one-variable-many-variable difference is critical for psychophysical analysis.

The one-variable psychophysical law provides no constraint against monotone transformation. The controversy between log and power laws, in particular, is unsolvable in principle, for they are monotonically equivalent. The central concept of classical psychophysics is too narrow to resolve its own central problem (Anderson, 1970).

The many-variable psychological law does provide constraint against monotone transformation. An inherently nonadditive inegration rule, for example, cannot be made additive by monotone transformation. Manipulation of two or more stimulus variables can thus provide proper tests of the additivity hypothesis, for it implies an additive structure in the data matrix. The same approach applies to other forms of integration function. With due regard to monotone indeterminacy (Anderson, 1974, Section IIA.6.f, 1982, Section 5.9), it may be said that the central concept of integration psychophysics is in principle sufficiently broad to resolve its own central problem.

The idea that nature obeys mathematical laws has long been prominent in physics, and Fechner, himself a physicist, bequeathed a similar idea to psychology. Integration psychophysics is an heir to Fechner, although it seeks for mathematical law within the mind itself.

Integration psychophysics also provides a new approach to the study of consciousness (Anderson, 1975). The concept of psychophysical law implies a direct relation between the physical stimulus and the conscious sensation that has simple form and unitary structure. Integration psychophysics envisages more complex cognitive processing. One example was noted in the size–weight illusion, which requires heaviness sensation to exist at both preconscious and conscious levels, and a similar case appeared in the cited study of categorical perception (see also Anderson, 1989).

Integration psychophysics is not really new. Innumerable investigators have been concerned with problems of stimulus integration in all areas of psychophysics and perception. What is new is the theory of functional measurement, which has provided a general approach to the study of stimulus integration, and the associated empirical studies of cognitive algebra.

Summary

Integration psychophysics involves a conceptual shift from classical psychophysics: a shift from *psychophysical* law to *psychological* law. Whereas psychophysical law is concerned with the relation between the physical stimulus and psychological sensation, psychological law is concerned with relations among sensations themselves. Whereas classical psychophysics sought simplicity and lawfulness at the psychological–physical interface, integration psychophysics seeks simplicity and lawfulness within the psychological domain.

Integration psychophysics is necessary to handle *multiple determination*: sensations and perceptions are typically integrated resultants of multiple stimulus determinants. But stimulus integration, especially integration across different sensory systems, generally cannot be handled in terms of psychophysical law. Most stimulus integration occurs within the psychological domain. Hence, the conceptual framework of classical psychophysics is too narrow for analysis of multiple determination.

The cutting edge of integration psychophysics resides in *algebraic models*. In many common psychophysical tasks, multiple determination has been found to obey algebraic rules. To establish these rules required solution of two problems of psychological measurement: measurement of subjective stimulus sensation and measurement of quantitative response. *Functional measurement* provided a practicable resolution to this interlocked set of three problems — by making the algebraic integration rule the base and frame for measurement. As one aspect of this tripartite problem, functional measurement provides validated measures of subjective sensation — and thereby resolves the classical problem of determining the psychophysical law.

Empirical applications are illustrated for a number of psychophysical tasks.

– Size–weight illusion shows how sensation can be measured at both conscious and unconscious levels.
– A study of optical illusions presents the first effective attempt to incorporate both assimilation and contrast processes in quantitative theory.
– Context effects become a tool for psychophysical analysis.
– A successful solution is obtained for the classical problem of psychophysical bisection.
– Mixture suppression in the taste senses illustrates a threshold–difference model.
– Auditory-visual integration demonstrates that speech perception is not categorical but continuous.
– Extensions to commonsense physics are illustrated with time–speed–distance judgments, which lead to a new theory of perceptual–cognitive development.

Integration psychophysics builds on a new foundation, as illustrated in these applications. This allows a solution to some old problems, including the classical problem of the psychophysical law, and an advance to new classes of problems.

Acknowledgement. I wish to thank Peter Petzold for assistance and the organizing committee of the Fechner Symposium for their gracious hospitality. This work was supported by NSF grant BNS82−07541.
Correspondence should be addressed to Norman H. Anderson, Psychology Department, University of California, La Jolla, CA 92093−0109, U.S.A.

References

Algom, D., Raphaeli, N., & Cohen-Raz, L. (1986). Integration of noxious stimulation across somatosensory communications systems: A functional theory of pain. *Journal of Experimental Psychology: Human Perception and Performance, 12*, 93−102.

Anderson, N. H. (1970). Functional measurement and psychophysical judgment. *Psychological Review, 77*, 153−170.

Anderson, N.H. (1972). Cross-task validation of functional measurement. *Perception & Psychophysics, 12*, 389−395.

Anderson, N.H. (1974). Algebraic models in perception. In E.C. Carterette & M.P. Friedman (Eds.), *Handbook of perception* (Vol. 2). New York: Academic Press.

Anderson, N.H. (1975). On the role of context effects in psychophysical judgment. *Psychological Review, 82*, 462−482.

Anderson, N.H. (1976). Integration theory, functional measurement and the psychophysical law. In H.-G. Geissler & Y.M. Zabrodin (Eds.), *Advances in psychophysics*. Berlin: VEB Deutscher Verlag der Wissenschaften.

Anderson, N.H. (1980). Information integration theory in developmental psychology. In F. Wilkening, J. Becker & T. Trabasso (Eds.), *Information integration by children*. Hillsdale, NJ: Erlbaum.

Anderson, N.H. (1981). *Foundations of information integration theory*. New York: Academic Press.

Anderson, N.H. (1982). *Methods of information integration theory*. New York: Academic Press.

Anderson, N.H. (1983a). Cognitive algebra in intuitive physics. In H.-G. Geissler (Ed.), *Modern issues in perception*. Amsterdam: North-Holland.

Anderson, N.H. (1983b). Intuitive physics: Understanding and learning of physical relations. In T.J. Tighe & B.E. Shepp (Eds.), *Perception, cognition, and development: Interactional analyses*. Hillsdale, NJ: Erlbaum.

Anderson, N.H. (1986). A cognitive theory of judgment and decision. In B. Brehmer, H. Jungermann, P. Lourens & G. Sevón (Eds.), *New directions in research on decision making*. Amsterdam: North-Holland.

Anderson, N.H. (1989). Information integration approach to emotions and their measurement. In R. Plutchik & H. Kellerman (Eds.), *Emotion: Theory, research, and experience* (Vol. 4). New York: Academic Press.

Anderson, N.H., & Cuneo, D.O. (1978). The Height+Width rule in children's judgments of quantity. *Journal of Experimental Psychology: General, 107*, 335−378.

Birnbaum, M.H. (1982). Controversies in psychological measurement. In B. Wegener (Ed.), *Social attitudes and psychophysical measurement*. Hillsdale, NJ: Erlbaum.

Bogartz, R.S. (1980). Some functional measurement procedures for determining the psychophysical law. *Perception & Psychophysics, 27*, 284−294.

Carterette, E.C., & Anderson, N.H. (1979). Bisection of loudness. *Perception & Psychophysics, 26*, 265−280.

Carterette, E.C., & Anderson, N.H. (1987). Setting straight the record. *Perception & Psychophysics, 42*, 409−410.

Clavadetscher, J.E. (1977). *Two context processes in the Ebbinghaus illusion*. Unpublished doctoral dissertation, University of California, San Diego.

Clavadetscher, J.E. (in press). Studies of a two process theory for geometric illusions. In N.H. Anderson (Ed.), *Contributions to information integration theory*.

Clavadetscher, J.E., & Anderson, N.H. (1977). Comparative judgment: Tests of two theories using the Baldwin figure. *Journal of Experimental Psychology: Human Perception and Performance, 3*, 119−135.

Cuneo, D.O. (1982). Children's judgments of numerical quantity: A new view of early quantification. *Cognitive Psychology, 14*, 13−44.

De Graaf, C., Frijters, J.E.R., & van Trijp, H.C.M. (1987). Taste interaction between glucose and fructose assessed by functional measurement. *Perception & Psychophysics, 41*, 383−392.

Farley, J., & Fantino, E. (1978). The symmetrical law of effect and the matching relation in choice behavior. *Journal of the Experimental Analysis of Behavior, 29*, 37−60.

Fechner, G.T. (1968). *In Sachen der Psychophysik*. Amsterdam: E.J. Bronset. (Originally published, 1877.)

Hawkins, R.D., Roll, P.L., Puerto, A., & Yeomans, J.S. (1983). Refractory periods of neurons mediating stimulation-elicited eating and brain stimulation reward: Interval scale measurement and tests of a model of neural integration. *Behavioral Neuroscience, 97*, 416−432.

Helson, H. (1964). *Adaptation-level theory*. New York: Harper & Row.

Hommers, W., & Anderson, N.H. (1985). Recompense as a factor in assigned punishment. *British Journal of Developmental Psychology, 3,* 75 – 86.

Hommers, W., & Anderson, N.H. (1989). Algebraic schemes in legal thought and in everyday morality. In H. Wegener, F. Lösel & H.J. Haisch (Eds.), *Criminal behavior and the justice system.* New York, Berlin: Springer.

Jones, B., & Gwynn, M. (1984). Functional measurement scales of painful electric shocks. *Perception & Psychophysics, 35,* 193 – 200.

Klitzner, M.D. (1975). Hedonic integration: Test of a linear model. *Perception & Psychophysics, 18,* 49 – 54.

Kovac, D. (1987). From psychophysically based experiments to experimentation from the psychoregulation point of view. Paper presented at the Fechner Symposium, Leipzig, July 1987.

Krantz, D.H., Luce, R.D., Suppes, P., & Tversky, A. (1971). *Foundations of measurement* (Vol. 1). New York: Academic Press.

Massaro, D.W. (1987). *Speech perception by ear and eye: A paradigm for psychological inquiry.* Hillsdale, NJ: Erlbaum.

McBride, R.L. (1983). A JND-scale/category-scale convergence in taste. *Perception & Psychophysics, 34,* 77 – 83.

McBride, R.L. (1986). Sweetness of binary mixtures of sucrose, fructose, and glucose. *Journal of Experimental Psychology: Human Perception and Performance, 12,* 584 – 591.

McBride, R.L., & Anderson, N.H. (in press). Integration psychophysics in the chemical senses.

McBride, R.L., & Johnson, R.L. (1987). Perception of sugar-acid mixtures in lemon juice drink. *International Journal of Food Science and Technology, 22,* 399 – 408.

Petzold, P. (1984). Information integration: A review of the literature in German-speaking countries since 1970. *The German Journal of Psychology, 8,* 312 – 322.

Pfanzagl, J. (1968). *Theory of measurement.* New York: Wiley.

Scheerer, E. (1987). What happened to Fechner's inner psychophysics? Historical issues and prospects for the future. Paper presented at the Fechner Symposium, Leipzig, July 1987.

Silverman, I.W., & Paskewitz, S.L. (1988). Developmental and individual differences in children's area judgment rules. *Journal of Experimental Child Psychology, 46,* 74 – 87.

Stevens, S.S. (1961). To honor Fechner and repeal his law. *Science, 133,* 80 – 86.

Stevens, S.S. (1974). Perceptual magnitude and its measurement. In E.C. Carterette & M.P. Friedman (Eds.), *Handbook of perception* (Vol. 2). New York: Academic Press.

Wilkening, F. (1980). Development of dimensional integration in children's perceptual judgment: Experiments with area, volume, and velocity. In F. Wilkening, J. Becker & T. Trabasso (Eds.), *Information integration by children.* Hillsdale, NJ: Erlbaum.

Wilkening, F. (1982). Children's knowledge about time, distance, and velocity interrelations. In W.J. Friedman (Ed.), *The developmental psychology of time.* New York: Academic Press.

Wilkening, F., & Anderson, N.H. (1982). Comparison of two rule-assessment methodologies for studying cognitive development and knowledge structure. *Psychological Bulletin, 92,* 215 – 237.

Wilkening, F., & Anderson, N.H. (in press). Representation and diagnosis of knowledge structures in developmental psychology. In N.H. Anderson (Ed.), *Contributions to information integration theory.*

Wolf, Y., & Algom, D. (1987). Perceptual and memorial constructs in children's judgments of quantity: A law of cross-representation invariance. *Journal of Experimental Psychology: General, 116,* 381 – 397.

Psychophysical Explorations of Mental Structures
Edited by H.-G. Geissler
in collaboration with M.H. Müller and W. Prinz
© 1990 by Hogrefe & Huber Publishers

Chapter 6

The Context for Evaluative Judgments: Psychophysics and Beyond

Allen Parducci and Douglas H. Wedell
Department of Psychology
University of California, Los Angeles, U.S.A.
and
Department of Psychology
University of South Carolina, Columbia, U.S.A.

It is easier to predict category ratings once their context is known than to know what goes into the context. In the laboratory, we try to achieve experimental control of the stimuli determining the judgments; outside the laboratory, we can only speculate about these determining stimuli, that is, about what constitutes the context for any particular judgment. Such is the harsh reality facing our attempts to apply the fruits of laboratory research. After reviewing experimental findings on contexts for category ratings, we will present some speculative possibilities, not always encouraging, concerning the context everyday value judgments.

Simple Laboratory Experiments

It would be reassuring to believe that in our simplest experiments we achieve complete control of the context for judgment, complete control of those stimulus values that determine the judgment. Achieving this ideal would simplify the discovery of useful judgmental principles: given the context, the judgment of each stimulus could be accurately predicted. Although we never achieve such complete control, it is something to work toward.

Range-Frequency Compromise on the Presented Stimuli

In what may be our simplest experiments, the context for judgment seems representative of the various stimuli actually presented by the experimenter; ratings of individual stimuli are roughly predictable from the frequency distribution of presented values. For example, when the stimuli to be rated form a list of numbers, ordered by magnitude and printed on a single page, the size-rating of each number can be predicted from its range position, i.e., from the proportion of the difference between the largest and smallest numbers that it cuts off, and also from its frequency position, i.e., from its percentile rank in the list (e.g., Birnbaum, 1974; Parducci, Calfee, Marshall & Davidson, 1960). These are the range and frequency principles, with the actual judgment falling half-way between the two.

The same range-frequency principles apply, though with added complications, when psychophysical stimuli are presented successively, in random order. Again, the entire frequency distribution of stimulus values suffices to predict the individual ratings, at least approximately (Parducci & Perrett, 1971; Parducci & Wedell, 1983). This suggests that the context for judgment must be fairly representative of the set actually presented over the series of trials.

Sequential Effects and the Size of the Context

Although there are reliable trial-to-trial sequential effects (e.g., Ward & Lockhead, 1970), these are small enough in comparison with the effects of the overall distribution so that the context for judging any particular presentation cannot be reduced to just the last several presentations. Consider the effects of shifting the stimulus range. Subjects adjust quickly to an extension of the range, but the context continues to include a dropped endpoint dozens of trials after a restriction of range (Parducci, 1956).

Frequency considerations also extend back beyond the last several presentations. Our recent research on nonrandom series (e.g., concatinations of five-stimulus blocks, each from either the top or bottom half of the range) indicates that the context on which the frequency principle operates includes at least the 10 most recent presentations. This seems to rule out models in which the frequency principle operates on smaller numbers of trials, e.g., on only the last two trials (Haubensak, 1983) or on as few as 5 or 10 (Ward & Lockhead, 1971). However, the effective context on which the frequency principle is applied may include fewer than 20 presentations, as suggested by Wedell's transfer experiment in which the rate of readjustment of the ratings following an unannounced reversal in the direction of skewing of the stimulus set was largely independent of the number of pre-shift trials beyond 20 (Wedell, 1984). Readjustment to the reversed skewing reached an asymptote by between 10 and 20 post-shift presentations.

Systematic Distortion of Context

Even without this short context of 10 to 20 items, overly-frequent re-presentations of the same stimulus may be discounted. Our favored explanation of the decreasing effect of skewing with increasing number of categories, what we call the "Category Effect," assumes that the frequency of a contextual stimulus is limited by a principle of consistency, not using more than one category for the same stimulus (Parducci & Wedell, 1986). This then implies that with a large number of categories (e.g., nine) the context for judgment may be much less skewed than the distribution of stimulus values actually presented by the experimenter. With the large number of categories, there also appears to be, under some conditions, an extension of the contextual range further beyond the stimulus extremes of the set actually presented. This extension also appears for judgments of the attractiveness of faces (Wedell, Parducci & Geisselman, 1987). To these modifications in the representation of the presented distribution must be added various classically-identified shifts in the context, including the Hollingworth central-tendency effect and also the time-order errors (Helson, 1964) which appear as general shifts up or down.

Unjudged or Segregated Context

In the simple psychophysical experiments on category ratings, each stimulus is rated by the subject as it enters his context for judgment. In a type of anchoring experiment studied by Helson (1964) and much more thoroughly by Sarris (1971, 1976), the subject is instructed to rate only every other stimulus; if the unrated stimuli are more extreme than any of the regular series, they extend the contextual range — just as though they had been rated along with the regular series (Sarris & Parducci, 1978).

Control by subjects. However, subjects can establish separate scales for odd and even trials of the experiment when instructed (and helped) to do so. For example, when small squares of varying size were presented on odd trials and larger circles were presented on even trials, ratings of the sizes of each were completely independent of the frequency distribution of the other's sizes; but when instructed to ignore the difference in shape, all stimuli were incorporated into a single context for judgment (Parducci, Knoebel & Thomas, 1976). Subjects in these simple experiments seem to have considerable control over what they will include in the context. This may also be the case for Wedell's (1984) transfer experiments in which some subjects adapted completely to the post-shift distribution, others not at all. Resistance to sudden changes in context can be interpreted as a directed retrieval of the much earlier frequencies. This seems consistent with memory research in which the earlier stimulus frequencies could be retrieved separately (Hintzman & Block, 1971).

Response averaging? Alternatively, the resistance to postshift adaptation can be interpreted as a hanging on to old responses, as though the response were a weighted average of what it would have been in the new context and what it was in the old context. It is as though the subject said to himself, "This square now looks small, but I had been calling it 'large'; I'll compromise by calling it 'medium.'" When the entire distribution is shifted upward (as in Johnson, 1949), subjects rapidly shift their context to the new set of stimulus values. In this case, it may seem clear to subjects that they should restrict their context to the new set.

Unjudged background. The context may also include unjudged background features, as emphasized by Helson in generalizing from his experiments on induced color (Helson, 1964). Background context can be particularly evident on the first trials of the experiment when the subject has not yet seen the entire set of stimuli that will be presented for judgment. In some of our square-judging research, the height of the largest square is little more than half the height of the lighted background area; if this largest square is presented first, it is rated "average"; other sizes in the first position are assigned smaller categories, as though the initial contextual range extended from the smallest discriminable size to the largest size possible against the background. Later, the upper-endpoint of the context shifts to a value closer to the size of the largest square but remains above it − as though the contextual range were still extended toward the larger background area (Parducci & Perrett, 1971).

With the method of simultaneous presentation, the entire distribution of presented values (e.g., a list of numbers) can serve as an unjudged background. For example, a single stimulus can be identified by the experimenter for rating by the subject. In unpublished work, we have found that this single rating follows range–frequency principles just as though all contextual stimuli had been rated.

Unjudged counterfactuals. Another condition producing extension of the contextual range occurs in experiments with what seems like a natural "neutral–point." In one of our pseudo–gambling experiments (Marsh & Parducci, 1978), subjects were presented with a set of outcomes of gambles for which they were to rate how pleased or displeased they would be with each outcome. In one condition, outcomes ran as high as a $200 win, with no loss greater than $100. If the effective contextual range matched the actual range of outcomes, losing $100 should have been as bad as winning $200 was good. However, the subjects' ratings suggested that the contextual range extended the same amount in both directions; losing $100 was rated less disappointing than it was when the outcomes ran from −$100 to +$100. The hypothetical but never–experienced possibility of losing $200 appears to have entered the context determining the judgments.

Contexts Outside the Laboratory

Entry of these unjudged stimuli into the context suggests possibilities for applications outside the laboratory. There is a practical interest in conditions that maximize the mean of all the judgments, particularly if one identifies judgments with experienced values (Parducci, 1984). When each stimulus is judged as it enters the context, range–frequency theory implies that this overall mean is proportional to the skewing of the contextual stimuli (Parducci, 1983). Because of the moderating influence of the frequency principle, the overall mean of the ratings always seems disappointingly closed to "average", i.e., to the middle value of the rating scale. For example, when stimuli from the top half of the range are presented four times more frequently than stimuli from the bottom half, the mean of all the ratings will be only 10% of the way up from the midpoint of the scale, e.g., at the limen between "5 − −average" and "6 − −slightly above average" on a nine–category scale. However, if unjudged stimuli of much lower value also enter the context, the overall mean of the ratings could be "7 − −satisfying" or higher on the same nine–point rating scale. The reminder of this paper presents speculations about possible entry of unjudged events into the context for everyday value judgments.

Identifying the context. Identifying the context for judgment sometimes seems hopelessly difficult outside the laboratory, but often one can make an educated guess. For example, if in the tropics there are complaints of the cold when the temparature is 25° C, one can be pretty sure that a context has been established by temparatures experienced right there in the tropics. One can have a similar experience in a temperate climate when a summer day seems cold even though the temparature is far above what it would be in winter. But unlike the context in psychophysical experiments, the context for everyday judgments of temparature is not always restricted to recent experiences. We evaluate the summer as "very cold" when our context consists mainly of much warmer summers from years back and does not include the intervening winters. Clearly, what gets included in the context depends on what it is that is being evaluated (cf., Kahneman & Miller, 1986).

One might try to make a cold summer seem warmer by reading adventure stories about trips to the Antarctic. This probably would not work. Fiction, fairy tales, movies − these seem to form their own contexts. However absorbed we become in them, whether or not we shiver in empathy with the frozen explorers, judgments of our own physical world seem scarcely affected.

Social comparisons. This type of contextual segregation is illustrated by the literature on social comparisons, in particular the research on "relative deprivation" (Crosby, 1976). You can read about some Arabian oil sheik being worth millions or billions of dollars without feeling any more impoverished yourself. However, if a colleage is sufficiently indiscrete to boast of having received a remarkable bonus, your own salary may suddenly seem inadequate − particularly if you evaluate your colleage as no more deserving than yourself. These potential events that are not experienced directly themselves have to seem like real possibilities before they can be incorporated in our contexts. Evoking dreadful comparisons is often ineffective. The mother can assert that the starving children of Bangladesh or Ethiopia would be delighted to eat the Brussels sprouts, but that does not make them any more palatable to children who cannot conceive being that starved themselves.

Scale changes. The literature on social comparisons raises an interesting question for contextual interpretations of judgment. When we hear of a rival's good fortune, we are not likely to experience empathically the thrill of success. More often, our immediate experience is a pang of disappointment. Has this higher level of success extended our contextual range upward without being judged itself?

Upward extension would mean that if we had judged the new event, our judgment would have been extremely positive. It seems more likely that hearing of the rival's success changes the meaning or scale value of our own situation, its position in an unchanged context: our rival's good news is our bad news. Mellers and Birnbaum (1982) have shown how such changes in scale value can be separated analytically from changes in context.

Drifts and biased sampling. Judgments of present events could be greatly enhanced if the contextual sampling of past events were distorted systematically downward. The negative time-order errors of psychophysics (Helson, 1964) can be interpreted as a downward drift in the values of contextual stimuli. Judgments would also be enhanced if representations of good events were dropped more quickly from the context than representations of bad events. Although neither of these two possibilities seems consistent with the literature on memory, the context for judgment is not the same as the set of remembered events. One can recall a dreadful experience without thereby feeling better about one's present situation, and our own pilot work on recall or recognition of the frequencies of previous presentations of squares does not encourage identification of the context with memory. Systematic distortion of contexts in the negative direction seems a happy (if somewhat unlikely) possibility, but one that we shall not discuss further in this paper.

Goals as context. The context for evaluating outcomes often seems to include goals or ambitions. Our intuitive theories of motivation tell us that we achieve more when we aim high. But the higher we aim, the further short of our goal we are likely to fall — so that we are more disappointed with our actual level of achievement. This ironical sense of failure may sometimes plague even the most successful.

How might goals enter the context for such self-evaluations? Initially, we may experience the goal in pleasing anticipation as we envision a future triumph. Though it is still in the future, we are already judging it positively. A new goal becomes the upper-endpoint of a context that it has extended upward. When we repeatedly experience this anticipation of success, we are skewing the distribution more negatively, i.e., with more of the experienced events, real or imaginary, near the top of the contextual range. But this works only insofar as our delusions of grandeur outweigh in experience the awareness of our lesser levels of actual achievement.

Alternatively, we sometimes anticipate the failure of our efforts. If this possibility of failure could establish a lower endpoint for the context without having to be experienced (even in anticipation), we could be enjoying a "free ride." It would be free in the sense of enhancing our judgments of what does occur without our having to pay with suffering for this lower endpoint. Adding an unjudged lower-endpoint to the context could greatly increase the overall mean of the judgments, producing a level more consistent with the glowing self-avowels that people regularly produce in response to surveys of happiness (cf., Andrews & Withey, 1976; Parducci, 1984).

Unjudged, evoked contexts. Contextual elements that are neither judged nor experienced may sometimes be evoked by the logic of those events that we do experience and judge. In the pseudogambling experiment, winning $200 evoked the possibility of losing $200. The likely symmetry of wins and losses in gambling makes it a special type of situation; this and a similar experiment with judgments of morality (Marsh & Parducci, 1978) are among the very few demonstrations of "neutral-point anchoring," in which the middle of the scale remains unchanged in spite of large contextual effects produced by extending the range in one direction or the other. However, it raises the question of whether other types of inferred counterfactuals may have some generality, as suggested in a recent article on "norm theory" by Kahneman and Miller (1986). For example, surpassing a goal may evoke the possibility of having fallen short of that goal.

Models of evoked events. We have begun to explore algebraically the implication for judgment of various models of how this might work. For example, in addition to the more recent past events (or some representative sampling of past events) in the same domain, the context can include unjudged elements temporarily evoked by the event being judged. The values of these temporary additions to the context may be either below, equal to, or above the currently experienced event, in any combination determined probabilistically. Current goals and extreme counterfactuals can also be included.

The effects permitting these additional, evoked elements in a temporary context, events that are not themselves judged and whose effects are only upon the judgment of the event that evoked them, depend upon the respective probabilities with which they are evoked and also on the frequency distribution of those events that are judged. As would be expected, the overall mean rating is higher when the evoked elements tend to be below whatever event evokes them.

As an illustrative example, consider the context elicited by a negatively-skewed distribution of "experienced events" for which stimulus values above the midpoint are sampled four times as often as those below the midpoint. Let the stimulus value of each event be represented on the dimension of judgment by a number from 20 to 39. With a context of 10 recent events, a representative contextual sample for an event with the stimulus value of 35 might be:

$$23\ 27\ 30\ 33\ 34\ \underline{35}\ 36\ 37\ 37\ 38\ .$$

Assuming equal weighting of range and frequency principles, the category rating of Stimulus 35 in this particular context would be 6.2 on a scale from 1 to 9 — according to the simple range-frequency model described in Parducci (1983) or in Parducci and Wedell (1986). If the rated event had been 25 (instead of 35), its rating in this same context would have been 2.0. Sampling all possible contexts of 10 items within these probabilistic constraints, the expected value of the mean of all ratings (including ratings of items as low as 20 or as high as 39) would be only 5.4 on the nine-point scale.

If one assumes, as suggested by our psychophysical research, that the two most extreme endpoints remain always in the context, the values 20 and 39 should be added, expanding the number of contextual items to 12. Adding these endpoints produces a greater average change in the less frequent, in this case lower, endpoint, raising the expected mean rating from 5.4 to 5.7. This is still not very far above an even balance at the midpoint of the scale, viz., 5.0.

This expected value can be raised appreciably by substituting a much lower endpoint, representing perhaps a very low goal or a hypothetical failure; for example:

$$21 \ 26 \ 30 \ 32 \ 33 \ 35 \ 35 \ \underline{35} \ 37 \ 38 \ (5 \ 39) \ .$$

The unjudged 5 raises the overall mean rating to 6.2, precluding any rating below 3. Although this is much more encouraging, how likely is it that one's goal could remain so far below one's achievements or that the logical possibility of a great failure would be added to the context without adding the possibility of a great success (e.g., an evoked value of 54)?

It seems much more likely that a particular event evokes as unjudged context other events that are closer to its own level on the dimension of judgment. A particular achievement evokes (perhaps unconsciously) the possibility of having done not quite as well but also the possibility of having done somewhat better. Suppose that to the context of 12 past events (including the two endpoints) one adds a temporarily evoked context of five items that are all close in value to the event being judged. In one such model, each of these five has an equal chance of being determined by one of three rules: (1) equal to S, the value of the event being judged; (2) equal to S plus a random, single-digit value; or (3) equal to S minus a random, single-digit value. A representative sample context for a stimulus with the value 37 might be:

$$25 \ 28 \ 31 \ 32 \ 32 \ 34 \ 34 \ 36 \ \underline{37} \ 39 \ (20 \ 39) \ (31 \ 37 \ 37 \ 43 \ 44) \ .$$

In addition to the sample of previously experienced events and the two extreme endpoints, the five temporary additions include, in this example, two equal values and also one value below and two above its own value. If the rated event had a value of 22, sample sets of evoked items might be:

$$(15 \ 21 \ 22 \ 25 \ 30) \ \text{or} \ (16 \ 19 \ 22 \ 22 \ 22) \ .$$

The net effect of these additions is a modest reduction in the expected value of the overall mean judgment (down to 5.4 from 5.7). Much more striking is its attenuation of extreme judgments. The simple range-frequency model implies that without these evoked items, about 20% of the ratings would be in the extreme categories (either "very very satisfying" or "very very disappointing"); addition of the evoked neighboring items virtually eliminates these extreme ratings! This dramatic attenuation is due primarily to the evocation of unjudged events that are more extreme than the most extreme of the events actually experienced; by temporarily adding values at or beyond the judged event, these evoked values make its rating less extreme.

The possibility of this attenuation may be seen as either good or bad, depending on one's view of life. If life seems "a vale of tears," including a strong portion of misery, one might be consoled by the thought that it would have been even worse without these evoked, but unjudged contextual elements. However, if life includes a lot of satisfying experiences, it might be discouraging to think of how much more ecstasy we could have had without the dampeners.

These models of evoked contexts are still in an early stage of exploration. It would be difficult to test them experimentally. But if this direction of application of range–frequency theory has intuitive appeal, one must be struck by how close the predicted overall mean of the ratings always seems to an even balance between positive and negative judgments.

Summary

Although range–frequency theory predicts the judgments when the context is under experimental control, it cannot predict what gets into the context for judgments made outside the laboratory. In psychophysical research, the context seems largely limited to the most recent 10 to 20 stimulus presentations, with the two endpoints enduring much longer. Contexts for everyday judgments may also include temporarily evoked values close to the stimulus being judged, and also more distatnt values, such as goals, social comparisons, and counterfactuals. Various models for representing these possibilities suggest that the overall mean of the judgments remains discouragingly close to the neutral–point of the scale.

Correspondence should be addressed to Allen Parducci, Department of Psychology, University of California, Los Angeles, CA 90024, U.S.A.

References

Anderson, N.H. (1981). *Foundations of information processing.* New York: Academic Press.

Andrews, F.M., & Withey, S.B. (1976). *Social indicators of well-being: Americans' perceptions of life quality.* New York: Plenum.

Birnbaum, M.H. (1974). Using contextual effects to derive psychophysical scales. *Perception & Psychophysics, 15,* 89–96.

Birnbaum, M.H. (1982). Controversies in psychological measurement. In B. Wegener (Ed.), *Social attitudes and psychophysical measurement.* Hillsdale, NJ: Erlbaum.

Crosby, F. (1976). A model of egoistical relative deprivation. *Psychological Review, 83,* 85–113.

Haubensak, G. (1983). *Absolutes und vergleichendes Urteil.* Berlin: Springer.

Helson, H. (1964). *Adaptation-level theory.* New York: Harper & Row.

Hintzman, D.L., & Block, R.A. (1971). Repetition and memory: Evidence for a multiple-trace hypothesis. *Journal of Experimental Psychology, 88,* 297–306.

Johnson, D.M. (1949). Learning function for a change in the scale of judgment. *Journal of Experimental Psychology, 39,* 851−860.

Kahneman, D., & Miller, D.T. (1986). Norm theory: Comparing reality to its alternatives. *Psychological Review, 93,* 136−153.

Marsh, H.W., & Parducci, A. (1978). Natural anchoring at the neutral point of category rating scales. *Journal of Experimental Social Psychology, 14,* 193−204.

Mellers, B.A., & Birnbaum, M.H. (1982). Loci of contextual effects in judgment. *Journal of Experimental Psychology: Human Perception and Performance, 8,* 582−601.

Parducci, A. (1956). Direction of shift in the judgment of single stimuli. *Journal of Experimental Psychology, 51,* 169−178.

Parducci, A. (1983). Category ratings and the relational character of judgment. In H.-G. Geissler & V. Sarris (Eds.), *Modern trends in perception.* Berlin: VEB Deutscher Verlag der Wissenschaften.

Parducci, A. (1984). Value judgments: Toward a relational theory of happiness. In R. Eiser (Ed.), *Attitudinal judgment.* New York: Springer.

Parducci, A., Calfee, R.C., Marshall, L.M., & Davidson, L.P. (1960). Contexts effects in judgment: Adaptation level as a function of the mean, midpoint, and median of the stimuli. *Journal of Experimental Psychology, 60,* 65−77.

Parducci, A., Knobel, S., & Thomas, C. (1976). Independent contexts for category ratings: A range–frequency analysis. *Perception & Psychophysics, 20,* 360−366.

Parducci, A., & Perrett, L.F. (1971). Category rating scales: Effects of relative spacing and frequency. *Journal of Experimental Psychology Monograph, 89,* 427−452.

Parducci, A., & Wedell, D.H. (1986). The category effect with rating scales: Number of categories, number of stimuli, and method of presentation. *Journal of Experimental Psychology: Human Perception and Performance, 12,* 496−516.

Sarris, V. (1971). *Wahrnehmung und Urteil.* Göttingen: Hogrefe.

Sarris, V. (1976). Effects of stimulus range and anchor value on psychophysical judgment. In H.-G. Geissler & Y.M. Zabrodin (Eds.), *Advances in psychophysics.* Berlin: VEB Deutscher Verlag der Wissenschaften.

Sarris, V., & Parducci, A. (1978). Multiple anchoring of category rating scales. *Perception & Psychophysics, 24,* 35−39.

Ward, L.M., & Lockhead, G.R. (1970). Sequential effects and memory in category judgments. *Journal of Experimental Psychology, 84,* 27−34.

Ward, L.M., & Lockhead, G.R. (1971). Response system processes in absolute judgment. *Perception & Psychophysics, 9,* 73−78.

Wedell, D.M. (1984). *A process model for psychophysical judgment.* Unpublished doctoral dissertation. University of California, Los Angeles.

Wedell, D.H., Parducci, A., & Geisselman, R.E. (1987). A formal analysis of ratings of physical attractiveness: Successive contrast and simultaneous assimilation. *Journal of Experimental Social Psychology, 23,* 230−249.

Psychophysical Explorations of Mental Structures
Edited by H.-G. Geissler
in collaboration with M.H. Müller and W. Prinz
© 1990 by Hogrefe & Huber Publishers

Chapter 7

Primacy Effects in Absolute Judgments

Gert Haubensak
Fachbereich Psychologie
Justus Liebig Universität
Gießen, F.R.G

Among the various theories of absolute judgments Parducci's range-frequency theory (Parducci, 1963, 1965; Parducci & Perrett, 1971; Parducci, Knobel, & Thomas, 1976) has been rather influential in recent years. The theory assumes that two principles determine the judgments. The range principle postulates that the Ss match their end categories to the end stimuli which define the stimulus range. The frequency principle postulates that each of the available categories is used equally often, or, alternatively, that the same number of stimuli is placed in each category. According to Parducci and Perrett (1971), the overt judgments reflect a compromise between these two principles.

Range-frequency theory has been notably successful in predicting the effects of stimulus range, spacing, and frequency on category ratings. Particularly, it is the only theory that accounts for the joint effects of all three variables. Nevertheless, Parducci's interpretation of the frequency phenomena may be questioned. Parducci ascribes the frequency phenomena to the Ss' inclination to use the missing or infrequent categories more often. The same position is taken up by Stevens and Galanter (1957) who assert that the Ss "inevitably" have expectations regarding the relative frequencies with which they should use the various categories. According to Stevens and Galanter, the

Ss' normal expectation is that they would be required to use the categories approximately equally often.

The difficulty with that interpretation is that some kind of counting, or representation, of stimulus frequencies is involved, even though Parducci is not quite clear on that point (cf. Parducci, 1963; Parducci & Perrett, 1971; Parducci, Knobel, & Thomas, 1976; Parducci, 1983). There are various findings which cast doubts on such an interpretation. For example, the Ss' ability to assess absolute stimulus frequencies is surprisingly poor. Parducci (1963) had his Ss record the number of stimuli which they recalled having been shown. Only 10% of the estimates were exactly correct. Individual estimates ranged from 4 to 45 stimuli, the correct number being 7 or 9 stimuli, depending on the stimulus distribution. As Parducci (1983) points out, these estimates might only reflect crude inferences from the Ss' own category ratings. Supporting evidence for this hypothesis has been provided by Neumann (1964). In his experiments he shifted the range of the stimuli from lower to higher values. Those of his Ss who were not aware of the shift adjusted their scale to the range of the poststhift series, whereas those who reported they had recognized the stimulus shift did not. A reasonable explanation for this rather curious finding might be that the verbal reports are based on the Ss' own category ratings, i.e., the Ss have no direct access to the stimulus values, much less the stimulus frequencies.

Further evidence against frequency counting or representation has been adduced by Parducci himself. In two supplementary experiments (Parducci, 1963; Parducci & Perrett, 1971) he forced his Ss to keep a cumulative record of how many stimuli they had placed in each category. The expectation was that the frequency tendency would be more pronounced when the Ss had a continuous record of their own response frequencies. There was, however, but little shift in the judgments both times.

The most conclusive evidence against frequency counting, or representation, has been provided by Schüssler (1981). Repeating Parducci's 1956 experiments with judgments of squares, Schüssler found that the Ss' category ratings displayed the so-called frequency tendency after only three stimulus presentations. This held true for both positively and negatively skewed frequency distributions. The data from an experiment formerly done at our laboratory confirmed Schüssler's results. In this experiment (Haubensak, 1984, 1985) the frequency distribution was positively skewed (i.e., the smaller stimuli were presented more often than the larger stimuli). On the very first trial most Ss selected a category that was close to the middle of the category scale but on the next two or three trials the Ss' category ratings reached or even overshot their final level. After such a small number of presentations the Ss could not be fully cognizant of the stimulus distribution. For that reason it seems highly improbable that the shifts in their category ratings were due to an inclination to use the missing or less frequent categories more often.

Primacy Effects

The early occurrence of frequency phenomena suggests a number of alternative interpretations. One is in terms of sequence effects (Haubensak, 1984, 1985). Still another is in terms of primacy effects (Haubensak, 1981, 1985). The primacy model assumes that the judgment scale is formed very early in the series and subsequently becomes hard to change.

Frequency phenomena arise from the fact that the more frequent stimuli are likely to come first when order is random. The judgment scale will therefore be centered on the range of the more frequent stimuli. With skewed distributions the centering produces a frequency bias. This may best be illustrated by an example. With multiple presentations of the smaller stimuli, the largest stimulus makes its first appearance relatively late in the presentations. By that time the upper end of the judgment scale will have been anchored to some smaller stimulus leaving only the more extreme categories to the larger stimuli. These stimuli will therefore be judged larger than they should be.

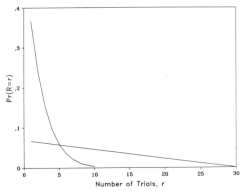

Figure 1. Probability distributions of the number of trials needed to obtain the largest and the smallest stimulus. The stimuli are presented in a random order with frequencies $11-7-5-3-2-2$. Flat curve: largest stimulus. Steep curve: smallest stimulus.

The most common procedure is to present the stimuli in random order without replacement. Hence each trial block can be compared to an urn from which balls of different colors are drawn, one at a time, without returning the chosen ball to the urn. The probability that it will take exactly R trials until the first occurrence of a prespecified stimulus is given by the negative hypergeometric distribution (cf. Johnson & Kotz, 1977, pp. 84−85). In most of our experiments we used a distribution with consecutive stimulus frequencies $11-7-5-3-2-2$. For this distribution the expected number of trials until the first occurrence of the largest stimulus is $E(R) = 10.33$ ($s = 6.94$), whereas it takes only 2.58 trials ($s = 1.86$) until the first occurrence of the smallest stimulus. Figure 1 shows the separate distributions of the number of trials needed to obtain the largest and the smallest stimulus of the series.

Experiment I

The primacy model rests on the assumption that the judgment scale forms after a small number of presentations and subsequently becomes hard to change. To test this assumption, a change was made in the range of the stimuli presented for judgment.

Method. The stimuli were 16 luminous outline squares whose widths varied from 1.0 cm to 16.0 cm, each step by 1.0 cm in an arithmetic series. The squares appeared, one at a time, on a 14 inch dark-tint screen viewed by the S seated at a distance of approximately 60 cm.

The Ss were 20 young students of psychology at the Justus Liebig University of Giessen. They were divided up into two groups. For Group L the shift was from the lower half of the stimulus range to the total stimulus range (i.e., from stimuli 1 − 8 to stimuli 1 − 16). For Group U the shift was in the opposite direction (i.e., from stimuli 9 − 16 to stimuli 1 − 16). There were two blocks of preshift trials followed by ten blocks of postshift trials. The temporal arrangement of the presentation series is diagrammed in Figure 2. There was no break in the presentation sequence. Within each block, order of presentation was random without replacement. A different random order was used for each S.

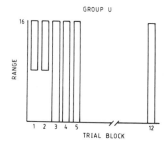 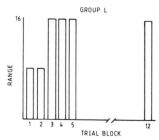

Figure 2. Schematic representation of the temporal arrangement of the presentation series.

The following instruction was administered to the Ss: "This is a study of how people judge the size of different squares. A series of squares will appear on the screen in front of you. Your task is to put each square in the categories numbered 1 through 6, according to its size. '1' is the undermost and '6' is the topmost of the six categories. There may or may not be more than one square in each category. This experiment concerns subjective impressions only, thus, there can be no right or wrong answers.

When you have made your judgments, press the appropriate response key on the calculator field of the keyboard in front of you. Once you have pressed the key, the presented square will disappear. To continue, press the space bar with your left hand. The next square will then appear on the screen immediately. Of course, your choices will seem arbitrary at first, but make one of the six responses anyway. After a number of presentations, you will have more confidence in your judgment."

Results and Discussion. A comparison was made between the two groups on the basis of the Ss' combined mean ratings of the stimuli. The group means are plotted in the upper part of Figure 3 as a function of the amount of postshift exposure. Inspection of this figure indicates that there is some adjustment to the postshift series but it is incomplete. At the last trial block (i.e., after 160 postshift presentations) the group means are still 1.5 category units apart. A trend analysis performed upon the mean ratings across the last six trial blocks indicated that the difference is extremely significant ($F(1, 18) = 33.51$, $p < 0.000$).

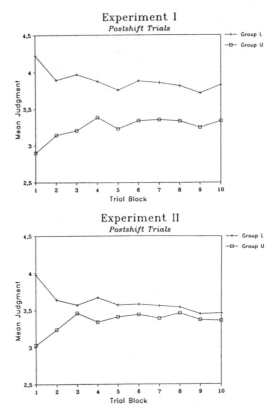

Figure 3. Upper part: Effect of different preshift series on subsequent mean rating of stimuli 1–16. Group U received two presentations with the upper half of the postshift series and Group L with the lower half, respectively. Adjustment to the postshift series is rapid but incomplete. Lower part: The same as above, but this time for Experiment II. Adjustment to the postshift series is fairly complete.

Inspection of Figure 3, upper part, suggests that the adjustment process is never complete. Accepting the hypothesis that the mean rating by Group L will never be the same as the mean rating made by Group U is tantamount to accepting the null hypothesis of no change in the difference between the group means. In order to minimize the type II error we used a level of $a = 0.10$ for a test of significance. Even at this level the null hypothesis of no change in the differences could not be rejected for the last six blocks of trials (approx. $F(5,14) = 0.06$, $p < 0.99$).

There was also no change in the combined mean of the two groups (approx. $F(5,14) = 2.12$, $p < 0.12$). Taken together, the results provide support for the hypothesis that the judgment scale forms after only few presentations and subsequently becomes stabilized.

An implication of the fixation of scale is that stimuli falling outside the initial range will be assigned to the extreme categories. This implication can be tested by comparing the frequencies with which the extreme categories were used by the two groups. In Figure 4, upper part, the percentage frequencies are plotted for the first block of postshift trials. The bars indicate that Group L used the highest categories (i.e., categories 5 and 6) far more frequently than Group U. For the two lowest categories (i.e., categories 1 and 2) the trend was in the opposite direction. This is just what should be expected when the range of the initial set of stimuli is transferred to the subsequent stimuli (cf. Poulton, 1979). Figure 4, lower part, shows that the transfer effects are still there in the last block of postshift trials (i.e., after 160 presentations).

Experiment II

The only difference between Experiments I and II was in the amount of experience Ss had with the preshift series. In Experiment II, there was only one block of preshift trials (instead of two as in Experiment I). The expectation was that with a smaller amount of preshift exposure the Ss would show more adjustment to the postshift series. The group means are shown in the lower part of Figure 3. Again a trend analysis was performed upon the mean rating across the last six blocks of trials. The differences between the group means were clearly not significant ($F(1,18) = 1.07$, $p < 0.32$). Again there was no change in the combined mean of the two groups across the last six trial blocks (approx. $F(5,14) = 1.62$, $p = .21$). From these results it may be concluded that with a smaller amount of preshift exposure the readjustment of the judgment scale is fairly complete.

General Discussion

Resistance to change of scale has been repeatedly found. To mention just a few examples, Parducci (1954, Experiment I) had his Ss judge ten different separations of two line. In order to create an initially false impression of the stimulus distribution, he postponed the presentation of the upper half of the stimulus series (stimuli $6-10$) until the 16th trial. To his great surprise, 5 of the 13 Ss showed no shift at all in their judgments.

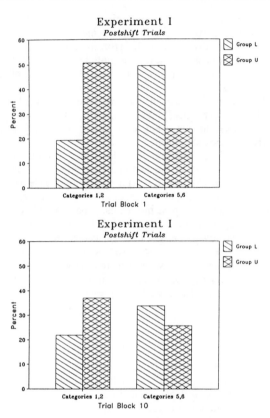

Figure 4. Upper part: Experiment I. Percentage frequencies of categories 1 and 2, and 5 and 6, respectively, as a function of preshift exposure. Group U received two presentations with the upper half of the postshift series and Group L with the lower half. First block of postshift trials is shown. Group U uses categories 1 and 2 more frequently than Group L. For categories 5 and 6 the opposite is true. Lower part: Same as above, except that the last block of postshift trials is shown. The effects of different preshift exposure can still be observed.

Two years later, Parducci (1956, Experiment I) again found a surprisingly small amount of shift when the postshift series was a restricted range of stimuli drawn from the lower half of the preshift range. Varying the amount of experience Ss had with the preshift distributions he found that the rigidity of the judgment scale was not a simple, increasing function of the amount of preshift experience.

Finally, reviewing Johnson's (1949) experiments with judgments of pitch, Guilford (1954, pp. 315−316) noted that there was considerable resistance to change of scale. This was brought out especially well by Johnson's mathematical formulation. Johnson proposed the hypothesis that the limen or transition point between the categories "high" and "low", $L(n)$, at any moment during the adjustment process should be a weighted average of the preshift limen, $L(1)$, and the limen, $L(2)$, that should be expected if there were complete adjustment to the new series. In terms of an equation

$$L(n) = \frac{wL(1) + nL(2)}{w + n} .$$

The postshift limen, $L(2)$, is weighted by the number of postshift trials, n, and the preshift limen, $L(1)$, is weighted by w, an empirical constant indicating the weight of the preshift series in hindering readjustment to the postshift series. There was more resistance to change with a shift from the lower–pitched to the higher–pitched tones than in the opposite direction. Some extra predisposing resistance against readjustment of the scale was indicated by the fact that, with five presentations of the preshift series, the weight given to the preshift limen relative to the weight of one trial in the postshift series became greater than 1.00. From this result Guilford (1954) concluded that the old impressions were more powerful than the more recent ones.

Using Johnson's equation, we determined the weight of the preshift limen for the data of Experiment I and II. The asymptotical value of the postshift limen, $L(2)$, (i.e., the value that should be expected if there were complete adjustment to the postshift series) was calculated from the data of Experiment II. The asymptotical value happened to be quite close to the midpoint of the total stimulus range, i.e., half–way between stimulus *8* and *9*. Fitting the empirical data with Johnson's equation by the method of least squares we obtained for w the values presented in Table 1.

Table 1. Weight given to preshift limen relative to weight of one trial in postshift series.

	Group L	Group U
Experiment 1	5.95	1.60
Experiment 2	0.75	0.65

The results exactly parallel those cited above. In Experiment I greater weighting had to be given to the preshift than to the postshift limen. With an extension of the range at the upper end of the series there was much more resistance against a change of scale than with an extension of the range at the lower end.

Summary

The results of the two experiments reported in the present paper indicate that the initial experiences with a series of stimuli can be more potent than the recent ones. The findings may be used as an explanation for frequency effects in judgments. The explanation is based on the fact that the less frequently presented stimuli seldom come first. Thus, the subject's initial scale is centered on the range of the more frequently presented stimuli, leaving only the extreme categories for the stimuli outside this range. Frequency effects may be due to the persistence of the initial judgments of the stimuli. Other frequency effects may exist (cf. Parducci & Wedell, 1986) but they have to be disentangled from the anchoring or centering effects reported in the present study.

It would be very important to conduct further studies, attempting to find out those characteristics of the situation which might be responsible for the persistence of the initial judgments. One is tempted to speculate that with a smaller number of categories the judgment scale forms even more rapidly because less subranges or boundaries have to be learned. Hence, the primacy effects should be even more pronounced with fewer categories.

One important characteristic of absolute judgment tasks is that Ss are given no information feed-back. The only criterion they can use is the internal consistency of their judgments (cf. Petzold, 1981). The lack of external information feed-back might contribute to the earlier anchoring and subsequent stabilization of the judgment scale.

Correspondence should be addressed to Gert Haubensak, Fachbereich Psychologie, Justus Liebig Universität, Otto–Behagel–Str. 10, 6400 Giessen, F.R.G.

References

Guilford, J.P. (1954). *Psychometric methods* (2nd ed.). New York: McGraw–Hill.

Haubensak, G. (1982). Eine weitere Vereinfachung der Range-Frequency Theorie des absoluten Urteils. *Psychologische Beiträge, 24,* 352–355.

Haubensak, G. (1984). Die psychologischen Grundlagen des Häufigkeitseffektes in absoluten Urteilen. *Psychologische Beiträge, 26,* 136–141.

Haubensak, G. (1985). *Absolutes und vergleichendes Urteil.* Heidelberg: Springer.

Johnson, D.M. (1949). Learning function for a change in the scale of judgment. *Journal of Experimental Psychology, 39,* 851–860.

Johnson, N.L., & Kotz, S. (1977). *Urn models and their application.* New York: Wiley.

Neumann, O. (1964). Wahrnehmungs– oder Urteilsänderung bei Anpassung eines Bezugssystems an eine veränderte Reizserie? Unpublished manuscript.

Parducci, A. (1954). Learning variables in the judgment of single stimuli. *Journal of Experimental Psychology, 48,* 24–30.

Parducci, A. (1956). Direction of shift in the judgment of single stimuli. *Journal of Experimental Psychology, 51,* 169–178.

Parducci, A. (1963). Range-frequency compromise in judgment. *Psychological Monographs, General and Applied, 77,* 1–50.

Parducci, A. (1965). Category judgment: A range-frequency model. *Psychological Review, 72,* 407–418.

Parducci, A. (1983). Category ratings in the relational character of judgment. In H.G. Geissler & V. Sarris (Eds.), *Modern issues in perception* (pp. 262–282). Berlin: VEB Deutscher Verlag der Wissenschaften.

Parducci, A., Knobel, S., & Thomas, C. (1976). Independent contexts for category ratings: A range-frequency analysis. *Perception & Psychophysics, 20,* 260–366.

Parducci, A., & Perrett, L.F. (1971). Category rating scales: Effetcs of relative spacing and frequency of stimulus values. *Journal of Experimental Psychology, 89,* 427–452.

Parducci, A., & Wedell, D.H. (1986). The category effect with rating scales: Number of categories, number of stimuli, and method of presentation. *Journal of Experimental Psycho logy: Human Perception and Performance, 12,* 496–516.

Petzold, P. (1981). Distance effects on sequential dependencies in categorical judgments. *Journal of Experimental Psychology: Human Perception and Performance, 6,* 1371–1385.

Poulton, E.C. (1979). Models for biases in judging sensory magnitude. *Psychological Bulletin, 86,* 777–803.

Schüssler, S. (1981). *Range-Frequency Theorie und Orientierungstheorie.* Phil. Dissertation, Universität Würzburg, Würzburg, F.R.G.

Stevens, J.J., & Galanter, E.H. (1957). Ratio scales and category scales for a dozen perceptual continua. *Journal of Experimental Psychology, 54,* 377–411.

Psychophysical Explorations of Mental Structures
Edited by H.-G. Geissler
in collaboration with M.H. Müller and W. Prinz
© 1990 by Hogrefe & Huber Publishers

Chapter 8

A Psychophysical View
of Equity Theory

Barbara Mellers
Department of Psychology, University of California
Berkeley, U.S.A.

This chapter examines the question of what is psychologically "fair" or equitable. In the last twenty years, equity judgments have been investigated by a number of researchers interested in descriptive models of fairness (Adams, 1965; Anderson, 1976; Harris, 1976, 1980; Messick & Sentis, 1979). The purpose of this chapter is to point out some connections between psychophysical judgment and equity judgment. Equity judgment can be thought of as a special case of comparison across stimulus dimensions. Theories developed to account for comparisons of psychophysical stimuli also appear successful at describing judgments of equity and inequity.

Cross Dimensional Comparison

Two theories of cross dimensional comparison are mapping theory and relation theory (Krantz, 1972; Shepard, 1978). According to mapping theory, stimuli from different modalities are mapped onto a common scale of sensation. Cross-modality matches occur when the values of the two sensations are equivalent. In contrast, relation theory asserts that relations between sensations, rather than sensations themselves, are compared. For example, the ratio of the heaviness of two weights might be compared to the ratio of the loudness of two tones. When these ratios are equal, a cross-modality match is obtained.

Mellers and Birnbaum (1982) proposed another theory of cross dimensional comparison referred to as relativity theory. This theory asserts that people consider the relative position of a stimulus in its distribution along one dimension and compare it to the relative standing of a stimulus on another dimension. To illustrate, consider the question, "Was Fechner as good at psychophysics as Bach was at musical composition?". According to relativity theory, people compare the relative position of Fechner in a subjective distribution of psychophysicists to the relative standing of Bach in a distribution of composers. The stimulus with the higher relative standing is judged to be "better."

In a psychophysical task, subjects might be asked, "Is the tone as loud as the weight is heavy?". According to relativity theory, people compare the relative position of the heaviness of a weight in the distributions of weights to the relative standing of the loudness of a tone in the distribution of tones. The common denominator along which comparisons are made is the relative position of a stimulus in its distribution.

Defining Relative Position

The relative position of a stimulus in its distribution is assumed to be the range–frequency value of that stimulus, according to Parducci's (1968, 1974, 1982) range–frequency theory. Range–frequency theory predicts how the judgment of a stimulus depends on its subjective value and the surrounding stimulus distribution. The range–frequency value of a stimulus is a compromise between two relative standings: the rank of a stimulus (the frequency principle) and the position of a stimulus relative to the endpoints (the range principle).

Range–frequency theory has been quite successful at describing contextual effects of numerous psychophysical continua (see Parducci & Perrett, 1971). Mellers and Birnbaum (1982) asked subjects to rate the subjective darkness of

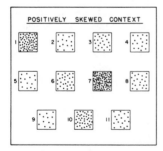
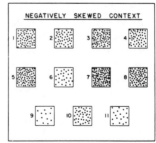

Figure 1. Two stimulus distributions. Patterns 9, 11, 6, 10, 1, and 7 are identical in both contexts; these stimuli have 12, 18, 27, 40, 60, and 90 dots, respectively. From Mellers and Birnbaum (1982).

dot patterns in one of two contexts. Figure 1 shows the two distributions which are positively skewed and negatively skewed with six patterns common to each of the contexts. The range of the two distributions is identical, but ranks of the six common stimuli vary across contexts.

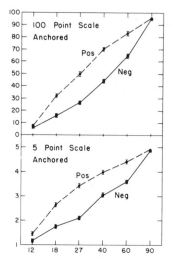

Figure 2. Mean category ratings for the common dot patterns plotted against number of dots. Dashed curves show ratings for the positively skewed distribution. Upper and lower panels show results for the 1 to 100 and 1 to 50 rating scales, respectively. Brackets represent plus and minus one standard error. From Mellers and Birnbaum (1982).

Figure 2 presents mean ratings of the common dot patterns using two anchored category rating scales (1 to 100 and 1 to 5) with a separate curve for each stimulus distribution. If there were no contextual effects, the curves would be identical. However, judgments of the same stimulus differ depending on the stimulus distribution. For example, in the upper panel, the 40 dot stimulus is rated "50" in the positively skewed distribution and "27" in the negatively skewed distribution. The curve from the positively skewed distribution is concave downward relative to the curve from the negatively skewed distribution, consistent with a range–frequency interpretation.

These types of contextual effects occur not only in category ratings, but have also been demonstrated in magnitude estimations and so-called "absolute" scales. Some researchers have argued that when subjects are allowed to choose their own standards and moduli in magnitude estimation tasks, the resulting judgments are an "absolute" scale of sensation (Zwislocki & Goodman, 1980; Zwislocki, 1983). Figure 3 shows "absolute" scales and magnitude estimations for the same stimuli as in Figure 1.

Panel A presents results using the "absolute" scaling procedure of Zwislocki and Goodman (1980). Responses to the same stimuli are assigned quite different numerical values as a function of the context. Although the freedom of the "absolute" scaling procedure increases individual differences, effects of the context still remain.

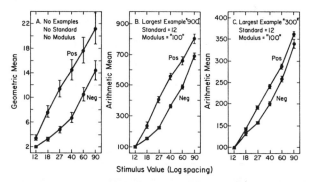

Stimulus Value (Log spacing)

Figure 3. Magnitude estimations plotted against number of dots. Panel A presents geometric means for subjects who were given the absolute scaling instructions of Zwislocki and Goodman (1980). Panels B and C show arithmetic means for subjects who were told to use the 12 dot pattern as the standard and "100" as the modulus. The two curves in Panel B are results when the instructions included an example response as high as "900"; Panel C shows results when the highest example is "300". Brackets represent plus and minus 1/12.5 of a standard deviation in all three panels. Pos = positively skewed distributions; Neg = negatively skewed distributions.

Panels B and C show magnitude estimations for subjects who were told to use lightest dot pattern as the standard and "100" as the modulus. Effects of the context appear similar in all three panels.

"Fair" Reward Allocations

Mellers (1982, 1986) has shown quite similar contextual effects in "fair" reward allocations. She asked subjects to distribute a fixed annual salary budget among a group of hypothetical faculty members given their merit ratings. The task was to determine the yearly salaries in as "fair" a way as possible.

Figure 4 presents the distributions of faculty merit ratings used by Mellers (1982, 1986). Longer dashes represent merit ratings common to all of the distributions (0.5, 1.0, 1.5, 2.0, 2.5, 3.0, 3.5), and shorter dashes are additional filler stimuli that were included to vary the contexts. For example, in the positively skewed distribution, there are additional faculty members with lower merit ratings; in the negatively skewed distribution, there are additional faculty members with higher merit ratings. Annual budgets were either $130,000, $260,000, or $520,000 (with an average of $10,000, $20,000, or $40,000 per faculty member).

Figure 5 presents mean salary allocations plotted as function of the merit ratings common to all of the distributions with a separate curve for each context. Upper panels are salaries from the bimodal and unimodal distributions;

lower panels are salaries from the positively skewed and negatively skewed distributions. "Fair" salaries assigned to the same merit value differ as a function of the stimulus distribution. For example, a faculty member with a merit rating of 3.0 in a positively skewed distribution is assigned a higher salary than the same faculty member in a negatively skewed distribution for all three levels of budget.

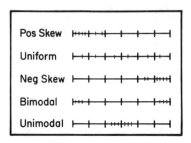

Figure 4. Stimulus distributions used for experiments on "fair" salaries and taxes. Longer lines represent common stimuli (merit ratings or salaries); shorter lines are the contextual stimuli. For merit ratings, the endpoints are 0.5 and 3.5; for salaries, the endpoints are $15,000 and $45,000. Pos Skew = positively skewed distribution; Neg Skew = negatively skewed distribution. From Mellers (1986).

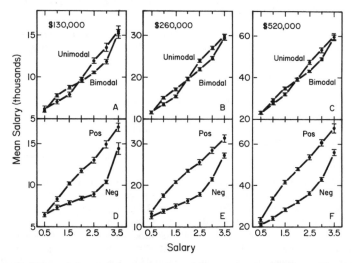

Figure 5. Mean salaries plotted as a function of the common merit ratings with a separate curve for each merit distribution and a separate panel for each amount to distribute. Upper panels show the bimodal and unimodal merit distributions; lower panels show the positively and negatively skewed merit distributions. Brackets represent plus and minus one standard error. Pos = positively skewed context; Neg = negatively skewed context. From Mellers (1986).

A Relativity Theory of Equity

Mellers (1982, 1986) argued that judgments of equity and inequity can be described by a theory which derives from the relativity theory of cross dimensional comparison. In particular, an equitable state is one in which the relative position of a person's input in the distribution of inputs matches the relative position of his or her outcome in the distribution of outcomes. When making judgments of inequity, people compare the two relative positions using a subtractive operation. When assigning "fair" outcomes to a set of individuals, people consider the relative position of each person's input and generate an outcome with the same relative standing.

According to the relativity theory of equity, variations in the stimulus distribution produce changes in the relative standing of a stimulus. Because the relative position of a stimulus is assumed to be its range-frequency value, the curves in Figure 5 should be nonlinearly related. The curve from the unimodal distribution should be steeper in the center than at the ends, and the curve from the bimodal distribution should show the opposite result. Similarly, the curve from the positively skewed distribution should be concave downward relative to the curve from the negatively skewed distribution. The results in all three panels are consistent with this prediction.

An alternative theory of cross dimensional comparison that might account for equity judgments is relation theory. According to relation theory, equity occurs when inputs are proportional to outcomes. Interestingly, this notion is closely related to one proposed over 2200 years ago by Aristotle who said, *"The problem ... is to divide the distributive honor or reward into parts which are to one another as the merits of the persons who are to participate."* (Ross, 1966, p. 1131). Many different forms of the Aristotelian theory of equity have subsequently been proposed (Adams, 1965; Anderson, 1976; Walster, Walster & Berscheid, 1978).

Relation theory implies that the curves in Figure 5 should be linearly related to each other. Although a small percentage of subjects assigned salaries that were consistent with this rule, the majority of the subjects made judgments that violated this asumption.

"Fair" Reward Allocations with Unspecified Budgets

It might be argued that the data in Figure 5 do not reflect what subjects consider to be "fair" salaries, because the salaries were constrained by a fixed budget. When a budget is specified, the salary given to one person necessarily depends on the salary given to other people. When the budget is unspecified, the salary can, in principle, be independent of the other salaries, and contextual effects might disappear.

To investigate this possibility, Mellers (1986) examined "fair" reward allocations in three additional conditions (positively skewed, uniform, and negatively skewed) without specifying a budget. The results are shown in Figure 6. By relaxing the constraints of the task, subject variability increases. Nonetheless, there are still effects of the stimulus distribution. The shape of the curves is similar to that found with fixed budgets in Figure 5. Thus, the effects of the context still remain even when the budget is unspecified.

Figure 6. Mean salaries plotted as in Figure 5 for conditions in which no budget is specified. Brackets represent plus and minus one standard error. Pos = positively skewed distribution; Unif = uniform distribution; Neg = negatively skewed distribution. From Mellers (1986).

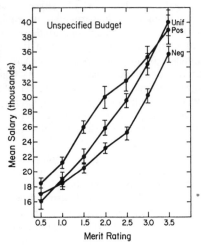

"Fair" Cost Allocations

Related to the question of "fair" reward allocations is that of "fair" cost allocations. What is a "fair" method for distributing shared costs among a group of individuals, each of whom benefits from the cooperative effort? For example, how should the costs of an airport be divided among airline companies that fly different types of planes and schedule different numbers of flights? Or how should a government assign taxes to its citizens in order to generate a fixed amount of revenue?

In order to investigate whether "fair" cost allocations could also be accounted for by the relativity theory of equity, Mellers (1986) used the same stimulus spacings as in Figure 1 to represent the salaries of hypothetical persons. Subjects were asked to assign "fair" salaries to generate a fixed amount of revenue. Longer dashes represent salaries common to all of the distributions ($15,000, $20,000, $25,000, $30,000, $35,000, $40,000, and $45,000); shorter dashes are additional filler stimuli that were included to vary the context.

One third of the subjects generated taxes consistent with the Aristotelian version of relation theory. Figure 7 shows means for the remaining subjects plotted as a function of the common salaries with a separate curve for each salary distribution. Panels on the left show conditions in which the amount of revenue to generate was 10% of the total salaries; panels on the right show conditions in which the amount of revenue was 30% of the salaries.

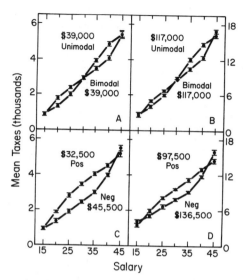

Figure 7. Mean taxes plotted as a function of the common salaries with a separate curve for each salary distribution and a separate panel for each percentage of the total salary to generate in revenue. Brackets represent plus and minus one standard error. Pos = positively skewed context; Neg = negatively skewed context. From Mellers (1986).

"Fair" taxes also depend on the stimulus distribution. Someone with a salary of $30,000 is assigned a higher tax in the positively skewed distribution than in the negatively skewed distribution, regardless of the amount of revenue to generate. Furthermore, effects of the context appear quite similar to those found for "fair" reward allocations. The slopes of the curves are steepest in regions of greatest density, consistent with the relativity theory of equity.

"Fair" Cost Allocations with Unspecified Revenues

Mellers (1986) also examined two conditions in which there was no specified amount of revenue to generate. The results are presented in Figure 8. Although the differences between the curves are less pronounced, there are still effects of the context; the positively skewed curve is concave downward relative to the negatively skewed curve.

Conclusions

What is "dark" or "loud" or "heavy" depends on the frame of reference used for comparison. In the same way, what is "fair" or "equitable" also depends on the other stimuli used for comparison. Both psychophysical judgments and equity judgments show similar effects of the stimulus distribution. An extension of range–frequency theory, which has been successful at describing contextual effects for numerous psychophysical continua, can also account

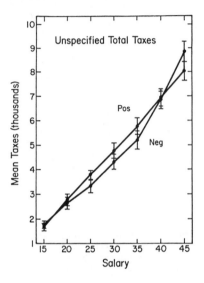

Figure 8. Mean taxes plotted as in Figure 7 for conditions in which no revenue was specified. Brackets represent plus and minus one half of a standard deviation. From Mellers (1986).

for comparison of psychophysical stimuli across different dimensions. Furthermore, equity judgment is a special case of cross dimensional comparison. The present results are consistent with a relativity theory of equity. In equity judgments, subjects consider the relative position of an input in the distribution of inputs and assign an outcome with the same relative standing in the distribution of outcomes. In judgments of inequity, the relative position of inputs and outcomes in their respective distributions are contrasted by means of a subtractive operation. The dimension along which subjects match or compare stimuli is neither sensation nor ratios of sensation, but rather the relative position of the stimulus with respect to its distribution.

Summary

Research on psychophysical judgment has shown that category ratings and magnitude estimations are susceptible to a variety of different contextual effects. Many of these effects can ve described by Parducci's range–frequency theory. According to this theory, judgments are a compromise between the rank of a stimulus in its distribution and the position of the stimulus relative to the endpoints. The present paper demonstrates that certain types of social judgments are also prone to contextual effects in a fashion similar to that found with psychophysical judgments. In particular, "fair" allocations of rewards (salaries) and costs (taxes) vary as a function of the range and spacing of the surrounding stimulus distribution. A theory of "fair" allocations is presented to account for the data. An equitable state is assumed to be one in which the relative position of an outcome in the distribution of outcomes matches the relative position of an input in the distributions of inputs. The relative standing of a stimulus is assumed to be its value based on the range–frequency compromise.

Correspondence should be addressed to Barabara Mellers, Department of Psychology, University of California, Berkeley, CA 94720, U.S.A.

References

Adams, S.J. (1965). Inequity in social exchange. In L. Berkowitz (Ed.), *Advances in experimental social psychology* (Vol. II). New York: Academic Press.

Anderson, N.H. (1976). Information integration applied to equity judgments. *Journal of Personality and Social Psychology, 33*, 291–299.

Harris, R.J. (1976). Handling negative inputs: On the plausible equity formulae. *Journal of Experimental Social Psychology, 12*, 194–209.

Harris, R.J. (1976). Equity judgments in hypothetical four-person partnerships. *Journal of Experimental Social Psychology, 16*, 95–115.

Krantz, D.H. (1972). Magnitude estimations and cross-modality matching. *Journal of Mathematical Psychology, 9*, 168–199.

Mellers, B.A. (1982). Equity judgment: A revision of Aristotelian views. *Journal of Experimental Psychology: General, 111*, 242–270.

Mellers, B.A. (1983). Evidence against "absolute" scaling. *Perception & Psychophysics, 33*, 523–526.

Mellers, B.A. (1986). "Fair" allocations of salaries and taxes. *Journal of Experimental Psychology: Human Perception and Performance, 12*, 80–91.

Mellers, B.A. & Birnbaum, M.H. (1982). Loci of contextual effects in judgment. *Journal of Experimental Psychology: Human Perception and Performance, 8*, 582–601.

Messick, D.M. & Sentis, K.P. (1979). Fairness and preferences. *Journal of Experimental Social Psychology, 15*, 416–434.

Parducci, A. (1968). The relativity of absolute judgment. *Scientific American, 249*, 84–90.

Parducci, A. (1974). Contextual effects: A range–frequency analysis. In E.C. Carterette & M.P. Friedman (Eds.), *Handbook of perception* (Vol. II). New York: Academic Press.

Parducci, A. (1982). Category ratings: Still more contextual effects! In B. Wegner (Ed.), *Social attitudes and psychophysical measurement*. Hillsdale, N.J.: Erlbaum.

Parducci, A & Perrett, L. (1971). Category rating scales: Effects of relative spacing and frequency of stimulus values. *Journal of Experimental Psychology, 89*, 427–452.

Ross, W.D. (Ed.). (1966). *The works of Aristotle* (Vol. IX). London: Oxford University Press.

Shepard, R.N. (1978). On the status of "direct" psychological measurement. In C.W. Savage (Ed.), *Minnesota studies in the philosophy of science* (Vol. IX). Minneapolis: University of Minnesota Press.

Walster, E., Walster, G. & Berscheid, E. (1978). *Equity: Theory and research*. Boston: Allyn & Bacon.

Zwislocki, J.J. (1983). Absolute and other scales: The question of validity. *Perception & Psychophysics, 33*, 593–594.

Zwislocki, J.J. & Goodman, D.A. (1980). Absolute scaling of sensory magnitudes: A validation. *Perception & Psychophysics, 28*, 28–38.

Psychophysical Explorations of Mental Structures
Edited by H.-G. Geissler
in collaboration with M.H. Müller and W. Prinz
© 1990 by Hogrefe & Huber Publishers

Chapter 9

The Influence of Class Membership of Stimuli on Judgment

Andreas Hinz and Hans-Georg Geissler
Sektion Psychologie, Karl-Marx-Universität
Leipzig, G.D.R.

Context effects in judgment processes are accounted for by various theories on frames of reference (Helson, 1964; Sarris, 1971; Parducci and Perrett, 1971; Witte, 1960). Research based on these theories of frames of reference is characterized by the fact that the set of stimuli making up the frame of reference varies only in terms of one continuous dimension. The question of the influence that similar or qualitatively related stimuli have on the formation of a frame of reference remains open. One approach to this question was developed by Wilhelm Witte (1960, 1975; cf. Zoeke and Sarris, 1983). Witte considers objects of everyday experience. The frame of reference is assumed to be formed by all those objects which belong to the same natural conceptual class as the object to be judged. There is also taken account of a sub-class membership of objects. One example Witte himself provided pertains to the sounds produced by a violin. In judging the pitch of violin sounds the set of all sounds of an orchestra forms the total system, the subset of all violin sounds forming the partial system. The judgment is modelled as a compromise between assignment to the total system on the one hand, and the partial system on the other.

This modelling has the disadvantage that the frames of reference of related or similar sub-classes are not taken into account in modelling the frame of reference. For instance, the influence of viola sounds cannot be captured in the example pertaining to the violin sounds. Furthermore, the frequency of the occurrence of the sub-classes is not taken into consideration.

Sub-Classes of Stimuli as a Frame of Reference

For one of the theories of frame of reference, namely the range-frequency theory, we now want to examine a generalization for the case that the stimulus set consists of different sub-classes where the similarities as well as the frequencies of the sub-classes are to be taken into account. Firstly, we present results of an experiment which demonstrates the influence of the sub-classes on the formation of the frame of reference. Secondly, we show how these effects may be explained on the basis of assumptions about the representations and the similarities of the sub-classes. The procedure is described in more detail in Hinz (1987). The reference to the representation is motivated by the principle of 'guided inference' (Geissler & Puffe, 1983).

Method

The stimuli used consisted of four different types of patterns: circles, squares, ovals, and rectangles. There were ten graduations of the size of the patterns corresponding to a linear progression of length and diameter. The subjects were asked to judge the size of the patterns on a five-point rating scale.

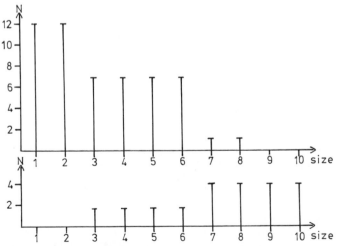

Figure 1. Frequency distributions for condition (a). Upper part: Distribution of the circles. Lower part: Distribution of squares, ovals, and rectangles.

The experiment consisted of two sub-experiments, (a) and (b), that differed in the frequency distribution of the patterns. Figure 1 illustrates the distributions for condition (a).

In condition (a) the distribution of the circles was positively skewed, whereas the distributions of the remaining patterns were negatively skewed. In condition (b) the distributions were reversed, that is, the distribution of the circles was negatively and those of the remaining patterns were positively skewed. In either condition each size level occured with almost equal frequency (12 or 13 times). The frequency of occurrence of the circle was 43%, while that of each of the other patterns was 19%. This choice represented a compromise between equal frequency of the four patterns on the one hand, and equal frequency of the types of distribution on the other hand.

Results

In condition (a) the distribution of the circles was positively-skewed. Mean ratings, in accordance with range-frequency theory, are higher under this condition than for the remaining patterns. It is just the other way round in condition (b). Figure 2 shows the mean ratings for medium-sized patterns.

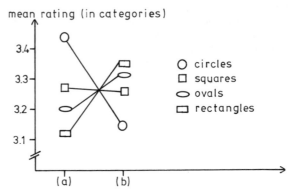

Figure 2. Mean ratings for conditions (a) and (b).

It is apparent that the circle shows the greatest variation between conditions (a) and (b). Among the remaining patterns, the ratings of the rectangle differ most strongly from those of the circle, the difference being less pronounced with the oval, and minimal with the square. Square, oval, and rectangle have the same distributions, thus the differences can be due only to the differential relationship to the pattern that has a different distribution, i.e., the circle.

Witte's theory of partial systems is unable to account for this result. But if we also consider the relationship of the patterns in terms of their similarities, these effects can be explained. A frame which allows for these effects is provided by the following model.

Modelling the Judgment

Our starting point is the basic formula of range-frequency theory.

$$J(x) = w \cdot R(x) + (1-w) \cdot F(x) .$$

This formula is extended so that the individual patterns constitute the frame of reference on the basis of their similarities to the pattern to be judged and the frequencies of their occurrence. The new formula reads as follows:

$$J_i(x) = w \cdot R(x) + (1-w) \cdot \sum_j \frac{h_j \cdot s(i,j)}{\sum_k h_k \cdot s(i,k)} \cdot F_j(x) .$$

$J_i(x)$:   Judgment of pattern i of size level x
$R(x)$:   range value of size level x
$F_j(x)$:   frequency value of pattern j of size level x
$s(i,j)$:   similarity of the patterns i and j
h_j: relative frequency of pattern j

The range value $R(x)$ is almost the same for all sub-classes. Thus we do not need a specifying index for the patterns. The frequency component consists of the frequency values for all sub-classes j, weighted by the similarity of the pattern i to be judged and by the relative frequency of the occurrence of pattern j. The denominator is necessary to force the weights to sum up to 1.

With these formulae we now want to determine the similarities of the patterns. For that purpose we need some specification of the similarities. We assume that each of the four patterns is represented by a set of features that consists of four components, as illustrated in Figure 3.

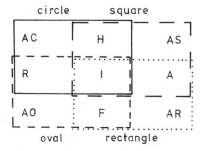

Figure 3. Representation of the four patterns. I: intersection; R: round; A: angular; H: high; F: flat. AC, AS, AO, AR: additional components peculiar to the patterns.

Each segment denotes a certain set of features. The circle, for example, is characterized by the following components: intersection (features that are common to all patterns, like symmetry and closedness), round (features that are common to the circle and oval), high (features that are common to the circle and the square), and AC (features that in addition to those mentioned are peculiar to the circle).

In order to approximately describe the similarity of the patterns on the basis of the features we adopt a special form of Tversky's contrast model (Tversky, 1977). We assume that the measure f is additive, and that only the set of common features is relevant to similarity. For the purpose of standardization we assume that the measure for each pattern equals 1. On the basis of the experimentally obtained rating data $J_i(x)$ and the formulae shown above the $s(i,j)$ and the parameters of the representation were estimated by means of an iterative procedure. For the measures f the equations yielded:

$$f(I) = .32$$
$$f(H) = f(F) = .31$$
$$f(R) = f(A) = .17$$
$$f(AC) = f(AS) = f(AO) = f(AR) = .20 .$$

By means of these values and the specifications mentioned above we can determine the similarities of the patterns. For example, the similarities of the circle (c) and the square (sq), oval (o), and rectangle (r) have the following values:

$$s(c,sq) = .63; \qquad s(c,o) = .49; \qquad s(c,r) = .20; \qquad s(c,c) = 1 .$$

Summary and Conclusion

The range-frequency theory describes contextual effects of stimulus range and frequency distribution for stimulus sets which vary only in terms of one continuous dimension. In this paper the problem of the frame of reference is examined under the aspect that the stimuli also vary in terms of discrete parameters by which different sub-classes of the stimulus set may be defined. An experiment has been presented which demonstrates different influences of the sub-classes on judgment. The greater the similarities of the sub-classes, the stronger the mutual influence of the frame of reference. We presented a mathematical model by which this result is derived theoretically on the basis of a representation of the sub-classes.

Two disadvantages of the procedure should be briefly mentioned. Firstly, the assumptions underlying the model are not tested yet. Such tests would be feasible if different kinds of distribution were examined. Secondly, no further methods for the determination of the representation and similarity of the patterns were used to prove the results obtained. Here we want to emphasize that we were not so much interested in the precise calculation of the special values of the relationship of similarity. Rather, for the case of continuously and discretely varying stimulus material we wanted to offer a possible way to link quantitative theories about frames of reference on the one hand, and set-theoretic ideas for the representation on the other hand.

Correspondence should be addressed to Hans–Georg Geissler, Sektion Psychologie, Karl–Marx–Universität Leipzig, Tieckstr. 2, Leipzig, DDR – 7030.

References

Geissler, H.-G., & Puffe, M. (1983). The inferential basis of classification: From perceptual to memory code systems. In H.-G. Geissler & V. Sarris (Eds.), *Modern issues in perception*. Berlin: Deutscher Verlag der Wissenschaften. Amsterdam: North-Holland.

Helson, H. (1964). *Adaptation level theory. An experimental and systematic approach to behavior*. New York, Evanston, and London: Harper & Row.

Hinz, A. (1987). *Mathematische Modellierung von Kontexteffekten bei Erkennungs- und Beurteilungsprozessen auf der Grundlage der internen Repräsentation von Mustermengen*. Unpublished Doctoral Dissertation, Karl–Marx–Universität, Leipzig.

Parducci, A., & Perrett, L.R. (1971). Rating scales: Effects of relative spacing and frequency of stimulus values. *Journal of Experimental Psychology Monograph, 89*, 427–452.

Sarris, V. (1971). *Wahrnehmung und Urteil*. Göttingen: Hogrefe.

Tversky, A. (1977). Features of similarity. *Psychological Review, 84*, 327–352.

Witte, W. (1975). Zum Gestalt- und Systemcharakter psychologischer Bezugssysteme. In S. Ertel (Ed.), *Gestalttheorie in der modernen Psychologie*. Darmstadt: Steinkopff.

Zoeke, B., & Sarris, V. (1983). A comparison of "frame of reference" paradigms in human and animal psychophysics. In H.-G. Geissler & V. Sarris (Eds.), *Modern issues in perception*. Berlin: Deutscher Verlag der Wissenschaften. Amsterdam: North-Holland.

Psychophysical Explorations of Mental Structures
Edited by H.-G. Geissler
in collaboration with M.H. Müller and W. Prinz
© 1990 by Hogrefe & Huber Publishers

Chapter 10

The Chemical Senses and Aging: Applications of the Method of Magnitude Matching

Joseph C. Stevens
John B. Pierce Foundation and Yale University
New Haven, U.S.A.

Some years ago at the XXII International Congress of Psychology in Leipzig I described a new method, called magnitude matching, for generating cross-modalitiy matching functions by means of magnitude estimation (Stevens & Marks, 1980; Stevens, 1982). In regular cross-modality matching subjects adjust the stimulus intensity in one modality (say loudness) to match various stimulus intensities in another modality (say brightness) and *vice versa*. The new alternative method was especially needed for the study of taste and smell because it is usually impractical to vary the concentrations of chemical stimuli continuously. The purpose of the present paper is to illustrate several applications of magnitude matching in the study of how aging affects the chemical senses. It had been known that aging tends to elevate both taste and odor thresholds (for a review see Bartoshuk, Rifkin, Marks & Bars, 1986), but we wanted to know whether aging also affects the perception of everyday suprathreshold levels of stimulation. As we shall see below, aging tends to spare suprathreshold tastes but to depress suprathreshold odors.

Essentially, in the present context, the method was adapted to work as follows. Two sensory modalities are selected, one for which there is no reason to believe that subjects are abnormal (the standard modality), another for which we might have reason to suspect a sensory abnormality (the target modality). Various stimulus levels are presented alternately to the two modalities but in random order with respect to level. The subjects' task is to make magnitude estimations of the subjective strength of all stimuli on a common scale of sensory magnitude. Then all the estimations of a given subject are normalized by multiplication by a number that makes the average estimation of the standard modality equal a constant across subjects (usualy 10 — an arbitrary but convenient choice). The effect of this procedure is to discount the inclination of some subjects to use large numbers, others small numbers in magnitude estimation. The normalized estimations can then be averaged across groups of subjects (in the present paper young and old subjects) and plotted, usually as straight lines in log–log coordinates (i.e., the data often take the form of a power function). In this way, then, the method of magnitude matching is used to compare a young group's and an old group's psychophysical functions relating perceived magnitude to the target stimulus magnitude.

One of our first applications of this method (Stevens, Plantinga & Cain, 1982) compared a group of 20 elderly persons (over 65 years) with a group of 20 young persons (under 25) for the strength of a fruity odor, iso–amyl butyrate, the target continuum. The standard continuum was loudness of noise. Of course, deafness is common in old age. To control this we used a low–pitched noise (140–500 Hz) — aging is hardest on the high frequencies — and excluded from further testing those persons who failed to meet a threshold criterion.

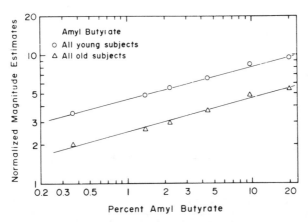

Percent Amyl Butyrate

Figure 1. A comparison in log–log coordinates of the average perceived intensity for 20 young (18–25 yrs) and 20 elderly (65–83 yrs) subjects for various concentrations of iso–amyl–butyrate, expressed as percentages of saturated vapor.

Figure 1 shows the results of this early study. The normalized estimations of the young were on the average 1.8 times larger than those of the elderly, and the differences are highly reliable stastically. Aging here seems to manifest itself in the up–down position of the power function, having little or no effect on the slope (exponent) of the power function. The slope of the functions in Figure 1 is 0.25. Low slopes characterize the world of odors (Cain, 1975; Moskowitz, Dravnieks & Klarman, 1976; Hyman, 1977). Another way to interpret Figure 1 is to note that the average elderly person needed about 10 times greater concentration than did the average young to get equivalent odor strength. I emphasize "average" because there are large individual differences (discussed below).

At about the same time, my colleague Linda Bartoshuk undertook a similar experiment for the four taste qualities, also using loudness as the standard modality (Bartoshuk et al., 1986). Although taste thresholds were typically elevated in her subjects the suprathreshold magnitudes for sweet, sour, and salty seemed to remain remarkably intact, even into very old age (bitter did seem to show some abnormality). As an example, Figure 2 shows the data for saltiness of NaCl. Except at the very low end, the functions for young and old are virtually identical. The curious divergence at the two lowest concentrations may reflect a strong tendency, studied later in some detail (Stevens & Cain, 1985; 1986a), on the part of the elderly to respond false positively to stimulus blanks and to stimuli that are below the measured threshold of the individual subject. This is shown by the symbols at the left end of the figure.

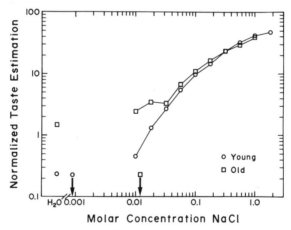

Molar Concentration NaCl

Figure 2. A comparison of average perceived taste intensity for 18 young (20–30 yrs) and 18 elderly (74–93 yrs) subjects as a function of molar concentration of NaCl. Symbols at the left are responses to deionized HOH alone. (Re-drawn from Bartoshuk et al., 1986.)

Because some colleagues expressed skepticism concerning the difference we found between taste and smell as regards aging we made a direct comparison by magnitude matching of smell (amyl–butyrate again) and taste (NaCl solutions), thereby by-passing loudness as the standard continuum (Stevens,

Bartoshuk & Cain, 1984). People find it quite natural to estimate taste and odor strengths on a common scale. Figure 3 shows the outcome for three groups of subjects — young, old, and very old. Here the data were normalized by means of the saltiness estimates, just as earlier by means of the loudness estimations. The results square well with those obtained with loudness: the elderly subjects showed depressed magnitude at all concentration levels tested.

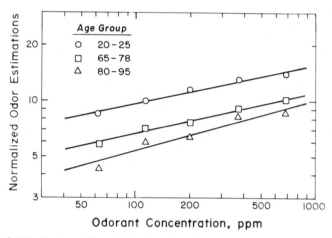

Figure 3. Magnitude matching of odor intensity of iso-amyl-butyrate as a function of parts per million in air. The comparison continuum was saltiness of NaCl. Each group contained 20 or more subjects.

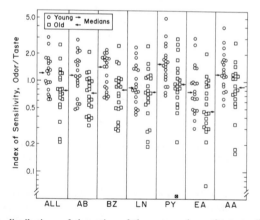

Figure 4. The distributions of the ratios of the mean odor estimate to the mean taste estimate for each subject and each compound: iso-amyl-butyrate (AB), benzaldehyde (BZ), d-limonene (LN), pyridine (PY), ethyl alcohol (EA), iso-amyl alcohol (AA), and the average ratios across compounds for each subject (ALL). Based on 20 young (19–25) and 20 elderly (70–89) subjects.

A weakened sense of smell shows itself not only in depressed magnitude and elevated thresholds but also in poorer ability to identify common odors (Schemper, Voss & Cain, 1981; Doty et al., 1984; Stevens & Cain, 1987). Depressed magnitude also characterizes most, if not all, odorants. One study (Stevens & Cain, 1985) examined six odorants, some pleasant (e.g. the fruity compounds amyl–butyrate, d–limonene, and benzaldehyde), an unpleasant one (pyridine), and two more or less neutral ones, amyl and ethyl alcohol. Saltiness again served as the standard continuum, and the normalized results look much like those in Figure 3. Limonene gave extremely flat functions that were not significantly different across age; a subsequent study, however, did reveal a significant difference between young and old (Stevens & Cain, 1986a).

Figure 4 presents the results in an alternative form in order to highlight individual differences. For each compound and for each subject is plotted the ratio of the mean odor estimate to the mean taste estimate. The average ratio is significantly higher for the young subjects, for all compounds except limonene. The individual ratios should not, however, be taken too seriously since both numerator and denominator are subject to flux. That they have some meaning, however, is proven by the fact that in every other study we have conducted the average index for the young turned out to be significantly higher than that for the elderly.

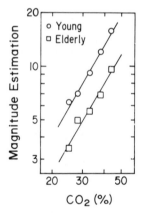

Figure 5. Magnitude matching of the perceived intensity of CO_2 as a function of concentration in air. There were 20 young (19–31) and 20 elderly (67–93) subjects.

Many people are unaware that the nasal cavity houses two kinds of chemical receptors. In addition to olfactory receptors, a population of common chemical receptors line the cavity. These receptors, which are served by the trigeminal, rather than the olfactory nerves, mediate sensations of pungency and irritation. Horseradish, ammonia, and smelling salts serve as examples of effective stimuli; but most, if not all, odorous substances in high enough concentration also trigger these receptors. The common chemical sense, which also has receptors in the oral cavity, pharynx, eyes, and trachea, protects against the inhalation and ingestion of caustic substances. Human beings learn to like moderate stimulation of this sense, and this helps to account for why people eat spicy food and smoke irritating tobacco.

To study sensations mediated by this sense we had subjects sniff various concentrations of CO_2 (Stevens & Cain, 1986b). This gas has little or no odor but triggers common chemical sensations very effectively. The method was again magnitude matching using saltiness as the standard continuum. The results appear in Figure 5, which shows that aging also depresses the sensation of nasal irritation. Note also the interesting difference between the slopes for CO_2 and typica odorants. The slopes in Figure 5 are 1.7, compared to 0.25 for amyl-butyrate in Figure 1. Thus, whereas odor sensation grows very slowly, common chemical sensation grows very rapidly as a function of gaseous concentration.

Many people are also unaware that odorous molecules reach the olfactory receptors not only via the nostrils but also, as in eating and drinking, by way of the nasopharynx. Characteristically odors aroused by this route are frequently referred to the mouth and often attributed to taste (Murphy, Cain & Bartoshuk, 1977; Murphy & Cain, 1980). We deemed it important to learn whether aging weakens nasopharyngeal smelling to comparable degree as it does smelling through the nostrils. For this purpoe we had subjects sample liquid solutions of ethyl butyrate, a compound having little taste but potent odor (resembling fruit-flavored chewing gum). They first sampled the solutions with the nose unpinched, then pinched to prevent odorous molecules from reaching the nose.

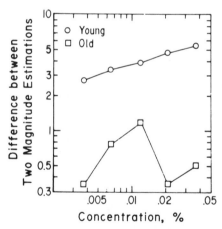

Figure 6. Comparison of 20 young (19–24) and 20 elderly (67–93) subjects for the mean difference of the magnitude matches of liquid solutions of ethyl butyrate with and without the nose pinched. The data shown were normalized using NaCl estimations, but the unnormalized estimates furnish virtually the same picture.

Figure 6 shows the average difference between the overall perceived difference with the nose pinched and unpinched. For the young this difference was large and orderly with respect to concentration, for the elderly small and irregular. Young subjects usually commented spontaneously on how much pinching the nose mattered; only one elderly subject so commented.

What practical implications does the weakening of nasal sensation have for the well-being of the elderly? For one thing, the flavor of food and drink is surely attenuated and may help to explain the frequent complaining about the food in homes for the aged (Cohen & Gitman, 1959). Others factors, such as the quality of the food and social setting in which it is consumed, also undoubtedly come into play. The sensory loss appears to come on so gradually that many persons never become aware of it.

The nasal senses serve not only to give pleasure but also to alert us to danger. A common example is the chemical warning agents added to otherwise odorless natural and liquid petroleum gases. We studied the capacity of the elderly to smell ethyl mercaptan, the agent usually mixed with the fuel gas propane (which in the USA alone annually causes several thousands of explosions, several hundreds of injuries, and several scores of fatalities). Stevens, Cain, and Weinstein (1987) found that the elderly's average detection threshold was 10 times higher than the young's. Some elderly subjects were unable to detect ethyl mercaptan at levels associated with concentrations of propane that would be potentially explosive. Suprathreshold odor strength was also typically attenuated in the aged, as measured by the method of magnitude matching. This may be important, as it is one thing to detect an odor and another to recognize it for what it is, assess the associated danger, and act accordingly.

Summary

This paper reviews studies in which a new method – magnitude matching revealed age-related changes in the chemical senses – taste, smell, and the common chemical sense. This method calls upon elderly and young subjects to estimate the strengths of stimuli applied to a "standard continuum," believed to be normal, interspersed with stimuli applied to a "target continuum," suspected of arousing abnormally weak strengths in the elderly.

Applied to taste (loudness of low-frequency noise as the standard continuum), the method reveals that the qualities of salt, sweet, sour (but not bitter) seemed largely impervious to the effect of old age.

Applied to smell, the method revealed that aging weakens smell magnitude at all concentrations; this proved true whether loudness or saltiness served as the standard continuum. The older the age group, the greater was the weakening revealed. Many odorants, ranging from pleasant to offensive, revealed the loss, and smelling through the nostrils and through the nasopharynx (as in eating) revealed approximately equal loss. The losses have practical consequences for the aged – notably in the failure to detect gas warning agents.

Applied to common chemical sensation (saltiness as the standard continuum), the method revealed substantial loss when the target continuum was several concentrations of nasally inhaled CO_2 — a practically odorless but highly pungent substance.

Acknowledgment. Preparation of this paper was supported by NIH Grant No. AG04287. Correspondence should be addressed to Joseph C. Stevens, John B. Pierce Foundation Laboratory, 290 Congress Avenue, New Haven, Connecticut 06519, U.S.A.

References

Bartoshuk, L.M., Rifkin, B., Marks, L.E., & Bars, P. (1986). Taste and aging. *Journal of Gerontology, 41*, 51−57.

Cain, W.S. (1975). Odor intensity: Mixtures and masking. *Chemical Senses and Flavor, 1*, 339−352.

Cohen, T., & Gitman, L. (1959). Oral complaints and taste perception in the aged. *Journal of Gerontology, 14*, 294−298.

Doty, R.L., Shamon, P., Applebaum, S.L., Giberson, R., Siksorski, L., & Rosenberg, L. (1984). Smell identification ability: Changes with age. *Science, 226*, 1441−1443.

Hyman, A.M. (1977). Factors influencing the psychophysical function for odor intensity. *Sensory Processes, 1*, 273−291.

Moskowitz, H.R., Dravnieks, A., & Klarman, L.A. (1976). Odor intensity and pleasantness for a diverse set of odorants. *Perception & Psychophysics, 19*, 122−128.

Murphy, C., & Cain, W.S. (1980). Taste and olfaction: Independence vs. interaction. *Physiology and Behavior, 24*, 601−605.

Murphy, C., Cain, W.S., & Bartoshuk, L.M. (1977). Mutual action of taste and olfaction. *Sensory Processes, 1*, 204−211.

Schemper, T., Voss, S., & Cain, W.S. (1981). Odor identification in young and elderly persons: Sensory and cognitive limitations. *Journal of Gerontology, 36*, 446−452.

Stevens, J.C. (1982). Magnitude matching: A new method to assess sensory magnitude. In H.-G. Geissler & P. Petzold (Eds.), *Psychophysical judgment and the process of perception* (pp. 17−24). Berlin: VEB Deutscher Verlag der Wissenschaften.

Stevens, J.C., Bartoshuk, L.M., & Cain, W.S. (1984). Chemical senses and aging: Taste versus smell. *Chemical senses, 9*, 167−179.

Stevens, J.C., & Cain, W.S. (1985). Age-related deficiency in the perceived strength of six odorants. *Chemical Senses, 10*, 517−529.

Stevens, J.C., & Cain, W.S. (1986a). Smelling via the mouth. *Perception & Psychophysics, 40*, 142−146.

Stevens, J.C., & Cain, W.S. (1986b). Aging and the perception of nasal irritation. *Physiology & Behavior, 37*, 323−328.

Stevens, J.C., & Cain, W.S. (1987). Old-age deficits in the sense of smell as gauged by thresholds, magnitude matching, and odor identification. *Psychology and Aging, 2*, 36−42.

Stevens, J.C., Cain, W.S., & Weinstein, D.E. (1987). Aging impairs the ability to detect gas odor. *Fire Technology, 23*, 198−204.

Stevens, J.C., & Marks, L.E. (1980). Cross-modality matching functions generated by magnitude estimation. *Perception & Psychophysics, 27*, 379−389.

Stevens, J.C., Plantinga, A., & Cain, W.S. (1982). Reduction of odor and nasal pungency associated with aging. *Neurobiology of Aging, 3*, 125−132.

Psychophysical Explorations of Mental Structures
Edited by H.-G. Geissler
in collaboration with M.H. Müller and W. Prinz
© 1990 by Hogrefe & Huber Publishers

Chapter 11

The Influence of Anchor Stimuli on Judgments of Attributes

Peter Petzold
Sektion Psychologie, Friedrich-Schiller-Universität Jena, G.D.R.

If a particular attribute of a stimulus is to be assessed, the judgment depends not only on this stimulus. Other stimuli previously or simultaneously presented affect this judgment as well and form a context in which the stimulus to be judged will be embedded. A special context effect is the contrast produced by an anchor stimulus. That means if a constant stimulus is presented prior to each stimulus to be assessed, the mean judgment shifts in the direction away from the scale value of the anchor stimulus. Helson (1964) explained the influence of anchor stimuli by his adaptation level theory, according to which a neutral point at the mean of the stimulus distribution reflects the context. Judgments then are related to the difference between the stimuli and the neutral point. There is a lot of evidence that the adaptation level theory is not appropriate to describe the context–influence in categorical judgments. Rather than the mean of the stimulus distribution the extremes of the range seem to serve as internal standards (Parducci, 1965; Petzold, 1981a,b,; Witte, 1975). Additionally, the frequency and the distribution of stimuli within the range are to be taken into account (Parducci, 1965). Models based on the range and the frequency of stimuli have turned out to be capable of predicting essential features of categorical judgments (Haubensak, 1985; Parducci, 1965; Petzold, 1981a,b). It is to be asked whether the contrast produced by anchor stimuli can also be accounted for by a range frequency model. If so, typical properties of the contrast should be explained by the model. Such properties will be described first. Then a range model will be suggested which predicts these properties. After that further implications of the model will be derived and an experiment meant to test these implications will be described.

Properties of the Contrast Effect Produced by Extraserial Anchor Stimuli

It seems to be appropriate to distinguish between extraserial and intraserial anchors. While for extraserial anchors the value of the stimulus variable is lower or higher than the value of the serial stimuli, the value of an intraserial anchor lies within the range of the serial stimuli.

First, we will consider extraserial anchor stimuli. For this case two properties of contrast seem to be especially important.

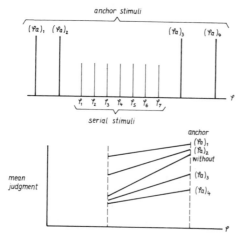

Figure 1. Influence of the position of anchor stimuli on mean judgments of serial stimuli.

Property 1: The shift of judgment due to an anchor stimulus is not equal for all serial stimuli. As some experimental findings show (Helson, 1964; Steger, Wilkinson & Carter, 1973; Sarris, 1976), the less the distance between the anchor and the serial stimulus is, the higher is the extent of contrast. This negative distance effect is illustrated in Figure 1. If the anchor is situated below the serial stimuli, the shift of judgment is higher for stimuli of lower scale values than for those of higher scale values. In other words, the slope of the function describing the relation between mean judgments and the stimulus variable decreases with decreasing position of the anchor. However, if the anchor lies above the serial stimuli, the opposite trend can be observed. In this case the slope decreases with increasing value of the anchor.

Property 2: The range of serial stimuli affects the extent of contrast produced by an anchor stimulus. The smaller the range is, the more influential is
the anchor. This interaction can be demonstrated, for example, by the results of
an experiment by Sarris (1976), in which categorical judgments of pitch were
studied with and without the presentation of an anchor stimulus for different
ranges. As can be seen in Figure 2, the extent of contrast is higher for the
smaller range. It should be emphasized that the distance effect is stronger for
the large range than for the small range.

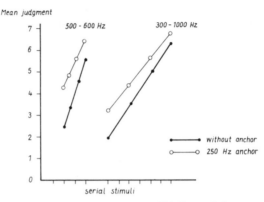

Figure 2. Influence of an anchor stimulus of 250 Hz on judgments of pitch for two
different frequency ranges according to Sarris (1976).

This interaction between range and influence of anchor stimuli is a crucial
point for models of the process underlying the effect of anchors. Neither the
adaptation level theory nor the similarity–classification model by Sarris (1976)
can explain this interaction. A range model will be described now from which
all the properties of contrast mentioned can be deduced.

A Range Model of Anchor Effects

According to Braida and Durlach (1969) a three stage process is assumed
to underly categorical judgments. In the first stage the relevant stimulus variable
is mapped into an internal "sensory" variable X, where X is a random variable
with a Gaussian distribution.

In the second stage the sensory variable X is transformed into a decision
variable Y. This transformation is essentially a calibration of the range of the
sensory variable experienced by the subject. Thus we have

$$Y = F(X) = \frac{X-K}{G-K},$$

where K is the lower extreme of the range and G the upper one.

In the third stage the value of the decision variable is compared with limen c_1, c_2, ... which subdivide the range into areas. The response is determined by the area the actual value of Y falls in.

This model, especially the transformation F has been generalized in former papers in order to explain some characteristics of categorical judgments, such as the edge effect of discriminability (Petzold, 1981a) and sequential effects (Petzold, 1981b).

For purpose of simplicity only one aspect of the generalization relevant to the effect of anchor stimuli will be mentioned here.

The lower extreme of the range, K, is replaced by a lower standard l and the upper extreme G by an upper standard u in the transformation. Thus we have

$$Y = F(X) = \frac{X-l}{u-l} \, .$$

In the simplest case, apart from the range no other context conditions exert an influence. Thus the lower standard corresponds to the lower extreme of the range and the upper standard is equal to the upper extreme.

$$l = K \text{ and } u = G \, .$$

But in general, the standards are composed of several variables. Especially, if an anchor stimulus is presented which lies below the serial stimuli, then it is integrated into the lower standard following an averaging rule. Thus we have

$$l = aK + bA \, , \quad a + b = 1 \, , \quad u = G \, .$$

Both anchor stimulus A and lower extreme K participate in forming the lower standard. This is an information integration process on the level of internal standards.

If the anchor is situated above the serial stimuli, it operates as a constituent of the upper standard and we obtain

$$l = K \, , \quad u = aG + bA \, , \quad a + b = 1 \, .$$

Because of the symmetry of the results we will only consider the case in which the anchor is below the serial stimuli. Then the decision variable corresponds to the following relation

$$Y = \frac{X - aK - bA}{G - aK - bA} \, .$$

This tranformation reflects the influence of anchor stimulus and range on the judgment. If we assume that the overt response is a linear function of the decision variable Y then Property 1 follows immediately from the transformation. Because the slope of the curve is proportional to the denominator of the transformation, the slope should decrease with decreasing anchor position. This corresponds to Property 1 found in experiments.

To derive the interaction between range and anchor position as formulated in Property 2 requires a lengthy calculation. I will confine myself to mention here that the predictions of the model correspond exactly to the data found by Sarris (1976).

According to the model suggested the anchor stimulus operates in an equivalent manner to the extremes of the range. Both the anchor and the extremes form internal standards and determine the psychological range. If so, all range effects should also be found for the influence of anchor stimuli. Especially, it has been found out in several studies (e.g., Braida & Durlach, 1969) that the discriminability of two stimuli increases with decreasing range. This effect is demonstrated in the left part of Figure 3. Moving the lower extreme of the range towards the upper extreme yields a higher discriminability of the stimuli s_1 and s_2. Changing the position of an anchor, as shown in the right part of Figure 3, should have the same effect. From this follows Hypothesis 1: *The nearer the anchor stimulus is to the range of serial stimuli the higher is the discriminability of the serial stimuli.*

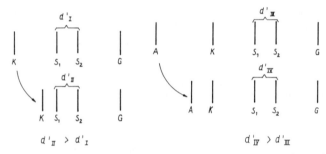

Figure 3. Influence of range and anchor position on the discriminability of two stimuli.

It is assumed that the anchor is integrated into an internal standard and that this process follows an averaging rule. The weight t of the anchor can be supposed to differ for different subjects. From the relation $a+b=1$ follows that the weight a of the extreme should be high for subjects with a low weight of the anchor and *vice versa.* In other words, subjects showing a high influence of the anchor should be less affected by the range. Thus we can formulate Hypothesis 2: *There exists a negative correlation between the increase of discriminability produced by decreasing range and by decreasing distance of the anchor stimulus from the range.*

An Empirical Test of Both Hypotheses

An experiment was conducted to test both hypotheses. Subjects were presented a random sequence of lines of seven different lengths and they made categorical judgments of the length on a 10–point scale. Prior to each line an anchor stimulus was presented that was shorter than all serial lines. Three sets of stimuli were used in the experiment which is shown in Figure 4. These sets were constructed in such a way that sets I and II differed only in the position of the anchor, whereas the ranges of sets II and III differed from each other, the anchor being invariant. The presentation time of the stimuli and the intervall between anchor and serial stimuli were 1 sec, respectively. 18 subjects participated in the experiment. Each subject was run under all conditions. Three subjects were randomly assigned to each of the six sequences of the experimental sets I, II, and III.

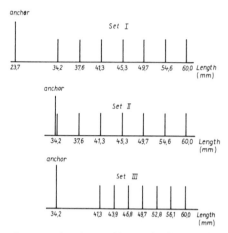

Figure 4. Influence of range and anchor position on the discriminability of two stimuli.

Using operative characteristics d' as a measure of discriminability was determined for adjoining pairs of stimuli separately for each subject and for the three sets of stimuli.

In order to test Hypothesis 1 the values of discriminability were compared between sets I and II. Because the anchor is less distant from the range of serial stimuli in set II the discriminability should be higher in this condition. The overall means of d' averaged over stimulus pairs and subjects are 1.22 for set I, 1.51 for set II, and 1.67 for set III. The higher value of d' in condition II is significant ($p=.05$) according to the Wilcoxon–test. This result corroborates Hypothesis 1. In order to test Hypothesis 2 the increase of d' produced by the approach of the anchor to the range from set I to set II and the increase of d' caused by decreasing range from set II to set III were to be correlated across subjects.

$$r_1 = \frac{(d'_{II})_1}{d'_I} \text{ and } r_2 = \frac{d'_{III}}{(d'_{II})_2}$$

were used as a measure of increase ratios of discriminabilities.

The correlation coefficient between r_1 and r_2 equals $-.59$. This result corresponds to the predicted negative correlation between the influence of the anchor and the effect of the range on discriminability.

Taken together, the results of the experiment described corroborate the assumption that an extraserial anchor operates as a constituent of internal standards and thus participates in determining the psychological range. Further support is provided by studies of similarity judgments. For instance, King and Atef Vahed (1986) have recently shown that the perceived similarity is increased by an extraserial anchor. This is in line with the notion that the anchor increases the range and that the perceived distance between two stimuli will decrease.

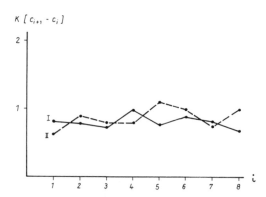

Figure 5. Difference between adjoining limens separating areas of different responses on the dimension to be judged for different anchor positions (set I and set II).

We have considered extraserial anchor stimuli to operate as constituents of internal standards. Additionally, the influence of anchor stimuli might be mediated by the shift of limens that subdivide the range into areas of different responses. Because the frequency of the anchor stimulus is much higher than that of the serial stimuli, the anchor could cause a considerable shift of limens according to the range–frequency model. It can be shown that this additional mechanism would not change the predictions of the model concerning the dependence of mean judgments on the anchor position and the range. Properties 1 and 2 can also be derived, even to a higher extent, because the frequency principle amplifies the effects. Therefore, by analyzing only mean judgments, it is hard to decide whether or not the anchor is implicitly judged and included in the subjective frequency distribution. But this question can be answered by considering the distance between the limens. If the anchor is not included in the frequency calculation, the distance is nearly constant if the serial stimuli are equally spaced and equally frequent. But if the anchor is included, then there is a tendency for the distance between adjoining limens to decrease towards the anchor.

The distance between limens can be determined from the experimental data by constructing criterion operating characteristics on the basis of conditional response frequencies. The results of this analysis for the experiment described are shown in Figure 5.

As can be seen no significant trend appears. The distance between adjoining limens seems to be constant. From this follows that extraserial anchors are not included in the calculation of the frequency of stimuli.

Intraserial Anchor Stimuli

Now we will consider briefly the influence of intraserial anchor stimuli. They also produce contrast, but the distance effect is more complicated. There exists a nonmonotone relation between the extent of contrast and the distance of the serial stimulus from the anchor. Near the anchor the contrast increases with increasing distance. Farther away from the anchor the opposite trend can be found as the results by Sarris (1976) indicate (Figure 6).

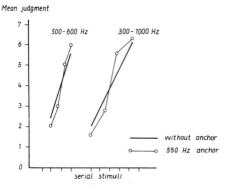

Figure 6. Influence of an intraserial anchor stimulus on the judgment of pitch for two different frequency ranges according to Sarris (1976).

This tritone trend which varies from the distance effect of extraserial anchor stimuli suggests that the mechanism underlying the influence of extraserial and intraserial anchors might differ from each other.

It can be shown that this pattern of results is predicted by the range-frequency model in which the range and the frequency of stimuli determine the limens between areas of different responses. Because the anchor is presented prior to each stimulus its frequency is comparatively high. Therefore, the anchor heavily influences the position of the limens.

Without going into the details of the mathematical derivation it should be mentioned that three characteristics of the influence of intraserial anchors follow from the model.

First, the tritone trend of the contrast effect, second, the higher extent of the influence in the small range, and third, the effect that there is a tendency for extreme stimuli of the range to exhibit a small contrast effect only in large ranges. In the small range however, a distinct contrast effect appears also for extreme stimuli.

Taken together, anchor stimuli seem to operate in two ways. First, they may be integrated into internal standards and participate in the formation of the psychological range. Secondly, they may be included in the calculation of the frequency distribution and with that in the determination of limens which subdivide the range into areas of different responses. The first mechanism seems to mediate the influence of extraserial anchors, whereas the second one is operative in case of intraserial anchor stimuli.

Summary

According to a model suggested anchor stimuli operate in two ways. Extraserial anchors are integrated into internal standards and participate in the formation of the psychological range like the extremes of the range of serial stimuli. From this follows that the discriminability of two serial stimuli increases with decreasing distance of the anchor from the range of serial stimuli. This prediction was supported by an experiment in which the length of lines was to be judged. A further corroboration of the model was the finding of a negative correlation between the increase of discriminability produced by decreasing the range of serial stimuli on the one hand, and by decreasing the distance of the anchor stimulus from the range on the other hand. Intraserial anchor stimuli seem to be included in the calculation of the frequency distribution and thus in the determination of limens which subdivide the psychological range into areas of different responses.

Correspondence should be addressed to Peter Petzold, Friedrich-Schiller-Universität, Sektion Psychologie, 6900 Jena, G.D.R.

References

Durlach, N.I., & Braida, L.D. (1969). Intensity perception. I. Preliminary theory of intensity resolution. *Journal of the Acoustical Society of America, 2,* 372–383.

Haubensak, G. (1985). *Absolutes und vergleichendes Urteil.* Berlin, Heidelberg, New York: Springer.

Helson, H. (1964). *Adaptation level theory.* New York, Evanston, London: Harper & Row.

King, D.L., & Atef Vahed, M.-K. (1986). Two extensions of the anchor–range effect. *Perception & Psychophysics, 39,* 96–104.

Parducci, A. (1965). Category judgment: A range–frequency model. *Psychological Review, 72,* 407–418.

Petzold, P. (1981a). The effect of discriminability in categorical judgments. In H.-G. Geissler, P. Petzold & H.F. Buffart (Eds.), *Psychophysical judgments and perceptual processes.* Berlin: VEB Deutscher Verlag der Wissenschaften.

Petzold, P. (1981b). Distance effects on sequential dependencies in categorical judgment. *Journal of Experimental Psychology: Human Perception and Performance, 7,* 1371–1385.

Sarris, V. (1976). Effects of stimulus range and anchor value on psychophysical judgment. In H.-G. Geissler & J. Zabrodin (Eds.), *Advances in psychophysics.* Berlin: VEB Deutscher Verlag der Wissenschaften.

Steger, J.A., Wilkinson, J., & Carter, R. (1973). Test of integration theory and adaptation level theory in anchored judgments. *Perceptual and Motor Skills, 36,* 271–274.

Witte, W. (1975). Zum Gestalt- und Systemcharakter psychischer Bezugssysteme. In S. Ertel (Ed.), *Gestalttheorie in der modernen Psychologie.* Darmstadt: Steinkopff.

II. Multidimensional Psychophysics

Psychophysical Explorations of Mental Structures
Edited by H.-G. Geissler
in collaboration with M.H. Müller and W. Prinz
© 1990 by Hogrefe & Huber Publishers

Chapter 12

Psychophysical Maps for Rectangles

Peter H. Schönemann
Department of Psychological Sciences
Purdue University
West Lafayette, U.S.A.

By "psychophysical maps" are meant maps which carry a number of physical measures of perceptual stimuli, such as line length, or area of rectangles or circles, into numerical responses which have been obtained from the subjects in some operationally defined way, e.g., by asking. In the specific context considered here, the maps carry a pair of physical measures suitable for defining rectangles (such as physical height and width) into category ratings of the dissimilarity of pairs of rectangles.

Some Background

I became interested in the question how people judge rectangles not because I have any strong feelings about rectangles, but rather because many other people have dealt with it before (see references). Over the years, there have been many different answers to this simple question. Here is a sample:
Q1: What are the relevant judgment dimensions?
Answers: (a) perceived area and shape, not height and width; (b) some subjects use area and shape, others use height and width.
Q2: Are these dimensions independent?

Answers: (a) no, they interact; (b) yes, they are independent.
Q3: How do people combine the subjective dimensions?
Answers: (a) they first use the Euclidean metric and then apply an unspecified monotone transformation; (b) they first use the city-block metric and then apply a well-defined monotone transformation.
Q4: Do all subjects deal with the rating task in the same way?
Answers: (a) yes; (b) no.

Answers (a) have been given by Krantz and Tversky (1975), answers (b) by Schönemann, Dorcey and Kienapple (1984). Needless to say, other investigators, e.g., Borg and Leutner (1983), or Wiener-Ehrlich (1978), have arrived at still other answers.

Krantz and Tversky did not address the individual difference question Q4 explicitly, but implied it because they derived the other three answers from an MDS (multidimensional scaling) analysis of group averages. Answer 3 to the metric question is also implied by their method of analysis: they preprocessed their data with an MDS program which maps the observed dissimilarity rating into Euclidean distances via a monotone tranformation and then analyzed them with an MDS model (Horan, 1969) based on the Euclidean metric.

The answers to the above four questions are interrelated. The two main conclusions, answers 1 and 2, rest on the validity of the two subsidiary conclusions, answers 3 and 4. In particular, whether the dimensions can be identified as area and shape (answer 1) depends on the metric of the scaling model, i.e., on answer 3. Similarly, answer 2 depends on the validity of answer 1: if subjects had actually used some other pair of dimensions, e.g., subjective height and width, then the interaction might disappear (Schönemann, 1977; Schönemann & Borg, 1981).

The most critical question is Q1, which can only be answered on the basis of the individual data, not just group averages. As Schulz (1971) and Schönemann (1971) have shown, the scaling model used by Krantz and Tversky guarantees uniquely identifiable dimensions only if a certain diagonality condition is met by all subjects. Since Krantz and Tversky did not report the individual data, and did not answer my repeated requests for information about these data, it seemed premature to consider the matter closed. We, therefore, collected our own data, arriving at answers (b).

It may surprise some of you that all these years we still cannot be sure how people judge rectangles. Some may say this is not a very important question – as long as psychologists can answer the really big questions we have nothing to worry about. One reason for our difficulties with this little question may be that we have approached it in the wrong way: typically, investigators start with the premise that a particular pre-conceived scaling model is appropriate for their data. Then they check it in some global way. Finally, they try to infer the judgment process from the properties of the model.

Foundations of Human Behavior

Let us now try the alternative route, reasoning from the judgment process to the model. We first ask what the experimental task implies about the subject's behavior. Then we ask whether our conclusions are compatible with any metric model, and if so, which one. Finally we ask whether this geometric model will be useful. To anticipate, our data suggest that a metric model may be appropriate but will probably not be very useful.

When we ask subjects to rate the dissimilarity of pairs of rectangles on a scale from 0 to 9, we confront them with a difficult and boring task. I propose the following axiom scheme for inferring some results we can expect from such a task:

Axiom 1 (human nature): Most people do not like to make fools of themselves.

Axiom 2: (least effort): People try to get difficult and boring tasks over with as soon as possible.

Axiom 3 (limited competence): Most people are capable of only rudimentary cognitive achievements. They can tell whether two stimuli are very similar or very different on certain sensory dimensions, but can concatenate differences from distinct dimensions only in the simplest possible way.

Axiom 4 (upper bound): By definition of the category rating task, subjects have to find a way that their numerical answer never exceeds the upper bound the experimenter imposed on the response scale (9 in our case).

Since we never tell subjects what we mean by the ambiguous term "dissimilarity", they are faced with a difficult task akin to concept formation. Axiom 1 implies they will make some effort to come up with a consistent strategy so they don't look foolish giving different numerical answers if the same pair of rectangles is presented twice. Axioms 2 and 3 imply that this strategy will be simple, but do not rule out the possibility that different subjects may come up with different judgment strategies. So we should be prepared for qualitative individual differences.

Once a subject has decided on the type of perceptual information he wants to use in his rating, he has to combine it in some way. Axiom 3 implies that if subjects try to combine the perceived differences on whatever stimulus dimensions they attend to, they will do this in the simplest possible way. They will shun all exponents larger or smaller than 1. For example, they will not use the Euclidean or any of the other, even fancier Minkowski metrics because this is much too difficult for them. Try it yourself: what is the cube root of $3^3 + 5^3$? Therefore, if they pick apparent height (H) and width (W) as their two dimensions, and perceive the difference on H to have magnitude a, and the difference on W magnitude b, then they will simply add both magnitudes and want to give $a + b$ as their dissimilarity rating.

Subadditivity

However, Axiom 4 implies that, for this simple rating strategy to work, they must modify the sum $a + b$ somehow so that the answer always stays below the upper bound of the rating scale. Suppose we present three collinear stimuli, *A*, *B*, and *C*. If the subject has assigned dissimilarity $a=5$ to the pair (A,B), and $b=6$ to the pair (B,C), then, to be consistent, he may wish to assign $a+b=5+6=11$ to the pair (A,C). However, since all responses must be between 0 and 9, he is forced to contract this sum a little, e.g., assign

$$d(A,C) = 9 < 11 = 5+6 = d(A,B)+d(B,C)$$

instead. In this case we say the dissimilarity ratings are "(segmentally) subadditive."

The same problem also arises for non-collinear triples. If a subject assigns magnitude 5 to the height difference, and magnitude 6 to the width difference, then he will also have to contract the sum before he can use it as a rating. In short, our axiom scheme suggest that (a) many category ratings will be segmentally subadditive, and, therefore, (b) satisfy the triangle inequality as they stand.

We now ask which dimensions subjects might use. As long as we use only rectangles as stimuli, we give them basically two choices: subjects can base their rating either on subjective height and/or subjective width, or they can base them on subjective area and/or shape. By "subjective height" I mean some variable which relates monotonically to physical height, and similarly for subjective width and area.

Since shape is more tricky to define when the design contains both tall and flat rectangles, assume for now it contains only flat rectangles. Then we could define physical shape as a ratio of height over width and subjective shape as something monotonically related to it. However, it will simplify matters if we define "physical shape" simply as half the difference of height and width. This could be justified as a linear approximation to log(*shape*) as long as height and width are not too small and don't vary too much. Similarly, we define physical size by the average of height and width as an approximation to log(*area*). A more cogent reason for working with these particular definitions of the physical measures will be given shortly.

To be concrete, let us use the numbers from 1 to 9 to identify 9 rectangles varied systematically on height and width in a 3x3 (*H/W*) orthogonal design:

$$
\begin{array}{ccc}
7 & 8 & 9 \\
\text{height} \quad 4 & 5 & 6 \\
1 & 2 & 3 \\
\end{array}
$$

$$\text{width}$$

where 1 is the smallest and 9 the largest rectangle. Then the pair (1,9) defines the "area diagonal", and the pair (3,7) the "shape diagonal" of the design.

We then can test for subadditivity with the simple function

$$f = a+b-c$$

where, e.g., $a=d(1,2)$, $b=d(2,3)$, $c=d(1,3)$ (collinear triple for width), or $a=d(1,5)$, $b=d(5,9)$, $c=d(1,9)$ (collinear triple for area). If the data are subadditive, the mean of f will be positive. If they are additive, it will be zero.

If it is negative, the triangle inequality is violated. On computing this function f for a number of studies (our own 3x3 and 4x4 studies, as well as data reported by Noma & Johnson, 1977; and Borg & Leutner, 1983), we invariably found that the mean of f is positive, in the vicinity of .2 on a scale from 0 to 1, and that it is positive in all four directions which seem plausible as dimensions for judging rectangles: parallel to H and W and also along the area and shape diagonals. In Figure 1, the distributions for f are given for 3 subgroups. The vertical lines indicate $f=0$. The three distributions on the left are for height and width triples, and those on the right for area and shape triples. The means of all six distributions are clearly positive. Thus dissimilarity ratings tend to be consistently subadditive, regardless whether subjects employ an H/W or an A/S

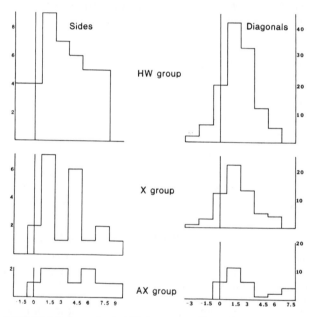

Figure 1. MBR: Distributions of subadditivity measure $f := a + b - c$.

system. This finding implies: (a) dissimilarity ratings can always be modelled as distances as they stand (because they satisfy the triangle inequality without any need for adding a constant or some other monotone transformation) and, (b) dissimilarity rating of rectangles are not well described by the city-block metric, because this metric stipulates

$$f = a + b - c = 0$$

along all lines regardless of their direction.

Thus our data are compatible with a metric, but we do not yet know which. We should note, at this point, that segmental additivity is not a defining

requirement of metrics, only the three distance axioms (non–negativity, symmetry, and triangle inequality) are. A simple metric which is not segmentally
additive is the chord–metric, e.g., for 3 points on a circle.

Metric for Bounded Response Scales

To model such data geometrically, we need a metric which (a) is segmentally subadditive and (b) respects (i.e., never exceeds) the upper bound of the
response scale. Since there are innumerable metrics with these two properties,
we add that it should also be relatively "simple", i.e., compatible with our
laziness and limited competence axioms.

In a number of previous publications we have suggested that a simple
modification of the strictly additive city–block metric,

$$d_c = a + b,$$

may be a promising candidate, viz. the metric

$$d_m^* = (a^* + b)/(1 + a^* b^*/k^2), \qquad 0 \le d_m^* \le k ,$$

where a^*, b^* are the dimensional projections in the metric of the observations,
and k is the upper bound. On dividing the observed distances by this bound,
one obtains as a standardized version

$$d_m = (a + b)/(1 + ab), \qquad 0 \le a, b, d_m \le 1 .$$

We have called this map a "Metric for Bounded Response scales" (MBR)
because (a) it is a metric and (b) it respects the upper bound k (or 1, in the
rescaled case). Viewed as a subadditive binary operation $\oplus$ on a and b in the
half-open interval $[0,1)$,

$$a \oplus b := (a + b)/(1 + ab) \qquad a, b \in [0,1) ,$$

the MBR has a number of pleasing formal properties which distinguish it from
several other subadditive metrics we have investigated as possible alternatives.
As a metric, it is segmentally subadditive along all lines except those exactly
parallel to one of the coordinate axes (so that either a or b are 0). More
generally, the MBR will approximate the city–block metric when either a or b,
or both, are small, the sup–metric when either a or b are close to one (and
both are non–zero), and the Euclidean metric when both a and b are in the
middle range.

The numerator satisfies the laziness and limited competence axioms. The
denominator provides a contraction to fit the city–block metric into the scale so
that it never exceeds the upper bound (Axiom 4). We do not expect subjects to
do this literally, but we know they must make some contracting adjustment if
they want to use the simple city–block addition rule.

The MBR can be approximated very closely by the city–block metric when
the data are pre–processed with "Fisher's z–transformation" (see any elementary statistics book). Mathematicians call it the "inverse hyperbolic tangent"
transform and denote it $\tanh^{-1}(x)$ $(:= .5 \ln[(1 + x)/(1 - x)])$. As the name and

notation suggest, this tranformation is the inverse of another transformation, the hyperbolic tangent transformation,

$$\tanh(x) := [exp(2x) - 1]/[exp(2x) + 1] .$$

In terms of these maps, the (standardized) MBR can be written

$$d_m = (a+b)/(1+ab) = \tanh[\tanh^{-1}(a) + \tanh^{-1}(b)]$$

which readily generalizes to $m > 2$ dimensions, as

$$d_m = \tanh \sum_k \tanh^{-1}|x_{ik} - x_{jk}| .$$

On taking the inverse hyperbolic tangent tranformation (which expands large intervals relative to small ones), one arrives at an additive decomposition of the data

$$\tanh^{-1}(d_m) = \sum_k u_{ijk} , \quad k=1, \ m,$$

which can be analyzed with a program for fitting the city-block metric. This indirect solution is convenient computationally. It differs little from a direct least squares solution of the MBR, even though it is based on the transformed segments

$$u_{ijk} := \tanh^{-1}|x_{ik} - x_{jk}| ,$$

instead of the segments $|x_{ik} - x_{jk}|$. The reason is that the tanh-transformation is close to the identity tranformation for segments smaller than .4. In Table 1 the computational aspects of the MBR are illustrated with a numerical example.

Schönemann and Kienapple (1984) and Schönemann, Dorcey and Kienapple (1985) gave more detailed evidence that the MBR indeed describes the observed dissimilarity rating reasonably well and, in particular, better than the city-block metric and several other metrics which might be viable alternatives.

The upper bound k of the unstandardized version could be treated as an individual difference parameter, on the premise that different people may employ different self-imposed upper bounds. However, we found empirically that this additional parameter does not improve the fit by much for group averages. On the other hand, we also found that within subjects the fit does improve if the upper bound is reduced by roughly 20% (i.e., to 7.2 for a scale bounded by 9). This suggests people use such rating scales conservatively (s.a. Parducci, 1982).

Overall, then, our first study confirmed that the MBR does a reasonable job in describing both the individual data and the averages for different strategy groups. In this study, we found 3 such strategy groups: half the subjects used the design dimensions (H and W), about a quarter used predominantly area and the rest predominantly shape. The MDS configurations turned out quite different for these 3 strategy groups.

Table 1. A numerical example illustrating the computational aspects of the MBR.[1]

Computational Illustrations of the MBR

generating origin at 0		coordinates at centroid		abscissa projections						ordinate projections			city-block metric (CB)		
x1	x2	z1	z2	A	B	C	D	A	B	C	D	A	B	C	D
A	.2	.2	−.375	−.275	.0	.2	.6	.7	.0	.1	.3	.7	.0	.3	.9	1.4
B	.4	.3	−.175	−.175		.0	.4	.5		.0	.2	.6		.0	.6	1.1
C	.8	.5	.225	.025			.0	.1			.0	.4			.0	.5
D	.9	.9	.325	.425				.0				.0				.0

x_{ik} z_{ik} $(a_{ij} = |x_{i1} - x_{j1}|)$ $(b_{ij} = |x_{i2} - x_{j2}|)$ $(c_{ij} = a_{ij} + b_{ij})$

	MBR (exact)				inverse hyperbolic tangent transforms of MBR			
	A	B	C	D	A	B	C	D
A	.000	.294	.763	.940	.000	.303	1.003	1.738
B		.000	.556	.846		.000	.627	1.242
C			.000	.481			.000	.524
D				.000				.000

$(d_{ij} = [a_{ij} + b_{ij}]/[1 + a_{ij}b_{ij}])$ $(\tan^{-1}[d_{ij}])$

e.g., $d(A,B) = (.2 + .1)/[1.0 + (.2)(.1)] = .3/1.02 = .294$
$= \tanh[\tanh^{-1}(.2) + \tanh^{-1}(.1)] = \tanh(.203 + 100)$

City-Block Solution Based on Inverse Hyperbolic Tangents of MBR

CB coordinates			estimated MBR coordinates		coordinate residuals		reproduced MBR above diagonal			
	y1	y2	z1	z2			A	B	C	D
A	−.437	−.348	−.371	−.296	.004	.021	.000	.337	.753	.945
B	−.190	−.186	−.162	−.158	.013	.017	.043	.000	.512	.836
C	.221	.048	.188	.041	.038	.016	.010	.044	.000	.501
D	.406	.486	.346	.413	.021	.012	.005	.010	.020	.000

(y_{ik}) $(\hat{z}_{ik} = .85 y_{ik})$ $|z_{ik} - \hat{z}_{ik}|$ residuals below

---

[1]   The 3 points A, B, C are collinear in the affine sense (i.e., without invoking any metric), since $-2(.2 \cdot .2) + 3(.4 \cdot .3) = pA + qB = (.8 \cdot .5) = C$, with $p + q = 1$. Hence the CB distances are additive: $c(A,B) + c(B,C) = .3 + .6 = .9 = c(A,C)$. However, the MBR distances are subadditive: $d(A,B) + d(B,C) = .294 + .556 = .850 > .763 = d(A,C)$. Since the coordinates are defined only up to translations, the x_{ij} are carried into the z_{ij} with origin at the centroid to identify them. The y_{ik} are the CB coordinates based on the $\tanh^{-1}(d)$ transforms. They relate to the MBR coordinate estimates by a multiplicative constant (.85) which can be ignored if only a spatial representation is sought. However, it is needed to assess the fit of the MBR solution relative to the actual ratings. This is preferable over evaluating the fit indirectly, e.g., in terms of stress, because this would suppress an unspecified monotone transformation.

Psychophysical Maps

In a second study (Schönemann & Lazarte, 1987) we replicated these results with a larger stimulus set and more subjects, using a 4x4 H/W design. This time, we deliberately included both flat and tall rectangles, and thus also, squares.

Our basic subadditivity prediction was again satisfied. An MBR with slightly reduced upper bound did again better than any of the other 7 metrics we investigated for comparison.

From the bivariate frequency plot of the 2 main design diagonals, we found 3 subject clusters: for the largest strategy group the dissimilarity ratings assigned to the endpoints of both main diagonals were both large (HW group), for a second group they were both small ("eccentricity", X group), and for a third group they were large for the shape diagonal but small for the area diagonal ("area and eccentricity", AX group).

For a consistency check, we split each of the two larger groups into halves and analyzed the resulting five subgroups separately. The main objective of this second study was to relate the average dissimilarity rating in each group directly to the physical coordinates defining the rectangles (in terms of H and W in cm).

As a first step, we looked at squares because they vary only along one dimension ("size"). Since we already knew from our previous study and also from the within subject analyses of the 4x4 replication that the $\tanh^{-1}$ transformation restores additivity, we applied it to the 4x4 dissimilarity matrices for the four squares. As expected, the matrices for all five groups could be well described in one dimension. On plotting the scale values u_i of "subjective size" against the widths of the four rectangles we obtained four linear plots (Figure 2). This enabled us to discard the subjective u_i and replace them by physical width. Denoting the stimulus with the larger physical coordinate by W_l and that with the smaller coordinate by W_S (to avoid absolute value signs), the following maps related physical width of squares, in cm, to the average ratings on a scale from 0 to 9:

$$\text{HW group 1: } d = 9 \tanh[.26(W_l - W_S)]$$
$$\text{HW group 2: } d = 9 \tanh[.22(W_l - W_S)]$$
$$\text{AX group 1: } d = 9 \tanh[.20(W_l - W_S)]$$
$$\text{AX group 2: } d = 9 \tanh[.22(W_l - W_S)]$$
$$\text{X group : } d = 9 \tanh[.03(W_l - W_S)]$$

Evidently the single parameter we estimated (the slopes of the lines in Figure 2) is essentially constant across the first four groups. It is much smaller in the fifth, eccentricity group. This suggests subjects in this group effectively ignore "size."

We then extended these maps from squares to rectangles. For the two HW groups, it seemed logical to consider physical height as the second dimension. To estimate the weights, we used the General Linear Model, $y = Xb + e$, where $y_i = \tanh^{-1}(d/9)$, obtaining the following maps for the two H/W subgroups:

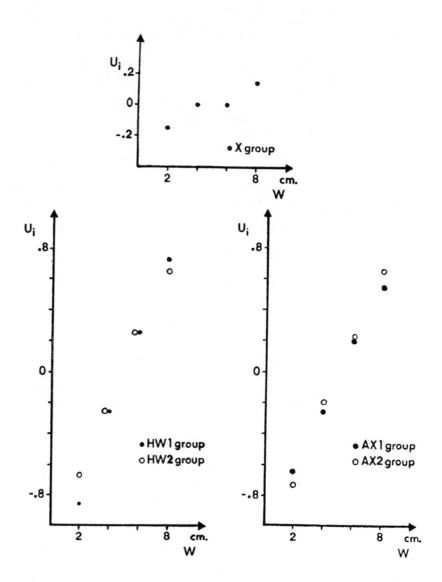

Figure 2. MBR: 1-dimensional psychophysical maps of physical width into subjective "size."

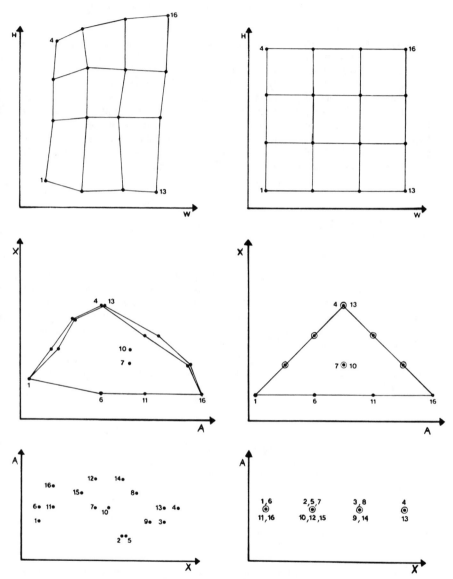

Figure 3. 2-dimensional psychophysical maps. Left: MDS configurations for three strategy groups based on MBR transformed dissimilarities. Right: Corresponding physical designs for the same three strategy groups.

HW group 1: $d = 9 \tanh[.09W_1 - .04W_S + .16H_1 - .19H_s]$
HW group 2: $d = 9 \tanh[.10W_1 - .07W_S + .11H_1 - .10H_s]$.

Subjects in the AX groups gave large ratings to the area diagonal and relatively smaller ratings to the shape diagonal. This suggests they use departure from squareness, "eccentricity", as an index of shape, i.e., they did not distinguish between tall and flat rectangles of the same eccentricity. Since we already knew from the subanalyses with squares that subjective size is a linear, not a quadratic function of width, we defined "physical area" (a better term would have been "size", but it starts with "s" as does shape) as the average of H and W, and "physical eccentricity" as half the magnitude of the H/W difference betwen H and W. Thus, our independent variables for the AX groups were $A: = (H + W)/2$ (physical) area, $X: = |H - W|/2$ (eccentricity). With this choice, we obtained for the two AX subgroups the maps:

AX group 1: $d = 9 \tanh[.15X_1 - .11X_s + .17A_1 - .15A_s]$
AX group 2: $d = 9 \tanh[.12X_1 - .09X_s + .23A_1 - .20A_s]$.

Finally, on fitting only eccentricity to the rating in the X group, we obtained the map

X group : $d = 9 \tanh[.37X_1 - .24S_s]$.

To assess the fit we computed squared η's and correlations (see Table 2). Note that we estimated only four parameters to describe 120 data points in each of the HW and AX subgroups, and only two parameters for the X group. Thus, both in terms of consistency between equivalent strategy subgroups, as well as in terms of global measures of fit, these maps describe the data quite well. To avoid misunderstandings, it should be noted that the expected value for η^2, which we consider more appropriate as a measure of fit (since we did not fit any overall effects), is not 0 for non−negative random data, but approximately .56.

Table 2. For explanations, see text.

group	4 parameter maps		weighted 2 parameter maps	
	η^2	r	η^2	r
HW1	.97	.92	.89	.73
HW2	.98	.92	.98	.90
AX1	.95	.82	.83	.79
AX2	.95	.84	.67	.77
X	.95	.78	.86	.66

We further found that these four−parameter maps can be replaced by even more parsimoneous weighted two−parameter maps, after weighting the larger, more pronounced stimulus projection up by a constant amount (by 1.2) and the smaller down (by .8, "Saliency effect", see, e.g., Rosch, 1977) without drastic deterioration in fit (see Table 2, right, and Schönemann & Lazarte, 1987).

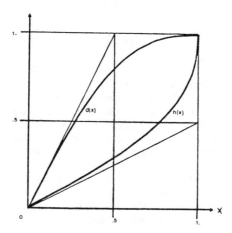

Figure 4. MBR: MBR norm for halving and doubling tasks.

Finally, we compared the results of the MDS analyses, based on the MBR, with those we predicted directly from the psychophysical maps. The results are summarized in Figure 3 for the three strategy groups. The plots on the right show the configurations predicted by the psychophysical maps, in terms of the physical measures. The plots on the left show the configurations obtained with an MDS program which fits the MBR to the observed dissimilarity ratings. The upshot is that, once the psychophysical maps are known, such MDS analyses essentially become superfluous, because they tell us nothing new above and beyond what we already know from the maps.

Adaptation of the MBR to 1-Dimensional Production Methods

The limited competence Axiom 3, and hence the MBR, account for subadditivity in terms of the concatenation, not in terms of the perception of stimulus differences which, instead, is assumed to be approximately veridical. Thus the MBR predicts that dissimilarity ratings tend to be subadditive across dimensions, whenever segments from different continua must be combined. In 1-dimensional, classical psychophysics we often prescribe experimental tasks, such as doubling, where perceived differences of the same sense modality must be combined. The basic logic of the MBR is easily adapted to predict subadditivity for such 1-dimensional production methods:

$$c^* = a^* \oplus b^* = (a^* + b^*)/(1 + a^* b^*/k^2) < a^* + b^*, \quad 0 \le c^* < k,$$

where now $a^* := |x_i - x_j|$, $b^* := |x_j - x_k|$ are two contiguous line segments. This 1-dimensional subadditive norm predicts overestimation for halving, and underestimation for doubling (see Figure 4). Given several doubling (or halving) settings, the upper bound k can be estimated.

Discussion

The main message is that any scaling model implies a prefabricated theory of behavior. It is unrealistic to expect that this theory remains psychologically plausible across widely differing experimental tasks. Whether it is plausible can be ascertained, to some extent at least, by a preliminary study of the task characteristics. In the present instance, the task consisted (a) of figuring out some meaning of the ambiguous phrase "Please indicate the dissimilarity between the 2 rectangles on a scale from 0 to 9," and (b) of repeatedly assigning numbers from 0 to 9 to pairs of rectangles, one pair at a time.

I have tried to capture the demand characteristics of this particular task with three axioms about human behavior and one axiom describing the task. This fourth Axiom virtually forces the subject into making segmentally subadditive numerical assignments. By the same token, it also virtually guarantees that the actually observed rating will satisfy the 3 formal distance axioms prior to any preprocessing, whether subjects actually use a geometric representation of the stimuli or not. Finally, we were led to expect individual differences in judgment strategies.

Hence, if we employ this particular, widely used rating task, we may primarily learn something about the problem solving behavior of different subjects, but probably very little about their sensory or perceptual capabilities. I see no reason why a similar caveat should not also apply to classical, 1-dimensional psychophysics. There the assumption is often implicit that different experimental methods (e.g., magnitude estimation, "ratio scaling", doubling, halving and middling), if only used properly (e.g., by judicious stimulus spacing etc.), are equivalent methods for arriving at all-encompassing "psychophysical laws."

This expectation may be unrealistic. To give a specific example: For the subadditive norm, $c^* = a^* \oplus b^*$, halving h and doubling d are inverse to each other only if the upper bound k is the same. We found empirically that this condition is violated for the production of circular area, i.e., for our subjects, $h[d(x)] \neq x$.

More generally, just as in the multidimensional case, different psychophysical methods involve different levels of processing. As more higher level, cognitive processes enter, it becomes more likely that qualitative individual differences will emerge and different judgment strategies confound the perceptual processes we try to study. In short, if we are not careful, we may learn more about the confounding aspects of the experimental task than about the sensory processes they were designed to measure.

Summary

Simple geometric forms, such as rectangles, have been used as stimulus material in MDS experiments at least since Attneave (1950). Investigators asked whether the Euclidean or the city–block metric was better suited for describing dissimilarity ratings obtained for such stimulus pairs. Most of them favored the simpler city–block metric. As a secondary question they asked whether, for judging the dissimilarity of rectangles, subjects use a height/width or an area/shape frame of reference. The consensus tended towards area/shape.

More recently, doubts have arisen whether *any* of the Minkowski metrics qualifies as a plausible judgment model: Schönemann (1982), Schönemann and Kienapple (1984), and Schönemann, Dorcey and Kienapple (1985) have consistently found that such dissimilarity ratings of geometric stimuli tend to be segmentally subaddtive, regardless whether a height/width or an area/shape system is assumed. This finding rules out all Minkowski metrics because they are all additive within dimensions. A closer analysis of the individual data, moreover, revealed systematic differences in judgment strategies. Some subjects use height/width, others area/shape, and still others only shape.

To reconcile these findings, a simple judgmental process model is derived from three basic axioms about human nature (vanity, laziness, and incompetence) and one constraint imposed by the rating task (an upper bound). The key ingredient of this process model is a subadditive metric, called MBR, which describes the observed data better than any of the Minkowski metrics. An immediate implication of the model is the expectation of qualitative strategy differences, which necessitates separate analyses by strategy groups. In a more recent paper, Schönemann and Lazarte (1987) extended these earlier findings to incorporate explicit psychophysical maps to predict the numerical dissimilarity ratings, and thus the outcome of any subsequent MDS analysis, from the physical stimulus characteristics and knowledge of the strategy group. Although these maps depend only on a very small number of parameters $(2-4)$, they recover the observed ratings with squared η's in the high nineties.

These findings point towards the need for greater caution in interpreting the results of MDS studies, which typically impose some arbitrary scaling model on averaged data without any serious effort to test the implied assumptions at the individual subject level. The results of past MDS studies may tell us more about the confounding aspects of the experimental task than about the perceptual processes they were designed to reveal.

Correspondence should be addressed to Peter H. Schönemann, Department of Psychological Sciences, Purdue University, West Lafayette, Indiana, 47907 U.S.A.

References

Attneave, F. (1950). Dimensions of similarity. *American Journal of Psychology, 3,* 516–556.

Birnbaum, M.H. (1982). Controversies in psychological measurement. In B. Wegner (Ed.), *Social attitudes and psychological measurement.* Hillsdale, NJ: Erlbaum.

Borg, I., & Leutner, D. (1983). Dimensional models for the perception of rectangles. *Perception & Psychophysics, 34,* 257–267.

Horan, C.B. (1969). Multidimensional scaling: Combining observations when individuals have different perceptual structures. *Psychometrika, 34,* 129–165.

Krantz, D., & Tversky, A. (1975). Similarity of rectangles: An analysis of subjective dimension. *Journal of Mathematical Psychology, 12,* 4–34.

Noma, E., & Johnson, J. (1977). Constraining nonmetric multidimensional scaling configurations. Technical Report. No. 60, Human Performance Center, The University of Michigan.

Parducci, A. (1982). Category ratings: Still more contextual effects. In B. Wegner (Ed.), *Social attitudes and psychophysical measurement.* Hillsdale, N.J.: Erlbaum.

Rosch, E. (1977). Human categorization. In N. Warren (Ed.), *Advances in cross cultural psychology* (Vol.1). London: Academic Press.

Schönemann, P.H. (1972). An algebraic solution for a class of subjective metrics models. *Psychometrika, 37,* 441–451.

Schönemann, P.H. (1977). Similarity of rectangles. *Journal of Mathematical Psychology, 16,* 161–165.

Schönemann, P.H. (1982). A metric for bounded response scales. *Bulletin of the Psychonomic Society, 15,* 317–319.

Schönemann, P.H. (1983). Some theory and results for metrics for bounded response scales. *Journal of Mathematical Psychology, 27,* 311–324.

Schönemann, P.H., & Borg, I. (1981). On the interaction between area and shape. In I. Borg (Ed.), *Multidimensional data representations: When and why.* Ann Arbor: Mathesis.

Schönemann, P.H., Dorcey, T., & Kienapple, K. (1985) Subadditive concatenation in dissimilarity judgments. *Perception & Psychophysics, 38,* 1–17.

Schönemann, P.H., & Kienapple, K. (1984). Artefakte in der mehrdimensionalen Skalierung. *Zeitschrift für Experimentelle und Angewandte Psychologie, 31,* 483–506.

Schönemann, P.H., & Lazarte, A. (1987). Psychophysical maps for subadditive dissimilarity ratings. *Perception & Psychophysics, 42,* 342–354.

Schulz, U. (1971). *Über zwei Modelle der multidimensionalen Skalierung unter Berücksichtigung individueller Differenzen.* Doctoral Dissertation, Phillips–Universität, Marburg, F.R.G.

Sixtl, F., & Wender, K. (1964). Der Zusammenhang zwischen multidimensionalen Skalieren und Faktorenanalyse. *Biometrische Zeitschrift, 6,* 251–261.

Wender, K. (1971). A test of independence of dimensions in multidimensional scaling. *Perception & Psychophysics, 10,* 30–32.

Wiener-Ehrlich, W.K. (1978). Dimensional and metric structures in multidimensional stimuli. *Perception & Psychophysics, 24,* 399–414.

Psychophysical Explorations of Mental Structures
Edited by H.-G. Geissler
in collaboration with M.H. Müller and W. Prinz
© 1990 by Hogrefe & Huber Publishers

Chapter 13

Representations of Dimensional Models of Similarity

Hannes Eisler
Department of Psychology, University of Stockholm
Stockholm, Sweden
Ralf Lindman
Department of Psychology, Åbo Akademi
Turku, Finland

This paper deals with similarity models with the restriction that only models with dimensional representations are considered, excluding, e.g., tree models. Furthermore, it contains mainly observations by the authors rather than giving an overview of the literature. In general, the data taken into consideration constitute similarity estimates. A study of iso-similarity (equidistance) contours (Shepard, 1964) seems to be one of the most efficient ways to compare representations of similarity models and will be used extensively here. An iso-similarity contour is the locus of points (stimulus, or better, percept coordinates) with a given similarity to (distance from) a standard stimulus.

Individual Differences, the Stimulus Universe, Strategies

The degree of agreement among observers seems to depend strongly on the stimulus universe. When the judgment of similarities is a simple, natural task, the similarity of a pair of stimuli appears to correspond directly to a percept of similarity. An example is an experiment with patterns of two luminous points

(Eisler & Roskam, 1977a), in which, with the exception of two out of 40 observers, the correlations between the grand mean and any one observer exceeded 0.78.

An example of a stimulus universe for which similarity does not come naturally is Shepard's (1964) figures of circles with radii ("spokes") where circle size and radius inclination varied. Observers differed vastly in their similarity estimates (Eisler & Knöppel, 1970; Shepard, 1964). The same finding will be demonstrated below. Clearly, for these stimuli with their distinct features the similarity estimates are generated by some cognitive strategy, and different observers apply different strategies.

Disagreement Between Experimenter and Observer

Most often the experimenter has preconceptions as to the structure of the subjective space that is to be revealed by processing the similarity estimates. And, likewise most often, these preconceptions are at fault. This tendency of the experimenter, usually expressed as a blind faith in the physical dimensions, constitutes what has been called the "physicalistic trap" (Eisler, 1982). There might be disagreement between experimenter and observer as to (a) the number of dimensions (cf. Eisler & Roskam, 1977b), (b) the nature of the dimensions, and (c) the scale of any one dimension (e.g., logarithmic instead of linear) as well as of the dimensions relative to each other (their relative saliency).

Metricity of Dimensional Models

The most common dimensional similarity models adhere to the Minkowski metric, where the distance d_{ij} between two points (stimuli) i and j in n dimensions is defined as

$$d_{ij} = \left[\sum_{1}^{n} |x_{ik} - x_{jk}|^r \right]^{1/r} \tag{1}$$

where x_{ik} is the coordinate of point i in dimension k and $1 \le r \le \infty$. $r=1$ corresponds to the city-block metric, $r=2$ to the Euclidian metric, and $r=\infty$ to the suprenum (dominance) metric, yielding iso-similarity contours in the shape of a diamond, a circle, and a square, respectively. One of the properties of a metric is that an iso-similarity contour must be convex. This is also the case for the three special cases of the Minkowski metric mentioned above. We obtain the suprenum metric (with a square as iso-similarity contour) when the observer in a similarity judgment only takes the dimension with the largest distance into account; accordingly there is only one term on the right hand side of Equation 1, though the particular dimension (*k*) may change from point pair to point pair. The opposite would be obtained when the observer only takes the dimension with the greatest similarity into account. This strategy entails an *r* value <1, *viz.* −∞, and thus no metric. Figure 1 shows iso-similarity contours for this case. The point in the middle is the standard. We see that the contours are concave.

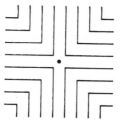

Figure 1. Theoretical iso-similarity contours for *r*= − ∞ in Equation 1. The dot is the standard stimulus.

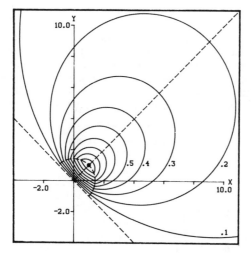

Figure 2. Theoretical iso-similarity contours for the content model. The dot is the standard stimulus, the numbers are the similarity values. (From Eisler, 1989. Copyright 1989 by Springer. Reprinted by permission.)

A further point regarding Minkowski models is that the shape of the iso-similarity contours may depend on the magnitude of the similarity and thus vary for the same stimulus universe (Schönemann, 1983).

The distance model as expressed in Equation 1 considers distances to be monotonically decreasing functions of similarities. These functions may or may not be specified. The content model (see, e.g., Eisler & Roskam, 1977a,b; Ekman & Sjöberg, 1965; Gregson, 1975) starts out instead from similarity s_{ij} ($0 \leq s_{ij} \leq 1$) for the two percepts i and j which correspond to stimuli I and J:

$$s_{ij} = \frac{2 \, \text{MIN}(h_i, h_j)}{h_i + h_j} \cos v_{ij}. \tag{2}$$

In Equation 2 percepts i and j are considered as vectors passing through the origin, with lengths h_i and h_j, and v_{ij} as the angle between the pair of vectors.

The content model for similarity is not metric. Figure 2 shows iso-similarity contours for this model (cf. also Gregson, 1975, p. 123). It can be seen that they are not symmetric around the standard (the point). The larger curves to the right, resembling circles, are inner loops of Pascal's limaçon, the smaller curves to the left are hyperbolas. The straight line at $45°$ examplifies the unidimensional case with only quantitative variation ($v_{ij} = 0$), whereas the half-circle around the standard shows the case with only qualitative variation (all vectors are of the same length).

Empirical Exemplifications

The iso-similarity contours to be shown here derive from a similarity estimation experiment with Shepard's circle-and-spoke figures as stimuli. At the end of the experiment, it became obvious that the points (combinations of circle size and inclination angle of the radii) were too few, so the iso-similarity contours were rather crude and the plots obtained (DISSPLA's contouring program was used) may occasionally not give a completely correct picture.

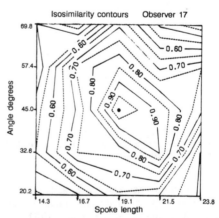

Figure 3. Empirical iso-similarity contours exemplifying closed curves in accordance with Equation 1.

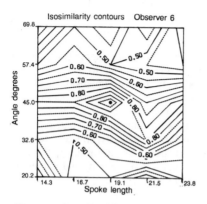

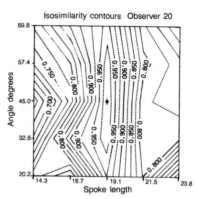

Figure 4. Empirical iso–similarity contours. This observer attended only to angle and disregarded circle size.

Figure 5. Empirical iso–similarity contours. This observer attended to only the circle size and disregarded angle.

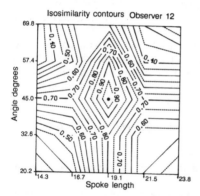

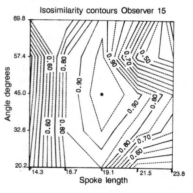

Figure 6. Empirical iso-similarity contours. This observer tended to take only the dimension with the greatest similarity into account. Accordingly, the contours are concave and resemble those of Figure 1.

Figure 7. Empirical iso-similarity contours. This observer shows asymmetries in the contours in accordance with Equation 2, and thus the contours have certain features in common with those of Figure 2.

Perhaps the most striking finding is the great individual differences between the 26 observers. Obviously, different observers used different strategies in their attempt to comply with the instruction to judge the similarity (between 0, no similarity at all, and 10, identity) of pairs of Shepard's figures. (For the data treatment, all estimates were divided by 10. These similarities are the numbers shown in the following plots).

Figure 3 shows an instance with closed contours. It is obvious that because of the scarcity of points it is impossible to determine the value or r in Equation 1, which was the intention of plotting the data.

Figures 4 and 5 show examples where the observers clearly did not obey the instructions, they attended to only one of the two features of the stimuli. In Figure 4 the observer discriminated the angle only, disregarding circle size, Figure 5 shows the opposite case.

Figure 6 demonstrates concave iso-similarity contours, approximating the crosses shown in Figure 1 and explained as corresponding to $r = -\infty$, i.e., observers who for every judgment attended only to the dimension with the greatest similarity. Figure 6 can also be seen as an instance where the shape of the contour depends on the magnitude of the similarity.

Good instances of iso-similarity contours according to the content model are difficult to find. Their most prominent feature is their asymmetry, but this may be concealed by the physical scale used in the plots. Rigorously, the axes should be scaled according to *subjective* circle size (spoke length) and *subjective* angle. Anyhow, Figure 7 shows features resembling Figure 2.

Summary and Conclusions

The theoretical part dealt with individual differences in similarity estimations implying varying strategies of the observers, and with experimenters' incorrect preconceptions regarding the subjective space from which these estimations supposedly are generated. Two theoretical iso-similarity contours are shown, one demonstrating the shape when an observer attends only to the dimension with the greatest similarity according to the distance model, and one for the content model. Neither is metric. The empirical part exemplifies different strategies by means of experimentally obtained iso-similarity contours. We may draw the following conclusions:

1. Studying iso-similarity contours may be an effective way to distinguish between similarity models.
2. Many points are necessary to obtain unique contours.
3. For heterogeneous stimuli we find great individual differences, because the observers apply different strategies.
4. Empirical examples can be found for observers not following instructions, for concave contours implying non-metric spaces, as well as for the typical closed iso-similarity contours.

Acknowledgement. This work was supported by the Swedish Council for Research in the Humanities and Social Sciences.
Correspondence should be addressed to: Hannes Eisler, Department of Psychology, University of Stockholm, S-106 91 Stockholm, Sweden.

References

Eisler, H. (1982). On the nature of subjective scales. *Scandinavian Journal of Psychology, 23*, 161–171.

Eisler, H. (1989). Data-equivalent models in psychophysics. In G. Ljunggren & S. Dornic (Eds.), *Psychophysics in action*. Berlin: Springer.

Eisler, H., & Knöppel, J. (1970). Relative attention in judgments of heterogeneous similarity. *Perception & Psychophysics, 8*, 420–426.

Eisler, H., & Roskam, E.E. (1977a). Multidimensional similarity: An experimental and theoretical comparison of vector, distance, and set theoretical models. I. Models and internal consistency of data. *Acta Psychologica, 41*, 1–46.

Eisler, H., & Roskam, E.E. (1977b). Multidimensional similarity: An experimental and theoretical comparison of vector, distance, and set theoretical models. II. Multidimensional analyses: The subjective space. *Acta Psychologica, 41*, 335–363.

Ekman, G., & Sjöberg, L. (1965). Scaling. *Annual Review of Psychology, 16*, 451–474.

Gregson, R.A. (1975). *Psychometrics of similarity*. New York: Academic Press.

Schönemann, P.H. (1983). Some theory and results for metrics for bounded response scales. *Journal of Mathematical Psychology, 27*, 311–324.

Shepard, R.N. (1964). Attention and the metric structure of the stimulus space. *Journal of Mathematical Psychology, 1*, 54–87.

Psychophysical Explorations of Mental Structures
Edited by H.-G. Geissler
in collaboration with M.H. Müller and W. Prinz
© 1990 by Hogrefe & Huber Publishers

Chapter 14

On Geometrical Analysis of Global Structure of Visual Space

Tarow Indow
Department of Cognitive Sciences
University of California Irvine
Irvine, U.S.A.

Visual space is the endproduct of a long series of processes: physical process from distant to proximal stimuli in the physical space (X), physiological process from retina to cortex in the physical body, and then visual space as a psychological phenomenon. If the retina is stimulated by homogeneous light of low intensity, we see completely unstructured mist of brightness (Ganzfeld). In ordinary conditions, however, we perceive highly articulated visual space extending in the three directions around the perceived self and visual space has a number of interesting geometrical features. Because we cannot perceive infinity, all distances we see are finite and hence visual space is closed. The horizon, when visible, always appears at the meridian of the visual space. We can directly perceive "straightness", "parallelness", etc.

Figure 1 gives such a configuration of stimulus points $\{Q_j\}$ in the horizontal plane (X) (see also Indow, 1982) at the level of eyes (R and L) that have been adjusted by the subject so as to generate the following geometrical forms in perception. The head of the subject was fixed but the subject was encouraged to scan Q's by moving the eyes. Two series of points (●) appear as straight lines parallel with each other, all pairs of points (o) appear to have lateral distances of the same length, and each set of 5 points along the y-axis appears to be fronto-parallel. Let us call these P(arallel)-alley, D(istance)-alley, and H(oropter)-curves. When one alley is being constructed, Q's for the other alley are not presented. The discrepancy between P-, and D-alleys, if real, shows that visual space under discussion is not structured according to Euclidean geometry. Genuineness of the discrepancy was discussed in Indow & Watanabe (1984a). Luneburg (1947) gave an interesting interpretation to the discrepancy and other geometrical phenomena in visual space, which is based upon two assumptions.

(1) Visual space is a Riemannian space (R) of constant curvature.

(2) Correspondence between perceived points P_j and stimulus points Q_j is as shown in Figure 2.

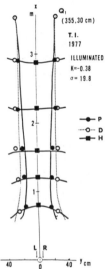

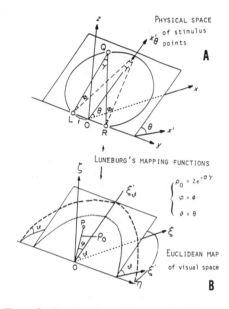

Figure 1. Parallel (P)- and distant (D)-alleys and fronto-parallel (H) curves.

Figure 2. Correspondence between physical space a Euclidean representation of visual space (EM: Poincaré's model).

According to the sign of Gaussian curvature K, R is either Euclidean (E) where $K=0$ or hyperbolic ($K<0$) or elliptic ($K>0$). When $K\neq0$, R cannot be represented without distortion in E of the same dimensionality. Let us take a particular representation of R in E (Figure 2B) and call it Euclidean map of R (EM) (Indow, 1979). All geometrical properties of R can be formulated in EM, e.g., equations for alleys and H-curves. This representation distorts length (non-isometric) but not angle (conformal). Denote by $\{P_j\}$ a configuration of points in *EM*. Luneburg assumed a simple form of correspondence as given in Figure 2. Then, as shown in Figure 1, we can have theoretical curves for P- and D-alleys and H-curves in *X* which can be compared with $\{Q_j\}$ constructed by the subject. The curves have two constants K and σ. The latter is in the third mapping function in Figure 2 and related to sensitivity for depth perception. The goodness of fit of the curves is always of the order as shown in Figure 1. If the horizontal plane of visual space is articulated in accordance with E, P-and D-alleys should coincide. On the contrary, P-alley is expected to lie outside D-alley when $K > 0$ and the reversed discrepancy when $K < 0$, provided an appropriate interpretation is given to "parallelness" (Indow, 1979). K always turned out to be negative. But its value changes according to the observing condition and size of $\{Q_j\}$ in X, and the same is true with σ (see Table 1 in Indow & Watanabe, 1984a). Hence, these are not universal constants to describe visual space of a subject under all circumstances. Visual space is not a solid box which can contain various configurations without changing its structure. Visual space is more dynamic and similar to a balloon. The subject sees nothing beyond the farthest point P_1 and the change of K actually suggests that visual space expands as a function of the perceptual distance to P_1 (Indow, 1984). Most alley experiments in the past have been conducted with configuration of small light points in the dark or of small objects in an illuminated space where no clear boundary is visible. This may be due to the following consideration. Luneburg's mapping functions are of egocentric form and, if this simple form holds, most likely it does in the frameless visual space. A way to explore geometry of visual space under more natural conditions is to rely upon the assumption (1) only, and to leave free the form of correspondence between visual space and X. In the approach proposed herein, it is expected that K is constant in visual space within a single glimpse, but its value and mapping functions may vary according to conditions. In order to take this more flexible approach, we need an additional set of data, scaled values of distances between points (Indow, 1982).

MDS to Construct $\{P_j\}$ in Euclidean Map with Riemannian Metric

Suppose a matrix D is given which consists of scaled values d_{ij} of visual distances δ_{ij} between points P_i and P_j. Notice that δ is a latent variable, but the subject can assign a positive value, $r_{jk.i}$, to ratio between two distances from a common point P_i; δ_{ij}/δ_{ik}. From these ratio judgments, d_{ij} are determined with an arbitrary unit (Indow, 1968; Indow & Ida, 1977). Then we can construct $\{P_j\}$ in EM such that Euclidean distances ϱ_{ij} in EM are related to geodesics in R and hence visual distance, δ_{ij}, and in turn, δ_{ij} is assumed to be related to the data d_{ij} by a power function with the exponent β.

Two programs have been developed. In the first program, δ is assumed to be proportional to d ($\beta = 1$) and d's for all combinations of points have to be given in D (Indow, 1982). In the second, DMRPD (Direct Mapping according to Riemannian metrics from Powered Distances), D can be incomplete and the optimum valaue of β is determined (Indow, 1983). In both programs, K is systematically varied to find out its optimum value. In order to define the value of K, we have to select an appropriate reference lenght by which K is defined (ϱ_{01} in Figure 3A). If two distances are to different, the subject feels difficulty in expressing the subjective ratio r, and hence it is better to leave D incomplete. It may well be the case that the subject is unable to assign r in proportion to the subjective ratio and the power function with unknown β will take care of this possible bias. Once $\{P_j\}$ is obtained in EM from the data D, we can compare it with theoretical equations in EM and also define the correspondence between EM and X by comparing $\{P_j\}$ with $\{Q_j\}$ (*a posteriori* definition of mapping functions).

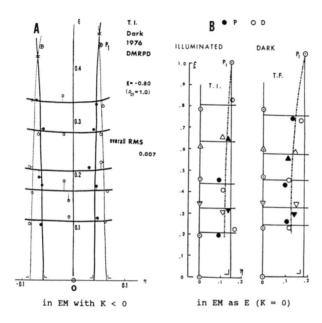

Figure 3. Alleys and fronto–parallel curves constructed in Euclidean map by multidimensional scaling according to hyperbolic metric (A) and Euclidean metric (B).

Figure 3A shows an example: $\{P_j\}$ constructed by DMRPD from D as to $\{Q_j\}$ similar to that in Figure 1 and theoretical curves in EM which are based on K only (Indow, 1983). Figure 3B shows two examples: $\{P_j\}$ constructed in E where K was constrained to be 0 (the result on the right side of the median only) (Indow, 1982). The results of other subjects are exactly the same in pattern, which is clearly against the view, often tacitly assumed, that visual space is Euclidean. If $K=0$ and hence EM directly represents visual space,

filled symbols for P-alley and unfilled symbols for D-alley in Figure 4B
have to be, not on the broken curve, but on the straight line, parallel to the
median line, because $\{Q_j\}$ has been adjusted so as to appear in that way in
visual space. On the other hand, when $K < 0$, theoretical curves in EM are as
shown in Figure 3A.

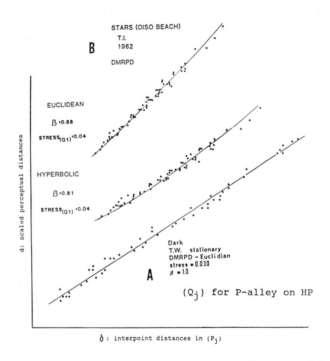

Figure 4. Relation between perceptual distances scaled by ratio judgment and distances
in constructed space: Alleys in fronto–parallel plane (A) and stars in the night sky represented in Euclidean and hyperbolic spaces (B).

Geometry of Fronto–Parallel Planes

Insofar as alleys and H–curves in the horizontal plane of eye level are
concerned, we have to conclude that this subspace of visual space is not
described by Euclidean geometry. It not necessarily implies that it is structured
in accordance with a mathematically familiar geometry such as R. If we take
the assumption (1), then we can say that the structure of the horizontal plane is
closer to hyperbolic geometry. In our daily life, we never come across patterns
like P– and D–alleys. Tracks of railroad are physically parallel and hence
appear to converge in visual space to a point on the horizon (vanishing point).

On the other hand, P-alley consists of two perceptually straight lines which are parallel up to the horizon, if the horizon is visible. Parallel lines we frequently perceive are either in a horizontal or vertical direction in front of the self. If visual space is hyperbolic as a whole, we can expect a discrepancy between P-and D-alleys when these are constructed on a plane which appears to be fronto-parallel. Let us call that plane horopter plane (HP). Equations in EM (Indow, 1979) for HP as well as P- and D-alleys on it have been obtained (Indow, 1988a) and two experiments have been performed (Indow & Watanabe, 1984b, 1988). No discrepancy was found between two { Q_{j}}'s for the P- and D-alleys on a HP. When $\{P_j\}$ is constructed by DMRPD from D with regard to $\{Q_j\}$, K turned out to be 0, and the data and δ, distances in EM as E, are proportional (see Figure 4A). Hence, we have to conclude that figures we see on a plane in front of us have Euclidean structure. If that were not the case, perhaps human beings would never have created Euclidean geometry.

Geometry of Night Sky Being Perceived

The approach based upon D can be extended to visual space under more natural conditions. A set of eleven stars of the same brightness level are taken as $\{Q_j\}$ and subjects, at the beach with an unobstructed view, made ratio judgments $r_{jk.i}$ where i, j, k denote the stars or the self (Indow, 1968). The night sky we see is an endproduct of the series of processes as discussed in the first section. An example obtained by DMPRD is given in Figure 5: $\{P_j\}$ constructed in three different spaces from the same data D (P_0 represents the self in visual space) (Indow, 1983). The correspondences between the data d and geodesics δ of $\{Q_j\}$ constructed in Euclidean and hyperbolic spaces are given in Figure 4B. In Figure 4B, the trend is slightly concave upwards ($\beta < 1$) in contrast to Figure 4A where $\beta = 1$. The embeddings in three spaces give indistinguishable results and hence we cannot pinpoint R by which the night sky is spanned. This failure to differentiate R suggests insensitivity of MDS when $\{P_j\}$ of unknown structure is at issue. In previous sections, $\{P_j\}$ having an intrinsic structure was dealt with, and hence the analysis was more powerful.

The perceived form of night sky in Figure 5 is different from that we see in a town where objects are visible in directions of ξ and η. The sky is most flattened in the direction of zenith. In this experiment, the subject faced toward the open sea in which nothing was visible. Lights from houses were visible far out in the direction of η, and stars in the zenith. Under this condition, all S's noticed that the sky was flattened most in the direction toward the horizon. the dynamic character of visual space is obvious in this example, too. The assumption (1) implies isotropy of visual space and hence EM. If the night sky in a given situation deviates in any form from a sphere, it may be interpreted as being due to the mapping functions between EM and X under the condition, not to anisotropy of visual space. Similarly, the assumption (1) is not contradictory with phenomena such as overestimation of vertical length, size constancy, etc. The phenomena can be ascribed to mapping functions which vary according to direction.

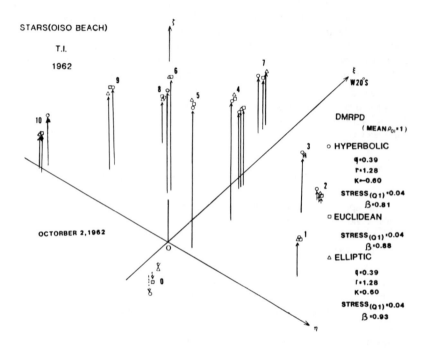

Figure 5. Configuration of stars embedded in three Riemannian spaces by multidimensional scaling.

Scaled Perceptual Distance d as Metric

When D is used as a set of data, how to scale latent variable δ is always a problem. In experiments referred to above, d's were obtained from ratio judgments. One way to check how consistently the subject assigns r to subjective ratios and whether d obtained from r behaves as metric is as follows. Once P-alley has been constructed, there are two series of Q's, each Q being on a perceptually straight line (Indow & Watanabe, 1988). Let us focus on such d's between points all of which are on the same perceptual line. Then, if d is metric, the additivity $d_{ik} = d_{ij} + d_{jk}$ for P_i, P_j, P_k in this order has to hold among these collinear d's. The additivity has been shown to hold for d's for visual distance. On the other hand, when perceptual difference δ between two colors is scaled by the same ratio judgment, a systematic deviation from the additivity has been found with d's for colors collinear in the color space. Since d's for perceptual distances can be regarded as metrics, the application of MDS to visual space and the results from it are really meaningful to the study of vision.

Summary and Conclusion

A somewhat unusual application of MDS has been discussed. Perhaps, physics and psychology are only two empirical sciences that have spaces which really exist: universe and visual space. Psychophysics has one more space of interest; color space (Indow, 1988b). However, this is not a space to exist by itself but a space as a means to represent relationships, as in most applications of MDS in cognitive, semantic, and social researches. On the contrary, visual space exists as a perceptual reality. Hence, how visual space is structured when we have it as the endproduct of the series of processes will be a question vital to psychophysicists: a question that Fechner might have been interested in. In order to take a flexible approach to this problem and to go beyond the frameless visual space, MDS will be a powerful tool, provided it is appropriately adjusted for this problem. We do not yet have MDS or other methodology to deal visual space as a more general Riemannian space in which curvature is not a constant or as a manifold, more general than Riemannian geometry.

It is a substantive question for the study of vision to ask why two kinds of subspaces in visual space, the horizontal plane and fronto-parallel planes, are differently structured. The key motive for assuming a constant K consists in the possiblility of free mobility in visual space. The problem will be discussed elsewhere.

Correspondence should be addressed to Tarow Indow, Department of Cognitive Sciences, School of Social Sciences, University of California Irvine, Irvine CA 92717, U.S.A.

References

Indow, T. (1968) Multidimensional mapping of visual space with real and simulated stars. *Perception & Psychophysics, 3*, 45−53.

Indow, T. (1979). Alleys in visual space. *Journal of Mathematical Psychology, 19*, 221−258.

Indow, T. (1982). An approach to geometry of visual space with no a priori mapping functions: Multidimensional mapping according to Riemannian metrics. *Journal of Mathematical Psychology, 26*, 204−236.

Indow, T. (1983). Multidimensional mapping in Riemannian space and its applications. Presented at the Annual Meeting of the Psychometric Society, University of California, Los Angeles.

Indow, T. (1984). On finiteness of visual space. Presented at the Mathematical Psychology Meeting, University of Chicago.

Indow, T. (1988a). Alleys on an apparent frontoparallel plane. *Journal of Mathematical Psychology, 32,* 259–284.

Indow, T. (1988b). Multidimensional studies of Munsell color solid. *Psychological Review, 95,* 456–470.

Indow, T., & Ida, M. (1977). Scaling of dot numerosity. *Perception & Psychophysics, 22,* 265–276.

Indow, T., & Watanabe, T. (1984a). Parallel- and distance-alleys with moving points in the horizontal plane. *Perception & Psychophysics, 35,* 144–154.

Indow, T., & Watanabe, T. (1984b). Parallel-alleys and distance-alleys on horopter plane in the dark. *Perception, 13,* 165–182.

Indow, T., & Watanabe, T. (1988). Alleys on an extensive apparent fronotparallel plane: A second experiment. *Perception, 17,* 647–666.

Luneburg, R.K. (1947). *Mathematical analysis of binocular vision.* Princeton University Press.

Psychophysical Explorations of Mental Structures
Edited by H.-G. Geissler
in collaboration with M.H. Müller and W. Prinz
© 1990 by Hogrefe & Huber Publishers

Chapter 15

Multidimensional Scaling of Line and Angle Discrimination

Chingis A. Izmailov and Evgenij N. Sokolov
Department of Psychophysiology
Moscow State University
Moscow, U.S.S.R.

From a geometrical point of view the angle is a combination of two lines. It is in accordance with intuitive thinking that angles are more complex perceptive stimuli than lines, and perception of angles is accomplished at a higher level of information processing than perception of lines. This claim is supported by both neurophysiological (Hubel & Wiesel, 1962) and psychophysical (Granovskaya, Bereznaya & Grigoreva, 1981; Selfridge & Neisser, 1974) evidence.

However, later results (Sillito & Versiani, 1977; Supin, 1981) permit to suggest an alternative idea, namely that lines and angles are equally specific percepts, and discrimination of angles is neither more complex nor simpler than discrimination of lines.

Some computer programs which recognise three-dimensional objects represented by contour drawings (Guzman, 1968; Waltz, 1975) have been based on a set of 8-10 stimuli. The stimuli were combinations of two, three, four or five lines. This set of basic combinations can be considered as an alphabet of contour scenes.

It may be assumed that the basic combinations of lines are perceptually equivalent, as letters of an alphabet are semantically equivalent. This suggestion was tested by applying multidimensional scaling analysis to discrimination data for lines and angles.

Method

In the first experiment 18 lines of different orientations (from 0° up to 162° in relation to visual horizontal axis) were used as a 153 pair combination of lines. Each pair was sequentially presented on the screen of a color TV–set. The subjects were instructed to rate perceived differences between the stimuli of each pair by an integer number that ranged from 0 (identical orientations) to 9 (most different orientations).

In the second experiment 12 angles (from 23° up to 165°) each having 2 − 4 different orientations (Table 1) in a frontal plane were presented on a TV monitor. Each pair of angles was displayed sequentially and the subjects were to estimate the perceived differences between pair members using rank evaluations from 0 (identical angles) up to 9 (most different angles).

Table 1. Geometrical characteristics (values and orientations) of angles. Orientation of angle was defined as the angle between bisector and an assumed horizontal line in the frontal plane of observation.

value of angle (degrees)	angle orientation (degrees)					
	0	45	90	135	180	315
25		1	2	3		4
28					5	
42		6	7	8		
60					9	10
75	11		12			
75	11		12			
90		13		14		15
105			16			
120	17			18		
125		19			20	
152	21	22	23		24	
155		25		26	27	28
165	29					30

The duration of stimulus presentation was 0.5 s. The intervals between pair members and pairs were set at 1 s and 3 s, respectively. Stimuli were presented in conditions of darkness adaptation. Each pair of stimuli was presented five times in quasi–random order. Subjects were instructed to estimate configurative differences only without analysing values of angles and orientations in the frontal field. The estimates for each pair were summed up across two subjects and five presentations.

Results

The matrixes of subjective differences for both sets of lines and angles (Tables 2 and 3) were analysed by the metric multidimensional scaling procedure. The scaling procedure yielded representations of the lines and angles as points in a euclidean space. In both cases two axes were required for representation of points in the space. The euclidean distances between points obtained from the calculated coordinates closely correspond to the subjective differences ($r = 0.972$ for lines, and $r = 0.974$ for angles).

Table 2. Estimates of perceived differences between lines, summed up across subjects and presentations.

orientation of lines (degrees)	N	1	2	3	4	5	6	7	8	9	10	11	12	13	14	15	16	17	18
0	1		30	38	38	42	49	52	61	70	90	69	56	53	44	38	34	38	36
23	2			5	13	12	20	32	31	40	55	62	65	69	65	63	60	65	63
25	3				6	12	20	32	32	41	56	64	67	68	65	67	64	67	63
30	4					10	16	25	33	43	55	65	73	71	69	68	70	63	63
35	5						5	14	31	38	47	70	70	72	71	70	67	65	65
42	6							6	23	34	50	67	76	72	70	65	71	66	66
53	7								12	25	46	61	73	73	74	74	70	69	71
72	8									28	43	62	70	71	68	68	70	69	69
90	10										36	42	47	60	62	67	66	67	68
110	11											30	42	50	52	52	51	57	55
127	12												17	27	33	31	41	37	45
140	13													17	17	30	26	33	37
145	14														9	15	18	25	30
150	15															6	12	16	22
153	16																3	10	14
158	17																	9	9
160	18																		4

The points representing line orientations are located in a two-dimensional space in such a way that the first axis intersects the points representing line-orientations of 0° and 90°, and the second axis intersects the points representing line orientations of 45° and 135° (Figure 1). The trajectory of points on the X_1, X_2-plane forms a circle centred in the origin of the axes X_1, X_2. The standard deviation of radii is only 10 per cent of the mean radius. This means that polar coordinates of points in the subjective space of line orientations (φ_i) are represented by double the geometrical angle of line orientations (α_i). The psychophysical function for the perception of a line orientation is derived as:

$$\varphi_i = 2\alpha_i, \tag{1}$$

where α_i varies from 0 to 180 degrees.

Table 3. Estimates of perceived differences between angles, summed up across subjects and presentations.

N	1	2	3	4	5	6	7	8	9	10	11	12	13	14	15	16	17	18	19	20	21	22	23	24	25	26	27	28	29	30
1																														
2	2																													
3	5	5																												
4	2	4	3																											
5	19	17	12	13																										
6	23	24	24	14																										
7	30	19	28	27	18	13																								
8	26	24	31	26	14	8	8																							
9	32	27	30	25	21	9	8	6																						
10	32	36	28	35	27	16	13	15	19																					
11	33	30	30	32	25	29	14	14	13	25																				
12	32	30	36	28	28	15	24	15	11	11	13																			
13	55	55	55	56	44	47	42	43	34	35	28	35																		
14	51	48	53	55	50	46	40	41	30	33	24	29	9																	
15	53	55	49	53	48	48	39	40	32	29	29	35	0	9																
16	61	59	61	54	49	40	40	38	52	46	44	34	31	26	22															
17	60	61	60	60	47	48	44	39	50	29	33	31	31	31	24	18														
18	62	73	68	61	58	47	53	44	42	35	36	36	41	27	17	3														
19	76	72	84	85	67	60	65	59	58	53	39	54	34	44	46	14	11	10												
20	80	77	77	67	74	63	58	57	64	63	36	44	38	43	32	12	11	8	1											
21	78	68	78	78	64	72	63	60	60	68	57	44	43	36	32	11	19	19	8	6										
22	76	83	79	78	63	71	68	78	68	54	64	54	49	44	43	29	22	10	4	7	2									
23	79	79	82	77	71	71	64	71	46	56	50	44	52	47	21	11	27	16	14	3	9									
24	80	71	72	76	72	59	65	60	55	55	44	43	46	47	37	14	12	10	6	9	14									
25	80	84	88	88	73	79	69	74	63	60	55	52	59	31	21	37	9	16	8	8	11	5								
26	82	86	81	82	79	69	65	66	63	56	54	49	55	31	26	27	9	6	5	7	6	4								
27	76	88	81	85	78	61	70	67	64	74	56	42	53	30	31	31	20	18	13	22	11	10	7	2						
28	88	83	89	89	84	80	71	68	74	53	58	56	53	53	48	37	30	25	19	25	9	7	7	13	3	4	9			
29	80	88	89	83	73	79	71	69	75	71	64	72	55	64	57	39	38	37	19	21	14	5	15	5	10	4	3			
30	87	87	88	88	84	79	77	78	66	57	58	56	56	46	30	16	20	10	9	11	6	4	3	4	0	8				

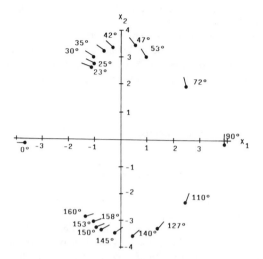

Figure 1. Two-dimensional euclidean space, representing discrimination of line orientations. The numbers near the points characterize the angles (in degrees) of line orientations on a frontal plane of observation. Horizontal angles of the points (φ) characterize perceived orientation of lines.

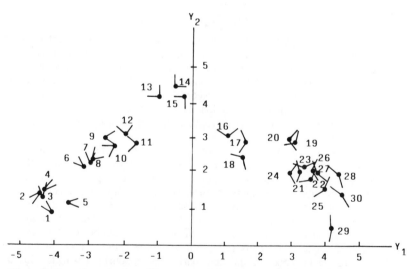

Figure 2. Two-dimensional euclidean space, representing discrimination of angles. The numbers near the points correspond with the numbers of stimuli in Table 1. Horizontal angles of the points (ψ) characterize subjective values of angles.

The points representing angles are also located on a plane (Figure 2). But in this case points form a semicircle from 0 to 180 degrees. The stimuli having the same values of angles but different orientations are located in the same area of the X_1, X_2-plane. The standard deviation of radii for points representing stimuli is 9 per cent of the mean radius. The polar coordinates of the points of this semicircle (ψ) in a clockwise direction are defined by direct values of stimuli (β). Thus,

$$\psi_i = \beta_i, \qquad (2)$$

where β_i varies from 0 to 180 degrees.

Discussion

The discussion will be concerned with a major problem that can be expressed by the following questions:

Can the detection of the angle be independent of discrimination of the lines? Or can we consider this outcome as a result of a two line–discrimination?

In the latter case the angle configuration will be defined by a subtractive function of the orientation of two lines — α_1 and α_2:

$$\beta = |\alpha_1 - \alpha_2|. \qquad (3)$$

The symbols in this equation have the same meanings as in equations (1) and (2). By using equations (1) and (3) we are now in a position to write:

$$\psi(\beta) = \varphi(\alpha_1) - \varphi(\alpha_2)$$
$$\psi(\beta) = 2\alpha_1 - 2\alpha_2 = 2\alpha_1 - \alpha_2 = 2\beta. \qquad (4)$$

The obtained equation (4) does not coincide with experimental psychophysical function (2). Thus one can assume that the detection of an angle is a separate visual processing rather than result of a two–line discrimination.

Point configurations of lines and angles in two–dimensional euclidean space (Figures 1 and 2) are in very good accordance with the color–point configuration obtained from color discrimination data (Sokolov & Izmailov, 1983). The similarity between color and line perception phenomena has been pointed out by Gibson (1933).

Therefore we can interpret the obtained data in terms of a spherical detector model of color discrimination as described in general form by Sokolov and Izmailov (1983). In terms of this model a three–stage neuronal network performs color analysis of lights (Figure 3). At the first, the receptor, stage, information on stimulus intensity is extracted from the short-, middle-, and long-wave ranges of the spectrum. At the second, predetector, stage, this information is analysed by chromatic and achromatic double–channel systems. The chromatic system contains red–green and blue–yellow opponent channels, and the achromatic one bright and dark non–opponent channels. In each double–channel system one of the channels has a sine characteristic in relation to light intensity and the other a cosine characteristic. The double–channel system forms the specific sensory quality, which is perceived, e.g., as hue.

Thus, each of the basic sensory characteristics of stimuli is coded by two reciprocally interconnected neuronal channels. At the third, detector, stage, the information from different double-channel systems is transmitted to the color-selective detectors. The strengths of synaptic connections between each detector and predetectors are governed by the spherical law. At the detector stage the information is integrated into a unitary sensation which is characterized by hue, brightness, and additionally arising saturation.

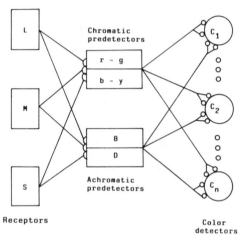

Receptors　　　　　　　　　　　　　　　　　　　Color
　　　　　　　　　　　　　　　　　　　　　　　 detectors

Figure 3. Schematic representation of a neural network suited for color analysis. At the first, receptor, stage, the intensity information is extracted from short-, middle-, and long-wave ranges in the spectrum. At the second (predetector) stage, this information is processed by a pair of independent double-channel systems. The chromatic system contains red-green and blue-yellow opponent channels and the achromatic system is built up of the non-opponent bright and dark channels. At the third, detector, stage, the information is integrated into a unitary sensation. The structure of the synaptic connections between each detector and the predetectors is submitted to the spherical law. Thus, unitary sensation characterizes hue, brightness, and additionally arising saturation.

An important characteristic of the spherical model is the integration of neurophysiological and psychological aspects of perception into a unitary structure. Thus, each stimulus point in the spherical model defined in terms of Cartesian frame of reference can be interpreted as a state of neurophysiological channels and the same point defined by spherical coordinates can be interpreted as psychological characteristics of the stimulus.

From this point of view the perception of line orientations is determined by two opponent channels converging on the set of selective orientation detectors (Figure 4). The perception of angles is determined by one opponent and other non-opponent channels converging on the set of selective angle detectors (Figure 5). The spherical models of the same types obtained for discrimination

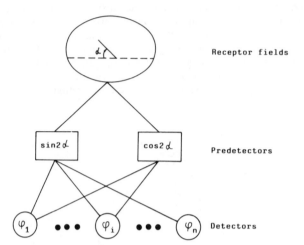

Figure 4. The structure of a sensory analyzer detecting line orientations. The stimulus is the angle between the line and the visual horizontal axis, measured in clockwise direction. The double-channel system of the predetectors provides both a sine-, and a cosine-transformation of the stimulus for each of the orientation detectors. Each detector is characterized by a specific pattern of synaptic inputs from the predetectors which defines its selectivity for a given line orientation.

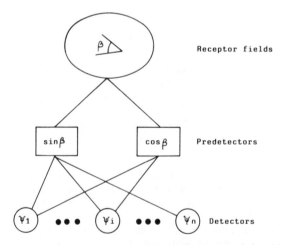

Figure 5. Schematic representation of sensory analyzers suited for the detection of angles. The angle between two lines, irrespective of its sign and orientation, serves as stimulus. The double-channel predetector system provides both a sine- and a cosine-transformation of a stimulus for each of the angle detectors. Coefficients of the synaptic connections between each detector on the one hand and the predetectors on the other hand correspond to the spherical law.

of lines and angles can be interpreted as a result of the activity of independent neuronal nets, accomplishing line and angle detection and giving an opportunity to relate both of them to identical basic characteristics of configurations. This means that extraction of lines as well as angles from a configuration pattern is accomplished by parallel rather than hierarchical information processing systems.

As a general conclusion it is suggested that the construction of a spherical model on the basis of judged large differences using multidimensional scaling procedure provides us with a useful psychophysical approach to identify basic sensory qualities.

Summary

In previous work a spherical model of color perception was suggested. Its basic structure, which accounts for both psychological and neurophysiological aspects, is claimed to be of relevance for other domains of perception. In the paper, the model is specified for the perception of lines and angles. Application to judged similarity of lines and angles suggests that their subjective representation reflects a parallel operation of independent neural systems rather than a hierarchical process that would give rise to angle representation following line detection.

Correspondence should be addressed to E.N. Sokolov, State University of Moscow, Psychological Faculty, Department of Psychophysiology, Prospekt Marksa 18/5, Moscow, U.S.S.R.

References

Gibson, J.J. (1933). Adaptation, after-effect and contrast in the perception of curved lines. *Journal of Experimental Psychology, 16,* 1−31.

Granovskaya, R.M, Bereznaya, I.Ya., & Grigoreva, A.N. (1981). *Perception and features of form* (in Russ.). Moscow.

Guzman, A. (1968). *Computer recognition of three–dimensional objects in a visual scene.* Ph. D. Thesis, AI–TK–258, Artificial Intelligence Laboratory, MIT, Cambridge, Mass.

Hubel, D.H., & Wiesel, T.N. (1962). Receptive fields, binocular integration and functional architecture in the cat's visual cortex. *Journal of Physiology, 160,* 106−154.

Selfridge, O., & Neisser, U. (1972). *Computer pattern recognition.* (In Russian. Translation from R. Held & W. Richards (Eds.), *Perception. Mechanisms and models.* San Francisco: Freeman.

Sillito, A.M., & Versiani, V. (1979). The contribution of excitatory and inhibitory inputs to the length preference of hypercomplex cells in layers II and III of the cat's striate cortex. *Journal of Physiology, 289,* 33−53.

Sokolov, E.N., & Izmailov, Ch.A. (1983). Conceptual reflex arc and color vision. In In H.-G. Geissler, H. Buffart, E.L.J. Leeuwenberg & V. Sarris (Eds.), *Modern issues in perception.* Amsterdam: North–Holland.

Supin, A.Ya. (1981). *Neurophysiology of mammaliaes vision* (in Russ.). Moscow.

Waltz, D. (1975). Generating semantic descriptions from drawings of scenes with shadows. In P.H. Winston (Ed.), *The Psychology of Computer Vision.* New York: McGraw-Hill.

III. Psychophysical Aspects of Time and Structure

Psychophysical Explorations of Mental Structures
Edited by H.-G. Geissler
in collaboration with M.H. Müller and W. Prinz
© 1990 by Hogrefe & Huber Publishers

Chapter 16

Foundations of Quantized Processing

Hans-Georg Geissler
Karl-Marx-Universität Leipzig
Leipzig, G.D.R.

Thinking of mental activities in terms of discrete time units has a relatively strong tradition in psychology (cf. Neumann, 1983). Early relevant work derived from the idea of a smallest unit of which psychological time is made up, the so-called moment, as first defined by the biologist von Baer (1864). Later findings suggest that, depending on various conditions and on the aspect of analysis, quanta of different size may play a role. In this respect most conclusive results have been obtained with perceptual tasks (Allport, 1968; Kristofferson, 1980, 1984; Latour, 1967; Lebedev, 1976, 1980; McReynolds, 1953; Michon, 1965, 1967; Stroud, 1955; Uttal, 1970; Vanagas, Balkelite, Bartusyavitchus & Kiryalis, 1976; among others). For these quantal time periods we will adopt Allport's (1968) term of "perceptual intermittency" or, for short, "intermittency." The various contributions to the issue differ as to their main goal. As perhaps nothing is as easy as to wash out quantal effects from experimental findings, most efforts have been concentrated on experimentation to furnish proof of the existence of quantal time units and to measure them. Only a few studies attempted to define a theoretical rationale for lawful relationships between different observable periods (cf. e.g. Kristofferson, 1980, 1984; McReynolds, 1953; Stroud, 1955). In view of a small data base from arbitrarily selected paradigms with widely differing ranges of intermittencies, the scope of these approaches, however, remained rather limited.

These limitations may account for the fact that theorizing based on the discreteness of internal timing had so little impact on modern chronometric research although it should be expected to bear on nearly all its issues.

The present paper seeks to develop a system of assumptions providing a new framework for analyzing quantal effects within a broad range of variation, bringing together phenomena from quite different experimental paradigms. To avoid the shortcomings of earlier approaches we will make a major attempt to establish a set of most basic assumptions by reanalyzing experimental facts which seem to be of general significance.

The assumptions themselves are propositions about sets of possible intermittencies which may emerge as a function of stimulus properties, task, and other factors. The advantage of this kind of formulation is its generality and independence of particular processing assumptions. Thus it may apply to aspects of serial and parallel processing as well and may even admit of conceptually different interpretations of the intermittencies themselves. On the other hand, application to concrete paradigms will always involve some complementary assumptions. In the present paper we will demonstrate this for a few typical specimens in the hope of encouraging attempts at incorporating time quantum assumptions into processing theories proper.

Logically, the system under consideration is independent of any reference to physiological mechanisms. However, as physiological interpretaions of the postulated periodic activities are straightforward, we will in some cases refer to physiological evidence as well.

The totality of assumptions involved in the proposed system represents a more elaborate version of a model advanced elsewhere (Geissler, 1987), for which the introduced term "time quantum model" (TQM) will be retained.

Foundations of the Time Quantum Model (TQM)

Reanalysis of a Former Model: Stroud's Hypothesis

The only approach which as an analytic formulation can be compared with TQM is the moment hypothesis advanced by Stroud (1955). A critical discussion of this theory is, therefore, particularly suited for a first heuristic characterisation of TQM.

According to Stroud (1955), some moment or "reference input interval" D is active under certain conditions. The most basic relation of the moment hypothesis implies that some internal quantity d, which is induced by the stimulus input, assumes preferred values which are either integer multiples $d = k \cdot D$ or integer fractions $d = D/l$ of D.

In general, the relation of d to stimulus parameters may be complex. It gets simplified in the case of sensations caused by low frequency sound where d can be equated with external period duration. With reference to data reported by von Békésy (1936) for absolute thresholds of low frequency sound sensations which show sharp breaks at characteristic frequencies, preferred period durations are found, in accordance with the hypothesis, at $d = D/4$, $D/3$, $D/2$, D, and $2D$, leading to an estimate of 111.82 ms[1] for D.

The assumption fits the data rather well ($R^2 = 0.99995$). That it cannot be entirely correct, despite this agreement, follows from the fact that it predicts only less than half of the observed breaks.

There are two shortcomings of a more general nature, Perhaps the most serious one is that the very fundamental intermittencies D, instead of having a proper place within a general theoretical framework, are obtained by data fitting using different *ad hoc* assumptions from one set of data to the other. This may (and indeed does) yield different estimates depending on the particular data.

A second shortcoming of Stroud's formulation is that its predictions, as in the Békesy case, may extend to both sides of D and, thus, do not involve lower and upper bounds (as theoretical constructs). Therefore, any $k \cdot d$ and D/l with integers $k > 2$ and $l > 4$, which lack an empirical correspondence, agree with it, too.

In the last part of his 1955 paper Stroud introduced the notion of "moment train" as an additional assumption. It is motivated by the fact that individually preferred tapping rhythms can be sustained up to some 40 taps and must be initiated anew after that. To be sure, this moment train assumption, which refers to a wider range, provides a new source of evidence of discrete intermittencies. The approach, however, provides no rationale for predicting the tapping rhythms and number of consistently executed taps.

Taking account of the weak points mentioned, the following general postulates can be stated for any forthcoming approach:

1. Dimensional numerical parameters should be universal, i.e. invariant across tasks and other conditions.

2. Any other numerical constituents must be elements of sets of integers derivable from the theory.

A Heuristic Outline of TQM Assumptions

The Operative–Set Assumption. The accumulated evidence suggests the existence of sets of intermittencies, acting like time windows of different sizes, which seem to be characteristic of classes of operative conditions to which they are adjusted. We define "operative sets" of intermittencies by $T^o = \{T_i^o\}$, where o indicates operative conditions such as task, critical stimulus properties, level of activation, and so forth. The principal goal of TQM can be defined as the specification of admissible operative sets of intermittencies. The above considerations suggest that the lower and upper bounds T_{Li}^o and T_{Ui}^o form the main constituents of an operative set T_i^o. The interval $T_{Li}^o \leq T_i^o \leq T_{Ui}^o$ will be

---

[1] A corrected estimate on the basis of von Békesy's data. Stroud's original estimate was 106.1 ms.

called "operative interval." A major task of TQM will thus be to specify the set of admissible bounds T^o_{Li} and T^o_{Ui} and the selection rules for admissible T^o_i belonging to the given operative intervals.

In what follows, we will for simplicity's sake omit the index o from all expressions.

The Time Quantum Assumption. As a most basic axiom TQM adopts the assumption of an elementary time quantum T. Consistent with the classic concept of "moment", T is supposed to represent an absolute lower bound of temporal resolution, hence the smallest possible lower bound of an operative interval. In keeping with the above postulate (1), T is claimed to be the only universal, numerical parameter of TQM. Universality in the sense of invariance need not necessarily exclude minor variations across individuals and even within individuals. In the latter case changes could be expected to occur, for instance, as a function of body temperature and biochemical factors like drug effects.

T is claimed to be universal in still another functional sense, namely that irrespective of the processes under consideration admissible intermittencies T_i are always multiples of T:

$$T_i = k_i \cdot T , \quad k_i \text{ integer.} \tag{1}$$

In order to maintain this fundamental time quantum assumption we can put forward several formal and empirical arguments.

Table 1. Empirical and predicted values of T_i.

f_{emp} [a]	38	32	28	22	18	14	11	9
$T_{i\ emp}$ [b]	26.31	31.25	35.71	45.45	55.55	71.43	90.91	111.11
$k_{i\ hyp}$	6	7	8	10	12	16	20	24
$T_{i\ pred}$ [b]	26.51	31.16	35.81	45.10	54.40	72.99	91.58	110.18

[a] in Hz   [b] in ms

Formally, as compared with Stroud's description, reference to a lower bound has the general advantage of a more parsimonious formulation because otherwise the lower bound would have to be introduced as an additional parameter. Using the largest common denominator $D_o = D/12$ Stroud's predictions could then be transformed into $d = 3D_o, 4D_o, 6D_o, 12D_o$, with $D_o = 9.32$ ms. However, complete inclusion of the lowest eight break frequencies leads to the estimate $D'_o = 4.648$ ms with an intercept $a = -1.38$ ms. Table 1 compares the empirical and predicted values ($R^2 = 0.99918$). The largest difference between empirical and predicted T_i values is close to 1 ms. If a is forced to become zero, D'_o becomes 4.558 ms.

Although the tempting simplicity of Stroud's fractionating rule has vanished from the present formulation, the assumed relation (1) to a lower bound proves quite useful.

An incidental conclusion we come to is that a time period of some 4.5 ms (an unexpectedly small value as compared with earlier formulations) may function as a basic time quantum in mental processes. Although we are on somewhat shaky ground when claiming that the smallest possible intermittency is just of that size (since any theory based on that value would remain essentially unchanged by introducing integer fractions of it as the "true" quantum values), it is fair to say that the further direct evidence known to us is compatible with the assumption that it indeed represents the largest common denominator of observed periods.

Let us now state in brief some of the most important sources of evidence:

1. The visual masking data of Vanagas et al. (1976) showing a clear periodicity of the percent correct curves are particularly impressive. On the basis of a re-evaluation of the results for 8 Ss a quantum value of 9.13 ms was proposed (Geissler, 1985a,b). Occasionally, however, a good fit was found for values close to 5 ms. An attempt to replicate the Vanagas et al. experiments (Buffart, Geissler & van Leeuwen, 1984) yielded less pronounced periods clustering at around one half of the Vanagas et al. period. Thus $T = 4.56$ ms may be a good guess at the "true" value, assuming that a doubled period can play the role of quantal processing time unit.

2. Quantal steps in thresholds of duration discrimination that show up after extended practice were described by Kristofferson (1980, 1984). A first quantal level is found at about 13.5 ms, which is three times 4.5 ms.

3. In an earlier paper by Latour (1967), integer relationships between RT periodicities in motor responses of the eye to horizontal position changes of a fixation light, on the one hand, and EEG rhythms during and prior to the experiment, on the other, were reported.

4. As will be shown below, TQM can be applied to data obtained in item–identification tasks. However, there are only few reports on stable identification rates which could be taken as direct evidence for elementary quantal operation times. The scanning rate for digits in Sternberg tasks (cf. Sternberg, 1966, 1967a,b) of 37.2 ms seems to be a notable exception. A similar value (36 ms, $SD = 0.9$ ms) was reported by Krol and Tanengolz (1976) as minimum presentation time in visual pattern recognition. This duration corresponds to eight time quanta or four double quanta and yields estimates for T of 4.65 ms ($SD = 0.12$ ms) and 4.50 ms ($SD = 0.11$ ms), respectively.

At present, it seems difficult to directly demonstrate periodic activities of such high frequency (about 200 Hz) within the cortex. There are, however, at least signs of convergent evidence worth mentioning. Some direct support comes from duration estimates for interhemispheric transfer (Roth, 1986, personal communication), clustering at small multiples of 4.5 ms, and for brain stem transmission, which stabilizes at this level in early childhood (Fabiani, Schmer, Tait, Gafni & Kinarti, 1979). Interestingly enough, time periods consistent with those suggested above on psychological grounds play the role of central constructs within two physiologically motivated theories. Lebedev (1976, 1980), for instance, refers to "relative refractoriness" as defined by Livanov (cf. Livanov, 1972), an assumed quantal period of about 10 ms by which phases and frequencies of brain waves are claimed to differ. Hendrickson, who speculated about neural pulse–train codes, adopted minimum interspike intervals, lasting somewhat longer than 4 ms, as critical constituents of his theory (cf. Hendrickson, 1972; Hendrickson & Hendrickson, 1980).

The Coherence Assumption. From the basic quantum axiom (1) it follows that lower and upper bounds must be integer multiples of T. Thus for any T_L and T_U we have:

$$T_L = q \cdot T \quad \text{and} \quad T_U = Q \cdot T \qquad (2)$$

with integers q and Q.

However, what are the possible sizes of the operative interval? Are there any lawful relationships between q and Q?

The appearance of periodic EEG patterns for limited spans of time is a well-known general phenomenon. A plausible reason for this temporal boundedness are limitations in the syncronization of local oscillatory activities caused by small differences in frequencies. TQM adopts this as a fundamental property of carrier oscillations assumed to be inherent in intermittency structures. In terms of intermittencies the coherence limitations of carrier oscillations may be represented as follows:

$$T_{iL} = L \cdot T_i \leq M \cdot T_i \; ; \quad L, M \text{ integer.} \qquad (3)$$

Here, T_{iL} denotes the duration of a chain of intermittencies T_i. M is the maximum length or "coherence length" of such chains. M could depend on the individual S and on the particular index i. It will be assumed below that M is characteristic of any individual as a whole. This requires, as one condition, that admissible T_i should have the same status of unique entities as T in (1). (2) also implies that the T_{iL} represent higher–order intermittencies. The interval $T_i \leq T_{iL} \leq T_{iM}$ will be called "coherence interval."

The treatment of the T_{iL} as functional units calls for detailed justification (see below). With respect to content (an issue that we cannot discuss in detail here), the notion of unit will certainly differ for T_i and T_{iL}. It may, for instance, imply execution of one cognitive operation in the case of small periods T_i, whereas for T_{iM} it may mean continuation of one and the same sequence of operation (or mode of operation) without referring to intervening results. (3) corresponds formally to the "moment train" as suggested by Stroud. The same is true for the pulse train hypothesis of Hendrickson (1972), and for the period of coherent processing defined by Lebedev (1976, 1980), calculated on the basis of relative refractoriness.

The most straightforward way of combining (2) and (3) is to assume

$$T_L = q \cdot T \quad \text{and} \quad T_U = L \cdot q \cdot T, \qquad (4)$$

putting $Q = L \cdot q \leq M \cdot q$.

This would yield a simple ratio law for the relation of upper and lower operative bounds.

Some more complex alternatives to (4) do not result in such lawful relationships. Assume, for instance, $T_{i+1} - T_i$ as being unrelated to T_L. An alternatively possible relation would then read: $T_U = q \cdot T_L \cdot v \cdot T$. This would automatically uncouple T_L and T_U. Evidence for the tenability of (4) for low values of q comes from an interesting finding of Cavanagh (1972). When compiling scanning times estimated from Sternberg tasks and STM spans for the same types of items taken from the literature, Cavanagh found a linear relation between scanning times and reciprocal span values with a nearly vanishing intercept. Thus the slope of 243 ms of the regression line represents an invariant for scanning a full memory. As the shortest scanning time per item ever found in Sternberg-type experiments comes close to 10 ms (cf. Atkinson & Juola, 1974), this would lead to an estimate of some 25 for M. To the extent that data pooled together from various sources admit of such a conclusion, relying on the above estimate for T (4.5 ms) q may be assumed to equal two.

The corresponding relations for individuals deviate markedly from the average outcome (cf. also Puffe, this volume). Results reported by Puckett and Kausler (1984), however, show typical series of slope clusters for groups of individuals, with the means of one series being 510.3 ms (500, 511, 520), 250 ms (241, 249, 257, 259, 263, 272) and 118.7 ms (101, 122, 133), and those of another being 351.0 ms (314, 338, 351, 373, 379) and 178 ms (172, 180, 186). The ratios of the first three means are close to 1:2:4, and those of the second ones are close to 1:2. The first series is compatible with the assumption of $L=28$ and $q=4$, 2, and 1, the second with $L=20$ and $q=4$ and 2, leading to an estimate of 4.6 ms for T.

Of course, such calculations do not lend themselves to establishing the quantal charater of the underlying processes. However, they provide evidence that, given the basic quantal law, (4) is a reasonable assumption about operative intervals, and they yield estimates of L. On the basis of these results it seems justified to assume that the constraint $M \leq 30$ holds true of the coherence length.

Further evidence for a coherence length of this order follows from cognitive operation times estimated on the basis of assumed algorithms of performance. For sentence–picture comparisons and analogue reasoning, for instance, maximum operation times of some 250 or 220 ms were repeatedly found (Klix & Hoffmann, 1978; Klix & van der Meer, 1978; among others). This value agrees with the recognition time of 226 ms as determined by Krol and Tanengolz (1976).

The Cavanagh finding has another aspect of great potential interest in that it relates processing speed and short-term recall. A rough analysis suggests that M restricts not only the time of coherent processing but also the number of elementary information units that can be stored in short-term memory (cf. Geissler, 1985a,b, 1987). If we accept $\log_2$ of the alphabet size A as an estimate of the information content I of an element, we get $I=3.33$ for single digits. Given a range of spans from 7 to 8, the number of stored units should be somewhere between 24 and 27, which is in good agreement with L values estimated above.

Lebedev's and Hendrickson's theories try to directly incorporate the relation between processing speed and storage capacity into the initial assumptions of their approaches (cf. also Weiss, 1986). Integration of both aspects is certainly imperative for TQM too. This would entail an expansion of the approach beyond the time domain, something that goes beyond the scope of the present paper.

Our considerations so far have left two important problems unresolved: In contrast to observations pointing to a strong clustering, no particular intermittency values within a given operative interval seem to be preferred to others. Are there further rules for narrowing down the number of admissible values? Furthermore, the theory (1) through (4) applies to time periods of arbitrary length. Preliminary evidence considered so far concerns ranges up to a limit of some 250 ms. Is there any real evidence indicative of expansion far beyond that value?

Grouping and Hierarchy Assumptions. Preferred Upper Boundary Values. Operation times as estimated from different cognitive tasks clearly show a band structure with distances across bands increasing with absolute duration (cf. Geissler & Buffart, 1985). Such bands seem to be located around 220 ms, 110 ms, and 55 ms, and values ranging about 36 ms were also reported. Previous papers (Geissler, 1985a,b, 1987) advanced a simple fractionating principle which in combination with the fundamental quantum axiom considerably restricts the number of admissible multiples. According to this principle, the k_i must also be integer fractions of the upper bound multiple L defined by (3):

$$k_i = L/lj .\qquad (5)$$

Assume, for instance, $L=24$. Then the set of admissible multiples $k_i=1$, 2, 3, 4, 6, 8, 12, and 24 follows from (5). If, in line with the above consideration for cognitive operations, the assumed size of q is 2, we get the final values 9.13 ms, 18.26 ms, 27.39 ms, 36.52 ms, 54.78 ms, 73.04 ms, 109.56 ms, and 219.12 ms. (Here, as in the examples below, we use the $\neq$ideal" estimate from the Vanagas et al. experiments.) Apparently, at least four of those predictions agree with the empirical operation times cited.

Possible L values within an interval 16...L...30 which exhibit more than four integer divisors are 16, 18, 20, 24, 27, 28, and 30. In this sense, these L values may be regarded as preferred operative boundaries. Although calculations as in the example above agree with the idea of operative intervals insofar as q and L can be operatively chosen, there is some degree of arbitrariness in the applied fractionating rule because it assumes that the multiples of the different periods must always exactly coincide at $T^q = L \cdot q \cdot T$.

This assumption can be weakened somewhat by the following "grouping assumption." According to the grouping assumption longer chains of partial intermittencies are divided into sub-chains of equal length, relaxing at the same time the strong condition of an identical termination point. If the group is of length g, the chain may be assumed to terminate after $k \cdot g$ groups for any k:

$$L = k \cdot g \leq M .\qquad (6)$$

Within this frame it is necessary to suppose a maximal chain length H so that $g \leq H$ where $H=7$ represents a reasonable bound.

A main consequence of this assumption of maximum operative boundaries is that L can vary as a function of g. Thus, admissible pairs for $H=7$ and

$M=24$ are: $k=1$, $g=24$; $k=2$, $g=12$; $k=3$, $g=8$; $k=4$, $g=6$; $k=5$, $g=4$; $k=6$, $g=4$; $k=7$, $g=3$ (to account for multiples $k_i>7$ involves the assumption of hierarchical grouping, i.e., the formal splitting up of g into products $g=m \cdot n$ with integers m, $n>7$). We get the admissible multiples $k_i=1$, 2, 3, 4, 5, 6, 7, 8, 12, 20, 21, and 24, i.e., four more admissible values (underlined) than predicted by the strong fractionating axiom. These multiples (assuming $q=2$) would correspond to the intermittencies of 45.65 ms, 63.91 ms, 182.60 ms, and 191.73 ms.

The set of admissible multiples even increases f they are not restricted to the maximal possible values for a given M. The only constraint on the k_i which can then be established as a theorem is that no primes $T_j \geq H$ and integer multiples of them can occur. Thus, these numbers represent "forbidden multiples."

It should be noted in passing (as this might be of interest for further steps of theoretical development) that a grouping boundary H together with a maximum hierarchy depth could even be used to replace a simple coherence length assumption. Thus, for $H=7$ and a hierarchy depth of 2 there is a proper set of multiples $k_i=1$, 2, 3, 4, 5, 6, 7, 8, 9, 10, 12, 14, 15, 18, 20, 21, 24, 25, 28, 30, 35, 36, 42, and 49.

The weak constraints of the "grouping assumption" hold if only one carrier oscillation at a time is assumed to operate. The selection rules become considerably strengthened if different oscillations are assumed to co-operate. In this case it again seems possible to assume preferred bounds L in the sense that multiples of different periods match exactly at K. This leads back to the intermittencies specified by the fractionating rule. Any subset of admissible multiples yielding L as their product can be interpreted as a system of intermittencies induced by a hierarchy of carrier oscillations. Multiples 4 and 6, for instance, can be interpreted to represent either six groups of four elementary periods or four groups of six elementary periods. Hierarchies containing the maximum number of hierarchically related carrier oscillations will be called complete synchronization hierarchies. As can easily be seen, complete hierarchies are generated by any permutation of the prime factors of L. For instance, the sequence 3, 2, 2, 2 for $L=24$ yields the admissible multiples $k_i=3$, 6 (3×2), 12 ($3 \times 2 \times 2$), and 24 ($3 \times 2 \times 2 \times 2$). Altogether, there are four different complete hierarchies.

Thus co-operative synchronization of carrier oscillations considerably restricts the number of admissible carrier oscillations. On the basis of the number of different possible hierarchies (in brackets) the upper bound values $L=18$, 20, 24, 28, and 30 can be regarded as preferred: 18 (8), 20 (8), 21 (3), 22 (3), 24 (20), 25 (2), 26 (3), 27 (4), 28 (8), 30 (13).

For fast EEG rhythms approximately harmonic relations of the main frequencies of different bands have long been used for definitions of fundamental spontaneous brain rhythms. Assuming that these bands are based on hierarchical synchronizations, as considered above, for $q=2$ and 4, and $L=24$ the predicted admissible intermittencies are $k_i^1=6$, 12, 24, and 48; $k_i^2=12$, 24, 48, and 96, respectively. This converts into the possible frequencies $\nu_i^{1,2}$ of about 36, 18, 9, 4, and 2 Hz. The corresponding empirical standard definitions of formations of brain waves are: gamma−40 Hz, beta−20 Hz, alpha−10 Hz, theta−5 Hz, and delta−2.5 Hz.

The Chunking Assumption and Coherence Interval Expansion. Grouping as defined in the proceeding section leaves the existence of the constituent grouped time units untouched. Base multiple q, as introduced by (4), on the other hand, treats these subordinate units actually as something vanishing in that it becomes completely integrated into the higher-order unit. Otherwise, it would make no sense to resort to a coherence length M as an upper limit of chain length. M should, at least approximately, be independent of the duration of the time units to which it refers.

The emergence of this kind of "intermittency chunking" is tantamount to substituting one system of carrier oscillations for another which really lacks some oscillation of higher frequency.

If we accept this as a fundamental constructive principle of "intermittency chunking", we are likely to get a lot of astonishing results. Suppose that modules q are subject to the same constraints as any integer multiples occuring in TQM, we should have

$$q \leq M . \qquad (7)$$

If (4) is conceived as a genuine recursive rule, it can be used to define a hierarchy of operative intervals, the first ranging from T to $L \cdot T$, the second from $L \cdot T$ to $L^2 \cdot T$, the third from $L^2 \cdot T$ to $L^3 \cdot T$, and so forth. To each of these base intervals a rule of the form (4) can be applied. In general, a rule

$$T_L^R = q \cdot L^{R-1} \cdot T \leq T_{iL}^R \leq T_U^R = L^R \cdot T \qquad (8)$$

for intermittencies T_{iL}^R of the R-th order should hold.

We shall not go into details here. However, if (8) contains any truth, the same simple ratio rule should hold for slow, long-lasting processes as well as for fast ones, provided processing continues without arbitrary interruptions.

For a rough check of this prediction we used reaction time data of Buffart and de Swaart (1985) obtained in perceptual problem tasks of various difficulties. The simple idea behind the analysis is that the longest RTs that occur provide some estimate of T_U^R for a given individual. The smallest RTs of the same individual could be above, but should never fall below some lower characteristic of the individual under the operative conditions. In other words, it is expected on the basis of the ratio law that the lowest RTs as plotted against the highest ones form a distribution with a straight cut ending at the bottom. The results, which are in good agreement with the expectation, will be published elsewhere.

Summary of Formal Assumptions

The assumptions considered above can be restated in the following condensed way:

1. Time quantum assumption:
Admissible intermittencies are integer multiples of a time quantum T:

$$T_i = k_i \cdot T , \quad k_i \text{ integer.} \qquad (1')$$

The size of T is about 4.5 ms.

2. Intermittency–chunking assumption:
Multiples of T can play the role of indivisible quantal time units or "pseudo–quants":[2]

$$T^q = q \cdot T , \quad q \text{ integer,} \qquad (2')$$

such that periods

$$T_i^q = k_i^q \cdot T^q , \quad k_i^q \text{ integer,} \qquad (1'')$$

again represent admissible intermittencies. q is called an "operative module."

3. Coherence assumption:
The T_i^q form "operative sets" belonging to operative intervals:

$$T^q \leq T_i^q \leq L \cdot T^q \leq M \cdot T^q , \quad \text{with integers } L \text{ and } M. \qquad (3')$$

M represents some upper limit of chain length which is assumed to be characteristic of an individual. A rough estimate is: $M \leq 30$. L is called an "operative boundary."

4. Hierarchical grouping assumption:
Within the constraints given by (3') the set of admissible intermittencies is restricted by the additional condition that the k_i^q form groups of equal length g such that

$$L = k \cdot g , \quad \text{with integer } g \leq H . \qquad (4')$$

The size of H is 7.
Hierarchical grouping is a possibility that must be considered. Grouping hierarchies induced by prime factorizations of L are called complete.
The admissible operative boundaries differ markedly by the number of possible hierarchical groupings. In this respect the values $L = 18$, 20, 24, 28, and 30 are preferred.

---

[2] Note that q is used as an index of T, not as an exponent.

Some Applications

In what follows, three typical examples taken from different experimental paradigms will be explained with the aid of TQM assumptions. Before we embark on this, however, an account on the basis of the model itself, of the conditions under which quantal effects are likely to show and under which they are unlikely to show directly, seems in place.

To begin with the latter, the obvious limitations of quantal structuring of mental processes are twofold. First, strict periodicities are limited by coherence length M. Second, local carrier oscillations must not be synchronized internally nor must they show any simple relation to external timing, for instance the beginning of stimulation.

The possible causes of observable quantization are apparent from these limitations. One of them is external driving: If the stimuli themselves show temporal periodicities, internal synchronization may occur as a function of external periodicity. Another may have to do with the nature of a cognitive task, namely if it involves repeated application of one and the same routine. Finally, preferred periods of easily observable size should result from intermittency chunking, irrespective of the psychological content of the processes under consideration.

Let us return to the cited von Békesy paradigm (an example of the first type) and subject the available data to a somewhat deeper analysis. Data of the Sternberg paradigm will serve as a repeated routine. In a final section duration discrimination phenomena will be treated as typical examples of intermittency chunking.

Preferred Values of Low Frequency Sound Thresholds

The fundamental difference between the present approach and Stroud's treatment of von Békesy's data rests on the basic TQM position which views intermittencies as genuine quantal units in the sense that they, once fixed, cannot be divided by externally induced periods. Therefore, in contrast to Stroud, external periods $t_f = 1/f$ are disallowed to be fractions of intermittencies. Rather, a preferred period should always be equal to some intermittency T_i or should be an integer multiple of it:

$$t_{fi} = k_f \cdot T_i . \qquad (9)$$

To get a reasonable set of predictions we must assume that only for $L = 24$ values of $k_f > 1$ are admissible. A possible reason for this absolute preference of this number is the preferred structure of synchronization hierarchies based on $L = 24$ which permit a recursive expansion of operative intervals. This point will become more obvious when discussing hierarchies of timing and cascades of intrinsic rhythms in the next section.

Thus, using the notation $T_i(L)$ for intermittencies from the interval $T \leq T_i(L) \leq L \cdot T$, the prerequisite for preferred external periods beyond the preferred L values 20, 24, 28, and 30 can be stated as follows:

$$k_f \cdot T_i(24) > 24 . \tag{10}$$

Admitting of small factors $k_f \leq 3$ only results in the set of multiples $72 = 3 \times 24$, $36 = 3 \times 12$, and $48 = 2 \times 24$.

For $T_i(24) < 24 \cdot T$ consistency with

$$k_f \cdot T_i(24) \leq 24 \tag{11}$$

in each case implies $k_f \leq 2$. From this follows the set of multiples: 1, 2, 3, 4, 6, 8, 12, 16, and 24.

Table 2. Empirical and predicted period durations t_f of low frequency sound at which thresholds change discontinuously.

K_f	6	7	8	10	12	15/16	20	24	28/30	36	48
$t_{f\ emp}$ [a]	26.31	31.25	35.71	45.45	55.55	71.43	90.91	111.11	133.33	166.66	222.22
$t_{f\ pred}$ [a]	26.70	31.36	36.02	45.33	54.64	70.94	91.89	110.53	133.81	166.41	222.29
$|\Delta|$ [a]	0.39	0.11	0.31	0.12	0.91	0.51	0.91	0.58	0.48	0.25	0.07

[a] in ms

The union set of multiples is as follows: 1, 2, 3, 5, 6, 7, 8, 10, 12, 14, 15, 16, 20, 24, 28, 30, 36, 48, and 72. Of these multiples the values 1 to 5 and 72 lie outside the range of von Békesy's observations, which, of course, does not rule out their empirical significance. An empirical correspondence cannot be found for 14. For the rest of the multiples there are excellent predictions if we assume that the pairs of closely adjacent multiples 15, 16, and 28, 30 cannot be separated by the measurement procedure. Table 2 juxtaposes the empirical values and the predictions obtained by linear regression ($R^2 = 0.99993$). The resulting estimate for the time quantum is $T = 4.657$ ms with an intercept of -1.239 ms.

Scan–Rate Clustering in Item Recognition

Preliminary evidence from Sternberg's item–recognition tasks was used above for the heuristic introduction of basic TQM assumptions. In general, the scanning rates, as estimated by RT-slopes, are highly variable. Therefore, an analysis of a larger body of data based on TQM assumptions seems desirable. Slopes obtained by Staude (1985) were reanalyzed on the assumption that any kind of bias limiting the validity of slopes as measures of scanning rates would result in deviations from predicted intermittencies which are unrelated to the quantum value. On the other hand, the presence of quantal structures should result in a denser packing of slopes in the neighbourhood of the predicted intermittency values. The reanalysis was based on data from 18 subjects and involved experiments with three types of items and separate slope estimates for positive and negative responses. A total of $18 \times 3 \times 2 = 108$ slopes was included.

To detect clusters of densely packed slopes a procedure using a function

$$a_i = \sum_{j \neq i} \frac{T_i}{(T_i - T_j)^2 + \epsilon}$$

with a small positive ϵ (to avoid singularities) was performed.

Regression based on cluster means using the assumed integer multiples of a common divisor yielded $T = 4.571$ ms and an intercept of 0.212 ms ($R^2 = .998$). The results are given in Table 3.

Table 3. Empirical and predicted values of slope cluster means across different tasks and subjects.

assumed multiple	5	7	8	9	10	12	16	18	20
number of data	2	2	5	8	12	12	13	9	3
$T_{i\,exp}$ [a]	23.15	32.30	37.68	40.64	45.15	55.72	73.24	81.20	92.77
SD [a]	0.07	0.14	0.28	0.97	1.00	2.18	2.33	0.95	0.15
$T_{i\,pred}$ [a]	23.06	32.20	36.78	41.35	45.92	55.06	73.35	82.49	91.62
$|\Delta|$ [a]	0.09	0.10	0.90	0.71	0.77	0.66	0.11	0.29	1.15

[a] in ms

Since the slopes were sampled from different individuals it seems pointless to speculate on the particular multiples detected. However, there are at least two implications of the outcome which seem important. First, the occurrence of clusters consistent with a basic quantal time close to 4.5 ms supports the notion that interindividual variation of the time quantum is small as compared with differences attributable to the hypothetical module sizes q and bound values L. Second, as was the case with the von Békésy data, such "forbidden" prime multiples as 11, 13, 17, and 19 do not occur.

Hierarchies of Timing and Cascades of Intrinsic Rhythms

An issue that is associated with the original notion of a psychological moment in a very direct way is that of duration discrimination. TQM assumed a whole hierarchy of "time windows." That normally duration discrimination conforms to Weber's Law without any sign of discreteness may be attributed to the fact that under most circumstances time is estimated on the basis of brief, unrelated chains of intermittencies (cf. Geissler, 1987). Kristofferson and co-workers demonstrated in several studies that practice may lead to very high accuracy in subjective timing which remains constant within large base intervals. In an experiment he performed upon himself, Kristofferson discovered that after extended practice the discrimination characteristics turned into a step function (Kristofferson, 1980). For the quantal periods of the duration threshold changing from about 10 to about 100 ms a simple doubling rule seems to hold.

The corresponding ranges of base durations also seem to conform to a doubling rule. They are about 16 times as large as the quantal discrimination thresholds.

The principle account of TQM for quantal discrimination periods is very straightforward: Unlike most other theories of duration discrimination it does not refer directly to processing assumptions. Rather, discreteness of thresholds is seen as a natural consequence of the mode in which time is internally represented, namely in the form of discrete chains of quantal periods. Within the time interval $q \cdot T \leq D \leq M \cdot q \cdot T$ a given duration D can be represented with an accuracy of $q \cdot T$. However, discriminating durations D_1 and D_2 with this precision would imply identification and comparison of M levels of different durations without any further organization of the interval. A sensible complementary assumption (in the sense defined in the introduction) implies that comparison is based on hierarchical representation mediated by hierarchically co-operating oscillations. The corresponding intermittencies can be considered as code units for comparison similar to different units of currency.

If we adopt this complementary assumption, two more postulates suggest themselves. The first is that optimum discrimination is assumed to be based on the finest hierarchical organization possible which is induced by the prime factors of a given bound L. The value L should be 24 because 24 provides the finest structuring among the possible alternatives.

The shortest quantal period identified by Kristofferson is about 13.5 ms, i.e., $3T$. Compatible with this value is for $L=24$ a tree-like structure with a trifurcation at the bottom. The nodes at the different levels of the tree correspond to intermittencies T, $3T$, $6T=2\times3T$, $12T=2\times6T$, $24T=2\times12T$.

If strict hierarchical organization is assumed, each of these values becomes a period that can be represented as a node at the bottom of a new, "expanded" hierarchical tree. This hierarchical organization does not permit full expansion up to $M \cdot T_i$. As can easily be seen the only size of q which can be used recursively within expanded trees compatible with the grouping tree for 24 is $q=2$. Therefore, expansion is possible up to $N=2^n < M$. For $M \leq 30$ it follows that $N=16$. The predicted sequence of operative intervals is therefore as follows: $I_1=[T,24T]$; $I_2=[3T,48T]$; $I_3=[6T,96T]$; $I_4=[12T,182T]$; $I_5=[24T,364T]$. For optimum performance there must always be jumps in the size of quantal discrimination periods when the end of an operative interval is reached. Accordingly, the observable base duration intervals must be $B_1=[T,24T]$; $B_2=[24T,48T]$; $B_3=[48T,96T]$; $B_4=[96T,182T]$; $B_5=[182T,364T]$. This restores Kristofferson's doubling rule. If we let $T=4.5$ ms, the predicted quantal duration thresholds as well as base intervals come very close to values reported by Kristofferson (1980, 1984) with the exception of B_1. Apparently, the quantal size T belonging to B_1 was not observable because of the duration of the signals used (which was 10 ms).

There are two doubtful points about this analysis. First, Kristofferson's estimates of mean quantum sizes have so far been taken at their face value without giving consideration to the evaluation procedure applied. Second, the base intervals were fixed prior to the experiment. One may suspect that both, calculation procedure and choice of intervals, might have led to a coincidence with TQM-assumptions merely by chance. This objection can be weakened, at least partly, by an analysis which uses single estimates of the quantal threshold values instead of the means of six series underlying Kristofferson's analysis. If the operative adjustment to the base ranges fixed in advance is imperfect, other quantum values that deviate from Kristofferson's levels are likely to occur which can be compared with TQM-expectations.

Table 4. Empirical and predicted quantal levels of duration discrimination from clustering of single estimates.

n_{typ}	3	5	6	8	12	14	15	21	24	26
number of data	3	4	8	2	4	2	2	2	2	5
$T_{i\,exp}$ [a]	13.35	23.40	27.40	37.40	53.55	63.40	67.40	95.85	108.10	117.30
$T_{i\,pred}$ [a]	13.98	22.97	27.47	36.47	54.45	63.44	67.90	94.91	108.40	117.40
$|\Delta|$ [a]	0.63	0.43	0.07	0.93	0.90	0.04	0.50	0.94	0.30	0.10

[a] in ms

Table 4 represents the result of using the procedure for detecting preferred quantal values that was suggested above. As was expected, 50 per cent of the estimated intermittencies are at levels that deviate considerably from Kristofferson's quantum values. On the other hand, the fit to TQM is fairly good ($R^2 = .9907$), yielding $T = 4.5$ ms. Again, "forbidden" multiples do not occur. Thus, TQM analysis which puts together Kristofferson's (1980, 1984) experimental evidence, provides arguments for intermittency chunking which leads to operative intervals of at least 800 ms. An analysis of slower rhythmical activities seems to suggest that this kind of adjustment may even extend to ranges of seconds and minutes (cf. Geissler, 1987).

Summary

This paper is based on the notion that the investigation of temporal structure of mental activity, in order to yield convergent results, must refer to the guidance of fairly general conceptual frameworks. One of the most fundamental options to be explored proceeds from the assumption of discrete temporal units or "psychological moments" as elementary building blocks of psychological time. Although the concept of a moment has a relatively strong tradition in psychology, it is shown that even the formally most developed approaches do not meet the requirements of a consistent theoretical framework.

Elaborating on previous versions of the so-called Time Quantum Model (TQM), the paper proposes a set of assumptions which seems suitable both from a point of view of powerful formal constraints of a consistent formal theory and from its account to established empirical facts.

It is demonstrated that from a relatively small set of "axioms" a large net of relations can be constructed that, via complementary specifying assumptions, applies to various empirical phenomena, e.g., discontinuities in sound detection, duration discrimination, recognition frequency in pattern masking, and phenomena of periodic driving. Apparently, it also accounts for laws of reaction time as established for item recognition and other paradigms including the observed range of variation.

The most fundamental assumptions involve: (1) Any admissible time periods are integer multiples of some elementary time period T_o or of fixed "packages" $q \times T_o$ with q being a small integer. (2) Admissible periods are ordered in "operative intervals" such that any admissible period belonging to an interval I is an integer multiple of its lower bound T_i, the upper bound being $L \times T$ with integer L smaller than a maximum value M. (3) The admissible periods T_i can be hierarchically organized using three possible ways of hierarchical structuring: (a) constraining the upper bound ("fractionating rule"); (b) between-period hierarchization within a given operative interval; (c) between-interval hierarchization, leading to an extension of quantal structures to longer periods of time.

From several sources of empirical evidence follows an estimate for T_o of some 4.5 ms and for M (the "coherence length") of 30 ms.

Correspondence should be addressed to Hans-Georg Geissler, Sektion Psychologie der Karl-Marx-Universität Leipzig, Tieckstr. 3, Leipzig, DDR – 7030.

References

Allport, D.A. (1968). Phenomenal simultaneity and the perceptual moment hypothesis. *British Journal of Psychology, 59*, 395 – 406,

Buffart, H., Geissler, H.-G., & van Leeuwen, K. (1984). *Unpublished experiments on quantized processing in perception.* Nijmegen.

Buffart, H., & de Swaart, S. (1985). *Unpublished experiments*, Nijmegen.

Cavanagh, J.P. (1972). Relation between immediate memory span and the memory search rate. *Psychological Review, 79*, 525 – 530.

Fabiani, M., Schmer, H., Tait, C., Gafni, M., & Kinarti, R. (1979). A functional measure of brain activity: brain stem transmission time. *Electroencephalography and Clinical Neurophysiology, 47*, 483 – 491.

Geissler, H.-G. (1985a). Sources of seeming redundancy in temporally quantized information processing. In G. d'Ydewalle (Ed.), *Cognitive information processing and motivation. Selected/revised papers, 23rd International Congress of Psychology* (Vol. III). Amsterdam: North-Holland.

Geissler, H.-G. (1985b). Zeitquantenhypothese zur Struktur ultraschneller Gedächtnisprozesse. *Zeitschrift für Psychologie, 193*, 347 – 362.

Geissler, H.-G. (1987). The temporal architecture of central information processing: Evidence for a tentative time-quantum model. *Psychological Research, 49*, 99 – 106.

Hendrickson, A.E. (1972). An integrated molar/molecular model of the brain. *Psychological Reports, 30*, 343 – 368.

Hendrickson, D.E., & Hendrickson, A.E. (1980). The biological basis of individual differences in intelligence. *Personality and Individual Differences, 1*, 3 – 33.

Klix, F., & Hoffmann, J. (1978). The method of sentence-picture comparison as a possibility for analyzing representation of meaning in human long-term memory. In F. Klix (Ed.), *Human and artificial intelligence* (pp. 171−192). Berlin: Deutscher Verlag der Wissenschaften.

Klix, F., & van der Meer, E. (1978). Analogical reasoning − An approach to mechanisms underlying human intelligence performances. In F. Klix (Ed.), *Human and artificial intelligence* (pp. 193−212). Berlin: Deutscher Verlag der Wissenschaften.

Kristofferson, A.B. (1980). A quantal step function in duration. *Perception & Psychophysics, 27,* 300−306.

Kristofferson, A.B. (1984). Quantal and deterministic timing in human duration discrimination. *Annals of the New York Academy of Sciences, 423,* 3−15.

Krol, W.M., & Tanengolz, L.J. (1976). The presentation time threshold and the time of recognition for object drawings (in Russian). In V.D. Glaser (Ed.), *Information processing in the visual system.* Leningrad: Academy of Sciences of the USSR.

Latour, P.L. (1967). Evidence of internal clocks in the human operator. *Acta Psychologica, 27,* 341−348.

Lebedev, A.N. (1976). On the neurophysiological basis of quantitative regularities in psychology. In H.-G. Geissler & Zabrodin, Y u. M. (Eds.), *Advances in Psychophysics* (pp. 411−416). Berlin: VEB Deutscher Verlag der Wissenschaften.

Lebedev, A.N. (1980). Note on the equations for speed and capacity of perception. The skeleton of a psychological theory. In H.-G. Geissler & P. Petzold (Eds.), *Psychophysical judgment and the process of perception.* Amsterdam: North-Holland.

McReynolds, P. (1953). Thinking conceptualized in terms of interacting moments. *Psychological Review, 60,* 319−330.

Michon, J.A. (1967). *Timing in temporal tracking.* Assen: van Gorcum.

Neumann, O. (1983). Moment. In J. Ritter & K. Gründer (Eds.), *Historisches Wörterbuch der Philosophie,* Vol. VI (pp. 108−114). Basel, Stuttgart: Schwabe.

Puckett, J.M., & Kausler, D.H. (1984). Individual differences and models of memory span: A role for memory search rate? *Journal of Experimental Psychology: Learning, Memory and Cognition, 10,* 72−82.

Staude, A. (1985). *Zur Prüfung der Cavanagh−Hypothese über den Zusammenhang von Gedächtnissuchrate und Gedächtnisspanne durch intraindividuellen Vergleich.* Unpublished diploma thesis, Karl-Marx-Universität, Leipzig.

Stroud, J.M. (1955). The fine structure of psychological time. In H. Quastler (Ed.), *Information theory in psychology* (pp. 174−207). Glencoe, Ill: The Free Press.

Sternberg, S. (1966). High-speed scanning in human memory. *Science, 153,* 652−654.

Sternberg, S. (1967a). Two operations in character recognition: Some evidence from reaction-time experiments. *Perception & Psychophysics, 2,* 45−53.

Sternberg, S. (1967b). Scanning a persisting visual image versus a memorized list. Paper presented at the *Annual Meeting of the Eastern Psychological Association,* Boston, 1967.

Vanagas, V., Balkelite, O., Bartusyavitchus, E., & Kiryalis, D. (1976). The quantum character of recognition processes in human vision (in Russian). In V.D. Glezer (Ed.), *Information processing in the visual system.* Leningrad: Academy of Sciences of the USSR.

Weiss, V. (1986). Memory as a macroscopic ordered state by entrainment and resonance in energy pathways. In V. Weiss et al. (Eds.), *Psychogenetik der Intelligenz.* Dortmund, Basel, Paris, London: Verlag Modernes Lernen.

Psychophysical Explorations of Mental Structures
Edited by H.-G. Geissler
in collaboration with M.H. Müller and W. Prinz
© 1990 by Hogrefe & Huber Publishers

Chapter 17

Temporal Dispersion in Natural Receptors and Pattern Discrimination Mediated by Artificial Receptors (Cochlear Implants)

Gerald S. Wasserman, Lolin T. Wang-Bennett
Department of Psychological Sciences
Purdue University, West Lafayette, U.S.A.
Richard T. Miyamoto
Department of Otolaryngology
Indiana University Medical School
Indianapolis, U.S.A.

A circular disk that is painted to produce a black–and–white pattern may produce quite vivid color sensations if it is rotated slowly. This so-called subjective color phenomenon has been independently reported (cf. Cohen and Gordon, 1949) by many amateur and professional observers. G.T. Fechner (1838) was one of the first to examine this phenomenon. More importantly, he offered an explanation which was endorsed by Helmholtz (1860/1962, Vol. III, p. 258) and which has since become quite prevalent as the accepted interpretation; hence these sensations are commonly called "Fechner colors."

In contemporary terminology, his explanation has two general parts: First, no matter what the objective time course of a stimulus, the sensory signal evoked by it is spread out in time. Second, the degree of this temporal dispersion is not fixed but variable. Adding to these generalities the particular concept that the degree of dispersion varies among the fundamental mechanisms that mediate our perception of color leads to the explication of the phenomenon. On this view then, a single achromatic moving contour evokes parallel responses with varying time courses in the several color mechanisms. Hence the relative activities of the color mechanisms vary leading to perceived differences in color. Certain additional influences have been recognized, such as the important role played by interactions among the various stimulus elements (cf. Wasserman, 1966) but Fechner's concept still gives a fair account of these striking sensations.

Behavioral Assessments of Temporal Dispersion

Systematic behavioral investigations of temporal dispersion have been conducted ever since Fechner's time. There have been many approaches: Some have studied responses to single stimuli as a function of some stimulus characteristic(s). Others have looked at interactions between stimulus pairs, calling this summation or masking depending on circumstance. Recently it has become fashionable to use approaches that depend from Fourier's Theorem. All of these approaches have their points of advantage and disadvantage. In the present context, our choice of approach was strictly determined by one over-riding constraint: We needed a methodology that would cover the entire response range of sensory systems. This constraint ruled out approaches that are useful only in that portion of the response range that is quasilinear (i.e., Fourier approaches) or that depend too heavily on near-threshold phenomena (i.e., most interaction experiments). Accordingly, the present discussion is restricted to those data produced by experiments in which (temporally) single stimuli are utilized.

Such experiments produce two reliable results: The first is that the index of dispersion is influenced by the observer's task even when identical stimuli are used. Consider the experiment of Kahneman and Norman (1964). They presented targets made of 1's and 0's which formed numbers (e.g., 101 or 011). If they asked observers to identify the number seen, then they found that temporal summation extended out as far as about 350 msec. On the other hand, if they asked the same observers to detect brightness differences between the stimuli, then summation was found to extend only out to about 100 msec. Comparable task-dependencies are found in many other studies of temporal processing and an extensive review of these data has been given elsewhere (Wasserman and Kong, 1979).

The second important result is that the form of the summation function varies with the task. Sometimes the summation is time dependent and can be characterized by the relation $I \cdot t^n = k$ where I is the stimulus intensity, t is the stimulus duration, k is a constant, and n is a number greater than one. If n gets very large (and it has been measured to be above 7.0) then very small changes in duration have a grossly disproportionate influence on summation which is why such data are said to be time dependent. On the other hand if $n = 1.0$, then intensity and duration trade reciprocally and their product (i.e., the total energy) governs summation. Such data are said to be energy dependent. In an important experiment on perceived numerosity, Hunter and Sigler (1940) found that numerosity influenced the form of summation: low numerosities were energy dependent while high numerosities were time dependent. Similar results have been reported by others and reviews have been given in Wasserman and Kong (1979) and in Wasserman (1978).

Physiological Data

An initial report (Kong and Wasserman, 1981) noted that exactly parallel phenomena could be observed in intracellular recordings from sensory neurons when the sensory code (i.e., the feature of the neural response chosen for measurement) was varied. Some features gave time–dependent results while others, drawn from the identical neural responses, gave energy–dependent responses. Further, we confirmed and extended Hartline's (1934) suggestion that summation would be determined by the latency of the sensory code. Hence, identical neural responses had not one summation interval but a family of summation intervals.

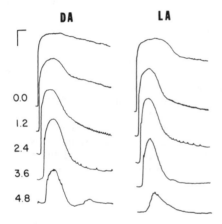

Figure 1. Intracellular photoreceptor potentials evoked by an 80 msec light flash in dark (DA) and light (LA) adaptation as a function of light intensity (given as log attenuation re 250 W/m^2). Traces start at stimulus onset. Calibration is 10 mV by 100 msec.

The Kong and Wasserman data were quite incomplete and can now be seen to represent a fairly preliminary examination of this problem: The limitation stemmed in part from the fact that those data were drawn from a limited range of durations and sensory codes. Far more importantly, they were drawn from only one state of adaptation. Since the powerful influence of adaptation on time- and energy-dependent phenomena is well known, a more complete experimental analysis of the physiology of temporal dispersion was executed. We present here previously unpublished data drawn from a thesis by Wang (1981).

Methods

Microelectrodes were used to obtain intracellular recordings of photo-receptor potentials from cells in the eye of *Limulus*. The methods were conventional. Details have been published in Wang and Wasserman (1985) and full particulars can be found in Wang (1981). The most important methodological features were: (a) The state of adaptation was strictly controlled (to ± 5%) by monitoring the response of the cell to a fixed stimulus and (b), the condition of the cell was strictly constant (±5%) for the ten-hour period required to complete the experiment.

Representative receptor potentials evoked in dark and light adaptation are shown in Figure 1 as a function of flash intensity. The complex time and energy dependencies of these potentials are obvious from inspection. We characterized these responses by measuring the following sensory codes: (a) The 5 mV latency, meaning the time from stimulus onset to the point where the receptor potential rose from baseline by 5 mV, (b) the C_l latency where C_l stands for the subpeak that can be seen on the rising phase of the response at medium intensities, (c) the C_l amplitude, meaning the potential difference between the C_l subpeak and baseline, (d) the peak amplitude, meaning the maximum amplitude of the whole response, and (e), the area under the response integrated for 10 seconds or until the response returned to baseline, whichever came first.

For each sensory code, we determined the intensity needed at each duration to produce a response of a criterion amount. The criterion was varied to cover the usable response range of the sensory code. These data were plotted as a function of intensity and duration for each sensory code for each state of adaptation. From these plots, the critical duration was extracted by the conventional technique of intersecting asymptotes. While more than one approach to the problem of characterizing the summation period is possible, as long as a single consistent and objective procedure is used throughout, one can obtain useful measures of temporal dispersion for further analysis.

Results

Figures 2a through 6b are plots of temporal dispersion as a function of sensory code. Each pair of plots shows the effect of adaptation on a given code. Within each plot, the effect of criterion is a parameter. Two results are compelling on mere inspection:

First, the form of the results varies drastically as a function of sensory code. In these double logarithmic plots, a line with slope of -1.0 represents an energy-dependent reciprocity result while lines with greater slopes represent time-dependent results. Using this guide, it is obvious that both of the peak codes and both of the latency codes are energy dependent until summation fails (Figures 2a through 5b) However the identical responses contain strongly time-dependent characteristics when an areal code is used as Figures 6a and 6b show.

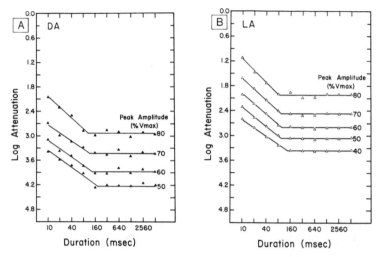

Figure 2. A: Dark adapted (DA) temporal summation functions relating the logarithm of the duration to the logarithm of the intensity (re 250 W/m²) required to evoke a response with a peak that is a criterion fraction of the saturated response (Vmax). B: Light-adapted (LA) peak temporal summation functions.

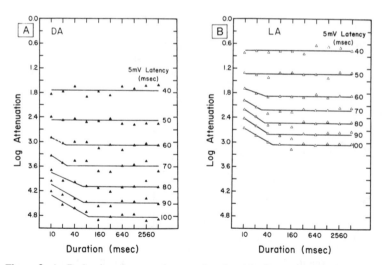

Figure 3. A: Dark–adapted temporal summation functions for a response that reaches 5mV at a criterion latency. B: Light–adapted 5 mV latency temporal summation functions.

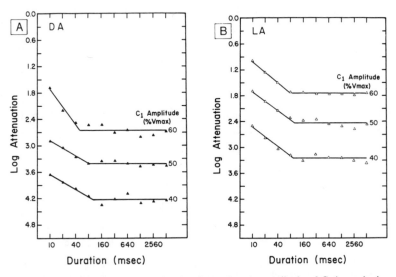

Figure 4. A: Dark-adapted summation functions when the amplitude of C_1 is a criterion fraction of Vmax. B: Light-adapted C_1 temporal summation functions.

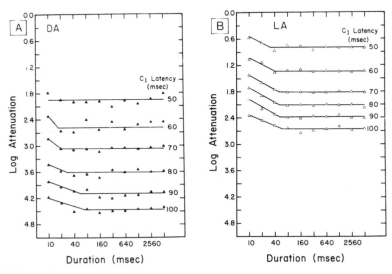

Figure 5. A: Dark-adapted temporal summation functions for a criterion latency of C_1. B: Light-adapted C_1 latency temporal summation functions.

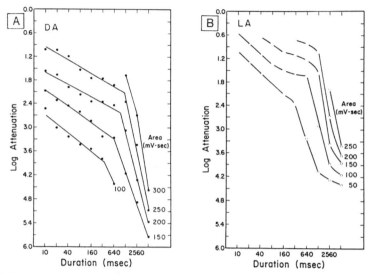

Figure 6. A: Dark–adapted temporal summation functions for a criterion area. B: Light–adapted areal temporal summation functions.

Second, the temporal dispersion is by no means constant. The plots clearly show that the degree of dispersion varies with the criterion even within a particular adaptation state and sensory code. Closer inspection makes it obvious that dispersion varies between plots as well which means that the sensory code and the adaptive state are both important quantitative determinants of summation.

These relations have a quite orderly character within any adaptation state. They are related, in an incompletely understood way, to the latency of the response feature measured. Figures 7a and 7b show the critical durations as a function of the latencies of their corresponding responses. In both states of adaptation, the data can be characterized by the relation: $CD = aL + b$ where CD is the latency, L is the latency, and both a and b are constants that are a function of adaptation. The difference between the data in these two plots was tested by a method that was independent of the just–given linear characterizations of the data. The test was done as follows: First, the distance between each point and the symmetry axis (i.e., the dashed lines in Figures 7a and 7b) was calculated. Then the differences between the distances of points with corresponding codes and criteria were computed. A t–test of these differences gave a clearly significant result ($t = 2.56$, df $= 12$, $p = .025$).

Discussion

Temporal dispersion is clearly not a fixed property of neurons; instead it depends on the way it is characterized. One and the same response can have a short or long summation interval. One and the same response can be energy or time dependent. These code–dependent changes in cellular summation parallel the task dependent changes in behavioral studies of dispersion.

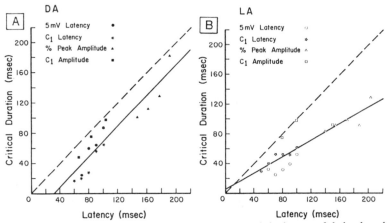

Figure 7. A: The relation between the critical duration and the latency of dark–adapted responses. Dashed line represents the tautologic upper limit for the critical duration. Solid line gives the best linear characterization of the data. B: Light–adapted relation between the critical duration and the latency.

An Hypothesis and an Interim Critique

This correlation between physiology and behavior invites the attractive hypothesis that the sensory code is task dependent. On this hypothesis, the behavioral variations in the form and extent of summation are linked to changes in the sensory code. Sensory information is not represented as a snapshot; instead sensory information is resident in a waveform which can be interrogated in many different ways. The form of the interrogation is concatenated with the time and energy dependencies of the waveform to yield the observed behavioral dispersion.

Two criticisms readily apply to this hypothesis. The first would be particularly compelling if one believed there might be a significant difference between human and animal nervous systems — were such the case, the hypothecated similarity between animal physiology and human behavior would merely be fortuitous. The second criticism would be of more general concern for it would question the correlative basis of the hypothesis. Spurious correlations are a not infrequent occurance in any domain. They are particularly worrisome in the difficult area of correlating brain with behavior. The phenomenological difference between brain and behavior leads many scholars to adopt an extremely cautious stance (cf. Teller, 1984).

But an experimental approach to this question that avoids the cross–species difficulty has recently become available in a most attractive form: Millions of human victims of sensorineural deafness are deaf because they have lost their auditory receptors or hair cells. While a few of them have also lost their auditory nerve, most retain enough nerve fibers to permit the surgical fitting of an implant in or near the cochlea. This cochlear implant transduces sound into electrical stimuli which are applied to the remaining nerve fibers and thereby produce an auditory sensation. We have given a review of this treatment elsewhere (Miyamoto et al., 1982) and recent symposia offer convenient summaries of current developments (e.g., Schindler & Merzenich, 1985). From our present standpoint, the important thing about a cochlear implant is that it is an artificial nerve cell. It is particularly an artificial receptor. Since the implant can be modified, one can change its coding and observe the effects of such changes on performance. Not only can such controlled experiments be done within a species, they can often be done within a single patient.

This permits us to test the task dependence hypothesis of sensory coding. Such a test should be robust with respect to the particular properties of either the domain that generated the hypothesis or the domain used for the test. The most robust prediction would be that the best way to encode information optimally for analysis by the brain would be to process the information so that any conceivable sensory code would be present. Without speculating about whether any particular behavioral performance is or is not mediated by any particular sensory code and without speculating about the enormous number of candidate codes that might be conceived, one can say that the hypothesis implicates the natural neural waveform in the optimal representation of information in the brain. This then formed the basis of our first investigations of artificial receptors: we added dispersion of the type produced by a simulated receptor neuron to the chain of natural and artificial neurons and we measured its effects on performance. For obvious practical reasons, the performance we chose to examine was the discrimination and recognition of human speech.

Artificial Receptor Properties

We simulated the receptor waveform with a computer program which had properties that have been described in detail previously (cf. Wasserman, 1981). It is a filter-feedback system composed of a rectifier and integrator, with gain-reducing feedback. For ease of reference, we have come to call this software system PAR which stands for Purdue Artificial Receptor or Prosthetic Auditory Receptor. Using PAR to simulate recordings from natural receptors indicated that a single integrator time constant would not adequately fit all of the recordings. Hence the PAR time constant was made a variable in our research and is referred to below as the dispersion time constant.

Natural speech stimuli were digitized and stored in the computer on disk. These tokens were the control stimuli in our research. The control tokens were then processed by PAR and the dispersed results were stored on the same disk. During any given experimental session, both the control and the dispersed representations of any token were transfered to memory for quick access.

Figure 8 shows the effect of PAR on a single syllable namely the word "fit." The traces are all plots of signal amplitude versus time. The top trace is a plot of the original natural speech token of "fit." The other traces are of the dispersed versions of the same token using dispersion time constants that extend from 0.1 msec to 10 msec. The quality of the simulation can be seen on inspection: it not only produces dispersion (most evident for larger time constants), but also produces response compression (compare the relative amplitudes of the vowel and consonantal portions), and adaptation (examine particularly the time course of the vowel portion).

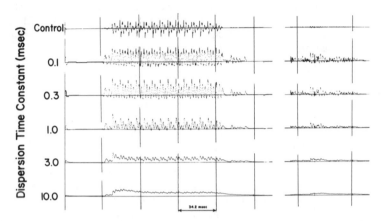

Figure 8. Waveform of the word "fit" before and after dispersion by PAR. A 100 msec silent stop has been excised.

PAR was used as a preprocessor acoustically coupled to a surgically-implanted 3M–House cochlear implant; the latter device has been described by Fretz and Fravel (1985). The 3M–House implant is a very simple signal processor which does not produce much change in the waveform of the transmitted signal. It does have input sensitivity and output level controls, however when these are set appropriately, the electrical stimulus at the auditory nerve should have a waveform that is a fair copy of that of the acoustic stimulus. The 3M–House device also has input filters that pre-emphasize the middle of the auditory spectrum. The bandpass of the acoustic coupling was therefore altered by using a compensating filter. The range of dispersion time constants actually used for experimentation (0.1 to 3 msec) was determined by the bandpass of the coupling spectrum.

Phonemic Differentiation Experiments

Patients. Patients were drawn from a population which has been described in detail elsewhere (Miyamoto, et al, 1982; 1986; Robbins, et al, 1985). This population includes children deafened at an age wherein linguistic competence is still undeveloped. It also includes adults deafened after they had fully matured. The ability of these patients to use speech as a communication vehicle varies considerably. Hence, all experiments were conducted as within-patient designs.

Patients were therefore selected that spanned the performance range. Patients were also selected for their motivation and cooperativeness.

Stimuli. Stimuli were CVC monosyllables chosen on the basis of their relative difficulty from the test devised by House, Williams, Hecker and Kryter (1965). They were enunciated by a natural speaker of English using a VU meter as a guide to sound level. They were grouped in sets of six; each set shared the same initial constant and vowel as follows:

Came, Cape, Cane, Cake, Cave, Case
Fill, Fig, Fin, Fizz, Fib, Fit
Map, Mat, Math, Man, Mass, Mad
Pun, Puff, Pup, Puck, Pus, Pub

Each set was stored on a separate disc. Hence the experiment used a blocked experimental design: Before each block, all of the stimuli from one dispersion of one word set were transfered from disc to memory. In random order, all of the dispersions of a given set were tested. Then a new disc was chosen and this process repeated until a session ended.

Procedure. Patients sat in a windowless acoustic booth which itself was placed inside a windowless soundtreated room. All experiments were under the control of a computer which could not be seen or heard by the patient. A closed-circuit TV system allowed the experimenter to see and hear the patient and to make a complete videotape recording of the experiment. The computer also generated a complete paper printout protocol of the experiment as well as a complete disc protocol.

The patients saw a video monitor controlled by the computer. All instructions were delivered as text on this monitor. The patient responded by pressing buttons on a box placed just below the monitor. Software button labels on the monitor were flashed by the computer to acknowledge patient responses.

A two-alternative forced choice procedure was used: On any given trial, two words were randomly sampled from the set of six in memory. Both were displayed as text on the patient's video monitor. One of these two words was then randomly sampled and presented acoustically. The patient heard the word only once. The patient had to press one of two buttons to indicate which of the two text words was closest to the heard word. This process was repeated for 20 trials and then a new block was begun. Self-paced rest periods were available between blocks.

Results

The largest source of variation was the patient. The control performance of patients varied from about 60% correct to about 85% correct. These large differences were clearly significant; hence we analyze the results within patients. The performance of a typical patient is shown in Figure 9 wherein performance is made a function of dispersion. This patient is typical in that his control performance is just about in the middle of the response range.

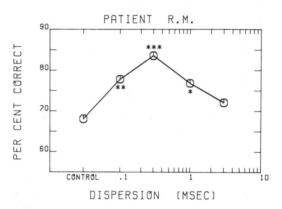

Figure 9. Phoneme discrimination in a two-alternative forced-choice task as a function of PAR dispersion. Data from a typical patient. Asterisks:* is $p<.05$, ** is $p<.01$, *** is $p<.001$.

There is no doubt that this patient is hearing better than chance even in the control condition. Standard errors are not shown in Figure 9 because they were about the size of the data points. Each data point is based on 400 trials. Both the binomial and between-block standard errors were only a few per cent. Hence the patient's control performance is many standard errors above the 50% chance level.

Dispersion improves performance with an optimum at 0.3 msec dispersion. This improvement was tested with Dunnett's (1955) test for making multiple comparisons of several treatments with a single condition. This test showed that there was little chance that the improvement was a chance fluctuation.

Every patient thus far tested has shown the same general pattern. However, the optimal dispersion varies across patients: It has varied from 0.1 msec to 1.0 msec. Further, the amount of improvement also varies; it is generally greatest for those patients whose control performance falls in the middle of the response range. Patients whose control performance is closer to either 50% or 100% show a smaller improvement; this is presumably a boundary condition effect.

Discussion

These data leave little doubt that passing speech signals through PAR improved discrimination between phonemes. But this does not tell us how the improvement occured. It could be that the patients are simply better able to hear out some primitive acoustic cue which can be used to distinguish between two phonemes more effectively. The patient, it will be recalled has perfect knowledge (from the video display of text) of the two possible phonemes that will actually be transmitted. It is not necessary for the patient to hear out the phoneme exactly; any property that distinguishes the one from the other could be utilized.

Sentence Comprehension Experiment

This experiment was designed to determine whether comprehension of the semantic content of speech could be improved by PAR dispersion. The design eliminated many primitive cues that could have been utilized in the phoneme discrimination experiment. By design, above-chance performance in this test is only possible if a patient understands the meaning of a sentence and uses that understanding to choose between two alternative words which themselves were never heard.

Stimuli. The stimuli were adapted from the SPIN test [devised by Kalikow, Stevens, and Elliot (1977) and modified by Bilger, Nuetzel, Rabinowitz, and Rzezckowski (1984)]. The sentences were recorded on tape by a professional announcer; copies of these tapes were kindly provided by Professor Robert Bilger. The sentences on these tapes were digitized and stored on disc with the following modification: the last word of each sentence was manually deleted from the file. To ensure that no trace of the last word was audible, the cut point sometimes had to be set so that it distorted the penultimate word. Text representations of possible last words were also stored. The truncated sentence was delivered to the patient as an auditory input; two possible last words were displayed on the monitor as visual inputs. One last word was connected closely with the main sentence; the other was not. The sentences were counterbalanced in pairs as follows:

Kill the bugs with this	spray vs. tea
Ruth poured herself a cup of	tea vs. spray
We shipped the furniture by	truck vs. roar
The lion gave an angry	roar vs. truck, etc.

Twenty-four counterbalanced pairs of sentences were prepared and presented in random order in each session. Half were control sentences; the other half were dispersed using the time constant that had turned out to optimize a given patient's phoneme discrimination performance. These same sentences were reversed in the next session so that those that had been the control became the dispersed sentences and vice versa. This process repeated until a total of four sessions had been run.

Procedure. The important aspects of the procedure remained much the same as in the previous experiment. The differences include the following: First, the patient never heard the target word and never saw the textual representation of the spoken material. Second, because of the difficulty of the task, a patient could push a button and replay a sentence repeatedly before making a decision.

Results

The sentence test was very difficult; it is more difficult than ordinary conversation since there are no contextual cues to aid in top-down processing. Many patients could not exceed chance in either the control or dispersed condition. A few of the patients who had had the highest scores on the phoneme test did produce results that were above chance in the sentence test but even these were often marginally significant. No conclusion can be reached from data that are not clearly out of the chance region. Therefore, we do not present the results from the typical patient here since that patient would have performed at chance in both conditions.

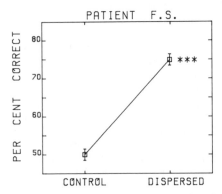

Figure 10. Sentence comprehension in a two-alternative forced choice task as a function of PAR dispersion (time constant = 1.0 msec). Error bars are between session standard error.

Figure 10 instead presents the results from the patient who gave the greatest deviation from chance. This patient was exactly at chance in the control condition but was correct on three out of four sentences in the dispersed condition. The results were extremely reliable; the error bars plotted in Figure 10 are the between-session standard errors. Using them to test the null hypothesis that the PAR-dispersed performance is a random variate with respect to chance gives a probability that is far below .0001. The data were this reliable because this patient had a strong response-key bias and almost always pressed the same button when he was guessing. The computer, of course, randomized the position of the button representing the correct choice so that both buttons were correct equally often. But even if the binomial standard error were used to test the null hypothesis more conservatively, the probability that this is a chance fluctuation would still be less than .0002.

Discussion

Under the most extreme conditions, with performance mediated by bottom-up auditory processing with no assistance from context or from lip reading, the data indicate that genuine comprehension of semantic content can be facilitated in some patients by PAR dispersion. But this finding, of course, has to be qualified by the fact that most patients can not get above the chance domain in this task.

Second Critique

The present results can easily be overinterpreted. It is important to note that the results do not prove the task-dependent hypothesis because both the treatment and the effect were quite complicated and therefore it is quite possible that other possibilities are valid. Future experiments are needed to address two critical questions:

What was the real treatment? PAR is a complex system with several subcomponents and several actions. It is obvious that it is possible the improvement produced by PAR could have been caused by only one or two of its components. It is also possible that the improvement could have been caused by PAR's compressive or adaptive properties.

What was the real effect? Did PAR produce its effect because it acted as a peripheral filter optimally coupled to the remaining nerve fibers or did it produce its effect because it encoded auditory information in a form optimally suitable for analysis by the brain? The latter alternative would have substantial implications for nerve net theory.

Experimental approaches to these questions are now in progress. But two things are quite clear: First, the sensorineural deaf patient offers a unique approach to answering questions of fundamental scientific importance. Second, the line of systematic thought and careful experimentation inaugurated by G.T. Fechner over a century ago has now borne fruit and may make it possible for his descendants to render rational assistance to the handicapped. Fechner, perhaps, would have been pleased to see the useful consequences of a deeper knowledge of the *"...factual limits, which are drawn by the universal laws of nature, to the mastery of* [man's] *will or* [man's] *mind..."* (Fechner, 1860/ 1966, p. 30).

Summary

Fechner's theory of subjective colors contained two fundamental concepts: First, sensory responses are dispersed in time relative to the stimuli that evoke them. Second, the degree of temporal dispersion is variable. Subsequent behavioral investigations of temporal dispersion have established that temporal dispersion is both quantitatively and qualitatively task-dependent.

We investigated the physiological correlates of temporal dispersion by investigating the properties of the most distal neural elements, the receptors. Intracellular recordings from photoreceptors showed that temporal dispersion was both quantitatively and qualitatively dependent on the sensory code (i.e., the feature of the neural response chosen for measurement).

The variation in these physiological measures of temporal dispersion was quite comparable to the variation in the behavioral measures. This observation suggested that behavioral task variation should be correlated with sensory code variation; this would imply that different features of the neural response mediated performance in different behavioral tasks.

The suggestion that the sensory code is task dependent is vulnerable on two grounds. First, the physiology comes from animals while the behavior comes from humans. Second, the suggestion is derived from correlational rather than experimental evidence.

A new preparation has recently become available which permits the direct test of such sensory coding hypotheses in within-species experiments: Some humans, who are deaf because they have lost their auditory receptors, have been surgically fitted with artificial receptors (cochlear implants). It is therefore possible experimentally to manipulate the properties of the implant and measure the effect of coding variations on behavior.

We have begun such investigations. Our initial experiments tested a proposition which is a robust deduction from the task-dependence hypothesis: Optimal performance depends on providing a sensory signal which simulates the characteristics of the natural neural response. The performance we chose to examine, for obvious practical reasons, was the pattern discrimination associated with speech communication.

Discrimination between isolated words and comprehension of whole sentences have been studied in controlled sensory-coding experiments. We have tested typical and extreme patients drawn from a population that includes post-lingually-deafened adults as well as prelingually-deafened children. In every case, the addition of dispersion to the sensory signal improved performance.

While this result supports the task dependence theory of sensory coding, it does not prove it. Many additional experiments remain to be done to determine the critical aspects of the treatment and to characterize the essential aspects of the performance.

Acknowledgements. Supported in part by the National Institutes of Health (EY − 07008), in part by the National Science Foundation (EET 87 − 07008), in part by the 3M Foundation, in part by the Trask Foundation, and in part by a David Ross Fellowship. Prof. Wang-Bennett is currently at the Otorhinolaryngology Department, Baylor College of Medicine, Houston, Texas, 77030 U.S.A.
Correspondence should be addressed to Gerald S. Wasserman, Department of Psychological Sciences, Purdue University, West Lafayette, Indiana, 47907 U.S.A.

References

Bilger, R.C., Nuetzel, J.M., Rabinowitz, W.M., & Rzezckowski, C. (1984). Standardization of a test of speech perception in noise. *Journal of Speech and Hearing Research, 27*, 32–48.

Cohen, J., & Gordon, D. (1949). The Prevost–Fechner–Benham subjective colors. *Psychological Bulletin, 46*, 97–136.

Dunnett, C.W. (1955). A multiple comparison procedure for comparing several treatments with a control. *Journal of the American Statistical Association, 50*, 1096–1121.

Fechner, G.T. (1838). Ueber eine Scheibe zur Erzeugung subjecktiver Farben. *Poggendorf's Annalen der Physik und Chemie, 45*, 227–232.

Fechner, G.T. (1860/1966). *Elements of psychophysics* (H.E. Adler, Translator). New York: Holt, Rinehart & Winston.

Fretz, R.J., & Fravel, R.P. (1985). Design and function: A physical and electrical description of the 3M House cochlear implant system. *Ear and Hearing, 6*, 14S–19S.

House, A.S., Williams, C.E., Hecker, M.H.L., & Kryter, K.D. (1965). Articulation testing methods: Consonantal differentiation with a closed–response set. *Journal of the Acoustical Society of America, 37*, 158–166.

Hartline, H.K. (1934). Intensity and duration in the excitation of single photoreceptor units. *Journal of Cellular and Comparative Physiology, 5*, 229–247.

Helmholtz, H.v. (1860/1962). *Physiological Optics* (J.P.C. Southall, Editor). New York: Dover.

Hunter, W.S., & Sigler, M. (1940). The span of visual discrimination as a function of time and intensity of stimulation. *Journal of Experimental Psychology, 26*, 160–179.

Kahneman, D., & Norman, J. (1964). The time–intensity relation in visual perception as a function of the observer's task. *Journal of Experimental Psychology, 68*, 215–220.

Kalikow, D.N., Stevens, K.N., & Elliot, L.L. (1977). Development of a test of speech intelligibility in noise using sentence materials with controlled word predictability. *Journal of the Acoustical Society of America, 61*, 1337–1351.

Kong, K.-L., & Wasserman, G.S. (1978). Changing response measures alters temporal summation in the receptor and spike potentials of the *Limulus* lateral eye. *Sensory Processes, 2*, 21–31.

Miyamoto, R.T., Gossett, S.K., Groom, G.L., Kienle, M.L., Pope, M.L., & Shallop, J.K. (1982). Cochlear implants: An auditory prosthesis for the deaf. *Journal of the Indiana State Medical Association, 75*, 174–177.

Miyamoto, R.T., Myres, W.A., Pope, M.L., & Carotta, C.A. (1986). Cochlear implants for deaf children. *Laryngoscope, 96*, 990–996.

Robbins, A.M., Osberger, M.J., Miyamoto, R.T., Kienle, M.J., & Myres, W.A. (1985). Speech–tracking performance in single–channel cochlear implant subjects. *Journal of Speech and Hearing Research, 28*, 565–578.

Schindler, R.A., & Merzenich, M.M. (1985). *Cochlear implants*. New York: Raven.

Teller, D.Y. (1984). Linking propositions. *Vision Research, 10*, 1233–1246.

Wang, L.T. (1981). *A study of visual system transformation and temporal summation rules as a function of dark and light adaptation*. Ph.D. Thesis, Purdue University.

Wang, L.T., & Wasserman, G.S. (1985). Direct intracellular measurement of non–linear postreceptor transfer functions in dark and light adaptation in *Limulus*. *Brain Research, 328*, 41–50.

Wasserman, G.S. (1966). Brightness enhancement in intermittent light: Methods of measurement. *Journal of Experimental Psychology, 72*, 300–306.

Wasserman, G.S. (1978). *Limulus* psychophysics: Temporal summation in the ventral eye. *Journal of Experimental Psychology: General, 107*, 276–286.

Wasserman, G.S. (1981). Cochlear implant codes and speech perception in the profoundly deaf. *Bulletin of the Psychonomic Society, 28*, 161–164.

Wasserman, G.S., & Kong, K.-L. (1979). Absolute timing of mental activities. *The Behavioral and Brain Sciences, 2*, 243–304.

Psychophysical Explorations of Mental Structures
Edited by H.-G. Geissler
in collaboration with M.H. Müller and W. Prinz
© 1990 by Hogrefe & Huber Publishers

Chapter 18

Binaural Adaptation and the Limitations on Localization of High-Frequency Sounds

Ervin R. Hafter
Department of Psychology
University of California
Berkeley, U.S.A.

Most theories of perception are simply transfer functions that describe the relation between stimulus and response. Directed at experimental control, these are typically derived using stimuli that differ on the fewest possible dimensions. The kind of model that emerges generally resembles a set of tuned filters that analyze an input by dividing it into separately coded segments along the dimension of interest. Examples include the long-accepted view of the auditory system as a kind of Fourier analyzer and more recent attempts to model the visual system in much the same way.

Unlike the simple stimuli used in the laboratory, those encountered in everyday life are often more complex, making it reasonable to suppose that our sensory systems have evolved ways of dealing with complexity. Thus, one might argue that the study of single dimensions in isolation, while powerful, can also be deceptive, promoting simplicity where it does not exist. This point will be illustrated by showing that a time-honored theory of hearing, derived using experiments with pure tones, is really quite limited, holding only for the special case of simple stimuli.

The Duplex Theory of Sound Localization

The physical bases for sound localization are Interaural Differences of Level (IDL) due to acoustic shadows cast by the head and pinnae and Interaural Differences of Time (IDT) produced by the longer path from the source to the distal than to the nearer ear (Blauert, 1983). Both of these factors were recognized in the last century, but it was thought that the IDT was of little use because of the ambiguities that can occur with all but the lowest of frequencies. Figure 1 shows a case of three different tonal frequencies presented from a single azimuth off the mid-sagittal plane. With low frequencies, the interaural phase difference (θ) can be used to compute $IDT = \theta/2\pi f$. But for $f = 1/2IDT$, neither channel leads nor lags, and for still higher frequencies, either side may lead or lag depending on f and the azimuth. For humans, ambiguity begins as low as 600 to 700 Hz for tones presented on the aural axis. This means that over most of the audible range, IDTs can be false cues to direction. To the nineteenth century theorists, this suggested a lack of sensitivity to time, with all localization based on IDLs. However, there is a problem with this position; as shown in Figure 2 (from Durlach & Colburn, 1978), the magnitude of the IDL declines with frequency, becoming negligible at very low frequencies. Yet listeners can readily localize low-frequency sounds. Thus, neither cue alone seems adequate to explain all of the empirical findings.

Figure 1. Exposition of three different tonal frequencies from a lateral source. It can be seen that only for lower frequencies the IDTs can be used as unambiguous cues for localization.

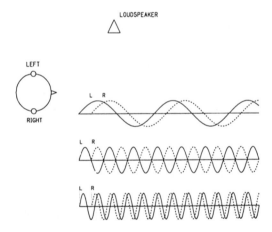

Rayleigh (1907) seemed to have solved these problems by proposing a duplex theory of localization which says that we are sensitive to IDLs in high frequencies and to IDTs in low. A variety of demonstrations have been offered in support of Rayleigh's position, especially of the notion that we do not encode IDTs in high frequencies, but perhaps none is more compelling than the percept of a pure tone presented through earphones with an interaural shift of phase. For low frequencies, an intracranial image is displaced toward the side of the leading channel but as the frequency is raised above 1200 to 1500 Hz, the image remains fixed in the center of the head, regardless of the value of θ. For a more detailed discussion of the duplex model and its antecedents see Hafter (1984).

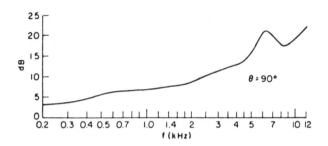

Figure 2. Interaural Differences of Level (IDLs) as a function of frequency. Note that, in contrast to IDTs, the IDLs provide good directional cues for high frequencies.

The idea that reliance on simple stimuli alone can lead to parsimonious but inadequate models of perception is well illustrated by the long term acceptance of insensitivity to interaural timing in high frequencies. Clearly, the low-frequency half of the duplex model holds for pure sinusoids, but these are special sounds, seldom heard outside of the laboratory. Recently, however, experimenters have focused increasingly on more complex stimuli, including acoustic transients (clicks), noise, harmonic sequences and amplitude modulation (AM). These have led to new perspectives on spatial hearing.

It has long been known that an IDT can be detected if presented in a high-frequency click (e.g., David, Guttman & van Bergeijk, 1959). Some have sought to reconcile this finding with the duplex theory by arguing that listeners are concentrating on information carried in the low-frequency filters (Hafter & De Maio, 1975; Yost, Wightman & Green, 1971). In support of this argument, Bernstein & Trahiotis (1982) found that subjects gave more weight to timing in the low-frequency end of a wideband signal, even when the levels of the high frequencies were much larger. We have found, however, that low-frequency noise does not prevent lateralization with such clicks, indicating that temporal information is available in the higher regions of the spectrum.

One might argue that transients are special, evoking discrete temporal responses that are uncharacteristic of the way high-frequency neurons react to sustained stimulation. However, more recent results have shown that IDTs can be detected in amplitude-modulated, high-frequency sinusoids, as long as the rate of modulation is not too high (e.g., Henning, 1974; Leakey, Sayers & Cherry, 1958; McFadden & Pasanen, 1976; Nuetzel & Hafter, 1976). Figure 3 depicts an example of Sinusoidal Amplitude Modulation (SAM) in both the time and the frequency domains. The temporal waveform is the product of two sinusoids, $f(t) = \cos f_c \cdot (1 + \cos f_m)$, where f_c and f_m refer to the carrier and modu-

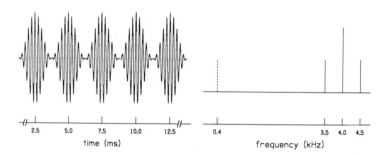

2.5   5.0   7.5   10.0   12.5   0.4   3.5   4.0   4.5

time (ms)   frequency (kHz)

Figure 3. Sinusoidal Amplitude Modulation (SAM) in the time and frequency domains. For explanations, see text.

lator frequencies, respectively. The amplitude spectrum consists only of the three spectral components at f_c and the two sidebands at $f_c - f_m$ and $f_c + f_m$; for the example shown, with 4000 Hz modulated by 400 Hz, these are represented by the solid lines. Whereas an interaural delay of the waveform's fine-structure alone (f_c) cannot be heard, IDTs in the amplitude-envelope are readily detected (Henning, 1980). One could argue that non-linear distortion in the auditory system produces an unwanted component at 400 Hz but this is readily refuted by measuring detection in the presence of a lowpass masker (e.g., Henning, 1974) or by showing that there is no sense of fusion or lateralization when one ear receives the SAM while the other is given the true 400–Hz tone depicted by the dashed spectral line (Nuetzel and Hafter, 1976).

Finally, results from psychophysics are often also used to postulate the workings of the sensory nervous system and, not surprisingly, the duplex theory has led to the assumption that neurons responsible for high frequencies do not process temporal differences between signals in the two ears. Following the behavioral observations with AM, physiologists have now sought and found single units in the central nervous system that encode IDTs in the envelopes of complex sound (Yin & Kuwada, 1984).

The Effect of Stimulus Variation on Lateralization

My own interest in high-frequency IDTs arose several years ago while attempting to model the binaural Masking-Level Difference MLD with a single mechanism for all frequencies. MLD refers to the improvement in detectability that can occur when an interaural difference of phase, time or level is introduced into either the signal or masker. Figure 4 shows one such example. A 500–Hz signal and noise-masker are presented to both earphones but the signal to one channel is first passed through an adjustable phase-shifting network. With the phase (ϕ) set to zero, inputs to the two channels are redundant, providing no advantage for binaural processing. This condition serves as the reference for the MLD. As ϕ is increased, the signals–plus–noise at the two ears become increasingly different from one another, adding information in the form of interaural differences of time and level. Detection becomes easier, to the point that in the most effective of these "binaural conditions," with $\phi = \pi$, the threshold is reduced by 15 decibels relative to the reference (Jeffress, Blodgett, Sandel & Wood, 1956); this is called an MLD of 15 dB.

Figure 4. Binaural presentation of a signal and a noise–masker with the signal being passed through a phase–shifting device. Shifting the phase of the signal for one channel results in increasing interaural differences in time and level for signal–plus–noise.

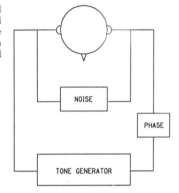

Various theories offered to explain the MLD all propose sensitivity to some aspect of the interaural information: (a) the Webster–Jeffress hypothesis says that the appropriate binaural cue is the signal–induced IDT (Webster, 1951; Jeffress et al., 1956); (b) the equalization–cancellation model proposes that the binaural nervous system adjusts the two inputs to best equalize the maskers and then compute the difference between the channels (Durlach, 1963); (c) the correlation model stresses sensitivity to the signal–induced change in the cross–correlation between the two channels (Osman, 1971); (d) the lateralization model argues that listeners compute a weighted sum of the IDT and IDL, combining the two cues with a time/level trading ratio (Hafter, 1971). For more discussion of MLDs, see Colburn and Durlach (1978) or Blauert (1983).

In an elaboration of the lateralization model, Hafter (1977) calculated the magnitudes of the trading ratios necessary to describe the MLDs found at various frequencies. In accordance with the duplex theory, he presumed that the ratio would be small for low frequencies, reflecting the special importance of IDT, but large for high frequencies, where the dominant cue is IDL. The surprising result was that the model fit well to a set of MLDs for frequencies from 250 to 4000 Hz (Hirsch & Burgeat, 1958) using a single trading ratio of 0 μs/dB. Wondering how this could be possible, I speculated that binaural neurons that adapt to high-frequency tones might recover and respond again if allowed sufficient time to recover between stimulation. Suppose that variation introduced by the noise masker provided the time for recovery. With ϕ in Figure 4 set to π, the IDT in the two signals–plus–masker constantly changes due to random fluctuations of the noise. Thus, even though the period of the high-frequency signal might be short relative to the refractory periods of single neurons, those units tuned to specific IDTs would have a much longer time between successive stimulations. This was thought to present yet another difficulty for Rayleigh's hypothesis, saying that for the duplex theory to hold, the interaural parameters should be free of noise.

A Different Paradigm: Trains of High–Frequency Clicks

In order to better understand the limitations on timing in high frequencies we began a series of experiments in which listeners would be asked to detect IDTs in trains of high-frequency clicks, each click made by passing a brief pulse through a bandpass filter centered on a high spectral frequency. The duration of a train would be the product of the Interclick Interval (ICI) and the number of clicks (n). Of special interest would be the effects of increasing the rate of stimulation (1/ICI).

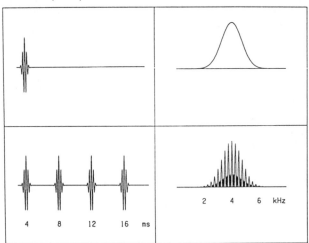

Figure 5. Effects of lengthening a train of clicks from $n=1$ to $n=4$ on energy and spectral envelope (lower part, right half). Each click passes a Gaussian filter with a center frequency of 4000 Hz and $\sigma = 700$ Hz. The ICI is 4ms.

Figure 5 describes the waveforms and spectra of a single click and a train of four presented with an ICI of 4 ms. For this example, the filter is Gaussian with a center frequency of 4000 Hz and $\pm 1\sigma$ points at 3300 Hz and 4700 Hz. Note that lengthening the train causes the energy to accumulate at integer multiples of the click-rate (250 Hz) while not affecting the spectral envelope, which is determined entirely by the filter. The skirts of realizable filters have finite attenuation, so a willingness to call these sounds "high–frequency" relies on the assumption that energies in the low frequencies are well below the threshold of audibility.

Binaural Information Limited by Internal Noise

Our first experience with these trains of clicks (Hafter, Dye & Nuetzel, 1980) showed that lateralization was excellent with click-rates of no more than about 100 per second but grew worse as the ICI was shortened. However, there was little or no effect if we changed the IDT from click to click. Thus, while diminishing the proposed importance of variation in the interaural parameter, the results did not offer a positive answer to the question, "What is it that makes slow presentations different from fast?" The answer would come from examination of the joint effects on threshold of ICI and n. For this we began with a notion from signal-detection theory that all thresholds can be thought of as masked-thresholds, regardless of whether the experimenter supplies the masker. For absolute thresholds, the masker is an internal noise added to the neural representation of the signal. From this point of view, IDTs are detected against a background of temporal variation or "jitter" introduced by the auditory system of the listener. When the criterion for threshold is a mean-to-sigma ratio (d') of 1.0, the threshold itself (ΔIDT) provides a direct measure of the standard deviation (across all of the neurons carrying the interaural information) of the internal noise:

$$\sigma\text{IDT}_n = \frac{\Delta\text{IDT}}{d'} = \frac{\Delta\text{IDT}}{1.0} = \Delta\text{IDT} . \qquad (1)$$

We assume that as the train is lengthened from 1 to n, the number of evoked neural responses is increased by a factor of N. If the samples of internal noise added to the representations of successive clicks are mutually independent, the amount of additional information should also increase by a factor of N and the standard error of the mean IDT-plus-jitter decline as the $\sqrt{N}$. If we call the threshold with only a single click ΔIDT_1, then when the IDT is adjusted to maintain a d' of 1.0, the threshold for n clicks (ΔIDT_n) becomes:

$$\Delta\text{IDT}_n = \frac{\Delta\text{IDT}_1}{N^{0.5}} . \qquad (2)$$

In its logarithmic form, this function is linear with an intercept at ΔIDT_1 and slope of -0.5.

$$\log \Delta\text{IDT}_n = \log \Delta\text{IDT}_1 - 0.5\log N . \qquad (3)$$

Stationary Processes

In search of an explanation for reduced sensitivity to IDTs presented at high rates, Hafter and Dye (1983) considered a variety of hypotheses including: (a) limitations of bandwidth set by the auditory filters, (b) non-independence between successive samples of the internal noise and (c) neural refractoriness. The first notes that, before binaural interaction can take place, the peripheral auditory system is organized into a series of bandpass filters. As seen in Figures 3 and 5, complex periodic signals are made up of the sums of more than one component of a harmonic series; a decrease in the ICI raises the fundamental frequency of the series, moving adjacent spectral components into increasingly separate auditory bands. This reduces the "depth of modulation" within the bands, so that the rise and decay of peaks in the temporal envelope are more gradual, an effect that should increase temporal variation in the internal noise. The second hypothesis points to the relatively low frequencies of some components of the internal noise such as respiration and heartbeat, factors which could increase the correlation between successive samples of the added jitter. Finally, there is the fact that individual neurons, having just fired, are in an absolute refractory period which precludes their response to ensuing stimulation.

For reasons that will become clear, only the neural refractoriness hypothesis will be discussed in detail. An idealization of this model describes the relation between n and the hypothetical variable N as:

$$N = 1 + P(n-1) \quad \text{where } 0 \le P \le 1 \text{ and } P = f(ICI) . \qquad (4)$$

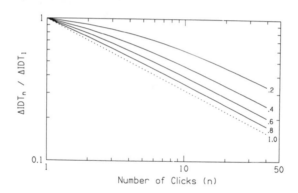

Figure 6. Relation between relative threshold and n (both logarithmical) for various values of P. P is the percentage of click duration not falling into the neural refractory period.

Here, (P) represents the percentage of time that clicks are informative, that is, do not occur during refractory periods. For slow rates, where the ICI is longer than all such periods, $P = 1$ and $N = n$; in that case, all clicks in the train are equally effective. But, when the ICI is shortened to the point that some of the clicks are lost, the effectiveness of the $n-1$ clicks beyond the first is reduced by a constant proportion $(1 - P)$. Figure 6 shows the effect of such a mechanism on performance, plotting the hypothetical relation between log relative threshold and log n for various values of P.

The lines radiating from the reference point at ΔIDT_1 represent solutions to Equation 3 with N computed as in Equation 4. The lowest (dashed) line

($P-1$) has the slope of -0.5 indicative of equal effectiveness throughout the train. Moving upward, we see that for large values of n where $N \sim pn$, the slopes approach -0.5 regardless of ICI. Since lengthening the train decreases the threshold in proportion to the $\sqrt{n}$, one may say that the statistics of the internal noise are stationary; that is, the expected values and variances of the added jitter are the same for each click.

A Non-Stationary Process: Adaptation

Only one of the three hypotheses, "bandwidth", "non-independence" and "refractoriness", is discussed here in detail because it has been shown that each of them is dominated by stationary statistics (Hafter & Dye, 1983). That is, each predicts log-threshold, log-n functions that reach an asymptotic slope of -0.5 for larger values of n, regardless of their effects on the overall level of performance. More important, however is the fact that the results from all of our work thus far have shown that the prediction of stationarity does not hold. Figure 7 shows an example of such data (reprinted from Hafter & Dye, 1983). The clicks had center frequencies of 4000 Hz and ICIs of either 10, 5, 2.5 or 1 ms. The data are averaged across four subjects.

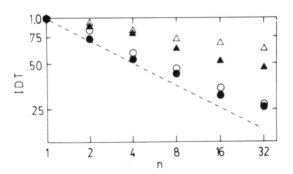

Figure 7. IDTs as a function of log n. ICIs: 10 ms (filled circles), 5 ms (open circles), 2.5 ms (filled triangles), 1 ms (open triangles).

The scale, in relative threshold, was computed by dividing each ΔIDT by the subject's ΔIDT_1. This allows one to combine data regardless of individual differences in absolute sensitivity. Rather than indicating a stationary process, these data are well described by straight lines with a common intercept at ΔIDT_1 but with slopes that grow more shallow with increasing rate:

$$\log \Delta \text{IDT}_n = \log \Delta \text{IDT}_1 - 0.5k \log n \qquad (5)$$

with $0 \le k \le 1$ and $k = \text{f}(ICI)$.

Relative thresholds are quite useful because they allow for direct comparisons, not only between individuals but also between signal parameters; for example, the spectral contents of the clicks, their sound–pressure levels or their interaural differences (IDT or IDL). To date, all such comparisons have found the relation expressed in Equation 5, making it necessary to propose an alternative to stationary processes.

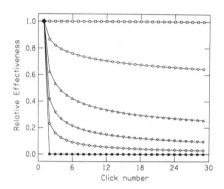

Figure 8. Possible solutions for *k* in Equation 6 yield differences in relative effectiveness for each click in a train. *k* can range from 0 (filled squares: only the first click is effective) to 1 (open squares: all clicks are equally effective).

In order to examine this process, we have applied a "method of subtraction" (Hafter, Buell & Richards, 1988) which assumes that any change in performance that accompanies an increase in duration is based on information carried in the added portion. By testing with many durations, one may then plot the effectiveness of each successive part. Substitution of the empirical results (Eq. 5) into the theoretical relation (Eq. 3) shows the relation between *N* and *n* to be a family of compressive power functions whose exponents depend on ICI:

$$N \propto n^k \quad \text{with } 0 \le k \le 1 \text{ and } k = f(ICI) . \qquad (6)$$

Since *N* is proportional to the information derived from any train, the derivative of Equation 6 describes the flow of information from the beginning of a train to its end. This is shown in Figure 8, which plots functions similar to the post–stimulus time histograms used by physiologists to describe the sequential firing patterns of neurons. From top to bottom, the separate curves represent solutions for values of *k* ranging from what a physiologist might call a "tonic" response ($k=1$), in which the clicks are equally effective, to a "phasic" response ($k=0$), in which only the first click is used. However, neither of those general classifications describes all of the data; rather, the process that we have called "binaural adaptation" (Hafter et al., 1988) reduces the effectiveness of successive elements by an amount dependent on the rate of presentation. Application of a similar analysis to various tests of lateralization reported in the literature has found good agreement with this result; that is, the

slopes of the log-threshold, log-duration functions are often more shallow than
-0.5, indicating a loss of information beyond the stimulus' onset (Yost &
Hafter, 1987). Thus it seems that "binaural" spatial hearing, limiting the rate at
which binaural processing can take place.

Where is the Information Lost?

We have by now learned many things about binaural adaptation by measuring its effects in conjuction with variations of other parameters. For example, it is unrelated to stimulus level. Thus, decreasing the audibility of the signal leads to higher interaural thresholds without affecting the slopes of the $\log - \Delta IDT$, $\log - n$ functions (Dye & Hafter, 1984).

In this section, I shall outline a set of studies intended to uncover the neurological site of the adaptation. The assumption is that the anatomical location of an operation can be inferred from its interaction with another behavior whose anatomy is known. This has been done using techniques like the "method of alternation" (Hafter, et al., 1988) in which interaural sensitivity is measured with trains consisting of two kinds of clicks that differ on some dimension and are presented in alternation.

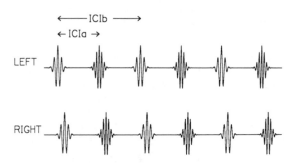

Figure 9. Binaural series of clicks with alternating frequencies. ICIa would be relevant if binaural adaptation took place after combination of disparate bands, ICIb, on the other hand, if adaptation took place prior to combining both bands.

For example, Figure 9 shows clicks which alternate in center frequency between 4000 Hz and 6000 Hz. If the mechanism of binaural adaptation were at a stage in the nervous system beyond the point where frequencies with the same interaural delay are combined into a perceptual unit based on common direction, no distinction would be made between the two types of clicks and the slope of the log-ΔIDT, log-n function would reflect ICI$_a$. However, if the operation were prior to the combination of disparate bands, the 4000-Hz clicks would interact only with 4000-Hz clicks and so on, producing the steeper slopes called for by ICI$_b$. Results from this experiment clearly support the latter

(Hafter & Wenzel, 1983), showing that multiple sites of the adaptation act separately within each spectral region.

Similar experiments with trains containing different types of clicks have pointed to the peripheral auditory system as the probable site. For example, an earlier study of interaural level (Hafter, Dye & Wenzel, 1983) had found that slopes of the log-ΔIDL, log-n functions closely resembled those with IDT. Since this suggested a stage at which the IDLs and IDTs are indistinguishable, discrimination was measured using a train that alternated between IDT and IDL. Unlike the case with alternating spectra, these two click-types interacted as though there were no difference between them (Hafter & Wenzel, 1983). In following up on this idea, a train was presented containing clicks that differed in their IDTs, such that either type heard alone would be lateralized at a different location in space (Hafter & Buell, 1984). Again, the adaptation seemed unaffected by the mixture of click-types, reinforcing our conviction that the site of the process is in the peripheral auditory system, even before the first stages of binaural interaction. This result says that the adaptation is actually a monaural process that reduces the effectiveness of post-onset information in the signal before it can be used to compute the signal's location.

As an addendum to this discussion of anatomy, one might wonder if all discrimination with high frequencies is based primarily on information in the onset of the stimulus and, if so, how does the listener monitor an ongoing stimulus enough even to know that it is still present? Puzzled by this, Hafter and Richards (1988) presented trains of clicks like those used for lateralization, but in a monaural situation in which the task was to discriminate between trains on the basis of differences in their ICIs (heard as differences of pitch). The result was that for ICIs as low as 2.5 ms, the slopes of the log-threshold, log-n functions remained at -0.5, indicative of equal effectiveness of the samples of ICI throughout the train. This suggests that there are two different kinds of pathways through the brain stem. The one that relays information about who or what made the sound based on its pitch monitors the acoustic environment continuously; the one that carries information to be combined with messages from the other ear for computation of where the sound is coming from tends to mark only the onset of the stimulus.

Why Adaptation?

Perhaps the most interesting question about binaural adaptation is, "Why have it?" One possibility is that sharpening of the onset does for hearing what edge effects do for vision, that is, highlighting the auditory stream with a kind of temporal "Mach band". From this perspective, it is tempting to relate binaural adaptation to the "Haas effect", in which perceptual precedence is given to onsets (Blauert, Canevet & Voiner, 1987), though the relation is debatable (Hafter et al., 1988). A different line of reasoning says that the non-adapting channels, such as those that carry information for pitch, make it unnecessary to monitor spatial information continuously. This is a kind of signal-to-noise argument, saying that the brain is willing to sacrifice some information in order to reduce clutter in its input.

Summary

This paper began with questions about the comparative usefulness of simple and complex stimuli for the study of perception. Unidimensional analyses have obvious advantages for ease of experimental control and direct connectability between independent and dependent variables but, by ignoring possible stimulus interactions, they can lead to deceptively simple theories. The lasting strength of Rayleigh's partially correct hypothesis about the inability to localize high-frequency sounds on the basis of time points to the danger of letting simplicity dominate one's thinking and research. Based as it was on observations with pure tones, the duplex theory ignored the basic fact that we live in a world in which useful information is carried in the interactions between stimulus components and the likelihood that we have evolved mechanisms capable of extracting that information. Fortunately, computer-based apparatus makes it possible to generate any definable stimulus, and from this ability will surely emerge other discoveries about complex sensory processes like those found in binaural interaction.

Correspondence should be addressed to Ervin R. Hafter, Department of Psychology, University of California at Berkeley, Berkeley, CA 94720, U.S.A

References

Bernstein, L.R., & Trahiotis, C. (1982). Detection of interaural delay in high-frequency noise. *Journal of the Acoustical Society of America, 71*, 147−152.

Blauert, J. (1983). *Spatial hearing: The psychophysics of human sound localization.* Cambridge, MA: MIT Press.

Blauert, J., Canevet, G., & Voinier, T. (1987). *The precedence effect: no evidence for an "active" release process found,* (pers. comm.).

Colburn, H.S., & Durlach, N.I. (1978). Models of binaural interaction. In E.C. Carterette & M.P. Friedmann (Eds.), *Handbook of perception,* Vol. IV (pp. 467−518). New York: Academic Press.

David, E.E., Guttman, N., & van Bergeijk, W.W. (1959). Binaural interaction of high-frequency complex stimuli. *Journal of the Acoustical Society of America, 31*, 774−782.

Durlach, N.I. (1963). Equalization and cancellation theory of binaural masking level theory of binaural masking level differences. *Journal of the Acoustical Society of America, 35*, 1206−1218.

Durlach, N.I., & Colburn, H.S. (1978). Binaural phenomena. In E.C. Carterette & M.P. Friedman (Eds.), *Handbook of Perception,* Vol. IV (pp. 365−466). New York: Academic Press.

Dye, R.H., Jr., & Hafter, E.R. (1984). The effects of intensity on the detection of interaural differences of time in high-frequency trains of clicks. *Journal of the Acoustical Society of America, 75*, 1593−1598.

Hafter, E.R. (1971). Quantitative evaluation of a lateralization model of Masking-Level-Differences. *Journal of the Acoustical Society of America, 50*, 1116−1122.

Hafter, E.R. (1977). Lateralization model and the role of time–intensity trading in binaural masking: Can the data be explained by a time–only hypothesis? *Journal of the Acoustical Society of America, 62*, 633–635.

Hafter, E.R. (1984). Spatial hearing and the duplex theory: How viable? In G.M. Edelman, W.E. Gall & W.M. Cowan (Eds.), *Dynamic aspects of neocortical function* (pp. 425–448). New York: Wiley Interscience.

Hafter, E.R., & Buell, T.N. (1984). Onset effects in lateralization denote a monaural mechanism. *Journal of the Acoustical Society of America, 76*, S91(A).

Hafter, E.R., Buell, T.N., & Richards, V.R. (1988). Onset-coding in lateralization: Its form, site and function. In G. Edelman, M. Cowan & E. Gall (Eds.), *Functions of the auditory system.* New York: Wiley.

Hafter, E.R., & De Maio, J. (1975). Difference threshold for interaural delay. *Journal of the Acoustical Society of America, 57*, 181–187.

Hafter, E.R., & Dye, R.H.Jr. (1983). Detection of interaural differences of time in trains of high-frequency clicks as a function of interclick interval and number. *Journal of the Acoustical Society of America, 73*, 644–651.

Hafter, E.R., Dye, R.H. Jr., & Nuetzel, J.M. (1980). Lateralization of high-frequency stimuli on the basis of time and intensity. In G. van den Brink & F.A. Bilsen (Eds.), *Psychophysical, physiological and behavioural studies in hearing.* Delft, The Netherlands: Delft University Press.

Hafter, E.R., Dye, R.H.Jr., & Wenzel, E. (1983). Detection of interaural differences of intensity in trains of high-frequency clicks as a function of interclick interval and number. *Journal of the Acoustical Society of America, 73*, 1798–1713.

Hafter, E.R., & Wenzel, E.M. (1983). Lateralization of transients presented at high rates: Site of the saturation effect. In R. Klinke & R. Hartmann (Eds.), *Hearing – Physiological basis and psychophysics* (pp. 202–208). Berlin: Springer.

Hafter, E.R., & Richards, V.M. (1988). Discrimination of the rate of filtered impulses. *Perception & Psychophysics, 43*, 405–414.

Henning, G.B. (1974). Detectibility of interaural delay in high-frequency complex waveforms. *Journal of the Acoustical Society of America, 55*, 84–90.

Henning, G.B. (1980). Some observations on the lateralization of complex waveforms. *Journal of the Acoustical Society of America, 68*, 446–454.

Hirsch, I.J., & Burgeat, M. (1958). Binaural effects in remote masking. *Journal of the Acoustical Society of America, 30*, 827–832.

Jeffress, L.A., Blodgett, H.C., Sandel, T.T., & Wood, C.L. (1956). Masking of tonal signals. *Journal of the Acoustical Society of America, 28*, 416–426.

Leakey, D.M., Sayers, B. McA., & Cherry, C. (1958). Binaural fusion of low- and high-frequency sounds. *Journal of the Acoustical Society of America, 30*, 322.

McFadden, D., & Pasanen, E. (1976). Lateralization at high frequencies based on interaural time differences. *Journal of the Acoustical Society of America, 59*, 63–69.

Nuetzel, J.M., & Hafter, E.R. (1976). Lateralization of complex waveforms: Effects of fine structure, amplitude, and duration. *Journal of the Acoustical Society of America, 60*, 1339–1346.

Osman, E. (1971). A correlation model of binaural masking level differences. *Journal of the Acoustical Society of America, 50*, 1126–1130.

Rayleigh, Lord (1907). On our perception of sound direction. *Philosophical Magazine, 13*, 214–232.

Webster, F.A. (1951). The influence of interaural phase on masked thresholds. *Journal of the Acoustical Society of America, 23*, 452–462.

Yin, T.C.T., & Kuwada, S. (1984). Interaural time sensitivity of high-frequency neurons in inferior colliculus. *Journal of the Acoustical Society of America, 76*, 1401–1410.

Yost, W.A., & Hafter, E. (1987). Lateralization. In W. Yost & G. Gourevitch (Eds.), *Directional hearing* (pp. 49–84). New York: Springer.

Yost, W.A., Wightman, F.L., & Green, D.M. (1971). Lateralization of filtered clicks. *Journal of the Acoustical Society of America, 50*, 1526–1531.

Psychophysical Explorations of Mental Structures
Edited by H.-G. Geissler
in collaboration with M.H. Müller and W. Prinz
© 1990 by Hogrefe & Huber Publishers

Chapter 19

Breaks in the Psychophysical Function for Duration

Hannes Eisler
Department of Psychology, University of Stockholm
Stockholm, Sweden

My interest in time perception grew out of an originally purely psychophysical problem: Is it the number behavior of observers, rather than their sensations, which determines the psychophysical function obtained, e.g., in a magnitude estimation experiment? Being pretty sure that number behavior in rats is negligible, I decided to carry out a duration reproduction experiment with rats. To get an idea of the possible data I carried out what I then considered a pilot study with human observers. The results (Eisler, 1975) were, however, so interesting that the focus was moved from animal to human experiments. But also the rat experiment was carried out (Eisler, 1984) — I had to discard three apparatuses built by different technicians until eventually the fourth worked as it should.

A characteristic of almost all temporal data are discontinuities in the function, which, as irregularities, were discovered as early as 1885 by Estel. In the present paper instances of such discontinuities or breaks are presented and a mathematical description will be given. Since the data stem from different experiments carried out over a long period, the methods of computation and plotting have become more sophisticated.

The theoretical starting point is Stevens' psychophysical power function of the form

$$\psi = \alpha(\phi - \phi_0)^\beta \tag{1}$$

where ψ stands for subjective and ϕ for physical duration, respectively; α, ϕ_0, and β are constants. This equation could be uniquely derived for ratio setting data (Eisler, 1974).

Figure 1 shows magnitude estimation data for durations varying between 1.3 and 20 s for 12 observers (Eisler, 1975). Breaks are clearly discernable for most of the observers. The exponent β was assumed equal on both sides of the break, and ϕ_0 was set 0 (to avoid fitting too many parameters to the ten points). The position of the break was judged by eye and it was described as a change in the scale unit α.

Figure 1. Log magnitude estimates as functions of log stimulus values for 12 observers. (From Eisler, 1975. Copyright 1975 by APA. Reprinted by permission.)

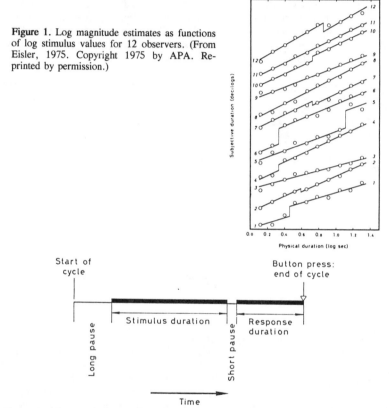

Figure 2. A cycle. For explanation see text. (From Eisler, 1975. Copyright 1975 by APA. Reprinted by permission.)

Of more interest are the reproduction experiments (which were checked by halving and doubling), because reproduction does not involve numbers. Figure 2 shows the main features of these experiments. The observers are presented a series of cycles, each trial (cycle) consisting of a quiet pause, followed at random by one of the ten standard durations (again varying between 1.3 and

20 s), indicated by a sound. At the end of the standard presentation the sound is interrupted fo 300 ms, whereafter it resumes and is terminated by the observer pressing a button when she/he experiences that the second sound had lasted equally long as (half as long as, twice as long as) the standard.

According to the model by Eisler (1975), the observer, rather than storing the standard duration in memory, "uses" two sensory registers. The contents of the first are the total subjective duration from the start of the standard to the moment of button press, i.e. subjective duration corresponding to the sum of standard and reproduced duration. The contents of the second register are the subjective reproduced duration. When the contents of the second register equal the difference between the contents of the first and the second register, the observer experiences the two durations (standard and reproduced duration) as being equal and presses the button. Figure 3 will elucidate this model. The model is called the "parallel–clock model", because two sensory registers ("clocks") are working simultaneously.

Figure 3. The duration reproduction task described in psychophysical terms. Subscripts S, V, and T refer to standard, variable, and total duration, respectively. (From Eisler, 1977. Copyright 1977 by Erlbaum. Reprinted by permission.)

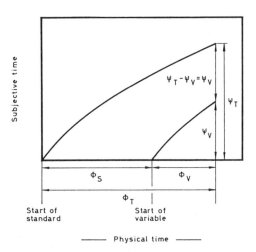

One of the implications of this model is that the parameters of Equation 1 can be computed from duration reproduction data, because what is reproduction ("equal setting") for the observer is duration halving from the experimenter's perspective (reproduced subjective duration is half the total subjective duration, i.e., the subjective duration corresponding to the sum of standard and reproduction). As is well known, the parameters of the power function can be derived from halving experiments. All following diagrams are plotted in accordance with this model, i.e. total duration (sum of standard and reproduced physical duration) in seconds is plotted on the abscissa.

A plot of reproduced duration vs. total duration is linear, which implies that the psychophysical function is a power function. When only one straight line is obtained the three parameters of Equation 1 are the same throughout the experimental range, from the longest total duration to the shortest reproduced duration. This case is exemplified in Figure 4. More than one straight line indicates a break in the psychophysical function; its upper segment differs from its lower one by either the scale unit α, the subjective zero ϕ_0, or both. The exponent β, on the other hand, has to be the same for both segments; otherwise the plot would be curvilinear.

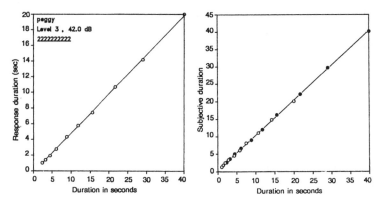

Figure 4. Duration reproduction. Left panel: Reproduced vs. total duration. Right panel: The psychophysical function. Filled circles: Standards (corresponding to total durations). Open circles: Variables (corresponding to reproductions).

Figures 5 and 6 show empirical examples of a break. Note that one break in the psychophysical function entails two breaks (three straight lines) in the plot of reproduced vs. total duration. The uppermost and lowermost straight lines must be parallel, since both standard and variable lie on the same segment of the psychophysical function with the same exponent β; for the middle line the standard (total duration) lies on the upper and the variable (reproduced duration) on the lower segment. For the middle line the slope is determined not only by the exponent, but also by the scale unit (Eisler, 1974, 1975).

If the experimental range for an observer is too small, one may get only two straight lines, or one of the "lines" may consist of only one point, as

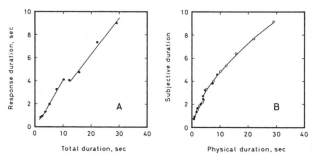

Figure 5. Duration reproduction. Panel A: Reproduced vs. total duration. Panel B: The psychophysical function. Note the break. (After Eisler, 1975. Copyright 1975 by APA. Reprinted by permission.)

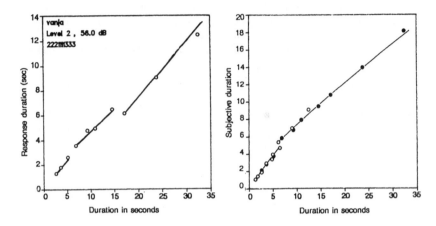

Figure 6. Duration reproduction. Left panel: Reproduced vs. total duration. Right panel: The psychophysical function. (From Eisler, 1989. Copyright 1989 by Springer. Reprinted by permission.)

shown in Figure 7. This observer also shows a "hole", not just a break, in the psychophysical function. Figure 8 exemplifies the appearance of breaks: sometimes there exists an overlap between the two segments, as can also be seen in Figure 9. Fig. 10 illustrates the case when the experimental range is insufficient to determine which of the two straight lines is the "middle" one, so that two different psychophysical functions are compatible with the data.

As Figure 11 demonstrates, the duration reproduction behavior of rats and humans is very similar, the breaks included.

In the learning phase of the rat experiment the rats had to learn to refrain from lever pressing during the standard. An investigation of the distribution of erroneous lever presses showed that almost all rats had a "hole" in the latency distribution, a period during which they never or almost never pressed the lever (Eisler, 1987). Figure 12 shows a variable which is monotonic to probability of lever pressing for certain intervals. Rat 1, for example, seemed never to press the lever in the interval 3.3−4.5 s. The same data are shown in Figure 13, where a horizontal segment in the plot indicates a latent duration of zero, a "temporal hole in the latency distribution."

Unfortunately the breaks seem to be all over the place. They might be a consequence of attempting to optimize performance by changing the scale unit in a way similar to changing the measurement range in a voltmeter to maximize accuracy. If timing behavior is governed by neural networks, the transition points may not be arbitrary for any one individual, and the transitions betwen different loops may involve "holes" in timing behavior of different kinds, as found in the duration reproduction experiments for both rats and humans, as well as in the learning phase of the rats.

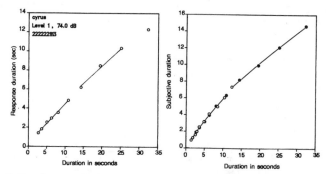

Figure 7. Duration reproduction.

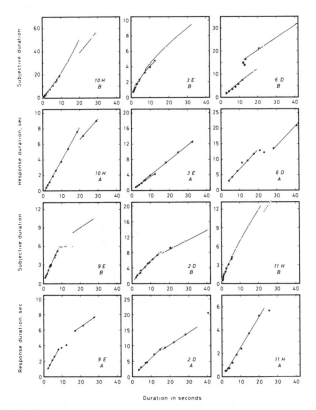

Duration in seconds

Figure 8. Duration halving (H), doubling (D), and reproduction (equal setting, E). These data show examples of overlap (10 H, 3 E), "holes" in the psychophysical function (6 D, 9 E), and just a single point for the longest duration (2 D, 11 H). Panels A: Reproduced vs. total duration. Panels B: The psychophysical function. Squares: Points that could not be determined uniquely. (Data from Eisler, 1975.)

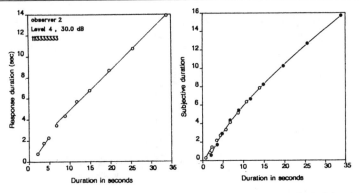

Figure 9. Duration reproduction data showing two overlapping psychophysical functions at the lower end.

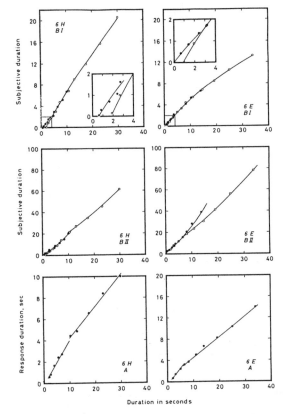

Figure 10. Duration halving (H) and reproduction (E) with two possible psychophysical functions, I and II. (Data from Eisler, 1975. Published in Eisler, 1989. Copyright 1989 by Springer. Reprinted by permission.)

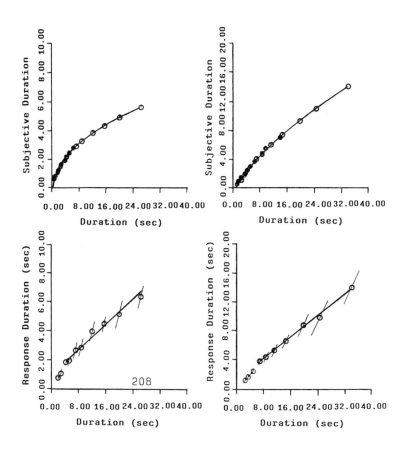

Figure 11. Duration reproduction from a rat (left) and a human observer (right). (From Eisler, 1984.)

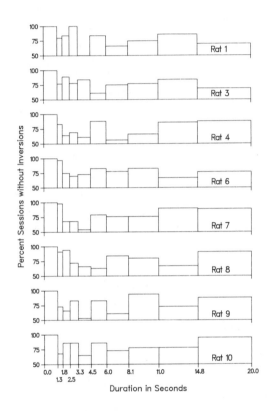

Figure 12. The height of the bars demonstrates the relative probability of one or more lever presses for the time intervals. (From Eisler, 1987. Copyright 1987 by Elsevier Science Publishers. Reprinted by permission.)

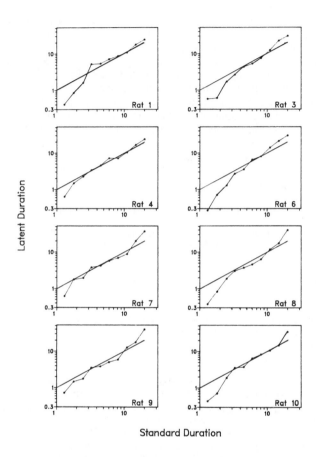

Standard Duration

Figure 13. Latency durations plotted against presented durations for eight rats. The straight line indicates agreement between the two variables. Its slope should be compared with the slope between adjacent points. A line segment parallel to the abscissa indicates "no lever presses" in that time interval, a "hole" in the latency distribution. (From Eisler, 1987. Copyright 1987 by Elsevier Science Publishers. Reprinted by permission.)

Summary

Discontinuities or breaks in the psychophysical function for duration (the function that relates experienced, sensed, duration to clock-time duration) are a general phenomenon. These breaks are found in human observers as well as in rats, they are demonstrated by using different psychophysical methods as magnitude estimation and ratio setting (halving, doubling, reproduction of time intervals). Application of the parallel-clock model (Eisler, 1975) makes it possible to determine the parameters of the psychophysical power function as well as the location of the break from duration reproduction data. Since such data are obtained without requiring numerical responses, rats can be employed as subjects, as well as the perhaps questionable use of numbers by human observers avoided. Discontinuities in the form of holes in latency distributions were found in the learning phase of rats, reminding of the breaks in psychophysical functions. A possible explanation is a shift from one loop to another in a neural network at a certain duration.

Acknowledgement. This work was supported by the Swedish Council for Research in the Humanities and Social Sciences.
Correspondence should be addressed to Hannes Eisler, Department of Psychology, University of Stockholm, S-106 91 Stockholm, Sweden.

References

Eisler, H. (1974). The derivation of Stevens' psychophysical power law. In H.R. Moskowitz, B. Scharf, & J.C. Stevens (Eds.), *Sensation and measurement* (pp. 61−64). Dordrecht, Holland: Reidel.

Eisler, H. (1975). Subjective duration and psychophysics. *Psychological Review*, 82, 429−450.

Eisler, H. (1977). Attention to visually and auditorily presented durations. In S. Dornic (Ed.), *Attention and performance VI* (pp. 247−259). Hillsdale, NJ: Erlbaum.

Eisler, H. (1984). Subjective duration in rats: The psychophysical function. (In J. Gibbon & L. Allan (Eds.), *Timing and time perception* (pp. 43−51). New York: New York Academy of Sciences. (*Annals of the New York Academy of Sciences, 423*.)

Eisler, H. (1987). Timing of rats' lever pressing when learning not to press: Temporal holes in the latency distributions. In E.E. Roskam & R. Suck (Eds.), *Progress in mathematical psychology*, Vol. 1 (pp. 219−232). New York: Elsevier Science Publishers B.V. (North-Holland).

Eisler, H. (1989). Data-equivalent models in psychophysics. In G. Ljunggren & S. Dornic (Eds.), *Psychophysics in action*. Berlin: Springer.

Estel, V. (1885). Neue Versuche über den Zeitsinn. *Philosophische Studien, 2*, 37−65.

Psychophysical Explorations of Mental Structures
Edited by H.-G. Geissler
in collaboration with M.H. Müller and W. Prinz
© 1990 by Hogrefe & Huber Publishers

Chapter 20

Prior Entry: Information Processing Requirements and the Judgment of Temporal Order

Robert B. Wilberg
Van Vliet Centre, University of Alberta
Edmonton, Canada
Richard D. Frey
Department of Psychology, University of Alaska

The order perception of simultaneous and closely sucessive stimuli in different sense modalities had been of experimental interest since the role of attention was first explored in such tasks at Wundt's Leipzig Laboratory in the last half of the 19th century.

Early experiments on both sides of the Atlantic (von Tchisch, 1885; Angell & Pierce, 1891; Geiger, 1902) employed different modifications of a basic methodology that precipitated at least one common finding among researchers engaged in temporal order perception. That is, selective attention could bias the subjective percept of an observer. To explain the common result of these earlier experiments, Titchener (1908) presented his Doctrine of Prior Entry. He offered this law of attention by stating that "the stimulus for which we are predisposed, requires less time than a like stimulus, for which we are unprepared, to produce its full conscious effect" (p. 251). Simply stated, the prior entry hypothesis maintains that when the onsets of two stimuli occur in close temporal proximity, the signal being attended to will enter conscious awareness prior to any other stimulus and thus will be subjectively perceived as having occured first, irrespective of the objective ordering of the signals.

Shortly after Titchener formulated his Doctrine, the phenomenon was somewhat discredited by Dunlap (1910) who concluded that the prior entry effects were due to artifacts associated with the experimental methodology of the earlier researchers. To further test the Doctrine of Prior Entry, and yet avoid the problems which Dunlap had associated with the earlier methodologies, Stone (1926) employed a different experimental paradigm. Subjects were presented auditory-tactual combinations at different stimulus intervals, with each pair of signals discretely presented after a warning signal. Subjects were given varying instructions of attentional set and were then required to report which stimulus occurred first. Titchener's work was supported by Stone's results indicating that subjects would perceive the attended stimulus as occuring first, even though the unattended signal preceded it by up to 50 ms in those discrete dual-stimulus ensembles.

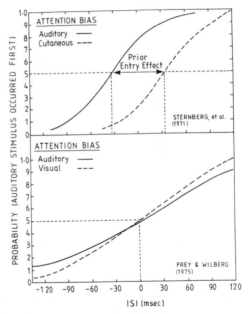

Figure 1. Comparison of results (idealized) on the Sternberg et al. (1971) and Frey and Wilberg (1975) prior entry investigations. The probability of the subject reporting that the auditory stimulus occurred first, is mapped along the ordinate. The various ISIs actually used, with the cutaneous signal becoming progressively delayed relative to the auditory signal, appear along the abscissa. The curve to the left shows the psychometric function when subjects were under an auditory attention bias (i.e. trials when subjects were reacting to the auditory signal); the right hand curve is the same function for the cutaneous bias.

Forty-five years after Stone's work, Sternberg, Knoll, and Gates (1971) repeated her experiment, only unlike Stone or any of the previous workers in this area, these authors attempted to control the attentional bias by something other than instructions, and measured their success by something other then the prior entry effect itself. To do this, they combined judgments of temporal order with a reaction time (RT) task in which subjects reacted to one of two stimuli while withholding a reaction to the other. The subjects in their study produced a mean prior entry effect of over 70 ms. In conjunction with the 50 ms effect found by Stone (1926), these data gave further support to Titchener's "law". Sternberg et al. (1971) concluded by stating that "...the same stimulus pair can be consistently perceived in two different orders, depending on the state of attention" (p. 12).

After Vanderhaeghen and Bertelson (1974) and later Cairney (1975a, 1975b) using signal detection methods failed to find support for the prior entry phenomena, we felt that an explanation for the elusiveness of the effect should be sought. One fairly consistent fact observed during a detailed literature search was that when a prior entry effect was shown, the subjects were either the experimenters themselves, or appeared to have had the phenomenon explained to them. Frey and Wilberg (1975) hypothesized that an a priori knowledge of the prior entry phenomenon predisposed subjects to "produce" the effect. A paradigm closely approximating the one used by Sternberg et al. (1971) was employed; however the naive subjects failed to produce a prior entry effect. The results of the Sternberg et al. study can be compared with those arising from the Frey and Wilberg investigations in the idealized graphs of Figure 1.

Sternberg et al. assigned the 50% point of the psychometric function as the point of subjective simultaneity in that condition, and the difference between the two 50% points (i.e. the distance between the curves) was considered the measure of the prior entry effect.

S. Sternberg (personal communication, February, 1976) suggested that the failure of the Frey and Wilberg (1975) study to find an effect was more likely due to procedural departures from the Sternberg et al. (1971) investigation than it was to the naivety of our subjects. The following experiment was designed to test that notion.

Experiment I

When Frey and Wilberg (1975) attempted to duplicate the paradigm and methods used by Sternberg et al., they assumed that the prior entry phenomenon was robust enough to survive certain procedural changes. These were as follows:

(a) The subjects were not rewarded for fast RT performances although they were provided with RT feedback on every trial.

(b) The cue signal was omitted and only one warning signal was presented to the subject prior to either a catch or a reaction trial.

(c) A reduced catch trial ratio was employed (10% catch trials versus a 50% catch trial ratio in the Sternberg et al. study).

Finally, auditory–visual pairs were used instead of the auditory–cutaneous ensembles.

The first three procedural differences were rectified in this experiment by conforming precisely to the Sternberg et al. format. As well, the equipment was modified so that auditory-cutaneous complication pairs could be used.

If following these modifications, the naive subjects' attention could not be made to bias their order perception, a case for an a priori knowledge effect or some other non-prior entry explanation would need to be entertained. On the other hand, if the data reflected the results obtained by Sternberg et al. the prior entry phenomenon would receive a direct confirmation.

Method

Subjects. Subjects were 6 volunteer graduate students, ages 23−30. They were naive with respect to the Doctrine of Prior Entry and were only told that the study was concerned with reaction time performance.

Task and apparatus. The experimental task was identical to that of Sternberg et al., namely to attend to the two sensory signals from different modalities, respond to the designated one (primary signal) while withholding the response to the non-designated one (auxiliary signal), and then to indicate which signal came first.

The subjects sat in a semidarkened room, with their preferred hands resting on a 24 by 13 cm platform. Immediately in front and mounted vertically was a reaction time lever switch requiring a minimum of 50 gm of force and 3 mm of travel to close. Subjects closed the switch by flexing the index finger on their preferred hand. Two micro-switches, one for each of the sensory modalities, located to the right of the reaction time lever were labelled "EAR" and "ARM" respectively. The subject used these to indicate which of the two signals came first. The time course of events was controlled by a series of interval timers, while the reaction time data was obtained from a digital read-out clock set to provide milliseconds.

Dependent variables. The main variable was the temporal order judgment itself (TOJ). Second, a simple RT complicated by requiring subjects to respond to a primary signal in the temporal presence of an auxiliary signal [Donders' (1868) C-type reaction] while keeping track of the signal order (TOJRT).

Preliminary procedures. Three major preliminary procedures were followed to ensure that the subjects were properly trained and that the actual experiment closely resembled the complication task of Sternberg et al. First, simple RT data was collected for each modality using a Donders' (1886) A-type reaction. These data were used to compute baseline RT performance, a necessary step when assessing the stability of the TOJRT and those complex RTs not involving the additional judgment of temporal order.

Second, to ensure that the attentional bias was both equal and stable in the auditory and cutaneous TOJ conditions, the TOJRT was tested for stability with respect to the complex RTs that occur when TOJs are not required. The up-and-down staircase procedure (Cornsweet, 1962) of adjusting the inter-stimulus interval (ISI) was used to obtain maximum RT stability for the various attentional conditions found in the experiment. A point system of pay–off incentives for fast RT performance was also used to further stabilize performance.

Third, each experimental session (one per day) started with each subject making a cross–modal match for intensity between an invariant 1 kHz, 72 dB SPL burst of white noise and a cutaneous signal, a mild electric shock to the forearm of the non–dominant hand.

Experimental Design

The TOJ from trial to trial was only considered if the RT related with it was equal to or faster than the sensory–related complex RT performance (control data) determined during a preliminary session prior to actual data collection each day. This selection ensured that the TOJ data were as true a reflection of the attentionally biased state as was possible. The examination of TOJ under the various attentional biases were repeated for all subjects. The 50% point of the psychometric function, or point of subjective simultaneity (PSS) were used as the relevant data in an analysis of variance. Within subject data were individually plotted (probit analyses) in accordance with the methodological procedures introduced by Sternberg et al. (1971).

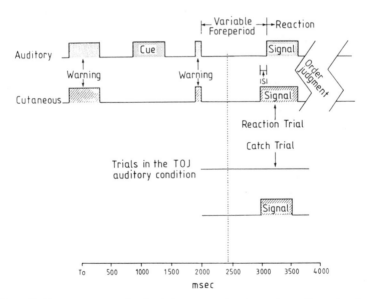

Figure 2. Concurrent temporal order judgment–reaction time task paradigm taken from Sternberg et al. (1971).

Procedure. Two sorts of trials were devised. Reaction trials required the subjects to respond to the primary signal and then make an order judgment. In the catch trial situation, only the auxiliary signal was given requiring no response. The 120 trials per subject were randomized with 50% being catch trials. A graphic representation of the concurrent reaction time task and temporal order judgment employed by Sternberg et al., and used in this series of experiments can be seen in Figure 2.

Both kinds of trials began with a 500 ms bimodal warning signal. There followed a 500 ms cue similar to the primary stimulus to remind the subjects that they were reacting to only the primary signal during that session. After the cue signal, there occured a final 40 ms bimodal warning, then a variable foreperiod followed by either a catch trial or a reaction trial. On a catch trial these preliminary signals were followed only by the auxiliary signal. Any reaction on these trials were penalized. On a reaction trial, both signals occurred with a positive or negative inter-stimulus interval (ISI) between them. For example, an ISI_{-90} indicated that the cutaneous signal preceded onset of the auditory signal by 90 ms, whereas an ISI_{30} indicated an auditory lead of 30 ms over the cutaneous signal. The subjects pressed the lever as quickly as was possible after the primary signal occurred and then indicated which of the two signals, auditory or cutaneous, seemed to have occurred first. Quick responses (speeded RT) were rewarded in an effort to ensure maximum attention towards the signal ensemble. Because the bimodal signals immediately ceased when the reaction time switch was pressed, the subjects may not have been be confident about the temporal order of the signals. In such instance, subjects were instructed to guess.

Results and Discussion

Reaction time performance remained fast and stable throughout the experiment, precipitating the assumption that attention was sufficiently biased towards the primary signal. With the exception of one subject who evidenced a 39 ms reversal effect, all subjects demonstrated a prior entry effect ranging from 11 to 69 ms. The average effect across subjects was 22 ms for the temporal order data (see Figure 3). However, when the inter-stimulus interval (ISI) points of subjective simultaneity for each subject in each attentional condition were analyzed, the prior entry effect was not supported (F $(1,4)=2.34$, $p>.10$).

The importance of this failure to gain significance should be tempered by the fact that Sternberg et al. did not statistically analyze the magnitude of their prior entry effect. Nor did Cairney (1975a) indicate observed PSS data for subjects in the different conditions he examined. Consequently it is difficult to assess the meaning of the various studies to each other. Of interest however was the fact that contrary to the Frey and Wilberg (1975) study, an individually reliable prior entry trend was realized in five of the six subjects.

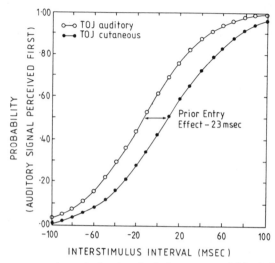

Figure 3. The mean psychometric functions for both sensory modalities is best exemplified by Subject 2 in Experiment 1.

Experiment 2

The one remaining difference between the Frey and Wilberg (1975) investigation which failed to obtain a prior entry effect, and those of Experiment 1 and Sternberg et al. (1971), was that of sensory modality. The former used auditory–visual pairs, the latter two had auditory–cutaneous pairs. Given the fact that other authors such as Stone (1926) found prior entry effects using auditory and tactile modalities, we considered the possibility that auditory-cutaneous complications were required for an optimal effect to occur. That is, if auditory–visual pairs, naive subjects, and the Sternberg et al. methodology were employed, would the prior entry effect occur?

Procedure. The experimental conditions were identical to that of Experiment 1 with the exception that the cutaneous signal was replaced by a visual stimulus (a 1 cm diameter neon light located 75 cm from the seated subject at eye level). Subjects, again were 6 graduate students with no a priori knowledge of the prior entry doctrine.

Results and Discussion

The reaction time performance remained fast and stable throughout all conditions of this experiment. Once again, five of the six subjects experienced a prior entry shift, with Subject 6 evidencing a reversal. A mean prior entry effect of 39 ms was obtained at the PSS, but it failed to be significant (*F*

(1,4)=3.50, *p*>.10) even though it exceeded a 30 ms shift for some of the auditory-visual pairs reported by Sternberg et al. (1971). The psychometric functions for the visual and auditory modalities of Subject 5 can be seen in Figure 4. The results are representative of those subjects who showed a prior entry shift.

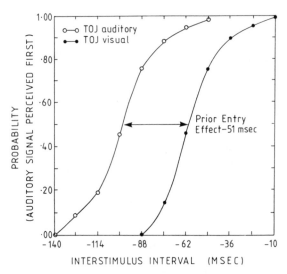

Figure 4. A prior entry effect of 51 ms produced by Subject 5 in Experiment 2.

Although a larger mean prior entry effect at the PSS was reached in this experiment using audiovisual pairs (22 ms in Experiment 1), a case cannot be made for or against an a priori hypothesis. That is, while the perceptual shift at the PSS for the total group was not significant in either experiment, ten of the twelve subjects demonstrated individually reliable prior entry effects. These results are interpreted as suggesting that neither the particular complication sensory pairs used, nor the presence or absence of knowledge about the Doctrine appeared to have any effect whatsoever upon the extent to which a prior entry effect could be observed.

Experiment 3

The results of the first two experiments and those of Sternberg et al. (1971), do not help define either the role or locus of the attentive processes in the biasing of order perception. There seems to be little evidence that the extent or direction of perceptual biasing can be controlled by further constraining the subject's attention to one signal or another. The exact cause of the prior entry phenomenon remains unclear.

Of the contemporary hypotheses put forward to account for the prior entry effect (see Sternberg & Knoll, 1973, for an overview) those whose themes involve the concept of unequal post-detection sensory channel processing have perhaps enjoyed the greatest attention. They hypothesize that subjective awareness of temporal RT task, processing subsequent to signal detection is not equal for the attended and unattended channels. The occurrence of the primary (attended) signal not only carries its onset information or "temporal marker" (Sperling & Reeves, 1980), but also the decision and directive to initiate a response. Consequently the attended signal requires more processing relative to the auxiliary (unattended) signal. The suggestion is that detection of the appropriate primary signal for a speeded response requires more of the limited processing capacity than does rejection of the unattended auxiliary signal.

The fact that an attended signal is more often perceived as occurrring first is viewed as a function of unequal post detection processing favouring the attended channel, and in turn affects a central temporal order decision mechanism. The hypothesis maintains that the actual arrival times of the two signals corresponds to the objective state of their onsets. The assumed mediator in the prior entry phenomenon is the relative amount of processing assigned to the two singals subsequent to detection.

A test of the unequal post detection signal processing hypothesis using the basic concurrent temporal order judgment RT task devised by Sternberg et al. would require that the following points be considered. First, the subjects must continue to be constrained such that they are maximally biased towards the primary signal. Second, that the subjects be forced to analyze both the primary and the auxiliary signal subsequent to detection. That is, the subjects must treat both signals in a more analytical manner than that of a simple trigger (which only requires that the subject acknowledge the simple occurence of a signal). Consequently the relative effects of the extra response initiation information in the attended channel would be lessened by forcing the subjects to consider the nature of the two signals more equally. Such a modification to the paradigm should, if the unequal processing hypothesis is correct, reduce or perhaps even eliminate the prior entry effect.

Task, apparatus, and subjects. The experimental task was similar to that used in the two previous experiments. The modified paradigm required that immediately after responding to the primary signal (the RT portion of the task) the subject had to indicate which one of two possible signal levels actually occurred in either the primary signal or the auxiliary signal. The experimenter randomly selected the particular modality to be interrogated. Three lamps of equal intensity coloured white (cue), red, and amber, housed under a common diffusion lens (8 mm wide), were used to provide the cue and the two signal levels in the visual modality. The complementary auditory signals were cue (1,000 Hz), low (750 Hz), and high (1500 Hz). Subjects were 6 volunteer graduate students with no previous experience in psycho-motor research nor had any knowledge of the Doctrine of Prior Entry.

Preliminary procedures. The preliminary procedures described in Experiment 1 were modified to account for the various tone and light signals and their combinations. The same stringent requirements constraining the subjects, and the necessary RT performance stabilities needed to ensure maximal biasing, were adhered to.

Procedure. The usual preliminary warning signal, appropriate primary stimulus cue, final bimodal warning signal, and variable foreperiod were given. Following this sequence, one of the visual–auditory signal ensembles with incorporated ISI occurred. These ensembles consisted of equiprobable pairings of high or low tone with red or amber lamps. As usual, immediately upon closing the RT switch, the light–tone ensemble used in that particular trial disappeared. The experimenter then verbally indicated which signal, primary or auxiliary was to be interrogated further. The subjects verbally responded with the nature (level) of the specified signal and whether it came first or last. All other procedures, catch trial ratios, etc. were identical to those used earlier.

Results

As in previous experiments, RT performance remained fast and stable throughout all trials. A 1.25% error rate for all subjects, spread equally over all ISI conditions and in both modalities led to the assumption that post detection processing was relatively equal in both channels. Contrary to the predicted prior entry attenuation postulated by an unequal post detection processing model, a massive prior entry effect of 116 ms surfaced. Unlike the results of Experiments 1 and 2, there was a significant difference between the points of subjective simultaneity of the different attentional conditions (F $(1,4)=9.86$, $p<.05$). The graphs of the psychometric functions shown by Subject 1 in Figure 5 are typical of most subjects. One subject exhibited a very small (10 ms) reversal effect.

Discussion

The results of Experiments 1 and 2 demonstrate that a prior entry effect in the positive direction can be realized in most naive subjects providing their attentional efforts can be made to bias perception. To this end, the concurrent temporal order judgment RT task devised by Sternberg et al. (1971) appears effective when using either auditory–cutaneous or auditory–visual pairs, if the attentional constraints on the subjects are strictly maintained. These constraints require at the outset that the subjects attain speeded responses to signal ensembles that are faster on average when a TOJ is also required than when no such judgment is required (see preliminary procedure, Experiment 1). As well, an extremely high catch trial to true trial ratio, such as 1:1 is imperative in order to maintain levels of event uncertainty that force the subjects to attend maximally to the "cued" primary signal.

However, even when the experimental constraints on the temporal order RT task are met, there is no guarantee as to either the extent or direction to which the attentive processes can be seen to bias attention. For example, the grouped data in Experiments 1 and 2 measured at the 50% point of the psychometric functions (PSS) did not reach significance whereas the individual subject effect was reliable. While this failure may not by itself be of much importance, it does point to the uniqueness of the effect as experienced by various individuals. This observation is underscored by the negative prior entry effects (reversals) perceived by some subjects.

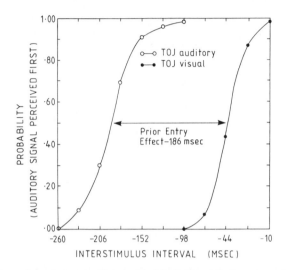

Figure 5. A massive prior entry effect produced by Subject 1 in Experiment 3.

The third experiment arose out of a general dissatisfaction with the lack of experimental control over the prior entry effect. From the results of the first two experiments it seemed that simply forcing subjects to expend the bulk of their attentive energies towards a cued primary signal was a necessary but insufficient experimental condition. That is, the concurrent temporal order judgment task and associated paradigm might allow the phenomenon to occur; but by itself was incapable of controlling either the direction of magnitude of the effect. According to Kahneman (1973), there is a limit to the effectiveness of attentional effort, in that only a certain amount can be allocated from a finite attentional pool and applied to the task situation.

The modifications made to the basic concurrent temporal order judgment RT task achieved two goals. First, the changes forced the subjects to process the two signals in the ensemble more equally following detection. Secondly, it increased the amount of information that had to be errorlessly processed while at the same time maintaining the fast and stable reaction time performances evidenced in the first two experiments (see Table 1). Though not statistically testable, the control (trials taken before each session, not requring the TOJ) and experimental RT data are comparable, both within and between experiments.

The modifications to the task and the resultant performances taken together suggest that the extent and direction of the prior entry effect can be controlled by the amount of information being processed. However, the role played by the information processing act in the biasing of temporal order remains unclear.

Table 1. Concurrent temporal order judgment—RT task performance with (Experimental) and without (Control) the TOJ.

	Auditory		Cutaneous/Visual[d]	
Experiment	Mean[a]	Std.Dev	Mean	Std.Dev.
Control Trials[b]				
1	208	36	242	38
2	201	31	230	28
3	220	18	280	36
Experimental Trial[c]				
1	201	31	237	31
2	195	32	206	23
3	212	36	280	37

[a] RT given in msec
[b] 40 trials per subject
[c] 120 trials per subject
[d] Cutaneous used in Experiment 1 only

Laming (1979), commenting on errors produced by responding to the incorrect signal in two-choice RT experiments, raises the possibility that subjects may respond to (process) the pre-exposure field (for example, a non-biased first occurring signal) because it "may look like a correspondingly brief sample from the reaction stimulus" (p. 214). As such, it could interfere with the subsequent decision-making. Shaw (1978) suggests that the order in which stimuli are processed from a display, may very well depend upon the relative magnitudes of their respective probabilities. That is, subjects would preferentially order the processing of highly probable (highly biased) signals. Sperling and Reeves (1980), on the other hand, report two separate factors to account for the preservation of order information. When the informational requirements are low (they used varying rates at which sequences of numerals were presented), subjects establish temporal markers which can be used later, in conjunction with signal strength, to reconstruct the actual order of the numeral sequence. At high numeral presentation rates, only the single factor of signal strength is available to preserve item order.

These possible accounts for the biasing temporal order through the act of information processing are not compelling explanations for the temporal order effects found in the Sternberg et al. paradigm. The low error rates in all the experiments reported here indicate that the number of reaction errors and the speed of response are independent of the order in which the biased stimulus appears in the stimulus ensemble. A high rate of sequential presentation seems unlikely to be the information processing factor, operating in the judgment of temporal order. Finally, the stimuli used in the ensemble were matched for equality of intensity. These possibilities can therefore be eliminated as factors that may have biased the judgments of temporal order in the above experiments.

If the perception of temporal order is controlled by the biasing of attention to one signal over another, three hypotheses are likely; two of them requiring an unequal signal processing hypothesis subsequent to detection.

First, the relative amount of channel processing remains the prime determiner as to which signal will rise to consciousness first. However the effect is incremented by the amount that must be processed in the biased channel. Processing demands in the unbiased channel are not essential to the phenomenon. That is, the relatively unequal signal processing (attentionally directed) biases the central temporal order mechanism; but only increasing the processing demands in the biased channel will elongate the effect.

Second, again the relative amount of post detection signal processing under maximal attentional bias is the basic determiner of temporal order. However since the subjects may be interrogated about either channel, they must process both, and it is this total load that suppresses the unattended signal's rise to consciousness. Unequal signal processing following detection creates the bias; but total processing load extends it.

Finally, subsequent to detection, the total amount of information in both the biased and unbiased channels together enhance a subject's predisposition to perceive the attentionally biased signal as occurring first. In this instance, the biasing of attention towards the primary signal is the theoretical imperative, and not the relative amount of post detection processing. That is, it is the attentional factors that bias the temporal order mechnism and not post detection processing. Attentional constraints predispose the subject; total processing requirements extend the effect.

The third alternative is perhaps the most acceptable because it supports the unidirectional relationship between attention and processing not readily discernable in the unequal post detection processing varieties. That is, "controlled" processing requires attention, but the act of selectively attending does not mean that one is actually processing information. The fact that maximum attention is a basic requirement of the prior entry phenomenon can be seen in the failure to observe the effect (see Figure 1) when the attentional constraints were insufficient. Yet maximum attention when coupled with low signal processing demands only resulted in marginal prior entry effects and a high degree of variability between subjects (see Experiment 1 and 2).

However, when subjects were forced to analyze the precise nature of both the biased and unbiased signals in the ensemble (Experiment 3), a massive prior entry effect was produced. This increase was not due to a trade-off in time spent analyzing the ensemble prior to its disappearance, because the TOJ reaction time (TOJRT) in all three experiments and their controls were comparable. Because the subjects knew they could be interrogated about the nature of either signal, processing had to be relatively equal in both sensory channels. This would militate against any hypothesis which uses relative unequal post detection processing as its prime tenant.

The extra processing involved in Experiment 3 did not arise from making the twin signal ensemble physically more complex. The signal display itself in each of the experiments was similar, but in the third experiment subjects knew that either signal could be interrogated. Consequently we believe it is the addition of the processing demands to the predisposition, enabled by maximally biasing attention to the primary signal, that is responsible for the extent and direction of the prior entry phenomenon. Whether this relationship is interactive in more than a simple additive sense remains to be seen.

Summary

When two asynchronous events occur closely together in time, we perceive the event to which our attention has been biased as having occurred first, regardless of their actual empirical order. Titchener (1908) used this phenomenon as the basis for his Doctrine of Prior Entry. The assumed cause of this mistake in temporal order perception is the unequal post-detection processing of the attended (biased) signal, relative to the unattended signal. Strong, reliable prior entry effects however have been difficult to obtain, even when subjects are maximally constrained towards the imperative signal.

In a series of experiments, based upon a paradigm used by Sternberg, Knoll and Gates (1971), we examined the prior entry effect using naive subjects and auditory/tactile or auditory/visual stimulus pairs in a reaction time procedure complicated by a temporal order judgment. The results of the experiments compel us to reject the unequal post-detection processing hypothesis in favor of one which reflects the combined processing load of both the attended and unattended channels, in the presence of a channel specific attentional constraint.

Correspondence should be addressed to Robert B. Wilberg, Van Vliet Centre, University of Alberta, Edmonton, Alberta, Canada T6G 2H9.

References

Angell, J., & Pierce, A. (1891). Experimental research upon the phenomena of attention. *American Journal of Psychology, 4,* 528–541.

Cairney, P.T. (1975a). Bisensory order judgment and the prior entry hypothesis. *Acta Psychologica, 39,* 329–340.

Cairney, P.T. (1975b). The complication experiment uncomplicated. *Perception, 4,* 255–265.

Cornsweet, T. (1962). The staircase-method in psychophysics. *American Journal of Psychology, 75,* 485–491.

Donders, F. (1868/69). Over de snelheid van psychishe processen. *Ondezalkingen geddan in her Physiologisch Laboratorium der Utrechtache Hoogeschool, Tweede reeks, II,* 92–120.

Dunlap, K. (1910). The complication experiment and related phenomena. *Psychological Review, 17,* 157–191.

Frey, R.D., & Wilberg, R.B. (1975). Selective attention and the judgment of temporal order. *Movement, 7,* 63–65.

Geiger, M. (1902). Neue Complikationsversuche. *Philosophische Studien, 18,* 347–435.

Kahneman, D. (1973). *Attention and effort.* Englewood Cliffs, NJ: Prentice-Hall.

Laming, D. (1979). Choice reaction performance following an error. *Acta Psychologica, 43,* 199–224.

Shaw, M.L. (1978). A capacity allocation model for reaction time. *Journal of Experimental Psychology: Human Perception and Performance, 4,* 586–598.

Sperling, G., & Reeves, A. (1980). Measuring the reaction time of a shift of visual attention. In R.S. Nickerson (Ed.), *Attention and Performance VIII.* Hillsdale, NJ: Erlbaum.

Sternberg, S., & Knoll, R.L. (1973). The perception of temporal order: Fundamental issues and a general model. In S. Kornblum (Ed.), *Attention and Performance IV* (pp.629–685). New York. Academic Press.

Sternberg, S., Knoll, R., & Gates, B. (1971). Prior entry reexamined: Effect of attentional bias on order perception. Paper presented at the meeting of the Psychonomic Society, St. Louis, LA, 1971.

Stone, S. (1926). Prior entry in the auditory-tactile complication. *American Journal of Psychology, 37,* 284–287.

Titchener, E. (1908). *Lectures on the elementary psychology of feeling and attention.* New York: Macmillan.

Vanderhaeghen, C., & Bertelson, P. (1974). The limits of prior entry: Non-sensitivity of temporal order judgments to selective preparation affecting choice reaction time. *Bulletin of the Psychonomic Society, 4,* 569–572.

von Tchisch, W. (1885). Ueber die Zeitverhaeltnisse der Apperception einfacher und zusammengesetzter Vorstellungen, untersucht mit Huelfe der Complicationsmethode. *Philosophische Studien, 2,* 603–634.

Psychophysical Explorations of Mental Structures
Edited by H.-G. Geissler
in collaboration with M.H. Müller and W. Prinz
© 1990 by Hogrefe & Huber Publishers

Chapter 21

Timing Mechanisms and the Threshold for Duration

Alfred B. Kristofferson
Department of Psychology, McMaster University
Hamilton, Canada

There are several reasons why the time sense is an ideal object of study using the methods and logic of threshold psychophysics. The stimulus can be controlled easily and precisely and it is one-dimensional, except for very brief durations. The afferent part of the system appears to be highly stable and there is no distortion due to transduction, at least for certain uses to which the stimulus may be put. It is a noise-free system, at least for simple discriminations, when the subject is highly practiced. Because of these features, under certain conditions the form and parameters of the psychophysical data appear to be determined entirely by central timing mechanisms. Those mechanisms can also be identified in behavioral data which are not usually thought of as psychophysical and an integrated set of concepts and multiple behavioral operations is gradually being established.

While the time sense is an ideal object for psychophysical study, it is probably not a very satisfactory model of sensory systems in general. One reason for saying this is that the form of the psychometric function which is appropriate for the duration dimension may be unique to it. Another reason is that the detection of differences in duration is strongly influenced by practice and the practice effects may extend over thousands of trials, as well as being specific to a particular value of the stimulus. Other sensory systems do not seem to have this property, and in this respect the time sense resembles motor skills more than it does other sensory processes.

The Duration Threshold

The duration threshold is defined here as one-half of the minimum difference in duration between two stimuli which yields perfect discrimination between them. This definition is possible because the psychometric function appears to be fully-bounded, as shown in Figure 1.

The probability of a response "long", plotted against stimulus duration, is a sigmoidal function, as shown in the upper part of the figure. Instead of a normal ogive, it is the cumulative form of the isosceles triangle shown in the lower part of the figure. For a highly-practiced subject, perfect performance is achieved for stimuli which differ from the mean by plus or minus one quantum or more.

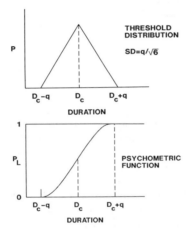

Figure 1. An isosceles triangle is an adequate representation of the distribution of duration thresholds. The cumulative form of the triangle (below) is the psychometric function which is fitted to data. The parameter q, so obtained, is the time quantum and the duration threshold.

The psychometric function is very similar to a normal ogive and it is difficult to distinguish between them empirically. However, we were able to present evidence favoring the triangle in 1971 (Allan, Kristofferson, & Wiens, 1971) and further support has accumulated since.

The threshold distribution which generates the psychometric function is a triangle spanning two time quanta and the size of the quantum measures its variability, the standard deviation being the quantum size divided by the square root of 6. The threshold is an internal threshold; all of the variability is generated internally, the afferent latencies of the stimuli marking the stimulus duration being deterministic (Kristofferson, 1977, 1980, 1984).

Two duration stimuli which differ by two quanta, or more, can be discriminated perfectly. The time quantum is the threshold and with good experimental control it can be measured free of distortion by noise, response bias and effects of irrelevant variables. It can be measured using other behavioral methods as well (see, e.g., Kristofferson, 1967, 1983) and it is this general quantitative agreement, rather than curve–fitting, which supports the strong statements I have made above about threshold measurement.

Laws of Behavioral Timing

The timing of events within the central nervous system shows great precision and flexibility. Michon (1985) emphasizes the flexibility, arguing that the organism can construct a time base appropriate for a task by selecting among multiple options. I agree, and from my narrower and more empirical viewpoint, I have recently proposed three theoretical laws or principles of timing which may provide some of those options (Kristofferson, 1984).

The Quantal Law

Central timing is sometimes controlled by a fast, stable periodic process with a period which is the time quantum. This process controls the flow of information by determining the instants at which information can move from A to B within the system, including the instants at which attention can switch from one input channel to another. Quantum size varies a little between individuals and is stable within one individual. It is not a single value. Instead, quantum sizes form doubles set with nominal values of 12.5, 25, 50, 100, and probably 200 msec. The mean value of q_{50} over individuals is actually 48 msec and it varies about 10% between individuals. The quantum was first identified in experiments on reaction time and on successiveness discrimination and first reported in 1967 (Kristofferson, 1967).

The quantum introduces uniform distributions of waiting times into the flow of information. The convolution of two such element distributions is an isosceles triangle, as in Figure 1.

The Deterministic Law

The time which elapses between A and B in the flow of information sometimes is timed perfectly so that repetitions of the internal time interval all have the same value. Increasing the length of the interval introduces no added variability, in such cases. This principle was first reported in 1976, based upon experiments on response–stimulus synchronization (Kristofferson, 1976).

The Statistical Law

Sometimes, increasing the time interval between *A* and *B* is accompanied by a continuous increase in variability. Figure 2 is an example from inter-response timing in tapping experiments by Wing and Kristofferson (1973). The standard deviation of the central timekeeper appears to be directly proportional to the mean and the ratio of SD to mean, the Weber ratio, is 0.023.

The question of whether it is the standard deviation, rather than the variance, which is proportional to the mean is not answered by the data in Figure 2 because the range of means is too narrow. On the basis of experiments now underway, I am convinced that Weber's Law is the correct statement of the Statistical Law, as I will show below.

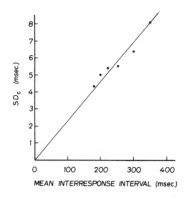

Figure 2. SD_c is the standard deviation of the intervals timed by the central timekeeper which controls interresponse intervals in isochronous tapping. Ratio of this SD to the mean interresponse time $= 0.023$. Means for five subjects. (Wing & Kristofferson, 1973)

Threshold and Base Duration

In two papers (Kristofferson, 1980, 1984), I have shown that threshold as a function of base duration sometimes obeys the strict form of Weber's Law and sometimes is a quantal step function. These results are summarized schematically in Figure 3.

The upper dashed line is the result obtained when the subject has had no prior practice at each base duration (Kristofferson, 1980) or when base duration is changed from session to session so that no specific practice is possible (Getty, 1975). The Weber ratio of standard deviation to mean of the threshold distribution is 0.05, in these cases. Others have obtained a similar result (see Macar, 1985).

The crucial condition for obtaining the quantal step function is prolonged practice at each specific base duration. As practice proceeds, steps swing down from the Weber's Law line and eventually become flat when practice is complete. The quantum sizes, which are shown as standard deviations in the figure, are then the members of the doubles set from 12.5 to 200 msec. As base duration increases, quantum size doubles each time base duration reaches 16 times the current quantum size. Thus, the step at 800 goes from $q=50$ to $q=100$.

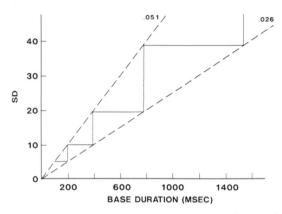

Figure 3. Schematic summary of the standard deviation of the duration threshold as a function of base duration. The dashed lines show that Weber's Law sometimes holds with a constant of proportionality of 0.051, sometimes one-half of that. Sometimes the function is the solid line, which is the quantal step function. The text discusses the conditions under which each of the three functions is obtained.

We see all three timing laws in this set of data. The full set of quantum values is present. So is Weber's Law. Deterministic timing is also represented, but it is less obvious. It resides in the flatness of the steps. We have shown that the mechanism of duration discrimination in these experiments is a race between the end of an internally–timed interval initiated by stimulus onset and the end of the stimulus. If the internally–timed interval ends before the stimulus ends, the stimulus is called "long". The isosceles triangle is the distribution of times of occurrence of the internal criterion. A flat step means that the internally timed interval can be increased in mean, as base duration increases, without increasing in variability. That is characteristic of deterministic timing according to Real–Time Criterion Theory (Kristofferson, 1977).

The diagram in Figure 3 is constructed using the mean value of q over individuals, 48 msec at the q_{50} level, and the $16q$ rule. That gives the Weber ratio of 0.051. The lower dashed line has a slope which is one-half that of the upper dashed line, as dictated by the quantum doubling. The lower line corresponds closely to the line we saw earlier in Figure 2 which describes inter-response timekeeping. Is this approximate halving of the Weber ratio a difference between motor and perceptual timing or can it be attributed to something else?

Explicit and Implicit Internal Standards

The quantal step function was obtained using the "many-to-few" psychophysical method (Allan & Kristofferson, 1974). One stimulus is presented on each trial, which the subject classfies as being long or short, and knowledge of results is provided. The stimulus is one out of a set like that is shown in Figure 4a. The time between two auditory pulses is the duration stimulus. The stimulus durations in a set are symmetrical around a midpoint; those less than the midpoint are short, the others long. The *MP* is the base duration.

Practice leads to the development of an internal standard against which presented stimuli are compared. This internal standard is the real-time criterion represented by the triangular distribution and its mean value comes to be set very close to the MP of the stimulus set. The internal standard is implicit, a stimulus equal to the *MP* is never presented. Instead, the internal standard must be computed from stimulus instances none of which is equal to the desired value.

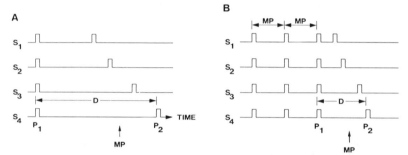

Figure 4. Sets of duration stimuli for (a) the many-to-few method and (b) the pulse train method. *D* is the duration of each stimulus and *MP* is the midpoint value of *D* for the stimulus set.

In the tapping experiments (Wing & Kristofferson, 1973), the desired internal standard is supplied to the subject as a stimulus, i.e., the standard is explicit. Each sequence of responses begins with a certain number of stimulus pulses in an isochronous series. Responses are synchronized to these, the desired rate is set, and then the stimulus pulses cease but the responses continue, hopefully at the desired rate. Thus the internal standard is made explicit. Motivated initially by an interest in the work in "stop reaction time" by ten Hoopen, Vos and Dispa (1982), we are now measuring duration thresholds using an explicit standard. A stimulus set for this "pulse train duration discrimination" method is shown in Figure 4b. The duration stimuli are the same as in the many-to-few method, except now the *MP* of the simulus set is given to the subject by an isochronous series which precedes each duration stimulus. Therefore, on each trial one stimulus is presented which consists of an isochronous series of pulses in which the final pulse is either slightly advanced or delayed. Knowing the number of pulses in advance, the subject must decide whether the final interpulse interval is long or short.

Our initial hypothesis was that the isochronous pulses would, on each trial, establish an internal rhythm and that the displacement of the final pulse would be detected as a disparity from a continuation of that rhythm. That is not what happens, as we have found in several different experiments. The most convincing of these is one by Jezdic (1986) who changed the number of pulses in the stimulus train from session to session but held it fixed within a session. Over the range $2-7$, the number of pulses does not affect discrimination. This is true even when $n=2$, which is the critical condition here. When $n=2$, the method is the same as the many-to-few method, and the internal standard established in sessions with $n>2$ transfers perfectly to $n=2$ sessions. Thus, the internal standard established by an isochronous pulse train is stored in memory and is not simply stimulus driven.

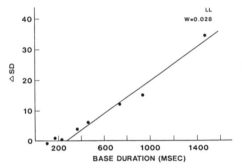

Figure 5. Pulse train duration discrimination results for Subject LL. The *SD* on the vertical axis is the *SD* corresponding to the increase in variance due to increasing base duration. Below base durations of 278 msec, changes in base duration have no effect upon threshold. Correlation coefficient above 278 msec = .987.

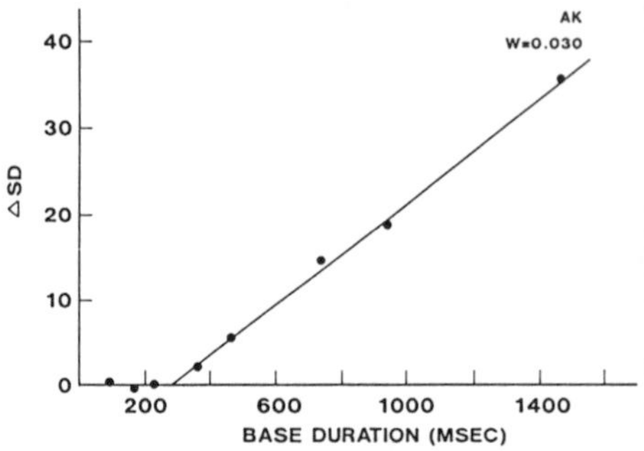

Figure 6. Same as Figure 5, but for Subject AK. Intercept at 286 msec, correlation coefficient = .999. Each data point is based upon at least ten experimental sessions (*N* = 3000) which follow extensive, specific practice.

Gary Foster and I now determine base duration functions using the pulse train method with $n=4$. Two subjects have been completed and the results are shown in Figures 5 and 6. Practice is a less significant factor with this method. Usually, ten sessions are sufficient to yield stable performance at each base duration and the improvement with practice over those ten sessions is only about 10%.

The base duration functions are the same in shape as the function obtained for response–stimulus synchronization (Kristofferson, 1976). For small base durations, timing is deterministic and the standard deviation of the threshold distribution in this deterministic region is 3.5 msec for LL and 4.2 msec for AK, respectively. That variance has been subtracted from the obtained variance at each base duration to derive the standard deviations plotted here in order to show that the variability increases above the deterministic level obeys Weber's Law, as is also the result of response–stimulus synchronization. In our case the Weber fraction is 0.03, as it is for response–stimulus synchronization, and is in good agreement with the lower dashed line in Figure 3.

Interresponse Timing

Foster and I are also working with motor timing over a wider range than in earlier work. One of our major interests is in the role of practice. We find that prolonged and specific practice is important here, too, at least for some subjects. Figure 7 is the first complete set of data. It agrees well with Figure 2, and the range is wide enough to enable us to conclude that *SD*, not variance, is linearly related to mean. However, we are facing some problems. For means in the middle range, stationarity is not achieved satisfactorily, even with extensive practice. The model which separates central timing from motor delay variance cannot be applied. The two data points above the line in Figure 7 reflect this fact. But there are some successful attempts to bring this under better experimental control.

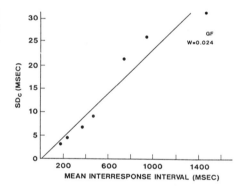

Figure 7. Tapping data obtained with the same continuation method as that in Figure 2. $SD_c = 0.024M - 0.32$.

Concluding Remarks

Figure 3 states an empirical generalization which should have considerable theoretical power if further evidence continues to support it. It suggests that the three laws of timing are interconnected and that all of them might be derived from a single logical mechanism.

There is now substantial support for Weber's Law as the proper statement for the statistical law of timing. The Weber ratio may exhibit the same doubling phenomenon as does the time quantum, although the evidence for that so far is weak and research explicitly directed at that proposition is needed. In this connection I point out that Snodgrass, Luce, and Galanter (1967) concluded that the Weber ratio for time estimates is about 0.10, so perhaps there is support for three values of a doubles set for the Weber ratio.

The memory representation of a time interval, which controls the internal timing of a reproduction of the interval, may differ depending upon the way in which the memory is encoded. Encoding by computation from dissimiliar instances may permit retrieval only via a quantal route. Encoding from exact stimulus instances is different. I cannot carry this theorizing further at present.

Summary

The quantal, deterministic, and statistical laws of timing are described briefly. These empirical principles arose from experiments on successiveness discrimination, reaction time, and response–stimulus synchronization, and it is shown that all these laws, with similar numerical constants, describes duration discrimination and the dependence of duration threshold upon base duration, as well.

The threshold measure base duration function follows the statistical law under some conditions, and the quantal–deterministic laws under other conditions. Among the important controlling conditions are the quantity and quality of practice, and the way in which the internal standard is encoded into memory.

Some current experiments dealing with these controlling conditions are described. These experiments are not yet complete. They include experiments on motor response timing and are attempting to bring the timing of inter-response interval within the framework of the three laws in order to compare motor timing with perceptual timing.

Correspondence should be addressed to Alfred B. Kristofferson, Department of Psychology, McMaster University, 1280 Main Street West, Hamilton, Ontario L8S 4K1, Canada

References

Allan, L.G., Kristofferson, A.B., & Wiens, E.W. (1971). Duration discrimination of brief light flashes. *Perception & Psychophysics, 9*, 327–334.

Allan, L.G., & Kristofferson, A.B. (1974). Judgments about the duration of brief stimuli. *Perception & Psychophysics, 15*, 434–440.

Getty, D.J. (1975). Discrimination of short temporal intervals: A comparison of two models. *Perception & Psychophysics, 18*, 1–8.

Jezdic, D.D. (1986). *The effects of varying pulse train length on apparent q-values in memory driven duration discrimination.* Honours thesis, Department of Psychology, McMaster University, Hamilton, Canda.

Kristofferson, A.B. (1967). Attention and psychophysical time. *Acta Psychologica, 27*, 93–100.

Kristofferson, A.B. (1976). Low–variance stimulus–response latencies: deterministic internal delays? *Perception & Psychophysics, 20*, 89–100.

Kristofferson, A.B. (1977). A real–time criterion theory of duration discrimination. *Perception & Psychophysics, 21*, 105–117.

Kristofferson, A.B. (1980). A quantal step function in duration discrimination. *Perception & Psychophysics*, *27*, 300–306.

Kristofferson, A.B. (1984). Quantal and deterministic timing in human duration discrimination. In J. Gibbon & L. Allan (Eds.), *Timing and time perception* (Annals of the New York Academy of Sciences, Vol. 423, 3–15). New York: The New York Academy of Sciences.

Macar, F. (1985). Time psychophysics and related models. In J.A. Michon & J.L. Jackson (Eds.), *Time, mind, and behavior*. Berlin: Springer.

Michon, J.A. (1985). The complete time experiencer. In J.A. Michon & J.L. Jackson (Eds.), *Time, mind, and behavior*. Berlin: Springer.

Snodgrass, J.G., Luce, R.D., & Galanter, E. (1967). Some experiments on simple and choice reaction time. *Journal of Experimental Psychology*, *75*, 1–17.

ten Hoopen, G., Vos, J., & Dispa, J. (1982). Interaural and monaural clicks and clocks: Tempo difference versus attention switching. *Journal of Experimental Psychology: Human Perception and Performance*, *8*, 422–434.

Wing, A.M., & Kristofferson, A.B. (1973). Response delays and the timing of discrete motor responses. *Perception & Psychophysics*, *14*, 5–12.

Psychophysical Explorations of Mental Structures
Edited by H.-G. Geissler
in collaboration with M.H. Müller and W. Prinz
© 1990 by Hogrefe & Huber Publishers

Chapter 22

The Structure of Internal
Representations and
Reaction–Time Related
Matching Task Phenomena

Klaus–Dieter Schmidt and Birgit Ackermann
Sektion Psychologie, Karl–Marx–Universität
Leipzig, G.D.R.

Studies in visual recognition usually seek to understand human perception in terms of underlying processes. In this respect matching task phenomena such as same–different or name–physical disparity which arise in a situation when subjects classify pairs of stimuli as the same or different, and in which reaction time is measured, are particularly informative. However, it is only fair to say that until now a unifying model is not yet in sight and that the discussion of specific phenomena is still rather controversial. This situation is reflected by approaches assuming processes behind same and different or identity and category matches (Bamber, 1969; Nickerson, 1978; Posner, 1978) by the reference to different principles of explanation such as levels of processing, facilitation vs. inhibition (for a review, see Proctor, 1981) or by attempts to attribute phenomena either to decision or response stages (Krueger, 1978; Ratcliff & Hacker, 1981).

In this paper it is assumed that the unsatisfactory situation is due to basic limitations of the kinds of approaches mentioned even though they are conceptually different. These limitations are: (1) the fact that the models are designed to cover a small set of phenomena, often no more than a single phenomenon; (2) the relatively large number of free parameters and their arbitrary choice involved in checking theoretical predictions.

This paper tries to explore a way out of these difficulties by relying on structure–theoretical methodology which serves as a common framework for designing experiments and conducting subsequent data analysis.

The most basic idea behind this methodology is the "guided inference" assumption maintaining that the course of information processing is mainly governed by task–specific internal representation of stimuli (Buffart & Geissler, 1984; Geissler & Buffart, 1985; Geissler & Puffe, 1983). As a corollary of this assumption, it follows that it is advisable to use sets of stimuli exhibiting constraints which can be formally described. As will be shown, the introduction of such constraints provides a powerful tool for the investigation of various phenomena and properties of the underlying processes as well as the mutual relationships of these phenomena.

A Structure–Theoretical Approach to Internal Representations

In the context of this approach, we consider internal representations to be homomorphic mappings of objects or events onto internal states of the observer. The homomorphic type of the mapping results from the information reduction which is necessary to restrict the apparent complexity of our environment so as to allow intelligent prediction and planning of behavior. An important source of information reduction by the observer is the discovery of environmental regularities. In this respect our approach is similar to Gibson's (1979) theory of perception. However, the main difference between Gibson's somewhat naturalistic view and a structure–theoretical approach consists in the assumption that environmental regularities cannot be grasped as physical invariances, but must be captured by applying internal operations to the perceivable states of the external world. These operations are as variform as the types of stimulus information discussed in the psychological literature (Cutting, 1987). The fact that there are various types of information assumed by researchers concerned with perception is not surprising. Perception operates as a very general, universal system. Therefore, it seems necessary to work out some form of a general theory of perceptual structuring using mathematical concepts which are sufficiently powerful to describe a large variety of information types.

In our opinion, an interesting approach to this problem is the description of perceptual information using the mathematical group theory. In an early paper, Cassirer (1944) showed that basic concepts of a perceptual theory can be developed in terms of group theory. He followed the ideas of Helmholtz and others who analyzed the constancy of form and size by means of the group of motions in the Euclidean space. Much later, an important work was done to apply mathematical group theory to the problems of form perception (Hoffman, 1966, 1978; Palmer, 1983; Leyton, 1986a, b). One aspect of this work is related to Garner's idea (Garner, 1962, 1974) that information and redundancy in perception do not reflect the properties of single stimuli, but of stimulus ensembles or sets. He was interested in the relation between the Gestalt concept of figural or pattern goodness and the structural property of redundancy. He emphasized that redundancy cannot be measured for individual stimuli, but that it pertains to a set of stimuli. The crucial question then is to obtain the perceptually relevant set. Garner's thinking includes the following points:

1. Each stimulus is an element of a total set.
2. Each stimulus can produce so-called inferred subsets on the part of the perceiving human.
3. The amount of redundancy of an individual stimulus is inversely related to the size of the inferred subset it belongs to.

The notion of inferred subsets seems so important because a stimulus can be perceived as a member of a class not only on the basis of some specific experience, but also with little need for prior experience. Such subsets inform us about the properties of perceptual systems.

Garner does not make explicit use of notion of group. Notwithstanding, to illustrate his idea about structural redundancy he chose as an example a set of patterns for which the inferred subsets are orbits of the well-known dihedral group D_4. He and his coworkers (see Garner, 1974; Clement, 1978; Ackermann, 1986; for a review of the main results) studied perceptual and memory phenomena for a set of five-dot patterns in which each dot is placed in one of nine cells of an imaginary 3×3 matrix. The psychologically relevant properties of these patterns are closely related to the size of inferred subsets which can be generated by a small set of internal operations: reflections about the horizontal, vertical or diagonal axis, rotations by 90 degree increments or combinations of these operations. Garner called them R(otation) & R(eflection) subsets.

To formalize the notion of inferred subsets we introduce the definition of an action of a (finite) group G on a (finite) set X (Suzuki, 1982). Let $X = (x, ...)$ be a finite set. The set of all one-to-one mappings of X onto X forms with respect to the composition $P_1 * P_2$ as binary operation a group, the symmetric group S_x. The elements of S_x are called permutations. Any subgroup of S_x is called a permutation group on X.

Definition (Suzuki, 1982; 7.5). *Let G be a group. A G-set is a pair $(X, \int)$ of a set X and a homomorphism $\int$ from G into the symmetric group S_x on X.*

The definition has two aspects. First, $\int$ is a permutation representation of G. However, this representation is not the regular representation of G. It reflects not only the group properties (corresponding to internal operations), but also the properties of the set belonging to. If we emphazise the set X, then we call $\int$ the action of G on X.

Now let us consider the set of Garner's five-dot patterns. It is easy to show that there are only eight distinct outputs for all combinations of the specified reflections and rotations. They are the symmetry operations of the quadratic grid which underlies the pattern generation. They form the dihedral group D_4. Let M be the total set of all five dot patterns on a 3×3 grid.

Thus, we construct the G-set (D_4, M). We say the dihedral group D_4 acts on M via the action $\int : g \rightarrow P(g \in D_4, P \in S_x)$. We know that the R&R-subsets show an interesting property: They are equivalence sets of a partition of the total set. In other words, two patterns belong to the same equivalence set if and only if the one pattern can be transformed by one of the specified reflections or rotations into the other. Using the notation of G-sets, we can demonstrate that the description of stimuli as G-sets and the concept of equivalence sets are inherently the same.

Definition (Suzuki, 1982; 7.7). *Let X be a G-set. A subset* $X^G =$ $(x^g | g \in G)$ *is called an orbit containing* $x \in X$, *we write it as* o_x. $|O_x|$ *is called the length of the orbit* O_x.

The definition of an orbit implies that for any x_1, $x_2 \in X$ the binary relation $R \subseteq X \times X$

$$x_1 R x_2 := \exists \ g \in G: x_2 = x_1^g$$

is an equivalence relation. In this way, we showed that the R&R-subsets are orbits of the G-set (D_4, M).

Another problem concerns the relation between the R&R-subsets and the symmetry operations forming the dihedral group. Here, the following theorem (Suzuki 7.9) is helpful. Let X be a G-set, and let O_x be the orbit containing x. Let H be a subset of G defined by

$$H = (g \ | \ g \in G, \ x^g = x) \ ,$$

then H is a subgroup of G.

It means that for every R&R-subset there exists a subgroup of G which is called the stabilizer of x, we write $H = S_G(x)$.

If O is a finite set, we have $|O| = |G:H|$. Thus, the size of the equivalence sets is a divisor of the group order and related to the stabilizer of x. If a pattern has only the identity as symmetry element, then the size of the R&R-subset of this pattern is 8. If a pattern has one additional symmetry element, a halfturn or a reflection, then this size is 4. If the pattern symmetries are the same as the whole group D_4, the R&R-subsets consist of one element. Although the dihedral group D_4 has subgroups of order 4, it is impossible to find appropriate five-dot patterns on a 3x3 matrix. Therefore, in this case there are no R&R-subsets of size 2.

As in the approach of Garner, the same set can be the underlying set of several distinct G-sets. The main problem with this kind of structure-theoretical approach is to find out the appropriate mathematical group(s) leading to the psychologically relevant partition(s) of the considered set of objects or events. In our opinion, there is no general solution to this problem. However, ideas concerning the contents of representation can help to determine the proper group.

Reaction-Time Related Phenomena in a Matching Task

It seemed to us that an anlysis of the structure of internal representations would offer a way to avoid some of the difficulties of reaction-time decomposition methods. To prove this suggestion, we conducted a series of matching task experiments with the described set of five–dot patterns. The subject was shown sequences of pairs of patterns, either side–by–side (perceptual match) or one after the other (sequential match). The task required the subject to judge as rapidly as possible whether the two stimuli were the same or different, but not to make errors. Two criteria of sameness were used: A pair of stimuli may be considered to be the same if the two stimuli are physically identical (identity match), or if the they were elements of the one equivalence set, i.e. were the same in form, but different in orientation (category match). In this paper, we will discuss only the case of the sequential category matching task (for other results, see Ackermann, 1986).

Method

Subjects. 17 university students participated in the experiment fulfilling a requirement of an introductory psychology course. All had normal or corrected to normal vision.

Stimuli and apparatus. The stimuli were so combined to pairs that all possible combinations of equivalence sets occurred in the experiment. On the basis of the equivalence set sizes (ESS's) and the type of the match (identity or category pairs) it was possible to distinguish 10 pair conditions in the experiment (see Table 1).

Table 1. Reaction times and errors as a function of pair conditions.

Condition	ESS 1. Stimulus	ESS 2. Stimulus	RT (ms)	Error rate (%)
Identity	1	1	544	–
	4	4	578	4.7
	8	8	639	6.5
Category	4	4	623	9.2
	8	8	743	19.1
Different	1	4	582	2.5
	1	8	584	3.1
	4	8	661	5.8
	4	4	630	6.2
	8	8	720	14.3

The stimuli were printed on slides and were back–projected in a two–field projection tachistoscope with stimulus and interval durations regulated by the control unit of the tachistoscope. The size of the white background was 32×32 cm, the size of the invisible grid was 13.5 cm $\times$ 13.5 cm. The diameter of the points was 0.5 cm. The subject was sitting at a distance of 2.25 m from the screen. The experiment was conducted under daylight conditions to minimize the effects of afterimages.

Procedure. In a single trial, the first stimulus was presented for 250 ms, followed by an interstimulus interval (ISI) of 250, 500, 1000, or 2000 ms. The second stimulus appeared on the right side of the first stimulus. Its presentation ended with the response of the subject or after 3000 ms. Each subject participated in four sessions. Within an experimental session the ISI was held constant. A session consisted of 272 trials, one half requiring "same" responses, and one half "different" responses according to the category matching instruction. The order of the four experimental sessions was varied between subjects, no feedback regarding the correctness of the responses was given. Before the first session the subjects received a training consisting of 40 trials.

Results

Error rate data. The proportion of errors was obtained for each subject as a function of the 10 pair conditions. The mean error rate for the whole experiment was 8.0%. The highest error rates were found for category matching pairs. A comparatively high error rate was also obtained for different pairs from one equivalence set size. An analysis of the relation between error rates and reaction times showed a highly significant positive correlation.

Reaction time data. Only reaction times for correct responses are considered in the further analysis. Mean reaction times were obtained as a function of the 10 pair conditions and ISI. In an analysis of variance with subjects as a repeated factor, there was a highly significant main effect of the pair conditions ($F(9,144)=27.24$, $p<0.01$). In this analysis, the effect of ISI does not reach significance. The interaction between the pair condition and ISI was also insignificant. Reaction time differences between the same and different pairs were only small, and in a t-test insignificant. Therefore, the further analysis was concentrated on reaction time differences between the 10 pair conditions shown in Table 1.

Discussion

The main result is the demonstration of a systematic effect of the ESS on the reaction time in a seqeuential category matching task. In order to perform a finer analysis of the observed effect we created a model predicting reaction times as a function of ESS. The ESS's are regarded as measures of the costs for the internal representation of the stimuli in the pair. If the stimuli in the pair are physically different, then, we assume, the comparison evokes two internal representations with common costs according to a simple additive rule $C(\text{Pair}) = C(S1) + C(S2) = ESS(S1) + ESS(S2)$. If the stimuli in the pair are physically identical, then the representation of the second stimuli within some time interval does not evoke a second representation. The costs of a pair do not differ from the costs for the representation of a single stimulus. On the basis of these considerations, we obtained the predictors given in Table 2.

The resulting model is relatively simple. It does not take in account a variety of other factors, for instance priming effects between geometrically transformed shapes. Nevertheless its fit to data is very good. The squared coefficient of correlation for same responses is $B=0.993$, the linear regression equation is $RT_{same} = (626.3 + 13.4C)$ ms. The prediction of reaction times for different responses seems to be a more complicated problem because one can think about other types of internal representations which can be used to detect a non-match. However, if one defines the predictors in an analogous manner, the squared coefficient of correlation is $B = 0.846$, and the corresponding equation $RT_{different} = (508.3 + 12.7C)$ ms. The agreement in the estimated parameters is reasonably good.

Table 2. Predictors and results of regression analysis.

Condition	ESS 1. Stimulus	ESS 2. Stimulus	Predictor	Predicted RT (ms)
Same				
Identity	1	1	1	540
	4	4	4	580
	8	8	8	633
Category	4	4	8	633
	8	8	16	740
$R^2 = .993$	$R_{same} = (526.3 + 13.4C)$ ms			
Different	1	4	5	572
	1	8	9	623
	4	8	12	661
	4	4	8	610
	8	8	16	712
$R^2 = .846$	$RT_{different} = (508.3 + 12.4C)$ ms			

Additionally, a pattern–specific analysis was attempted. Only the reaction times for same responses were considered. First, we investigated the relation between the stabilizers of the patterns and the mean reaction times. The results are presented in Table 3.

Table 3. Mean same reaction time as a function of the pattern stabilizers H in the dihedral group D_4. v: vertival axis, h: horizontal axis; d1/d2: diagonal axes.

Stabilizer	$|H|$	$|H:G|$	Mean reaction time
Identity (1)	1	8	641.5
1, reflection v	2	4	
1, reflection h	2	4	560.8
1, reflection d1	2	4	
1, reflection d2	2	4	584.8
1, inversion	2	4	589.5
D_4	8	1	542.4

In a next step, we computed the correlations between the mean reaction times over all experimental conditions and the ESS's, and also between these reaction times and the goodness ratings from Garner and Clement (1963), for the 17 pattern classes. The product–moment correlation coefficient for ESS was $r=0.81$ for identity matches, and $r=0.69$ for category matches. An even closer relationship was found between the mean reaction times and the corresponding goodness rating ($r=0.89$ for identity pairs and $r=0.85$ for category pairs). This finding can easily be understood, because Garner and Clement identified the number of straight lines in a pattern as a second determinant of goodness ratings. If we include the number of lines as a second predictor in our analysis, then we find the expected higher correlation: a multiple correlation coefficient $R=0.87$ for identity matches, and $R=0.79$ for category matches. The number of lines is strongly related to the mathematical group of collineations, i.e., there exists another group acting on the pattern set which was used in the experiment. The corresponding permutation group has the order 9, and it is isomorphic to $C_3 \times C_3$. Their orbits reflect cyclic changes of rows or columns in the 3×3 grid. Because this transformation no longer left the shape of a pattern invariant, all patterns belonging to an orbit are physically different. Therefore, the size of the orbit itself is not a measure adequate to our purpose. But, if the stimuli of one R&R–subset are considered as inherently the same, the orbits of the collineation group contain different number of nonequivalent patterns. These numbers form a measure (COL) that is analogous to ESS measure. A multiple linear regression with ESS and COL as predictors leads to a somewhat better fit to the reaction time data: $R=0.90$ for identity matches, and $R=0.91$ for category matches.

Relations Between Reaction–Time Prediction in A Structure–Theoretical Approach and the Temporal Architecture of Central Information Processing

The prediction of reaction times on the basis of relatively simple characteristics of internal representations shows some interesting relations to the temporal architecture of central information processing. Current views on this topic are most completely described by the new, elaborated version of the time–quantum model (TQM, cf. Geissler, 1987a,b). This model assumes the existence of an absolute lower bound for intermittencies, the time quantum T, which has a duration of approximately 4.5 ms. Intermittencies of central processing must be multiples of T or of small packets $T^*=k \cdot T$, $k=1,2,\ldots$, which play the role of pseudo–quantal units. A second assumption states that for any given individual there is a maximal value M, the so–called coherence length, such that k is less than, or equal to, M. In our experiment, the identified slope can be seen as an integer multiple of the time quantum T with $k=3$, $T^*=13.5$ ms. In accordance with our model, the operative upper boundary $L \cdot T^*$ can be estimated at $16 \cdot 13.5$ ms or 216 ms. This value appears to play an important role in the chronometric exploration of visual recognition tasks (Geissler, 1985). Interestingly enough, a very similar value can be obtained by a reanalysis of the data found by Checkosky and Whitlock (1973), who conducted a memory search experiment using a subset of the Garner and Clement dot patterns. This subset consisted only of patterns of ESS 4 (good patterns) and ESS 8 (bad patterns). The sizes of the positive set in the memory search task were two and three. Additionally, the discriminability of the stimuli was varied on two levels (intact vs. degraded, Table 4). Positive responses were made only to test stimuli which are physically identical to one of the elements of the memory set. Reflected or rotated patterns of the same R&R-subset, and also patterns of other R&R-subsets, required negative responses.

Table 4. Reaction times in the memory search task (from Checkosky & Whitlock, 1973) as a function of positive set size and ESS.

Size of the positive set	ESS	Discriminability	Reaction time Empirical	Predicted
2	4	Intact	580	583
	8		658	654
3	4		620	619
	8		722	724
2	4	Degraded	689	683
	8		751	753
3	4		711	718
	8		827	824

Because a homogeneous structuring for negative responses could not be expected we analyzed only the positive responses.

As a predictor which is comparable with that in the matching task model we computed the product of the size of the positive set in the memory search task s and the equivalence set sizes ESS. The resulting equations we:

$$RT = (512.6 + 8.83(s \cdot ESS)) \text{ ms}, \quad r = 0.998, \text{ for intact stimuli,}$$
$$RT = (611.8 + 8.84(s \cdot ESS)) \text{ ms}, \quad r = 0.995, \text{ for degraded stimuli.}$$

Both equations are a nearly perfect fit to the empirical data. Besides, the slope in both equations is equal and can be easily interpreted as double the size of the time quantum T ($k=2$, $T^*=9$ ms). Consequently, the upper bound can be estimated at $24 \cdot 9$ ms or 216 ms.

For a more complete understanding of this subjects, the problem of upper boundaries should be considered in greater detail. Upper boundaries in central information processing apparently express preferred hierarchies of intermittencies (cf. Geissler, 1987b). They correspond to the prime factorization $16 = 2 \cdot 2 \cdot 2 \cdot 2$ and $24 = 2 \cdot 2 \cdot 2 \cdot 3$ which allow for a large number of different hierarchizations. In the case of our experiment, the occurrence of such upper boundaries could be related to the discrete group structure of the operations playing a role in the build-up of the internal representations.

Summary and Conclusion

The purpose of the present study was to demonstrate the possibility of applying group-theoretical characteristics of internal representations to the problem of reaction–time decomposition in a matching task. We used a set of patterns for which the psychologically relevant groups, and also the partitions of the whole set into equivalence sets, could easily be inferred from geometrical considerations. In a more general way, any attempt to describe internal representations on the basis of groups mainly depends on the identification of the appropriate groups. Our knowledge of this subject has not been sufficiently systematic about this topic. Therefore, a central problem of further theoretical thinking must be the investigation of criteria which effectively limit the range of relevant groups or structures.

Besides the groups which play a role in perception, it may be appropriate to pay attention to the group–theoretical analysis of logical thinking in the work of Piaget. In his opinion, subgroups of order two, the so–called involutions, are of special interest. He erroneously assumed that formal thinking includes only such groups. As shown by Ascher (1984), on a formal level this would mean a confusion of groups and their generators. Nevertheless, specific products of such groups could play an important role in a deeper understanding of the structuring of internal representations. Ascher (1984, p. 310) refered to so–called wreath products (Polya, 1937, 1940) of the group C_2 and the symmetric group S_x. For logical expressions he computed the following isomorphisms:

$$K_1 - C_2 \text{ order 2,}$$

$$K_2 - D_4 \text{ order 8,}$$

$$K_3 - S_4 \times C_2 \text{ order 48.}$$

It would be useful to investigate the actions of these groups in a broader range of situations.

Another proposal to determine psychologically relevant groups was made by Buffart (1986). He postulated that a representation which is a subgroup of S_x is a psychologically acceptable representation only if it is a hierarchy and if it does not contain two elements that are also elements of one and the same element of another hierarchy belonging to S_x. This postulate characterizes the internal representation as a so–called formal Gestalt quality which by definition is invariant under transformations. In some ways, the proposal of Buffart is complementary to our analysis of internal representations. Further considerations are necessary to work out the common and the different proprties of these frameworks.

Finally, the present study tried to connect assumptions about internal representations and formal time structures. Our analysis of the matching task and the memory search task illustrates that under certain circumstances both domains can be related to each other by very simple assumptions. For the development of specific models on an algorithmic level, the study of inter-individual differences in task performance should be useful.

Correspondence should be addressed to Klaus-Dieter Schmidt, Sektion Psychologie, Karl-Marx-Universität Leipzig, Tieckstr. 2, 7030 Leipzig, G.D.R.

References

Ackermann, B. (1986). *Strukturanalysen visueller Erkennungsleistungen am Beispiel des Vergleichens einfachen geometrischen Materials.* Unpublished doctoral dissertation. Leipzig: Karl-Marx-Universität.

Ascher, E. (1984). The case of Piaget's group INRC. *Journal of Mathematical Psychology, 28,* 282–316.

Bamber, D. (1969). Reaction times and error rates for "same"–"different" judgements of multidimensional stimuli. *Perception & Psychophysics, 6,* 169–174.

Buffart, H.F.J.M. (1986). Gestalt qualities, memory structure, and minimum principles. In F. Klix & H. Hagendorf (Eds.), *Human memory and cognitive capabilities.* Amsterdam: North-Holland.

Buffart, H.F.J.M., & Geissler, H.-G. (1984). Task-dependent representation of categories and memory guided inference during classification. In E. Degreef & J. van Buggenhaut (Eds.), *Trends in mathematical psychology.* Amsterdam: North-Holland.

Cassirer, E. (1944). The concept of group and the theory of perception. *Philosophical and Phenomenological Research, 5,* 1–35.

Checkosky, S.F., & Whitlock, D. (1973). The effects of pattern goodness on recognition time in a memory search task. *Journal of Experimental Psychology, 100,* 341–348.

Clement, D.E. (1978). Perceptual structure and selection. In E. Carterette et al. (Eds.), *Handbook of perception. Vol. IX: Perceptual processing.* New York: Academic Press.

Cutting, J.E. (1987). Perception and information. *Annual Review of Psychology, 38,* 61–90.

Garner, W.R. (1962). *Uncertainty and structure as psychological concepts.* New York: Wiley and Sons.

Garner, W.R. (1974). *The processing of information and structure.* Potomac, Md.: Lawrence Erlbaum Associates.

Garner, W.R., & Clement, D.E. (1963). Goodness of pattern and pattern uncertainty. *Journal of Verbal Learning and Verbal Behavior, 2,* 446–452.

Geissler, H.-G. (1985). Zeitquantenhypothese zur Struktur ultraschneller Gedächtnisprozesse. *Zeitschrift für Psychologie, 193,* 347–362.

Geissler, H.-G. (1987a). Hierarchien periodischer Vorgänge als Grundlage zeitlich–diskreter Strukturen psychischer Prozsse. In H.G. Geissler & K. Reschke (Eds.), *Psychophysische Grundlagen mentaler Prozesse.* Leipzig: Karl-Marx-Universität.

Geissler, H.-G. (1987b). The temporal architecture of central information processing: Evidence for a tentative time-quantum model. *Psychological Research, 49,* 99–106.

Geissler, H.-G., & Buffart, H.F.J.M. (1985). Task dependency and quantized processing in classification. In G. d'Ydewalle (Ed.), *Cognition, information processing and motivation.* Amsterdam: North-Holland.

Geissler, H.-G., & Puffe, M. (1983). The inferential basis of classification: From perceptual to memory code systems. In H.G. Geissler et al (Eds.), *Modern issues in perception.* Amsterdam: North-Holland.

Gibson, J.J. (1979). *The ecological approach to visual perception.* Boston: Houghton Mifflin.

Hoffman, W.C. (1966). The Lie algebra of visual perception. *Journal of Mathematical Psychology, 3,* 65–98.

Krueger, L.E. (1978). A theory of perceptual matching. *Psychological Review, 85,* 278–304.

Leyton, M. (1986a). A theory of information structure. I. General principles. *Journal of Mathematical Psychology, 30,* 103–160.

Leyton, M. (1986b). A theory of information structure. II. A theory of perceptual organization. *Journal of Mathematical Psychology, 30,* 257–305.

Nickerson, R.S. (1978). On the time it takes to tell things apart. In J. Requin (Ed.), *Attention and Performance VII.* Hillsdale, NJ: Lawrence Erlbaum Associates.

Palmer, S.E. (1983). The psychology of perceptual organization: A transformational approach. In J. Beck et al (Eds.), *Human and machine vision*. New York: Academic Press.

Posner, M.J. (1978). *Chronometric explorations of mind*. Hillsdale, NJ: Lawrence Erlbaum Associates.

Proctor, R.W. (1981). A unified theory for matching task phenomena. *Psychological Review, 88*, 291–326.

Proctor, R.W. (1986). Response bias, criteria settings, and the fast-same phenomenon: A reply to Ratcliff. *Psychological Review, 93*, 473–477.

Ratcliff, R., & Hacker, M.J. (1981). Speed and accuracy of same and different responses in perceptual matching. *Perception & Psychophysics, 30*, 303–307.

Suzuki, M. (1982). *Group theory I*. Berlin: Springer.

Psychophysical Explorations of Mental Structures
Edited by H.-G. Geissler
in collaboration with M.H. Müller and W. Prinz
© 1990 by Hogrefe & Huber Publishers

Chapter 23

Quantized Speed–Capacity Relations in Short–Term Memory

Martina Puffe
Karl–Marx–Universität Leipzig
Leipzig, G.D.R.

Information from the sensory input and from permanent memory must somehow be stored and processed together in order to meet cognitive demands. It is widely accepted that short-term retention is accomplished by the short-term memory (STM). However, there is a controversy on whether the model of one homogeneous memory system is adequate to describe short-term storage of information and its task-dependent processing (e.g. Klapp, Marshburn & Lester, 1983). Thus, the defining properties and mechanisms of STM are still under discussion.

Nevertheless, there is basic agreement on at least two properties, namely that the amount of information storable in STM is limited, and that information processing in STM is predominantly serial. It seems worth analyzing the relationship between speed of serial processing and STM storage capacity, as was initiated by Cavanagh (1972) in order to learn more about this memory system.

Cavanagh analyzed the relationship between the speed of serial processing and STM storage capacity by comparing data obtained in so-called item-recognition tasks (Sternberg, 1969) and studies of memory spans (Jacobs, 1887). In the recognition task the subject has to decide whether an item presented is a member of a memorized item set. The commonly found linear and parallel dependence of reaction time (RT) on memory set size for positive and negative responses (Sternberg, 1969, 1975) has been interpreted by an exhaustive serial scanning. Thus the slope of the regression lines fitting the RT is considered to be an estimate of the processing time per item. Memory span as a measure of storage capacity is usually defined by the maximal length of an item list a subject can correctly reproduce after one presentation in half of the trials.

Using data collected in several investigations for seven types of items (e.g. digits, words, random forms) and plotting mean slopes against reciprocal spans, Cavanagh obtained a strong linear dependence. The slope of the best fit was 243 ms per span with an intercept near zero and $r^2 = 0.995$. In other words, for all types of items the processing time per item multiplied by the span is in the neighbourhood of the constant time period of 243 ms.

The aim of this paper is to show that the kind of recognition task used by Burrows and Okada (1975) lends itself to a more detailed investigation of the relationship found by Cavanagh. On the basis of their method we will present evidence for a discrete variation of the estimated time constant.

Interpretation of Cavanagh's Result — Implications of a Time Quantum Model

How can we interpret the dependence of search time per item on the reciprocal of span? Because of its simplicity the first of three interpretations presented by Cavanagh seems to be most attractive. According to Cavanagh, there is a fixed integer number T of storable elementary information units and a fixed elementary duration t for processing each unit. So the duration C of a complete search through STM is

$$C = T \cdot t .$$

For different types of items, different numbers of elementary units are needed for storing one item. The more units are needed the smaller should be the number of storable items, i.e., the span. On the other hand, the processing time per item should become longer with an increasing number of units per item. We thus get the above-mentioned inverse relationship between the search time per item and the span. Put in different terms, search time per item multiplied by the span should be a constant for all types of material.

This interpretation puts two complementary constraints on the efficiency of STM: the limitation of storage capacity determined by a limited number of storable elementary information units, and a speed limitation for serial processes determined by an elementary processing time. Cavanagh's interpretation does not involve assumptions about the values of the hypothetical parameters T and t and its variability. Further constraints may be derived from theories about the timing of mental processes including time quantum assumptions. In the following the Time Quantum Model (TQM) proposed by Geissler (1985a,b; 1987a,b) will be considered.[1]

---

[1] For a detailed and complete introduction into the theoretical assumptions see Geissler (1987a,b).

1. TQM postulates a discrete variation of time periods in which the processing mode does not change. Intermittency intervals of such periods are defined by a lower boundary D_L and an upper boundary D_U with D_U being an integer multiple of D_L. All admissible intermittencies are integer multiples of D_L and integer fractions of D_U.

2. The shortest lower boundary is given by a time quantum t of about 4.5 ms. Integer multiples of t, called pseudoquants t', can be shortest lower boundaries, too, representing the shortest time period for an individual or for special task demands. The upper boundary is given by the lower boundary multiplied by the maximal length of prefixed chains of operations, called coherence length M. M is in the order of 30. Depending on the state of an individual or a special task demands, operative limits $L \leq M$ may become fixed.

3. Each upper boundary is assumed to be the lower boundary for the next broader intermittency interval. Thus, a hierarchy of intermittency intervals is proposed.

According to the TQM, the duration C of a complete search through STM suggested by Cavanagh corresponds to the upper boundary of the shortest intermittency interval which is

$$D_u = M \cdot t' \quad \text{with } t' = q \cdot t \text{ and an integer } q > 0.$$

The maximal number T of information units storable in STM equals the maximal length of prefixed chains of operations M. In both approaches there is an elementary processing time t. From this it follows that the time period C should be an integer multiple of 4.5 ms, regardless of the variation of M, where M is an integer. Furthermore, if M and the pseudoquant t' are independent determinants of C, this period should vary discretely across subjects and task demands.

Before presenting some data supporting the TQM assumption of a discrete variation of the time period C, we want to introduce the method used to collect the data.

Measuring STM Storage Capacity and Processing Rate Within One Task

For his analysis Cavanagh used group means for spans and processing rates that were obtained from different tasks (recall and recognition) for different subjects. Although his interpretation calls for identical coding for the two tasks, the occurrence of task–dependent coding differences cannot be ruled out. This is due to difficulties in demonstrating the intra–individual relationship between processing rate and the reciprocal of span that occurred in the experiments of Puckett and Kausler (1984), Brown and Kirsner (1980) and in those conducted by Staude (1985) and Kühnel (1986) in our own laboratory. The storing format may depend on the task: in the case of recall, item information should be stored completely for item reproduction (Drewnowski, 1980; Levy & Craik, 1975), whereas in recognition storage of features distinguishing between positive and negative items will do. If we want to investigate different determinants of STM capacity, our measure of determinants should be based on a comparable memory load. Therefore, we have proposed that storage capacity and processing rate should be measured jointly within one and the same task (cf. Puffe, 1987).

A recognition task with short and long lists seems to serve this purpose. By using short and long lists of words in the recognition task Burrows and Okada (1975) demonstrated that there is a break in the linear relationship between RT and the size of the memorized set if the set size becomes longer than 7 items. A bilinear function provides a good fit to the data. The break was found in several investigations using words and pictures (Okada & Burrows, 1978; Franklin, Okada, Burrows & Friendly, 1980; Hockley & Corballis, 1982; Corballis, Katz & Schwartz, 1980; Banks & Fariello, 1974; Schmidt, 1982).

Burrows and Okada suggested that the break indicates a change of the processing strategy caused by the limit of STM storage capacity. This conclusion is supported by research evidence obtained by Adams and Collins (1978) who analyzed visual evoked potentials and RT obtained in a recognition experiment with digits. They found a change in the morphology of evoked potentials corresponding to a break in the RT function for supraspan lists.

As Burrows and Okada (1975) supposed, the obtained bilinearity could be explained by assuming a mixture of two strategies for long lists: a more direct decision based on familiarity and serial search. Another explanation is that subjects structure the list if the set size exceeds the memory span. Franklin et al. (1980) suggest that in recognizing items of supraspan lists a serial search between categories and a parallel one within them is performed.

If one accepts (a) that the intersection point of the two regression lines yields an estimate of the number of storable items for the item material used, and (b) that the slope for short lists represents an estimate of the processing time per item, the relationship between the two measures obtained from one task is analogous to the Cavanagh relation for recall and recognition data.

We performed an experiment in order to replicate the general effect reported by Burrows and Okada (1975). A subject was asked to learn a list of two–syllabled German words. The set size was 2, 3, 4, 6, 8, 10, 12, 16, respectively. After correct written recall without paying attention to item order the subject had to decide for a set of successively presented test items whether a test item was a member of the learned list. Half of the decisions were positive, the other half negative. All subjects had to learn two lists of each set size. A word that was a member of one list could be a negative test item for other lists. There were four sessions for the recognition task, and the order of lists was balanced across sessions and subjects.

Figure 1 shows the mean RT aggregated for positive and negative decisions plotted against the memory set size. The data of the two response types were combined in order to enable comparison of our data with those of other investigations. Only data for correct responses and RT's below 2 s were included. The mean proportion of errors was 2.3%.

A break of the linear dependence of RT on set size appears between eight and ten items. The best fit is given by a bilinear function yielding $r^2 = 0.9951$.[2] The two regression lines are defined by the equations

$$RT = 19.86 \text{ ms} + 486.30 \quad \text{for set sizes } 2-8$$
$$RT = 3.11 \text{ ms} + 636.64 \quad \text{for set sizes } 10-16.$$

In general, our experiment confirmed Burrows' and Okada's finding of a bilinear trend of RT as a function of set size although there were marked differences of estimated parameter values.

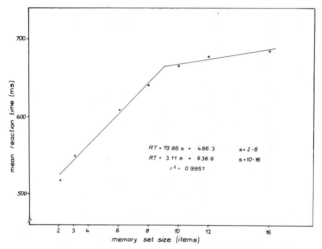

Figure 1. RT as a function of set size and the bilinear function fitting the data.

Burrows and Okada performed two experiments using the same subjects and set sizes (2, 4, 6, 8, 10, 12, 16, 20 items) for both, varying only the composition of the test item set. In Experiment 1, each item of the memorized set was tested only once. As in our experiment, a standard fixed set procedure was used in Experiment 2, that is to say, each positive item could be tested more then once, particularly for small set sizes.

The slopes that Burrows and Okada obtained for short lists amounted to 57 ms/item and 37 ms/item and the intersection points of the two fitting regression lines 6.71 items and 6.83 items for Experiment 1 and 2, respectively. From this it follows that the hypothetical period C for a complete search through STM estimated by the intersection point mulitplied by the slopes for short lists was 382 ms and 253 ms for Experiment 1 and 2, respectively. In our experi-

---

[2]   As in the Burrows and Okada (1975) experiment, a logarithmic function also fits the data, yielding $r^2 = 0.986$.

ment, the slope for short lists was 20 ms/item, the intersection point 8.99 items and the period C 180 ms.

Obviously, there is a variation of the parameters which seems to depend on special task demands. By analyzing our data together with data collected in other investigations we will now demonstrate a discrete variation of C that is in line with the assumptions of the TQM.

Evidence for a Discrete Variation of the Time for a Complete Search through STM

Table 1 shows data collected in 11 experiments sampled from five studies using short and long word lists. The parameter estimates are based on the equations for the bilinear function reported in the studies.

Table 1. Estimated parameters from recognition experiments using short and long word lists.

Source	Exp. No.	max. set size s_{max} (items)	slope for short lists sl (ms/item)	intersection point of the regression lines i (items)	slope × intersection point C (ms)
Burrows &	1[a]	20	57	6.71	382
Okada (1975)	2	20	37	6.83	253
Okada &	1[b]	20	47	7.50	352
Burrows	2a	16	29	6.19	180
(1978)	2b[c]	16	53	5.24	278
Franklin	1	20	28	9.78	274
et al. (1980)	2	24	47	7.58	356
Corballis et al. (1980)		16	30	3.43	103
Hockley &	1	16	20	5.10	102
Corballis (1982)	2[d]	16	38	6.52	248
Puffe		16	20	8.99	180

[a] modified set of test items: each item of the learned set was tested only once.
[b] additional task: the subject had to count backward from a two-digit number for 3−5 sec before presentation of the test item.
[c] additional task: the subject saw a varied set of 2, 4, or 6 items before seeing the test item and had to give a positive answer if either the fixed or the varied set contained the test item.
[d] modified set of test items: negative test items were repeated as often as positive test items.

In general, the experiments used a fixed set recognition task as described above, the maximal set size being 16, 20 or 24 items. In some experiments, however, either a different composition of the test item set was used or the subjects had to perform an additional task before seeing the test item. These experiments are marked, and an explanation for this is given below.

The mean of the eleven estimated C–values amounts to 246 ms which is in good agreement with Cavanagh's constant of 243 ms. Cavanagh used group means of data from different investigations, so his estimate may represent an average value.

Figure 2 shows the processing time per item, i.e., the slope for short lists as a function of the reciprocal of the intersection point (cf. Table 1).

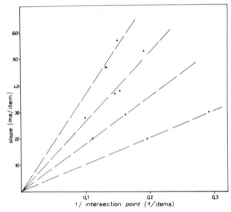

Figure 2. Slope for short lists as a function of the reciprocal of the intersection point (full circles). The slope of the broken line indicates the cluster means of the C–values given in Table 2.

Cavanagh found a linear dependence of the processing time per item on the reciprocal of span interpreting the slope of the fitting regression line to be C. In our analysis obviously no single regression line fits the data but a fan pattern does. Thus, there is no single time constant estimating the duration of a complete search through STM. Instead a discrete variation of C can be found.

Table 2. Ordered estimates of C collected from eleven experiments.

Cluster	1	2	3	4
C(ms)	102	180	248	352
	103	180	253	356
			274	382
			278	
Mean (ms)	102.5	180	263	363

Table 2 shows the ordered estimates for C sampled from Table 1. At least four clusters can be separated. For the two clusters containing the large C-values another separation seems to be possible.

Note that C-values obtained in different investigations may belong to one cluster and that there is surprisingly good agreement. On the other hand, the same subjects can belong to different clusters, produced by the same intersection point but different processing rates (Burrows & Okada, 1975, Experiment 1 and 2).

This fact supports independency of the number of storable units M and the elementary time period $t' = q \cdot t$ as hypothesized by the TQM. The cluster means are nearly in the proportion of 1:2:3:4 with a difference of about 90 ms between them, that is $20 \cdot 4.5$ ms. The proportion obtained can be predicted by assuming q to be 1, 2, 3, or 4 with M being constant. But of course a variation of M might contribute to the variation of C, too.

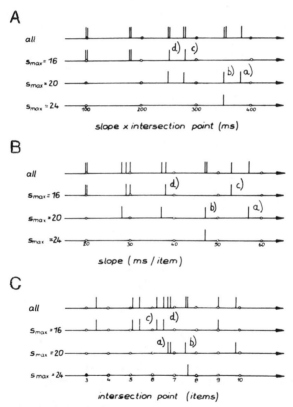

Figure 3. Estimated parameters for eleven experiments aggregated and separated for the maximal set size used in the experiments.
a) time period C (slope for short lists × intersection point,
b) slope for short lists,
c) intersection point of the two regression lines of the bilinear fit.
Experiments with modified task conditions are marked (for explanations, see Table 1).

Figure 3 shows the estimated values for C, i and sl, taken together for all maximal set sizes (top row) and separately for the maximal set size used in the experiments. Experiments with modified task conditions are marked again.

In Figure 3A, the clear discrete variation of C is demonstrated once more. As can be seen, the C-values obtained for experiments with the same maximal set size s_{max} may belong to different clusters and those for different s_{max} to one cluster. However, the lowest C obtained for a given s_{max} seems to correlate with s_{max}. The highest C for a given s_{max} is obtained for modified task conditions (i.e., modified test item set or additional tasks). Thus, the data suggest that C is affected by special task conditions, but we need more data for a detailed analysis.

Now let us consider the variation of the components of C. As can be seen in Fig. 3B, there is a clear discrete variation of the slopes for short lists. Table 3 shows the ordered slopes taken from Table 1. Apparently there are five clusters of slope values.

There is a difference of about 9 ms/item between the means of the clusters. So all processing times per item, estimated by the slopes, seem to be multiples of 9 ms. Figure 4 shows the slopes for short lists given in Table 3 as a function of a hypothetical number of steps per item n, beginning with $n = 2$ and adding one step per cluster.

Table 3. Slopes for short lists obtained from eleven experiments.

Cluster	1	2	3	4	5
slopes	20	28	37	47	53
(ms/item)	20	29	38	47	57
		30			
mean (ms/item)	20	29	37.5	47	55

The fitting linear regression line yielding $r^2 = 0.993$ has a slope of 8.8 ms/item and an intercept near zero. This result is compatible with the TQM assuming that all processing times per item are always multiples of the double of 4.5 ms. This result is also consistent with estimates of the time quantum Geissler (1985b) found by analyzing data collected in visual masking and recognition experiments. The estimated values for the time quantum were about 9 ms.

A clear discrete variation for the intersection points shown in Figure 3C cannot be found although a broad variation of i is noticeable. Nevertheless, the intersection point contributes to the discrete variation of the C-values because the clustering of C cannot be explained by the slope variation only. Experiments yielding different slopes may belong to the same cluster of C. Special task conditions seem to affect both the slopes and the intersection points. The maximal set size used in a given experiment tends to determine a lower limit for the lowest slope or intersection point that can be obtained for that s_{max}. Additional tasks or modified test item sets seem to lead to an increase of slope values. But we should mention again that these tendencies need further investigation.

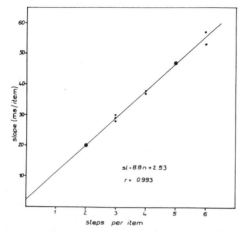

Figure 4. Slopes for short lists as a function of hypothetical steps per item (full circles) and the fitting regression line.

In summary we may say that the data presented support the assumption that there is a quantal time structure of serial processes operating in STM. A discrete variation of the estimated time period for a complete search through STM was found. The mean, however, was in good agreement with the Cavanagh constant. Special task demands seem to affect this period. The estimated processing time per item varied discretely, too. The obtained discrete variation and the parameters estimated are compatible with the TQM.

Capacity Limits or Optimization of Processing Strategy?

The idea of estimating parameters of storage capacity and processing rate of serial processes within one task is based on the assumption that there should be a change in the strategy of information processing if the item set to be compared serially with the test item exceeds the storage capacity of STM. This change of strategy is indicated by the break in the linear dependence of RT on memory set size in the recognition task. The analysis of individual data (discussed elsewhere) gives considerable support to the assumption that in performing the task subjects structure the list. However, the question of whether categorization is used only beyond the capacity limits of STM remains to be answered. Perhaps there is an optimization of the processing strategy depending on special task demands. So the number of items in which there is a change of strategy need not necessarily correspond to the maximal number of items that can be stored in STM.

McGregor (1987) suggests that the use of a hierarchical strategy is to be expected if the set size exceeds four or six items depending on the use of an exhaustive or self–terminating serial search, respectively. The number of items where the Directed Entry Model of Naus (1974) proves more effective than a linear serial search depends on the number of categories a subject needs to organize the items of the learned list (Puffe, 1987).

Of course one should assume that there exists an upper limit of chunks storable in STM, but below that limit the subject either can organize the item set according to the properties of the items or is constrained by special task demands. There is an analogous assumption in the TQM. Depending on the state of an individual or special task demands operative limits $L \leq M$ are used that allow construction of a suitable processing hierarchy in performing the task.

However, the data presented suggest that there are discrete intermittencies typical of STM processes, and that these intermittencies are affected by task demands. Therefore, we should try to find real limits that are constraints for STM processes and factors set by task demands that determine the preferred strategy without violating these limits. The method used seems to lend itself to an investigation of the relationship between processing rate and storage capacity provided we succeed in modeling the processing strategies applied in a differentiated way.

Summary

Short–term memory seems to have at least two basic properties: the amount of storable information is limited, and information processing is predominantly serial. Cavanagh (1972) demonstrated that the number of items storable in STM multiplied by the time needed to process on eitem in serial search is a constant of about 243 ms, which he interpreted as the time needed for a complete search through STM.

Cavanagh's finding was based on the analysis of data collected in Sternberg's item–recognition task and the memory span task for several types of material. In our subsequent investigations of the relationship between scan rate and span a different methodological approach was adopted which tried to estimate the two parameters merely in one task in order to avoid task–dependent coding differences. We used the item–recognition task with short and long lists of words (Burrows & Okada, 1975) in which the slopes of the regression line fitting the RT for short lists were taken as an estimate of the time needed to process one item on the one hand, and, on the other hand, the number of items where the linear dependence of RT on memory set size broke down as an estimate of the storage capacity of STM.

The data of eleven experiments performed by several investigators and, in addition, our own data were analyzed. The results were as follows:
1. There was a considerable variability in the estimated parameters even within one type of material. A constant time period for a complete search through

STM was not found. However, the mean time period calculated from eleven experiments was in good agreement with the Cavanagh constant.

2. A clear discrete variation of the calculated time period for a complete search through STM was demonstrated. At least four clusters could be distinguished. The cluster means amounted to 102.5, 180, 263, and 363 ms, respectively. The estimated processing time per item also varied discretely.

3. Special task demands seemed to affect the estimated parameters. These results were discussed against the background of Geissler's Time Quantum Model (Geissler, 1985a,b; 1987a,b). which assumes quantal timing of mental processes. This model allows for predictions of admissible time periods in central information processing based on a universal time quantum and a limited maximal length of prefixed chains of operations. The results presented support for this model.

Acknowledgement. I want to thank Klaus-Dieter Schmidt for helpful discussion promoting this investigation.
Correspondence should be addressed to Martina Puffe, Karl-Marx-Universität Leipzig, Sektion Psychologie, Tieckstr. 2, 7030 Leipzig, G.D.R.

References

Adam, N., & Collins, G. (1978). Late components of the visual evoked potential to search in short-term memory. *Electroencephalography and Clinical Neurophysiology, 44,* 147−156.

Banks, W.P, & Fariello, G.R. (1974). Memory load and latency in recognition of pictures. *Memory and Cognition, 2,* 144−148.

Brown, H.L., & Kirsner, K. (1980). A within−subjects analysis of the relationship between memory span and processing rate in short−term memory. *Cognitive Psychology, 12,* 177−187.

Burrows, D., & Okada, R. (1975). Memory retrieval from long and short lists. *Science, 188,* 1031−1033.

Cavanagh, J.P. (1972). Relation between the immediate memory span and the memory search rate. *Psychological Review, 79,* 525−530.

Corballis, M.C., Katz, J, & Schwartz, M. (1980). Retrieval from memory sets that exceed the memory span. *Canadian Journal of Psychology, 34,* 40−48.

Drewnowski, A. (1980). Attributes and priorities in short-term-recall: A new model of memory span. *Journal of Experimental Psychology: General, 109,* 208−250.

Franklin, P.E., Okada, R., Burrows, D., & Friendly, M.L. (1980). Retrieval of information from subjectively organized lists. *Journal of Experimental Psychology: Human Learning and Memory, 6,* 732−740.

Geissler, H.-G. (1985a). Sources of seeming redundancy in temporally quantized information processing. In: G. d'Ydewalle (Ed.), *23rd International Congress of Psychology*(Revised Papers, Vol. 3). Amsterdam, New York, Oxford: North-Holland.

Geissler, H.-G. (1985b). Zeitquantenhypothese zur Struktur ultraschneller Gedächtnisprozesse. *Zeitschrift für Psychologie, 193,* 347−362.

Geissler, H.-G. (1987a). Temporal architecture of task dependent information processing: Evidence for a time-quantum model. *Psychological Research, 49,* 99−106.

Geissler, H.–G. (1987b). Hierarchien periodischer Vorgänge im Zentralnervensystem als Grundlage zeitlich diskreter Strukturen psychischer Prozesse. In: H.–G. Geissler & K. Reschke (Eds.), *Psychophysische Grundlagen mentaler Prozesse*. Leipzig: Karl–Marx–Universität.

Hockley, W.E., & Corballis, M.C. (1982). Tests of serial scanning in item recognition. *Canadian Journal of Psychology, 36*, 189–192.

Jacobs, J. (1887). Experiments on "prehension". *Mind, 12*, 75–79.

Klapp, S.T., Marshburn, E.A., & Lester, P.T. (1983). Short–term memory does not involve the memory of information processing: The demise of a common assumption. *Journal of Experimental Psychology: General, 112*, 240–264.

Kühnel, R. (1986). *Verarbeitungsgeschwindigkeit in Sternbergaufgaben und Kurzzeitbehalten in Abhängigkeit von der Komplexität individueller Items*. Unpublished manuscript, Karl–Marx–Universität, Leipzig.

Levy, B.A., & Craik, F.I.M. (1975). The coordination of codes in short–term–retention. *Quarterly Journal of Experimental Psychology, 27*, 33–35.

McGregor, J. (1987). Short–term memory capacity: Limitation or optimization. *Psychological Review, 94*, 107–108.

Naus, M.J. (1974). Memory search of categorized lists: A consideration of alternative self–terminating search strategies. *Journal of Experimental Psychology, 30*, 221–233.

Okada, R., & Burrows, D. (1978). The effects of subsidiary tasks on memory retrieval from long and short lists. *Quarterly Journal of Experimental Psychology, 30*, 221–233.

Puckett, J.M., & Kausler, D.H. (1984). Individual differences and models of memory span: A role for memory search rate? *Journal of Experimental Psychology: Learning, Memory and Cognition, 10*, 72–82.

Puffe, M. (1987). Ein methodischer Ansatz zur gleichzeitigen Bestimmung von Speicherkapazität und Informationsverarbeitungsgeschwindigkeit im Kurzzeitgedächtnis. In: H.–G. Geissler & K. Reschke (Eds.), *Psychophysische Grundlagen mentaler Prozesse*. Leipzig: Karl–Marx–Universität.

Schmidt, K.–D. (1982). *Untersuchungen zur Mikrostruktur des visuellen Wiedererkennungsgedächtnisses*. Unpublished manuscript, Karl–Marx–Universität, Leipzig.

Staude, A. (1985). *Zur Prüfung der Cavanagh–Hypothese über den Zusammenhang von Gedächtnissuchrate und Gedächtnisspanne durch intraindividuellen Vergleich*. Unpublished manuscript, Karl–Marx–Universität, Leipzig.

Sternberg, S. (1969). Memory scanning: Memory processes revealed by reaction–time experiments. *American Scientist, 57*, 421–457.

Sternberg, S. (1975). Memory scanning: New findings and current controversies. *Quarterly Journal of Experimental Psychology, 27*, 1–32.

Psychophysical Explorations of Mental Structures
Edited by H.-G. Geissler
in collaboration with M.H. Müller and W. Prinz
© 1990 by Hogrefe & Huber Publishers

Chapter 24

Cyclical Neural Codes of Human Memory and Some Quantitative Regularities in Experimental Psychology

Arthur N. Lebedev
Institute of Psychology
Academy of Sciences of the U.S.S.R.
Moscow, U.S.S.R.

The idea that memory functions might be based on cyclic brain processes is an old one and has been explored by many investigators. However, despite much effort devoted to it, there has been little success in determining significant parameters such as memory capacity, speed of processing, precision of judgment and other characteristics of memory processes.

This paper is based upon the previously suggested assumption that information stored in human memory is coded by groups of cyclically recurrent neural impulses (cf. Lebedev, 1982) which are generated by coherent discharges of central neurons. Chains of these code elements are proposed to form "code words." It is asserted that code words are generated by ensembles of neurons located in different brain structures and that they can recur cyclically with a frequency equal to the well-known alpha rhythm of about 10 c/s.

For such an approach the observation is crucial that power spectra within the alpha range quite often exhibit two different peaks changeable in magnitude but usually of stable position on the frequency axis. As can be seen in Figure 1, the typical distance between neighbouring peaks is approximately one cycle per second.

A typical steplike difference between neighbouring peak frequencies within the alpha range is approximately one decimal fraction of the maximal peak frequency. The reciprocal value defines the period of alpha-wave beating. One can estimate this period from the duration of the single alpha spindle (about one second). To set the bounds of the spindle, however, is difficult because all other bioelectrical waves mask the bounds of the alpha spindle. This is a possible source of artificially lowered estimates of the spindle duration T obtained if an analysis of spindles is carried out by direct visual inspection.

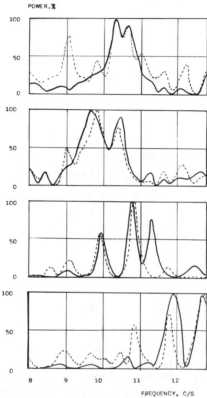

Figure 1. Fourier (solid lines) and Walsh (dotted lines) spectra of power within the alpha band frequencies of four subjects. Horizontal axis: frequency in c/s; vertical axis: power in percent. The power of the dominant peak in each spectrum is equal to 100 percent.

The depression of spectral density between neighbouring peaks can be described as an attraction of intermediate frequencies to both peak frequencies. This attraction is expected to occur if neighbouring frequencies differ from one another by less than $1/aT$, where a is their mean frequency value, and T is the period of the alpha beating.

Likewise, the waves of identical or just equal frequencies are attracted if the phase difference between them is less than $1/aT$. Further, according to our hypothesis, the period of alpha-wave beating is interconnected with the code word duration and the alphabet size of code letters is interrelated with the critical phase difference $1/aT$. The product of the mean peak alpha frequency a and the period T is assumed to be equal to the number of code letters within one code word (not necessarily different) as well as to the alphabet size of code letters:

$$N = aT - 1. \qquad (1)$$

In (1) one of the letters is subtracted because it points only to the beginning of the code word. Under these conditions the maximal number C of different code words is equal to the number of all possible combinations of code letters within one code word:

$$C = N^N. \qquad (2)$$

It was mentioned above that neurons which by virtue of their acitvity generate single code words are located in different brain structures, such as the neocortex, paleo- and archicortex, diencephalon, the reticular structures and others. All these neurons are excited coherently, involving into their own rhythms the neurons of other ensembles. The neural ensembles compete with one another. Each new sequence of memorized signals forms a new ensemble, that is to say, a new code word.

The number of elements within one memorized sequence is equal to the short-term memory capacity H or less. The short-term memory span H is a function of the alphabet size M of memorized signals and of the alphabet size C of all code words:

$$C = M^H. \qquad (3)$$

Approximately $M = A$ can be assumed to hold, where A is an objectively given alphabet span of signals, but in the general case a more complex relation will apply.

The implications of (3) can be tested experimentally. If the given alphabet of memorized signals is fixed, then the higher the short-term memory span, the larger the product aT in line with equations (1) and (2).

A.V. Pasynkova and I.V. Maltseva from our laboratory have established the short-term memory span for decimal digits in dozens of adults. The mean frequency of alpha-rhythm and the mean duration of single alpha-spindles of the same subjects were measured in a resting state with their eyes closed. As expected memory span increased as the values of the product aT increased. But the empirical relation deviated markedly from the quantitative prediction (1) yielding:

$$N = 0.3aT + 5.7 \qquad (4)$$

Nevertheless, we can now calculate the theoretical value of the short-term memory span using equations (2) and (3). The theoretical and experimental data are shown in Table 1.

In accordance with formula (3), if the alphabet span M is changed the short-term memory span changes also. This consequence was examined by our collaborators M.N. Syrenov and N.A. Skopintseva. In his experiments M.N. Syrenov identified the short-term memory spans of 11 chess-players. The memorized strings were randomly composed of chess pieces excluding pawns. The figures were either white or black in color. The given alphabet size corresponded to the 5 different chessmen. The number of figures to be memorized within one string was 10. The number of different strings was 20. The mean value of the short-term memory span turned out to be equal to 6.76 figures with a standard deviation of 0.70.

Table 1. Short-term memory span for decimal digits as a function of alpha-rhythm parameters.

Number of of subjects	Alpha-rythm frequency, a (in c/s)		Product aT		Memory span, H calculated* experimental		
	mean	st.dev.	mean	st.dev.		mean	st.dev.
5	9.32	1.11	4.28	0.60	5.89	5.68	0.42
12	10.64	1.22	5.50	0.28	6.37	6.42	0.89
7	10.86	1.47	6.55	0.18	6.78	6.50	0.64
4	11.00	0.65	7.41	0.28	7.12	7.10	1.48
4	9.98	0.46	8.62	0.37	7.61	7.18	0.48

$^*H = (0.3aT + 5.7) \lg(0.3aT + 5.7)$

Formula (3) predicts that in the case of memorizing two-colored figures memory capacity is shortened in accordance with the solution to the equation:

$$5^{6.76} = 10^x, \qquad (5)$$

where x is the calculated short-term memory span for chess figures of both colors, yielding $x = 4.73$. In actual fact the experimental mean value of the short-term memory span for two-colored chess pieces was 4.76 (standard deviation 0.73).

Other experiments of the same kind confirmed these findings. In his experiments with 30 adults our co-worker V.K. Oshe compared the short-term memory span for decimal digits ($M = 10$) with the short-term memory span for marks randomly placed along a horizontal axis on a computer screen. Each of the five marks was a short vertical line, the length of the horizontal axis being 180 mm. The distances between neighbouring marks were randomly chosen multiples of a "grid" distance of 18 mm. As is well-known, the differential threshold between neighbouring mark positions is approximately 0.01 in total length yielding an alphabet size of distinguished marks of 100. According to (3) we have

$$10^H = 100^P, \qquad (6)$$

where H is the short-term memory span for decimal digits and P the short-term memory span for mark positions. (5) can be simplified yielding:

$$P = H/2. \tag{7}$$

The theoretical values calculated in line with (7), and experimental data are shown in Table 2. The difference between data and predictions is about 5%.

Table 2. Short-term memory capacity for digits and random marks.

Number of subjects	Memory capacity for digits, H	theoretical*	experimental mean	st.dev.
4	4.46	2.13	2.12	0.22
6	5.66	2.83	2.58	0.34
13	6.57	3.28	3.33	0.22
7	7.81	3.90	3.99	0.13

* $P = H/s$

Let the identification of one signal from among K simultaneously perceived signals take t_K milliseconds. The next formula predicts this duration as a function of the alphabet span M of perceived signals as well as the period of alpha-wave beating T:

$$t_K = T(1-p^K)(1-p)^K/(K+1), \tag{8}$$

where p is the probability of undelayed identification during one period T:

$$p = (1 - 1/aT)/KM. \tag{9}$$

The derivation of equations (8) and (9) from the above-mentioned premises was given earlier (Lebedev, 1982). Formula (8) permits prediction of the visual search speed as a function of the short-term memory span $H=K$ according to the adopted designations.

O.J. Kondratjeva in our laboratory carried out experiments of this kind using 12 adult subjects. Table 3 contains experimental data as well as theoretical calculations with the parameter T put at 1 s.

The results confirm the predictions qualitatively: the larger the short-term memory span, the higher the visual search speed. But the difference of about $10-20$ per cent in these experiments between theoretical and experimental data is by no means small. The problem of the determination of visual search speed is thus far from being resolved.

The experimental task relating to the problem of memory search speed involves a comparison of the M memorized signals (the memory set) with the K simultaneously perceived signals. Then the quantity n of all possible comparisons is

$$n = MK(K+1)/2. \tag{10}$$

We have supposed that within some channels these comparisons occur simultaneously. The number of these channels must be equal to the number H

of signals stored within short-term memory. Each single comparison takes a t_K delay calculated in accordance with (9). An exhaustive procedure of comparing all perceived signals with the given memory set should, then, take $t_K n/H$ ms, whereas a self-terminating procedure for positive items should last $(n+1)t_K/2H$ ms on average.

Table 3. The dependence of visual search speed on short-term memory span for items of different type.

Types of items	Memory span	Visual search time (ms/item)		
		According	with instruction to search	
	mean	to (8)	rapidly	accurately
numbers (371,856,...)	2.1	322	192	289
syllables (ron,geb,...)	2.3	303	173	270
words (dog,cab,...)	3.5	221	152	246
triple letters (aaa,ccc,...)	5.3	155	120	195
triple digits (111,555,...)	6.3	132	116	189

In the case of one perceived signal $(K=1)$ and a maximal number of memorized signals $(M=H)$ one can calculate the time delay which is needed for a positive comparison according to:

$$t_1 = T(H+1)(1-(1-1/aT)/H)^2/4H. \qquad (11)$$

According to (11), the time needed for a short-term memory scan is about 250 ms if the memory span H is much more than one unit. This value coincides with the time constant discovered by Cavanagh (1972).

Table 4. The dependence of memory search speed on the short-term memory span.

Elements of memory	Memory	Memory search time (ms/element)	
		experimental data	according to
		(Cavanagh, 1972)	Formula (12)
syllables	3.4	72	73
random forms	3.8	68	66
geom. figures	5.3	50	48
words	5.5	47	46
letters	6.3	40	40
colors	7.1	38	36
digits	7.7	33	33

Analyzing the experimental data published by Cavanagh we have found that the scanning time per memory signal is equal to the right-hand part of (12)

$$t = t_1/(H-1), \qquad (12)$$

where t_1 is calculated according to (11) and H is considerably greater than 1.

The theoretical and experimental data published earlier are given in Table 4. There is reasonably good agreement between theoretical and experimental data.

In short, the larger the short-term memory span, the shorter the intervals between comparisons of perceived and prememorized signals. There is some reason to assume that the same intervals relate to the duration estimates of perceived signals and that they can be considered as time quanta.

Analyzing the experimental data of N.D. Bagrova (Bagrova, 1980) relating to time differential thresholds we have found that the alphabet size M in such experiments depends on the test duration D in accordance with

$$M = 2aD, \qquad (13)$$

where a is again the mean frequency of alpha–rhythm, 10 c/s. Using this value M we calculated the short-term memory span and the identification time according to (8) with $K=H$, $a=10$ c/s and $T=1$s. The results of calculations as well as experimental data are given in Table 5.

Table 5. The dependence of differential time threshold on test durations of acoustical stimuli (data from Bagrova, 1980).

Test duration	Differential thresholds (ms)	
(in ms)	Experimental	According to (8)
100	26	22
200	54	52
300	76	71
500	109	95
700	102	110

The theoretical and experimental data are closely interrelated. The smallest T_k predicted from (8) for $K=M=1$ and $T=1$ s is about 5 ms which perhaps not accidentally falls close to a quantal value suggested at some 4.5 ms (cf. Geissler, this volume).

Summary

Cyclically recurrent patterns of coherent neural discharges are assumed as hypothetical code elements of human short-term memory. The specific approach based on this idea provides a quantitative account of basic characteristics like STM spans, speed of visual and memory search as well as duration discrimination. Predictions are made using only two parameters which can be interpreted in terms of electroencephalogram periods, the mean alpha period and the period of alpha wave beating. For a most fundamental hypothetical variable, the number of storing states, N, prediction involves a linear readjustment.

Correspondence should be addressed to Arthur N. Lebedev, Institute of Psychology, Academy of Sciences of the USSR, Yaroslavskaya 13, Moscow 128366, USSR.

References

Bagrova, N.D. (1980). *Time factor in human perception.* Leningrad: Nauka.

Cavanagh, J.P. (1972). Relation between the immediate memory span and the memory search rate. *Psychological Review, 79,* 525–530.

Geissler, H.-G. (1987). Hierarchien periodischer Vorgänge im Zentralnervensystem als Grundlage zeitlich diskreter Strukturen. In H.-G. Geissler & K. Reschke (Eds.), *Psychologische Grundlagen mentaler Prozesse. In memoriam G.T. Fechner* (pp. 27–85). Leipzig: Karl-Marx-Universität.

Lebedev, A.N. (1982). Note on the derivation of equations for speed and capacity of perception. The skeleton of a physiological theory. In H.-G. Geissler & P. Petzold (Eds.), *Psychophysical judgment and the process of perception* (pp. 282–285). Berlin: VEB Deutscher Verlag der Wissenschaften. Amsterdam: North-Holland.

Psychophysical Explorations of Mental Structures
Edited by H.-G. Geissler
in collaboration with M.H. Müller and W. Prinz
© 1990 by Hogrefe & Huber Publishers

Chapter 25

Task-Dependent Structuring of Motor Programs

Stephan Haake
Sektion Psychologie, Karl-Marx-Universität Leipzig
Leipzig, G.D.R.

A movement sequence is said to be planned in advance if a representation of the entire sequence is generated, which contains some essential features of the upcoming sequence of movements, such as their serial ordering (Keele, 1981, 1986).

The motor program begins at a very abstract level, and after passing through successive levels it ultimately produces detailed action. The program that guides movement is abstract in the sense of independence from the articulators that execute it.

Such a conceptual division separates a motor level from a conceptual level (Raibert, 1977; MacKay, 1982). The conceptual level embodies the timing and sequencing of activity. The global sequence is not directly "known" by the muscle system.

A Short Review of Some Task-Dependent RT Results that Argue for a Multilevel Representation of Motor Programs

Certain reaction time results argue for a multilevel representation of motor programs. This hierarchic representation of a sequence is revealed in the preparation time for rapid movement sequences but also in the on-line production of sequences.

First I will make some remarks on preparation time for rapid movement sequences like speech and typewriting revealed in experiments with the simple reaction time paradigm. In these experiments sequence complexity was manipulated in terms of the number of movement parts — and a systematic dependence of preparation time on sequence complexity was shown (Henry & Rogers, 1960; Henry, 1980; Sternberg, Monsell, Knoll & Wright, 1978). In the experiments conducted by Sternberg and co-workers in 1978 on rapid movement sequences, subjects made responses composed of short sequences of equivalent response elements, that were either spoken words or keystrokes. The response length (number of elements) over a range from one to five, and element size, i.e., duration, were varied. The two main measures were response latency and response duration, from the first element to the last. The main results from the experiment were as follows:

First, mean latency increased with response length, and the increase was approximately linear (see Table 1). Mean latency also increased with the number of constituents per unit. The effects on mean latency of number of units and number of constituents per unit were additive.

Table 1. Fitted latency functions in the sequence production task for different kinds of items (from Sternberg et al., 1978).

Task	mean latency function, $L(n)$
Speech	
Ascending numbers	$263.3 + 12.6(n-1)$
Weekdays	$259.9 + 8.8(n-1)$
Monosyllabic nouns	$261.5 + 11.1(n-1)$
Disyllabic nouns	$267.4 + 10.1(n-1)$
Typewriting	
Alternating hands	$229.7 + 14.9(n-2)$
One hand	$231.2 + 4.1(n-2)$

Second, the mean time interval from one unit to the next also increased with response length (Table 2). The increase was approximately linear. The effects of number of units and unit size were additive.

Third, the rate at which mean latency and mean time interval from one unit to the next increased with response length was similar.

Sternberg et al. accounted for these results with a buffer search model. The idea was that the program for the entire sequence of motor responses consists of discrete subprograms which correspond to each of the responses in the sequence. According to the model, the entire program is loaded into a buffer which must be searched to find the subprogram for each response regardless of its serial position in the sequence. On the assumption that the search proceeds at a uniform rate and that the duration of all nonsearch processes (e.g. stimulus processing and efferent signalling) is constant, the timing results of Sternberg et al. can be explained. Assuming that the buffer search model is correct, how are the subprograms for the required responses initially determined and loaded into the buffer?

Table 2. Fitted duration functions in the sequence production task for different kinds of items (from Sternberg et al., 1978).

Task	mean duration function, $D(n)$
Speech	
Ascending numbers	$101.1 + 57.6(n-1) + 12.2(n-1)^2$
Weekdays	$168.8 + 183.1(n-1) + 12.6(n-1)^2$
Monosyllabic nouns	$122.4 + 91.9(n-1) + 13.6(n-1)^2$
Disyllabic nouns	$173.4 + 180.4(n-1) + 12.0(n-1)^2$
Typewriting	
Alternating hands	$71.9(n-1) + 15.2(n-1)^2$
One hand	$142.9(n-1) + 14.1(n-1)^2$

Rosenbaum, Saltzman and Kingman (1984) attended to this question and conducted experiments in which they employed a simple extension of Sternberg's task. Instead of telling subjects exactly what response sequence to perform, they required subjects to choose between two possible response sequences. The main empirical question was how the time to perform each response in the ultimately required sequence depends on the number of responses in the sequence to be performed, the number of responses in the sequence that does not have to be performed, and the relationship between the two.

In a first experiment subjects made choices between keyboard sequences which are shown in Table 3.

Table 3. Choice reaction conditions in the experiments from Rosenbaum, Saltzman and Kingman (1984). i, r, m: left index, ring, and middle finger, respectively. I, R, M: right index, ring, and middle finger, respectively.

Experiment 1	Experiment 2
i vs. I	i vs. I
ir vs. IR	i vs. IRM
irm vs. IRM	I vs. irm
	irm vs. IRM

The main independent variable was the number of responses in the sequence to be performed. The main dependent variable was choice reaction time, termed *T1* and the time between the responses (*T2, T3*). The main findings were as follows:

— mean *T1* increased approximately linearly with number of responses in the sequence;

—mean *T2* increased with *n* (for *n*=2 and *n*=3) at approximately the same rate as mean *T1*;

—mean *T3* approximately equalled mean *T2* (for *n*=3).

In a second experiment subjects chose between sequences that contained sometimes unequal numbers of responses. The main findings of these experiments were twofold.

First, mean T1 for single responses was considerably longer when the alternative sequence consisted of three responses than when the alternative sequence consisted of just one response.

Second, mean *T1* was longer for three-response sequences than for single responses, but mean *T1* for three-response sequences was only slightly longer when the alternative sequence consisted of three responses than when the alternative sequence consisted of just one response.

Rosenbaum, Saltzman and Kingman accounted for these results with a hierarchical decisions model. According to the model, plans for possible response sequences are hierarchically organized, and performing one of the two possible response sequences is based on two types of decisions. The first is a decision between the two response sequences, which is necessary only after the choice reaction signal is presented, and is achieved by selecting the superordinate control element corresponding to the required sequence. The second is a decision about which response to perform at each serial position within the initially selected sequence; this decision is achieved by selecting the subprogram corresponding to that serial position. The results of the first experiment reported by Rosenbaum, Saltzman and Kingman can be accounted for by assuming that the time to choose among the subprograms for a given response sequence increases with the number of subprograms from among which to choose. To account for the results of the second experiment of Rosenbaum, Saltzman and Kingman two elaborations of the model are needed. One is that choices can only be made between or among elements at the same functional level. Despite the success of the hierarchical decisions model it fails to account for the fact that subjects can often choose more quickly between similar responses than between dissimilar responses. For example, Heuer (1982a,b) found that subjects can choose between oscillatory movements of one hand or the other more quickly if the movements are of the same form (i.e., both vertical or horizontal) than if the movements are of different form (i.e., one vertical and one horizontal).

To accommodate these facts, Rosenbaum and Saltzman (1984) proposed a motor-program editor model. This model says that subjects prepare for a choice between two sequences by constructing an ordered set of motor subprograms each of which has a list of the motor features shared by the alternative responses at the corresponding serial position; the subsequent choice time is assumed to depend on the number of features to be supplied to the initially readied feature lists. A second series of experiments was designed to distinguish between the two models of response selection. In five experiments reported by Rosenbaum, Inhoff and Gordon (1984), subjects chose between response sequences consisting of one to four button presses. Among the phenomena found are the following:

−systematic effects of the serial positions of uncertain responses in the alternative sequences;
−effects of the structural similarity of the two sequences, both on the time to choose between the sequences and on the time to perform responses within them;
−effects of the requirement to cancel some responses depending on the structural relationship between those responses and the other responses in the same sequence and in the other sequence.

On the basis of these results, Rosenbaum, Inhoff and Gordon (1984) proposed a hybrid of the motor−program editor model and the hierarchical decisions model − the Hierarchical Editor Model (HED).

A Formal Discussion of the Hierarchic Concept: Rosenbaum's HED Model

HED assumes that under speeded conditions motor plans are hierarchically structured, abstract programs that take the form of a phrase structure grammar. Subjects prepare for a choice between response sequences by readying responses shared by the two possible sequences. The essential new ideas in the HED model are that the physical production of planned motor sequences is controlled by the successive "unpacking" of nested subprograms and that before this unpacking process begins, it is gone through once in advance to ensure that all uncertain nesting relations are resolved. Two passes are made through the program:

The first, the edit pass ensures that all initially uncertain compositions in the program are fully specified, and proceeds by successively unpacking high−level codes into their constituents, beginning with the first uncertain composition and ending when all constituents have been fully unpacked. To minimize the duration of the edit pass during the choice RT interval, the edit pass proceeds up to the first uncertain composition before the choice reaction signal is presented. Then after the choice reaction signal is presented, the edit pass continues. The second, the execution pass, governs performance of the programmed sequence by means of the same unpacking process, except that unpacking always begins at the highest level of the program and results in response execution whenever terminal elements are encountered. The characteristics of the HED can be summed up in the following five points:

1. programs for motor sequences are hierarchically structured;
2. an edit pass specifies all initially uncertain compositions;
3. an execution pass governs performance of the programmed sequence;
4. the edit and execution passes proceed by unpacking the programs into successively smaller units;
5. each unpacking operation, whether it occurs in the edit pass or execution pass, takes a finite and measurable amount of time.

Each unpacking operation, whether it occurs in the edit pass or execution pass, takes a finite and measurable amount of time; so the number of steps preceding a response can be used to predict its latency.

Table 4 illustrates the application of the HED model to the choice IiMm (right index finger, left index finger, right middle finger, left middle finger) vs. Mm (right middle finger, left middle finger). In terms of a phrase structure grammar, the following processes and structures are deployed:

1. Sequence definition: In preparation for the choice reaction signal a plan is defined in a manner consistent with the phrase structure representation shown in Table 4.
   ($\neq$ denotes a terminal element; $\varnothing$ denotes the null set).
2. Rule definition: To interpret the reaction signal when it is presented, the following rule is established: If the reaction signal is X then A $-$ $\varnothing$; otherwise (O), A $-$ Ii.
3. Rewriting up to the first uncertain juncture: In this case A $-$ Ii or $\varnothing$.
4. Completion of the edit pass after the reaction signal is identified.
5. Completion of the execution pass.

Table 4. Application of the HED model to choice IiMm vs. Mm (from Rosenbaum, Inhoff & Gordon, 1984).

IiMm vs. Mm

1. sequence definition   2. rule definition

sequence $-$ AB	if reaction signal is X	then A $-$ $\varnothing$
A $-$ Ii or $\varnothing$	if reaction signal is O	then A $-$ Ii
I $-$ $\neq$		
i $-$ $\neq$		
B $-$ Mm		
M $-$ $\neq$		
m $-$ $\neq$		

3. rewriting up to the first uncertain juncture
(before the reaction signal)

sequence $-$ AB (O)

4. completion of the edit pass
(after the reaction signal)

if O then $-$ IiMm	if X then $-$ Mm
A $-$ Ii (1)	A $-$ $\varnothing$ (1)
I $-$ $\neq$ (2)	B $-$ Mm(2)
i $-$ $\neq$ (3)	M $-$ $\neq$ (3)
B $-$ Mm(4)	m $-$ $\neq$ (4)
M $-$ $\neq$ (5)	
m $-$ $\neq$ (6)	

5. completion of the execution pass

sequence $-$ AB (7)	sequence $-$ AB (5)
A $-$ Ii (8)	A $-$ $\varnothing$ (6)
I $-$ $\neq$ (9)	B $-$ Mm(7)
i $-$ $\neq$ (1)	M $-$ $\neq$ (8)
B $-$ Mm(1)	m $-$ $\neq$ (1)
M $-$ $\neq$ (1)	
m $-$ $\neq$ (1)	

We can now count the number of unpacking operations preceding each response to see whether the time to produce that response increases with the number of unpacking operations that immediately precede it. For IiMm, the number of steps preceding I is nine, whereas for Mm the number of steps preceding M is eight.

When mean response time is plotted against the number of unpacking operations (Figure 1), a straight line is shown to provide a good fit to the mean response times of the initial responses. These results suggest that the time to carry out all rewrite steps was the same on the average, an outcome not required by the model.

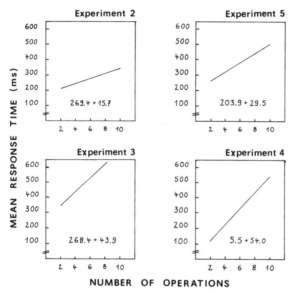

Figure 1. Mean response time as a function of number of unpacking operations for initial responses (adapted from Rosenbaum, Inhoff & Gordon, 1984).

Interpreting the Data of Rosenbaum, Inhoff and Gordon in Terms of the Time Quantum Model

However, there are interexperimental differences in the estimate of processing speed during the movement onset-time ($T1$) — in Table 5, upper half, shown as the slope of the best-fitting linear function relating $T1$ to the number of steps. These differences cannot be explained by Rosenbaum and co-workers within the scope of their model. The estimate of processing speed ranged from 10 ms and 16 ms per step in experiments 1 and 2 to 44 ms, 55 ms and 29 ms per step in experiments 3, 4 and 5. The explanation that Rosenbaum and his co–workers offer is that the overall speed of decoding was higher in the first experiments because of motivational factors.

Table 5. Upper half: Slopes of fitted functions for mean response time of the initial responses plotted against number of unpacking operations (from Rosenbaum, Inhoff & Gordon, 1984). Lower half: Slopes predicted by Time Quantum Model (Geissler, 1985a,b).

Experiment	slope (ms per step)
1	10
2	16
5	29
3	44
4	55

Experiment	predicted slope in ms (L: 30; n: 2)
1	9.13
2	18.26
5	27.39
3	45.65
4	54.78

Another possible explanation emerges from the conceptual framework of discrete time periods in mental processes. According to Geissler, discrete time periods are based on hypothetical carrier processes. The Time Quantum Model (TQM) proposed by Geissler (1985a,b) states the general properties of such carrier processes. The TQM is based on the following assumptions:

First, all admissible discrete time periods are integer multiples from the lowest possible operation time or "time quantum" T (T equals 4.5 ms).

Second, admissible time periods are able to form chains to the point of $M \leq 30$. Within the coherence length M of such cycles, mental information processing occurs in a deterministic, discrete and strictly timed manner. The value of M is specific to each subject and his state.

Third, the discrete time periods are ordered in intervals whose boundaries may vary in a task–dependent manner.

Fourth, there exists a tendency towards hierarchical organization of discrete time periods. From this tendency there follows the so–called fractionation rule, according to which admissible time periods are integer values of an actual, task–dependent maximum value $L \leq M$.

Fifth, L-values with a high number of integer dividers are emphasized in accordance with their possibilities for multiple hierarchic organization. Stressed values of L are 16, 18, 20, 24, 28, and 30 in correspondence with the estimation of $M \leq 30$ as an upper boundary.

Sixth, the model assumes a hierarchic metaorganization of discrete time periods with preferred binary structure, which may bring about regular time relations between fields of phenomena which are diverse in content and timing characteristics.

Based on these assumptions the TQM allows to predict discrete time periods.

Sofar, TQM has been applied to mental processes in perception and visual short-term processing like the time course of masking phenomena or search rate in Sternberg's item-recognition procedure (Geissler, 1985a,b); preliminary attempts focus on relations extending to periodicities in physiological systems like the course of heart-rate. Now we want to show that TQM can lead to a better understanding of the aforementioned results which Rosenbaum and co-workers obtained about the timing of organizational processes in the production of motor sequences. Table 5, lower half, shows an estimation of slopes based on the predictions of TQM. The predicted slopes are in agreement with the really obtained slopes.

Thus, TQM provides a tool for the proper understanding within information processing of interexperimental differences in terms of task-dependent shifts, the amount of time needed for each hypothesized step, and within the constraints set by TQM assumptions.

TQM provides also a good fit to the data reported by Sternberg et al. (1978), especially if we look at the individual data (Table 6). So we think that the concept of discrete time periods can also contribute to a better understanding of shifts in the timing of information processing in the motor domain.

Table 6. Slopes of individual latency functions in the sequence production task for ascending numbers (from Sternberg, Monsell, Knoll & Wright, 1978).

Subject	slope (ms/word)
1	10.1
2	9.5
3	11.3
4	19.4

Summary

Task-dependent structuring of motor programs expresses itself in two ways. First, if movement sequences have to be generated under speeded conditions there will be a need for planning processes which establish a representation of the entire sequence in advance. Second, the representation itself and the generation process which is guided by the representation depend upon the essential features of the upcoming sequence and external and/or internal contextual constraints, e.g., other representations which may be similar or dissimilar. Effects of movement onset time and timing within sequences are related to task-specificity. In a first approximation timing effects were described with reference to task-complexity. This was followed by explanatory approaches at the model level such as the HED which accounts for the process structure of the generation of rapid movement sequences. However, such models do not serve to explain task-specific differences in time estimates of each processing operation. The time needed for each operation obviously does not assume arbitrary values but is, in accordance with Geissler's TQM predictions, restricted to certain ranges of values. A problem that remains to be resolved is why these operation times assume certain values as a function of demands. A possible course might be individual physiological constraints.

Correspondence should be addressed to Stephan Haake, Sektion Psychologie, Karl–Marx–Universität Leipzig, Tieckstr. 2, Leipzig, DDR – 7030.

References

Geissler, H.–G. (1985a). *Sources of seeming redundancy in temporally quantized information processing* (Report No.63/1985). Research Group on Perception and Action at the Center for Interdisciplinary Research (ZIF), University of Bielefeld.

Geissler, H.–G. (1985b). Zeitquantenhypothese zur Struktur ultraschneller Gedächtnisprozesse. *Zeitschrift für Psychologie, 99,* 347 – 363.

Henry, F.M., & Rogers, D.E. (1960). Increased response latency for complicated movements and a "memory drum" theory of neuromotor reaction. *Research Quarterly, 31,* 448 – 458.

Henry, F.M. (1980). Use of simple reaction time in motor programming studies: A reply to Klapp, Wyatt & Lingo. *Journal of Motor Behavior, 12,* 163 – 168.

Heuer, H. (1982a). Binary choice reaction time as a criterion of motor equivalence. *Acta Psychologica, 50,* 35 – 47.

Heuer, H. (1982b). Binary choice reaction time as a criterion of motor equivalence. Further evidence. *Acta Psychologica, 50,* 49 – 60.

Keele, S.W. (1981). Behavioral analysis of movement. In V.B. Brooks (Ed.), *Handbook of physiology, Section 1: The Nervous System. Vol. II: Motor control, Part 2* (pp.1391 – 1414). Baltimore: American Physiological Society.

Keele, S.W. (1986). Motor control. In L. Kaufmann, I. Thomas & K. Boff (Eds.), *Handbook of perception and performance.* New York: John Wiley & Sons.

MacKay, D.G. (1982). The problem of flexibility, fluency, and speed–accuracy trade–off in skilled behavior. *Psychological Review, 89,* 483 – 506.

Raibert, M.H. (1977). *Motor control and learning by the state–space model* (Technical Report AI–TR–439). Artificial Intelligence Laboratory, MIT.

Rosenbaum, D.A., Inhoff, A.W., & Gordon, A.M. (1984). Choosing between movement sequences: A hierarchical editor model. *Journal of Experimental Psychology: General, 113,* 372 – 393.

Rosenbaum, D.A., & Saltzman, E. (1984). A motor–program editor. In W. Prinz & A.F. Sanders (Eds.), *Cognition and motor processes.* Berlin, Heidelberg: Springer Verlag.

Rosenbaum, D.A., Saltzman, E., & Kingman, A. (1984). Choosing between movement sequences. In S. Kornblum & J.Requin (Eds.), *Preparatory states and processes.* Hillsdale, NJ: Lawrence Erlbaum Associates.

Sternberg, S., Monsell, S., Knoll, R.L., & Wright, C.E. (1978). The latency and duration of rapid movement sequences: Comparisons of speech and typewriting. In G.E. Stelmach (Ed.), *Information processing in motor control and learning.* New York: Academic Press.

IV. Towards Inner Psychophysics

Psychophysical Explorations of Mental Structures
Edited by H.-G. Geissler
in collaboration with M.H. Müller and W. Prinz
© 1990 by Hogrefe & Huber Publishers

Chapter 26

On the Regulation of Excitability in Cerebral Cortex – A Bridge Between EEG and Attention?

Brigitte Rockstroh and Thomas Elbert
Abteilung für Klinische und
Physiologische Psychologie
Universität Tübingen
Tübingen, F.R.G.

It is a common approach in psychophysiology to relate brain waves, i.e., parameters extracted from the EEG, to psychological constructs. Aspects of event-related potentials (ERP), for instance, have been linked to attention (such as the terminal, CNV [Tecce & Cattanach, 1982] or the processing negativity, Nd, Näätänen, 1982), readiness to respond (the Bereitschaftspotential, BP, Deecke, Bashore & Brunia, 1984), or memory function (such as the P3, Donchin, 1981, Rösler, 1982). Such an approach has been questioned repeatedly even by ERP researchers. Donchin, Ritter and McCallum (1978) argued that "one gains very little understanding by assigning to a poorly understood phenomenon an equally poorly defined concept as a label" (p. 359). The development of complementary approaches seems to be an urgent challenge. However, we believe that an alternative approach should be based on neurophysiological or neurocybernetic considerations taking advantage of new methods of EEG analysis which have been provided by nonlinear science. Such methods – sometimes referred to under the heading of "chaos" – currently revolutionize scientific thinking about origins and causes. Mathematics alone, however, will be insufficient to understand the nature and causes of the "deterministic chaos" suspected in the EEG time series. In the present chapter, we will there-fore develop a model in a deductive manner and suggest ways to evaluate its goodness of fit with data. We will describe how regulatory circuits within the brain might generate electrical activity underlying spontaneous EEG fluctuations and certain ERP components. Our line of argument starts with the biocyberneti-cal view advanced by the group of Braitenberg, Palm, and Schüz (Braitenberg, 1978, 1984; Palm, 1982) that thresholds of cortical activity are regulated in a feedback loop. This idea is coupled with the hypothesis that a regulation of excitability thresholds in cortical neuronal networks is realized via a modulation of the depolarization in dendritic trees of cortical pyramidal neurons. The degree of depolarization manifests itself as surface negativity as recorded in the EEG. Depending on the attentive behavior the enhancement of excitability is directed to different neuronal circuits and consequently related to EEG activity.

Cell Assemblies

A central concept in models about the functioning of the brain is that of cell assemblies (Hebb, 1949) or neuronal networks, defined as assemblies of neurons connected with one another by synaptic junctions that serve to trans-mit information and that may be involved in memory storage. Since the contents of memory depend on experience, the synapses between neurons cannot be determined in a complete genetical way. The strengthening of the connections between neurones is considered to be the physiological basis of learning and memory storage. It has been suggested that within the networks the ability of simultaneously active synapses to depolarize the postsynaptic membrane is increasd above a certain level of postsynaptic activity, while insufficient activation weakens active synapses (Bienenstock, Cooper & Munro, 1982). The question of how synapses become modified by experience has been approached by Bear, Cooper and Ebner (1987), who suggest that the membrane potential at which Ca^{2+} enters the postsynaptic membrane through NMDA channels should vary with the history of prior cell activity. Accordingly, a good proportion of the excitatory NMDA synapses become strengthened through learning while others degenerate or remain unchanged.

Feedback–Control of Cortical Excitability

Threshold control of excitability within and across networks can be ex-pected for different reasons. Firstly, there is a danger of interconnected networks becoming activated beyond control (Braitenberg, 1978). If the number of active networks reaches a certain critical level, there is a high probability of the remaining ones becoming activated too – up to a final stage of maximal activation as seen in an epileptic seizure. Such an overactivation might be prevented by a threshold control that can rapidly detect an explosive ignition among cell assemblies and that would then regulate cortical excitability by raising thresholds. Furthermore, threshold control would enable the brain to interrupt ongoing activity, when relevant information is received (Elbert & Rockstroh, 1987). If thresholds are set high consequent upon the presentation of relevant information, previous activity will instantaneously drop to a low level, and activity will survive only in elements pertaining to the concept of the incoming stimulus. If the brain can adjust thresholds in advance, threshold control can be considered a mechanism for directing attention to future action. Cortical tuning would then improve the processing of an expected event.

Brain Systems Involved in the Feedback Control of Cortical Excitability

According to the model of Skinner and Yingling (1977) the interplay of both the mediothalamic-frontocortical system (MTFCS) and the mesencephalic reticular formation (MRF) regulate bioelectric activity related to attentive behavior, EEG, and ERP-components. Both systems converge upon the Nucleus Reticularis Thalami (R) which "gates" thalamocortical activity. The regulation is realized from excitation by the MTFCS and inhibition by the MRF on R-cells, which has inhibitory control over the transmission through sensory relay nuclei. Inhibition of R opens the thalamic "gates" so that excitation is transferred to the frontal cortex (FC) via the medial thalamus (MT). This leads to a general readiness for information intake and is reflected by a slow negative wave such as the initial CNV (Rockstroh, Elbert, Birbaumer & Lutzenberger, 1982). If the event that inhibited R is irrelevant, the FC will activate R in turn, thereby interrupting its own excitation − closing the "gate". Thus, the ability to focus attention occurs by way of inhibition in the thalamocortical circuits carrying irrelevant information. Otherwise a distinct pattern of R activation throughout the FC will release thalamic activation to specific cortical regions. Skinner and Yingling conclude that the MTFCS regulates bioelectric activity selectively because "it operates as a specifically organized system with phasic control" (p. 53).

Excitability of cortical regions can be tuned by nonspecific thalamocortical fibers which synapse with the apical dendrites. This process might be considered a candidate for the regulation of thresholds of neuronal excitability. However, such a tuning of nonspecific thalamocortical afferents can only be effective if information about ongoing activity in the networks to be regulated is taken into account. A "measurement device" must be assumed that receives information about ongoing activity of cortical neuronal networks and which transmits this information to the thalamus. Neuroanatomical structures that fulfill these requirements are the basal ganglia (Braitenberg, 1984; Scheibel & Scheibel, 1966; Marsden, 1982; Brooks, 1986; Schneider & Lidsky, 1987).[1]

---

[1] There is ample evidence indicating the importance of the basal ganglia for attentive behaviour; e.g., by Hassler (1978, 1980), Marsden (1982), Cairus (1952), Schmidt (1983), as well as for the importance of basal ganglia in the regulation of slow potentials such as the Bereitschaftspotential (e.g., Deecke, Kornhuber & Schmitt, 1976; Tsuda, 1982).

The ventral system of the basal ganglia contains the limbically innervated Nucleus accumbens, while the dorsal system receives input from major areas of the cerebral neocortex, the thalamus, and the Raphe nuclei in the reticular formation (Marsden, 1982; Brooks, 1986). We can assume a regulatory loop as illustrated in Figure 1, comprising cortex — striatum — pallidum — thalamus — cortex. This assumption is in line with the conclusion drawn by Brooks (1986) that "the basal ganglia are parts of a control circuit that may operate somewhat like those of the cerebellum, that is, by comparing intended outputs with their actual execution" (p. 294).

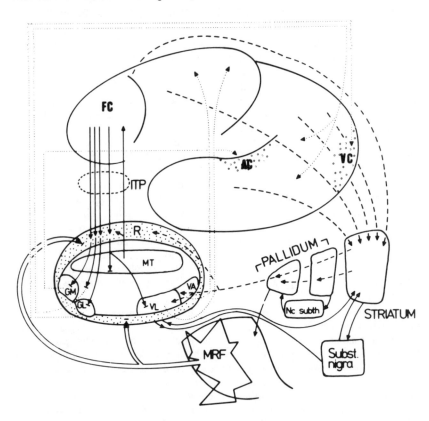

Figure 1. Schematic illustration of brain structures assumed to be involved in threshold regulation. All cortical regions send information about the actual excitation via the basal ganglia (striatum, pallidum) to the thalamus (dashed lines). From there, thalamocortical afferents project back to all cortical regions (dotted lines) being modulated by the MTFCS (solid lines). ITP: inferior thalamic peduncle. The pole of the temporal lobe receives no thalamocortical afferents, and, hence, does not participate in the described regulatory loop. (Adopted from Elbert & Rockstroh, 1987).

Representation of Cortical Excitability in the Spontaneous EEG

The connections between cortical pyramidal cells are believed to be primarily excitatory. The "nonspecific" thalamic fibers, that is, the fibers which do not carry specific sensory input information, synapse with the dendritic trees of pyramidal neurons at locations rather distant from their cell bodies, primarily in layer I. A depolarization of the apical dendrites modulates the excitability of the neurons which can be interrupted through inhibitory synapses closer to the soma, since the depolarization at the axon hillock is essential. This suggests that the apical dendritic tree may be a candidate for the regulation of cortical excitability thresholds. Depolarization of the apical dendrites causes an efflux of negative charges into extracellular space and back into the neuron in the deeper layers. This results in a polarization of the cortex with the negative pole near the surface. A lowering of thresholds for cortical excitability will hence result in an increase of surface negativity, while a positive wave will be generated when thresholds are set high. In acute focal epilepsy — during the (inter)ictal spike discharges — thousands of neurons in the focus undergo an unusually large depolarization (PDS) synchronously, on which a burst of APs is superimposed. The PDS is followed by a hyperpolarizing potential and neuronal inhibition (Ayala, Dichter, Gumnit, Matsumoto & Spencer, 1973). In areas surrounding the focus many neurons are inhibited during the PDS. Even in distant projection areas, neurons can be excited only briefly, but are more often inhibited during the PDS (Schwartzkroin & Wheal, 1984; Dichter & Ayala, 1987). That means that the controlling loop "tries" to increase thresholds but obviously does not succeed in doing so in the epileptic focus.

The following examples should illustrate the functioning of threshold regulation as represented by scalp–recorded brain potentials. Let us first give an example of "automatic" threshold regulation largely unaffected by incoming stimuli. Activity at time t will determine activity at the very next moment $t + \tau$, τ denoting the time required for the regulatory loop cortex — striatum — pallidum — thalamus — cortex to transform the information received from the cortex and to transmit it back readjusting its excitability. The nonspecific thalamocortical input to the cortex will be large for small amounts of ongoing activity (A) but will be set to very low values when much activity is circulating. A possible relationship is illustrated by the function

$$A(t+\tau) \; = \; f(A(t)) \; = \; e^{-A(t)} \cdot A(t) \cdot constant \;.$$

Figure 2 illustrates that the trajectories of nearby points separate exponentially, resulting in two complete time series — which limits prediction for future development. There are certainly numerous other possible relationships and the feedback is certainly not so simple. The global control of excitability is probably organized in a topographical manner (the caudate nucleus at least preserves required information), and additionally local autoregulation might exist, e.g., realized via GABAergic interneurons (basket cells). However, Figure 2 illustrates that even such a simple feedback system can generate rather irregular or chaotic time series looking very much like an EEG.

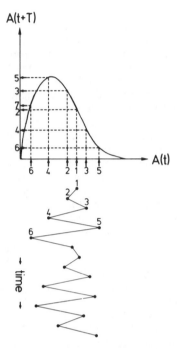

Figure 2. Relationship between activity at time t ($A(t)$) and activity at the next moment $A(t+1)$ and examples of a time series of $A(t)$ generated by the successive iterates, starting with the arbitrary point '1', the next iterate would be '2', then '3', etc.

Consequences of the Regulation of Cortical Excitability for ERPs

An external event or stimulus produces additional input to the cortex. Consequently, the momentary activity ($A(t)$) and all subsequent activity will be changed. Stimulus input activates the primary projection areas via specific thalamic fibers, enhancing $A(t)$. The feedback control will cause a compensatory increase in threshold, which should show itself in the EEG as a transient positive shift. Indeed, modality nonspecific positive EP components develop after a latency of 100 – 150 ms (P2) in response to every enhancement of cortical activity. The reflexive limiting of cortical excitability allows for the interruption of ongoing activity, while incoming activity fed through specific afferents is maintained. Therefore, strong inputs enable the initiation of activity in specific cortical networks and block previously active elements. If the event is relevant, cortical input may be enhanced through brain stem and/or limbic activity. If attention is to be directed actively towards the relevant stimulus, the working of the feedback loop can be controlled via the MTFCS. Stimuli can activate MTFCS operation directly via brain stem collaterals feeding into R and releasing FC activity. A pronounced dampening of cortical activity can then be achieved by a longer-lasting increase in firing threshold, which would manifest itself as a P3b-like wave in the ERP. Storage of relevant events in memory may require ongoing reverberation for a little while without much additional disturbing activation. If this down-regulation of excitability is controlled by the FC, a frontal negative shift is superimposed on the widespread positivity. The resulting potential shift, known as slow wave, has been related by a number of authors (e.g., Rösler, 1982; Roth, Rothbart & Kopell, 1978) to memory load.

Whenever an event is anticipated (i.e., signalled, as in the two-stimulus paradigm, or self-induced), it is advantageous to the organism to adjust certain thresholds in advance. We may assume the following process: The input from the signal stimulus activated the MTFCS. However, the contingency between S1 presentation and MTFCS activity is favoured when the excitation reverberating in the MTFCS is maintained. This becomes possible when the imperative stimulus (S2) is presented within an adequate time interval. This contingency may be conditioned, i.e, the neuronal representation of S1 acquires the capacity to elicit threshold regulation in networks that might be involved in S2-associated processing. Furthermore, in order to prevent premature activation, i.e., a "false start", threshold regulation should start late in the anticipatory interval. This process of threshold regulation is reflected by the time course of negative SPs (CNV) within the anticipatory interval. While the negative peak early in the anticipatory interval may represent activation of the MTFCS, the "late" or "terminal" CNV represents the trade-off between efficient preparation – enabled by threshold reduction – and the avoidance of a "false start" by means of threshold balance.

Such a relationship was demonstrated by Lutzenberger, Elbert, Rockstroh and Birbaumer (1979): Subjects were trained to induce different levels of negativity "by command" (see below). The performance in a signal detection task was measured consequent upon the self-induced SP-shift. Subjects performed best on trials with an intermediate level of negativity, whereas increasing negativity was accompanied by an increasing number of "false alarms", and zero or positive shifts (as compared with a pretrial baseline) decreased the number of detected signals. Support for the functional significance of threshold regulation for attentive behavior can also be derived from the relationship between surface negative SPs and behavioural responses. For example, response latency was shorter when the reaction time task was presented with high CNV amplitudes than when following decreased negativity (Rockstroh, Elbert, Lutzenberger & Birbaumer, 1982). Spontaneous slow potential shifts were found to covary with performance efficiency in various tasks in the "potential related event" paradigm (Stamm, 1984; Bauer, 1984).[2] This admits of the following interpretation: Tasks presented during increases in negativity are presented when activity is low and consequently thresholds have been lowered. Hence, the task is pre-

---

[2] In this paradigm task onset is triggered by the detection of slow negative or positive shifts in the EEG. Tasks were performed faster, and subjects made fewer errors, following increases in negativity than when the task onset was triggered by positive SP-shifts.

sented to an easily excitable brain with little ongoing activity and is consequently processed efficiently. When subjects learned to systematically modify their SPs within an operant feedback procedure (Elbert, Rockstroh, Lutzenberger & Birbaumer, 1980), performance in various tasks was more efficient after self-induced increase in negativity, as compared to self-induced negativity suppression (for a summary of results see Birbaumer, Elbert, Rockstroh & Lutzenberger, 1981; Rockstroh, Elbert, Lutzenberger & Birbaumer, 1989; Rockstroh, Birbaumer, Elbert & Lutzenberger, 1984).

Several recent theories have proposed different "modes" of processing within the brain (e.g., Cooper, McCallum & Papakostopoulos, 1979; Posner & Snyder, 1975; Norman & Shallice, 1985; Shiffrin & Schneider, 1977). In line with these theories, we may conclude from the preceding statements that in one "mode" of brain functioning the EEG reflects excitability under extensive MTFCS modulation. During this mode, event-related slow potentials are generated and EEG synchronization vanishes. In the other mode, threshold regulation should be automatic, which might become manifest in more synchronous EEG oscillations. Both modes may be present at the same time in different brain regions. The EEG recording will then reflect an integration of both modes modulated by the effects of incoming stimuli and consequent activities in reafferent pathways. Experimentally, however, it should be possible to evoke either of the modes and to test predictions for EEG and SPs in order to elaborate the present model.

Summary

A model is proposed which describes the regulation of cortical excitability. It is based on the fact that pyramidal neurons have firing thresholds which can be modulated via lasting depolarizations of the dendritic tree. It is suggested that modification of excitability takes place separately in the different neuronal networks, constituing one physiological basis of attentive behavior.

Depolarizations of apical dendrites give rise to surface-negative scalp potentials which appear in the DC-records of the EEG. Hence, the extent of excitability in one brain region can be measured as amplitudes of slow potential shifts arising from the corresponding region.

Distinct information processing requires the overall amount of neural activity to be kept within limits at any given moment. A feedback loop is postulated which regulates the overall amount of neural firing thresholds. Consequences of this regulation for the EEG as well as for attentive behavior are outlined.

Acknowledgement. Research was supported by the Deutsche Forschungsgemeinschaft (SFB 307) and the Max-Kade Foundation (grant to the second author).
Correspondence should be addressed to Brigitte Rockstroh, Psychologisches Institut, Abteilung Klinische & Physiologische Psychologie, Gartenstr. 29, 7400 Tübingen, F.R.G.

References

Ayala, G.F., Dichter, M., Gumnit, H., Matsumoto, H., & Spencer, W.A. (1973). Genesis of epileptic interictal spikes: New knowledge of cortical feedback system suggests a neurophysiological explanation of brief paroxysms. *Brain Research, 52*, 1 – 17.

Bauer, H. (1985). Regulation of slow brain potentials affects task performance. In T. Elbert, B. Rockstroh, W. Lutzenberger & N. Birbaumer (Eds.), *Self-regulation of the brain and behaviour* (pp. 216 – 226). Heidelberg: Springer.

Bear, M.F., Cooper, L.N., & Ebner, F.F. (1987). A physiological basis for a theory of synapse modfication. *Science, 237*, 42 – 48.

Bienenstock, E.L., Cooper, L.N., Munro, P.W. (1982). Theory for the development of neuron selectivity: Orientation specificity and binocular interaction in visual cortex. *Journal of Neuroscience, 2*, 32 – 48.

Birbaumer, N., Elbert, T., Rockstroh, B., & Lutzenberger, W. (1981). Biofeedback of event-related slow potentials of the brain. *International Journal of Psychology, 16*, 389 – 415.

Braitenberg, V. (1978). Cell assemblies in the cerebral cortex. In R. Heim & G. Palm (Eds.), *Theoretical approaches to complex systems.* Heidelberg: Springer.

Braitenberg, V. (1984). *Vehicles. Experiments in synthetic psychology.* Cambridge, Mass.: The MIT Press.

Brooks, V.B. (1986). *The neural basis of motor control.* Oxford: Oxford University Press.

Cairus, H. (1952). Disturbances of consciousness with lesions of the brainstem and diencephalon. *Brain, 75*, 109 – 145.

Cooper, R., McCallum, W.C., & Papakostopoulos, D. (1979). A bimodal slow potential theory of cerebral processing. In J.J. Desmedt (Ed.), *Cognitive components in cerebral event-related potentials and selective attention* (pp. 182 – 186). Basel: Karger.

Deecke, L., Kornhuber, H.H., & Schmitt, G. (1976). Bereitschaftspotential in Parkinsonian patients. In W.C. McCallum & J.R. Knott (Eds.), *The responsive brain* (pp. 169 – 171). Bristol: Wright.

Deecke, L., Bashore, T., Brunia, C., Grünewald-Zuberbier, E., Grünewald, G., & Kristeva, R. (1984). Movement-associated potentials and motor control. In R. Karrer, J. Cohen & P. Tueting (Eds.), *Brain and information* (pp. 398 – 428). New York: The New York Academy of Sciences.

Dichter, M.A., & Ayala, G.F. (1987). Cellular mechanisms of epilepsy. Status report. *Science, 237*, 157 – 164.

Donchin, E. (1981). Surprise!...Surprise? *Psychophysiology, 18*, 493 – 513.

Donchin, E., Ritter, W., & McCallum, W.C. (1978). Cognitive psychophysiology: The endogenous components of the ERP. In E. Callaway, P. Tueting & S. Koslow (Eds.), *Event-related brain potentials in man* (pp. 349 – 411). New York: Academic Press.

Elbert, T., Rockstroh, B., Lutzenberger, W., & Birbaumer, N. (1980). Biofeedback of slow cortical potentials. *Journal of Electroencephalography and Clinical Neurophysiology, 48*, 293 – 301.

Elbert, T., & Rockstroh, B. (1987). Threshold regulation – A key to the combined dynamics of EEG and event-related potentials. *Journal of Psychophysiology, 1*, 317 – 334.

Hassler, R. (1978). Striatal control of locomotion, intentional actions and of integrating and perceptive activity. *Journal of Neurological Sciences, 36*, 187 – 224.

Hassler, R. (1980). Brain mechanisms of intention and attention with introductory remarks on other volitional processes. In H.H. Kornhuber & L. Deecke (Eds.), *Motivation, motor and sensory processes of the brain* (pp. 585 – 614). Amsterdam: Elsevier.

Hebb, D.O. (1949). *The organization of behavior.* New York: Wiley.

Lutzenberger, W., Elbert, T., Rockstroh, B., & Birbaumer, N. (1979). Effects of slow cortical potentials in a signal detection task. *International Journal of Neuroscience, 9*, 175 – 183.

Marsden, C.D. (1982). The mysterious motor function of the basal ganglia: The Robert Wartenberg Lecture. *Neurology, 32,* 514−539.

Näätänen, R. (1982). Processing negativity: An evoked potential re-reflection of selective attention. *Psychological Bulletin, 92,* 605−640.

Norman, D.A., & Shallice, T. (1986). Attention to action. In R.A. Davidson, G.E. Schwartz & D. Shapiro (Eds.), *Consciousness and self-regulation* (pp. 1−18). New York: Plenum Press.

Palm, G. (1982). *Neural assemblies. An alternative approach to artificial intelligence.* Heidelberg: Springer.

Posner, M.I., & Snyder, C.R. (1975). Attention and cognitive control. In R.L. Solso (Ed.), *Information processing and cognition: The Loyola Symposium.* Hillsdale, NJ: Erlbaum.

Rockstroh, B., Elbert, T., Birbaumer, N., & Lutzenberger, W. (1982). *Slow brain potentials and behavior.* Baltimore: Urban & Schwarzenberg.

Rockstroh, B., Elbert, T., Lutzenberger, W., & Birbaumer, N. (1982). The effects of slow cortical potentials on response speed. *Psychophysiology, 19,* 211−217.

Rockstroh, B., Birbaumer, N., Elbert, T., & Lutzenberger, W. (1984). Operant control of EEG and event−related and slow brain potentials. *Biofeedback & Self-Regulation, 9,* 139−160.

Rockstroh, B., Elbert, T., Lutzenberger, W., & Birbaumer, N. (1989). Biofeedback produced hemispheric asymmetry of slow cortical potentials and its behavioural effects. *International Journal of Psychophysiology,* in press.

Rösler, F. (1982). *Hirnelektrische Korrelate kognitiver Prozesse.* Berlin: Springer.

Roth, W., Rothbart, R.M., & Kopell, B.S. (1978). The timing of CNV resolution in a memory retrieval task. *Biological Psychology, 6,* 39−49.

Roth, W.T., Ford, J.M., & Kopell, B.S. (1978). Long latency evoked potentials and reaction time. *Psychophysiology, 15,* 17−23.

Scheibel, M.E., & Scheibel, A.B. (1966). The organization of the nucleus reticularis thalami. A Golgi study. *Brain Research, 1,* 43−62.

Schneider, J.S., & Lidsky, T.I. (Eds.) (1987). *Basal ganglia and behavior: Sensory aspects of motor functioning.* Toronto: Huber.

Schmidt, W. (1983). Involvement of dopaminergic neurotransmission in the control of goal-directed movements. *Psychopharmacology, 80,* 360−364.

Schwartzkroin, P., & Wheal, H. (Eds.) (1984). *Electrophysiology of epilepsy.* New York: Academic Press.

Shiffrin, R.M., & Schneider, W. (1977). Controlled and automatic human information processing: II. Perceptual learning, automatic attention and a general theory. *Psychological Review, 84,* 127−190.

Skinner, J.E., & Yingling, C.D. (1977). Central gating mechanisms that regulate event−related potentials and behavior. In J. Desmedt (Ed.), *Attention, voluntary contraction and event-related cerebral potentials* (pp. 30−69). Basel: Karger.

Stamm, J.S. (1984). Performance enhancements with cortical negative slow potential shifts in monkey and human. In T. Elbert, B. Rockstroh, W. Lutzenberger & N. Birbaumer (Eds.), *Self-regulation of the brain and behavior* (pp. 199−215). Heidelberg: Springer.

Tecce, J.J., & Cattanach, L. (1982). Contingent negative variation. In E. Niedermeyer & F. Lopes da Silva (Eds.), *Electroencephalography* (pp. 543−562). Baltimore: Urban & Schwarzenberg.

Tsuda, T. (1982). Contingent negative variation in parkinsonism. *Tokushima Journal of Experimental Medicine, 29,* 87−94.

Psychophysical Explorations of Mental Structures
Edited by H.-G. Geissler
in collaboration with M.H. Müller and W. Prinz
© 1990 by Hogrefe & Huber Publishers

Chapter 27

Toward a State-Dependent Psychophysiology of Visual Perception and Cognition

Jirina Radilova
Institute of Physiology
Czechoslovak Academy of Sciences
Prague, Czechoslovakia

Psychophysiological approaches are a relatively new and valuable tool in trying to understand perceptual and cognitive processes in the human brain. Among them, event-related brain potentials (ERPs) – the electrical responses to external stimuli, when amplified and averaged scalp-recorded EEG, provide a non-invasive method. One of the most interesting ERPs components is the so-called P300 wave (Sutton, Braren, Zubin & John, 1965). When recorded from the human scalp it is a large-amplitude positive evoked potential component which appears with a latency of about 280 ms up to about 750 ms. It has been studied mainly in experiments concerning human cognitive processes (Sutton, Tueting, Zubin & John, 1967; Donchin, Kubovy, Kutas, Johnson & Herning, 1974; Radilova & Radil, 1982). This wave was supposed to be related to the quality of the stimulus, its significance and utility (Sutton et al., 1965; Näätänen, 1975), the certainty of its occurrence (Squires, Hillyard & Lindsay, 1973), the complexity of signal detecting procedures (Cooper, McCallum, Newton & Papacostopoulos, 1977), the internal state of the perceiving system (level of attention; Hillyard, Hink, Schwendt & Picton, 1973), the current state of decision making mechanisms or of following processes (Posner & Boies, 1971; Donchin, 1974), "conscious awareness", "relevance" and probability

(Picton, 1984). The negative or positive emotional impact on cognitive processes which we studied in different experimental situations (Radilova, 1982) also seems to be a relevant factor.

Forty-one healthy subjects aged 18 – 45 years participated in the experiment. They were university students, postgraduates, scientists or staff. Recordings of the EPs were made from O_z with reference to the left earlobe. A special technique based upon the DEC LAB 8/E computer and on an electronic programming device was developed which enabled single evoked potentials induced by geometrical stimuli to be classified into two groups according to a binary psychological criterion, and to be averaged separately. Using this method and adopting a modification of Miller's (1956) "7 ± 2" paradigm, we had found previously that when the number of simultaneously presented items, light squares, was recognized correctly, the late positive component, P300, showed in the majority of cases a higher amplitude (Radilova, Radil & Maras, 1979). In this experiment an important factor determining the differences in P300 might have been the subject's certainty or uncertainty about the correctness of his judgment.

In this series of experiments each subject was seated in an armchair in a darkened, electrically and partially acoustically shielded chamber. Communication with the experimenter was via an Intercom device. The subjects had received prior training and were instructed to remain relaxed, but to watch carefully the center of the screen which was placed in front of them at a distance of 90 cm. Randomly placed white light quares (3 x 3 cm), from 6 to 9 in number, were projected on the screen by a Kodak–Carousel Tachistoscope. The subjects had to tell the experimenter the number of projected squares, and whether they were certain or uncertain about their judgments. The ERPs were classified according to their subjective criterion, but also according to the objective one, the number of squares. The experiments usually took place between 9 a.m. – 1 p.m. and lasted about 40 minutes.

Every trial started with a warning 200 ms beep followed, after 1200 ms, by the opening of the tachistoscope shutter for 200 ms. The total number of projected slides was 200 for each subject, the interflash interval was 7 s to allow recovery from the previous flash.

By storing each potential in the computer's memory until the subject reported the number of items, and whether he was certain or not, the system described solved the problem of longer latency of subject's evaluation in comparison with that of ERPs. By pushing one of two knobs, the experimenter then sent the single EP waiting in the operational memory of the computer into one of its two averaging systems. The averaged P300 amplitudes of two different groups were measured peak-to-peak. A clear P300 was visible in all recordings. We performed four groups of the described experiments and three groups of modfied ones in which their emotional impact was manipulated.

In the first group of 19 subjects, in which stimuli were classified according to the subjects' certainty or uncertainty irrespectively of the objective correctness of their statements, the P300 showed a higher amplitude in ERPs correcponding to certainty during recognition in 58% of all cases; in 32% no difference was found, and in 10% P300 was higher for ERPs corresponding to uncertain judgments. The differences in amplitude exceeding 20% of the total amount were considered significant.

In the second group of 22 subjects only a part of ERPs was processed: In subgroups 1 and 2 only those corresponding to the situation, i.e., whether the subject was certain or uncertain, respectively. In both groups ERPs were classified according to the criterion whether the number of items was judged correctly or incorrectly, whereas in subgroups 3 and 4 only those ERPs were classified which corresponded to correct or incorrect recognition, respectively (the criterion being whether the subject was certain or uncertain in this judgment).

It was found that P300 was of higher amplitude when the subjects were both certain and correct, whereas no differences were found when they were uncertain and responded incorrectly, i.e., both factors contributed to the difference in the P300 amplitude.

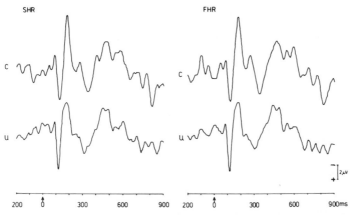

Figure 1. Averaged ERPs induced by randomly distributed light squares in the stimuli. Classification according to the binary cognitive criterion (C: certain, U: uncertain judgment), and according to current heart-rate. P300 amplitudes are usually higher than when heart-rate increases.

In the first group of subjects this conclusion was supported by the fact that in the case of certain recognition the subjects were more likely to be right than wrong, and that in the case of correct answers they were more likely to be certain rather than uncertain about their judgments. In the second group of subjects similar results were found concerning the coincidence of subjective certainty or uncertainty with objective correctness or incorrectness of the subjects' evaluation of stimuli. The conclusion can be drawn that both factors influence the amplitude of P300, and that they are interrelated.

The aim of another experiment was to analyse whether the emotional (stress-inducing) impact of the visual stimuli on healthy subjects would also be reflected in the P300 amplitude. Twenty-five healthy, paid subjects (aged

17−55 years) participated in this experiment. The same technical system as the one mentioned above was adopted, but as an additional device, a monitoring system (for details, see Maras, Javorsky & Radil, 1984) was used to record the instantaneous heart-rate of subjects during the experiment.

The subjects watched slides projected for 300 ms, representing bodies of murdered people, suicides (hanged people), corpes of people who died in car accidents, burnt bodies, bodies in adipocere, etc. or white squares. They had to tell the experimenter the number of squares, and whether or not they were certain about their statements. ERPs were automatically classified into four groups according to their certainty or uncertainty concerning the numbers of items and according to their high or low instantaneous heart-rate. P300 was again found to be of higher amplitude when the heart-rate was elevated (Figure 1). This experiment demonstrates that the subjects' current physiological state combined with vegetative-emotional factors influences perception and cognition.

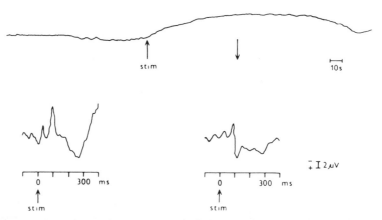

Figure 2. Plethysmographic recording of penile erection induced by an erotic picture (upper curve), and the P300 of averaged ERPs induced by geometrical stimuli, 7±2 light squares, presented simultaneously during sexual arousal (lower curves). P300 is of lower amplitude (right) in the comparison with the relaxed state (left).

In other experiments the task of the subject was to judge the number of simultaneously presented and randomly distributed elements in the visual field either in a relaxed state or during penile erection. Sexual arousal was induced by presenting erotic slides to the subjects (16 male university students, aged 19−29 years) and detected by means of a plethysmographic device. It was possible to average and compare only evoked potentials corresponding to correct responses, as only a binary evoked potential classification procedure was available. In this study (Radilova, Figar & Radil, 1983), it was found that the amplitude of the late positive evoked potential wave was usually lower during penile erection than in the relaxed state (Figure 2).

During sexual arousal the geometrical stimulus used and the cognitive visual task performed undoubtedly become less relevant for the subject, reflected in the low amplitude of the P300 wave. On the other hand, erotic stimuli themselves evoke higher amplitudes of the P300 wave under similar conditions in comparison with indifferent ones (Figure 3), like horrifying pictures in comparison with indifferent ones (Radilova, 1982). The emotional impact of visual stimuli increased the amplitude of the P300 irrespectively of the positive or negative nature of the emotion induced. Complex mechanisms of motivation and selective attention might be involved here. Thus, it seems that the "trajectory" of information processing during cognition is greatly influenced by both the psychological and physiological state of the subject, is state–dependent (see also Radil, Bohdanecky and Indra, this volume), and that it interacts with other mental processes (motivation, attention, emotion, etc.) in a complex manner.

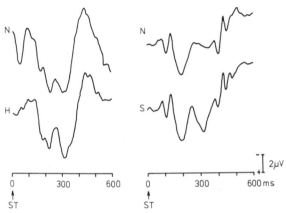

Figure 3. Averaged ERPs corresponding to horrifying (H) and control (N) (left) and erotic (S) and control (N) (right) pictures in two typical subjects. P300 amplitude is higher for both relevant horrifying and erotic pictures in comparison with the control (irrelevant ones).

Summary and Conclusions

We may summarize by stating that:

1. The amplitude of the P300 component of the event–related potentials evoked by 7 ± 2 randomly distributed geometrical patterns, presented simultaneously by means of a tachistoscope, was higher when subjects were certain in their judgments (cognitive–psychic state).

2. Current heart rate was increased by presenting horrifying pictures. Higher heart rate, reflecting negative emotional feeling, was accompanied by a higher P300 amplitude.

3. The emotional-vegetative state of male subjects was altered by inducing sexual arousal by means of erotic slides. Under this condition, when geometrical slides were presented, P300 showed a decrement in amplitude.

The results of our investigations indicate that a subject's current physiological and psychic state influences his perceptual and cognitive processes and that these states can be determined objectively by psychophysiological methods.

Correspondence should be addressed to Jirina Radilova, Institute of Physiology, Czechoslovak Academy of Sciences, Videnska 1083, 14000 Prague, Czechoslovakia.

References

Cooper, R., McCallum, W.C., Newton, P., Papacostopoulus, D., Pocock, P.V., & Warren, W.J. (1977). Cortical potentials associated with the detection of visual events. *Science, 196,* 74−77.

Donchin, E., Kubovy, M., Kutas, M., Johnson, R., & Herning, R.I. (1974). Graded changes in evoked response (P300) amplitude as a function of cognitive activity. *Perception & Psychophysics, 14,* 319−324.

Donchin, E., Ritter, W., & McCallum, W.C. (1978). Cognitive psychophysiology: The endogenous components of the ERP. In E. Callawy, P. Tueting & S.H. Koslow (Eds.), *Event-related potentials in man.* New York, London: Academic Press.

Hillyard, S.A., Hink, R.F., Schwent, V.L., & Picton, T.W. (1973). Electrical signs of selective attention in the human brain. *Science, 182,* 171−180.

Maras, L., Javorsky, S., & Radil, T. (1984). A monitoring system for feedback control of psychophysiological parameters in man. *Physiologia bohemoslovaca, 33,* 545.

Miller, G.A. (1956). The magical number seven, plus or minus two. Some limits in our capacity for processing information. *Psychological Review, 63,* 81−97.

Näätänen, R. (1975). Selective attention and evoked potentials in humans − a critical review. *Biological Psychology, 2,* 237−307.

Picton, T.W. (1978). The ERP and decision and memory. In E. Callawy, P. Tueting & S.H. Koslow (Eds.), *Event-related potentials in man.* New York, London: Academic Press.

Posner, M.I., & Boies, S.J. (1971). Components of attention. *Psychological Review, 78,* 391−408.

Radilova, J., Radil, T., & Maras, L. (1979). Detection of the number of stimuli and evoked potentials. *Activitas Nervosa Superior, 21 (Suppl.),* 25−26.

Radilova, J. (1982). The late positive components of visual evoked responses sensitive to emotional factors. *Activitas Nervosa Superior, 24 (Suppl.),* 334−337.

Radilova, J., & Radil, T. (1982). Some EEG correlates of perception and cognition. In R. Sinz & M.R. Rosenzweig (Eds.), *Psychophysiology 1980* (pp. 349−353). Amsterdam: Elsevier.

Radilova, J., Figar, S., & Radil, T. (1983). Sexual arousal and visual perception. *Activitas Nervosa Superior, 25 (Suppl.),* 168−170.

Squires, K.C., Hillyard, S.A., & Lindsay, P.H. (1973). Cortical potential evoked by confirming and disconfirming feedback following an auditory discrimination. *Perception & Psychophysics, 13,* 25−31.

Sutton, S., Braren, M., Zubin, J., & John, E.R. (1965). Evoked potentials correlates of stimulus incertainty. *Science, 150,* 1187−1188.

Sutton, S., Tueting, P., Zubin, J., & John, E.R. (1967). Information delivery and the sensory evoked potentials. *Science, 155,* 1436−1439.

Psychophysical Explorations of Mental Structures
Edited by H.-G. Geissler
in collaboration with M.H. Müller and W. Prinz
© 1990 by Hogrefe & Huber Publishers

Chapter 28

Toward State–Dependent Psychophysics

Tomas Radil, Zdenek Bohdanecky
and Miroslav Indra
Institute of Physiology
Czechoslovak Academy of Sciences
Prague, Czechoslovakia

Human performance is apparently contingent both upon the current physiological and psychological state of the subject. Different aspects of perceptual–cognitive and voluntary–motor activity can be measured objectively by means of psychophysical methods based upon the conceptual and methodological achievements of G.T. Fechner and his followers (see Radil, 1987).

This paper presents various experimental procedures exemplifying the state–dependent approach to psychophysics that relates performance, as measured psychophysically, to the subject's current physiological state.

Sensory Thresholds Contingent upon EEG

A computer system and additional electronic circuits have been developed for detecting the presence/absence of alpha activity in the EEG recorded from the occipital scalp. The EEG signal passes through band–pass filters, an amplitude level is set with respect to the distribution of alpha amplitude maxima prior to the experiment, and the presence of alpha waves above the present level is detected.

In relaxing subjects sitting in a dark room, alpha and non–alpha periods alternate spontaneously. Sensory thresholds were established using the "staircase" technique either during alpha or non–alpha periods. Each measurement took 20 – 25 min; stimulus intensity gradually decreased in consecutive trials until it ceased to be detectable, then it started to increase automatically, and so on. The values at 7 – 8 threshold reversals were established and averaged. Each alpha– and non–alpha periods took at least 500 ms, shorter periods were omitted. For the estimation of acoustic thresholds (the measuring steps were 0.5 dB), the subject had to press a button whenever she/he heard the tone (30 ms, 100 Hz). For the estimation of visual thresholds the steps were $7 \cdot 10^{-3}$ lx. Due to the distance of the eye from the screen and the diameter of pupil the actual illumination was correspondingly lower. The size of stimulus was 1.5 angular degrees and duration was 20 ms. The subject again had to press a button whenever she/he detected the light spot. Together with the threshold values, reaction time (the interval lasting from stimulus presentation until the button was pressed) and the duration of alpha– and non–alpha periods were measured automatically and were separately stored for trials in which the subject detected or failed to detect the stimulus, respectively.

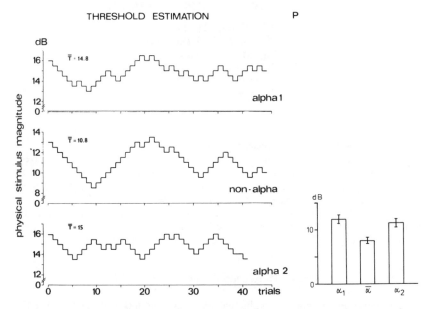

Figure 1. Acoustic threshold estimation during alpha (two sessions – alpha 1, alpha 2) and non–alpha periods. Left: threshold measurement by means of the staircase method. Right: Average values of the threshold for the whole group of subjects.

When the acoustic thresholds were inspected (Bohdanecky, Bozkov & Radil, 1984), a difference was found for alpha and non–alpha sessions, the threshold always being higher during alpha periods (Figure 1). Neither the latencies during alpha and non-alpha periods nor the duration of the alpha- and non-alpha periods corresponding to detected or undetected stimuli showed any difference. In the visual experiments (Bohdanecky, Bozkov & Radil-Weiss, 1983) no differences in thresholds were found. However, the latency periods of responding were significantly longer for the alpha periods.

It follows from these experiments that some aspects of stimulus detection are to a certain degree inhibited during the alpha periods of EEG, commonly associated with a more relaxed state of the brain, in comparison with the non-alpha periods, which are mostly characterized by desynchronized EEG activity corresponding to a higher level of vigilance.

Visual-Motor Tracking Errors Related to Cardiac Activity

The subjects sat in a semidark chamber in a distance of 120 cm from a computer-controlled CRT. For one-dimensional tracking we used two parallel short vertical lines moving contiuously over the screen in horizontal direction. The whole range of target displacement was 5 angular degrees. The movement of a joystick was accompanied by corresponding movements of a light spot over the screen. The task of the subjects was to maintain the light spot within the moving target. Eight tasks, each lasting for three minutes and differing in target speed, type of tracking movement (sine or ramp, circular or square) and in type of tracking (normal or reversal), were performed by each subject (Indra, Bohdanecky & Radil, 1987).

An analysis of variance was run for the results of one-dimensional tracking and indicated that most of the differences in tracking error (TE) incidence among separate tasks were due to target speed (being higher at 2 s stimulus periods in comparison with 3 s ones) and the type of stimulus movements (being higher for ramp than for sine).

It was obvious that TE incidence over target trajectory was higher in positions where target acceleration was maximal, i.e., at both ends of ramp trajectory and at the middle of sine trajectory. The cardiac cycle was determined on the basis of the R-waves of ECG. The total R-R intervals were normalized and divided into 10 classes. The TE incidence was found to be significantly lower in the middle of R-R interval (approximately). Higher heart rate was usually accompanied by increased TE incidence (Figure 2).

Results concerning the type of stimulus movements indicate that regular sine-type tracking was easier to adopt and follow. It seems that pendulum-like types of movements are more usual and thus better tracked due to evolutionary circumstances. The observed, but less pronounced, differences between normal and reversal tracking (the joystick had to be moved with appropriate speed but in opposite direction with respect to the target), could be explained by the relatively fast training on the easy task, and the regular nature of the movements during performance.

The main finding was that TEs are time-locked with respect to the phase of the cardiac cycle, irrespectively of the type of task, i.e. slow or fast, sinusoidal or ramp target movement, etc. All one-dimensional tracking experiments were ranked according to the mean incidence of TEs and the mean value of heart rate expressed for each of them. It was found that higher TE incidence was accompanied by higher heart rate (Radil, Indra & Bohdanecky, 1987; Figure 2).

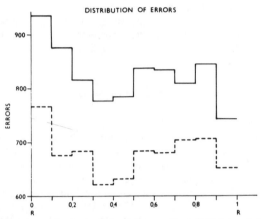

Figure 2. Tracking error distribution over the normalized R–R interval (derived from neighbouring R waves of ECG). Solid line: high actual heart rate. Dashed line: low actual heart rate.

In additional experiments (Bohdanecky, Indra & Radil, 1987), a computer–controlled feedback design was adopted. Either the mutual distance between the two vertical lines representing the horizontally moving target, or the speed of the target movement became contingent upon the instantaneous TE. TE incidence above a preset value increased the distance between the vertical lines, while TE incidence below the preset value decreased the distance. In other experiments, an amount of TE incidence above the criterion led to a decrease of target speed whereas the target moved faster when TE incidence was below the criterion value.

The results demonstrated that TE incidence in the case of feedback control of the target size was higher than in experiments involving feedback control of target speed. Under feedback condition, when the task of the subject was more complex in the sense that she/he had to follow the target and to influence one of its parameters, no statistical differences were found in TE incidence during different phases of R–R intervals (Figure 3). Similarly, there were no marked differences in mean TE incidence relating to average heart rate.

Experiments with two–dimensional tracking (Mates, Indra & Radil, 1988) confirmed the above results in the sense that TE incidence is highest in those parts of the target trajectories where the speed of one coordinate and/or the direction of target movement change. However, no significant dependence of TE on the cardiac cycle phase was found.

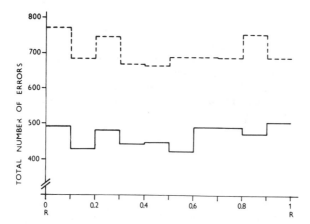

Figure 3. Tracking error distribution over the normalized R-R intervals for the two feedback conditions: variable target size (dashed line) or speed (solid line).

It follows from the above experiments that TE incidence is time–locked with respect to the cardiac cycle in the case of easy tracking tasks, whereas this correlation disappears or weakens during complex (feedback modulated or two–dimensional) tracking.

Differential Temporal Threshold Related to Cardiac and Respiratory Cycle

Here our aim was to examine whether the differential perceptual threshold of two successive brief visual stimuli (i.e. minimal time interval between them required for seeing them as one) bears any connection to the phase of cardiac and respiratory cycle. The stimuli were presented by means of two diodes emitting red light and mounted side by side on a black panel and covered by a plastic transparent disc (9 mm in diameter). The sequencing of stimuli, recording of responses and data analysis were controlled by means of a computer. The experiment started after a period of relaxation and dark adaptation, when the ECG electrodes or the transducer for recording respiration were attached and the subject was instructed. The presentation of double pulses was either contingent upon the occurrence of an R-wave or delayed with respect to the R-wave for 400 ms. In other experiments, stimulus presentation occured during the inspirium or exspirium, respectively. Four light pulse durations, 20, 10, 5 and 2 ms, were chosen. Interstimulus interval duration was changed in linear 10 ms steps. A special version of simultaneous threshold measurement was applied.

No significant changes in threshold estimates contingent upon the particular phase of the cardiac or respiratory cycle were found in the experimental situation described. No differences were seen between the upper and lower points of threshold reversals.

However, there exists a highly significant difference between the situation with the shortest pulse duration (2 ms) and all other pulse durations, the former requiring a marked increase in the unfilled time interval between both stimuli. In 30% of the sessions the increasing difficulty of the cognitive task was followed by an increase in heart rate.

It follows from the above experiments that temporal differentiation of two successive visual stimuli, which is a rather complex task, is not contingent upon the current phase of the cardiac and respiratory cycle.

Summary and Conclusions

The results mentioned demonstrate that some types of human performance detected by means of experimental procedures, which might be called psychophysiological, do depend on the current state of the subject. This, however, is not the case for other situations. Thus, both the type of performance and the paramters defining the state of the subject seem to be important factors from the point of view of state-dependence of processes measured by psychophysical means. So far, we have analyzed only a few processes which we mentioned in the present paper (others dealing with psychophysiological approaches are included in another contribution in the present volume − Radilova, this volume). Nevertheless, it is obvious that the current state of the subject is an important aspect to be taken into consideration in psychophysics. Contemporary experimental techniques enable us to explore different physiological parameters and "correlates" of a person's current psychic state on-line, and to classify the results of psychophysical and other measurements accordingly (Radil, Radilova, Bohdanecky & Bozkov, 1985; Radil, Bohdanecky, Lansky, Radilova & Spacek, 1986; Radil, Indra, Franek & Bohdanecky, 1987).

So far, however, the state of the subject has been neglected in the majority of psychophysical experiments. This is true both of short and of many long-term psychophysical measurements (as, e.g., of psychometric functions lasting for several days, when the state of the subject is very likely to change). Thus, natural variability, i.e, the modulation of the processes under study − a brain phenomenon of considerable functional significance − is being unnecessarily excluded from the scope of our heuristics.

The variability-modulation of phenomena studied by psychophysical means should become the subject of objective analysis and should not be discarded as meaningless "noise" by means of statistical methods used from this particular point of view. Thus, the development of state-dependent psychophysics might represent a progressive step from the methodological point of view. When we have a closer look at the experiments discussed, it seems that epochs covered by spontaneously appearing alpha acitvity in the EEG are accompanied by a lower level of vigilance. We should, however, add experiments concerning other types of performance that can be measured psychophysically. Excitability changes over the cardiac cycle do not seem to be caused by general phasic shifts of vigilance. Such a hypothesis was suggested by experiments on rats demonstrating that a considerable amount of mesencephalic reticular neurons generated "spontaneous" impulse activity that was time-locked with respect to the cardiac cycle (Radil-Weiss & Sykova, 1977). The processes studied in the above-mentioned experiments, however, were influenced in a different way. A hypothesis to be tested is that only the "easy" automatized tasks are being modulated during the cardiac cycle, but not the more "difficult" ones engaging more complex brain mechanisms. This assumption might help explain conflicting experimental evidence concerning correlations of cardiac activity and other functions (details are given in Indra et al., 1987).

A final remark pertaining to a more general point and to the topic of the present conference seems in order.

The founding of psychophysics by G.T. Fechner was an extremely important step in the objective analysis of subjective psychic phenomena. Another ingenious approach, having the same aim, was that developed by J.E. Purkyne (see Radil et al., 1988). It was based upon objectivation of perceptual and cognitive processes through self-observation of the researcher. Further development of experimental methods and technology made it possible to add sophisticated recordings of neuroelectric, polygraphic, motor and other processes. The objective analysis of subjective-psychic phenomena is characterized presently by a combination of the three approaches mentioned. Thus, the basic drawbacks peculiar to each of them are compensated to some extent. In spite of its effectiveness in gaining relevant information, classical psychophysics neglects the nervous processes going on in the human brain and the underlying phenomena studied in a similar way as behaviorism neglects those taking place in the animal brain during behavior. The stimulus-response nature of psychophysical methodology, which is prevalent now, is certainly not independent of the underestimation of modulatory influences upon the phenomena studied which may have been caused by complex regulative brain processes. Objective self-observation requires a great deal of knowledge about the process studied, special talents and considerable skill and experience. In spite of its power in objectivation of the subjective aspects of the processes investigate, it will clearly remain an exclusive method accessible only to few researchers with exceptional capacities and providing information concerning only some phenomena. Even the most advanced recording techniques inform us "only" about the physiological aspects of the ongoing processes. Their interpretation requires additional objective information on their subjective psychic aspects provided either by psychophysical means or by objectivized introspection (other possibilities not being available). The combination of all three approaches is an unavoidable condition of further scientific progress in neuroscientific research on the most complex human nervous activities. Bringing these three approaches together in order to achieve a higher level of efficiency represents one of the typical methodological features of contemporary psychophysiology.

The following conclusions might be derived from our results: The alternation of alpha activity and desynchronized EEG activity was detected on-line, and sensory thresholds were measured in both conditions. The acoustic threshold was higher and reaction time to visual stimuli was longer during alpha activity in comparison to desynchronized activity. In a simple unidimensional visual–motor tracking task (light spot, controlled manually by means of a joystick, out of target moving over the screen of a computer scope) the error rate depended on the actual phase of the cardiac cycle. Besides, the error rate was positively correlated with heart rate. This was not the case for complex (modulated one–dimensional and two–dimensional feedback) tracking. The threshold of temporal discrimination of light stimuli did not depend on the phase of cardiac and respiratory cycle. The results indicate that current physiological processes determining the state of the organism probably influence various types of performance in different ways.

Correspondence should be addressed to Tomas Radil, Institute of Physiology, Czechoslovak Academy of Sciences, Videnska 1083, 14000 Prague, Czechoslovakia.

References

Bohdanecky, Z., Bozkov, V., & Radil, T. (1984). Acoustic stimulus threshold related to EEG alpha and non–alpha epochs. *International Journal of Psychophysiology*, 2, 63–66.

Bohdanecky, Z., Bozkov, V., & Radil–Weiss, T. (1983). Visual stimulus threshold related to EEG alpha and non–alpha epochs. *Acta Neurobiologiae Experimentalis*, 43, 215–220.

Bohdanecky, Z., Indra, M., & Radil, T. (1987). The one–dimensional tracking task under feedback conditions. *Activitas Nervosa Superior*, 29, 140–141.

Bohdanecky, Z., Dimitrov, G., Indra, M., & Radil, T. (1987). Perception of brief visual stimuli and the cardiac cycle. *Activitas Nervosa Superior*, 29, 304–305.

Indra, M, Bohdanecky, Z., & Radil, T. (1987). Tracking errors related to cardiac cycle: A new approach. *International Journal of Psychophysiology*, 5, 161–166.

Mates, J., Indra, M., & Radil, T. (1988). Two–dimensional visual motor tracking. *Activitas Nervosa Superior*, 30, 272–273.

Radil, T. (1987). 100 years after the death of Gustav Fechner (1801–1887). (in Czech). *Czeskoslovenska Psychologie*, 87, 480–482.

Radil, T., Bohdanecky, Z., Lansky, P., Radilova, J., & Spacek, M. (1986). The psychophysiology of memory operation during visual cognition. In F. Klix & H. Hagendorf (Eds.), *Human memory and cognitive capabilities* (pp. 687–711). Amsterdam: Elsevier.

Radil, T., Bohdanecky, Z., Radilova, J., Indra, M., Lansky, P., Maras, L., Mates, J., & Paus, T. (1988). J.E. Purkyne and psychophysiology of perceptual cognitive and sensory–motor processes. In J. Purs (Ed.), *Jan Evangelista Purkyne in Science and Culture* (pp. 825–837). Prague.

Radil, T. Indra, M., & Bohdanecky, Z. (1987). Errors in one–dimensional tracking to depend on actual heart rate. *Physiologia Bohemoslovaka*, 36, 553.

Radil, T., Indra, M., Franek, M., & Bohdanecky, Z. (1987). Sensory–motor coordination studied by means of visual and acoustical tracking. In E. van der Meer & J. Hoffmann (Eds.), *Knowledge aided information processing* (pp. 275–281). Amsterdam: Elsevier.

Radil, T., Radilova, J., Bohdanecky, Z., & Bozkov, V. (1985). Psychophysiology of unconscious and conscious phenomena during visual perception. In F. Klix, R. Näätänen & K. Zimmer (Eds.), *Psychophysiological approaches to human information processing* (pp. 97–127). Amsterdam: Elsevier.

Radil–Weiss, T., & Sykova, E. (1977). Vegetative Prozesse in der Aktivität retikulärer Neurone – Mögliche Beziehungen zur Entstehung von Neurosen. In R. Baumann & K. Hecht (Eds.), *Stress, Neurose, Herz–Kreislauf* (pp. 109–113). Berlin: VEB Deutscher Verlag der Wissenschaften.

Chapter 29

Psychophysiological Identification of Working-Memory Subsystems

Bernd Schönebeck
Bereich Psychologie
Zentralinstitut für Kybernetik und
Informationsprozesse
Akademie der Wissenschaften der DDR
Berlin, G.D.R.

Cognitive scientists still lack a satisfactory method for measuring mental load. Even though psychophysiological techniques have to some extent proved of value in that they enable temporal courses to be measured, and avoid interference with the processes to be investigated (which occurs when using the secondary task technique), they have been incapable of bridging this gap. According to Wickens (1984), "These (psychophysiological) measures are highly sensitive and reflect the total resource demands imposed on the system but are undiagnostic with regard to the locus of demand."

We consider that this lack in specificity is a general problem with event-related physiological responses as reflections of how the organism as a whole copes with the demands made on it. The modulation of internal spontaneous rhythms through external stimuli, however, should be much more selective. Let me illustrate this, taking spontaneous oscillations of the cardiac rhythms as an example, which were analysed with the help of the cardiac interval signal power spectrum.

Our subjects were instructed to recall in writing as accurately as possible a number of short texts. Recording of physiological parameters was carried out in the reading phase. The following recall parameters were registered:

1. The number of accurately recalled propositions — the replication score;
2. The number of adequately paraphrased propositions — the reconstruction score.

Reconstruction items were assumed to derive from long-term memory, whereas the replication items were considered to represent the short-term memory component of recall.

In 3 experiments the material was varied in different ways:
a) with regard to text coherence (Kintsch & van Dijk, 1978),
b) with regard to the emotional content of texts, with coherence being kept constant, and,
c) in terms of concreteness and imaginability, coherence again being kept constant.

In spite of wide differences along these lines we were able to identify throughout two alternative reading strategies: an elaborative and a rehearsal strategy. According to Presley, Levin and Ghalata (1984) as well as Aaronson and Ferres (1984), the rehearsal strategy is based on controlled subvocalisation. Reading time is determined by the formation of small articulation–related chunks. The elaborative strategy involves semantic processing, and reading time depends on integrative semantic activities resulting in the formation of larger, meaningful units.

Table 1. Correlations between text difficulty (numbers of reinstatements and inferences) and reproduction scores. Averaged data for the elaborative and rehearsal strategies (*: $p < .10$; **: $p < .05$).

Elaborative Reading

reproduction scores	inferences	reinstatements
replication	−.39*	−.33*.
reconstruction	−.18	−.55**
total reproduction	−.40*	−.09

Rehearsal Reading

reproduction scores	inferences	reinstatements
replication	−.18	.07
reconstruction	−.06	.10
total reproduction	−.19	.09

Variation of Text Coherence

In the first experiment a total of 16 texts was used, whose difficulty was varied as suggested by Kintsch and van Dijk (1978). For the maintenance and generation of text coherence Ss had to perform a varying number of cognitive operations, viz. reinstatements and inferences. To distinguish elaborative and rehearsal readers among the Ss we examined whether reading time related to semantic processing operations, that is, whether there was a significant correlation between reading time and the cognitive operations to be performed. Wherever elaborative reading was practised, specific effects of inferences and reinstatements on recall performance were found (Table 1).

Reinstatements, which according to Kintsch and van Dijk (1978) are searches in long-term memory for propositions previously read, led to selective strengthening of the long-term memory component reconstruction. Inferences, however, impaired short-term memory performance (i.e., the replication score). If coherence generation and reading time are unrelated, there is no evidence of reinstatements and inferences effects on recall. Instead, we then find a positive correlation between short-term memory performance (replication) and reading-time, which is indicative of rehearsal processes.

Rehearsal and elaborative strategies result in significant differences for all recall parameters, which is due to strategy-specific use of working-memory. We share Bourne's and his coworkers' (Bourne, Young & Angell, 1986) idea of variable resource allocation during reading. One major fundamental difference between the strategies in our view concerns the use of controlled processing operations for subvocalisation in the rehearsal strategy and for fext integration for elaborative reading. Furthermore, to achieve replication with the rehearsal strategy, it is sufficient to assume a phonological short-term store as is usually done (e.g. Baddeley, 1982; 1983). For the elaborative reading, however, significantly improved replication has been obtained. Therefore, the involvement of another memory store has to be postulated. The latter would be required to account for the inhibitory effect of the inferences too (Table 1), because a mere phonological memory system would be insensitive to semantic factors.

In several studies Klapp, Marshburn and Lester (1983) demonstrated the existence of a short-term store whose capacity is, unlike that of the phonological store, capable of considerable extension owing to grouping and chunk formation effects. Of crucial importance for optimum usage of this system appears to be semantic preprocessing which results in the formation of bigger units. This is why what I refer to as "semantic short-term memory" is only efficient with elaborative-type reading. In the rehearsal strategy the formation of a large number of small chunks soon results in store overflow.

Do these alternative strategies give rise to different physiological patterns? I am going to examine this for the relation between demand and replication performance (I cannot deal here with demand relating to the long-term memory recall component reconstruction). To predict replication on the basis of the psychophysiological demand that was analyzed with the help of the power spectrum, separate backward multiple regression analyses were carried out for elaborative and rehearsal reading (Table 2).

Comparing with the rehearsal strategy which only involves the phonological store, for elaborative reading, where replication is achieved through both the phonological and semantic short-term store, only half of the variance is accounted for. Moreover, correlation analyses have revealed qualitatively different relationships of replication to cardiac arrhythmia for the two strategies (Table 3).

Usage of the phonological store in the rehearsal strategy is associated with a rise in the spectral energy of the range up to 0.25 Hz. The range $0.15-0.25$ Hz is of special importance, since frequencies around 0.05 Hz and 0.10 Hz are influenced by additional processes.

Table 2. Multiple backward regression analysis for prediction of the replication scores on the basis of the cardiac interval signal power spectrum (non-averaged data; $p < .05$).

Elaborative Reading

predictors (in Hz)	weight (r^2)	variance (R^2)
0.06	.06	
0.10	.07	26%
0.28	.15	

Rehearsal Reading

predictors (in Hz)	weight (r^2)	variance (R^2)
0.10	.07	
0.21	.09	
0.25	.13	51%
0.38	.11	

Table 3. Significant ($p < .05$) correlations between power spectrum amplitudes and replication scores (non-averaged data).

frequencies (in Hz)	Rehearsal Reading	Elaborative Reading
0.06	.36	
0.10	.53	
0.13	.31	
0.15	.46	
0.18	.36	
0.21	.54	
0.25	.54	−.26
0.28		−.42
0.31		−.24
0.34		−.21
0.37		−.23

Involvement of semantic short-term memory in elaborative reading is demonstrated by the amplitude decrease in the range of higher frequencies upwards of 0.25 Hz (Table 3).

Regarding the allocation of resources, I should say that according to Mulder (1980) the controlled processing load is reflected in the 0.10 Hz amplitude reduction. To establish its relation to coherence generation, polynomial regression analyses with the 0.10 Hz amplitude were done for both strategy groups (Figure 1).

For elaborative reading, which includes coherence generation, we obtained a significant linear relation for inferences: the larger the number of inferences, the higher the controlled processing load. Reinstatements, however, have no effect on cardiac arrhythmia but are characterised by lower heart rates. Thus the processing load associated with inference generation can be physiologically recorded and distinguished from long-term memory search processes, i.e., reinstatements.

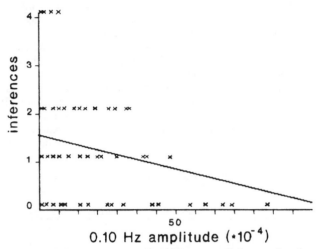

$$0.10 \text{ Hz amplitude } (*10^{-4})$$

Figure 1. Polynomial regression analysis between controlled processing demand (0.10 Hz amplitude) and inferences. Elaborative reading, non–averaged data, $p < .05$.

For rehearsal reading there was, however, no evidence of a relation between coherence generation and controlled processing.

According to Aaronson and Ferres (1984) the rehearsal strategy is based on directed subvocalisation. Therefore a relation was expected between controlled processing load and the demands made on the phonological short-term store or between the physiological parameters reflecting them. Table 4 shows that, indeed, only with the rehearsal strategy there are significant correlations between phonological store usage (0.15 − 0.25 Hz) and controlled processing (0.10 Hz).

Table 4. Correlations between controlled processing (0.10 Hz amplitude) and the demand on phonological short-term memory (0.15–0.25 Hz) for both reading strategies (*: $p < .05$).

frequencies (in Hz)	Rehearsal Reading	Elaborative Reading
0.15	−.24*	−.18
0.18	−.17	−.17
0.21	−.49*	−.07
0.25	−.21*	−.03

Variation of Emotional Content

Twelve texts of varying emotional content were used: cruel, neutral and sexual texts. Just as in the first experiment, we were able to identify elaborative and rehearsal readers. Interestingly enough, only with elaborative reading of cruel and sex-centred texts could we record measurable emotional responses (namely significant changes in electrodermal activity and pulse transmit time), wheres a significant drop in controlled processing load[1] with emotional rather than neutral texts was found for either of the reading strategies.

Due to strategy-specific use of working memory, which we have described, different consequences of this impairment of controlled processing are predictable for the two strategies.

Subvocalisation processes are an essential component of the reading process and become more automatic as reading skills improve (Sokolov, 1963; Mc Guigan, 1984). Therefore, with the rehearsal strategy, impairment of controlled processing will have a limited effect only, because subvocalisation can also proceed autonomously so that the phonological store does not break down. With

Table 5. Mean replication scores for the neutral and emotional texts and both reading strategies.

Text group	Rehearsal Reading	Elaborative Reading
neutral	27.1%	41.6%
emotional	21.4%	28.2%

Table 6. Correlation between power components, reflecting the demand on semantic short-term memory, and replication scores for the elaborative reading (non-averaged data; *: $p < .05$).

Frequencies (in Hz)	Text groups neutral	cruel	sex-centered
0.25	−.25*	−.16	−.20
0.28	−.20	−.18	−.03
0.30	−.45*	−.10	−.06
0.34	−.37*	−.06	−.04
0.38	−.44*	−.24	−.25*
0.40	−.38*	−.15	−.04

elaborative reading, where controlled processing is employed for text integration, the associated formation of larger units is impaired. Efficient use of semantic short-term memory should therefore not be possible. If these con-

---

[1] These observed reductions of demand for controlled processing correspond to the temporal trade-off hypothesis (Ellis, 1982) of aversive information processing (for detailed discussion, see Schönebeck, 1988; Zimmer & Schönebeck, 1987).

siderations prove correct, it should be expected that replication performance for emotional texts is slightly impaired in the case of rehearsal reading, but markedly in the case of elaborative reading.

As Tables 5 and 6 show, significant impairment for emotional texts indeed occurs only in elaborative reading.

The replication rate falls to a level as low as that for the rehearsal strategy with neutral texts. Besides, the decreased importance of semantic short-term memory for replication with elaborative processing of emotional texts is associated with a corresponding change in the psychophysiological demand: for emotional texts the significant relation between replication and the demand on semantic short-term memory, which we have always found for elaborative reading, disappears.

Variation of Concreteness and Imaginability

In this experiment using 16 texts of varying abstractness and imaginability, evidence of intraindividual strategy variation was obtained. It was only with concrete and high imaginable texts that subjects were able to employ the elaborative strategy. Consistent with our assumptions, a significant relation between semantic short-term memory demands (that is, a drop in spectral energy between 0.25 and 0.40 Hz) and replication should therefore occur only for high-imaginable concrete texts. For the sake of simplicity I am using spectral energy sums of this frequency range.

Table 7. Correlations between replication scores and the demand on semantic short-term memory (spectral energy sums from $0.25-0.40$ Hz) for all three experiments (non-averaged data; *: $p < .05$).

	Elaborative Reading	Rehearsal Reading
Experiment 1	$-.37^{*}$	$.51^{*}$
Experiment 2	$-.32^{*}$ (neutral texts)	$-.07$ (neutral texts)
Experiment 3	$-.28^{*}$ (concrete high imaginable texts)	$.05 \quad .09 \quad -.07$ (abstract and low imaginable texts)

Table 7 summarizes the results of all three experiments. Both intraindividually (in experiment 3) and interindividually (experiments 1 and 2) elaborative reading leads to significantly higher replication scores. This is due to the semantic short-term memory being used in an optimum manner. Physiologically, the demand on semantic short-term memory is characterised by a drop in the spectral energy of the higher frequency range upwards of 0.25 Hz.

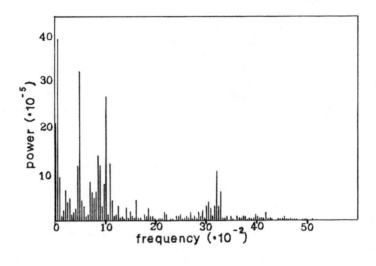

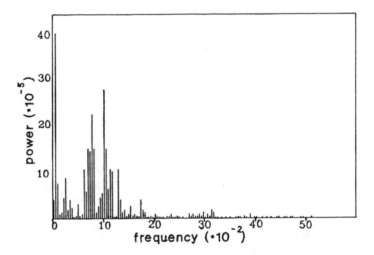

Figure 2. Cardiac interval signal power spectrum, reflecting the cognitive strain in performing a Sternberg–task (subject No. 15) with categorized (Figure 2a) and uncategorized (Figure 2b) lists.

Summary and Conclusions

The rehearsal strategy yields no negative correlations of replication performance with the higher-frequency part of the power spectrum. Especially the first experiment, however, suggests that demand on phonological short-term memory links up with increased spectral energy in the low frequency range up to 0.25 Hz. Since we are dealing here with the modulation of whole frequency ranges, the following conclusions can be derived for medically oriented investigations into the cardiac interval signal power spectrum.

1. Nonsemantic phonological short-term storage or processing is associated with increased sympathetic cardiovascular activity.
2. Demands on the semantic short-term store involves a decrease in parasympathetic activity.
3. Moreover, our findings confirm the results of Mulder (1980) that controlled processing results in an amplitude reduction at 0.10 Hz.

Results from a recent experiment allow us to generalize these conclusions. We used a Sternberg-task with categorized (two categories of three items) each vs. uncategorized (six items from distinct categories) lists (derived from Naus, 1974). An optimal usage of the semantic short-term memory is possible only with categorized lists. Therefore, we predicted that the application of categorized lists would lead to a selective amplitude reduction in the faster frequency range (upwards of 0.25 Hz) of the heart period power spectrum. Indeed, we were able to demonstrate such an effect (Figure 2).

We were able to show that elaborative and rehearsal strategies give rise to a different recall performances as well as different psychophysiological demands. We have suggested that this is due to stragey-specific usage of different working–memory subsystems. We suggest, as Klix (1984) did, that working memory characteristics are not narrowly specified but vary with the task. The demands made on the various subsystems which can be selectively measured with the aid of the cardiac interval signal power spectrum constitute the overall mental load which occurs when subjects have to cope with task requirements.

Correspondence should be adressed to Bernd Schönebeck, Bereich Psychologie, Zentralinstitut für Kybernetik und Informationsprozesse, Akademie der Wissenschaften der DDR, Kurstr. 33, 1086 Berlin, G.D.R.

References

Aaronson, D., & Ferres, F. (1984) Reading strategies for children and adults: Some empirical evidence. *Journal of Verbal Learning and Verbal Behavior, 23*, 189–220.

Baddeley, A.D. (1982). Reading and working memory. *Bulletin of the British Psychological Society, 35*, 412–414.

Baddeley, A.D. (1983). Working memory. *Philosophical Transactions of the Royal Society London B, 302*, 311–324.

Bourne, L.E. Jr., Young, S.R., & Angell, L.S. (1986). Resource allocation in reading: An interactive approach. *Zeitschrift für Psychologie, 194*, 155–176.

Ellis, M.E. (1982). Evolution of aversive information processing: A temporal trade-off hypothesis. *Brain, Behavior, and Evolution, 21*, 151−160.

Klapp, S.T., Marshburn, E.A., & Lester, P.T. (1983). Short-term memory does not involve "working memory" of information processing: the demise of a common assumption. *Journal of Experimental Psychology: General, 112*, 240−264.

Klix, F. (1984). Über Wissensrepräsentation im menschlichen Gedächtnis. In F. Klix (Ed.), *Gedächtnis, Wissen, Wissensnutzung.* Berlin: VEB Deutscher Verlag der Wissenschaften.

Kintsch, W., & van Dijk, T.A. (1978). Toward a model of text comprehension and production. *Psychological Review, 85*, 363−394.

Mc Guigan, F.J. (1984). How is linguistic memory accessed−A psychophysiological approach. *The Pavlovian Journal of Biological Sciences, 19*, 119−136.

Mulder, G. (1980). *The heart of mental effort. Studies on the cardiovascular physiology of mental work.* Groningen: Rijksuniversiteit.

Naus, MA. J. (1974). Memory search of categorized lists: a consideration of alternative self-terminating search strategies. *Journal of Experimental Psychology, 102*, 992−1000.

Presley, M., Levin, J.R., & Ghalata, E.S. (1984). Memory strategies monitoring in adults and children. *Journal of Verbal Learning and Verbal Behavior, 23*, 270−288.

Schönebeck, B., Zimmer, K.W., & Kniesche, R. (1985). Cognitive strain in text comprehension and heart rate variability. In F. Klix, R. Näätänen & K. Zimmer (Eds.), *Psychophysiological approaches to human information processing.* Amsterdam: Elsevier.

Schönebeck, B. (1988). *Zur strategiespezifischen Beanspruchungsmessung beim Lesen und Reproduzieren von Texten unterschiedlicher Kohärenz, Anschaulichkeit und Abstraktheit sowie emotionalen Gehaltes.* Unpublished Doctoral Dissertation, Akademie der Wissenschaften, Berlin.

Sokolov, A.N. (1963). *Inner speech and thought* (in russ.). Moskau: Prosweshtchenie.

Wickens, C. D. (1984). Processing resources in attention. In R. Parasuraman & D.R. Davies (Eds.), *Varieties of attention.* New York: Academic Press.

Zimmer, K.W., & Schönebeck, B. (1986). Emotional excitement in text comprehension: Recall and autonomic response patterning. In F. Klix & H. Hagendorf (Eds.)., *Human memory and cognitive capabilities. Mechanisms and performance* (Part B). Amsterdam: Elsevier.

Psychophysical Explorations of Mental Structures
Edited by H.-G. Geissler
in collaboration with M.H. Müller and W. Prinz
© 1990 by Hogrefe & Huber Publishers

Chapter 30

A Psychophysiological Study of Perception and Retrieval after Repeated "Subliminal" Stimulation

Norbert Roth and Günther Roscher
Institut für Physiologie, Medizinische Akademie
Institut für Neurobiologie
Akademie der Wissenschaften
Magdeburg, G.D.R.

It is a trivial fact that perception is not simply the uptake of information into the "central processor", but a highly active and very intricate function. Any systematic approach to the study of behavior more or less directly faces the problem of memory retrieval processes (Anochin, 1967; Grossberg & Stone, 1986; Roth, 1980). A number of external variables, as physical characteristics of stimuli (e.g., intensity, duration, contrast, extent of the receptor area stimulated), or of internal factors (arousal level, organic state, motivation and the like) may affect the processing of input information at any given instant. In almost all cases, the intake of information from the surrounding world is "selective", i.e., the behavioral meaning of stimuli is judged and this appraisal in turn acts on the perceptual process.

This assumption of control mechanisms working at a very early stage of processing is supported by a large number of empirical reports (see Dixon, 1981; Emrich, 1983; Kostandov, 1983). Most of these authors deal with the problem of so-called subconscious or preconscious perception and the relevant control mechanisms which may or may not activate a memory content and thus lead to conscious identification of an event.

Dixon (1981) postulates that because of different control mechanisms "the brain can monitor and analyse sensory inflow which may never achieve phenomenal representation" and "... in brief then, selective processes operating preconsciously may be initiated by conscious volition and/or parameters of the external stimulus. By the same token, preconscious responses to these two sorts of influence are also interactive with four organismic variables – need state, the disposition to emotional reactions to particular items of sensory inflow, information stored in unconscious long-term memory and organic state."

Our present study is devoted to the investigation of these "interface"-function between (unconscious) long-term memory (LTM) and conscious experience. Since very short or degraded stimuli are known to affect the processing of information (e.g., in semantic priming experiments, Neely, 1976), we developed a paradigm in which extremely short stimuli had to be repeatedly presented for conscious recognition.

Method

Subjects. Ten healthy paid volunteers (mean age: 23.4 years), all graduate students of medicine, participated in the experiments. Each subject (S) underwent one training and two experimental sessions. All of them had normal or corrected to normal visual acuity, and no one had a history of neurological disease. The experiments were carried out on three consecutive days in the forenoon hours.

Stimulus material. Ninety-six German nouns were used describing concrete things from everyday life and without obvious emotional impact. Words were printed in a 6×10 dot matrix (capitals) on white paper and photographed. They were projected as white–on–black slides. A word consisting of six letters subtended a horizontal visual angle of 2.5 degrees. A hatched area (3.5×1.8 degrees) was projected as a masking slide.

Procedure. The time course of one trial block, i.e., the repeated exposure of one target stimulus, is shown in Figure 1.

Following a "ready" signal given by the experimenter, the S pressed a microswitch and thus started repeated projection of the target word, which continued until the switch was released, i.e. until the S reported target recognition. As shown in Figure 1, continuous forward and backward masking was applied. The exposure time of the single target stimuli was adjusted to fit the following criterion: For conscious recognition of the word a minimum of five and a maximum of 12 repetitions were desired. If after 12 repetitions the S did not identify the word, single exposure times were increased in steps of 1.6 ms to enable recognition until the 20th repetition. These trial blocks were discarded from evaluation, but this procedure appeared to be necessary for maintaining the S's motivation. In the first experimental session, the inter–stimulus–interval (ISI) for all trial blocks was 2.0 s. In the second experiment, the ISI was varied over trial blocks: every 16 words were projected with ISIs of 0.5, 1.0,

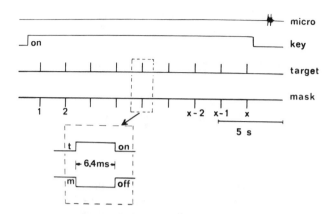

Figure 1. Stimulus–response arrangement in one trial block. While S presses the key, the target word is repeatedly projected. After recognition, the key is released and a verbal response is given. The onset demonstrates the temporal relationship of target and mask. EEG–epochs related to the first two and the last three stimuli within the block are taken for ERP analysis.

2.0, 4.0, and 8.0 s, respectively. The order of different ISIs was randomized over the task, and the Ss were informed whether the ISI would be shorter or longer that the preceding one (at the same time they were given the "ready signal" for the next trial). The timing of stimulation was controlled by a CAMAC computer system which also served for data acquisition.

Data acquisition and analysis. The S's performance was assessed on the basis of stimulus repetitions necessary for word recognition, i.e. the cumulative exposure time per trial block. False reports and trial blocks with no response after 20 repetitions were counted separately.

During the entire experiment, the EEG (Fz, Cz, O1, O2) was monitored (low-pass filter: 30 Hz, time constant: 1 s), epochs of 1.0 s prior to and 0.9 s after each single stimulus were digitized at a rate of 200 cps and stored on magnetic tape. Collodium secured Ag/AgCl electrodes were used with interelectrode resistance less than 5 kOhms. The vertical EOG was picked up by electrodes above and below the left orbita, horizontal EOG from both outer canthi.

The off-line analysis included averaging of the EEG epochs No. 1, 2, $x-2$, $x-1$, and x (see Figure 1) over trial blocks and graphic display of mean blink distribution during stimulus repetition.

Results

Task performance. All our Ss were able to identify target words after repeated presentation. The single exposure times were in the range from 4.8 to 9.0 ms (mean: 6.4 ms). In the first experiment (ISI constant, 2.0 s), the mean number of repetitions was 8.3 (SD: 2.4). If stimuli were selected according to word length and word frequency in common language, no significant influence of these variables upon recognition rate could be found (see Table 1).

Table 1. Mean cumulative exposure times (n = 10) as a function of word frequency in spoken language, and of word length. Values in ms.

Class of words	mean	SD
frequent/short	70.8	11.6
frequent/long	74.5	10.2
rare/short	74.0	15.1
rare/long	74.6	11.4

In the second session, the effect of different ISIs on word identification was examined. Figure 2 demonstrates, for three Ss, that with shorter ISIs, the number of repetitions neccessary for recognition increases.

The optimum ISI, wich requires the least number of repetitions, amounts 2.0 s for 8 Ss. Two Ss performed best when words were presented at intervals of 4.0 or 8.0 s, respectively. Note that for all Ss the 1.0 s ISI does not fit into the monotonous trend between 0.25 and 2.0 s.

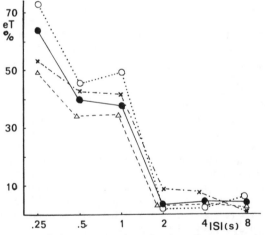

Figure 2. Relative cumulative exposure times for three Ss as a function of the ISI. Individual values of optimal performance (least number of repetitions). Black circles represent the group mean (n = 10).

Subjective reports. After the last session, all Ss reported their subjective impressions. They stated unanimously that words could not be read but stimuli were perceived as a "flicker or flashing" of the mask. Even assessment of word length was reported to be difficult or impossible. Concentrating attention on the physical properties of the stimuli, i.e., attempting to identify letters, hindered recognition. Most Ss reported that "undirected, rather passive attention was best" and that "words came to mind like during spontaneous remembering." For all Ss the perception of a virtually unreadable word was a "strange experience." Except for the direction of attention, no cognitive strategy was reported.

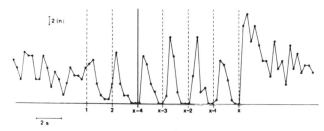

Figure 3. Mean eye blink distribution during word recognition. Male subject, 22 years. Vertical lines show the moment of target stimulation. Numbering of single trials as in Figure 1.

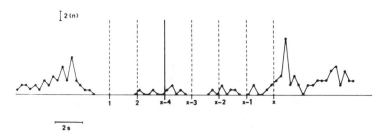

Figure 4. Eye blink distribution in a subject with very low baseline blink rate. Male subject, 24 years. Note that despite a significantly different baseline level, blink pattern is essentially identical with that of Figure 3.

Blink distribution. Eye-blink distribution during trial blocks was analyzed from the vertical EOG. Only data from the first experiment (ISI: 2.0 s) will be presented here. Typical examples are shown in Figures 3 and 4. It is evident that, with the "ready signal" before a new trial block, the number of blinks considerably decreases with respect to baseline values. Immediately prior to each stimulus, blinks are completely suppressed. This suppression may reflect visual attention, virtually no stimulus in the whole experiment is left unattended. After word recognition (x), the number of blinks increases significantly for a few seconds and declines again to resting level. These changes of blink rate during trial blocks were similar in all our Ss, independent of individual baseline values.

Event-related potentials (ERP). The averaged ERPs for one S during experiment 1 are shown in Figure 5. The shape of ERPs varies with electrode

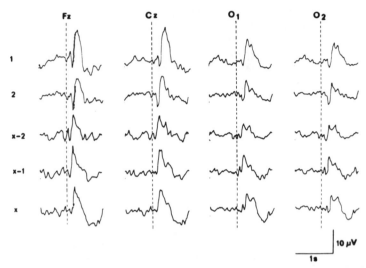

Figure 5. Averaged ERP from male subject, 22 years. The numbers refer to stimulus position within trial blocks (see Figure 1). Negativity upwards, broken lines indicate the moment of stimulus (word) exposure.

localization as well as with the position of stimuli within one trial block. Whereas in fronto-central derivations mainly the negative wave peaking at approximately 260 ms and a late positive complex varied during target recogniton, in occipital regions most Ss revealed an increasing amplitude of the second positive peak (P 230) that was superimposed on the larger negative wave. Dynamic changes of the large negative and positive waves are demonstrated in Figure 6. The group mean for six Ss was calculated for stimuli 1, 2, and x − 1 only. For the last stimulus prior to recognition (x), only four Ss had a sufficient number or artefact-free EEG epochs due to the rebound of blinks. Prominent components which vary consistently during trial blocks, are the large negative (N 260) and positive (P 480) deflections. There are only minor changes of the amplitudes, but a significant reduction of their peak latencies, mainly between the first and the second stimulus of a trial block.

Discussion

The stimulus setting employed in this study allowed our Ss to retrieve relevant memory contents after repeated exposure of target words. Due to extremely short stimulus duration and masking, a single stimulus failed to produce conscious recall. On the basis of this observation it seems reasonable to suppose that the single stimulus in a trial block conveys only partial information. Since in our experiments Ss performed with high accuracy (error rate 5%), the repetition of this partial input information must provide the basis for successful retrieval, i.e., the activation of LTM contents is realized as a piece-meal process. This may be the main difference to other studies with short stimulus exposure, where inspection time is the main measure of performance (Deary, 1986; Garnett, 1985; Nettelbeck, Edwards & Vreugdenhil, 1986).

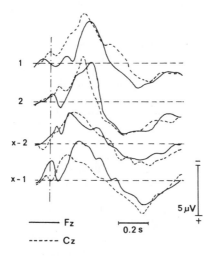

Figure 6. Group mean of ERP (n = 6) in Fz and Cz during word recognition. Broken vertical lines indicate stimulus onset.

There are at least two possible explanations for the phenomenon observed, one of them based on the properties of the "iconic memory" (Sperling, 1960) and the other on the assumption of direct access of partial information to LTM.

Iconic memory (Sperling, 1960; Neisser, 1967) has been attributed to visible persistence as a basis for phenomenological report and/or a precategorial representation ("informational persistence"; Coltheart, 1980). An alternative explanation, the "dual–buffer model" (Mewhort, Campbell, Marchetti & Campbell, 1981) takes into consideration a feature buffer (pre–identification) and a character buffer (post–identification). This model envisages an "iden-tify–then–select" mode of operation (Chow, 1986). In experiments of Eriksen and Collins (1967), the successive–field paradigm, in which two subsequently presented (incomplete) dot patterns were integrated into letters, recognition of these letters was possible until approximately 300 ms after the first stimulus. Holding and Orenstein (1983) failed to replicate these results. Orenstein and Holding (1987) emphasized "that information from non–attended locations is unavailable for report by subjects." On the basis of their results, they reject the dual–buffer model. A "select–then–identify" mode of processing seems most likely for the processes related to "iconic" memory (Chow, 1986; Orenstein & Holding, 1987).

Under our experimental conditions, an accumulation or completion of partial information on the basis of "iconic" storage should improve performance, i.e., reduce the number of required stimulus repetitions with shortest ISIs (250 ms), whereas stimuli delivered at ISIs of 4 or 8 s should not be identified because the iconic storage is supposed to decay until 250 or 300 ms. Our results with variable ISIs contradict the hypothesis of a kind of "iconic accumulation" and support the conclusions of Haber (1983) and Orenstein and Holding (1987) "that the traditional view on iconic memory needs rethinking." The optimum recognition performance of our Ss with ISIs of 2.0 s may be explained only with another type of memory access. Since the blink suppression during trial blocks suggests that Ss paid attention to all singel stimuli (Stern, Walrath & Goldstein, 1984), we assume that every stimulus contributes to the eventual identification of the target word. Several authors suppose that very early control mechanisms affect the processing of verbal information (Kosslyn, 1980; Molfese, Papanicolaou, Hess & Molfese, 1979; Zimmer, 1987), and that control must not be conscious. These mechanisms might play an important role in our task: If the first stimulus of a trial block causes a "spreading activation" (Posner & Snyder, 1975) in a given network, then the subsequent stimuli should find a facilitated structure which enables faster processing and enhances activation persisting from the preceding step. With every further stimulus repetition, the activation of information in LTM is narrowed down to the relevant semantic representation (Keele & Neill, 1978) which eventually becomes a conscious experience. This type of processing and memory activation is very close to semantic priming which – under certain conditions – reveals a similar dependency on the time interval between stimuli (Sudevan & Taylor, 1987).

ERP findings reported in this study also lent support to this explanation: During a trial block the latency of ERP components decreases parallel to the stepwise item recognition. If we assume a focussing or "narrowing-down" of spreading activation (Neill & Westberry, 1987), then the netto effect of neural activation must not change during stimulus processing within trial blocks, i.e., amplitude changes must not occur. The faster processing of later stimuli (2, $x-2$, $x-1$, x) will appear only in latency shifts. The findings by Boddy and Weinberg (1981) of an enhancd N 130/P 210 component after priming with semantically related words was replicated in our experiments only for occipital derivations, where a P 230 was superimposed in most Ss on the large negative wave (N 200 – 400) and revealed an increasing amplitude towards stimulus recognition. This confirms also a result of Boddy (1985) in a priming paradigm with variable stimulus onset asynchrony (SOA).

Semantic priming was reported to occur also with degraded or backward masked stimuli (McCauly, Parmelee, Sperber & Carr, 1980), and "it is generally accepted that performance can be affected by stimuli that are not completely and unambiguously identified" (Purcell, Stewart & Stanovich, 1983). The priming effect is time-dependent, as was demonstrated by Fowler, Wolford, Slade and Tassinary (1981). They found no semantic priming with a SOA of 200 ms, but a facilitated processing (faster reaction times) when prime and target were 2 s apart.

In our experiment, the slow negative wave (see Figure 6) is similar to that observed by Polich, Vanasse and Donchin (1980) to out-of-category words, non-words and incongruous sentence completions and which also appeared in fronto-central rather than posterior localizations. In our case it might reflect memory scanning on the basis of partial input information which (at least at the beginning of a trial block) must include a broad area of semantic categories. There may be a close functional relationship to a "processing negativity" (Näätänen, Alho & Sams, 1985). In priming experiments, the spreading activation dissipates as a function of semantic distance (DenHeyer & Briand, 1986). We used an identical stimulus within each trial block which is supposed to be scanned first over brod categories. With repeated presentations the semantic distance between the perceived stimulus and the target word representation in LTM is assumed to decrease.

The interpretation of the late positive wave's functional significance is difficult at the present state of our experiments. This prominent component which occurs in the time range of the P300 (Donchin, Karis, Bashore, Coles & Gratton, 1986), varies with a number of external and internal factors. Since this positive wave is already present at the very beginning of each trial block, i.e., when the meaning of the stimulus is not yet known to the S, it may be related to ability (Johnson & Donchin, 1978) and to "updating" of memory contents as well (Rösler, 1982). The latency of the P300 is reported to be delayed when the target is difficult to discriminate (McCarthy & Donchin, 1981). The decreasing peak latency in our experiments then could be explained in terms of an enhanced discrimination during the trial block. Mechanisms of activation and inhibition relating to selective attention during our task (Neill & Westberry, 1987; Algarabel et al, 1987; Hillyard & Hansen, 1986) could be related to the time course of ERP changes.

The data give evidence that even stimuli which are too short for conscious identification after a single presentation may cause long-lasting changes of excitability in neural networks associated with LTM and thus may perhaps affect later perception and performance even in another behavioral context (Yaniv & Meyer, 1987).

The procedure employed in our investigation seems to be a useful tool for further research on memory retrieval mechanisms.

Summary

Perception of external signals is affected by a number of control processes: Motivation, emotion, prior experience, and organic state may modulate the "uptake" of information at a very early state of processing; and this influence need not be conscious. In the present study, an experimental design was chosen which allows to "split" the retrieval process into several steps.

Our results may be explained in the context of the "spreading activation"-theory (Posner & Snyder, 1975): With repetition of ultra-short stimuli, the preceding exposure causes activation (below conscious threshold) of semantic representations. This persisting activation facilitates the processing of the subsequent exposure, hence, the activated field is narrowed down, and eventually the conscious threshold is reached. An "iconic" storage is very unlikely to be involved in this process, but our results add support to the assumption that the uncomplete information delivered by single, short stimuli probably are processed up to the level of long term memory representation.

Correspondence should be addressed to Norbert Roth, Institut für Neurobiologie, Bereich Psychophysiologie, Akademie der Wissenschaften, Leipziger Str. 44, 3090 Magdeburg, G.D.R.

References

Algarabel, S., Pitarque, A., Soler, M.S., Ruiz, J.C., Baixauli, J.M., & Dasi, C. (1987). Effect of prime type on lexical decision time. *Perceptual and Motor Skills, 64,* 119–125.

Anochin, P.K. (1967). *Das funktionelle System als Grundlage der Architektur des Verhaltensaktes.* Jena: Fischer.

Boddy, J. (1985). Brain event related potentials in the investigation of language processing. In D. Papakostopoulos, S. Butler & I. Martin (Eds.), *Clinical and experimental neuropsychophysiology* (pp.173–203). London: Croom Helm.

Boddy, J., & Weinberg, H. (1981). Brain potentials, perceptual mechanisms and semantic categorisation. *Biological Psychology, 12,* 43–62.

Chow, S.L. (1986). Iconic memory, location information, and partial report. *Journal of Experimental Psychology: Human Perception and Performance, 12,* 455–465.

Coltheart, M. (1980). Iconic memory and visible persistence. *Perception & Psychophysics, 27,* 183–228.

Deary, I.J. (1986). Inspection time: Discovery of rediscovery? *Personality and Individual Differences, 7,* 625–631.

Den Heyer, K., & Briand, K. (1986). Priming single digit numbers: Automatic spreading activation dissipates as a function of semantic distance. *American Journal of Psychology, 99,* 315–340.

Dixon, N.F. (1981). The conscious/unconscious interface: Contributions to an understanding. *Psychological Research Bulletin, 5,* 1–15.

Donchin, E., Karis, D., Bashore, T.R., Coles, M.G.H., & Gratton, G. (1986). Cognitive Psychophysiology and human information processing. In M.G.H. Coles, E. Donchin & S.W. Porges (Eds.), *Psychophysiology* (pp. 244–265). Amsterdam: Elsevier.

Eriksen, C.W., & Collins, J.F. (1967). Some temporal characterisctics of visual pattern perception. *Journal of Experimental Psychology, 74,* 476–484.

Fowler, C.A., Wolford, G., Slade, R., & Tassinary, L. (1981). Lexical access with and without awareness. *Journal of Experimental Psychology: General, 110,* 341–362.

Garnett, P.D. (1985). Intelligence measurement by computerized information processing using inspection time. *Journal of General Psychology, 112,* 325–335.

Grossberg, S., & Stone, G. (1986). Neural dynamics of word recognition and recall: Attentional priming, learning, and resonance. *Psychological Review, 93,* 46–74.

Haber, R.N. (1983). The impending demise of the icon: A critique of the concept of iconic storage in visual information processing. *Behavioral and Brain Sciences, 6,* 1–54.

Hillyard, S.A., & Hansen, J.C. (1986). Attention: Electrophysiological approaches. In M.G.H. Coles, E. Donchin & S.W. Porges (Eds.), *Psychophysiology* (pp. 227–243). Amsterdam: Elsevier.

Holding, D.H., & Orenstein, H.B. (1983). Sensory storage of fragmentary displays. *Perceptual and Motor Skills, 57,* 1283–1294.

Johnson, R.Jr., & Donchin, E. (1978). On how P300 amplitude varies with the utility of the eliciting stimuli. *Electroencephalography and Clinical Neurophysiology, 44,* 424–437.

Keele, S.W., & Neill, W.T. (1978). Mechanisms of attention. In E.C. Carterette & M.P. Friedman (Eds.), *Handbook of Perception* (pp. 3−47). New York: Academic Press.

Kosslyn, S.M. (1980). *Image and Mind*. Cambridge, Mass.: Harvard University Press.

Kostandov, E.A. (1983). *Funcionalnaya asimmetriya polusharii mosga i neososnavayemoye vospriyatiye*. Moscow: Nauka.

McCarthy, G., & Donchin, E. (1981). A metric for thought: A comparison of P300 latency and reaction time. *Science, 211*, 77−80.

McCauly, C., Parmelee, C.M., Sperber, R.D., & Carr, T.H. (1980). Early extraction of meaning from pictures and its relation to conscious identification. *Journal of Experimental Psychology: Human Perception and Performance, 6*, 265−276.

Mewhort, D.J.K., Campbell, A.J., Marchetti, F.M., & Campbell, J.I.D. (1981). Identification, localization, and "iconic memory": An evaluation of the bar probe tasks. *Memory and Cognition, 9*, 50−67.

Molfese, D.L., Papanicolaou, A., Hess, T.M., & Molfese, V.J. (1979). Neuroelectrical correlates of semantic processes. In H. Begleiter (Ed.), *Evoked Brain Potentials and Behaviour* (pp. 89−106). New York: Plenum Press.

Näätänen, R., Alho, K., & Sams, M. (1985). Selective information processing and event-related potentials. In F. Klix, R. Näätänen, & K. Zimmer (Eds.), *Psychophysiological approaches to human information processing* (pp. 73−93). Amsterdam: North-Holland.

Neely, J.H. (1976). Semantic priming and retrieval from lexical memory: Evidence for facilitatory and inhibitory processes. *Memory and Cognition, 4*, 648−654.

Neill, W.T., & Westberry, R.L. (1987). Selective attention and the suppression of cognitive noise. *Journal of Experimental Psychology: Learning, Memory and Cognition, 13*, 327−334.

Neisser, U. (1967). *Cognitive Psychology*. New York: Appleton−Century−Crofts.

Nettelbeck, T., Edwards, C., & Vreugdenhil, A. (1986). Inspection time and IQ: Evidence for a mental speed-ability association. *Personality and Individual Differences, 7*, 633−641.

Orenstein, H.B., & Holding, D.H. (1987). Attentional factors in iconic memory and visible persistence. *Quarterly Journal of Experimental Psychology, 39A*, 149−166.

Polich, J., Vanasse, L., & Donchin, E. (1980). Category expectancy and the N 200. *Psychophysiology, 18*, 142.

Posner, M.I., & Snyder, C.R.R. (1975). Attention and cognitive control. In R.L. Solso (Ed.), *Information Processing and Cognition: The Loyola Symposium* (pp. 55−85). Hillsdale, NJ: Erlbaum.

Purcell, D.G., Stewart, A.L., & Stanovich, K.E. (1983). Another look at semantic priming without awareness. *Perception & Psychophysics, 34*, 65−71.

Rösler, F. (1982). *Hirnelektrische Korrelate kognitiver Prozesse*. Berlin: Springer.

Roth, N. (1980). Psychophysiological indices for a hierarchic organisaiton of functional systems. *Wissenschaftliche Zeitschrift Karl-Marx-Universität Leipzig, 29*, 230−234.

Sperling, G. (1960). The information available in brief visual presentations. *Psychological Monographs, 74*, No.11 (Whole No. 498).

Stern, J.A., Walrath, L.C., & Goldstein, R. (1984). The endogenous eyeblink. *Psychophysiology, 21*, 22−23.

Sudevan, P., & Taylor, D.A. (1987). The cueing and priming of cognitive operations. *Journal of Experimental Psychology: Human Perception and Performance, 13*, 89−103.

Yaniv, I., & Meyer, D.E. (1987). Activation and metacognition of inaccessible stored information: Potential bases for incubation effects in problem solving. *Journal of Experimental Psychology: Learning, Memory, and Cognition, 13*, 187−205.

Zimmer, K. (1987). Psychophysiologische Experimente zur Wirkung emotionaler Reize auf die Gedächtnisaktivierung. *Wissenschaftliche Zeitschrift Humboldt-Universität Berlin, 36*, 407−413.

Psychophysical Explorations of Mental Structures
Edited by H.-G. Geissler
in collaboration with M.H. Müller and W. Prinz
© 1990 by Hogrefe & Huber Publishers

Chapter 31

Some Aspects of Interpreting the ERP as a Spatio-Temporal Function

Peter Bartsch
Institut für Physiologie der Charité
Humboldt-Universität
Berlin, G.D.R.

What are the differences between the neuronal excitations of the occipital, temporal, and postcentral cortex which are reflected in our conscious experience of light, sound, and feeling, respectively? Following current knowledge of the functional topography of the cortex (Creutzfeldt, 1976, 1983; Jones & Powell, 1970; Penfield & Jasper, 1954) and taking account of the concept of distributed cerebral systems (Mountcastle, 1957), the discrepancy can be expected to be found in the spatio-temporal function of unspecific elementary processes which reflect the content of the message.

This bears the problem of relating the topographically different signals of simultaneously recorded evoked potentials with the distributed cerebral systems mentioned above. The basis for the interpretation of ERPs put forth in this paper was, on the one hand, derived from generally accepted physiological evidence, and, on the other hand, by essential problems in current EEG and ERP methodology.

Physiological Evidence. First, according to Lorente de Nó (1947), neurons which form open electrical fields are suitable candidates for non-invasively recorded electrophysiological potentials. The dendrite-soma-axon configuartion of these neurons appears long and thin. Consequently, generation processes in the cortex are essentially limited to pyramidal cells, the main type of neurons having a columnar structure. Second, the postsynaptic potential inputs of the pyramidal cells have an amplitude up to 8 mV and a duration of 15−40 ms (Creutzfeldt, 1983). Thirdly, during suprathreshold excitation, the pyramidal cells produce a biphasic action potential which is conducted via the axon towards the white matter within 1−2 ms and via cell soma and dendrites towards the cortex surface within 4−6 ms. In this process the potential fields are spread in a rotationally symmetric way around the transmission axis with the amplitude fluctuating perpendicularly to the axis (Creutzfeldt, 1983).

Finally, under the condition of fast axonal AP-conduction, the free pathway length accessible to conduction is a manifold of the AP's geometric length. The de- and repolarisation vectors are generated at different locations, yet simultaneously, so that they overlap to a great extent in the resulting reflection. This applies to all axonal fibers ending in the cortex, even though the soma-dendritic spikes leading towards the cortex surface have only a theoretical length of 20 − 30 mm (since the free-pathway-length takes up only a small fraction of this distance), and de-and repolarisation occur successively and do not overlap. The amplitude can exceed 15 mV.

Some Methodological Problems in EEG and ERP Research. The first problem concerns the traditional bandpass of an EEG-amplifier ranging from 1 up to 70 Hz. The aforementioned points make evident, that this bandpass falls clearly within the infrafrequency range of cellular responses. As a second problem, ERP recordings are ambiguous sources of information, because various information processes are characterized by a certain spatio-temporal pattern of activity. This activity is measured between two spatially distinct electrode sites and, thus, cannot be tapped neither by analyzing the shape of the ERP, nor by interpolations of the potential's extent over the scalp (Homan, Herman & Purdy, 1987); Vieth, 1984).

Inner Relationships between Simultaneously Recorded ERPs

The inner relationships between two and more simultaneously recorded evoked potentials have been studied in our laboratory during the last years. These investigations have involved three levels of analysis: the occurence of probability of ERP components, the relationships between simultaneously recorded parent populations of ERPs (interchannel coincidence), and potential phenomena related to this interchannel activity (Subpotential-Units, SPU).

The Probability of Occurrence of ERP Components

Two auditory evoked potentials were recorded simultaneously from a normally hearing subject at Cz and C4 (Figure 1) and averaged in the traditional way, however by using 250 single potentials. Of the two potentials the Cz derivation clearly showed larger amplitudes. A prerequisite for studying the relationships between two potentials is the knowledge of the probabilities of

occurence for each of their components. For this purpose, the amplitude histo-
graphy of the statistical parent populations of the potentials at Cz and C4 was
studied.

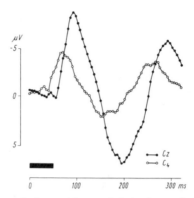

Figure 1. Auditory evoked potentials recorded simultaneously from a normally hearing
subject at Cz (solid circles) and C4 (open circles), averaged over 250 single potentials.
Stimulus: 85 dB HL, 1000 Hz, 50 ms, interstimulus interval 5 s.

These amplitudes were classified in such a way that the baseline corresponded to the mean value of the averaged potential and that, on the premise
of normal distribution of the values, to pass across this baseline meant that the
occupation of all classes was equal. In order to obtain a strong statement of
class occupation large parent populations were necessary. In Figures 2 and 3
the X–axis was rotated at the coordinate origin by 180 degrees so that positive
and negative classes would be placed over each other. The negative classes
were drawn facing upward. Accordingly, the absolute probabilities of occurrence of the potential at Cz (Figure 2) are 15% for P1, 65% for N1, 55% for
P2, and 40% for N2.

After calculating the squared correlation coefficient of the averaged EP and
the occupation of corresponding pairs of classes it also became evident that the
larger amplitudes of the single potentials were more relevant to the averaged
EP. A signal–free probe of the EEG at Cz showed a markedly smaller occupation of the central, i.e., middle amplitude, classes. The analogous study of
the C4 parent population (Figure 3) showed larger probabilities of occurrence
for all components, although the averaged potential exhibited smaller amplitudes: 18% for P1, 70% for N1, 58% for P2, and 58% for N2.

Likewise, in this population the central classes were occupied to a greater
degree than in the corresponding EEG probe.

The absolute probability of all components is less than 100% and decreases
to 5–20% when the probability of the EEG is included in the calculation procedure. Therefore, we cannot conclude that, when comparing two or more
derivations, the same component must be found in all of them. The inner
relationships existing between two parent populations of simultaneously derived

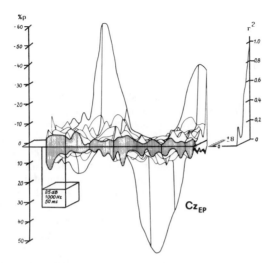

Figure 2. Amplitude histogram of the statistical parent population of all 250 single potemtials, recorded at Cz. Left scale: percentage of probability; right horizontal scale: number of amplitude classes between 0 and ±8; right vertical scale: squared cross correlation coefficient between the averaged EP (see Figure 1) and the occupation of corresponding classes.

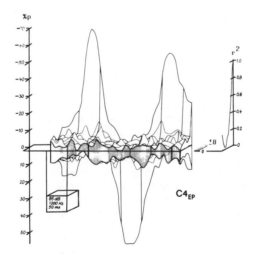

Figure 3. Amplitude histogram of the statistical parent population of all single potentials recorded at C4.

potentials can only be studied adequately on the level of simultaneously generated single potentials.

The Interchannel Coincidence

Interchannel coincidence was introduced as a new parameter into our studies of inner relationships. It reflects a coupling between simultaneously generated single potentials, which is significant in regard to concurrent background changes in the EEG. By analyzing the EP and the above described EEG histograms statistically with highest possible resolution, a characteristic pattern of amplitude classes for the EP parent population can be attained. Only those classes which are occupied with a significantly greater frequency form the "matrix." A subsequent comparison was made between each single EP and this matrix. Three values per dwell time could be appointed: -1 refers to the coincidence of as single EP with a negative amplitude class, $+1$ to the coincidence with a positive amplitude class, and 0 refers to no coincidence. In this way, each single EP is transformed into a time series with -1, $+1$ and 0.

These calculations reveal the coincidence of sections of a single EP with classes of the matrix. The inner relationships were hidden until a comparison across time series of simultaneously generated potentials was made. Only interchannel coincident measures involving a delay are of interest, since information processing is defined by the amount of time needed for integration, conduction, and synaptic transfer between two or more locations. The determination of the maximal permissible time delay was difficult to accomplish. Experiments on rats conducted in our laboratory indicated that the maximal permissible time delay must be limited to 10 ms in order to exclude the influence of reverberation. Subsequent research has shown that a maximal delay of 15 ms applies to the human brain.

An essential limitation of this interchannel coincidence measure must be mentioned: this delay, hence our "interchannel" coincidence, is statistical, not causal in nature. Since evidence of a directed information flow from A to B is deduced from the recording of an initial occurrence in A and a second occurrence in B, it cannot be ruled out that A and B are influenced asymmetrically by some unknown third structure thereby only simulating an information flow from A to B, or *vice versa*. In other words, interchannel coincidence reflects maximum–probability coupling between two simultaneously generated single potentials. It is defined by delay, corresponding latencies, direction, and polarity. Adding the coincident occurrences of all single potentials belonging to one parent population yields a histogram in temporal synchronization with corresponding averaged EP. The following example illustrates some results of the coincidence analysis.

100 auditory evoked potentials were recorded at Cz and Fz. The bandpass of the amplifier was between 1 and 70 Hz. The upper part of Figure 4 shows the averaged potential at Fz; the histogram of interchannel coincidence, directed from Cz to Fz in temporal synchronization, is shown in the lower half. The dwell time is 1 ms. It is evident, that these coincident events or couplings have

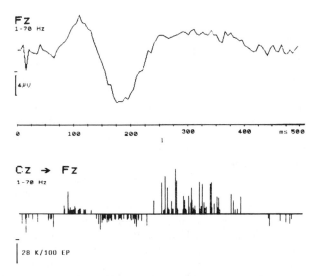

Figure 4. Auditory evoked potential at Fz (above), averaged over 100 single potentials, and histogram of interchannel coincidence directed from Cz to Fz (below).

equally abrupt beginnings and endpoints. The couplings are discontinuous to a large degree, but comparable to the averaged EP-waves which reveal a similar trend. However, EP-amplitudes and coincident occurences are not proportional. The mean delay is 5.3 ms for negative and 4.8 ms for positive coincident occurences. Although the probability of coincident occurrence being lower, the temporal pattern of interchannel coincidence in the opposite direction, i.e., from Fz to Cz, was very similar. A comparison of coincident occurrences from Cz to Fz and *vice versa* reveals that the relationships between these two electrode sites are bidirectional.

The Subpotential–Units (SPU)

Interchannel coincident occurrences of topographically separate EP parent populations reflect inherent couplings and, as mentioned above, are characterized by delay, corresponding latencies, direction, polarity, and the probability of occurrence. However, they remain a formal statistical characterization as long as the neurophysiological correlates of each coincident event are unknown. Returning to the concept of columnar organization (Asanuma, 1975; Goldman-Rakic, 1984; Hubel & Wiesel, 1968; Merzenich, 1973; Mountcastle, 1957), an interchannel coincidence must reflect occurrences in the open electrical field of pyramidal cells, i.e., input relations reflect postsynaptic potential and output relations soma–dendrite spikes. In their duration, however, both potential phenomena differ from each other. The former requires 15 to 40 ms, the latter 4 – 6 ms. We have been evaluating an experimental series of different kinds of event–related potentials under varying conditions of bandpass. In this way we found potential phenomena which appear to be similar to those mentioned above. These potential phenomena, presumably the essence of inter-channel coincidence, will be referred to as Subpotential Units of Event–Related Potentials (SPUs). With the concept of columnar organization in mind, these SPUs are postulated to have the following properties:

1. In all cases, SPUs must show the same temporal pattern, regardless of the recording site, the type of the event–related potential, and the subject.
2. They differ only in time and probability of occurrence, currence, direction, and delay, which are all contingent upon the individual mechanisms of information processing.

So far, our empirical evidence does not lend support to, or refute, the above-mentioned assumptions. However, a new methodology for the detection of the SPUs had to be developed. The point in time at which coincidence was determined at the receiving structure, in respect to the sender, was defined as the trigger. The trigger released the selection of adjacent single EP–values (consisting of a maximum of 50 dwell times, 4 dwell times prior to, and 46 following coincident occurrence), separate storage, and averaging. This procedure included numerous and often complicated supplementary computer calculations, e.g., the suppression of manifold trigger releases by new coincident occurrences appearing within one and the same selected EP epoch.

Two examples will be presented to explain this analytic concept and its results. All data were obtained from one subject. If the bandpass of the amplifier was between 1 and 70 Hz, coincident occurrence- triggered SPUs could only be determined in exceptional cases.

Example 1. Parallel to the derivation previously shown, each of the 100 single potentials of both parent populations was also amplified at a bandpass of 32 to 200 Hz. In Figure 5, left side, the averaged potential of Fz is depicted above, the coincidence histogram of Cz to Fz in temporal synchronization below. Because of the higher bandpass, the amplitude of the averaged EP is reduced, the components N1 and P2 appear somewhat earlier. In the coincidence histogram a clear change in pattern is apparent, in addition, a greater similarity between potential amplitudes and coincident occurrences is evident.

Now the isolation of SPUs is successful, as can be seen on the right side of Figure 5. An almost complete mirror image of negative and positive courses appears: both have a short increase or decrease of 4 – 6 ms, followed by a continuous decrease or increase, respectively. The vertical lines show the standard deviation. In reference to the first value recorded, the duration of negative SPUs is 35 ms, and that of positive SPUs 50 ms. K marks the time of coincident occurance. SPUs' onset is apparently a bit earlier. It was not necessary to establish subgroups, since the square correlation coefficient was greater than 0.6. All delay–times were almost identical (5.6 ms). Data obtained from analysis in the reverse direction, i.e. from Fz to Cz, was similar. The SPUs do not differ from those previously shown, not even in their delay–times.

Example 2. In a third pair of amplifiers connected in parallel, the frequency range was set at 200 to 2000 Hz. Under these high–frequency condi-

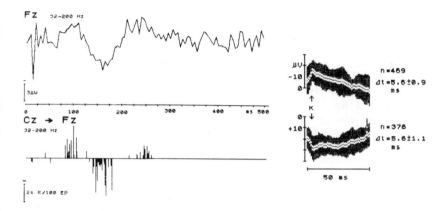

Figure 5. Left: The same auditory evoked potential as in Figure 4, recorded at Fz, but this time amplified at a bandpass of 32—200 Hz (above), the changed interchannel coincidence histogram directed from Cz to Fz (below). Right: SPUs with standard deviation (black lines) isolated from the Fz parent population with help of interchannel coincidence analysis. K marks the time of coincidence occurence.

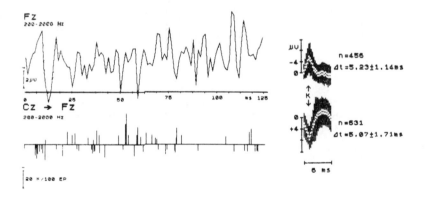

Figure 6. Left: The "evoked potential" at Fz amplified at a bandpass of 200—2000 Hz with a 4-fold higher time resolution (above), the histogram of interchannel coincidence directed from Cz to Fz (below). Right: SPUs of the Cz parent population.

tions (dwell time 250 ms) averaging does not lead to any evoked potential recognizable as such (Figure 6). The signal seems to fluctuate stochastically, as shown here at Fz. The coincident occurrences originating at Cz have lost their typical temporal pattern, but exhibit several grouping along the time axis. In this frequency range, however, a SPU of very short duration (5 ms) can be isolated. The sweep flank is somewhat steeper, the course has a biphasic trend. As in the previous example, a division into subgroups is not necessary. The delay-times are similar.

Both types of SPUs (mono- and biphasic), isolated from either an early or a late phase of the EP, have the same simple structure. They differ only in their latencies and probabilities of occurrence. Considering the two sites of derivation we investigated, their maximum lay at Cz. After repeated recordings on one subject the same kinds of SPUs were isolated, differing only in their latencies and probabilities of occurrence. In a comparison with another subject, no differences in the templates of biphasic SPUs were found.

Concerning the question of whether our SPU configurations really represent responses from pyramidal cells, it should be emphasized that this assumption is supported by the SPUs' apparent similarity to the biphasic and postsynaptic potentials obtained through direct derivation from the visual cortex of the cat (Goldman-Rakic, 1984). Furthermore, when using a bandpass of 32 – 200 Hz, the spatio-temporal summation of monophasic SPUs accounts for the amplitude-time template of summed potentials of the corresponding direction with a ten times larger amplitude.

Summary and Conclusions

A new methodology for ERP analysis was developed in order to achieve a better understanding of the underlying physiological processes. In a three-step analytic procedure, inner relationships between two parent populations of simultaneously derived, yet spatially distinct, ERPs could be revealed. This procedure included the investigation of the probability of occurence of typical ERP components, the assessment of coincident interchannel activity, as it is pertained to a physiological delay time, and the isolation of subpotential-units (SPUs). These investigations reveal inner relationships in the form of subpotential-units showing a replicable temporal pattern when the same bandpass is applied. The amplitude of the SPUs varies topographically and their shape is identical over subjects and the type of ERP. The influence of the bandpass on the temporal pattern of the SPU indicates, that the SPU is a replicable composition of several elementary potentials.

Correspondence should be addressed to Peter Bartsch, Institut für Physiologie der Humboldt-Universität zu Berlin, Hessische Straße 3/4, 1040 Berlin, G.D.R.

References

Asanuma, H. (1975). Recent developments in the study of columnar arrangement of neurons in the motor cortex. *Physiological Review, 55*, 149–156.

Creutzfeldt, O.D. (1976). The brain as a functional entity. *Progress in Brain Research, 45*, 451–462.

Creutzfeldt, O.D. (1983). *Cortex cerebri.* Berlin, Heidelberg, New York, Tokio: Springer.

Goldman-Rakic, P. (1984). Modular organization of prefrontal cortex. *Trends in Neurosciences, 7*, 419–429.

Homan, R.W., Herman, J., & Purdy, P. (1987). Cerebral location of international 10–20 system electrode placement. *Electroencephalography and Clinical Neurophysiology, 66*, 376–382.

Hubel, D.H., & Wiesel, T.N. (1968). Receptive fields and functional architecture of monkey striate cortex. *Journal of Physiology, 195*, 215–243.

Jones, E.G., & Powell, T.R.S. (1970). An anatomical study of converging sensory pathways within the cerebral cortex of the monkey. *Brain, 93*, 793–820.

Lorente de Nó, R. (1947). Actionpotential of the motoneurons of the hypoglossus nucleus. *Journal of Cellular and Comparative Physiology, 29*, 207–287.

Merzenich, M.M., & Brugge, J.F. (1973). Representation of the cochlear partition on the superior temporal plane of the macaque monkey. *Brain Research, 50*, 275–296.

Mountcastle, V.B. (1957). Modality and topographic properties of single neurons of cat's somatic sensory cortex. *Journal of Neurophysiology, 20*, 408–434.

Mountcastle, V.B. (1979). An organizing principle for cerebral functions: The unit module and the distributed system. In F.O. Schmitt & F.G. Worden, (Eds.), *Neurosciences* (pp. 21–49). Cambridge, London: MIT Press.

Penfield, W., & Jasper, H. (1954). *Epilepsy and the functional anatomy of the human brain.* Boston: Little, Brown & Company.

Vieth, J. (1984). Die Magnetenzephalographie, eine neue funktionsdiagnostische Methode. *Zeitschrift für Elektroenzephalographie, Elektromyographie und verwandte Gebiete, 15*, 111–118.

Psychophysical Explorations of Mental Structures
Edited by H.-G. Geissler
in collaboration with M.H. Müller and W. Prinz
© 1990 by Hogrefe & Huber Publishers

Chapter 32

Changes of Bereitschaftspotential
Due to Different Workload by
Muscular and Mental Activities

Gabriele Freude and Peter Ullsperger
Zentralinstitut für Arbeitsmedizin der DDR
Berlin, G.D.R.

The Bereitschaftspotential (Bp) is one of the most intensively investigated event-related slow brain potentials. Since the first publications in this field (Kornhuber & Deecke, 1964, 1965) the Bp has become a very well-accepted neurophysiological parameter when studying the different aspects of motor control. As the Bp appears in the period of preparation, i.e., before voluntary movements start, it is considered a most attractive neurophysiological tool for investigating the interaction between the organism and the environment at the stage of planning and programming movements.

Due to the time-locked appearance of Bp and the movement involved, Bp was preferably studied from different "motor" angles. There is much evidence in Bp-literature that this negative-going slow pre-movement potential reflects motor-specific changes in central nervous activation in preparation for self-paced voluntary movements.

Analyses of the topographic distribution of Bp over the scalp (Becker, Höhne, Iwase & Kornhuber, 1972; Deecke, Scheid & Kornhuber, 1969; Deecke, Grözinger & Kornhuber, 1976; Kornhuber, 1977; Kornhuber & Deecke, 1965; Vaughan, Costa & Ritter, 1968) or of the relation between Bp and the somatotopic representation (Brunia, 1984; Brunia & van den Bosch, 1984a,b; Vaughan et al., 1968) have shown that generally Bp is more pronounced over that hemisphere which is contralateral to the moving limb. This contralateral preponderance of negativity (CPN; Deecke, 1984) was confirmed by simultaneously registered changes in the magnetic field ("Bereitschafts-magnetfeld"; Deecke, Weinberg & Bricke, 1982). On the basis of these results, the contralateral primary-motor cortex seems to be more involved in the preparatory processes than the ipsilateral. This concurs with the general suggestions about the structure and the function of the motor cortex. Furthermore, the supplementary motor area (SMA) is considered to be critically involved in motor preparation, especially in the decision about the moment when a movement has to be performed (Deecke, Kornhuber, Lang, Lang & Schreiber, 1985).

The complexity of motor programs requiring the execution of movements was also discussed to influence the Bp. Kristeva (1984) found that the Bp prior to playing a melody on the piano was higher and began earlier compared to that for a single note. A more complex motor program for melody playing was assumed.

Another set of investigations supporting the Bp as a "motor" phenomenon involved studies relating to handedness (Deecke, Grözinger & Kristeva, 1978; Kristeva, Keller, Deecke & Kornhuber, 1979; Kutas and Donchin, 1974, 1977; Papakostopoulos, 1978). The general trend which can be derived from the various and not quite consistent results is that Bp is more lateralized in right-handed than in left-handed persons. That is in accordance with the assumed higher preponderance of one hemisphere in right-handed persons.

One may conclude from all these studies that Bp reflects neuronal processes which are mainly associated with the preparation of a motor act.

Otherwise, an interpretation of Bp as an exclusively motor-specific brain potential would lead to hasty conclusions on the functional significance of this brain potential. For a better understanding of this phenomenon it might be useful to consider further potential influences, some of them being described in more psychological terms.

Movements requiring a low force level but a high level of concentration (high precision of movements) produce a pronounced development of Bp (Freude & Ullsperger, 1987; Kristeva & Kornhuber, 1980).

Kornhuber and Deecke (1965) have shown that Bp is influenced by factors characterized by the subjects as concentration and expectation on the one hand, and fatigue and indifference, on the other. A higher intentional involvement when preparing a movement results in an increase of the Bp amplitude. A decrease of the Bp amplitude was found in the course of repetitive movements, which is due to the monotony in the process of movements (Freude & Ullsperger, 1987; Kornhuber & Deecke, 1965). Even the levels of motivation (McAdam & Seales, 1969) and attention (McAdam & Rubin, 1971) have a significant influence).

One may conclude that Bp is sensitive to all factors which influence the level of central-nervous activation in the period of preparing a self-paced voluntary movement. It should be taken into account that both "motor" and "nonmotor" factors seem to be significant for the occurrence of slow potential changes preceding a movement.

The anticipated workload of a planned activity also has an important effect on Bp. On the basis of this general assumption, the effect of the varied workload both during muscle activity and mental activity will be discussed in the following sections.

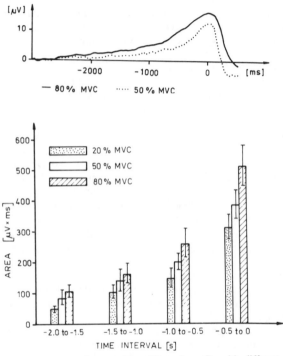

Figure 1. Mean Bps, averaged over nine subjects from Cz with different forces and mean areas of Bp negativity with standard errors at four consecutive time intervals. Zero time represents the movement onset.

Bereitschaftspotential — Changes Due to Variations of Muscle Activity

To study the influence of different movement parameters on Bp, the force and speed of movements were varied in several experiments. Becker, Iwase, Jürgens and Kornhuber (1976) found that the Bp starts earlier and tends towards larger amplitudes preceding slow smooth movements compared to rapid ballistic movements. It was suggested that these differences reflect a different organization of slow and rapid voluntary movements.

Becker and Kristeva (1980) investigated Bp prior to simple finger movements which were carried out on two different force levels. In all derivations a higher negativity of Bp was found prior to movements of a higher force level.

In line with these findings, Figure 1 shows results obtained in investigations of the influence of force on Bp prior to squeezing a hand-grip dynamometer (Freude & Ullsperger, 1987). The experiments were carried out at three different force levels: 20%, 50% and 80% of maximum voluntary contraction (MVC). The results confirm that the Bp amplitude is a function of the expected force level. An increase in force results in an increased negativity of Bp. As demonstrated in Figure 1, the dependence of Bp on the force level is pronounced in the early phases of Bp (area analysis was made for the intervals −2000 ms to −1500 ms, −1500 ms to −1000ms) as well as in the following ones (−1000 ms to −500 ms, −500 ms to 0 ms).

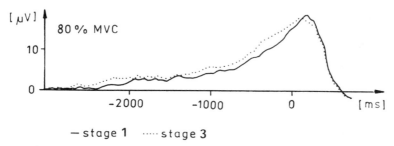

− stage 1   ⋯⋯ stage 3

Figure 2. Comparison of the mean Bps at Cz location from nine subjects for the first and third stages of the experiment for muscular fatiguing contraction at 80% MVC.

These results are consistent with those obtained by Becker and Kristeva (1980) and Kutas and Donchin (1977) who found that the Bp amplitude varied as a function of force. It was postulated that the greater negativity of Bp prior to strong rather than slight isometric contractions reflected a higher activity of the cortical structures involved. Possibly, the preparation for isometric contractions with greater muscular effort evoke more cortical activation than contractions with low effort. CNV-investigations (Contingent Negative Variation) of Rebert, McAdam, Knott and Irvin (1967) showing a higher negative shift when expecting movements that require higher forces can be discussed in the same context.

Kutas and Donchin (1977) investigated the influence of force on the distribution of Bp over both hemispheres. Contrary to what might have been expected from studies of Evarts (1968) a more pronounced lateralization of Bp was not found. It was concluded that force affected especially the symmetric component of Bp (cf., Hillyard, 1973).

A more expressed negativity due to a higher muscle activity was also found during fatiguing hand contractions with 80% MVC (Figure 2; Freude & Ullsperger, 1987). To analyze the influence of muscular fatigue, the whole experimental period in this study was divided into three equal stages. An increase of Bp that was found at the last stage of the experiment reflected a higher degree of cortical activation or, in psychological terms, the effort was higher when working with fatigued muscles.

These examples of Bp studies support the hypothesis that Bp is influenced by the degree of muscular effort. Here the question arises as to the extent to which the anticipated effort must be connected with physical workload, or in other words, whether or not the anticipation of a mental task following a self-paced movement will influence the Bp.

Bereitschaftspotential and Mental Load

Unlike the investigations mentioned before (Becker & Kristeva, 1980; Freude & Ullsperger, 1987; Kutas & Donchin, 1977), muscle activitys was held constant in the experiment described now. The mental load was modified by varying the time pressure for the solution of arithmetical tasks (three categories of tasks). The motor act consisted in a simple finger movement, i.e., a key was pressed to call a task on a computer display. The time of task display was varied to obtain the different categories of time pressure (Freude, Ullsperger, Krüger & Pietschmann, 1988).

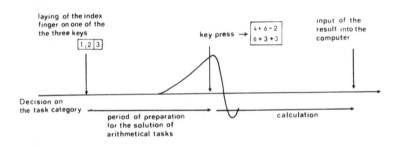

Figure 3. Sequence of activities (for explanations, see text).

The subjects were instructed to proceed as follows (see Figure 3): They had to decide on the category of task they wanted to solve and to lay the index finger of the right hand on one of the three defined keys. The Bp was analysed 1.5 s before the key was pressed. Having finished their calculations, the subjects had to feed the result into the computer via a keyboard. Altogether 200 tasks were presented. The tasks of different categories were to be solved in a mixed sequence and at almost the same frequency.

Figure 4 shows the grand mean Bps separately for the three categories of tasks. The higher the self-chosen time pressure, the higher was the Bp.

Analyses of variance of the Bp areas have shown that the influence of the category is significant for the last phase of Bp (time interval: −350 ms to 0, 0 is the moment of movement onset). That especially the late phase of Bp is influenced by the expected mental performance is in accordance with several results of CNV-investigations (Birbaumer, Lutzenberger, Elbert, Rockstroh & Schwarz, 1981; Simons, Öhman & Lang, 1979; Rockstroh, Elbert, Birbaumer & Lutzenberger, 1982) and provides evidence for similar neuronal processes underlying the genesis of premovement slow potentials.

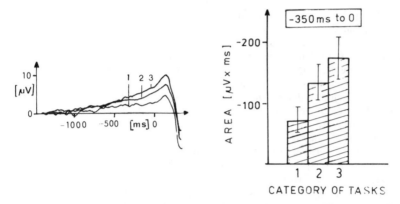

Figure 4. Grand mean of Bps at Cz across all 14 subjects before calculation of tasks of the three categories and the areas of Bp with standard errors for the time interval, immediately before the key press (-350 ms to 0, 0 is the moment of key press).

Obviously, the premotor Bp was influenced by the expected time pressure, although the motor act, i.e., pressing a key for presentation of tasks, was practically the same.

Unlike the well-known CNV-paradigm (Walter, 1964), in our experiment the task category was not announced by an external stimulus (Birbaumer et al., 1981; Simons et al., 1979), through, e.g., different modalities of a warning stimulus, but the subjects had to decide themselves which degree of mental load they wanted. Thus, the augmentation of the Bp preceding higher mental load might be interpreted as an expression of appropriate self-activation according to the expected workload.

A more intense "motor preparation" does not seem to be responsible for the described increase in Bp. Firstly, according to subjective estimation, the pressing force for the three different keys was equally independent of the category of tasks. Secondly, Bp investigations of the influence of force on Bp have shown that relatively high differences in the expected force level are necessary to induce such pronounced differences in Bp as described in the present study.

Thus, one may conclude that the anticipated greater mental effort influences the level of central nervous activation which is assumed to be responsible for the increase in the negativity of the Bp.

Summary and Conclusion

The results described here suggest that the Bp is influenced by the workload of a planned activity. It is not surprising that the higher motor strain, i.e., a higher force of a movement, results in a higher negative shift of Bp. We assume that this increase in the negativity of Bp, although induced by a higher muscular effort, is not primarily "motor-specific". When the motor activity, e.g., the pressing of a key to initiate further information processing, was held constant, but the preparatory set was modified by a graduated time pressure for the solution of mental tasks, the Bp increased as well. The increase in the negativity was related to the effort of the expected performance. One may argue that a differential motor set could be produced by changing the mental strain. From our point of view, this can be excluded due to the subjective estimation of force developed during the pressing of keys and due to results of experiments about the relation between Bp and the force applied.

The increase in the negativity due to higher workload seems to be independent of the specificity of the actual demand. In the first place, the higher central nervous activation when preparing muscle and mental activities seems to be responsible for the higher negativity of Bp.

According to the Bp paradigm, the planned activity is self-paced and not announced by an external stimulus (CNV-paradigm). Thus, the different degrees of negativity developed prior to graduated motor and mental activities can be considered an expression of appropriate self-activation aiming at an effective performance for information processing and motor command.

A lot of findings from other pre-event slow potential investigations agree with these Bp results. Generally, the slow cortical negativity is associated with the state of becoming "attentive", "motivated" or "prepared" for particular performances (see Rockstroh et al., 1982, ch. 4). In the same context, an increased excitability of cortical structures involved in the tasks to be solved is thought to be responsible for the increased negativity of slow potentials (Bauer & Nirnberger, 1980; Deecke et al., 1976; Elbert, 1978; Weber & Bauer, 1986).

We may conclude by saying that the results described here are a contribution to the discussion of the functional significance of Bp. They confirm that Bp is influenced also by factors which are not closely connected with motor functions. Since Bp always appears in connection with a motor activity, and most information processing in real life is connected with motor acts, the Bp will become a useful neurophysiological parameter in investigations of processes of central nervous activation in preparation for mental performances, e.g., during work with visual display terminals.

Correspondence should be addressed to Gabriele Freude, Zentralinstitut für Arbeitsmedizin der Deutschen Demokratischen Republik, FB Psychophysiologie, Nöldnerstr. 40–42, Berlin, DDR – 1134.

References

Bauer, H., & Nirnberger, G. (1980). Paired associate learning with feedback of DC-potential shifts of the cerebral cortex. *Archiv für Psychologie, 132*, 237–238.

Becker, W., Höhne, O., Iwase, K., & Kornhuber, H.H. (1972). Bereitschaftspotential, prämotorische Positivierung und andere Potentialkomponenten bei sakkadischen Augenbewegungen. *Vision Research, 12*, 421–436.

Becker, W., Iwase, K., Jürgens, R., & Kornhuber, H.H. (1976). Bereitschaftspotential preceding voluntary slow and rapid hand movement. In W.C. McCallum and J.R. Knott (Eds.), *The responsive brain*. Bristol: Wright and Son, pp. 99–102.

Becker, W., & Kristeva, R. (1980). Cerebral potentials prior to various force deployments. *Progress in Brain Research, 54*, 189–194.

Birbaumer, N, Lutzenberger, W., Elbert, T., Rockstroh, B., & Schwarz, J. (1981). EEG and slow cortical potential in anticipation of mental tasks with different hemispheric involvement. *Biological psychology, 13*, 251–260.

Brunia, C.H.M. (1984). Contingent negative variation and readiness potential preceding foot movement. *Annals of the New York Academy of Sciences, 425*, 403–406.

Brunia, C.H.M., & van den Bosch, W.E.J. (1984). Movement–related slow potentials. I. A contrast between finger and foot movements in right–handed subjects. *Electroencephalography and Clinical Neurophysiology, 57*, 515–527.

Brunia, C.H.M., & van den Bosch, W.E.J. (1984). The influence of response side on the readiness potential prior to finger and foot movements. A preliminary report. *Annals of the New York Academy of Sciences, 425*, 434–437.

Deecke, L. (1984). Movement-asscociated potentials and motor control. Introduction. *Annals of the New York Academy of Sciences, 425*, 398–401.

Deecke, L., Grözinger, B., & Kornhuber, H.H. (1976). Voluntary finger movement in man: Cerebral potentials and theory. *Biological Cybernetics, 23*, 99–119.

Deecke, L., Grözinger, B., & Kristeva, R. (1978). Hemispherical differences of cerebral potentials preceding right and left unilateral and bilateral finger movements in right-handed subjects. *European Journal of Physiology, 373* (Suppl.), R 74.

Deecke, L. Kornhuber, H.H., Lang, W., Lang, M., & Schreiber, H. (1985). Timing function of the frontal cortex in sequential motor and learning tasks. *Human Neurobiology, 4*, 143–154.

Deecke, L., Scheid, W., & Kornhuber, H.H. (1969). Distribution of readiness potential, premotion positivity and motor potential of the human cerebral cortex preceding voluntary finger movements. *Experimental Brain Research, 7*, 158–168.

Deecke, L., Weinberg, H., & Bricke, P. (1982). Magnetic field of the human accompanying voluntary movement: Bereitschaftsmagnetfeld. *Experimental Brain Research, 48*, 144–148.

Elbert, T. (1978). *Biofeedback langsamer kortikaler Potentiale*. München: Minerva.

Evarts, E.V. (1968). Relation of pyramidal tract activity to force exerted during a voluntary movement. *Journal of Neurophysiology, 31*, 14–27.

Freude, G., & Ullsperger, P. (1987). Changes of the Bereitschaftspotential in the course of muscular fatiguing and non-fatiguing hand contraction. *European Journal of Applied and Occupational Physiology, 56*, 105–108.

Freude, G., Ullsperger, P., Krüger, H., & Pietschmann, M. (1988). The Bereitschaftspotential in preparation to mental activities. *International Journal of Psychophysiology, 6*, 291–297.

Hillyard, S.A. (1973). The CNV and human behavior. *Electroencephalography and Clinical Neurophysiology, 33* (Suppl.), 161–171.

Kornhuber, H.H., Deecke, L. (1964). Hirnpotentialänderungen beim Menschen vor und nach Willkürbewegungen, dargestellt mit Magnetbandspeicherung und Rückwärtsanalyse. *Pflügers Archiv für die gesamte Physiologie, 281*, 52.

Kornhuber, H.H., & Deecke, L. (1965). Hirnpotentialänderungen bei Willkürbewegungen und passiven Bewegungen des Menschen. Bereitschaftspotential und reafferente Potentiale. *Pflügers Archiv für die gesamte Physiologie, 284*, 1–17.

Kristeva, R. (1977). Study of the motor potential during voluntary recurrent movement. *Electroencephalography and Clinical Neurophysiology, 42*, 588.

Kristeva, R. (1984). Movement-Related Potentials with bilateral actions and with piano-playing. *Annals of the New York Academy of Sciences, 425*, 398–428.

Kristeva, R., Keller, E., Deecke, L., & Kornhuber, H.H. (1979). Cerebral potentials preceding unilateral and simultaneous bilateral finger movements. *Electroencephalography and Clinical Neurophysiology, 47*, 229–238.

Kristeva, R., & Kornhuber, H.H. (1980). Cerebral potentials related to the smallest human finger movement. *Progress in Brain Research, 54*, 177–182.

Kutas, M., & Donchin, E. (1974). Studies of squeezing: Handedness, responding hand, response force and asymmetry of readiness potential. *Science, 186*, 545–548.

Kutas, M., & Donchin, E. (1977). The effect of handedness, of responding hand and of response force on the contralateral dominance of the readiness potential. In J.E. Desmedt (Ed.), *Progress in Clinical Neurophysiology* (Vol. 1): *Attention, voluntary contraction and event related cerebral potentials* (pp. 189–210). Basel: Karger.

McAdam, D.W., & Seales, D.W. (1969). Bereitschaftspotential enhancement with increased level of motivation. *Electroencephalography and Clinical Neurophysiology, 27*, 73–75.

McAdam, D.W. & Rubin, E.H. (1971). Readiness potential, vertex positive wave, contingent negative variation and accuracy of perception. *Electroencephalography and Clinical Neurophysiology, 30*, 511–517.

Papakostopoulos, D. (1978). Electrical activity of the brain associated with skilled performance. In D.A. Otto (Ed.), *Multidisciplinary perspectives in event-related brain potential research* (pp. 134–137). Washington, DC: US Government Printing Office/ EPA 1978.

Rebert, C.S., McAdam, D.W., Knott, J.R., & Irwin, D.A. (1967). Slow potential change in human brain related to level of motivation. *Journal of Comparative and Physiological Psychology, 63*, 20–23.

Rockstroh, B., Elbert, T., Birbaumer, N., & Lutzenberger, W. (1982). *Slow brain potentials and behavior*. Baltimore, München: Urban und Schwarzenberg.

Simons, R.F., Öhman, A., & Lang, P.J. (1979). Anticipation and response set: Cortical, cardiac, and electrodermal correlates. *Psychophysiology, 16*, 222–233.

Vaughan, H.G. Jr., Costa, L.D., & Ritter, W. (1968). Topography of the human motor potential. *Electroencephalography and Clinical Neurophysiology, 25*, 1–10.

Weber, G., & Bauer, H. (1986). Informationsverarbeitung und Leistungsniveau in Abhängigkeit kortikaler Gleichspannungsschwankungen. *Zeitschrift für Experimentelle und Angewandte Psychologie, 1*, 164–176.

Psychophysical Explorations of Mental Structures
Edited by H.-G. Geissler
in collaboration with M.H. Müller and W. Prinz
© 1990 by Hogrefe & Huber Publishers

Chapter 33

The Dynamics of Vegetative Parameters During Mental Training

Lothar Beyer, Thomas Weiß and Ellen Hansen
Bereich Medizin, Institut für Physiologie
Friedrich–Schiller–Universität
Jena, G.D.R.

For many years we have been studying activation processes within the central nervous system by means of EEG, psychomotor, and vegetative parameters. In connection with these problems our laboratory investigates the neurophysiological laws that govern activating processes involved in physical exercise and the level of optimal activation (Ascheron & Beyer, 1982; Beyer & Schumann, 1981; Krause, Ullsperger, Beyer & Gille, 1983; Schober & Beyer, 1984).

Psychophysical studies of activation or arousal mainly deal with a hypothetical concept of activation specified originally in the classical activation theory (e.g., Duffy, 1962). According to the classical theory, there exists an optimal level of personal activation for many kinds of performance. Activation and performance may be related to each other according to the Yerkes and Dodson rule (Yerkes & Dodson, 1908). However, recent evidence is in strong contradiction to this idea (Fahrenberg, Foerster, Schneider, Müller & Myrtek, 1986; Helin & Hänninen, 1987).

The original theory appears to be too simple because it does not consider the different pattern of physiological activation in different conditions and situations. Total physiological activation is very difficult to determine because, as a

rule, significant correlations neither among different psychophysiological parameters nor between psychophysiological activation and subjectively estimated
mental tension during performance are observed. The most valid estimation of
activation and its relationship to performance is reached by examining the
relationship between activation and performance parameter by parameter (Helin
& Hänninen, 1987).

From a physiological point of view motor performances consist of two
components, energetic and metabolic processes, and processes of information
and motor control.

Physiological mechanisms and laws of adaptation concerning the second
component, i.e., the adaptation of central nervous information processing, require further extensive exploration. Adaptation processes of motor control and
information processing may occur on the motivational level, on the sensomotor
level, within the activation system and in accordance with the vegetative–homoeostatic level.

Of special importance for the subdivision of the different activation levels
is their strong relation to the external situation in which the given state takes
place (Ascheron & Beyer, 1982; Beyer & Schumann, 1981).

The changes and dynamics of vegetative phenomena which accompany
quantitative and qualitative changes of central nervous activation are dependent
on load and adaptation.

Figure 1 shows a subdivision into different CNS power or functional
domains. Quantitative and qualitative changes of central nervous activation may
be divided into six hierarchically organized groups:

– long-lasting reactions, as habituation to daily requirements, e.g., in trade,
  profession and sports;
– habituation to novel requirements, shown by slow or sudden decrease of
  changes induced by load during repeated exercise;
– tonic changes accompanying performance and restitution lasting some days,
  e.g. over one week;
– current tonic circadian activation;
– nonspecific phasic activation, depending on the duration of intensity and on
  pattern of exercise;
– specific phasic activation depending on the coordination, motivation and
  psychic load of the exercise (Beyer & Schumann, 1981).

Changes within the last two groups also occur during motor imagination.

A Study of Activating Processes and Motor Imagination

Motor imagination (or mental practice of motor skills) proves an interesting field of study at least for two reasons. The first reason is its applicability
in situations which do not allow physical practice. The second reason is of
theoretical nature because motor imagination constitutes an exemplary field of
research into the relation between movements and cognitive processes. In this
case, the central question concerns the mode of action of motor imagination
(Heuer, 1985).

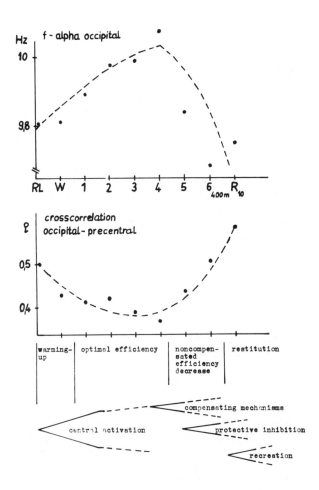

Figure 1. Schematic subdivision into different central nervous system power or functional domains demonstrated in an example consisting of six subsequent races of 400 m (RL: preload value, W: after warming up, 1−6: runs, R: recovery). Upper part: mean frequency of the alpha-range of EEG; lower part: cross-correlation of the EEGs from occipital and precentral area.

The aim of this study is to detect changes of vegetative parameters during motor imagination which could contribute to a better understanding of activating processes and the mode of action of motor imagination.

Methods

Eight subjects undergoing systematical training in swimming were requested to imagine their own swimming movements over a distance of 100 m in their preferred style, while sitting in a resting position without any real or imitated movement. The subjects started imagination as soon as the supervisor signalized the beginning of the registration. The start and the end of the mental exercise were signalized by the subjects pressing a button. One series consisted of three periods of mental training (MT) and a 3-minute rest between each two periods. Heart rate (HR), skin conductance (SC), respiration rate and EEG were recorded before, during and after each MT. Heart rate was analyzed from ECG as a tachogram. For each subject skin conductance was measured with electrodes placed on the index finger and middle finger of the left hand. We recorded respiration rate by means of a thermistor. The electrodes of the EEG pickup were of the Ag-AgCl type and were placed on the precentral and occipital region of the cortex contralaterally to the preferred hand. EEG was analyzed by power density spectrum.

Results

Imagination time was 25 per cent longer than the real swimming time. There was no significant difference between the three periods of mental training.

On the average, heart rate increased from approximately 70 beats per minute at rest to 90 beats per minute, in single cases up to 120 bpm. HR began to rise when the subjects were asked to start imagination. Thus, the highest HR-values were found during the middle range of the imagination period. These high values decreased after the imagination period. HR during both resting periods between the single trials of imagination was still attenuated immediately after the end of imagination. In the second third of the rest period there was no difference compared with the resting level before the first imagination. After the last imagination HR decreased at least to the initial level and in most cases to a lower level. We observed the highest HR during the middle of the first and the second period of imagination. All values during imagination were significantly higher in comparison with the resting level before the start (see Figure 2).

A number of cases showed the phenomenon of respiratory arhythmia during the resting period.

Skin conductance also showed a rapid enhancement at the start of each MT period followed by a continuous decrease during the whole MT period and the following rest interval. Maximal values decreased from the first to the third period of imagination (see Figure 3).

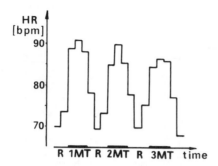

Figure 2. Average heart rate calculated for each minute during rest (R) and for three equal parts within the three periods of mental training (MT). The abscissa does not show the real time.

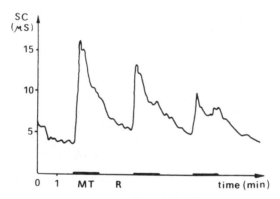

Figure 3. Skin conductance. MT = period of mental training. R = rest.

Respiration cycle doubles during MT as compared with breathing during rest interval. The imagined turns can be identified by single, longer periods of respiration. Considering the variation of duration of the respiration cycle, the lowest variability can be shown during the second MT period.

The EEG shows an increase of the middle frequency within the alpha-range during the imagination periods and also during the intertrial rest intervals. Figure 4 shows that, especially in the precentral region, there were more extreme changes in the second and the third period of imagination as compared with the initial level.

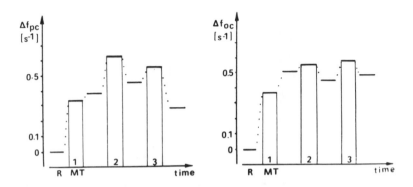

Figure 4. Mean frequency of the alpha-range of the EEG (difference to resting level before first imagination) from the precentral (pc) and occipital (oc) region during rest (R) and three periods of mental training (MT).

Discussion

We found different changes in the examined parameters. These changes are similar to those of physiological correlates in other forms of mental performance. Especially the respiration cycle of swimmers seems to be in accordance with the real motor pattern. There is a strong coupling between respiration cycle and arm movement and the position of the head, respectively. There are some remarkable differences between changes relating to the single periods of imagination. In most cases the maximum of HR lies in the middle of the imagination period. Its rise is less steep than that of SC at the start of imagination. Different systems show different courses of activation. In the occipital area mean alpha-frequency increases up to the third period and is enhanced during the rest period. In the precentral area mean alpha-frequency becomes maximal during the second period of imagination and is generally enhanced during the rest period. Skin conductance changes slow down from the first to the third imagination. These results confirm our opinion that there are different conditions for an effective imagination during the first, second or third period of mental training, whereas optimal conditions in our investigation seem to have prevailed during the second period.

The mean alpha-frequency (MAF) increases, relative to the previous resting periods, during the MT periods as well as during all periods following the rest before the first imagination. It is not surprising that the MAF is enhanced during MT. Ascheron and Beyer (1982) and Krause, Ullsperger, Beyer and Gille (1983) have reported similar changes of the MAF during motor performance. It is interesting that the examined changes of MAF during motor performance are higher for the precentral area, whereas larger increases of

MAF during MT were found for the occipital area. This is in accordance with different alpha–generators in the central and the posterior regions of the brain (Inouye, Shinosaki, Yagasaki & Shimizu, 1986; Ozaki & Suzuki, 1987). The significant increase of the MAF during all periods, as compared to the MAF in the course of the rest period preceding the first imagination, proves to be very interesting. None of the vegetative parameters under examination undergoes such an increase for the periods between MT. Further research into imagination phenomena must give evidence whether tonically increased MAF is only a sign for increased activation or, additionally, for good imagination.

The examined vegetative changes seem to be in accordance with real motor patterns. The situations remind of adaptation of vegetative parameters in connection with exercise. Thus, it seems possible that some structures (e.g., hypothalamus, see Hilton, 1986) are activated during real performance as well as during MT. This contrasts with the opinion that the activity of the central nervous system during motor imagination is likely to be entirely different from the activity during motor performance (Heuer, 1985). From a physiological point of view, however, the most relevant hypothesis for explaining the effect of MT is the programming hypothesis (Pickenhain & Beyer, 1979; Heuer, 1985) which implies that improvement in performance can be attributed to the effect of repetitions, on the one hand, and to the correction of the central processes by means of internal feedback, on the other hand. The changes of vegetative parameters examined in this paper give a further indirect evidence for this approach. If, in addition, data on regional cerebral blood flow (Roland, Larsen, Lassen & Skinkoj, 1980) will be considered, it seems obvious that imaginations of movements are movements with blocked final motor pathway. Therefore, MT might be a good model to examine activation processes which occur in a similar way during motor performance.

In conclusion we recommend vegetative parameters as valid tools for describing activating processes that occur when particular exercises must be performed. The differences in the courses of the investigated parameters can be interpreted as different states of activation caused by factors, such as attention, skill, adaptation, and motivation. Research into central nervous processes can become more objective with the help of vegetative parameters. Different processes in different systems can be coupled in different ways and with different efficiency by the brain stem and by the limbic system (Skinner, 1984).

In general, we can say that our results may contribute to an understanding of CNS activation during different kinds of behavior, such as motor imagination or voluntary movements.

Summary

Central nervous processes of sensorimotor and behaviour control are prerequisites of skilled action and motor performance. In such processes activation is in accordance with functional changes of neurons of the cerebral cortex. Psychophysiological studies of activation mainly deal with a hypothetical concept of activation which appears to be too simple in its original version.

Thus, qualitative and quantitative changes of central nervous activation may be subdivided into six hierarchically organized groups.

In the present study, mental training (MT, or mental practice) was chosen in order to examine activation processes. Moreover, MT itself proves an interesting field of investigation into the relation between movements and cognitive processes.

Eight subjects undergoing systematic training in swimming were tested during mental training. They were requested to imagine their own movements of 100 m swimming. EEG, heart rate, skin conductance, and respiration rate were recorded before, during and after one series of three periods of mental training. Different changes were found in the examined parameters. The results confirm the opinion that optimal conditions for central nervous activation during mental training seem to have prevailed during the second period of MT. The results provide indirect evidence for an interpretation of the effect of mental training in terms of the programming hypothesis.

Correspondence should be addressed to Lothar Beyer, Bereich Medizin, Institut für Physiologie, Friedrich-Schiller-Universität, Teichgraben 8, 6900 Jena, G.D.R.

References

Ascheron, R., & Beyer, L. (1982). Belastungsabhängige Veränderungen des ZNS auf der Grundlage rechnergestützter EEG-Analyse. *Medizin und Sport, 22,* 49–51.

Beyer, L., & Schumann, H. (1981). Möglichkeiten neurophysiologischer Untersuchungen in der Sportmedizin anhand von zwei ausgewählten Beispielen. *Medizin und Sport, 21,* 65–69.

Duffy, E. (1962). *Activation and behaviour.* New York: Wiley.

Fahrenberg, J., Foerster, F., Schneider, H.-J., Müller, W., & Myrtek, M. (1986). Predictability of individual differences in activation processes in a field setting based on laboratory measures. *Psychophysiology, 23,* 323–333.

Helin, P., & Hänninen, O. (1987). Relaxation training affects success and activation on a teaching test. *International Journal of Psychophysiology, 5,* 275–287.

Heuer, H. (1985). Wie wirkt mentale Übung? *Psychologische Rundschau, 36,* 191–200.

Hilton, S.M. (1986). Principles of organization of cardiovascular control. In H. Koepchen, C. Brooks & K. Koizumi (Eds.), *Neurovegetative control systems. Basic functions, integration and disorders* (pp. 115–119). Amsterdam: Elsevier.

Inouye, T., Shinosaki, K., Yagasaki, A., & Shimizu, A. (1986). Spatial distribution of generators of alpha activity. *Electroencephalography and Clinical Neurophysiology, 63,* 353–360.

Krause, G., Ullsperger, P., Beyer, L., & Gille, H.G. (1983). Changes in EEG power density spectrum during static muscle work. *European Journal of Applied Physiology and Occupational Physiology, 51,* 61–66.

Ozaki, T., & Suzuki, H. (1987). Transverse relationships of the alpha rhythm on the scalp. *Electroencephalography and Clinical Neurophysiology, 66,* 191–195.

Pickenhain, L., & Beyer, L. (1979). Beziehungen zwischen den hierarchisch organisierten Rückmeldekreisen und der Ergebnisrückmeldung als wesentlicher Faktor für die Ausbildung innerer Modelle von Arbeitshandlungen. In F. Klix & K. Timpe (Eds.), *Arbeits- und Ingenieurpsychologie und Intensivierung* (pp. 109–114). Berlin: VEB Deutscher Verlag der Wissenschaften.

Roland, P.E., Larsen, B., Lassen, N.A., & Skinkoj, E. (1980). Supplementary motor area and other cortical areas in organization of voluntary movements in man. *Journal of Neurophysiology, 43,* 118–136.

Schober, F., & Beyer, L. (1984). Die objektive Bestimmung der Flimmerverschmelzungsfrequenz zur Charakterisierung des aktuellen Aktivierungszustandes des ZNS. *Medizin und Sport, 24,* 245–252.

Skinner, J.E. (1984). Central gating mechanisms that regulate event-related potentials and behavior. In T. Elbert, B. Rockstroh, W. Lutzenberger & N. Birbaumer (Eds.), *Self-regulation of the brain and behavior* (pp. 42–55). Berlin, Heidelberg, New York: Springer.

Yerkes, R.M., & Dodson, J.D. (1908). The relation of strength of stimulus to rapidity of habit-formation. *Journal of Comparative and Neurological Psychology, 18,* 459–482.

Psychophysical Explorations of Mental Structures
Edited by H.-G. Geissler
in collaboration with M.H. Müller and W. Prinz
© 1990 by Hogrefe & Huber Publishers

Chapter 34

Heart Rate and Heart Rate Variability – Occurrence and Diagnostic Significance

Klaus Eckoldt and Volker Lange
Institut für medizinische Physik und Biophysik
Humboldt-Universität
Berlin, G.D.R.

The judgment of heart rate and its spontaneous irregularity already played a major role in old Chinese medicine. In modern times, the work done by Carl Ludwig (Ludwig, 1847) in Leipzig in the middle of the last century has led to renewed interest in this phenomenon among physiologists. The first exact continuous measurement, in the form of a cardiotachogram, was by Fleisch and Beckmann (1932). These authors emphasized the pathophysiologic significance of heart rate variability and gave first hints concerning its generation. They also found that with physical load the amount of sinus arrhythmia (SA) – as the physiologic irregularity of the heart beat used to be called in the clinically oriented literature – decreases with rising heart rate. Extensive investigations in a number of diseases were done by Schlomka and coworkers (Schlomka & Reindell, 1936; Schlomka, 1937; Schlomka & Christ, 1938; Schlomka & Dietrich, 1938; Schlomka & Overlack, 1938; Schlomka & Schmitz, 1938) who found a decrease of the SA in cardiac disturbances. From 1963 onward Kalsbeek and coworkers tried to apply the changes of SA to the measurement of mental load (Kalsbeek & Ettema, 1963, 1965; Kalsbeek, 1971). It was found that an increasing load was often associated with a decrease in SA that was much more pronounced than the increase of the mean heart rate. The early enthusiastic results were followed by a number of contradictory results in which no changes or even a rise in SA with mental load were found (Krause, Sowa & Gwozdz, 1977; Rohmert, Laurig, Philipp & Luczak, 1973).

In this paper we want to give the background of SA, point out measuring principles and problems in the quantification of SA with different measures, and discuss the main influences from factors other than mental load. Some of our own results will complete this account.

Generation of the Heart Beat

The action potential of the sinus node (SNAP) is characterized by the lack of the spike and plateau and above all by the inconstant diastolic resting potential. Between two action potentials we find a continuous decline of the membrane potential from the maximal polarization to the membrane threshold: a diastolic depolarization or the pacemaker potential. The time distance between two successive SNAPs depends on three conditions: the maximal polarization, the steepness of the diastolic depolarization and the position of the threshold. One or more of these conditions can be altered by temperature, mechanical stretch of the sinus node tissue, application of acetylcholine or vagal activity and application of epinephrine or sympathetic stimulation, respectively. The cause of the slow diastolic depolarization in potential pacemaker tissue is the inconstancy of the potassium permeability in connection with a relatively high sodium and/or calcium permeability of the cell membrane.

All changes of the heart rate must be generated by one of the mentioned influences. In relation to our problem, the tonizations of the efferent vegetative nerves are most important: increase of the vagal tone results, by means of an enhanced K^+-permeability, in a prolongation of the period duration, but increase of sympathetic tone or enhanced release of epinephrine lowers the period duration by reducing K^+-permeability. If both vegetative branches get a higher tonization, the vagal effect will predominate. Furthermore, the result of an altered vagal activity comes about much more quickly than that of a sympathetic one.

It must be kept in mind that the activity of the cardiac nerves results in bathmotropic, dromotropic and ionotropic actions, in addition to the above-mentioned chronotropic action, although the degree of coupling of these different effects is not quite clear.

After the discussion of measuring and processing synchronous events of the heart action we come back to the cardiac innervation.

Determination of the Heart Period Duration

Hitherto, it has been impossible to record the sinus node action potential noninvasively from the intact man. So we must use a signal which is closely related to the formation of the excitation. Because of the sharpness of the R-peak of the ECG this event is commonly used as a signal for the appearance of the heart action. Between the generation of the heart excitation in the sinus node and the maximum of the R-peak is a latency of about 300 ms due to the sinoatrial, the atrioventricular and the intraventricular conducting time. If the sum of these times were constant, the R-R distance would represent the precise interbeat interval. This is, however, not the case. All these intervals show a certain variability. Little is known about the sinoatrial conduction because it is commonly ascertained indirectly by overdrive pacing. The variability of the atrioventricular conduction under different conditions in man was estimated by us to be at ± 3 ms (Eckoldt & Eismann, 1977). Much higher values were found by Warner and coworkers (Warner, de Tarnowsky, Whitson & Loeb, 1986) in dogs. The mean total time variability between excitation formation and R-peak was estimated at ± 5 ms (error propagation law).

At present, the recording of the R-peak is done automatically by a suitable electronic device. The best trigger point is the maximum of the R-peak, ascertained with a peak detector. A suitable device for automatic determination of the the heart period duration (see Eckoldt, 1984) consists in a high-gain, low noise isolation amplifier, band-pass filter for the range of the main frequency of the R-peak (18-60 Hz), 50 Hz selective filter, peak detector, square impulse formation and a dead time circuit. The derived rectangular impulse opens the way for a 1000 Hz alternation voltage to a counter which counts the number of zero crossings between two such impulses. The result is the duration of one heart period in milliseconds. It is fed into a microcomputer where further processings are done. At first, possible artefacts are eliminated from extrasystoles or muscle potentials. Then an arrhythmia measure like the mean successive difference is calculated and the mean values of these data over ten seconds or one minute are plotted.

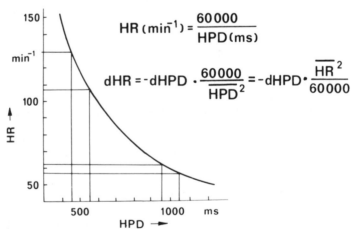

Figure 1. Connection between heart rate (*HR*) and heart period duration (*HPD*) as well as its changes *dHR* and *dHPD*.

Measures of Sinus Arrhythmia and their Dependencies

The most important reason for different results concerning the behavior of sinus arrhythmia is the use of different measures for its quantification. Even the application of the reciprocal bases of heart period duration (*HPD*) and heart rate (*HR*) gives different results if the mean values are inconstant. This is shown in Figure 1.

Any variability measure of *dHPD* may be transferred into the *dHR* scale by multiplication by the square of the *HR* mean value. Furthermore, we cannot predict how the variability behaves without changes of the innervation strength if only mean values of *HR* changes, for instance with temperature. If the rate variability remains constant, the variability of period duration falls with rising mean heart rate in correspondence to HR^2. On the other hand, if one assumes that the period variability remains constant, the variability of the heart rate rises with the square of the rate mean value. The variability quotients *dHR*/ *HR* = *dHPD*/*HPD* are likely to remain constant regardless of the mean values. This means that the rate variability and the period duration variability become greater with the rate mean and the period duration mean, respectively (Eckoldt, 1984).

A widely used variability measure is the standard deviation of *HR* or *HPD*, respectively. If there is a trend in the time series, which is commonly the case during physical load and sometimes under mental load, the standard deviation evaluates the long–term non–stationarity of *HR* and not its variability. By filtering the time series with a digital high–pass filter (time constant approximately 5 s) (Lange, 1987), this disadvantage can be avoided.

Nevertheless, no information concerning the frequency of irregularity is given by this measure, it depends on the amplitude of the oscillation only.

A further well–known measure is based on successive differences of instantaneous *HR* or *HPD*. Besides the amplitude this score is linearly dependent on the frequency of the oscillation and inverse of the mean value of *HR* (Eckoldt, 1984; Lange, 1987).

As we found, all the known measures can be attributed to a combination of an amplitude factor *A*, the centre frequency of oscillation f_c and the mean value of heart rate. Between the individual measures the exponents of these three main factors are different (Lange, 1987),

$$SA = A^k f_c^{-1} \overline{HR}^m .$$

Another approach is the evaluation of the spectral distribution of the variability by means of spectral analysis. Here the sum of the spectral power corresponds to the variance of the time series and that of the spectral amplitude — the square root of power — corresponds to the standard deviation (Catfield, 1982). This is of importance if the absolute spectral powers at different heart rates are compared. Sometimes we divide the total spectrum into the thre periodic main regions which represent the different physiological oscillation circuits (see below).

The Direct Efferent Influences upon the Generation of the Rhythms within the Sinus Node

As mentioned above, the different tonization of the vegetative heart nerves causes the adjustment of the mean heart rate and is mainly responsible for the generation of sinus arrhythmia.

By blocking both branches of the cardiac vegetative innervation by means of intravenous injection of propranolol plus atropine the so-called intrinsic heart rate (*IHR*) results. Its normal value can be calculated by the formula of Jose (1966): $IHR = 118.1 - (0.57 \cdot age)$. Deviations of the actual *IHR* of more than $\pm$ 15% from the predicted one indicate a disturbance of the sinus node function, as in the sick sinus syndrome. In this case all further connections between sinus arrhythmia and vegetative innervation are invalid.

During the total pharmacological blockade sinus arrhythmia disappears, as it does during heart transplantation.

Fleisch and Beckmann (1932) already found that the extent of the SA is reduced after administration of atropine alone, so especially the vagal branch of the heart nerves seems to be involved. Detailed informatiion resulted from the experiments on dogs performed by Koepchen and Thurau (1957, 1959). Our group (Eckoldt, 1974; 1975; Schwarz, 1976) carried out gradual pharmacological vagal denervation and studied its effect upon heart rate and integral sinus arrhythmia. The mean heart rate increased in a linear function, and sinus arrhythmia measured as successive differences of instantaneous heart rates decreased exponentially and was significantly related to doses of atropine. Administration of propranolol in order to block the sympathetic ß-receptors diminished the mean heart rate and had no significant effect upon arrhythmia. From this result we derived a 2-dimensional plot sinus arrhythmia over mean heart rate to evaluate the relative contribution of the cardiac vagal and sympathetic tones (see below).

Katona and Jih (1975) did experiments on dogs and also found a decrease in variability by cooling the cardiac vagal nerve and by atropine administration. A correlation coefficient of 0.91 between the mean period duration and its peak-to-peak variation was calculated.

Direct evidence of the connection between the amount of phasic cardiac vagal activity and heart rate variability is presented in a paper on rabbits by Koizumi (Koizumi, Terui & Kollai, 1983). The sympathetic phasic activity does not influence sinus arrhythmia because of the shorter reaction time of acetylcholine as compared with norepinephrine.

In most cases spectral analysis of the heart period duration variability shows 3 peaks of the power density. The high frequency peak in the range between 0.15 and 0.5 Hz (corresponding to period duration of $2-6$ s) is associated with respiration. It represents the well-known respiratory sinus arrhythmia (RSA). The medium frequency peak is in the range from $0.05-0.15$ Hz ($6-20$ s) around the centre of 0.1 Hz, and represents the well-known rhythmicity of blood pressure, the Mayer-waves. The low frequency peak below 0.05 Hz (>20 s) is interpreted as perfusion rhythmicity as found in plethysmographic or heat conductivity measurements in different organs and muscle parts, respectively. These variations of perfusion are not synchronous in the different regions so that they do not influence the arterial blood pressure and are not generated via the arterial pressoreceptors. All three periodic variabilities point to oscillatory systems that have resonance frequencies in the regions mentioned. The oscillation can be excited by suitable trigger signals. The CNS divisions which are involved in the oscillation circuits are different. It seems that the low frequency oscillation must be generated in interaction with the cortex because it fails completely in cases of brain death (Kero, Antila, Ylitalo & Valimaki, 1978) whereas the respiratory rhythmicity is absent in some patients and present in others.

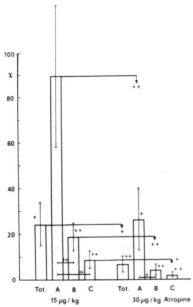

Figure 2. Influence of graded pharmacological blockage of the vagal transmission by atropine upon the total spectral power (Tot.) and the three main spectral divisions *A*, *B*, and *C* (+: *p*<.05; ++: *p*<.01).

In our experiments with gradual parasympathetic blockade by administration of atropine we found a nonuniform reduction of the three main frequency ranges (Figure 2). The respiratory range *C* was most affected, and the minute rhythm range *A* was hardly affected by a lower dosage. In accordance with the experimental results of Akselrod (Akselrod, Gordon, Ubel, Shannon, Barger & Cohen, 1981), we conclude that the mean and high frequency variations of heart beat (*B* and *C*) are mediated by the vagal nerve, while the low frequency range is mediated only partly by the vagus and partly by the sympathetic nerve, or by an indirect action via the perfusion of the sinus node artery.

From these experimental results we may infer that the mean heart rate is influenced by the cardiac vagal and sympathetic innervation, with a predominance of the vagal nerve at low heart rate, and that sinus arrhythmia is generated mainly by the vagal innervation, which is modulated rhythmically by the mentioned oscillatory circuits.

Furthermore, a lot of central interactions and reflexes from chemoreceptors, vegetative and somatic afferences, emotions, motor coinnervation, etc., influence vagal and sympathetic origin neurons of the brainstem and thereby the heart rhythm, as is depicted in Figure 3.

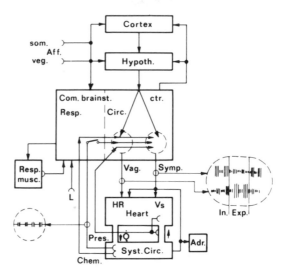

Figure 3. Scheme of the origins of cardiac control.

Sources of the Heart Rhythm Variability

Physiological Influences (Besides Mental Load). The first influence on HRV to be mentioned is the mean heart rate itself. As mentioned above, the degree of dependence is different when using different measures of HRV. All measures including integral spectral power (except presumably the variability coefficients s_{HR}/HR or s_{HPD}/HPD) are more or less dependent on HR. This must be kept in mind when HRV is to be compared at different HR.

The second important dependence is that of respiration. As we found (Eckoldt & Schubert, 1975), HRV increases with respiratory volume, and according to Angelone and Coulter (1964) and Hirsch and Bishop (1981), there is a strong dependence on the amount of RSA from the respiratory rate. Between 50 and 10 cycles per minute the amplitude of the respiratory related variability rises by the five-fold. Therefore it is advisable to control respiration, if possible.

Furthermore, HRV depends on the age of the subject. We found an increase of ΔHR from birth up to 6 years and thereafter a decrease to less than a quarter of the "juvenile" value by the age of 65 years (Figure 4). This is why HRV analyses in elderly people are of limited value.

Even low-intensity physical load, like the transition from the supine to sitting position, causes a decrease of HRV (Figure 4). Also orthostatic load influences HRV because of a changed pressoreceptor working point. At light ergometric load, HRV decreases drastically until heart rate is about 120 min^{-1}. Thereafter HRV remains nearly constant. After an exhausting piece of work HRV remains at a low level for a long time (approximately one hour) due to chemoreceptor interference.

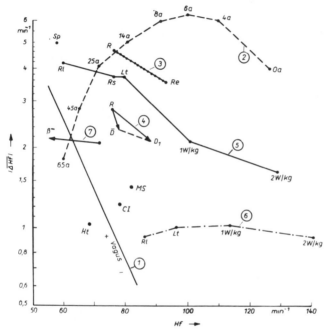

Figure 4. Tonus diagram: Heart rate variability against heart rate in different experimental situations:
1: pharmacological vagal blocking;
2: age dependence (0 – 65 years);
3: mental arithmetic task (R: rest; Re: test performance);
4: discrimination task (R: rest; D_1: reaction; $\overline{D}$: level);
5: ergometric load (Rl: rest, suppine; Rs: rest, sitting; Lt: pedalling without load; 1 W/kg and 2 W/kg: load intensity of 1 and 2 W per kg bodymass, respectively);
6: like 5, but with vagal blocking;
7: sympathetic blocking by propranolol;
Ht, CI, MS: cardiac patients suffering from hypertension, coronary insufficience, and mitral stenosis, respectively.

Pathophysiological Influences. Zwiener (1976) found differences in HRV spectra as well as in blood pressure and respiration spectra between normals and patients with neurovegetative disturbances. HRV is reduced in disturbances of the vagal transmission. This is the case in diabetic polyneuropathia where a reduction by nearly a half was found by Rabending, Klöckner and Reichel (1982). We found reduced integral HRV in cardiac patients (Figure 4) suffering from hypertension, mitral stenosis, coronary insufficiency (Eckoldt, 1984). The degree of reduction proved to be related to the severity and the duration of illness. Appropriate therapy could lead to a normalization of HRV. In such cases, cardiac control was influenced by the illness resulting in an altered parasympathetic tonization.

Mental Load and Heart Rate Variability. As we mentioned in the introduction, the results concerning the influences of mental load upon HRV and the reflection of load intensity in HRV are contradictory. If we bear in mind the multitude of possible influences besides the mental load, this fact is not surprising. The most common sources of error are the following: use of an inadequate measure (dependence of HR, sensitive to trend in mean HR), changes in respiration pattern (frequency, volume, regularity) possibly induced by the task frequency, inconvenient body position (additional static load).

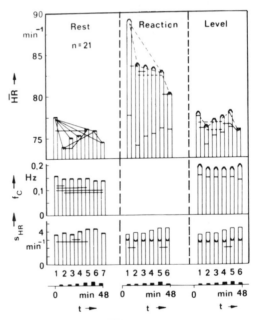

Figure 5. Reaction of mean heart rate $\overline{HR}$, the characteristic frequency f_c of the power spectrum of $HR-$variability, and the standard deviation s_{HR} of HR in repeated discrimination tasks with five rising load intensities.

In principle, an irradiation of the mental processes to the brain-stem circulatory centres is to be expected although from the energetic point of view circulatory rearrangement is not necessary to cope with the load. Therefore, the individual specificity of the reaction is very important. We doubt if there are general quantitative dependencies of HRV on mental processes, quite apart from the difficulties of quantifying mental work-load intensity at all (Firth, 1973).

In our own experiments, we set an optomotor discrimination task as introduced by Michel (1981), and made at first ten repetitions of the standard test in the same procedure to evaluate fatigue processes (repetition investigation). Then we reduced the decision time in steps in order to raise the task difficulty (investigation of increasing load).

The response of heart rate to the load was characterized by a sudden short rise followed by a decline lasting about 20 sec (called "reaction") and an adjacent constant level (called "level"). The same terms were used to describe HRV.

In the experiments with a repeated but constant load, the reaction and the level of *HR* fell continuously with the number of repetitions, whereas the high pass-filtered standard deviation from the *HR* mean, as a measure of HRV, remained at a significantly lower value with respect to resting conditions. This value, however, did not change with the repetitions. In the series with rising load, the course of *HR* and HRV is quite similar (Figure 5). This means that the rising load is responded to by *HR* and by HRV in a different way but in no case is that response proportional.

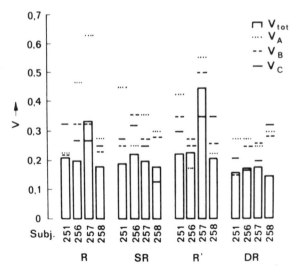

Figure 6. Variability coefficients $V = s/\bar{x}$ of total power V_{tot} and spectral parts V_A, V_B, V_C in four subjects in different phases of an optomotor discrimination test (R: rest; SR: single reaction, i.e., reaction without discrimination; R': second resting phase; DR: discrimination test phase).

In some recent investigations the usefulness of heart rate power spectral data for mental work-load measurements was anlysed. Mulder and Mulder (1981) showed that the spectral region near 0.1 Hz, the one related to blood pressure, was insensitive to respiratory changes in their experimental condition, but its amplitude was found to be inversely related to the task difficulty in a sentence comprehension task. These findings were not confirmed by Honzikova, Penaz and Fiser (1987) in experiments with controlled respiration in an acoustical discrimination task.

From our above-mentioned experiments, the variability coefficients of integral and spectral HRV out of the ten repetitions were calculated for four subjects in different test phases (Figure 6). The result was that the intrasubject variabilities of the spectral parts are higher than that of the integral measure. This means that because of lower reproducibility there is no advantage in using spectral analysis to evaluate mental processes.

Summary and Conclusion

Heart rate and heart rate variability are dependent on reflexogenic and central vegetative cardiac tonization. A two-dimensional plot of both parameters allows the judgment of the relative contributions of cardiac vagal and sympathetic activity. Prerequisites for this are: age of the subject less than 60 years, sinus rhythm (no pathological rhythm disturbances), sufficient recording time (more than 5 min), controlled respiration (frequency, tidal volume, regularity), convenient body position of the subject (no static load), elimination of artefacts from the time series of cardiac intervals, use of a set of independent parameters for the characterization of heart rhythm variability (like variability quotient of HR, mean spectral frequency and mean HR). We must take into account that there is a considerable intraindividual variability at rest in the order of $\pm$ 25% for the integral variability, and that the spectral one is even higher. Little is known as yet about the relation between the kind and strength of mental load and heart rate variability, mainly because of a great amount of individual specificity.

Correspondence should be addressed to Klaus Eckoldt, Institut für medizinische Physik und Biophysik, Humboldt-Universität, Invalidenstr. 42, Berlin, DDR−1040.

References

Akselrod, S., Gordon, D., Ubel, F.A., Shannon, D.C., Barger, A.C., & Cohen, R.J. (1981). Power spectrum analysis of heart rate fluctuation: A quantitative probe of beat-to-beat cardiovascular control. *Science, 213*, 220−222.

Angelone, A., & Coulter, N.A. (1964). Respiratory sinus arrhythmia: a frequency dependent phenomenon. *Journal of Applied Physiology, 19*, 479−482.

Catfield, C. (1982). *Analyse von Zeitreihen.* Leipzig: Teubner.

Eckoldt, K. (1974). Zur Beeinflussung der Herzfrequenz durch das vegetative Nervensystem. *Ergebnisse der experimentellen Medizin, 15*, 120−125.

Eckoldt, K. (1975). *Untersuchungen über die Wirkungen der vegetativen Herznerven mit Hilfe von unblutigen Meßverfahren.* Dissertation B., Mathematisch-Naturwissenschaftliche Fakultät, Humboldt-Universität, Berlin.

Eckoldt, K. (1984). Verfahren und Ergebnisse der quantitativen automatischen Analyse der Herzfrequenz und deren Spontanvariabilität. *Das Deutsche Gesundheitswesen, 39*, 856−863.

Eckoldt, K., & Eismann, V. (1977). Variability of RR, PR and RT of the ECG at rest and work. *Advances in Cardiology, 19*, 65−67.

Eckoldt, K., & Schubert, E. (1975). Zum Einfluß der Atemtiefe auf die Sinusarrhythmie des Herzens. *Acta Biologica Medica Germanica, 34*, 767−771.

Fleisch, A., & Beckmann, R. (1932). Die raschen Schwankungen der Pulsfrequenz registriert mit dem Pulszeitschreiber. *Zeitschrift für die gesamte experimentelle Medizin, 80*, 487−510.

Firth, P.A. (1973). Psychological factors influencing the relationship between cardiac arrhythmia and mental load. *Ergonomics, 16*, 5−16.

Hirsch, J.A., & Bishop, B. (1981). Respiratory sinus arrhythmia in humans: how breathing pattern modulates heart rate. *American Journal of Physiology, 241*, H620−H629.

Honzikova, H., Penaz, J., & Fiser, B. (1987). Power spectra of blood pressure and heart rate fluctuations during mental load. *Chronobiologica, 14*, 188.

Jose, A.D. (1966). Effect of combined sympathetic and parasympathetic blockade on heart rate and cardiac function in man. *American Cardiologist, 18*, 476−478.

Kalsbeek, J.W.H., & Ettema, J.H. (1963). Scored regularity of the heart rate pattern and the measurement of perceptual or mental load. *Ergonomics, 6*, 306.

Kalsbeek, J.W.H., & Ettema, J.H. (1965). Sinus arrhythmia and the measurement of mental load. Communication at the London Conference of the British Psychological Society.

Kalsbeek, J.W.H. (1971). Sinus arrhythmia and the dual task method in measuring mental load. In W.T. Singleton, J.G. Fox & D. Whitfield (Eds.), *Measurement of man at work.* London: Taylor & Francis Ltd.

Katona, P.G., & Jih, F. (1975). Respiratory sinus arrhythmia: Noninvasive measure of parasympathetic cardia control. *Journal of Applied Physiology, 39*, 801−805.

Kero, P., Antila, K., Ylitalo, V., & Valimaki, I. (1978). Decreased heart rate variation in decerebration syndrome: quantitative clinical criterion of brain death? *Pediatrics, 62*, 307−311.

Koepchen, H.P., & Thurau, K. (1957). Über die Rolle des Vagus bei den durch venöse Infusionen erzeugten Herzfrequenzsteigerungen (Bainbridge-Reflex). *Pflügers Archiv für die gesamte Physiologie, 264*, 573−584.

Koepchen, H.P., & Thurau, K. (1959). Über die Entstehungsbedingugnen der atemsynchronen Schwankungen des Vagustonus (respiratorische Arrhythmie). *Pflügers Archiv für die gesamte Physiologie, 269*, 10−30.

Koizumi, K., Terui, N., & Kollai, M. (1983). Neural control of the heart: significance of double innervation re-examined. *Journal of the Autonomic Nervous System, 7*, 279−294.

Krause, M., Sowa, K., & Gwozdz, B. (1977). Herzarrhythmie als ein Belastungsindex bei geistiger Belastung. *Medizin und Sport, 17*, 191−193.

Lange, V. (1987). *Individuelle psychophysiologische Beanspruchungen im Belastungsbewälti-gungsprozeß und deren Erfassung in testartigen Untersuchungen.* Dissertation B., Mathematisch-Naturwissenschaftliche Fakultät, Humboldt-Universität, Berlin.

Ludwig, C. (1847). Beiträge zur Kenntnis der Einflusses der Respirationsbewegungen auf den Blutlauf im Aortensystem. *Archiv für Anatomie und Physiologie, 13*, 242−302.

Michel, J. (1981). *Grundlagen, Methodik und Ergebnisse eines multivariaten dynamischen Untersuchungsverfahrens mit psychischer Belastung zur quantitativen Erfassung und Differenzierung von Systemeigenschaften des menschlichen Organismus − Ein Beitrag zur psycho-physiologischen Systemanalyse.* Dissertation B., Medizinische Fakultät, Humboldt-Universität,Berlin.

Mulder, G., & Mulder, L.J.M. (1981). Information processing and cardiovascular control. *Psychophysiology, 18*, 392−402.

Rabending, G., Klöckner, H., & Reichel, G. (1982). Quantitative Bestimmung der respiratorischen Herzarrhythmie für die neurovegetative Funktionsdiagnostik. *Ergebnisse der experimentellen Medizin, 41*, 391−393.

Rohmert, W., Laurig, W., Philipp, U., & Luczak, H. (1973). Heart rate variability and work-load measurement. *Ergonomics, 16*, 33−44.

Schlomka, G. (1937). Untersuchungen über die physiologische Unregelmäßigkeit des Herzschlages. 3. Mitteilung. *Zeitschrift für Kreislaufforschung, 29*, 510−524.

Schlomka, G., & Christ, J. (1938). Untersuchungen über die physiologische Unregelmäßigkeit des Herzschlages. 8. Mitteilung. *Zeitschrift für Kreislaufforschung, 30*, 637−653.

Schlomka, G., & Dietrich, H. (1938). Untersuchungen über die physiologische Unregelmäßigkeit des Herzschlages. 6. Mitteilung. *Zeitschrift für Kreislaufforschung, 30*, 453−461.

Schlomka, G., & Overlack, P. (1938). Untersuchungen über die physiologische Unregelmäßigkeit des Herzschlages. 9. Mitteilung. *Zeitschrift für Kreislaufforschung, 30*, 721−734.

Schlomka, G., & Reindell, H. (1936). Untersuchungen über die physiologische Unregelmäßigkeit des Herzschlages. *Zeitschrift für Kreislaufforschung, 28*, 473−492.

Schlomka, G., & Schmitz, G. (1938). Untersuchungen über die physiologische Unregelmäßigkeit des Herzschlages. 5. Mitteilung. *Zeitschrift für Kreislaufforschung, 30*, 41−54.

Schwarz, V. (1976). *Die Beeinflussung der Herzfrequenz und Sinusarrhythmie durch pharmakologische Blockade in Ruhe und bei Belastung.* Dissertation A, Medizinische Fakultät, Humboldt-Universität, Berlin.

Warner, M.R., de Tarnowsky, J.M., Whitson, C.C., & Loeb, J.M. (1986). Beat-by-beat modulation of AV-conduction. II. Autonomic neural mechanisms. *American Journal of Physiology, 251*, H1134−H1142.

Zwiener, U. (1976). *Pathophysiologie neurovegetativer Regelungen und Rhythmen.* Jena: G. Fischer.

V. Explorations of Complex Perception

Psychophysical Explorations of Mental Structures
Edited by H.-G. Geissler
in collaboration with M.H. Müller and W. Prinz
© 1990 by Hogrefe & Huber Publishers

Chapter 35

On Dynamic Pertinence Models

Wolfgang Prinz
*Abteilung für Psychologie, Universität Bielefeld
Bielefeld, F.R.G.*

This paper examines how we can account for phenomena of passive, or unintentional attention. More specifically, I will concentrate on a particular type of theory of these phenomena which claims that our cognitive systems are furnished with the capability of constructing and maintaining dynamic internal models of potential external events and, hence, of detecting discrepancies between these internal models and real events in the external world. In what follows I shall briefly discuss the concept of unintentional attention first, then turn to the notion of dynamic models, and finally discuss some related evidence from the paradigm of continuous search.

Unintentional Attention

Though the last thirty years have seen a tremendous increase in our knowledge about selective attention, it must be admitted that the range of phenomena that have come under study in this literature does not cover the full range of phenomena that have been traditionally subsumed under the heading of attention. The emphasis has been on what classic authorities like Wundt, James or Titchener have called active, voluntary, or intentional attention and not on passive, involuntary, or unintentional attention.

In the case of intentional attention there is always a specific intention preceding the information to be processed, and the issue is how the intention affects the processing of the information (cf., e.g., Prinz, this volume). More-over, in the typical experimental setting, the intention is implemented through an instruction that specifies which pieces or aspects of the stimulus information are relevant to the task under study (Heuer & Prinz, 1987; Neumann & Prinz, 1987). The nature of this class of attentional phenomena can be summarized in terms of three major features. First, intentional attention is directed inside-out (Bridgeman, 1987); i.e., intention comes first and information second; second, it is always specific in the sense of being selective with respect to certain prespecified aspects of input information (e.g., certain locations, certain colors, etc.), and third, it is based on the criterion of relevance, which implies that the to-be-selected information is required for the initiation and/or execution of intended actions (Allport, 1987; Neumann, van der Heijden & Allport, 1987; Prinz, 1983).

In the case of unintentional attention there is no specific intention preceding the information to be processed. Here the issue is how certain pieces, or aspects, of input information can get selected in the absence of explicit inten-tions directed toward them. It may be interesting to consider unintentional attention in terms of the three aforementioned features. First, unintentional attention is directed, or, more precisely, attracted in the outside-in direction. First comes the information, and second the intention to examine it, or the attention attracted by it. Second, unintentional attention is unspecific to a large extent. For any situation, we can think of a host of possible events that would unavoidably catch our attention, if they occurred in that situation, and there is no specific common attribute, neither physical nor semantic, shared by all of them, as would be required in the case of intentional attention.[1] Third, the selection criteria on which unintentional attention is based can be summarized under the concept of pertinence. This concept which is due to Norman (1968) implies the notion that information which is actually there catches our attention by virtue of the fact that it differs from information expected, or computed, on the basis of an anticipatory internal model of the ongoing external events. This model, it is assumed, specifies the limited range of stimulus events that pertain to a given situation and, by implication, thereby specifies the unlimited range of non-pertinent events that catch our attention.

At a rather primitive level, one could think of the pertinence model as specifying a certain constant pattern of stimulation. In this case any change of that pattern would be noticed as a non-pertinent event. At a somewhat more sophisticated level, where the model also incorporates changes over time, change *per se* would lose its non-pertinent character, except if the change leads to novel patterns of stimulation. At a still more sophisticated level, one could

---

[1] On the other hand, unintentional attention cannot be entirely unspecific. This is because one can also specify a couple of specific events that would attract one's attention nearly under all circumstances one can think of, like hearing one's name or seeing an object approaching one's body at high speed, etc. The following discussion will not consider these cases, where rele-vance and significance-related criteria come also into the play (cf., e.g., Bernstein, 1979, 1981; Maltzman, 1979; Neumann, 1990, Prinz, 1983, ch. 6), but rather concentrate on genuinely unspecific selection.

also think of a system that neither responds to change nor novelty *per se*, but rather to non-pertinence with respect to a given situation. A system like this would require a pertinence model that also incorporates the possible occurrence of specific novel events — in which case novelty, too, would lose its non-pertinent character. Change and novelty are known to be important factors in the mechanisms underlying, e.g., orienting reflexes (Bernstein, 1979, 1981; Rohrbaugh, 1984; Sokolov, 1963a,b), free choice preference judgements (e.g., Berlyne, 1960, 1969), or detection responses in search (e.g., Neisser & Lazar, 1964; Prinz, 1979, Exp. 1, Prinz, Tweer & Feige, 1974).

Dynamic Models

Crucial to the notion of unintentional, pertinence-based selection is the concept of an internal model that specifies the range of pertinent (stimulus-) events in a given situation. Stipulating internal models of external events has become widespread in modern theories of perception and cognition — though these models have not always been introduced with respect to attentional phenomena. A famous example is Sokolov's neuronal model hypothesis of the orienting reflex, which claims that an orienting reflex develops whenever the stimulus delivered fails to coincide with a previously created neuronal model of the stimulus (Sokolov, 1963a, p. 287). In the original form of the hypothesis, the neuronal model was "conservative" in the sense that, in order to avoid the development of an orienting reflex, the new stimulus had to be a repetition (or continuation) of the old one(s) from which the model was constructed. In a later version the neuronal model could also be "progressive" in the sense that it could involve extrapolations in time of expected stimulus values (Sokolov, 1963b; cf. Velden, 1978). In a similar vein, Norman introduced the concept of pertinence to denote the "class of events deemed to be pertinent to the ongoing analysis" of the input (Norman, 1969, p. 33; Norman, 1968).[2]

In order to be efficient, such internal models must be dynamic in the sense of continuously updating themselves to the actual state of external affairs. As far as movement control by real-event models is concerned, some properties of the updating mechanism have been studied (e.g., Arbib, 1981; Dean, 1990). However, as far as the guidance of attention through models of potential events is concerned, little is known about the underlying mechanisms.

These mechanisms can be studied at two levels, overt information sampling and covert information integration. The pattern of overt sampling behavior (e.g., eye movements) may give an indication of the strategies that subjects use for collecting the information needed to meet the requirements of given tasks (cf. Moray, 1984), but it does not tell us much about the covert operations of

---

[2] Other related approaches have stressed the importance of internal models for movement guidance and action control (e.g., Arbib, 1981; MacKay, 1984; Yates, 1985). However, under this viewpoint the emphasis has been on models as a means of representing real events (including their action-related potentialities), rather than potential events (in the sense of being pertinent to the situation specified through preceding events).

information integration through which task-specific dynamic models are constructed and maintained. How much time and effort is required for constructing, maintaining, and updating them? How much task-specific practice is required for a model to become effective for selection? How complex can models be? Under which circumstances can they become progressive, rather than merely conservative? And, to end up with the most radical query: Do we have reasons to believe that pertinence models exist at all?

Continuous Selection

In this section I will try to show that some of these questions can be answered on the basis of observations from continuous visual search tasks. In this paradigm which was introduced by Neisser (1963), the subject is required to scan through the lines of a list and search for a predefined target item (or for any item from a predefined set of targets). There is only one target interspersed among a large number of nontargets, and the subject is instructed to stop the scan immediately upon detecting the target (Figure 1).

Figure 1. Example of a search list as used in the continuous visual search paradigm. Subjects are instructed to scan the lists as in reading, i.e., row by row and from left to right within rows. A single target is contained in each list at an unpredictable location (Z in this list).

```
MKLXMNLHFWVNTMHWKLFWVTLNMVXNTMHKWVTF
VTFXVLNWVFNLWKVFWXHLNTVMKFXWLTXVNMLV
TXKFWLTXFVLMFTNXFMHNKFVHLTKNMHWTVMXT
TWVNKFXHVLFNVLXKMLHKXLNFXLNHWLXKWVLT
VFXHNLMWNTVWLXTFNLHVWTLNHKMNWHFNWLKT
WXMTWHVNTFKNWVTXFLWXTVMFHZVFTWXVNFLM
NXMWKVMXHLKVHTMNVHFKNMFHTXKLMFHKVTFX
WVTMFHKLTVNFMVXLWMHVWNFTMNKWVNTKFLVW
FTVMFNTLWKFVNWKTVHNWMXKLFVKXFNMWTNMH
HVKLWTFKHMVFXHLMKNHMTNHKLVFWTHFXKHLX
MKTNVMHWXLNMHXLFWTNLKWNMHXLWHTNLFWXT
NTWMNHKLFNMLHNFMHLWMTXHLNFMLHVFXHNKW
HMNTHMWXHTLNMHWTNMHTNXLHMVXKLTNMHWVF
```

Neisser (1967) has offered a model of search control in this task which comes close to what appears to be a common-sense account of search. The model postulates that, upon the instruction to search for a particular letter, an internal representation of that target letter is formed and put into a somehow activated condition. With this the activated representation "in mind" the searcher then scans through the list until she/he detects an object that matches the representation and is thus identified as the target to be searched. According to this view, target detection is based on matches and nontarget rejection is based on mismatches between the incoming stimulus information and the stored representation of the target (as formed on the basis of the instructions).

Yet, there is now much reason to believe that the story is reversed and that we have to assume that the critical comparisons are made between incoming stimulus information and stored representations of nontargets rather than targets so that target detection is based on mismatches and nontarget rejection on matches between these two pieces of information. These nontarget representations, it is assumed, are formed and maintained on the basis of the items encountered while scanning the list. According to this view, an internal model of the actual nontarget items is generated (or re-generated) on each trial, and the scan is continued as long as the items in the list match the items in the model. Targets are then detected by default, i.e., by virtue of the fact of not being nontargets.

Why should we believe that the system operates in such a counterintuitive and seemingly uneconomical mode? There are two ways to answer a question like this: by providing arguments to show that this might be a sensible mode of operation and by providing evidence to show that it is really used.

As far as arguments are concerned, one has to start from the fact that, under the conditions of the present task, targets are rare events, whereas nontargets are encountered and repeated all the time during the scan. Under this condition, the generation and maintenance of an internal model of potential nontargets appears to be a natural consequence of the processing of the input information. Note that this does not apply to targets. As there is only one target per list, there is no opportunity to refresh its representation on the basis of stimulus information.[3]

As far as evidence is concerned, space does not permit to go in detail through the experimental findings that support this view (for summary, see Prinz, 1977, 1986). There are two independent sources of such evidence, one supporting the notion that target detection occurs by default, i.e., without, or at least prior to, target identification, and the other one supporting the notion that nontarget rejection is based on matches with stored nontarget representations rather than mismatches.

In what follows, I will concentrate on one piece of evidence from this second source. In a couple of experiments, we compared performance with two different types of search lists, random and predictable. In random lists the nontarget background would consist of a random sequence of items drawn from a predefined pool of nontargets. In predictable lists the item string was constructed according to some arbitrary rules, thereby introducing kind of an artificial syntax and, hence, some degree of predictability across subsequent items in the string.

---

[3] Moreover, if one looks at the task in terms of the action decisions required for the control of the scan, another, somewhat related asymmetry becomes apparent: On the basis of each sample a decision must be taken to either stop the scan (if the sample contains the target) or to take another sample (if it contains nontargets only). As taking another sample is much more frequent than stopping the scan, it is certainly economical to set up the decision criterion in terms of the more frequent alternative and leave the infrequent one unspecified (cf. Heuer & Prinz, 1987).

If the supposed mechanism for short-term integration of nontarget information really exists, it should profit by the predictability built into the string —
provided, of course, that it is capable of acquiring the particular pattern of
sequential redundancy and using it to enhance processing. This expectation was
borne out in a couple of experiments showing that search speed increases and
error frequency decreases to the extent predictability is introduced (for details,
see Prinz, 1979, Exp. 2; Prinz, 1983; Prinz & Nattkemper, 1987; Prinz &
Prinz, 1985).

Figure 2. Results from an experiment by
Prinz & Nattkemper (1987). Filled circles:
Overall results. Open circles: Results for
predictable lists in two subgroups of subjects. For details, see Prinz and Nattkemper, 1987.

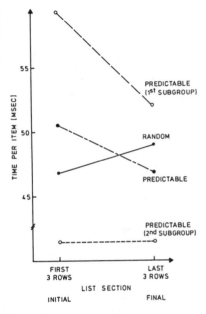

If one assumes that the supposed integration procedure that serves to build
up the internal model has to be started anew on each trial, one should expect
that the development of performance within trials is different with predictable
and random lists (Nattkemper & Prinz, 1984). When the item strings are
predictable, the system must first invest some costs in the acquisition (or
warm-up) of the pertinence model and will only later in the course of the trial
be able to benefit from it. Thus, in the initial phase of each trial, acquisition
costs should outweigh processing benefits whereas in the final phase this relationship should be reversed. With random lists, where the strings are unpredictable, no such development can be expected since there is no sequential
structure that has to be acquired before it can be used. If this reasoning is
valid, a comparison of the within-trial development of search speed should help
to uncover the supposed build-up of the pertinence model.

Figure 2 shows data from an experiment reported by Prinz and Nattkemper
(1987) that lend some support to this notion. In the random condition there was

some decrease of search speed in the course of the trial, which is probably due to trivial factors like fatigue, saturation, etc. In the predictable condition the reverse development was observed. Here the scan was started at a lower speed and ended up at a higher speed as compared to random lists, indicating higher costs in the beginning and benefits in the end.

Unfortunately, however, this nice picture disappeared when we examined the data at the level of individual subjects. At this level we observed that subjects differed substantially and reliably with respect to the pattern of this interaction. Some subjects (particularly those who were, on the average, slower with predictable as compared to random lists) showed the expected within–trial development, whereas others (particularly those who were, on the average, faster with predictable as compared to random lists) exhibited no such pattern.

```
RANDOM        V T H F V N K L X V F W L T F K M T W H K T K V V L
              F M L F M M F L L T K X H M W H X T W N N H T W T F
              M K W L F N F H V V K K X H M M L V T W X T L T L X
              M L T N T L H W H L L T L H L K M H T X L F M V K V
              X M N T X N T H F H K M T W H X T H X H K N W H L K


PREDICTABLE   W N V V F K L X L W W T H M X L V W L T W M M H K X
              V W W N M K N M M K V W T M N T V F X V X W T T M N
              H F V V W W W W M K H F H X V X X T M T K V K F F L
              X T N H N K F V W W N M M H H H K L V F L L H M V F
              K F W X X T T T M V H L X T W T M M M H X X W L W W
```

Figure 3. Illustration of the difference between random and predictable lists in the experiment by Prinz and Nattkemper (1987).

This could suggest that there are different modes of making use of the structure in predictable lists. In fact, we observed that the algorithm for generating predictable lists produced item strings that exhibited two characteristic features, a conspicuous and an inconspicuous one (see Figure 3). The conspicuous feature was the increase in the frequency of repetitions in adjacent locations, and the inconspicuous feature was the creation of correlations among items across adjacent locations. Though these two features are formally equivalent (in the sense that they are two components of the autocontingency pattern built into the string; cf. Prinz, 1986) they are certainly not equivalent in functional terms.

Suppose, that there is one mode of forming a pertinence model that solely relies on item repetitions (repetition analysis). In this case the model would comprise a set of stored representations of the nontargets in the list. It is generated on the basis of the first nontargets encountered, and all later repetitions of these nontargets will serve to maintain and update it. When the lists are random this is the sole possible mode of constructing and maintaining a pertinence model. When the lists are predictable it must be assumed that the repetition–based pertinence model can be formed and maintained more efficiently, due to the increase in repetition frequency. Thus, when the search would exclusively rely on this simple mode of integration, the supposed cost/benefit reversal should not apply. Rather, one would have to expect some overall advantage of predictable lists, due to their increased repetition density.

Suppose, furthermore, that there is a second mode of forming a pertinence model that relies on item correlations (correlation analysis). In this case the model would have to be more complex, since it would have to comprise, in addition to the nontarget representations themselves, some kind of representation of the particular pattern of sequential dependencies across items at different locations. With random lists this mode cannot be used. It can be used, however, with predictable lists. In this case some costs for generating and maintaining it should arise, and these costs would have to be invested before any processing benefits could be obtained.

Though this account covers the findings quite nicely, there are two problems with it: It is a *post hoc* account, and it relies on hypothetical differences between subjects. Particularly, one would like to understand why some subjects supposedly rely on repetition analysis and some others on correlation analysis as their preferred modes of forming pertinence models (see Prinz & Nattkemper, 1987, for a discussion of this issue).

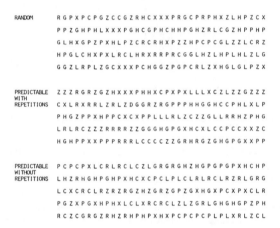

Figure 4. Illustration of the three list conditions used in the experiment by Prinz and Prinz (1985).

More direct evidence in support of the distinction between the two modes of integration comes from a study with primary school children (Prinz & Prinz, 1985). In this experiment three list conditions were used: random, predictable with repetitions and predictable without repetitions (see Figure 4). The two predictable lists exhibited the same basic pattern of sequential dependencies across adjacent string locations, but item repetitions at immediately adjacent locations could either be permitted or not. With repetitions permitted, the lists were basically similar to those in the first experiment (though the absolute amount of repetition density was somewhat higher). In this condition, it was assumed, both integration modes should be applicable. By the same token it was assumed that, with repetitions excluded, the efficiency of repetition analysis should be relatively weaker so that the data should more clearly exhibit the pattern of cost/benefit reversal considered indicative of correlation analysis.

Figure 5 shows that predictable lists with repetitions were scanned considerably faster than random lists throughout the course of the trial, with no indication of a cost/benefit reversal at all. Unlike in the first experiment this result was observed in virtually all subjects. Thus we may conclude that, for the children under study, repetition–based integration was clearly the prevailing mode of integration in this condition. Yet, when adjacent repetitions were excluded, the scan was initially slower and finally faster as compared to random lists. This is what must be expected on the assumption that correlation–based integration is applied in this condition.

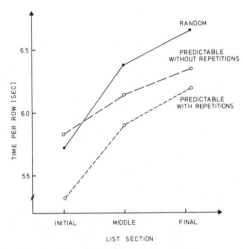

Figure 5. Results of the experiment by Prinz and Prinz (1985).

Summary and Conclusions

Dynamic pertinence models have been discussed with respect to the selection and the processing of information. Pertinence models are internal models of potential external events. In order to be effective such models have to be dynamic, i.e., they must be continuously updated according to the actual state of the external situation. With respect to information selection, these dynamic pertinence models account for phenomena of passive, involuntary, or unintentional attention. With respect to information processing they account for processing benefits due to the predictability of environmental events. Some illustrative findings from the continuous visual search paradigm have been discussed. These findings suggest that construction, maintenance, and updating of pertinence models may be based on different modes of information integration. At the one end there seem to be rather simple integration modes, like repetition analysis, yielding "conservative" pertinence models, that lead the system to expect still more of the same information that it has been processing before. At the other end there seem to be more sophisticated integration modes, like correlation analysis. These yield more "progressive" pertinence models, that lead the system to expect specific new information which is computed on the basis of the previously processed old information according to certain rules. Associated with these modes are their characteristic patterns of costs and benefits.

Correspondence should be addressed to Wolfgang Prinz, Abteilung Psychologie, Universität Bielefeld, P.O. Box 8640, 4800 Bielefeld, F.R.G.

References

Allport, D.A. (1987). Selection for action: Some behavioral and neurophysiological considerations of attention and action. In H. Heuer & A.F. Sanders (Eds.), *Perspectives on perception and action* (pp. 395 – 419). Hillsdale, NJ: Erlbaum.

Arbib, M.A. (1981). Perceptual structures and distributed motor control. In V.B. Brooks (Ed.), *Handbook of physiology, Sect. 1: The nervous system. Vol. II: Motor control, Part 2* (pp. 1449 – 1480). Bethesda, Md: American Physiological Society.

Berlyne, D.E. (1960). *Conflict, arousal, and curiosity.* New York: McGraw-Hill.

Berlyne, D.E. (1969). The development of the concept of attention in Psychology. In C.R. Evans & T.B. Mulholland (Eds.), *Attention in neurophysiology* (pp. 1 – 26). London: Butterworths.

Bernstein, A.S. (1979). The orienting response as novelty and significance detector: Reply to O'Gorman. *Psychophysiology, 16,* 263 – 273.

Bernstein, A.S. (1981). The orienting response and stimulus significance: Further comments. *Biological Psychology, 12,* 171 – 185.

Bridgeman, B. (1987). Relations between the physiology of attention and the physiology of consciousness. In O. Neumann, A.H.C. van der Heijden & D.A. Allport (Eds.), *Visual selective attention* (pp. 259 – 266). (*Psychological Research, 48*)

Dean, J. (1990). The neuroethology of perception and action. In O. Neumann & W. Prinz (Eds.), *Relations between perception and action: Current approaches.* Berlin: Springer.

Heuer, H., & Prinz, W. (1987). Initiierung und Steuerung von Handlungen und Bewegungen. In M. Amelang (Hrsg.), *Bericht über den 35. Kongreß der Deutschen Gesellschaft für Psychologie in Heidelberg 1986,* Bd. 2 (pp. 289 – 299). Göttingen: Hogrefe.

MacKay, D.M. (1984). Evaluation: The missing link between cognition and action. In W. Prinz & A.F. Sanders (Eds.), *Cognition and motor processes* (pp. 175 – 184). Berlin: Springer.

Maltzman, I. (1979). Orienting reflexes and significance: A reply to O'Gorman. *Psychophysiology, 16,* 274 – 282.

Moray, N. (1984). Attention to dynamic visual displays in man-machine systems. In R. Parasuraman & D.R. Davies (Eds.), *Varieties of attention* (pp. 485 – 513). Orlando, Fl: Academic Press.

Nattkemper, D., & Prinz, W. (1984). Costs and benefits of redundancy in visual search. In A.G. Gale & F. Johnson (Eds.), *Theoretical and applied aspects of eye movement research* (pp. 343 – 352). Amsterdam: North-Holland.

Neisser, U. (1963). Decision time without reaction time: Experiments in visual scanning. *American Journal of Psychology, 76,* 376 – 385.

Neisser, U. (1967). *Cognitive psychology.* New York: Appleton-Century-Crofts.

Neisser, U., & Lazar, R. (1964). Searching for novel targets. *Perceptual and Motor Skills, 19,* 427 – 432.

Neumann, O. (1990). Action-related aspects of visual selective attention. In O. Neumann & W. Prinz (Eds.), *Relations between perception and action: Current approaches.* Berlin: Springer.

Neumann, O., & Prinz, W. (1987). Kognitive Antezedentien bei Willkürhandlungen. In H. Heckhausen, P.M. Gollwitzer & F.E. Weinert (Eds.), *Jenseits des Rubikon.* Berlin, Heidelberg: Springer.

Neumann, O., van der Heijden, A.H.C., & Allport, D.A. (1986). Visual selective attention: Introductory remarks. In O. Neumann, A.H.C. van der Heijden & D.A. Allport (Eds.), *Visual selective attention* (pp. 185 – 188). (*Psychological Research, 48*)

Norman, D.A. (1968). Toward a theory of memory and attention. *Psychological Review, 75,* 522 – 536.

Norman, D.A. (1969). *Memory and attention.* New York: Wiley.

Prinz, W. (1977). Memory control of visual search. In S. Dornic (Ed.), *Attention and Performance VI* (pp. 441 – 462). Hillsdale, NJ: Erlbaum.

Prinz, W. (1979). Integration of information in visual search. *Quarterly Journal of Experimental Psychology, 31,* 287 – 304.

Prinz, W. (1986). Continuous selection. *Psychological Research, 48,* 231 – 238.

Prinz, W. (1983). *Wahrnehmung und Tätigkeitssteuerung.* Berlin: Springer.

Prinz, W., & Nattkemper, D. (1987). *Integrating nontarget information in continuous search.* Report No. 145 of the research group on Perception and Action, Center for interdisciplinary Research, University of Bielefeld, Bielefeld, F.R.G.

Prinz, W., & Prinz, U. (1985). Verarbeitung redundanter Zeichensequenzen durch Kinder im Grundschulalter. *Zeitschrift für Entwicklungspsychologie und Pädagogische Psychologie, 27,* 210 – 222.

Prinz, W., Tweer, R., & Feige, R. (1974). Context control of search behavior: Evidence from a 'hurdling' technique. *Acta Psychologica, 38,* 73 – 80.

Rohrbaugh, J.W. (1984). The orienting reflex: Performance and central nervous system manifestations. In R. Parasuraman & D.R. Davies (Eds.), *Varieties of attention* (pp. 323 – 373). Orlando, FL: Academic Press.

Sokolov, E.N. (1963a). *Perception and the conditioned reflex.* New York: Pergamon Press.

Sokolov, E.N. (1963b). Higher nervous functions: The orienting reflex. *Annual Review of Physiology, 25,* 545 – 580.

Velden, M. (1978). Some necessary revisions of the neuronal model concept of the orienting response. *Psychophysiology, 15,* 181 – 185.

Yates, J. (1985). The content of awareness is a model of the world. *Psychological Review, 92,* 249 – 284.

Psychophysical Explorations of Mental Structures
Edited by H.-G. Geissler
in collaboration with M.H. Müller and W. Prinz
© 1990 by Hogrefe & Huber Publishers

Chapter 36

Specific and Nonspecific Effects of Activation

*Georg Mandler, Carmen Overson
and Yoshio Nakamura
Center for Human Information Processing
University of California
San Diego, U.S.A.*

Prior activation of mental events (such as representation of words) leads to enhanced perception, comprehension, and production of the activated material. This phenomenon has been generally described as "priming." In this paper we present evidence for generalized priming effects in two contexts. First, we deal with specific priming in which a previously existing representation is directly or indirectly activated. We show parallel effects in two tasks: recognition and word stem completion. Second, we present a new phenomenon — nonspecific priming — which involves the establishment and activation of meaningless material which can then be related to any relevant dimension. The occurrence of automatic (activation dependent) priming is related to the nonconscious production of "memorial" material.

The distinction between deliberate (conscious) and automatic (nonconscious) access to memorial material has become increasingly important (see Mandler, 1989, for an overview). We present a further exploration of the mechanisms involved in two automatic phenomena within the context of dual process theory. Since its inception, dual process theory has been applied to a variety of different phenomena in a number of different guises. The general hypothesis (cf. Mandler, 1979) is that there are two processes that address the representation of an event: intra-event activation or integration which affects the relation among the features of the event, and inter-event elaboration which reflects relations between the event representation and other mental contents. The distinction has been variously called one between perceptual and conceptual information, between intra-item and extra-item information, and between event information and context information (cf. Mandler, 1980). It is generally assumed that activation/integration may have as one of its consequences an increase in phenomenal familiarity. Since its original development as an explanation of recognition phenomena (Mandler, Pearlstone, & Koopmans, 1969; Juola et al., 1971), dual process theory has been useful in a variety of other contexts, for example in connectionist theory (Hinton, 1981), and in understanding the accessibility of items due to "response bias."

As the term is generally understood, the process underlying priming phenomena can usually be ascribed to activation. Activation and integration are automatic processes that occur whenever the representation of an event (in this case a word) is accessed. Activation boosts the level of activation of all the constituent features of the event, and integration follows automatically as the previously established connections among the features lead to further selective activation of the specific features of the item and thus "integrate" and isolate the specific event that is activated. In Mandler (1980) we indicated that such processes may be found in a variety of different tasks. Specifically we suggested that activation affects the familiarity phenomenon in recognition as well as word priming in the stem completion task, where subjects are given the initial letters of a target word and required to complete the stem with the first word that comes to mind. Subjective experiences of familiarity occur in recognition in the absence of semantic search processes. Similarly, word priming in the completion task occurs in the absence of semantic processing both in normal subjects and in anterograde amnesic patients (Mandler, 1980; Graf, Mandler, & Haden, 1982; Graf, Squire & Mandler, 1984). In Mandler, Graf and Kraft (1986) we showed that direct activation, i.e., when a word is presented and later tested for recognition and for stem completion, produced high hit rates and completion rates for the targets. Indirect activation, where phonologically and semantically related items but not the target word itself are primed, produced short term effects in both priming and recognition for phonologically related items, but only recognition effects for semantically (categorically) related items. In a subsequent study (Overson & Mandler, 1987), where the target items and the indirect activation were generated in connected contexts (brief stories and rhymes), we found indirect activation of word completion for both phonologically and semantically related targets.

Specific Activation in Recognition and Word Priming

The present experiments are designed for a more sensitive exploration of the generalized role of activation in recognition and word priming. We extend our work on indirect activation and relate it to reaction time in both recognition and wordpriming. Despite wide uses of the stem completion task (Warrington

& Weiskrantz, 1970), and the general impression that it involves fast and automatic responding, no systematic data are available on processing times for the task.

The general hypothesis under test is that prior activation of specific target words (direct activation) and of related phonological or semantic contexts (indirect activation) should produce the fastest recognition and completion reaction times (RTs) for direct activation, followed by phonologically related targets, with the semantically related targets showing the slowest RTs. Activation of the target words during presentation makes it more likely that the presentation of a part of the word (the stem) will spread preferentially to the target word rather than other possible completions. When the target word is presented together with rhymes (e.g. chair, hair, tear, bare), then stems that have a possible completion with the rhyme (e.g., STA – – – –) will benefit from the activated phonological unit and produce rhyming targets (stare, stair) rather than other completions (stable, stage). In the case of semantic sets (chair, table, couch, bed), stems that have a possible semantically related completion (e.g., SOF – – – –) will be preferentially activated over other possible completions (sofa, rather than soft, soften). We assume that the phonological rhyming units are activated directly without any further mediation, while semantic representations require more complex representations and activations.

When testing follows immediately upon presentation the effects of activation are automatic, involving no or few search processes that depend on elaborative processing of the target items. We have shown that immediate recognition tests utilize little in the way of search processes; the latter are increasingly useful as time between presentation and testing increases (Mandler, 1980; Mandler, Graf, & Kraft, 1986). Stem completion is unimpaired by limited perceptual processing at input (Graf, Mandler, & Haden, 1982), and also unimpaired in amnesic patients (Graf, Squire, & Mandler, 1984). In both cases, elaborative processes are presumably inhibited, but automatic activation occurs unimpeded. In fact, instructing subjects to produce completions that match the words previously presented significantly impairs stem completion performance (Graf & Mandler, 1984; Overson & Mandler, 1987).

Two experiments were conducted. In Experiment 1 (Lists) subjects were initially presented with a list of word consisting of consecutive sets of words that either rhymed or were conceptually (categorically) related. In Experiment 2 (Passages) subjects read short stories and poems that contained categorically or phonologically related words, respectively. Following the presentation, one group in each experiment was given a recognition test and another group was given the completion test.

In Experiment 1 (Lists) subjects were given 18 sets of consecutive groups of 5 words that either rhymed or were categorically related. For a direct test the target word, which was part of the original set, was included in the test; when indirect activation was tested the target words were not originally presented but were phonologically (rhyming) or semantically related to the presentation set. Table 1 gives a schematic demonstration of the completion test. In this case if SPARROW was presented then the test of SPA – – – – – was a direct test, if it was not presented then it was an indirect test. Subjects were given the three letter stems individually and required to respond quickly with the first word that came to mind to complete the stem. In the recognition test they were given the full words and required to indicate whether they had seen the word before. In both tests distractors unrelated to the presentation set were included.

Table 1. Sample lists of rhymes and categories.

	Rhymes	Categories
presented	Arrow	Eagle
	Narrow	Canary
	Barrow	Robin
	Harrow	Bluebird
Target	SPArrow	

We start with the main question addressed in these experiments: Does activation have parallel effects for both recognition and word priming? The answer is an unqualified yes, as shown by the data in Figure 1. The effect of the four types of item is generally the same for both kinds of tests and both experiments. Theoretically more important is the effect for the three activated item types alone, with direct activation showing the faster reaction times followed by rhyming and then semantic indirect activation. In addition to the statistical analyses of the reaction times, we note the predicted ordering of the Target, Rhyming and Semantic items. The consistency of the ordering of the three primed item types for the four independent groups of subjects is highly significant ($p < .001$).

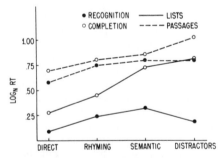

Figure 1. Logarithmic transformations of the reaction times for both stem completion and recognition following List and Passage presentations. The points on the abscissa are for direct target activation, indirect (rhyming and semantic) target activation and new distractors.

Overall we also find faster responses following activation by lists than following activation by passages, and also faster RTs for the recognition test.

The fast reaction times for recognition performance were, of course, to be expected. Recognition involves relatively little response preparation for the yes/no choice, while in the completion test the subjects do not hit the first key of the response until they have the entire completion response ready. However, the difference in response times to the two kinds of tests is not very large. Overall the difference was less than 1 sec, and for the "fast" list experiment the difference between recognition and completion for "correct" (i.e., activated) responses it is only 210 msec. Such a small difference further supports our argument that both of these automatic responses have similar underlying processes.

In previous experiments with the stem completion test we have been successful in leading subjects to believe that the test was unrelated to the preceding presentations. In fact, when subjects have difficulty in recalling the presentation items, instructions to complete the stems with items that first come to mind produce completions identical with the situation where the items can be recalled. However, instructions to produce items that were actually presented shows large decrements compared with the "first comes to mind" instructions (Graf & Mandler, 1984). In an experiment reported in Overson and Mandler (1987) we also found that subjects instructed to give completions that were part of the presentation passages took seven times longer to produce than subjects who gave the first response that came to mind. In the main Overson and Mandler study we tested only for indirect activation and produced significant priming effects. In the present experiments we did, however, for the first time, test direct target and indirect targets in the same experiments. In the case where the semantic categories and the rhyming set have been well encoded (as in the Passages experiment), it is reasonable to assume that some subjects, at least, made the connection between test and presentation and went into a search mode, rather than giving — as instructed — the first response that came to mind.

All of these arguments suggest that the source of the slow responses to the Passages test may be deliberate search processes on the part of some subjects. We examined questionnaires given to subjects at the conclusion of the tests, as well as the individual mean reaction times for the subjects in this experiment and selected 3 out of 12 subjects who had slow RTs as well as questionnaire scores that indicated that they had made the connection between presentation and test. We call the slow subjects "self-instructed" whereas the others are automatic responders. The first test was of the prediction that subjects who had "caught on" were not only slow but also gave fewer correct responses than the subjects who gave the first response that came to mind. The mean percent correct for "automatic" subjects was 28%, for self-instructed subjects it was 23% ($z = 1.27$, $p = .10$). This was true for both tests, for recognition the percentages were 40% and 33%, for completion the percentages were 16% and 12%. The data also show that the difference in response times is primarily due to those responses that were "incorrect", i.e., nontarget completions and "no" responses in recognition. These data suggest that the instigation of search processes, when subjects can make the "connection" between presentation and test produce worse performance as well as slower responses. Responses are particularly slowed when subjects try to recall a presented item, are then unable to find it and give an incorrect response.

Conclusions

Dual process theory postulates two representational processes: activation and elaboration. Activation and the ensuing integration of the representation make the mental event more easily and automatically accessible. Elaboration of a mental event produces, by establishing connections to other mental contents, access to the representation through search and retrieval processes. The experiments reported here addressed in the first instance the similarity between two tasks that draw primarily on item activation: immediate recognition and word priming in the stem completion task. We have shown that both tasks show similar and parallel effects of the direct and indirect activation of target items. These data argue for the generality of dual process theory and the importance of sheer activation in making material automatically accessible. In addition, we found that under conditions where search processes are invoked by the subjects, response times increase significantly and performance tends to suffer. It should be noted, however, that under conditions where the target material is easily accessible, search processes also take more time but also produce better performance (cf. Graf & Mandler, 1984; Overson & Mandler, 1987). The conditions under which automatic access or deliberate search are preferable strategies depends on the degree of activation and the adequacy of elaboration. If activation is high, as is the case shortly after prior presentation, automatic access will be useful and search process may be deleterious; if activation has dissipated and the target material has been well encoded then deliberate search is the preferred mode of access.

The prevailing mode in memory search for the first century after Ebbinghaus has been a stress on deliberate search and retrieval processes, even though Ebbinghaus was well aware of the importance of automatic access to memorial material (see Mandler, 1985). The upsurge of interest in automatic "memories" speaks not only to purely academic interests, but also recognizes the fact that the majority of everyday access to previously encountered material is automatic rather than deliberate, i.e., access is achieved without conscious intervention. Many things come to mind automatically and often unbidden. Immediate recognition and word priming are two experimental counterparts of such everyday occurrences.

Nonspecific Effects of Activation

Studies of the differential and preferential accessibility of higher order information following minimal exposure have used pattern masks and have generally appealed to spreading activation as an explanatory mechanism. On the other hand, an experiment by Kunst–Wilson and Zajonc (1980) employed very short exposures, without a mask, and suggested an entirely different process of direct access to affective information without any cognitive processing.

Kunst-Wilson and Zajonc presented subjects with ten irregular octagons each of which was exposed five times for 1 ms under conditions of lowered illumination and without a mask. In the test phase subjects were presented with ten pairs of octagons for 1 sec each. One member of the pair was new and the other one came from the exposed set. Subjects were required to judge either which of the pair they liked better (or preferred) or which had been shown previously. Overall recognition judgments were close to chance (47% correct), while preference judgments showed a significant preference for previously exposed stimuli (60%). The Kunst-Wilson and Zajonc effect has been replicated and extended, for example by Seamon, Brody, and Kauff (1983) and Bonnano and Stillings (1986). The latter demonstrated that subjects not only showed preference in the absence of recognition for the previously presented shapes, but that they also generated familiarity judgments for the presented stimuli that were equal in magnitude to the preference judgments.

We have explored these effects further in Mandler, Nakamura, and Shebo-Van Zandt (1987). Given that prior exposure can produce both preference and familiarity, we suggested that these effects are not specific to any feature of the stimulus, but depend on the sheer activation of the representation of the meaningless random shapes. Prior exposure generates the representation of the stimuli, and these initially rudimentary representations are further activated by successive presentations. Such activated representations may then apparently be related to any judgment about the stimuli that is stimulus-relevant. The notion of relevance is introduced only to indicate that subjects are unlikely to attempt to relate the activation of the representation to questions about such irrelevant dimensions as, for example, taste or odor. We showed that judgments both of brightness and of darkness are equally facilitated by prior minimal exposures.

The procedure used followed the Kunst-Wilson and Zajonc experiments with minor modifications. Of twenty irregular octagons, ten were randomly assignd to the exposure phase, and ten test pairs were constructed by randomly pairing exposed and unexposed octagons. The octagons were presented for 2 ms, followed by a dark field. The subjects were instructed that during the first part stimuli would be presented in the tachistoscope at durations so brief that they might not actually see what was being presented, but that they were to pay close attention to the flashes. They were then presented with the ten target octagons repeated five times in different random orders. Following the exposure phase, subjects were given the test phase in which pairs of exposed and unexposed (old and new) octagons were presented in the tachistoscope for 1 sec. The procedure was identical for all conditions, except for the test instructions. For the recognition test, subjects were instructed to choose the octagon that they recognized as having seen before. In the preference condition they were asked which shape they liked better; and in the brightness and darkness conditions they were instructed to report which of the two shapes seemed brighter or darker, respectively. Twelve different subjects were tested in each of the four conditions (recognition, preference, brightness, and darkness).

The results in Table 2 show mean percentages for recognition, and for identification of target shapes as preferred to, brighter than, or darker than the unexposed shapes. Recognition and preference results replicate of the Kunst–Wilson and Zajonc experiment. Preference percentages were significantly greater than recognition probabilities. Values for preference, brightness, and darkness judgments are significantly different from the chance recognition results.

Table 2. Mean percentages for four experimental groups.

Recognition	46.7
Preference(Liking)	61.7
Brightness	60.0
Darkness	60.1

The data are unequivocal in showing that judgments of brightness, as well as the opposite judgments of darkness, are generated with the same likelihood as preferences (liking) in the absence of stimulus recognition. We conclude that any relevant dimensions can be related to the activation of the stimulus representation. In contrast to Kunst–Wilson and Zajonc, these experiments do not permit any conclusion of unique, specific affective discriminations. If preferences bias the stimuli toward brightness judgments – as might be argued – they should not equally bias the stimuli toward darkness judgments. In contrast, the results can be reasonably assimiliated within the context of current information processing theory, which stresses the activation of, and subsequent access to underlying representations. No special affective processes need to be invoked. The exposure effect seems to depend on the integrity of the activated but meaningless perceptual pattern which is then related to any dimension of judgment (liking or brightness or darkness) imposed on it.

Summary

We conclude that priming as a function of prior activtion can be relatively easily demonstrated and shown to be a general effect across different kinds of tests when we deal with meaningful stimuli, i.e., that are already well represented and elaborated mental events. On the other hand, we have shown that newly developed representations, i.e., relatively meaningless ones, can produce nonspecific conscious events. In all cases the final product is a conscious content, but the preceding processes are automatic and nonconscious. In contrast, recall and long term recognition, as well as other kinds of retrieval dependent memorial events, are a function of conscious cues and other conscious initiators of search processes.

Acknowledgement. The research of this paper was supported by National Science Foundation grant No. BNS 84–04228.
Correspondence should be addressed to George Mandler, Center for Human Information Processing, University of California, San Diego, La Jolla, CA 92093, U.S.A.

References

Bonnano, G.A., & Stilling, N.A. (1986). Preference, familiarity, and recognition after repeated brief exposures to random geometric shapes. *American Journal of Psychology*, *99*, 403−415.

Graf, P., & Mandler, G. (1984). Activation makes words more accessible, but not necessarily more retrievable. *Journal of Verbal Learning and Verbal Behavior*, *23*, 553−568.

Graf, P., Mandler, G., & Haden, P. (1982). Simulating amnesic symptoms in normal subjects. *Science*, *218*, 1243−1244.

Graf, P., Squire, L.R., & Mandler, G. (1984). The information that amnesic patients do not forget. *Journal of Experimental Psychology: Learning, Memory, and Cognition*, *10*, 164−178.

Hinton, G.E. (1981). Implementing semantic networks in parallel hardware. In G.E. Hinton & J.A. Anderson (Eds.), *Parallel models of associative memory*. Hillsdale, NJ: Erlbaum.

Juola, J.F., Fischler, I., Wood, C.T., & Atkinson, R.C. (1971). Recognition time for information stored in long-term memory. *Perception & Psychophysics*, *10*, 8−14.

Kunst-Wilson, W.R., & Zajonc, R.B. (1980). Affective discrimination of stimuli that cannot be recognized. *Science*, *207*, 557−558.

Mandler, G. (1979). Organization and repetition: Organizational principles with special reference to rote learning. In L.-G. Nilsson (Ed.), *Perspectives on memory research*. Hillsdale, NJ: Erlbaum.

Mandler, G. (1980). Recognizing: The judgment of previous occurrence. *Psychological Review*, *87*, 252−271.

Mandler, G. (1985). From association to structure. *Journal of Experimental Psychology: Learning, Memory, and Cognition*, *11*, 464−468.

Mandler, G. (1989). Memory: Conscious and unconscious. In P.R. Solomon, G.R. Goethals, C.M. Kelley & B.R. Stephens (Eds.), *Memory: Interdisciplinary approaches*. New York: Springer Verlag.

Mandler, G., Graf, P., & Kraft, D. (1986). Activation and elaboration effects in recognition and word priming. *Quarterly Journal of Experimental Psychology*, *38A*, 645−662.

Mandler, G., Nakamura, Y., & Shebo-Van Zandt, B.J. (1987). Non-specific effects of exposure on stimuli that cannot be recognized. *Journal of Experimental Psychology: Learning, Memory, and Cognition*, *13*, 646−648.

Mandler, G., Pearlstone, Z., & Koopmans, H.J. (1969). Effects of organization and semantic similarity on recall and recognition. *Journal of Verbal Learning and Verbal Behavior*, *8*, 410−423.

Overson, C., & Mandler, G. (1987). Indirect word priming in connected semantic and phonological contexts. *Bulletin of the Psychonomic Society*, *25*, 229−232.

Seamon, J.G., Brody, B., & Kauff, D.M. (1983). Affective discrimination of stimuli that are not recognized: II. Effect of delay between study and test. *Bulletin of the Psychonomic Society*, *21*, 187−189.

Warrington, E.K., & Weiskrantz, L. (1970). Amnesia: Consolidation or retrieval? *Nature*, *228*, 628−630.

Psychophysical Explorations of Mental Structures
Edited by H.-G. Geissler
in collaboration with M.H. Müller and W. Prinz
© 1990 by Hogrefe & Huber Publishers

Chapter 37

Just Noticeable Impossible Patterns: An Exploration of the Capacities and Shortcomings of Perception

Emanuel Leeuwenberg
Institute for Cognition Research
and Information Technology (NICI)
University of Nijmegen, Netherlands
and
Johan Wagemans
Laboratory for Experimental Psychology
University of Leuven, Belgium

Propositions may be consistent or inconsistent with each other. The conscious verification of their (in)consistency usually occurs in successive steps, i.e., testing each proposition one by one. Also, a visual pattern can be consistent or inconsistent, i.e., possible or impossible. The conscious verification of its (in)consistency ususally occurs in successive stages too. The question is, however: does there exist another kind of (in)consistency–verification of visual patterns, namely, on a specific perceptual level, as distinct from a conscious level of slow reasonning. Our answer is yes. We believe that the perceptual verification takes many pattern parts into account in parallel, although its response is less decisive than a conscious response. Some considerations in favour of this view are the following:

In an objective sense, visual patterns are always possible. Several authors (Gillam, 1979; Pomerantz & Kubovy, 1981) show patterns that are clearly possible in three dimensions, but perceived as impossible. Kulpa (1983) demonstrates that almost all patterns perceived as impossible are possible in 3-D. In fact, all patterns are possible in two dimensions. Thus, only in a perceptual sense patterns might be impossible. What does this mean?

It is widely accepted that an impossible pattern is preferably organized in local parts that are incoherent in space, in the way they are interpreted (Kulpa 1983; Hochberg 1981; Pomerantz & Kubovy 1981). We share this opinion, but it implies that a rapid perceptual assessment of (in)consistency is not a primary goal of perception, but rather a consequence of processes involved in establishing perceptual preferences. Therefore, we will now consider these preference processes for understanding the perceptual sensitivity for pattern (in)consistencies. With respect to perceptual preferences, two views can be distinguished:

1. The preference for a specific pattern interpretation is based on decision rules, guided by local cues. All other alternative interpretations of a pattern are not taken into account. This view is more or less shared by Kanizsa (1979,1985), Pomerantz and Kubovy (1986) and Biederman (1987).

2. The perceptual system considers all possible interpretations. The preference of one interpretation of a pattern depends not only on the "quality" of this interpretation itself, but also on the qualities of alternative interpretations of the pattern (Gregory 1970, 1974, 1981). According to a more specific view, the "quality" of an interpretation is determined by its simplicity (Koffka, 1962; Hochberg & McAlisther, 1953; Kulpa, 1983; Buffart, Leeuwenberg & Restle, 1981; Leeuwenberg & Boselie, 1988). This view is in line with the "descriptive minimum-principle."

The second opinion, that seems to us more plausible for many reasons, is supported by explanations of impossible patterns by Boselie and Leeuwenberg (1986). Several of their demonstrations show that the local-"impossible"-interpretations of patterns are more simple (less information load) than the global-"possible"-interpretations. This obtains also for Figure 1A. The "impossible" interpretation of this figure is presumably slightly more simple than the "possible" interpretation. At first sight, Figure 1A is interpreted as impossible. Figure 1B and 1C are obviously possible variants of Figure 1A. However, after prolonged inspection, a more complex, but also more consistent interpretation of Figure 1A emerges in a faint and attenuated way (Van Leeuwen, Buffart & van der Vegt, 1988). This interpretation is depicted in Figure 1A', showing an elevation of the central rectangle and a slight displacement of this rectangle to the right. Thus the dominant local-"impossible"-interpretation, as well as the global-"possible"-interpretation play a role in perception. Probably the balance of the complexities of the two interpretations determines the preference for one above the other.

Thus, if the assessment of pattern (in)consistency depends on perceptual preference processes, and the latter depend on the balance of various pattern interpretations, the perceptual assessment of pattern (in)consistency depends indirectly on the balance of pattern interpretations. However, these interpretations, especially the global ones, account for all parts of a pattern. Therefore, the establishment of pattern (in)consistency will probably not occur in serial

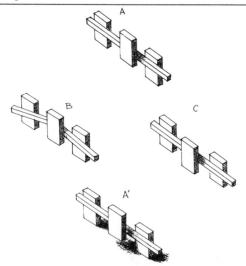

Figure 1. As opposed to Figure B and C, Figure A appears impossible at first sight. The impossibility of the pattern is not a geometric issue, but a perceptual one (Kulpa, 1983). The conflict in Figure A can be solved by seeing its middle rectangle as displaced and tilted. This solution is suggested by Figure A'.

Figure 2. Detail of a painting by Gerard Terborg. Pay attention to the complexity of the pleats and wrinkles of the dress. To calculate the consistency of such a complex pattern in a rational, "reasoninglike" manner would require a fair amount of processing time.

steps, but rather in a holistic way, i.e., many pattern parts are taken into account in parallel. Inspection of Figure 2, a painting of Gerard Terborg, may support this tentative conclusion: a single glance suffices to know that this picture is rather consistent in 3–D. Are we tracing this picture in a serial way, testing (in)consistencies? In our view, we do not. However, the immediate impression that this picture is consistent, does not prove that all parts are taken into account together. We can not exclude that the immediate impression is based on a parallel assessment of many isolated local cues for (in)consistencies. Therefore, we will set up experiments with possible and impossible patterns, that — hopefully — do not contain local cues for (in)consistencies. We will verify our hypothesis that, on a perceptual level, consistencies and "inconsistencies" in patterns are rapidly noticed accounting for many pattern parts in parallel.

(Im)Possible Patterns

The subjects' task is to judge whether a briefly presented complex pattern is possible or not. Figure 3 shows some of the patterns used in the experiments. Figures 3A and C are possible, whereas 3B and D are impossible. The (im)possibility of the figures can be checked by tracing the pattern. When the amount of forward bars equals the number of bars going backwards, the figure is possible, otherwise it is impossible. There are two levels of inconsistency,

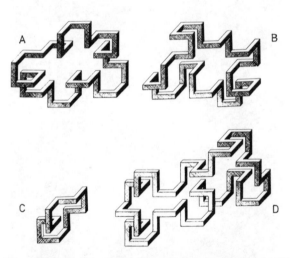

Figure 3. Some possible and impossible figures used in the experiments. (A) A possible figure consisting of 34 elements. (B) A pattern consisting of 34 elements, impossible because of a difference between forward and backward elements (namely, two). (C) A possible pattern consisting of 12 elements. This is the smallest experimental pattern. (D) The largest impossible pattern. It comprises an inconsistency level of four elements.

the difference between forwards and backwards being either two or four bars (see figure 3B and D, respectively). The complexity of the patterns increases with the number of bars ranging from 12 to 50 (see figures 3C and D, respectively).

A crucial characteristic of the figures is that they do not contain any local cues. This means, that the whole pattern must be scanned to detect its (im)possibility. Regardless of the exact point of departure of the tracing, the last part before coming back to the starting point reveals the (im)possibility of the pattern. In other words, when an arbitrary small part of the figure is occluded, one cannot exactly tell whether the pattern is possible or not.

Furthermore, attention has been paid to the regularity of the figures. In the most cases, the patterns show a typical sequence of variations in three-dimensional space (first height, then width, then depth, etc.). This means, that the amount of subsequent bars in one surface plane is often two, sometimes three or four. Both possible and impossible patterns are matched with respect to this particular feature. This is done in order to prevent irregularity being a cue for the figure's impossibility.

Presentation time of the figures is kept short in order to prevent subjects from calculating the figure's (im)possibility. Whether calculation was indeed prevented, should be revealed by the relation between the patterns' complexity and performance: "Calculation" processes should lead to more accurate results for simple patterns as compared to the more complex ones. The absence of such a relation between the patterns' complexity and the score level would support the parallel character of the information processing during the task. A cognitive problem solving strategy would certainly create a correlation between complexity and performance. A bright flash is used to mask the afterimage in order to control the presentation time of the figures.

Experiment 1

Material. The stimulus material consisted of three sets of 40 complex patterns. Each set contained 20 possible and 20 impossible patterns. Set 1 and set 2 were parallel sets consisting of different (im)possible figures. Set 1' consisted of mirror images of Set 1 patterns. All sets comprised 15 patterns with two, and five figures with four inconsistencies, respectively. The complexity, indicated by the number of bar-elements, ranged from 12, 14, 16, etc. up to 50 in each set. The patterns were copied on slides, resulting in dark figures against a bright background. Two projectors were used. The first one projected the figures under a visual angle of 12 degrees. The second one contained no slides, and, by producing bright flashes, served for masking the subject's afterimage. The presentation time of the figures was 1.5 seconds. This is very short, taking into consideration that trained subjects (such as the authors) need significantly more time to judge the figures adequately (see Experiment 4). The presentation time of the mask was 300 ms, the ISI was 200 ms.

Subjects. 54 Students of the University of Nijmegen participated in the experiment. They were all unfamiliar with the experimental figures.

Conditions. All subjects ran two series, each consisting of presentations of 20 possible and 20 impossible figures. Subjects were randomly divided into 3 experimental conditions which only differed with respect to the second series. Subjects ran two identical series of 40 possible and impossible figures in exactly the same order of presentation (1–1, Condition A). In Condition B, two series were presented, the second one consisting of the same set of patterns as in the first series shown in the same order of presentation, but this time mirrored (1–1'). Condition C comprised two different but parallel series (1–2) with the same order of complexity and possible–impossible alternations (e.g., first figure: 32 elements and impossible, shortly noted as 32 I, second figure: 24 elements and possible, noted as 24 P). Each condition was run by 18 subjects.

Procedure. Subjects entered the experimental room and took a seat in front of the projection screen. They were told what was meant with possible and impossible figures (in terms of the possibility to construct them with real world blocks). An example of each category was shown on a carton (the examples were not used in the experimental series). When the subjects understood the difference, they were informed that the figures used in the experiment would more complex and presented for a very short time. Subjects were instructed to rely on their intuition and to give an answer in all cases, even when they thought they had not seen the (im)possibility of the figure. Lights were dimmed and the examples were projected on the screen, in order to give an impression of the short presentation time, and to exercise the procedure of encircling the answers on a response-sheet. Following the examples, the first series of 40 experimental figures was successively presented. The whole procedure, including the instruction and the examples took about eight or nine minutes. After a short break of four or five minutes, the second series was run, without informing the subjects whether the figures were the same or different. Answers had to be filled in on a response-sheet.

Table 1. Means and standard deviations of the number of correct answers in Experiment 1 (1.5 s).

	Series		
Conditions	First Series	Second Series	Total
Condition A (1−1; n=18)	X̄=21.2778 SD=3.7855	X̄=20.6667 SD=3.0098	X̄=20.9722* SD=3.3847
Condition B (1−1'; n=18)	X̄=21.2778 SD=3.0833	X̄=21.0556 SD=2.7326	X̄=21.1667* SD=2.8735
Condition C (1−2; n=18)	X̄=19.7778 SD=2.8192	X̄=20.3333 SD=3.6622	X̄=20.0556 SD=3.2333
Total	X̄=20.7778* SD=3.2718	X̄=20.6852 SD=3.1131	X̄=20.7315** SD=3.1788

* *p<.05*
** *p<.01*

Results

The analysis of results is very straightforward. All correct answers are counted for each subject. These scores are averaged for each condition. Means and standard deviations can be found in Table 1. To evaluate these results, one has to compare them with chance–level, which is 20 in this case, because a series contains 20 possible and 20 impossible figures. The most important result is that human perceivers seem to be susceptible to small inconsistencies of complex patterns presented within a time as short as 1,5 s. The mean for the

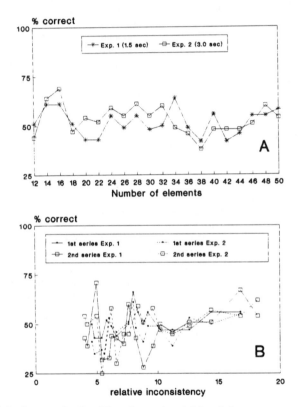

Figure 4. Performance levels of Experiments 1 and 2 in relation to pattern complexity. (A) Pattern complexity (number of elements). (B) Relative inconsistency (difference between the number of forward and the number of backward bars divided by the total number of bars).

first series (averaged over conditions) is 20.8 and differs significantly from chance–level ($t = 1.7469$, $d.f. = 53$, $p < 0.05$). One–tailed tests are used, because our prediction is that subjects will do better than chance. Performance does not improve in the second series. Thus, no learning effect is found. This can be interpreted as evidence for the absence of local cues. This interpretation is corroborated by the fact that the conditions do not differ significantly. It is a remarkable fact that even identical figures, in an identical order, do not yield better results. The global mean for the two series together (20.7) is significantly different from chance ($t = 2.3915$, $d.f. = 107$, $p < 0.01$).

In Figure 4 the scores are represented in relation to the complexity of the patterns. Figure 4A shows the results in relation to the number of bars, whereas figure 4B contains the score levels as plotted against the relative inconsistency of the figures (inconsistency level divided by the total number of bars). Trend analyses do not yield significant results. There is no correlation between complexity of the figures and accuracy of their perception. Again, this can be taken as evidence for the perceptual character of the discernment of the patterns' (im)possibility. The process involved does not seem to be a serial one, with each element of the visual input requiring a certain amount of information processing. Although the effect is rather faint (but statistically significant!), we considered it interesting enough to undertake some further explorations.

Experiment 2

Subjects. Subjects were 30 students of the University of Nijmegen. They had not participated in the previous experiment and were not familiar with the complex patterns.

Procedure. The procedure was the same as in Experiment 1, except for two differences. First, performance time was increased to 3 seconds in order to raise the mean score level, that was rather low in Experiment 1. Second, a third series of 40 figures was added to establish enhanced learning effects.

Conditions. Condition A consisted of three identical series of figures in exactly the same order of presentation (1-1-1). Condition B contained a first series of 40 figures, a second series of mirrored Set 1 patterns, and a third, parallel, series, all with a same order of complexity and possible–impossible variations (1-1'-2). Condition C is similar to Condition B, except that the second and third series are exchanged (1-2-1').

Results

Means and standard deviations are summarized in Table 2. As in Experiment 1, perceivers are capable to detect the (im)possibility of patterns. The general mean (averaged over conditions and series) is 21.5, which is significantly different from chance ($t = 4.2761$, $d.f. = 86$, $p < 0.001$). The mean for Experiment 2 does not diverge from the one found with a presentation time of 1,5 s in Experiment 1. Furthermore, repeated presentations of more figures again do not yield better results, which corroborates our previous statement concerning the inability to learn detecting the (im)possibility of patterns by experience. The question whether the task at hand is a learnable one will be subject of further investigations in Experiment 3.

Table 2. Means and standard deviations of the number of correct answers in Experiment 2 (3 s).

Conditions	First series	Second series	Third series	Total
		Series		
A (1−1−1) (n=10)	$\bar{X}=21.6$ SD=3.2	$\bar{X}=22.3^{*}$ SD=3.0	$\bar{X}=22.5^{*}$ SD=2.6	$\bar{X}=22.08^{**}$ SD=2.91
B (1−1′−2) (n=10)	$\bar{X}=22.6^{**}$ SD=2.7	$\bar{X}=21.6$ SD=4.3	$\bar{X}=22.5^{*}$ SD=3.6	$\bar{X}=22.23^{**}$ SD=3.52
C (1−2−1′) (n=10)	$\bar{X}=20.2$ SD=1.8	$\bar{X}=19.2$ SD=3.9	$\bar{X}=21.4$ SD=2.7	$\bar{X}=20.27$ SD=2.98
Total	$\bar{X}=21.47^{**}$ SD=2.76	$\bar{X}=21.03$ SD=3.89	$\bar{X}=22.08^{**}$ SD=2.99	$\bar{X}=21.50^{**}$ SD=3.25

* $p<.05$
** $p<.01$

The relationship between pattern complexity and performance of the subjects is shown in Figure 4. As in Experiment 1, there is no correlation between the complexity of the patterns and the accuracy of their perception. Again, this is interpreted as evidence against the serial visual information processing. The most important fact about Experiment 2 is the replication of the finding that the human visual system is faintly susceptible to small inconsistencies in complex patterns.

Experiment 3

Method. Ten subjects ran 24 series of 40 figures each (this is a total of 960 patterns!). Experimental sessions were distributed over two or three days, in order to give learning effects the highest chances and to minimize fatigue effects or attention decay. Subjects were free to participate and could themselves choose the distribution of the sessions. The only limitations were, that all sessions had to take place in the course of one week and on more than one day. During the experimental sessions (which maximally took about 1,5 hour), subjects were free to take a break whenever they wanted. Most of the subjects got three or four series of 40 figures non-stop after each other, followed by a short pause of about five minutes, again followed by three or four test series. This sequence was repeated three or four times on two or three different days.

All subjects were students from the University of Nijmegen who had not participated in the previous experiments. They were paid according to standard fees. Presentation time was handled as a between-subjects factor (either 1.5 or 3 seconds, N=5 for both conditions). Series were randomly chosen out of four possibilities (1, 1′, 2, 2′). The two presentation orders were used at random. Therefore, each subject got about three times the same figures in exactly the same order of presentation.

Results

Global means (averaged over subjects and series) are 20.13 and 20.59 for 1,5 and 3 seconds presentation time, respectively. Only the second mean differs from chance level ($t=2.3729$, $d.f.=119$, $p<0.01$). When the results for the 1.5 sec presentation time are pooled with the ones from Experiment 1, they reach significance ($\overline{X}=20.42$, $SD=3.1367$, $t=2.0059$, $d.f.=227$, $p<0.05$). Most important about these data is, first, that they are not better than after only two or three series of 40 figures and, secondly, that there is no serial effect when the data are ordered as subsequent series of 40 figures. The latter results are viewed as clear evidence against any improvement due to learning of the perceptual processes involved in the task at hand. Even after presentation of 960 figures their (im)possibility is by no means detected better than after the first presentation. In our view, this result evidences that the patterns do not contain (in)consistency cues to which subjects can become sensitive.

The experiments so far indicate that the human visual system is susceptible to small inconsistencies in complex patterns. This is taken as evidence for the large amount of information that can be taken into account. That we are dealing with perception as such is obvious for several reasons. First, our subjects were not aware of the figures' (im)possibility, second, they made no use of a serial strategy, and, third, their results did not improve by experience. Experiment 4 is intended to find out how (in)consistencies in patterns are established on a conscious level of cognitive processing.

Experiment 4

Method. Subjects (n=12) were again students of the University of Nijmegen, which had not yet participated in this series of experiments. The same figures as in the previous experiments were used, but, contrary to the former experiments, presentation time of the figures is under the subjects' own control. After the subjects were given the examples on the carton, they were instructed to judge the figures as fast and accurately as possible. It was stressed that both speed and accuracy are important. The subjects then got a response panel that was connected with the slide-projector. When subjects pressed the button, a figure appeared on the screen. As long as the button was held pressed, the projection lasted; when the pressure on the button diminished in a significant degree, the figure disappeared. In this way, the subjects were able to determine how long they wanted to view the figures before deciding upon their (im)possibility. The procedure was explained to the subjects and when they were supposed to understand, the same examples were shown again, but now by slide-projection. No subject ever experienced difficulties with the procedure. After the presentation of each figure, the answer and the presentation time were registered. An experimental session consisted of one single series of 40 patterns and lasted for about twenty minutes (instructions and examples included).

Results

The first surprising finding concerns the low score level ($\overline{X} = 23.33$, $SD = 6.4432$, $t = 2.0018$, $d.f. = 64$, $p < 0.05$). The average presentation time is 15.33 s. Notice that the level of significance of Experiment 1 is similar, but that the presentation time (1.5 sec) is ten times smaller than that of Experiment 4. A first, rather straightforward conclusion from these findings is that the information processing on a more conscious level is rather low and slow in comparison to that on a perceptual level.

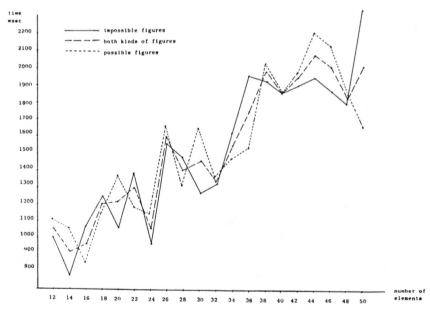

Figure 5. Presentation time (as chosen by the subjects) in relation to complexity of the figures (Experiment 4).

A qualitative analysis provides another interesting finding. When asked for the strategy that subjects eventually used, eight out of twelve said they had none. The performance of these eight subjects is remarkably worse

($\overline{X}$=20.125, SD=2.8504) than the general average and is not significantly different from the perceptual performance. These subjects watch the figures for 13.56 s. The other four subjects applied a stragegy and reach considerably better scores (X=30.75, SD=5.62) but take still more time (18.87, sec).

The relation between the complexity of the patterns and the time required to judge their (im)possibility is shown in Figure 5, making obvious that complex figures need more processing time. Statistical tests between the first and the last ten patterns (ordered according to complexity) reveal significant differences for both possible and impossible figures (see Table 3). In sum, it

Table 3. Analysis of differences between pairs which gives detailed evidence about a linear relation between reaction times and complexity of the patterns.

	Differences		
Figures	First two vs. last two	First four vs. last four	First half vs. last half
Impossible	$t=3.5132^{**}$ df=46	$t=4.1076^{**}$ df=94	$t=4.6962^{**}$ df=238
Possible	$t=2.3473^{*}$ df=46	$t=3.8219^{**}$ df=94	$t=3.8637^{**}$ df=238
Both kinds	$t=4.2360^{**}$ df=94	$t=5.6316^{**}$ df=190	$t=5.9465^{**}$ df=478

* $p<.05$
** $p<.01$

can be concluded that the cognitive processing required for consciously checking upon the (im)possibility of the complex patterns is rather low, slow and serial, but capable of dramatic improvement.

Discussion

The first three experiments indicate that the human visual system is susceptible to small insonsistencies in complex patterns. The effect, although actually faint and probably hardly convincing, proves to be significant. Besides, the perceptual performance is only slightly worse than the reasoning performance (about two times) although the stimulus exposure times in the perceptual experiments were much smaller (about ten times) than the exposure times in the conscious judgment experiment.

In effect, our main goal has been to show that the perceptual system accounts for many pattern parts simultaneously. Whether this goal is reached, depends on whether the patterns lack isolated cues for pattern (in)consistencies. We have done all effort to avoid such cues. In the construction of the patterns we have taken care that forward or backward moves of a pattern are not related with up-down or left-right moves of a pattern. An additional measure to exclude possible global cues is the use of mirror patterns in the experiments. Even after the construction of the patterns many single features have been tested, but none them appeared to be related with pattern (in)consistency. The lack of any learning effect in the perception experiments supports this conclusion.

We found, however, a complex cue for pattern inconsistency, namely the number of uninterrupted forward bars minus the number of uninterrupted backward bars. (Notice that a series of forward bars can be interrupted by backward bars.) This cue predicts about 60 per cent of the pattern (in)consistencies if used in an optimal way. Furthermore, the responses are equally well related with this cue as with pattern (in)consistency (no significant difference). Thus this cue can be regarded as equivalent with pattern (in)consistency, i.e., it might have been a subjective (in)consistency concept for the subjects in the experiments. On the other hand, the establishment of this cue requires at least as much effort as the establishment of the pattern (in)consistency. This opinion is based on our personal experience with specifying the complex cue on a conscious level. In our view, the presence of this complex cue does hardly tone down our conclusion that perception accounts for many pattern parts in parallel.

Summary

An attempt is made to explore the visual system's ability to distinguish possible from impossible patterns by means of parallel processing. Complex patterns were designed consisting of chains of orthogonal bar–elements. Half of the figures are possible, half of them impossible. The subjects' task is to judge whether each of the patterns is possible or not. Exposure time is held too short for judging on a conscious, rational level. Yet, the data reveal a significant but faint susceptibility to the (in)consistencies of the complex patterns. Care is taken to prevent that the (im)possibility of the patterns can be detected on the basis of local cues. The presence of a hidden local cue would presumably be revealed by a learning effect. However, such a learning effect is not found, not even after many repeated trials. Furthermore, no relationship is found between the complexity of the patterns and the score level. Both obsevations support that the perceptual system accounts for many pattern parts in parallel and reduces the plausibility that subjects have made use of a serial computational strategy. The perceptual susceptibility to small inconsistencies in complex patterns gives rise to notice some differences between perceptual and cognitive information processes.

Correspondence should be addressed to Emanuel Leeuwenberg, Institute for Cognition Research and Information Technology (NICI), Montessorilaan 3, P.O. Box 9104, 6500 HE Nijmegen, The Netherlands.

References

Biederman, J. (1987). Recognition by components: A theory of human image understanding. *Psychological Review, 94*, 115−147.

Boselie, F., & Leeuwenberg, E. (1986). A test of the mimimum principle requires a perceptual code system. *Perception, 15*, 331−354.

Buffart, H., Leeuwenberg, E., & Restle, F. (1981). Coding theory of visual pattern completion. *Journal of Experimental Psychology: Human Perception and Performance, 7*, 241−274.

Gillam, B. (1979). Even a possible figure can look impossible! *Perception, 8*, 229−232.

Gregory, R.L. (1970). *The intelligent eye*. New York: McGrawHill.

Gregory, R.L. (1974). Choosing a paradigm for perception. In E.C. Carterette & M.P. Friedman (Eds.), *Handbook of Perception, Vol. 1* (pp. 255−283). New York: Academic Press.

Gregory, R.L. (1981). *Mind in science: A history of explanations in psychology and physics*. London: Weidenfeld and Nicolson.

Hochberg, J.E. (1973). *Perception* (2nd edition). Englewood-Cliffs, N.J.: Prentice-Hall.

Hochberg, J.E, (1981). On cognition in perception: Perceptual coupling and unconscious inference. *Cognition, 10*, 127−134.

Hochberg, J., & McAlister, E. (1953). A quantitative approach to figural goodness. *Journal of Experimental Psychology, 46*, 361−364.

Kanizsa, G. (1979). *Organization in vision*. New York: Praeger.

Kanizsa, G. (1985). Seeing and thinking. *Acta Psychologica, 59*, 23−33.

Kanizsa, G., & Gerbino, W. (1982). A modal completion: Seeing or thinking? In J. Beck (Ed.), *Organization and representation in perception* (pp. 167−190). Hillsdale, NJ: Erlbaum.

Koffka, K. (1962). *Principles of Gestaltpsychology* (5th edition). London: Routledge & Kegan Paul.

Kulpa, Z. (1983). Are impossible figures possible? *Signal Processing, 5*, 201−220.

Leeuwenberg, E., & Boselie, F. (1988). Against the likelihood principle in visual form perception. *Psychological Review, 95*, 485−491.

Peterson, M.A., & Hochberg, J. (1983). Opposed-set measurement procedure: A quantitative analysis of the role of local cues and intention in form perception. *Journal of Experimental Psychology: Human Perception and Performance, 9*, 183−193.

Pomerantz, J., & Kubovy, M., (1981). Perceptual organization: An overview. In M. Kubovy & J. Pomerantz (Eds.), *Perceptual Organization* (pp. 423−456). Hillsdale, NJ: Erlbaum.

Pomerantz, J., & Kubovy, M., (1986). Theoretical approaches to perceptual organization. In K. Boff, L. Kaufman & J. Thomas (Eds.), *Handbook of Perception and Human Performance, Vol. 2* (pp. 1−46). New York: Wiley.

Rock, I., (1977). In defense of unconscious inference. In W. Epstein (Ed.), *Stability and constancy in visual perception: Mechanisms and processes* (pp. 321−373). New York: Wiley.

Rock I., (1985). Perception and knowledge. *Acta Psychologica, 59*, 3−22.

Van Leeuwen, C., Buffart, H., & Van der Vegt, J. (1988). Sequence influence on the organization of meaningless serial stimuli: Economy after all. *Journal of Experimental Psychology: Human Perception and Performance, 14*, 481−502.

Psychophysical Explorations of Mental Structures
Edited by H.-G. Geissler
in collaboration with M.H. Müller and W. Prinz
© 1990 by Hogrefe & Huber Publishers

Chapter 38

"Judgment" vs. "Response":
A General Problem and Some
Experimental Illustrations

Odmar Neumann and Jochen Müsseler
Abteilung Psychologie, Universität Bielefeld
Bielefeld, F.R.G.

Sometimes a theoretical problem becomes apparent when two different research traditions meet within the same empirical field of investigation. The meeting ground that we are concerned with in this paper is visual backward masking. The two experimental traditions are sensory psychophysics and information processing research. The problem that their encounter elucidates –or at least one of the problems that it sheds light upon – regards the concepts of "judgment" and "response".

First we describe the two research traditions, one of which was initiated under the direct influence of Gustav Theodor Fechner. Next we discuss some possible conceptualizations of the relationship between judgment-based and response-based research into visual backward masking. Finally, we present some data that suggest one particular view of this relationship, viz. that they represent mutually complementary, but not necessarily converging, operationalizations of backward masking.

Judgment–Based Research on Backward Masking

The concept of judgment is central to Fechner's psychophysics. At the beginning of chapter 8 of the "Elemente der Psychophysik", Fechner (1860/ 1964) discusses which kinds of measurement are required by psychophysics, and then goes on to say:

"*Die Ausführung des Masses auf Grund dieser Bestimmungen setzt voraus, dass wir die Gleichheit von Empfindungen und Empfindungsunterschieden unter verschiedenen Umständen wirklich genau zu beurtheilen und zu constatiren vermögen*" (Putting into practice the measure(ment) on the basis of these designations presupposes that we are indeed able to exactly judge and state the equality of sensations and of differences between sensations under various circumstances). (Fechner, 1860, p.70)

Thus, the subject in a Fechnerian experiment had the double task of first observing his sensations (introspection) and second of judging them (making an introspection–based decision).

Research on visual masking began within this methodological framework. The first masking experiment was published only eight years after Fechner's "Elemente der Psychophysik". The author was Sigmund Exner, then a medical student in the laboratory of Herrmann von Helmholtz (Exner, 1868). Later on, Exner became a professor of physiology himself, and still later his career led him into the Austrio–Hungarian Ministry of Education at Vienna, where he was one of the favorite targets of attacks by Karl Kraus (e.g. Kraus, 1900, 1901, 1903, 1907).

As Henri Piéron (1914) has noted, Exner was probably influenced by Fechner's book when he proposed a version of the logarithmic law to account for his data: According to Exner, if stimulus intensity grows in geometric progression, then the time needed for the sensation to reach its maximum (*Maximalzeit*) will grow in arithmetic progression. This possible influence of Fechner on Exner's theorizing is interesting, but more relevant to our present topic is Fechner's influence on Exner's method.

Exner worked with a very cleverly constructed and very precise tachistoscope, in which he could present a lighted semi–disk, followed by a lighted complete disk, followed by a dark interval. Using exposure durations between 14.5 and 19.3 msec for the first stimulus (in those days measurement was to the tenth of a millisecond!), Exner found that this stimulus became invisible when the second stimulus had a minimum duration of between 118.8 and 287.3 msec, depending on luminance.

Exner did not use the term "masking" for this effect. In fact he did not recognize that the second stimulus interfered with the perception of the first. (This was realized only almost half a century later by Exner's student Rudolf Stigler [Stigler, 1910]). Exner's interpretation was that the apparent disappearance of the first stimulus was due to the time course of visual sensations. In this he was wrong, but he had discovered visual backward masking.

He had discovered it by a strict application of Fechnerian methodology. By means of what was subsequently called the ascending and descending method of limits, Exner determined the mask durations at which the test stimulus became just invisible or just visible. (Incidentally, Fechner [1860/1964] himself did not use the term "method of limits." His name for this method was "Methode des ebenmerklichen Unterschieds" [method of the just noticeable difference]).

Exner's work was at the beginning of a research tradition that has been continued until the present. The psychophysical style of investigating visual backward masking was taken up and further developed by researchers such as Stigler (1910), Piéron (1914), Fry (1934), Werner (1935) and Alpern (1953) and is still flourishing (e.g. Reeves, 1982; for a review see Breitmeyer, 1984). The methodological characteristics of this line of research have remained remarkably uniform since the pioneer work of Sigmund Exner: A very precise control of stimulus parameters (in modern research with the help of devices such as an artificial pupil and a Maxwellian view); a small number of highly trained observers, usually including the experimenter himself; and careful judgments by these observers that provide the raw data for constructing, e.g., threshold functions.

Response-Based Research on Visual Backward Masking

Almost a century after Exner's discovery, visual backward masking was rediscovered within the research context of what was to become a powerful and influential movement, "Information Processing Psychology." Both George Sperling in his dissertation (Sperling, 1960) and Averbach and Coriell in independent work that was published one year later (Averbach & Coriell, 1961) were interested in the processing of briefly presented letter sequences.

Let us have a look at the work of Averbach and Coriell (1961). They were among the first investigators that used a television monitor to present their stimuli, two rows of 8 letters each. The subject's task was to report one of these letters, designated by a cuing stimulus that was either a bar marker or a circle indicator and that appeared at various temporal positions before or after the letter array. One of their discoveries was that the circle indicator reduced performance at certain delays, particularly around 100 msec; i.e. the number of letters reported correctly was much less than with the bar marker. Thus, they had rediscovered visual backward masking and more specifically metacontrast, a variant that had first been described by Stigler (1910).

Since Averbach and Coriell (1961) were unaware of this previous psychophysical research, they had to invent a new name for their masking effect, "erasure". In a way, this renaming was not unjustified, since there are many obvious differences between Averbach and Coriell's method of assessing erasure and the classical backward masking experiment in the tradition of Exner (1868).

The difference that deserves a closer examination in our present context concerns the subject's task and the dependent measure. Averbach and Coriell's subjects neither had to observe nor to judge anything. As the authors put it "The subject's task is to name the letter designated by the marker" (Averbach & Coriell, 1961, p.311). If the subject felt he could not do this − that is, if he was uncertain about the letter's identity −, he had nevertheless to come up with some answer, guessing the letter's identity if necessary.

Thus, Averbach & Coriell's subjects were not asked about their sensations or perceptions, but about the letter that was in fact presented. They were not required to carefully judge introspective evidence, but to be as good as they could in terms of percent correct, using any kind of information that they had at their disposal. They were required to produce a correct response, not to give a valid judgment.

This style of experimentation – using naive subjects, giving them a task that can be assessed objectively, and using a performance score (percent correct and/or response latency) as the dependent measure – has become a standard in present-day investigations of visual backward masking. Although there have been a few attempts in the early days of information processing research on backward masking to use subjective judgments in addition to performance measures (e.g. Liss, 1968; Haber & Standing, 1968), the methodological gap between the two traditions, judgment-based and a response-based research on visual backward masking, is fairly obvious.

Judgment vs. Response

How do the two methods relate? One possible answer is both trivial and unproductive, and therefore, we shall mention it only briefly: Some investigators from both fields would probably argue that their own approach is simply the correct one, whereas the other is outmoded or inadequate. Proponents of objective performance measures tend to view subjective psychophysics as a residual of unscientific introspectionism; whereas researchers who are used to the rigorous standards of psychophysics sometimes feel that putting a naive subject in front of a computer monitor and giving him a task that he is allowed to solve by any strategy that he happens to invent can provide only the crudest kind of data, especially in combination with the less than perfect control of parameters such as stimulus luminance and retinal locus that is typical of this kind of research.

If one does not resort to this kind of methodological solipsism, then there seem to be essentially two further, more interesting, answers to the question of how the two styles of research are related.

First, it might be that they provide converging operations for the same inferred internal process. Perhaps it is one and the same effect of a visual mask that is assessed by psychophysical judgments and by responses in an information-processing task. Possibly it is nothing more than a matter of convenience whether we ask the subject to observe the stimulus display and record his judgment about, say, apparent brightness, or whether we have him perform a letter identification task and record response latency and/or percent correct. Since both methods have their advantages and shortcomings, it would in this event be desirable to use both in conjunction, or at least to combine results from both for theory building.

The alternative possibility is that such a convergence does not exist, or is partial at best. It could be that the conscious representation that a psychophysical judgment refers to and the processing operations whose efficiency shows up in response accuracy and response latency measures are not necessarily correlated. In this case, we would again want to consider both kinds of data. The aim, however, would not be to merge them, but rather to contrast them. Perhaps this will provide us with insights into the functional architecture of the processing system and, more specifically, into the place and function of conscious representations within the system.

The possibility that judgment and response are not necessarily correlated seems indeed plausible, if one takes into account data from fields other than visual backward masking (see Neumann, 1989, for a review). To mention just two examples from the recent literature: Bridgeman, Kirch and Sperling (1981) had their subjects judge the position of a visual target and, in addition, respond manually by pointing to the target. When illusory motion was induced by means of a surrounding frame that jumped back and forth, this had a strong effect on position judgments, but pointing performance remained largely unaffected. Similarly, McLeod, McLaughlin and Nimmo–Smith (1985) have shown that manual performance in hitting a falling object is far superior to visual–coincidence judgments.

In the backward masking literature, dissociations between judgment and response have allegedly been demonstrated under headings such as "subliminal perception", "preconscious processing" or "unconscious perception" (e.g. Dixon, 1971, 1981; Marcel, 1983). Unfortunately, this line of research has been hampered by methodological problems ever since it started in the 1950s (see, e.g., Eriksen, 1960; Cheesman & Merikle, 1985; Holender, 1986). There are, however, other examples that do not suffer from these methodological difficulties. We will briefly describe two sets of results from our research.

Two Experimental Examples

Both examples point to a dissociation between judgment and response in metacontrast. As mentioned, this is a special kind of visual backward masking in which the mask is presented laterally adjacent to the test stimulus; e.g. the target is a disk and the mask is a surrounding ring or a larger disk.

The first example is the Fehrer–Raab effect. As first reported by Fehrer & Raab (1962), the latency of a simple key–pressing response (a–reaction) is unaffected by metacontrast masking, even if the target is completely obliterated by the mask, as assessed by the subjects' judgments. This effect has often been replicated in subsequent research (see Neumann, 1982, for a summary). At first glance, it seems to demonstrate a clear–cut dissociation between judgment and response. We became interested in it, however, because we were skeptical about this conclusion, which seems to imply that, counter–intuitively, the target can trigger a voluntary response although the subject does not consciously perceive it.

Our skepticism was based on a closer examination of the effect, which indicated that the standard finding as such does not yet provide any conclusive evidence. The reason is that the judgment is about detectability, brightness or some other non–temporal dimension, whereas it is, of course, latency that is reflected in reaction time measurement. Hence there is a logical possibility to explain the effect without implying any dissociation between judgment and response. All that has to be assumed is that the masked target reduces not only response latency, but also the latency of the subjective perception of the mask. In this case the Fehrer–Raab effect would occur even though the subject reacts not to the masked target, but to the mask. The reason why the masked target speeds up the processing of the mask could be that it acts as a kind of pacemaker that prepares the system for the processing of the mask. In fact, our model of masking predicts this to happen ("weather station model"; Neumann, 1979, 1982; Neumann & Müsseler, 1989).

If this is the correct explanation of the Fehrer–Raab effect, then the apparent dissociation between judgment and response should disappear if we ask the subject the right question, viz. not whether the target was detectable, but when the mask appeared. According to the hypothesis, the reduction in response latency that constitutes the Fehrer–Raab effect should be accompanied by a corresponding shift in the apparent temporal position of the mask.

This can be assessed by temporal order judgments (Cazin, 1981; Neumann, 1982). We presented subjects with two identical disks, one to the left and one to the right of fixation. One of the disks served as the standard. The other – the comparison disk – appeared either alone, or it was preceded by a smaller disk that was, however, masked by it. The task was to judge which of the two visible disks (the standard or the comparison disk) appeared first. As predicted, the masked target caused a systematic displacement of the psychometric function. The larger the SOA (Stimulus Onset Asynchrony) between target and the comparison disk that masked it, the more the comparison disk appeared shifted forward in time relative to the standard.

In a further experiment we measured the Fehrer–Raab effect, using exactly the same experimental conditions (Neumann, 1982; Rosengärtner, 1980). The result was equally clear-cut, but disappointing from the point of view of the hypothesis under investigation: The reduction in response latency was consistently larger than the shift in the judged temporal position of the mask/comparison stimulus. The data indicated that roughly half of the amount of the Fehrer–Raab effect can be accounted for by a shift in the apparent temporal position of the mask, but the other half cannot.

Hence the dissociation between response and judgment has survived our test. Judgment and response are both influenced by the masked target, but differently. Clearly, the response does not depend on the judgment.

The second example leads to essentially the same conclusion. It concerns an effect in metacontrast masking that we discovered several years ago, using a small black disk as the target and a surrounding ring as the mask (Neumann, 1979): If a target–mask sequence is presented to the left or right of fixation, and a second stimulus identical to the target – a distractor – is presented contralaterally, then the U–shaped masking function will be changed in a characteristic manner: While the descending part of the function remains unaffected, the ascending part is shifted towards longer SOAs due to the presence of the distractor.

This has been found reliably in several studies with a judgment task, using the method of constant stimuli (Neumann, 1979; Aufschläger, 1979) and the signal detection method (Adler, 1979). To our great surprise, this distractor effect disappeared, however, when we switched from judgment to response. In one experiment, we used four different variants of the target (disks slightly truncated on different sides), between which the subject had to discriminate in a forced-choice decision task. Though the experiment was identical to the previous ones in all relevant aspects, the distractor effect vanished (Milewski, 1980; Figure 1).

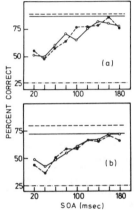

Figure 1. Percent correct forced-choice responses in a task in which 6 subjects had to decide on which side (left, right, bottom, or top) a target disk was slightly truncated. Abscissa: SOA target-mask. Open circles: no distractor. Filled circles: with distractor (an untruncated disk of the same size as the target). Horizontal lines: Data from a control condition without mask. The two panels represent two levels of difficulty of the task (b = very slight truncation, a = more pronounced truncation). (Data from Milewski, 1981).

In recent experiments we have replicated this result with other stimuli. Subjects had to discriminate between two arrowheads, that pointed either to the left or to the right and that were followed by a mask that consisted of two overlapping arrowheads. Performance was not reliably affected by any of the distractors used in this experiment (an arrowhead identical to the target, an arrowhead pointing in the other direction, or a disk of similar size; Figure 2).

Those who believe in "hard" response measures will probably interpret this as a proof that the subjective judgment method is flawed. However, we have no reason to regard the earlier results as invalid. To check for possible artifacts, we have recently replicated and extended the earlier research with the disk-ring paradigm. Instead of a small number of experienced observers, we used a large group of naive subjects. There were two different distractors, either a disk identical to the target or an arrowhead. Further, two groups of subjects received two different instruction that stressed either careful observation or fast, "automatic" responding. The task was always to judge whether the target was present. There was a highly significant distractor effect in all conditions, as can be seen in Figure 3.

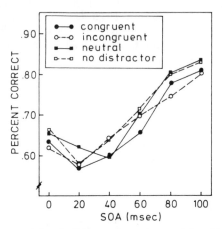

Figure 2. Percent correct forced-choice responses in a task in which subjects had to decide whether a masked arrow pointed to the left or to the right. The mask was a pattern that contained both kinds of arrows. The distractor was either a left–pointing or a right-pointing arrow (congruent or incongruent, with the direction of the target arrow) or neutral stimulus (a disk). Also shown are data from a no-distractor control condition. Data from 7 subjects averaged.

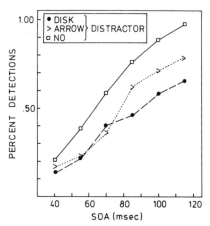

Figure 3. Detection of a target disk followed by a ring as a function of SOA. The distractor was either a disk identical to the target or an arrow. Data from two groups of 20 subjects who received different instructions (see text) have been combined since they did not differ statistically.

Thus, our data indicate that the crucial factor is indeed the kind of task that subjects are given. If we require them to detect a target stimulus, judgments about the presence or absence of the target will apparently be influenced by the distractor. (This is even the case if the instruction requires fast, "automatic" responding.) If we ask subjects to discriminate between alternative targets in a forced-choice task, then the distractor seems to have no reliable effect on the percentage of correct responses.

A discussion of the possible reasons for this dissociation is beyond the scope of the present paper. To mention just one possibility: Perhaps the subject in the forced-choice version of the experiment does not necessarily have to consciously perceive the target in order to discriminate it. This need not be "discrimination without awareness." Possibly the mask looks differently when different targets are presented, so that the subject can arrive at a correct forced-choice decision without seeing the target. Hence forced-choice performance would, according to this possibility, remain unaffected by the distractor, though the perception of the target is impaired.

Summary and Conclusions

Visual backward masking has been investigated within two research traditions: Fechnerian, psychophysical research based on judgments by experienced observers, and modern information processing research with performance scores (percent correct or reaction time) as the dependent variable. We have discussed the relationship between these two research traditions, using two experimental examples from metacontrast. One was the Fehrer-Raab effect, the other was the effect of a distractor on the masking function. Both examples show that objective performance measures and subjective judgments may lead to divergent results. Response latency may exhibit no effect of masking, while judgment measures do; and judgments may be affected by a distractor that leaves forced-choice performance unchanged. With respect to the methodological question that we have been concerned with in this paper, the conclusion is that the two kinds of measures do not necessarily converge.

Correspondence should be addressed to Odmar Neumann, Abteilung für Psychologie, Universität Bielefeld, 4800 Bielefeld, F.R.G.

References

Adler, A. (1979). *Die Wirkung eines zusätzlichen Reizes im Gesichtsfeld auf den Verlauf der Metakontrast-Funktion: III. Ein Kontrollexperiment mit objektiven Leistungsmaßen.* Unpublished Thesis, Ruhr-Universität Bochum.

Alpern, M. (1953). Metacontrast. *Journal of the Optical Society of America, 43,* 648–657.

Aufschläger, M. (1979). *Die Wirkung eines zusätzlichen Reizes im Gesichtsfeld auf den Verlauf der Metakontrast-Funktion: Aufblitzen und Erlöschen als Zusatzreize.* Unpublished Thesis, Ruhr-Universität Bochum.

Averbach, E., & Coriell, S. (1961). Short-term memory in vision. *Bell System Technical Journal, 40,* 309–328.

Breitmeyer, B.G. (1984). *Visual masking: An integrative approach.* New York & Oxford: Oxford University Press.

Bridgeman, B., Kirch, M., & Sperling, A. (1981). Segregation of cognitive and motor aspects of visual function using induced motion. *Perception & Psychophysics, 29,* 336–342.

Cazin, H. (1981). *Die Wirkung eines maskierten visuellen Reizes auf die zeitliche Verarbeitung des Maskierreizes: Psychophysische Messung.* Unpublished Thesis, Ruhr-Universität Bochum.

Cheesman, J., & Merikle, P.M. (1985). Word recognition and consciousness. In D. Besner, T. Waller, & G. McKinnon (Eds.), *Reading research: Advances in theory and practice,* Vol. 5. New York: Academic Press.

Dixon, N.F. (1971). *Subliminal perception: The nature of a controversy.* London: McGraw-Hill.

Dixon, N.F. (1981). *Preconscious processing.* Chichester: Wiley.

Eriksen, Ch.W. (1960). Discrimination and learning without awareness: A methodological survey and evaluation. *Psychological Review, 67,* 279–300.

Exner, S. (1868). Über die zu einer Gesichtswahrnehmung nöthige Zeit. *Sitzungsberichte der kaiserlichen Akademie der Wissenschaften zu Wien, Mathematisch-naturwissenschaftliche Classe, 58(2),* 601–632.

Fechner, G.Th. (1860). *Elemente der Psychophysik.* Leipzig: Breitkopf & Härtel. (Reprint: 1964. Amsterdam: Bonset).

Fehrer, E., & Raab, E. (1962). Reaction time to stimuli masked by metacontrast. *Journal of Experimental Psychology, 63,* 143–147.

Fry, G. (1934). Depression of the activity aroused by a flash of light by applying a second flash immediately afterwards to adjacent areas of the retina. *American Journal of Physiology, 108,* 701–707.

Haber, R.N., & Standing, L. (1968). Clarity and recognition of masked and degraded stimuli. *Psychonomic Science, 13,* 83–84.

Holender, D. (1986). Semantic activation without conscious identification in dichotic listening, parafoveal vision, and visual masking: A survey and appraisal. *The Behavioral and Brain Sciences, 9,* 1–66.

Kraus, K. (1900). Universitätsbummel. *Die Fackel, 1(31),* 12–19.

Kraus, K. (1901). Universitäts-Bummel. *Die Fackel, 3(89),* 17–19.

Kraus, K. (1903). Die Fakultät in Liquidation. *Die Fackel, 5(144),* 3–8.

Kraus, K. (1907). Medizinisches Familienidyll. *Die Fackel, 9(223/224),* 3–5.

Liss, Ph. (1968). Does backward masking by visual noise stop stimulus processing? *Perception & Psychophysics, 4,* 328–330.

Marcel, A.J. (1983). Conscious and unconscious perception: An approach to the relation between phenomenal experience and perceptual processes. *Cognitive Psychology, 15,* 238–300.

McLeod, P., McLaughlin, C., & Nimmo-Smith, I. (1985). Information encapsulation and automaticity: Evidence from the visual control of finely timed actions. In M.I. Posner & O.S. Marin (Eds.), *Attention and Performance XI*. Hillsdale, N.J.: Lawrence Erlbaum.

Milewski, R. (1980). *Untersuchung der Metakontrast-Funktion mit einem Zwangswahl-Konturidentifikationsverfahren*. Unpublished Thesis, Ruhr-Universität Bochum.

Neumann, O. (1979). Visuelle Aufmerksamkeit und der Mechanismus des Metakonstrasts. In E. Eckensberger (Ed.), *Bericht über den 31. Kongreß der Deutschen Gesellschaft für Psychologie*. Göttingen: Hogrefe.

Neumann, O. (1982). *Experimente zum Fehrer-Raab-Effekt und das "Wetterwart"-Modell der visuellen Maskierung* (Report No. 24/1982). Bochum: Ruhr-Universität, Psychologisches Institut, Arbeitseinheit Kognitionspsychologie.

Neumann, O. (1989). Kognitive Vermittlung und direkte Parameterspezifikation. Zum Problem mentaler Repräsentation in der Wahrnehmung. *Sprache und Kognition, 8*, 32 – 49.

Neumann, O., & Müsseler, J. (1990). Visuelles Fokussieren: Das Wetterwart-Modell und einige seiner Anwendungen. In C. Meinecke & L. Kehrer (Eds.), *Bielefelder Beiträge zur Kognitionspsychologie*. Göttingen: Hogrefe.

Piéron, H. (1914). Recherches sur les lois de variation des temps de latence sensorielles en fonction des intensités excitatrices. *Année Psychologique, 20*, 17 – 96.

Reeves, A. (1982). Metacontrast: U-shaped functions derive from two monotonic processes. *Perception, 11*, 415 – 426.

Rosengärtner, B. (1980). *Die Wirkung eines maskierten visuellen Reizes auf die zeitliche Verarbeitung des Maskierreizes: Reaktionszeitmessung*. Unpublished Thesis, Ruhr-Universität Bochum.

Sperling, G. (1960). The information available in brief visual presentations. *Psychological Monographs, 74* (Whole No. 498).

Stigler, R. (1910). Chronophotische Untersuchungen über den Umgebungskontrast. *Pflüger's Archiv für die gesamte Physiologie, 134*, 365 – 435.

Werner, H. (1935). Studies on contour: I. Qualitative analysis. *American Journal of Psychology, 47*, 40 – 64.

Psychophysical Explorations of Mental Structures
Edited by H.-G. Geissler
in collaboration with M.H. Müller and W. Prinz
© 1990 by Hogrefe & Huber Publishers

Chapter 39

The Latency Course of Feature Encoding Interfaced with Algorithm-Based Figure Classification

Uwe Kämpf and Joachim Hoffmann[1]
Zentralinstitut für Kybernetik
und Informationsverarbeitung
Akademie der Wissenschaften der DDR
Berlin, G.D.R.

Recent research has been broadly concerned with the question, how our central processing might be sequentially paced in order to fit with hierarchically relayed constraints due to some "top-down" classification. In the present paper, however, we ask for the consequences of interfacing the latter "bottom-up" with peripheral speeding constraints on parallel feature encoding. Perception we regard to be a matter of fascinatingly effective coordination between the evaluation of sensory data and their interpretation in terms of category hierarchies stored in memory. In light of this, we attempted to study what would happen in the conflict case of disturbing or even damaging the apparently tight structural interlock between both processual components by spatiotemporally manipulating the task lay-out. Consider, e.g., one of the famous paintings made by the 16th century italian manierist Guiseppe Arcimboldo (Figure 1A). What we easily see

---

[1] Now at the Max-Planck-Institut für Psychologische Forschung, München, F.R.G.

is a conflict between two concurrently emerging interpretations, a global one, the portrait of the king, at first glance and a local one, the fruits it consists of, at second glance.

Both depend on a rather contradictory way to use different aspects of the data made available by "bottom-up" feature encoding. From a phenomenological point of view, it seems to be even more obvious, what kind of data (e.g., color, edges, etc.) should be sensorily encoded in order to fit with the apparently "simpler" local level of category assignment. The global level, however, seems to depend on rather "complex" structural relations between the featural parts, being thus hierarchically defined "top-down" from the point of view of the whole. Nevertheless, as might be concluded from subjective experience as well as from the experimental evidence of numerous studies, it is the global picture level that has been shown to dominate over the local one not only in the spatial domain, but clearly to precede it in the temporal domain, too. Under tachistoscopic setting, a rough and global description for similarly conflicting, although featurally laid out much simpler, pictorial arrangements seems likely to be more quickly available for classificatory use than a fine and local one (Navon, 1977, 1981; Kinchla & Wolfe, 1979; Pomerantz, 1983; Hoffman & Kämpf, 1985; Hoffmann & Zießler, 1986).

Hierarchy of top-down postsensoric processing, due to some functional priority for globally coherent interpretation of the whole, in spite of some eventually conflicting information in the local detail, is generally regarded to account for the counterintuitive global-to-local precedence (cf. Miller, 1981; Boer & Keuss, 1982; Geissler & Puffe, 1983; Arend & Wandmacher, 1985). However, this must not necessarily mean that no precategorial cues for the "complex" global features, as opposed to the phenomenally more "simple" local features, could be encoded in the sensory data base. In fact, visual feature coding has been shown to be early mediated by spatio-temporal filtering of the retinal input, providing other criteria than that of phenomenal appearance for evaluating a feature to be simple or complex (Blakemore & Campbell, 1969; Harvey, Roberts, & Gervais, 1983). Thus, the ease of attending to interpretation levels might be interferred with by some speeding constraints due to spatio-temporal filtering on bottom-up feature encoding of different figural quality. Even, if we would not be able exactly to define the features actually used by the top-down processing in order to solve the classification task, we might well be able to predict what kind of features could be available in principle for a very early vs. a processing step later on, only knowing about some spatio-temporal restrictions on the availability of sensory data and assuming bottom-up processing to be tightly interfaced with top-down processing.

Consider, e.g., the well known reciprocal relationship between spatial and temporal resolution in our ability to selectively attend to channels of vision, as has been extensively studied in the framework of filter-channel approach (Kulikowski & Tolhurst, 1973; Breitmeyer & Ganz, 1976). Filtering out the spatial high-resolution base for feature encoding in Arcimboldo's painting, retaining thus only the spatial low-resolution one, leaves its global interpretation nearly unaffected, but suppresses the local one (Figure 1B). And precisely this is what happens, e.g., in the case of briefly glancing at a moving

Figure 1. Ambiguous picture by G. Arcimboldo, seen in normal acuity (A, upper part) and low-pass filtered (B, lower part).

car, or similarily, of tachistoscopic performance requiring, thus, high temporal resolution rather than low temporal resolution. In fact, the bottom–up output immediately after a tachistoscopic presentation might be regarded as a series of pulses allowing for increasing spatial acuity in the temporal range of some hundreds of milliseconds after presentation onset (Breitmeyer & Ganz, 1976; Di Lollo, 1980). Increased spatial resolution might be achieved, therefore, to the costs of decreased temporal resolution only, and vice versa. So the initiation of a top–down global stimulus description might be supported, too, simply by the initial absence of relevant local cues in the early bottom–up data streams. The aim of our investigation is, then, to ask whether the presumed spatio–temporal speeding constraints on bottom–up feature coding would influence, if brought into conflict with, first, the early initiation, and second, the further proceeding of hierarchical top–down classification.

What is the theoretical background for these inquiries? Interfacing bottom–up and top–down processing has been linked in cognitive tradition with the assumption about some peripheral data overflow having to be encoded initially in parallel, but then rather sequentially classified, in order to implement central hierarchy requirements. Unlike the early cognitivist models, having regarded the information exchange between both kinds of processing to proceed in a discrete and chunk–like fashion, contemporary theories favour the idea of a rather continuous stream–like data transfer between them. Therefore, they assume different processing stages not to be, as has been previously stated, separated one from another by layers of buffer storage (e.g., Sperling, 1960; Atkinson & Shiffrin, 1969). Rather the processing levels are conceived, now, to be closely interfaced in data cascades (McClelland, 1979; McClelland & Rumelhart, 1981; Rumelhart & McClelland, 1982). Within either of the cascade levels, as well as between different ones, processing is assumed to run in parallel over a considerable range of time, allowing for data transfer to be carried out at any particular moment of processual coexistence. Nevertheless, the concurrent data streams would be processed by different rates, thus resulting in synchronization lags between them. Appropriately tuning the latter should be essential, according to the theory considered, for sequentializing a structural hierarchy to be processually implemented.

From this type of model the prediction might be derived, that as early as an access to an encoded feature would be allowed for by the bottom–up speeding constraints discussed above, it should immediately be included in the hierarchy of the actual top–down classification task under way. In order to fulfill the preconditions for efficiently synchronized information processing, this must hold true regardless of whether or not the considered feature would be required for, logically, performing the actual step. So it would be of interest to compare the tachistoscopic performance latencies between hierarchically organized classification tasks, being in accordance with the feature coding priorities on the one hand, but in dissonance, on the other hand.

The basic idea for doing so is experimentally to assign the highest classificatory priority, commonly being associated with the presumedly most early encoded global feature, to the most lately encoded local feature, for now. Probably, such an inversion could hardly be achieved with the stimuli most common to studies of global–to–local precedence having only two conflicting interpretation levels in terms of highly overlearned patterns without explicitly given hierarchy for the underlying classification. So we constructed a set of stimuli involving features of potentially different spatial robustness against temporal deficiency. They had to be matched step-by-step with a set of categories on the base of an algorithm consisting of several hierarchically relayed connections similar to the "exclusive or" (XOR) type, that has been extensively studied in recent work on perceptual learning in distributed networks. In our experimental study, however, these between feature–level connections were laid out asymmetrically, in order to guarantee for hierarchy of performance.

Classifying Geometrical Stimuli into Hierarchically Relayed Categories

In a first experiment, we defined an algorithm aimed to classify geometrically featured figural stimuli into hierarchically relayed categories. Features might have been of either rectangular, semicircular or triangular shape at what we call, for sake of simplicity, a global (the outline), medial (the cut) and local (the pin) figure level, according to their potentially different spatial robustness against temporal deficiency in early visual processing (Figure 2). The features could be, thus, of figurally the same shape from level to level, or they could differ from one another between levels.

examples for possible figures

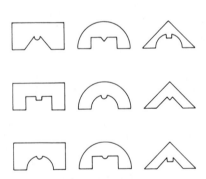

Figure 2. Examples of the geometrically featured stimulus patterns to be classified by the subjects.

In a first blocked experimental condition the stimuli had to be classified proceeding form global to local, in a second condition, however, vice versa, in order to obtain the desired priority conflict. Subjects were forced to follow the hierarchy of performance by asymmetrically laid out "exclusive-or" links between classes, making a lower level classificatory feature invaluable for the appropriate decision until having tested for an eventually conflicting higher order feature, that could probably appear concurrently within the same stimulus. The categories were given numbers according to their instructed ordering in the algorithm hierarchy. Stimuli belonged to a first category in case of a rectangular global feature, regardless of all other feature levels. They belonged to a second category in case of a semicircular medial feature, given however, not to be rectangular at the global level. They belonged to a third class with a triangular local feature, given there was no medial semicircular or even global rectangular feature present in the stimulus. They belonged to a fourth class, lastly, if none of these hierarchically relayed conditons were fulfilled. The best strategy to cope with the task would be, then, to check the hierarchy as has been sketched out so far, step by step, consecutively testing one feature after another.

This is just what should hold true for our second blocked experimental condition, too. Here, however, the hierarchy of performance was completely turned over, i.e., the stimuli were undertaken to an algorithm of essentially the same lay-out, except for proceeding from local to global now, rather than vice versa. First, they had to be tested for local rectangularity (category 1), second for medial semicircularity (category 2), then for global triangularity (category 3) and, lastly, for none of the above (category 4). Thus, the supposed priorities of bottom-up feature coding and of the top-down classification algorithm were forced to conflict.

Figure 3. Mean response latencies from the first experiment plotted against the categories for the global-to-local (filled circles) vs. local-to-global (open circles) series: the first (dotted lines) vs. the last (solid lines) ten trials.

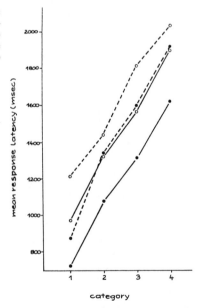

As a result, the mean response latencies over the first vs. the last ten trials (in order to control for training progress) of both experimental conditions are plotted against the category level to be answered, respectively (Figure 3). Obviously, from category to category, i.e., presumedly from step to step of performing the algorithm, we obtained a rather remarkable growth in decision latency, the latter being, however, constantly faster for the global–to–local performance, than for the local–to–global one. Regarding the straight lines of nearly the same slope, differing thus, only in their intercept, it would be tempting to assume them to quantify the supposed performance steps from category to category. Except for a shift to a generally shorter latency level, this pattern of results was not influenced by training progress. Accordingly, an analysis of variance (ANOVA), associated with, revealed significant effects of either factor classification rule ($F(1,18) = 4.82$; $p < 0.05$), category level ($F(3,54) = 152.76$; $p < 0.005$), but no significant interactions between either of the both factors classification × category ($F(3,54) = .16$; $p > 0.1$), classification × progress ($F(1,18) = 0.26$; $p > 0.1$), category × progress ($F(3,54) = 0.91$; $p > 0.1$), and no triple interaction ($F(3,54) = 1.98$; $p > 0.1$).

But the pattern of results, which seems so clearly to speak in favor of step–by–step performance so far, must be questioned for several reasons. Consider, e.g., the latency increment for the third to the fourth category. Logically, no further testing step should be predicted here, because no additional feature matching would be required. Having accepted a stimulus as a member of category three should be precisely the same as having rejected its memberhip to category four, and vice versa. No latency difference between them, therefore, should be expected. Whatever the reasons are, for obtaining one — they would be the same for both classification rules. This suggests the forthcoming of feature utilisation, in spite of the obtained latency difference in its early beginning supposedly mediated by feature availability, not further to depend on the latter later on, i.e., to be of the same case–independent layout.

That this is more than only a "surface effect" might be concluded from a split of the data for the last ten trials according to different possible degrees of identity between features of different levels. The rather complex pattern of interactions obtained, has not to be considered in full detail here. Let us pick up, instead, only two rather typical examples showing some remarkable deviations from linearity in their curvature (Figure 4). The latter are, obviously, repeated between the both conditons, suggesting thus, that classificatory, but not visually(!), equivalent features would be handled the same way for either case. Beyond that, the differential influences of the between feature–level identities indicate fulfilling the task demands not to be a matter of strictly sequentially matching feature by feature. Rather, there seem to be involved parallel process interactions too, as might be predicted from the cascading model, causing the answers to depend on between feature relations as well as on within level layout. Therefore, the latency relations between, e.g., the categories three and four, would fit sometimes rather the theoretically expected dependencies, other times rather the observed ones in the overall data, as has been discussed above, being mediated by feature relations between levels. We will return to this point later on.

For now let us consider, again, the question why, although being able to obtain remarkable feature availability effects on feature use initiation, we obtained no such effects on the proceeding of the latter further on. Possibly, this might be due to the relatively long latency differences from category to category reflecting supposedly the execution of distinct "steps" of feature use, lasting thus approximately about 300 msec. This is well above the approximate global-to-local feature availability difference of about 250 msec. So it could have prevented further interactions of feature availability with feature use beyond the first step. Subjects themselves reported the changes between the actual feature quality, proceeding from step to step of the algorithm, to be the most difficult and probably time-costing task demand. In a second experiment we tried to avoid this complication, keeping the feature to be matched of a constant quality from level to level.

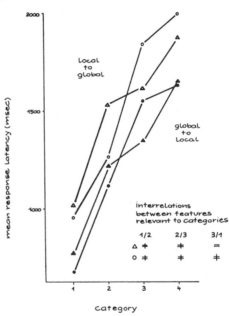

Figure 4. Latency data from the first experiment split for different between feature- level interrelations. Two illustrative examples taken from the last ten trials.

Our second experiment replicated the first one in most conditions, except for keeping the features to be matched, instead of changing them, constant from step to step of the algorithm for either of the both classification rules, i.e., of rectangular shape at any hierarchical level to be tested. Stimuli had to be rectangular at the relevant level in order to fit the appropriate category, given however, not to have been so at higher order level, regardless of whether the algorithm had to proceed from global to local, or vice versa.

Again, as a result, the mean response latencies over the first vs. the last ten trials are plotted for the both classification rules against the appropriate category level (Figure 5). The most striking result, here, is the dramatically reduced overall latency range required in order to fulfill the hierarchically relayed task demands. Obviously, this must be due, as has been expected, to avoiding the "on-line" controls for changing the matching feature step by step.

Keeping the latter, instead, constant to be of rectangular shape, resulted in more effective processing due to, possibly, a higher degree of task automation. In spite of the shortened overall latency range, the relative differences between initiating the classification in the both reversedly built-up hierarchies were maintained, qualitatively, in our second experiment. The obtained classification dynamics, however, differed considerably and in a nonlinear way between the level-reversed hierarchies, clearly indicating, thus, to have influenced not only the early beginning, but also the further forthcoming of top–down processing by bottom–up speeding constraints. The nonlinearities obtained in the data became even stronger with training progress. Accordingly, the analysis of variance revealed significancies not only for either of the factors classification rule $(F(1,11) = 12.82; p < 0.005)$ category level $(F(3,33) = 62.67; p < 0.005)$ and training progress $(F(1,11) = 21.36; p < 0.05)$ per se, but also for the interactions classification $\times$ category $(F(3.33) = 7.02; p < 0.01)$, classification $\times$ training $(F(1, 11) = 6.09; p < 0.05)$ and category training $(F(3,33) = 3.65; p < 0.05)$. No significant triple interaction was found $(F(3.33) = 2.41; p > 0.1)$.

Figure 5. Mean response latencies from the second experiment plotted against the categories for the global–to–local (filled circles) vs. local–to–global (open circles) series: the first (dotted lines) vs. the last (solid lines) ten trials.

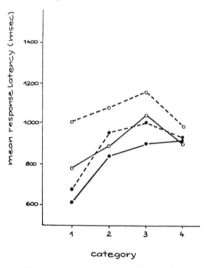

At the same time it is obvious even from the curvature of the latency dependencies per se, especially for the turned over local–to–global task, that a linear step–by–step model would be incapable in principle to account even for the surface structure of the data for both classification rules. Consider the results for the global–to–local condition. Here, the interrelations between the answer latencies are, except for some deviations from strong linearity, in reasonable accordance with a–priori expectations. The early available global feature, one might be forced to argue in order to explain the supraproportional fastness of category one latency, has got some process bonus by its early utilization. Even the third and fourth category are answered to by nearly the same latency, as may be well explained given that accepting the one of them just means rejecting the other, and vice versa, as has been discussed above. But not so in case of the local-to-global level reversed classification condition. Here, not only a linear, but any monotonic fit for the data, and therefore, the step-by-step model of performance, too, seems to be absurd for the reason that even in surface the plots strongly deviate from linearity. Mostly, this seems to be due to the surprisingly late classifying answers for the third category, depending on the global feature supposed to be encoded earliest. In fact the latencies obtained, however, were even slower than that to category four, i.e., the stimuli featurally not explicitly defined, but coming out in comparingly fast reactions.

Figure 6. Latency data from the second experiment split for difference between feature-level interrelations with examples for patterns fitting to category one in the last ten trials of the local-to-global series.

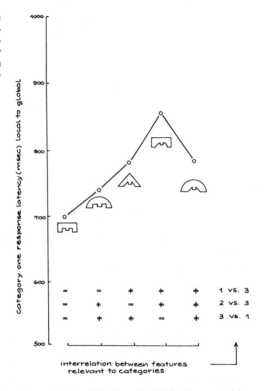

Crucial for understanding these results might be the following considerations. Keeping the feature to be matched figurally constant from level to level of the hierarchy, gave an a priori unexpected advantage for testing the quite uniformly laid out, now, last class of "all others" having no rectangular features at all. In order to decide whether or not an object could potentially belong to this category, it should be sufficient to test for the presence or absence at all of any rectangular feature in the stimulus, regardless of level. One might ask, what conditions must be met for obtaining deviations between the test for a certain feature per se, and the test for the appropriateness of its level. Interestingly, there seems to be no such deviation observable in the global-to-local condition. In the turned over local-to-global conditon, however, we well might have obtained one, explaining thus the faster answer latencies to category four as compared to category three. Suppose the decision system being tuned, preferably to use the local feature to test for rectangularity, in order either to come out in the highest priority answer, or to proceed further on. Preferably available from the coding system would be, however, another feature, the global one, signalizing rectangular shape or not, at an actually irrelevant level. This would clearly result in some Stroop-like interference, being potentially able to disturb performance.

The only way, appropriately to use this early available kind of information would be, then, to prime the system for two somewhat different kinds of performance. In case of no early (i.e., globally) detected rectangularity, it would be useful to develop some latent readiness for the fourth category to be answered, depending on completely non-rectangular figural layout that might have been matched in any, not only the consecutive, order. An early (i.e., globally) signalized rectangularity, however, would be ignored best, or even inhibited, perhaps, in order to avoid Stroop-like interference with the higher priority (local and medial) features of potentially the same shape. After having disproved the latter possibility, a new access to the already faded away category-three-relevant global data level would probably be required, what might at least partially explain the comparedly late answers of that type.

Branching of processing along the sketched two line depends, thus, strongly on the early detection of a rectangular feature. In light of our assumptions about cascaded processing, however, this is not intended to suggest an early decision about this point to be responsible for branching the processing cascade. Rather the latter might be laid out similarily to what has been described, commonly, as a "horse race" between parallel processes, those sequential chains would come out faster or later to an end, depending on the featural layout of the stimulus. Consider, again, the split of the data according to the between-level feature interrelations for the last ten trials of the local-to-global category-one responses (Figure 6). If the cascading would depend on an early decision about global rectangularity or not, then a rather clear and unequivocal difference between globally rectangular stimuli and others should be predicted by our "priming" model. In fact it depends, however, on the degree of between-level identities in the stimulus, whether the reactions would be speeded up or slowed down by global rectangularity, as compared to neutral shape. This might be clearly seen by inspecting the category one responses, illustrated by stimulus examples apropriate to the split data. Autonomous tests for between-level feature interrelations must mediate, therefore, the performance deep structure, being not represented in its surface flow chart. Generally, we are forced to argue, that the visual system tries to minimize the "costs" of structural mismatch between early sensory feature availability and priority of classificatory use by processual modifications: in order to compensate for the loss of efficiency by a somewhat different kind of "benefit" that might be gained in such cases.

Summary

So let us summarize to have been successful in experimentally replicating the well-known level effects of global-to-local precedence in visual cognition. Additionally, we found the synchronization between the earliest possible access to a feature level and the associated ones with priority of need for in hierarchical decision making to be crucial for the initiation (Experiment 1), as well as for the proceeding (Experiment 2) of cascaded processing. One might speculate, whether the great differences in the latency range to cope with the requirements of the first vs. the second experiment would be due to the level of process "control" vs. "automaticy" that might be achieved under the conditions of featurally forced to change vs. kept constant category structure. Further investigations are needed to clarify this point. Possibly, a different degree of structural "package density" into processual cycles, as has been extensively discussed in other context (Geissler, 1987) might account for the radical change in the results from the first to our second experiment.

Correspondence should be addressed to Uwe Kämpf, Zentralinstitut für Kybernetik und Informationsverarbeitung, Akademie der Wissenschaften der DDR, Kurstr. 33, Berlin, DDR – 1086.

References

Arend, J., & Wandmacher, U (1985). Superiority of global features in classification and matching. *Psychological Research, 47*, 143 – 157.

Atkinson, R.C., & Shiffrin, R.M. (1971). The control of short-term memory. *Scientific American, 224*, 82 – 90.

Boer, L.C., & Keuss, P.J.G. (1982). Global precedence as a postperceptual effect: An analysis of speed-accuracy tradeoff functions. *Perception & Psychophysics, 31*, 358 – 366.

Breitmeyer, B.G., & Ganz, L. (1976). Implications of sustained and transient channels for theories of visual pattern masking, saccadic suppression, and information processing. *Psychological Review, 83*, 1 – 36.

Blakemore, C., & Campbell, F.W. (1969). On the existence of neurons in the human visual system selectively sensitive to the orientation and size of retinal images. *Journal of Physiology, 203*, 237 – 269.

Di Lollo, V. (1980). Temporal integration in visual memory. *Journal of Experimental Psychology: General, 109*, 75 – 97.

Geissler, H.G. (1987). The temporal architecture of central information processing: Evidence for a tentative time-quantum model. *Psychological Research, 49*, 99 – 106.

Geissler, H.G., & Puffe, M. (1983). The inferential basis of classification: From perceptual to memory code systems. In H.G. Geissler (Ed.), *Modern issues in perception* (pp.87 – 124). Amsterdam: North Holland.

Harvey, L.O. Jr., Roberts, J.O., & Gervais, M.J. (1983). The spatial frequency basis of internal representation. In H.G. Geissler, (Ed.), *Modern issues in perception* (pp. 217 – 226). Amsterdam: North Holland.

Hoffmann, J., & Kämpf, U. (1985). Mechanismen der Objektbenennung – parallele Verarbeitungskaskaden. *Sprache & Kognition, 4*, 217 – 230.

Hoffmann, J., & Zießler, M. (1986). The integration of visual and functional classifications in concept formation. *Psychological Research, 48,* 69–78.

Kinchla, R.A., & Wolfe, J. (1979). The order of visual processing: "Top down", "bottom up", or "middle out". *Perception & Psychophysics, 25,* 225–231.

Kulikowski, J.J., & Tolhurst, D.J. (1973). Psychophysical evidence for sustained and transient detectors in human vision. *Journal of Physiology, 232,* 149–162.

McClelland, J.L. (1979). On the time relations of mental processes: An examination of systems of processes in cascade. *Psychological Review, 86,* 287–330.

McClelland, J.L., & Rumelhart, D.E. (1981). An interactive activation model of context effects in letter perception: Part 1. An account of basic findings. *Psychological Review, 88,* 375–407.

Miller, J. (1981). Global precedence in attention and decision. *Journal of Experimental Psychology: Human Perception and Performance, 7,* 1161–1174.

Navon, D. (1977). Forest before trees: The precedence of global features in visual perception. *Cognitive Psychology, 9,* 353–383.

Navon, D. (1981). The forest revisited: More on global precedence. *Psychological Research, 43,* 1–32.

Pomerantz, J.R. (1983). Global and local precedence: Selective attention in form and motion perception. *Journal of Experimental Psychology: General, 112,* 516–540.

Rumelhart, D.E., & McClelland, J.L. (1982). An interactive activation model of context effects in letter perception: Part 2. The contextual enhancement effect and some tests and extensions of the model. *Psychological Review, 89,* 60–94.

Sperling, G. (1960). The information available in brief visual presentations. *Psychological Monographs, 74,* 1–29.

Psychophysical Explorations of Mental Structures
Edited by H.-G. Geissler
in collaboration with M.H. Müller and W. Prinz
© 1990 by Hogrefe & Huber Publishers

Chapter 40

New Theoretical Results on
Testing Self-Terminating vs.
Exhaustive Processing in
Rapid Search Experiments

James T. Townsend
Department of Psychology, Indiana University
Bloomington , U.S.A.
Trisha Van Zandt
Department of Psychological Sciences
Purdue University
West Lafayette, U.S.A.

Two important questions in cognitive psychology concern how a subject "searches" through arrays of items to find a specific, predetermined item. One question involves how comparisons between a single (often visually) presented "probe" or "target" and a list stored in memory take place, a memory search (e.g., Sternberg, 1966). The second question deals with visual search, which involves the comparison processes between a display of several items and a single "target" item stored in memory (e.g., Atkinson, Holmgren, & Juola, 1969; Townsend & Roos, 1973). The difference between visual and memory search is illustrated in Figure 1. Mean reaction times to determine that a target is present (on "positive" trials) or absent (on "negative" trials) are used to try and determine the underlying processes involved in the search.

It is very difficult, however, to determine how the comparison process takes place between the target item and the items in the search set, especially when using mean reaction time data as the sole basis for determination. For instance, the complications arising from the tests of serial (one at at time) and parallel (simultaneous) processing are well known (e.g., Anderson, 1976; Townsend, 1972; Townsend, 1974; Townsend, 1976; Vorberg, 1977). Several procedures have been developed in recent years that are capable of diagnosing among a large class of serial vs. parallel models (Snodgrass & Townsend, 1980; Townsend, 1984; Townsend & Ashby, 1983). On the other hand, less is known concerning "self–terminating" vs. "exhaustive" search, although Ashby (1976), Townsend and Ashby (1983) and Townsend and Roos (1973) have made some progress on the problem. We say that a search is exhaustive if the subject must search through all items in the search set before making a positive or negative response, while self–terminating search takes place if the subject can discontinue the search after the detection of the target.

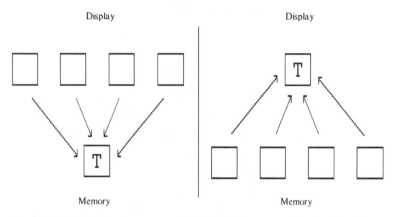

Figure 1. Visual (left) and memory search (right). Memory search takes place between several items stored in memory and single target presented visually, while visual search takes place between a single target held in memory and several items presented between a single target held in memory and several items presented visually.

Observation of mean reaction time with increased load has been the most popular method to test exhaustive and self–terminating processing, probably because of its ready intuition and the close tie between increasing mean reaction time and efforts to test serial and parallel processing (Sternberg, 1966). But, there are other techniques which can be used to make the exhaustive vs. self–terminating distinction. These include the use of redundant targets (e.g. Baddeley & Ecob, 1973; Bjork & Estes, 1971; Egeth, Folk & Mullin, 1988), reaction time variances (Schneider & Shiffrin, 1977), or keeping the expected number of items processed constant (Ashby, 1976; Townsend & Ashby, 1983). The emphasis in this paper is on the observation of slope differences between reaction time functions for target present (positive) and target absent (negative) trials, that is, parallelity vs. nonparallelity of positive and negative trial functions, to test for self–terminating or exhaustive processing. We will also consider the implications of exhaustive processing on position effects: the effects of target placement on mean reaction time (see below).

Consider the standard serial model as an example. The standard serial model postulates that the comparison process between the target and the items in the search set takes place serially, where mean processing times (comparison times) are equal for all target and nontarget items (Sternberg, 1966). This model predicts linear, increasing mean reaction time functions, since increasing the load by the addition of a single nontarget item to the search set produces a constant amount of processing time added to the overall mean reaction time.

The standard serial self-terminating model predicts that the positive mean reaction time function increases only half as fast as the negative process function; on the average the target will be found half-way through the comparison process and processing will then stop. This prediction depends, of course, on either random placement of the target among nontarget items by the experimenter, or a random pattern of search on the part of the searcher. Alternatively, the standard serial exhaustive model predicts equal-sloped mean reaction time functions, because the comparison process always continues through the entire search set, even after discovery of the target. These results depend entirely on the exact specifications of one's model, however. Many self-terminating models may not predict the two-to-one slope (rate of increase) ratio between positive and negative mean reaction time functions (Townsend & Roos, 1973), just as some exhaustive models may not predict equal slopes.

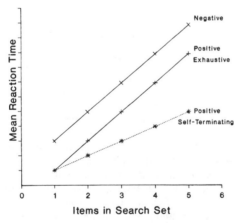

Figure 2. The standard serial model. The self-terminating search model predicts a positive mean reaction time function that has half the slope of the negative mean reaction time function.

Assuming that errors are not playing a major role in the experiment then the following postulate seems reasonable for the standard serial model. When mean reaction time is plotted separately for positive trials and for negative trials, the mean reaction time function for negative trials should be indicative of an exhaustive search. The subject must make an exhaustive search of all the items in the negative search set to be able to respond correctly that the target item is not present. If the slope (rate of increase) of the positive function is half that of the negative function, we might wish to take that as evidence for self-terminating search as suggested above. If, on the other hand, the two functions are equal-sloped, with equal rates of increase, an exhaustive search model might be favored (see Figure 2). (For more background on the self-terminating vs. exhaustive processing question, see Ashby, 1976; Townsend, 1974, or Townsend & Ashby, 1983).

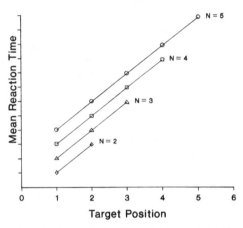

Figure 3. Position effects in the standard self-terminating model with a fixed order of processing (position 1 to position 5). For clarity, the position curves for different values of *N* have been separated, rather than plotted as a single line.

This sort of test is very easy to apply. However, overall mean reaction time data can mask other important aspects of the data which may be helpful in distinguishing between different processing models. For instance, the standard serial model above assumes that the individual mean processing times are equal for each of the items and positions in the search set. This is a strong and questionable assumption. Equal average processing times across all items implies that there can be no effect of target placement on mean reaction time unless search is self-terminating. We call the influence of target placement a "position effect[1]"; so, for the standard serial self-terminating model, mean reaction times will be faster when the target is processed very early in the

---

[1]   Our "position effect" has often been referred to as a "serial position effect." In an attempt to forestall any confusion between "serial" processing and "serial" position, and to generalize the concept of "position" to nonlinear display presentations, we adopt the shorter term "position effect" in this paper.

search, and slower when the target is processed near the end of the search. We can consider target placement in two ways: the target placement in the search set (either the set of items held in memory or the set of items presented visually), and the effects of target placement on the processing path, that is, the actual order in which items in the search set are processed, or processing location. If the serial processor were to always proceed from search set position one to position two, and on to position n, mean reaction time will increase when plotted against target placement in the search set (Figure 3). Position effects are manifested by an interaction of target search set location with processing path in self-terminating serial processing. In parallel systems, the speed at which an individual search set position is processed determines the position effects.

In this paper, we will present several new results concerning position effects and the form of the mean reaction time functions. However, let us first outline the present status of the use of mean reaction time functions and position effects to discriminate between self-terminating and exhaustive search strategies. Ashby (1976) and Townsend and Roos (1973) showed that reasonable serial and parallel self-terminating models can predict equal-sloped mean reaction time functions (itself a phenomenon previously attributed only to exhaustive serial process models, e.g., Sternberg, 1966, 1975) yet still permit position effects across target and nontarget items (which cannot be predicted by standard exhaustive serial models). It was demonstrated at that time that plausible process models (for example, models based on reasonable strategies, limited capacity and differential allocation of processing attention) of either the self-terminating or exhaustive variety could accommodate the often reported equal slopes of the positive and negative reaction time functions. These same models could handle the occasionally cited differential position effects which were earlier thought to imply self-termination, a result presumably at odds with the finding of equal slopes.

The upshot was (and is) that equal slopes are not very diagnostic with regard to exhaustive or self-terminating processing. However we know much less about the diagnosticity of unequal slopes (i.e., a slope ratio greater than one). Also, position effects, while certainly compatible with self-terminating processing, can be predicted to some extent by exhaustive models. To what extent exhaustive models can predict strong position effects (as compared to the predictions of self-terminating models) has never been determined. This paper will be devoted to the issue of the relative slopes of the negative and positive functions and to the prediction of such position effects.

The overall plan will be to consider serial exhaustive models and within that class, to address first the slope ratio question and second the question of ultimate position effects. Then we will consider parallel exhaustive models, presenting our somewhat more limited results with regard to these two questions.

Serial Exhaustive Models

Our strategy will be to work from more restricted cases to the most general. Hopefully, this strategy will whet the reader's intuition for the underlying dynamics of the process.

The Slope Ratio Issue

Let us then first formalize the standard serial model with exhaustive processing. To calculate the mean serial reaction times for a negative or positive trial, we need only add up the mean processing time for all of the items in the search set. Notice that "processing times" refer to the time taken for an individual comparison between target and search set, whereas "reaction times" refer to total time taken by the subject to make a response.[2] Call the mean reaction time for a negative trial with n items $E_n[RT^-]$, and for a positive trial with n items $E_n[RT^+]$. If, as above, we asume that all items, target and nontarget, are processed with the same individual mean processing time, then mean total reaction time for n nontarget items $(E_n[RT^-])$ is just $nE[T]$, where T is the random processing time for an individual nontarget item. Likewise, the mean reaction time for $n-1$ nontarget items and one target $(E_n[RT^+])$ is $nE[T]$, since targets and nontargets are processed identically, and all nontargets will also be processed in this exhaustive search. The rate of increase of these two functions is the same, predicting equal-sloped mean reaction time functions. This model can never predict any slope ratio other than one-to-one between the positive and negative mean reaction time functions.

The Before vs. After Model

Now allow the individual mean processing times to vary a bit. Assume that positive and negative processes take place in exactly the same way until the discovery of a target in the positive process. After the target is processed, all nontarget items can be processed with a different duration (not necessarily longer or shorter, just different). By making the distinction between "before" and "after" target processing, this model can predict a very limited range of position effects, but also fails to predict a slope ratio different from one-to-one.

---

[2]   We refer to the total mean comparison or processing time for all items as mean reaction time. For the present, we assume that the average "residual" processing time, such as the time required for stimulus encoding, motor responses, etc., is invariant (or of negligible variance) across different processing loads. The addition of this constant term to the total mean processing time does not affect our derivations or conclusions.

Before a target is processed, let the random processing time for a non-target be $T(B)$. Let the random target processing time be $T(t)$, and let random processing time for nontargets processed after the target be $T(A)$. Therefore, processing times vary with the order in which items in the search set are processed; in this way, we predict position effects in various types of displays (linear, circular, etc.) depending on the processing path taken through the search set. For a search set consisting of n items, there are $n!$ possible processing paths that could be taken. We will let the probability of a single processing path j ($j = 1,2,...,n!$) be represented by P_j. We assume for this model that all processing paths are equiprobable, that is, that the probability of any processing path is $1/n!$. The target item then appears in one of the n different processing locations along a path with probability $1/n$.

For negative trials with n items, mean reaction time is just $nE[T(B)]$, since the processor is looking for a target up until the last nontarget item. Mean reaction time for a positive trial can now depend on when or where the target is found:

$$E_n[RT^+] \;=\; 1/n \sum_{i=1}^{n} E[RT^+ \,|\, \text{target is in the } i^{th} \text{ search set position}]$$

$$=\; 1/n \sum_{i=1}^{n} [(i-1)E[T(B)] + E[T(t)] + (n-i)E[T(A)]]$$

$$=\; (n/2)(E[T(B)] + E[T(A)]) + E[T(t)] - (1/2)(E[T(B)] + E[T(A)]) \;.$$

Notice that the slope of the positive function is half that of the negative function when and only when $E[T(A)]$ is zero. If $E[T(B)] = E[T(A)]$ the equal slope result is produced. $E[T(A)]$ is zero when all nontargets after the target are left unprocessed, that is, a self-terminating search, or, unreasonably, when nontargets found after the target are processed with infinite speed.

Equal Average Increments Model

More generally, we may allow for position effects across targets and nontargets, across search set position and processing location. This allows a tremendous amount of freedom in the exhaustive model. Let $E[T_{ij}^-]$ be the mean processing time for a nontarget in search set position i on processing path j, and P_j represent the probability of processing path j as defined above. Likewise, let $E[T_{ij}^+]$ represent the mean processing time for a target item in the same serial position i, and on the same processing path j. Processing time for an individual item is now allowed to vary with search set position (i.e., where in the search set it is located), processing location (i.e., where on the processing path it is located), and its identity as a target or a nontarget.

At this point, we make the assumption of equal average increments (Townsend & Ashby, 1983; Townsend & Roos, 1973). The equal average increments assumption states that the average target or nontarget processing times across search set position and processing order is a constant with respect to *n*. That this average value might change with *n* could suggest that somehow the processor could know ahead of time how many items there are to be processed, and where a target is going to be found in any given display. Alternatively, it is not difficult to conceive of a serial (or parallel) model where individual processing times increase as load increases, perhaps due to a fixed amount of capacity spread across all items to be processed, or that an earlier subprocess could deliver more items for comparison but in a more degraded form. The assumption of equal average increments rules out such possibilities. Models which satisfy the constraint of equal average increments, however, are still very general. Reaction time is allowed to vary with both search set position and processing location, allowing for all conceivable position effects, without making restrictive assumptions about system capacity.

The assumption of equal average increments is defined by the equation

$$E[T] = \sum_{j=1}^{n!} P_j(1/n \sum_{i=1}^{n} E[T_{ij}]) \ .$$

Mean processing time $E[T]$ for an individual target or nontarget item is independent of overall load. Notice that this definition refers only to the processing times across individual target or nontarget items, and not to all the items intermixed within a search set. The processing times can vary with search set position, processing location, or both, but do not depend on search set size. Thus, in a limited capacity system, reaction time could increase with *n* across trials, but only because there are more items to be processed. The item processing times will be unaffected by the load change on the average. This prevents the processor from knowing how many items are in the display before processing all of them; for example, a system would not be able to change the processing rate for an item within a trial because the number of items to be processed had changed from the previous trial.

Using the assumption of equal average increments, we can now examine a general serial exhaustive model, where mean negative reaction time for *n* nontarget items is expressed as

$$E_n[RT^-] = \sum_{j=1}^{n!} P_j E[RT^- | \text{processing order } j]$$

$$= \sum_{j=1}^{n!} P_j \sum_{k=1}^{n} E[T_{kj}^-]$$

$$= n E[T^-] \ .$$

$E[T^-]$ is the weighted average of the individual nontarget processing times, assumed constant with respect to *n*.

For positive trials, we must examine the mean reaction time for any trial conditioned on where the target is found in the search set and where the target is placed in the search set. Let Q_j^* represent the probability (determined by the experimenter) that the target is placed in search set position j^*, where j^* varies from one to n. The overall mean reaction time is expressed as

$$E_n[RT^+] = \sum_{j=1}^{n!} Q_j^* P_j E[RT^+ | \text{processing order } j, \text{ target placement } j^*]$$

$$= \sum_{j=1}^{n!} P_j [Q_{j^*} \sum_{j^*=1}^{n} [\sum_{i \neq j^*}^{n} E[T_{ij}^-] + E[T_{j^*j}^+]]] .$$

We need to examine the change between $n=1$ and $n=2$ to show that a two-to-one slope ratio is impossible, even under these general conditions.

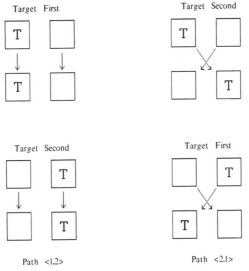

Figure 4. The two possible processing paths and different target placements in the search set. For either processing path $<1,2>$ or $<2,1>$, the target can be processed first or second in the search depending on its original position in the search set. For example, the target is processed first on path $<1,2>$ if it is first in the search set. On path $<2,1>$, the target is processed first if it is second in the search set.

The reasoning for larger n is completely similar. In the case where $n=1$, $E_1[RT^+]$ is just $E[T^+]$, the average processing time for a target item. When $n=2$, we must consider two possible target placements and two possible processing paths. These considerations can be seen in Figure 4. For processing path $<1,2>$, that is, search set position 1 processed first and search set position 2 processed second, the target can be placed in either the first or second position in the search set. Assume this is done by the investigator with probability 1/2. So, it can be processed first or second on this processing path depending upon where it is placed. Likewise, for processing path $<2,1>$, the target can be placed in either the first or second position. Considering all possibilities we write

$$E_2[RT^+] = P_1\{(1/2)(E[T_{11}^+] + E[T_{21}^-]) + (1/2)(E[T_{11}^-] + E[T_{21}^+])\}$$
$$+ P_2\{(1/2)(E[T_{12}^+] + E[T_{22}^-]) + (1/2)(E[T_{12}^-] + E[T_{22}^+])\}$$
$$= E[T^+] + E[T^-] .$$

The change in reaction time from $n=1$ to $n=2$ for the positive case can then be written as

$$\Delta E[RT^+] = E[T^+] + E[T^-] - E[T^+] = E[T^-] .$$

The negative case is simpler, since we know that $E_n[RT^-] = nE[T^-]$. We can write the change in reaction time from $n=1$ to $n=2$ as

$$\Delta E[RT^-] = 2E[T^-] - E[T^-] = E[T^-] .$$

Because $\Delta E[RT^-] = \Delta E[RT^+]$, a two-to-one slope is impossible.

As noted above, this result extends to the case where there are n items in the display, since $E_n[RT^+] = (n-1)E[RT^-] + E[T^+]$. Since the rate of change between both positive and negative trials is $E[T^-]$ for all n, mean reaction time curves cannot be anything but equal-sloped.

Unrestricted Exhaustive Serial Models

We now wish to examine the case where individual processing times are allowed to vary with no restrictions. In the present demonstration, we employ the reasonable postulate that, on the average, processing times do not become faster as the processing load increases. This outcome would imply a supercapacity process which is rarely found in the human information processing literature.

To begin, let us look at the change in the reaction time from $n-1$ to n items by averaging over search set position and processing location. In the positive case,

$$\Delta E[RT^+] = [(n-1)E[T^-,n] + E[T^+,n]] - [(n-2)E[T^-,n-1] + E[T^+,n-1]]$$

and in the negative case

$$\Delta E[RT^-] = nE[T^-,n] - (n-1)E[T^-,n-1] .$$

Notice that the average individual processing time $E[T,n]$ is now a function of the number of items n in the search set, whereas in the case of equal average increments, we assumed that it was independent of search set size.

For a given n, relate the change in positive reaction time $\Delta E[RT^+]$ to the change in negative reaction time $\Delta E[RT^-]$ by the ratio $n/n-1$, that is,

$$[n/n-1]\Delta E[RT^+] = \Delta E[RT^-] .$$

In this way, we specify that the change in the positive function is less than the change in the negative function by a ratio that is less than or equal to two. If we can show that this ratio is impossible, it will follow immediately that a two-to-one ratio (or for that matter, any ratio greater than or equal to $n/(n-1)$ is impossible.

By substituting the values for $\Delta E[RT^+]$ and $\Delta E[RT^-]$ into the above expression, we see that

$$E[T^+,n] - E[T^+,n-1] = [(n-2) - \{(n-1)^2/n\}]E[T^-,n-1]$$
$$= \{-1/n\}E[T^-,n-1] ,$$

or that the positive process must be of supercapacity, since the change in the average target processing time from $n-1$ to n must be negative. Processing time for target items must therefore be getting faster with increasing load to produce a negative reaction time function which increases more rapidly than the positive reaction time function, as given by the assumption

$$[n/n-1]\Delta E[RT^+] = \Delta E[RT^-] .$$

Ultimate Search Set Position Effects

To investigate further capacity restrictions within the serial exhaustive model, we now allow for the strongest reasonable position effects on positive trials. With "strong search set position effects," we allow the average conditional reaction time for a positive trial (conditioned on the placement of the target item within the search set) to equal the reaction time for a negative trial such that, if the target is placed in the jth position in the search set, then the mean conditional reaction time for that trial will equal the mean reaction time for a negative trial with j items; $E_n[RT^+|\text{target is } j^{th}] = E_j[RT^-]$. This is not an unreasonable assumption, since these are exactly the same position effects that would be predicted by the standard serial self-terminating model with a fixed search path starting at position one and proceeding through to position n (see Figure 3). While the specific calculations that we present here concern increasing position effects, that is, primacy effects, the results are identical for strong recency effects, assuming that the search takes place in the opposite direction through the search set.

Assume that we have already averaged over processing location, so that T_j denotes the processing time for an item in the jth position in the search set. The model on which the present results are based permits average processing times to vary with search set position or position on the processing path. However, as the processing load is increased by adding new items to the search set, the times for the previous search set positions are unchanged. Thus, for all search set sizes n greater than or equal to j, T_j^- will be the average negative processing time for search set position j. Then we can express the concept of strong search set position effects by the equation

$$E_n[RT^+|\text{target } j^{th}] = \sum_{i \neq j}^{n} E[T_i^-] + E[T_j^+] = E_j[RT^-] = \sum_{i=1}^{j} E[T_i^-] .$$

Solving for $E[T_j^+]$ we find that

$$E[T_j^+] = E[T_j^-] - \sum_{i=j+1}^{n} E[T_i^-] .$$

So that $E[T_j^+]$ will always be positive, it must be the case that

$$E[T_j^-] > \sum_{i=j+1}^{n} E[T_i^-] ,$$

for all j. So, for example, $E[T_1^-]$ must be greater than $E[T_2^-] + \cdots + E[T_n^-]$ to produce the position effect. Likewise, $E[T_2^-]$ must be greater than $E[T_3^-] + \cdots + E[T_n^-]$. Therefore, $E[T_i^-]$ is always considereably greater than $E[T_{i+1}^-]$, and $E[T_i^+]$ is very much less than $E[T_i^-]$. Notice also that $E[T_n^-]$, the change in negative reaction time from $n-1$ to n, goes to zero as n gets large. This means that this model predicts a negative reaction time function which is nonlinear, negatively accelerating toward an asymptote with large n. These effects are systematically extreme to the point of being absurd.

Defining the capacity of a system as the behavior of the mean individual processing time under increasing load, then these results also imply that the nontarget process is of supercapacity. The value for the mean individual nontarget processing time $E[T^-]$ as defined by

$$E[T^-] = (1/n) \sum_{j=1}^{n} E[T_j^-]$$

is strongly decreasing with n, that is, average processing time is speeding up under increased load.

We have examined a rather general serial exhaustive model which predicts strong position effects. We made no assumptions on processing capacity or on slope ratio, yet we showed that the exhaustive properties of this model make the prediction of strong position effects together with linearity of the mean reaction time functions and limited capacity processing impossible. When we allowed for position effects and examined conditions under which the positive function increases more slowly than the negative function, we found that the target processes must be of supercapacity.

We have shown that even in very general cases it is unreasonable to expect a serial exhaustive process to produce significant slope differences, or even strong position effects. We will now investigate the parallel exhaustive case.

Parallel Independent Process Models

Serial models were for many years the most preferred explanantion of human information processing. The major reason was probably the close relation of serial processing to the ubiquitous digital computer and the inevitable computer metaphors (see Roediger, 1980, for an excellent discussion of the use and misuse of metaphors in psychology). Another ancillary reason may be that for most purposes, mathematical representations of serial processes are also more tractable (for certain exceptions, see Vorberg & Ulrich, 1987). This is certainly the case here. Our results for parallel systems are more limited in scope than those for the serial systems. Yet, we believe they are reasonably convincing and bear the same message: slope ratios (negative to positive) of greater than one are unnatural, if not absurd, for most exhaustive systems. Another conclusion is that strong search set position effects lead to awkward or impossible consequences in exhaustive models.

While discussing serial models, mean individual processing times were used. More stochastic "power" is required for our theorem-proving machinery in the parallel situation (e.g., Townsend & Ashby, 1978; Townsend & Ashby, 1983, Ch.8). In the independent parallel case, we will use the individual processing time distribution functions. We will use the notation $G^+(t,n)$ and $G^-(t,n)$ to refer to the processing time distributions of targets and nontargets under load n respectively. Observe that within–trial temporal effects such as "before" vs. "after" are absent because of the assumption of independence on separate items.

The Slope Ratio Issue

As in the serial model case, we will look at the behavior of the distribution functions as n ranges from 1 to 2, varying the capacity requirements on the target or nontarget processes and varying the initial $(n=1)$ conditions of the process. We will see that the two–to–one slope ratio which we are trying to create will interact with the capacity of the independent process and the nature of the distribution functions. As in most of the serial demonstrations, any slope ratio greater than one will usually lead to an ill outcome. The two–to–one ratio is especially of note, however, because of its association with the self–terminating version of the standard serial model. Its use in some of our proofs will also simplify the notation, lessening the number of symbols to remember.

Notice first that mean reaction time for a single nontarget item is

$$E_1[RT^-] = {}_0\int^\infty (1 - G^-(t,1))dt \ ,$$

(see e.g., Townsend & Ashby 1983, pp.92–93, p.170) and mean reaction time for two nontarget items is

$$E_2[RT^-] = {}_0\int^\infty (1 - [G^-(t,1)]^2)dt \ .$$

Similarly, mean reaction time for a single target item is

$$E_1[RT^+] = {}_0\int^\infty (1 - G^+(t,2)G^+(t,1))dt \ ,$$

and mean reaction time for one target and one nontarget is

$$E_2[RT^+] = {}_0\int^\infty (1 - G^-(t,2)G^+(t,2))dt \ ,$$

when search is exhaustive. The change from $n=1$ to $n=2$ in the negative process can then be expressed as

$$\Delta E[RT^-] = {}_0\int^\infty (G^-(t,1) - [G^-(t,2)]^2)dt \tag{1}$$

and in the positive process as

$$\Delta E[RT^+] = {}_0\int^\infty (G^+(t,1) - G^-(t,2)G^+(t,2))dt \ . \tag{2}$$

Both Processes Are Unlimited in Capacity

Let both target and nontarget processes be of unlimited capacity, that is, $G^-(t,1)=G^-(t,2)=G^-(t)$ and $G^+(t,1)=G^+(t,2)=G^+(t)$ (see, e.g., Townsend & Ashby, 1983, Ch.8). This means that the individual processing time for a target or nontarget is independent of overall load, the same restriction that we examined in the serial case. We will show that, under these conditions, positive decisions must be slower than negative decisions. This result is rarely seen in typical memory and visual search tasks (e.g., Atkinson, et al., 1969; Briggs & Blaha, 1969; Clifton & Birenbaum, 1970; Townsend & Roos, 1973; Schneider & Shiffrin, 1977). Because our model has no mechanism by which to predict such a result, for example, no "rechecking" procedure as suggested in visual "same" vs. "different" judgments (e.g., Bamber, 1969; Krueger, 1978), we will conclude that the two–to–one slope ratio is impossible in this case.

The change from $n=1$ to $n=2$ for negative trials is

$$\Delta E[RT^-] = {}_0\int^\infty G^-(t)(1 - G^-(t))dt \ .$$

In the same way, the change in the positive process from $n=1$ to $n=2$ is

$$\Delta E[RT^+] = {}_0\int^\infty G^+(t)(1 - G^-(t))dt \ .$$

A two–to–one slope ratio (but any ratio greater than one will produce the same result, as noted) requires that $\Delta E[RT^-]=2\Delta E[RT^+]$, or that

$${}_0\int^\infty G^-(t)(1 - G^-(t))dt = 2 \ {}_0\int^\infty G^+(t)(1 - G^-(t))dt \ .$$

Therefore, $G^-(t)$ is greater than $G^+(t)$ for all t greater than zero. This suggests that negative processes are actually faster than positive processes in this case, since this restriction implies that $E[T^-]$ is less than $E[T^+]$. We have already discussed this situation as being very unlikely in visual or memory search. It appears, then, that this unlimited capacity independent parallel exhaustive search model cannot predict a two–to–one slope ratio.

To illustrate this, consider the case where individual processing times are distributed exponentially, i.e., $G(t) = 1 - e^{-v(n)t}$. Denote the processing rate for a target under load n as $v^+(n)$ and the processing rate for a nontarget under load n as $v^-(n)$. The change in the negative function from $n = 1$ to $n = 2$ is

$$\Delta E[RT^-] = [1/(v^-(2) + v^-(2)) + 1/v^-(2)] - 1/v^-(1) \quad (3)$$

and for the positive (but still exhaustive) function,

$$\Delta E[RT^+] = [1/v^-(2) + 1/v^+(2) - 1/(v^-(2) + v^+(2))] - 1/v^+(1) \quad (4)$$

Since both processes are of unlimited capacity in this case, i.e., independent of load n, processing rates simplify to v^+ and v^-. The change in the negative function $\Delta E[RT^-]$ becomes $1/2v^-$, while the change in the positive function is

$$\Delta E[RT^+] = v^+/((v^- + v^+)v^-) .$$

Setting $\Delta E[RT^-] = 2\Delta E[RT^+]$ and solving for v^+ gives $v^+ = v^-/3$. Therefore, v^+ is always less than v^-, or $E[T^+]$ is always three times greater than $E[T^-]$.

Only Negative Processes Are of Unlimited Capacity

Let's examine another case where only the nontarget process is of unlimited capacity, but where processing times are equal for targets and nontargets when $n = 1$. This is not a crazy assumption, as it is widely thought that the intercept difference between the positive and negative mean reaction time functions is due to subprocesses lying outside the search procedure (e.g., Sternberg, 1975). In any event, the target processing time is now free to vary in any way which might produce a two–to–one slope, as long as the processing time for a single target is equal to that for a single nontarget. We will show that for this case, the target process must be supercapacity, that is, must be faster with increased load, and that this model therefore cannot predict a two–to–one slope ratio.

Let $G^+(t,1) = G^-(t,1) = G(t)$, and $G^-(t,1) = G^-(t,2)$; $G^+(t,2)$ is free to vary in any way to produce a two–to–one slope ratio. Substituting into Equations (1) and (2), a two–to–one ratio is produced if

$$_0\int^\infty (G(t) - [G(t)]^2)dt = 2 \, _0\int^\infty (G^+(t,1) - G^+(t,2)G^-(t,2))dt$$

$$= 2 \, _0\int^\infty (G(t) - G(t)G^+(t,2))dt .$$

This holds only if $G(t) = G^+(t,1) < G^+(t,2)$, or that the positive process is of supercapacity. Any model which implies supercapacity must be deemed implausible.

Again looking at an exponential example of this condition, let $v^+(1) = v^-(1) = v^-(2) = v^- = v$, but $v^+(2) \neq v$. Then $\Delta E[RT^-] = 1/2v^- = 1/2v$ as before, and substituting into Equation (4) above,

$$\Delta E[RT^+] = v/(v^+(2)(v + v^+(2))) .$$

Setting $\Delta E[RT^-] = 2\Delta E[RT^+]$ and solving for $v^+(2)$ gives

$$v^+(2) = (v/2)(\sqrt{17} - 1)$$

so $v^+(2) > v = v^+(1)$, and the target process is of supercapacity.

Limited Capacity Processes

Finally, we will examine the case where the nontarget process is of limited capacity, again setting the processing time distributions for single targets to be equal to single nontargets when $n = 1$. In this way, the target process may not need to speed up as much to produce a two-to-one slope ratio as it would if the nontarget process was of unlimited capacity. Intuitively, since the nontarget process is slowing down, perhaps the target process will not need to "work as hard" to produce the two-to-one slope ratio. We will show that under these conditions, the processing time distributions of this model must be very carefully ordered to produce the desired slope ratio.

These conditions stated mathematically are $G^-(t,1) = G^+(t,1) = G(t)$, and $G(t) > G^-(t,2)$. The negative processing time distributions are ordered in this way to produce limited capacity processing for nontarget items, that is, mean processing time which increase as the processing load increases (see Townsend & Ashby, 1983, Ch.8). Substituting into Equations (1) and (2), we observe a two-to-one slope ratio if

$$_0\int^\infty (G(t) - [G^-(t,2)]^2)dt = 2\,_0\int^\infty (G(t) - G^-(t,2)G^+(t,2))dt .$$

Therefore, $G^+(t,2) > G^-(t,2)$, i.e., the positive processing time distribution must be greater than the nontarget processing time distribution when $n = 2$. This result predicts that mean target processing times will be less than mean nontarget processing times with a load of two. When we look at the implications for larger values of n, we see that $G^+(t,n) > G^-(t,n)$ for the condition that $\Delta E[RT^-] = 2\Delta E[RT^+]$. If we assume that the positive process is also of limited capacity, we can show that the positive and negative processing time distributions are ordered such that $G^+(t,1) = G^-(t,1) > G^+(t,2) > G^-(t,2) > \cdots > G^+(t,n) > G^-(t,n)$. Let the positive process become "maximally limited," that is, as limited in capacity as the negative process by letting $G^+(t,n) = G^-(t,n)$. Then, by substitution into the above integral, we can show that $G^-(t,1)$ must equal $G^-(t,2)^2$, or that $G^-(t,1)$ must be less than $G^-(t,2)$. This is a violation of the original assumption that the negative process be of limited capacity, and hence the positive process cannot be "as limited" as the negative process.

This is not as strong a result as those we have presented in the previous two models, yet it is very difficult to determine the relationships between these functions under such minimal restrictions as distribution ordering. We present below, however, an example of an exponential model which, under these restrictions, must predict supercapacity of the positive process.

We will only consider the case where the negative function is linear in n (Townsend & Ashby, 1983, p.89), e.g., the rates must then satisfy the equation

$$v^-(n) = 1/n \sum_{i=1}^{n} 1/i .$$

In this case, $v^-(1)=1$ and $v^-(2)=3/4$, and therefore $\Delta E[RT^-]=1$.

We express $v^+(2)$ as $av^+(1)$, so that we can consider the processor to be of limited capacity if $a<1$, of unlimited capacity if $a=1$, and of supercapacity if $a>1$. Substituting into Equation (4), the change in the positive function becomes

$$\Delta E[RT^+] = [\{1/av^+(1)\} + \{4/3\} - \{1/(3/4 + av^+(1))\}] - 1/v^+(1) .$$

Setting $\Delta E[RT^-]=2\Delta E[RT^+]$ and solving for $v^+(1)$ gives

$$v^+(1) = (3/40a)[(8a-5) + \sqrt{64a^2 + 80a - 135}] .$$

To avoid an imaginary $v^+(1)$, a must be greater than .956. If $a<1$, however, $v^+(1)$ is less than 1. This means that the intercept of the positive function is greater than that of the negative function, implying both slow positive responses and a crossover of the two reaction time functions. Restricting $v^+(1)$ to be greater than or equal to $v^-(1)$ so that positive responses are faster than negative responses, no value of $a \leq 1$ will work. Again, the positive function must be of supercapacity to produce the two-to-one slope ratio.

Ultimate Search Set Position Effects

As in the serial case, we now want to determine what kinds of position effects we could reasonably expect from an independent, exhaustive parallel model. Because of the intractabilities which arise from a "distribution-free" approach to this question, we are forced to consider only the exponential case as a suggestive example.

Recall from the serial case that the strongest position effects could be represented allowing the conditional positive reaction time (conditioned on target placement j within the search set) to be equal to the reaction time for a negative trial with j items. In the parallel case we will make the identical argument, examining the target processing rates for different target placements in terms of plausibility.

We will restrict the negative reaction time function to be linear by the same definition of processing rates as in the case of limited capacity processes above. We will also assume that position has no effect on negative processing rates. This yields $v^-(1)=1$ and $v^-(2)=3/4$ as observed before.

For positive processing rates, let $v_i^+(2)$ denote the processing rate for a target item in display position i. The conditional reaction times for two items can then be expressed as

$$E_2[RT^+|\text{target is } i^{th}] = [\{1/v^-(2)\} + \{1/v_i^+(2)\} - \{1/(v^-(2)+v_i^+(2))\}]$$

where $i=1,2$. By replacing the value 3/4 for $v^-(2)$ in this equation, and setting the conditional positive reaction time equal to the negative reaction time for i items, we can solve for $v_i(2)$. When the target is first ($i=1$), $E_1[RT^-]=1$. Solving for $v_1^+(2)$ yields the quadratic equation

$$(1/3)(v_1^+(2))^2 + (1/4)(v_1^+(2)) + (3/4) = 0 \ ,$$

which has no real solutions. In other words, no speed of processing given by $v_1^+(2)$ can satisfy the condition. The same procedure for $v_2^+(2)$ gives one positive solution, that $v_2^+(2)$ must equal 3/4. We see here the parallel analogue to the previous serial model, in that we may observe linearity of the negative function or strong position effects but not both.

Exhaustive parallel models with independent processing times apparently have great difficulty predicting significant slope differences between positive and negative reaction time functions. Similarly, our example suggests that exhaustive parallel models are incompatible with strong position effects and linearity, but more general results on this issue would be desirable.

Summary and Conclusion

We began with serial models, showing that when the search is exhaustive, sizeable slope differences between negative and positive mean reaction time functions are very difficult and usually impossible to predict. Even when allowed a wide range of position effects, where individual processing rates are independent of processing load or varying with processing load, exhaustive search models tend to predict parallel, or at least not steadily diverging, mean reaction time functions. The finding of equal-sloped mean reaction time functions is by no means uncommon (e.g., Atkinson, et al.,1969; Burrows & Okada, 1971; Sternberg, 1966). Townsend and Roos (1973) showed, however, how self-terminating models could predict such a result; these studies, therefore, provide little support for an exhaustive processing hypothesis. Other studies reporting significant slope differences between positive and negative mean reaction time functions (e.g., Briggs & Blaha, 1969; Briggs & Johnsen, 1973; Clifton & Birenbaum, 1970; Schneider & Shiffrin, 1977) are thus very strong evidence against exhaustive processing.

It is further difficult for a serial exhaustive model to predict strong search set position effects especially while preserving linearity of the negative reaction time function. A serial exhaustive process model predicting strong position effects also predicts that the negative function is very negatively accelerated, or concave, and consequently that the nontarget process is of supercapacity. Some concavity of positive and/or negative mean reaction time functions is not uncommon (e.g., Kristofferson, 1972; Townsend & Roos, 1973), but the above exhaustive model predicts that asymptotically the mean reaction time function levels out to a constant, an unlikely prediction indeed.

Parallel models appear to have similar limitations to serial models. Parallel exhaustive search models that predict slope differences between positive and negative functions imply supercapacity of target processing in many cases. Strong position effects are impossible to predict if the negative mean reaction time function is linear. Although an unlimited capacity, independent exhaustive parallel model could predict some degree of concavity, it could not generally predict the untoward result of a flat asymptote mentioned in the preceding paragraph (c.f., Townsend & Ashby, 1983, Proposition 4.9, p.92). Furthermore, it also could not predict significant differences between positive and negative functions, nor could it explain the conjunction of linearity and strong effects noted in several of Townsend and Roos' subjects.

A sizeable number of memory and visual search studies finding strong position effects has been reported. This causes us to be skeptical of exhaustive processing explanations in rapid memory and visual display search experiments. For instance, Burrows and Okada (1971) found quite dramatic primacy and recency effects in their memory search study. Also, Forrin and Cunningham (1973) found strong recency effects which decayed as the time target (probe delay) increased. Harris, Shaw and Altom (1985) found very strong recency effects in visual search of a large ($n = 10$) display.

Perhaps most convincing are the results of Clifton and Birenbaum (1970), who found a clear dichotomy of slope ratios between their subjects, nine of which had equal-sloped mean reaction time functions and the remaining three had two-to-one slope ratios, the negative function increasing twice as the positive function. They found a significant recency effect of target position when probe delay was short, averaging across subject data. These two findings of slope differences and position effects are impossible for any of the exhaustive models we have discussed to predict.

This brief discussion is not meant to serve as an exhaustive review of the vast visual and memory search literature. It is, in fact (and unfortunately), very difficult to condense and compare these works because of the differences in experimental conditions (varied vs. consistent mapping of stimulus materials, amount of practice, sequential or simultaneous presentation of the memory set in memory search, etc.) and the data which were not published in each case. For instance it was rare to find studies that reported both positive and negative mean reaction time functions as well as position effects (much less ancillary statistics such as error rates, reaction time variances, etc.). On the whole, however, the experimental literature suggests that exhaustive processing strategies are implausible in most memory and visual search paradigms. It should be recalled in this context that self-terminating models can accommodate equal or nonequal slopes. Further, the absence of position effects in a particular study may be due simply to equal probabilities of different search paths in serial processing or equal processing times on different positions in parallel processing, even though processing is self-terminating.

These facts, together with the damage done to the exhaustive hypothesis by the empirical occurrence of significant slope differences and position effects, provide strong evidence in favor of self-terminating and against exhaustive processing.

Acknowledgements. We thank Hans–Georg Geissler and Harry Schröder and their many colleagues for their hospitality and extensive efforts in organizing this valuable tribute to international scientific communication. We are indebted to Ronald J. Evans for inspiring the Before vs. After Model, and Helena Kadlec for proofreading the manuscript and checking out our theoretical work. The research herein was supported in part by a National Science Foundation — Memory and Cognitive Processes grant No.BNS 8319377.
Correspondence should be addressed to James T. Townsend, Department of Psychology, Indiana University, Bloomington, Indiana 47405, U.S.A.

References

Anderson, J.R. (1976). *Language, memory, and thought.* Hillsdale, NJ: Erlbaum.

Ashby, F.G. (1976). *Pattern matching: Self*-terminating or exhaustive processing? Unpublished master thesis, Purdue University.

Atkinson, R.C., Holmgren, J.R., & Juola, J.F. (1969). Processing time as influenced by the number of elements in a visual display. *Perception & Psychophysics, 6,* 321–326.

Baddeley, A.D., & Ecob, J.R. (1973). Reaction time and short-term memory: Implications of repetition effects for the high–speed exhaustive scan hypothesis. *Quarterly Journal of Experimental Psychology, 25,* 229–240.

Bamber, D. (1975). Reaction times in a task analogous to "same"-"different" judgement. *Perception & Psychophysics, 18,* 321–327.

Bjork, E.L., & Estes, W.K. (1971). Detection and placement of redundant signal elements in tachistoscopic displays of letters. *Perception & Psychophysics, 9,* 439–442.

Briggs, G.E., & Blaha, J. (1969). Memory retrieval and central comparison times in information processing. *Journal of Experimental Psychology, 79,* 395–402.

Briggs, G.E., & Johnsen, A.M. (1973). On the nature of central processes in choice reactions. *Memory and Cognition, 1,* 91–100.

Burrows, D., & Okada, R. (1971). Serial position effects in high–speed memory search. *Perception & Psychophysics, 10,* 305–308.

Clifton, C., & Birenbaum, S. (1970). Effects of serial position and delay of probe in a memory scan task. *Journal of Experimental Psychology, 86,* 69–76.

Egeth, H., Folk, C., & Mullin, P. (1988). Spatial parallelism in the processing of lines, letters, and lexicality. In B.E. Shepp & S. Ballesteros (Eds.), *Object perception: Structure and process.* Hillsdale, NJ: Erlbaum.

Forrin, B., & Cunningham, K. (1973). Recognition time and serial position of probed item in short–term memory. *Journal of Experimental Psychology, 99,* 272–279.

Harris, J.R., Shaw, M.L., & Altom, M.J. (1985). Serial position curves for reaction time and accuracy in visual search: Tests of a model of overlapping processing. *Perception & Psychophysics, 38,* 178–187.

Kristofferson, M.W. (1972). When item recognition and visual search functions are similar. *Perception & Psychophysics, 12,* 379 – 384.

Krueger, L.E. (1978). A theory of perceptual matching. *Psychological Review, 78,* 151 – 169.

Roediger, R.L.III. (1980). Memory metaphors in cognitive psychology. *Memory and Cognition, 8,* 231 – 246.

Schneider, W., & Shiffrin, R.M. (1977). Controlled and automatic human information processing: I. Detection, search, and attention. *Psychological Review, 84,* 1 – 66.

Snodgrass, J.G., & Townsend, J.T. (1980). Comparing parallel and serial models: Theory and implementation. *Journal of Experimental Psychology: Human Perception and Performance, 6,* 330 – 354.

Sternberg, S. (1966). High-speed scanning in human memory. *Science, 153,* 652 – 654.

Sternberg, S. (1975). Memory-scanning: New findings and current controversies. *Quarterly Journal of Experimental Psychology, 27,* 1 – 32.

Townsend, J.T. (1972). Some results concerning the identifiability of parallel and serial processes. *British Journal of Mathematical and Statistical Psychology, 25,* 168 – 199.

Townsend, J.T. (1974). Issues and models concerning the processing of a finite number of inputs. In B.H. Kantowitz (Ed.), *Human information processing: Tutorials in performance and cognition* (pp. 133 – 168). Hillsdale, NJ: Erlbaum.

Townsend, J.T. (1976). Serial and within-stage independent parallel model equivalence on the minimum completion time. *Journal of Mathematical Psychology, 14,* 219 – 238.

Townsend, J.T. (1984). Uncovering mental processes with factorial experiments. *Journal of Mathematical Psychology, 28,* 363 – 400.

Townsend, J.T., & Ashby, F.G. (1978). Methods of modeling capacity in simple processing systems. In J. Castellan & F. Restle (Eds.), *Cognitive theory,* Vol.3 (pp.200 – 239). Hillsdale, NJ: Erlbaum.

Townsend, J.T., & Ashby, F.G. (1983). *The stochastic modeling of elementary psychological processes.* Cambridge University Press.

Townsend, J.T., & Roos, R.N. (1973). Search reaction time for single targets in multiletter stimuli with brief visual displays. *Memory and Cognition, 1,* 319 – 332.

Vorberg, D. (1977). *On the equivalence of parallel and serial models of information processing.* Paper presented at the Tenth Annual Mathematical Psychology Meetings held at University of California at Los Angeles.

Vorberg, D., & Ulrich, R. (1987). Random search with unequal search rates: Serial and parallel generalizations of McGill's model. *Journal of Mathematical Psychology, 31,* 1 – 23.

Psychophysical Explorations of Mental Structures
Edited by H.-G. Geissler
in collaboration with M.H. Müller and W. Prinz
© 1990 by Hogrefe & Huber Publishers

Epilogue

Beyond Fechner[1]

Wolfgang Prinz
Abteilung für Psychologie, Universität Bielefeld
Bielefeld, F.R.G.

When talking about going beyond Fechner, I do not speak of Fechner as a historical figure. I rather use his name as a symbol that stands for a certain approach to the study of perception — an approach that has become known as the psychophysical paradigm. Though this paradigm has earned considerable merits in the time since, it has at the same time become obvious that, in order to be comprehensive, the study of perception has also to go beyond that paradigm in various ways.

I will briefly discuss three ways of going beyond Fechner. One way is to reverse the psychophysical program and to start the study of perception on the output side (in terms of perceptual experiences), rather than on the input side (in terms of physical stimulus dimensions). Another, independent way is to shift the emphasis from mental contents to actions as the relevant output of perceptual modules that really counts in terms of the system's achievements. These are two well-established ways of going beyond the psychophysical approach. Less established is a third way that arises from combining the two. In this approach the study of perception forms a part of the study of action control, one of the main issues being how the required action-specific selectivity of information processing is accomplished. At the end of my presentation, I will

---

[1] First presented at: Developments in psychophysical theory. Conference in honor of G.T. Fechner, Bonn, F.R.G., June 25–28, 1987.

outline what a theory would have to look like that meets this requirement. But before I come to this let me briefly sketch the first two ways of going beyond Fechner.

Perception and Knowledge

There are two broad traditions in the study of perception, knowledge-related and action-related. The knowledge-related tradition is rooted in philosophy, particularly in epistemology. In this tradition perception is viewed as a cognitive function that, under appropriate conditions, produces certain types of mental contents or perceptual experiences. Theories of perception have thus to account for the properties of these experiences, i.e., for what we perceive, and usually they do so by reference to the stimulus conditions under which we perceive what we perceive.

The Input-Oriented Approach

In the classic psychophysical approach for which I use Fechner's name, this program is realized in a straightforward way. Here the main interest lies on those aspects of perceptual experiences that can be accounted for in terms of physical input dimensions as well as the transformation rules and mechanisms that link one to the other: "Given a physically specified stimulus how is it represented in perceptual experience?"

Central to this notion is the understanding that the properties of perceptual contents are somehow derived by way of transformation from corresponding properties of physical stimuli. As a consequence, the study of perception has to take the form of a systematic investigation of psychophysical transformation rules and their underlying mechanisms. As has been noted by Bischof (1966) an approach like this is *reproductive* in the sense that it is predominantly concerned with those aspects of perceptual experiences that *re*-produce corresponding physical input dimensions.

Output-Oriented Approaches

With output-oriented approaches the issue is basically reversed. Here the interest is on the properties of perceptual experiences per se, and the main question is which of these properties can be accounted for in terms of corresponding physical input dimensions and which cannot. Correspondingly, the analysis starts from the output rather than from the input: "Given a certain perceptual experience – how can its properties be explained?" And, more specifically: "How can those of its properties be accounted for that cannot be directly mapped to physical input dimensions?"

When one adopts this view, it becomes obvious that there are some properties inherent in our perceptual experiences that cannot be traced back to corresponding stimulus properties, at least not in a simple and direct way. It rather appears that we have to take into account additional factors that enter into our percepts and furnish them with various kinds of properties that are not stimulus-dependent. This view has two major consequences. First, as far as theory is concerned, perception can then no longer be considered a reproduction of stimulus properties, but rather a *productive* construction on the basis of such properties (Bischof, 1966). Second, as far as method is concerned, the methods developed under the input-oriented approach are now considered incomplete because they account only for some part of the factors that contribute to perceptual experience. Therefore, they must be complemented with output-oriented methods.

If we want to have a slogan that captures much of the spirit of the output-oriented approach we can go back to Koffka's famous question "Why do things look as they do?", which, to this author, was the leading question of the psychology of perception. With respect to method it makes explicit that the study of perception has to start with a descriptive inventory of perceptual phenomena. With respect to theory it is not so much this question itself but rather Koffka's discussion of possible answers that has stressed the importance of those ingredients of perceptual experience that cannot be directly traced back to stimulus properties. For an author like Koffka the study of perception, at least in its more interesting parts, is the systematic investigation of those aspects of perceptual experience that *cannot* be accounted for by the classic psychophysical transformation rules and their underlying mechanisms.

If this is true there must be some further factors that determine the properties of experiences. These factors, it must be assumed, somehow originate from the perceiver, and they are effective as antecedent conditions of the processing of the input information. In the history of perception, two broad classes of such factors have been discussed which may roughly be termed form- vs. content-related.

Under the heading of form-related determinants I classify those factors that are considered general or formal rules of perception and perceptual organization. Without knowledge of these rules or principles one cannot predict the output on the basis of a particular given input. The laws of perceptual organization that were so thoroughly discussed by the Gestalt school early in our century are prominent examples of such principles. The same applies to the rules for the mapping of dimensions of subjective experience to dimensions of physical variation that were first captured in Müller's doctrine of specific nerves energies. As Helmholtz pointed out more than a hundred years ago in his treatise on *Die Thatsachen in der Wahrnehmung* one cannot know which perceptual experience will arise on the basis of a given stimulus (say, a tone of 1000 Hz), unless one knows that the perceptual system is constructed such that it "converts" vibrations of air pressure into sound.[2]

---

[2] It should be noted that Helmholtz and the early Gestaltists, though their approaches to perception differed deeply in many important respects, nevertheless joined in the claim that these formal conditions of perception, preceding the stimulus both logically and temporally,

Under the heading of content-related determinants I subsume all kinds of factors that contribute to the specific conditions of perceptual experience in a given perceiver at a given time. This applies, e.g., to the amount of the perceiver's knowledge. What we perceive is always coded in terms of what we know, and there are many demonstrations showing that the way we perceive objects and events depends on what we know about them. Though this may be both trivial and obvious, it is noteworthy that the systematical investigation of these relationships had to wait for a long time in the history of perceptual research until it was eventually taken up and systematically included into the framework of the information processing approach. Somewhat less trivial are content-related factors that are linked to the perceiver's dynamic states, like motives, intentions, sets, etc. The recognition of the importance of these determinants of perceptual experience was one of the central messages of the so-called New Look to perception in the early fifties.

To summarize, the first way to go beyond Fechner is to reverse the direction of inquiry and strive for stimulus-antecedent conditions of perception. The results of these reversed inquiries show that, in order to give a complete account of perceptual experience, it is indispensible to consider both input-related factors and input-antecedent conditions on the side of the perceiving system as well.

Perception and Action

In the action-related tradition that is rooted in biology rather than philosophy, perceptual functions are considered to play an important role in the control of behavior. Functionally speaking, the main achievement of perceptual modules is that they provide the animal with the information required for the initiation and guidance of its actions. According to this view, theories of perception must account for what we do rather than for what we perceive. More specifically, they have to explain how our actions are related to the information available from our environment. Again, there are two versions of the problem, input-oriented and output-oriented.

Input-Oriented Approaches

In the classic behaviorist program this notion is realized in a way essentially parallel to the psychophysical program in the knowledge domain. Here the emphasis is laid on the control of behavior through environment variables, i.e., on those aspects of an animal's behavior that can be accounted for in terms of corresponding physical input dimensions and in the rules that link environmental to behavioral variables. "What does the animal do, given a specified stimulus?"

(Footnote continued)
must be considered empirical equivalents of Kant's notion of a priori forms of intuition (Helmholtz, 1879, p. 19ff.; Metzger, 1963, p. 45ff.).

What are the rules, and which are the mechanisms that mediate between environment and behavior?

It is important to note that, with this approach, the achievements of perceptual modules cannot be studied in isolation. This is because whenever there is a rule linking environmental to behavioral variables it must be based on an interplay between perceptual and motor modules, perhaps including further ones. What can be concluded is that there must be an output of the perceptual module(s) that is related to some environmental properties in a systematic way, but there is no way of specifying the nature of this output any further. This is one of the main reasons why there is no separate systematic treatment of perception in theoretical programs like those of Hull or Skinner.

However, this does not mean that the input–oriented version of the action approach can (or even has to) relinquish processing models at all. For instance, much of the evidence we have from the motor control literature suggests that the gap between properties of stimuli and of stimulus–guided movements can indeed be bridged by modularly organized processing models. Another example comes from Braitenberg's "Vehicles" (1984) which demonstrate that a relatively simple processing system is necessary and sufficient to furnish a stimulus–driven device with rather complex forms of behavior.

An Output–Oriented Approach in Outline

When we want to adopt an output–oriented approach in the action domain we are going two steps beyond Fechner. First, we are dealing with the perceptual control of actions rather than perceptual experiences per se, and second we consider the case where the analysis starts on the output side (a given action) and then proceeds to the input side (the stimulus information available). "Given a specified action, to which extent can it be accounted for by the stimulus information available?" Which of its properties can be traced back to properties of the input information? Which properties cannot be traced back this way, and to what extent do these reflect antecedent conditions of perception that interact with the processing of the input information?

With this approach it becomes apparent that whenever an animal is engaged in some action only a small portion of the information available is used for controlling that action. In other word, the action–controlling system shows a high degree of selectivity with respect to the information available. Though the notion of selective attention is quite commonplace today and though we have rather sophisticated models of how selective processing is accomplished, we are still far from understanding how action–specific selectivity is implemented and maintained in perceptual systems as an antecedent condition of information processing. In other words, we know rather much about selective processes, as triggered by the presentation of stimulus information, but only little about the nature of the antecedent selective states on which these processes are based.

In conclusion let me sketch in outline some tentative ideas about how selective states could be realized. I will ask three questions. How can selective states be generated, maintained, and updated? In which formats can they be implemented? How can they affect the ongoing processing? I briefly go through these questions, not so much in an attempt to answer them, but rather to point out possible answers.

"How are action-specific selective states generated, maintained and updated?" Basically, there are two classes of such states, depending on the action phase considered. First, before the action is performed its accompanying selective states are specified by the intention to act. When a specific intention is built up (e.g., on the basis of the instruction in an experimental task), a corresponding selective state is generated, and it is maintained as long as the intention is kept active. This state, it is assumed, somehow specifies the environmental conditions under which the intended action gets initiated. Second, when the action is being carried out, a different set of accompanying selective states is generated, depending on the requirements of the ongoing action itself. These states, it is assumed, somehow specify the environmental information that has to be selected in order to carry the action on. In order to be effective this pattern must be permanently updated according to the actual state of affairs.

To illustrate the distinction, for a person waiting at a red traffic light, there are two different sets of selective states: a set of intentional states that prepares one to attent to the occurrence of a green light at a particular location in the environment, and a set of executional states that prepares one to pick up the information required to get the car moving, once the green light has given way to initiate that action (e.g., information about the position of the right hand relative to the geer shift or the right foot relative to the accelerator pedal, etc.).

"How are selective states implemented?" A convenient way of approaching this issue is to think of rules as the basic units of implementation (cf. Heuer & Prinz, 1987; Neumann & Prinz, 1987). These rules specify which information is required for the initiation and the execution of action units. Let me give three comments on this notion.

The first comment is that we have to distinguish between two basic types of such rules, discrete production rules and continuous transformation rules. A production rule specifies a pattern of information required to initiate an action. Conversely, a transformation rule specifies which information has to be selected for the control of action execution. Both types of rules generate and maintain selective states by way of specifying certain patterns of required information on their input side. At the same time, they, of course, also specify how that information has to be used, i.e. they specify on their output side the pattern of the action, or movement, to be executed. In a certain way, these rules form bridges over the gap between perception and action by linking patterns of action commands to patterns of environmental information.

The second comment is that there may be two possible views on the levels of representation at which these patterns are implemented. One possibility is, that they are implemented at separate coding levels, i.e., in terms of sensory and motor codes, respectively. According to this view, the rules pertain to sensory-motor coordination, i.e., they are considered rules linking movements (motor codes) to stimuli (sensory codes). Another possibility is that the two classes of patterns are both defined at the same level of coding. In this case the rules would not have to bridge a gap between two incommensurate forms of codes. They would rather connect certain individual codes within a common coding scheme, in which environmental events and actions are both coded in the same mental language (Prinz, 1990). A common coding view like this implies the notion of a common representational medium for environmental events and action. This does not apply to the sensory–motor coordination view, which relies on separate and incommensurate codes on the input and the output side.

The third comment is that there may be an interesting way to relate the distinction between these two views to the distinction between production rules for action initiation and transformation rules for action execution. This is suggested by an obvious difference between their respective selection requirements. On the one hand, the conditions of action initiation will usually be expressed in terms of certain categories of environmental events. As such categories can only be defined in semantic terms it is reasonable to assume that appropriate selective states can only be assembled at this level. An early version of a cognitive interpretation like this was inherent in Ach's theory of determining tendencies, particularly in his concept of "Zielvorstellung" (Ach, 1905). On the other hand, the conditons of the executional guidance of ongoing actions cannot be defined this way. Rather, the selection required in order to get the movements coordinated to the actual state of environmental conditions pertains to information from certain sources (sensory channels, locations within channels, etc.) at certain points in time – and can therefore be exclusively expressed in physical and, hence, sensory terms. This could suggest that the level at which action–specific selective states are maintained is different for initiation and execution. If this were true, we would not be surprised to find corresponding differences in the processing requirements of these two forms of selection (cf. Neumann, 1987).

"How can selective states interact with the processing of environmental information?" This is my last point and I do not have much to say about it. A commonplace notion is, that selective states are realized by way of selective preparation, or priming of the pertinent codes. Such priming, it is assumed, then serves to somehow privilege or facilitate the intake of stimulus information that matches these codes and, hence, to eventually realize the original intention through an action that gets initiated under appropriate conditions and is executed in accordance with the actual environmental conditions.

To summarize, the second way to go beyond Fechner is to regard action control as the relevant achievement of perception rather than perceptual experiences. In the input–oriented version of this approach the issue is how environmental information determines behavior. In the output–oriented version which essentially combines the two basic ways of going beyond the classic psychophysical paradigm, the issue is how the perceptual control of intended and ongoing actions is achieved. In order to account for this, we need a theory of action–specific selective states, of their generation and maintainance, their implementation and their interaction with incoming stimulus information.

Summary

Three ways of going beyond Fechner have been discussed. One way is to reverse the psychophysical program and to start the study of perception on the side of perceptual experiences. Another, independent way is to shift the emphasis from mental contents to actions as the relevant output of perceptual systems. A third way arises from combining the two. In this approach the study of perception forms part of the study of action control, and the question how action–specific selectivity of information processing is accomplished is one of the central issues. This approach is explored in some detail and some aspects of a theory of action–specific selectivity are discussed.

References

Ach, N. (1905). *Über die Willenstätigkeit und das Denken*. Göttingen: Vandenhoeck & Ruprecht.

Bischof, N. (1966). Erkenntnistheoretische Grundlagenprobleme der Wahrnehmungspsychologie. In W. Metzger (Ed.), *Handbuch der Psychologie*, Vol. I/1 (pp. 21−78). Göttingen: Hogrefe.

Braitenberg, V. (1984). *Vehicles. Experiments in synthetic psychology*. Cambridge, Mass.: MIT Press.

Helmholtz, H.v. (1879). *Die Thatsachen in der Wahrnehmung*. Berlin: Hirschwald.

Heuer, H. & Prinz, W. (1987). Initiierung und Steuerung von Handlungen und Bewegungen. In M. Amelang (Ed.), *Bericht über den 35. Kongreß der Deutschen Gesellschaft für Psychologie in Heidelberg, 1986*. Göttingen: Hogrefe.

Metzger, W. (1963). *Psychologie*. Darmstadt: Steinkopff.

Neumann, O. (1987). Zur Funktion der selektiven Aufmerksamkeit für die Handlungssteuerung. *Sprache & Kognition, 3*, 107−125.

Neumann, O., & Prinz, W. (1987). Kognitive Antezedentien bei Willkürhandlungen. In H. Heckhausen, P.M. Gollwitzer & F.E. Weinert (Eds.), *Jenseits des Rubikon*. Berlin, Heidelberg: Springer.

Prinz, W. (1990). A common coding approach to perception and action. In O. Neumann & W. Prinz (Eds.), *Relations between perception and action: Current approaches*. Berlin: Springer.

Author Index

Aaronson, D. 348, 351
Ach, N. 497
Ackermann, B. 10, 282
Aczél, J. 43
Adam, N. 293
Adams, S.J. 114, 119
Adler, A. 451
Akselrod, S. 401
Algarabel, S. 365
Algom, D. 86, 88, 89
Alho, K. 365
Allan, L.G. 269, 273
Allport, D.A. 193, 412
Alpern, M. 447
Altom, M.J. 487
Anderson, C.A. 54
Anderson, J.R. 470
Anderson, N.H. 4, 72−81, 83−86, 88−91, 114, 119
Andrews, F.M. 100
Angell, J. 253
Angell, L.S. 349
Angelone, A. 402
Anochin, P.K. 357
Antila, K. 401
Arbib, M.A. 413
Arend, J. 457
Asanuma, H. 373
Ascher, E. 287
Ascheron, R. 387, 388, 392
Ashby, F.G. 470, 472, 473, 475, 481, 482, 484, 485, 487
Atef Vahed, M.-K. 144
Atkinson, R.C. 459, 469, 482, 486
Attneave, F. 63, 65, 66
Aubert, H. 60
Aufschläger, M. 451
Averbach, E. 447, 448
Ayala, G.F. 327
Azzarello, M.A. 31

Baddeley, A.D. 349, 470
Bagrova, N.D. 309
Baird, J.C. 45
Balkelite, O. 193
Bamber, D. 278, 482
Banks, W.P. 293
Barger, A.C. 401
Bars, P. 130
Bartoshuk, L.M. 130, 132, 133, 135
Bartusyavitchus, E. 193
Bashore, T.R. 323, 365
Bauer, H. 329, 384

Bear, M.F. 324
Becker, W. 378, 380−382
Beckmann, R. 396, 400
Bereznaya, I.Ya. 181
Berlyne, D.E. 413
Bernstein, A.S. 412, 413
Bernstein, L.R. 230
Berscheid, E. 119
Bertelson, P. 255
Beyer, L. 387, 388, 392, 393
Biederman, J. 432
Bienenstock, E.L. 324
Bilger, R.C. 223
Birbaumer, N. 325, 329, 330, 383
Birenbaum, S. 482, 486, 487
Birnbaum, M.H. 3, 40, 46, 50−56, 77, 80, 95, 99, 115, 116
Bischof, N. 492, 493
Bishop, B. 402
Bjork, E.L. 470
Blaha, J. 482, 486
Blakemore, C. 457
Blauert, J. 229, 232, 239
Block, R.A. 97
Blodgett, H.C. 232
Boddy, J. 364
Boer, L.C. 457
Bogartz, R.S. 76
Bohdanecky, Z. 337, 340−342, 344
Boies, S.J. 333
Bonnano, G.A. 428
Borg, I. 150, 153
Boselie, F. 432
Bourne, L.E., Jr. 349
Bozkov, V. 340, 341, 344
Braida, L.D. 140, 142
Braitenberg, V. 324, 325, 495
Braren, M. 333
Breitmeyer, B.G. 447, 457, 459
Briand, K. 365
Bricke, P. 379
Bridgeman, B. 412, 449
Briggs, G.E. 482, 486
Brodhun, E. 60
Brody, B. 428
Brooks, V.B. 325, 326
Brown, H.L. 292
Brunia, C.H.M. 323, 378
Brysbaert, M. 3, 59−61, 66
Buell, T.N. 237, 239
Buffart, H.F.J.M. 9, 11, 197, 200, 202, 279, 287, 432

Burgeat, M. 232
Burrows, D. 291, 293−295, 297, 300, 486, 487

Cain, W.S. 131−136
Cairney, P.T. 255, 258
Cairus, H. 325
Calfee, R.C. 95
Campbell, A.J. 363
Campbell, F.W. 457
Campbell, J.I.D. 363
Canevet, G. 239
Carr, T.H. 364
Carterette, E.C. 76, 77, 83
Carter, R. 139
Cassirer, E. 279
Catfield, C. 399
Cattanach, L. 323
Cavanagh, J.P. 10, 199, 290−293, 296, 300, 301, 308
Cazin, H. 450
Checkosky, S.F. 285, 286
Cheesman, J. 449
Cherry, C. 230
Chow, S.L. 363
Christ, J. 396
Clavadetscher, J.E. 81−83
Clement, D.E. 280, 284, 285
Clifton, C. 482, 486, 487
Cobb, P.W. 60, 63
Cohen, J. 211
Cohen, R.J. 401
Cohen, T. 136
Cohen-Raz, L. 86
Colburn, H.S. 229, 232
Collins, G. 293
Collins, J.F. 363
Coltheart, M. 363
Cooper, L.N. 324
Cooper, R. 330, 333
Corballis, M.C. 293, 295
Coriell, S. 447, 448
Cornsweet, T. 256
Costa, L.D. 378
Coulter, N.A. 402
Craik, F.I.M. 292
Creutzfeldt, O.D. 368, 369
Crosby, F. 98
Cuneo, D.O. 88
Cunningham, K. 487
Cutting, J.E. 279

David, E.E. 230
Davidson, L.P. 95
Dean, J. 413

Deary, I.J. 363
Deecke, L. 323, 325, 378, 379, 384
de Graaf, C. 86
Delboeuf, J.R.L. 59
De Maio, J. 230
Den Heyer, K. 365
de Swaart, S. 202
de Tarnowsky, J.M. 398
Dichter, M.A. 327
Dietrich, H. 396
Di Lollo, V. 459
Dispa, J. 273
Dixon, N.F. 357, 449
Dodson, J.D. 387
Donchin, E. 323, 333, 365, 379, 381, 382
Donders, F. 256
Dorcey, T. 150, 155
Doty, R.L. 134
Dravnieks, A. 132
Drewnowski, A. 292
Duffy, E. 387
Dunlap, K. 254
Dunnett, C.W. 222
Durlach, N.I. 140, 142, 229, 232
d'Ydewalle, G. 3, 59−61, 66
Dye, R.H., Jr. 234, 236, 238, 239

Ebbinghaus, H. 82, 427
Ebner, F.F. 324
Eckoldt, K. 398−400, 402, 404
Ecob, J.R. 470
Edwards, C. 363
Edwards, W. 37, 44
Egeth, H. 470
Eisler, H. 166−168, 242−251
Eismann, V. 398
Ekman, G. 64, 168
Elbert, T. 325, 326, 329, 330, 383, 384
Elliot, L.L. 223
Ellis, M.E. 352
Elmasian, R. 56
Eriksen, C.W. 363, 449
Estel, V. 242
Estes, W.K. 470
Ettema, J.H. 396
Evarts, E.V. 381
Exner, S. 446, 447

Fabiani, M. 197
Fahrenberg, J. 387
Falmagne, J.-C. 36, 41, 42
Fantino, E. 77
Fariello, G.R. 293
Farley, J. 77
Fechner, G.T. 2, 16, 17, 19, 21, 36−42, 44, 46, 47, 49, 50, 55, 56, 58, 60, 69, 71, 76, 90, 211, 212, 225, 339, 345, 445−447, 453, 491, 492, 494, 495, 497, 498

Fehrer, E. 449, 450, 453
Feige, R. 413
Ferres, F. 348, 351
Figar, S. 336
Firth, P.A. 405
Fiser, B. 406
Fisher, R.A. 24
Fleisch, A. 396, 400
Foerster, F. 387
Folk, C. 470
Forrin, B. 487
Foster, G. 274, 275
Fowler, C.A. 364
Franek, M. 344
Franklin, P.E. 293, 295
Fravel, R.P. 220
Freeman, R.B. 66
Fretz, R.J. 220
Freude, G. 379, 381, 382
Frey, R.D. 254, 255, 258, 259
Friendly, M.L. 293
Frijters, J.E.R. 86
Fry, G. 447

Gafni, M. 197
Galanter, E.H. 36, 42, 58, 59, 63, 104, 275
Ganz, L. 457, 459
Garner, W.R. 10, 279−281, 284, 285
Garnett, P.D. 363
Gates, B. 254
Geiger, M. 253
Geisselman, R.E. 96
Geissler, H.-G. 12, 125, 194, 197, 199, 200, 206, 208, 279, 285, 286, 291, 298, 301, 309, 318−320, 457, 467
Gervais, M.J. 457
Getty, D.J. 271
Ghalata, E.S. 348
Gibson, J.J. 186, 279
Gillam, B. 431
Gille, H.G. 387, 392
Gitman, L. 136
Goldman-Rakic, P. 373, 376
Goldstein, R. 364
Goodman, D.A. 117
Gordon, A.M. 314−318
Gordon, D. 211, 401
Graf, P. 423, 424, 426, 427
Granovskaya, R.M. 181
Gratton, G. 365
Green, D.M. 17, 230
Gregory, R.L. 432
Gregson, R.A. 168
Grigoreva, A.N. 181
Grözinger, B. 378, 379
Grossberg, S. 357
Guilford, J.P. 110, 111
Gumnit, H. 327
Guttman, N. 230
Guzman, A. 181
Gwozdz, B. 397
Gwynn, M. 86

Haber, R.N. 364, 448
Hacker, M.J. 278
Haden, P. 423, 424
Hänninen, O. 387, 388
Hafter, E.R. 230−232, 234, 236−239
Hansen, J.C. 365
Harris, J.R. 487
Harris, R.J. 114
Hartline, H.K. 213
Harvey, L.O. 457
Hassler, R. 325
Haubensak, G. 95, 105, 106, 138
Hawkins, R.D. 77
Hebb, D.O. 324
Hecker, M.H.L. 221
Heinemann, E.G. 60, 63, 66
Helin, P. 387, 388
Helmholtz, H.v. 211, 493
Helson, H. 6, 59, 60, 66, 69, 80, 96, 97, 99, 124, 138, 139
Hendrickson, A.E. 197−199
Hendrickson, D.E. 198
Henning, G.B. 230, 231
Henry, F.M. 312
Herbart, J.F. 20
Herman, J. 369
Herning, R.I. 333
Heuer, H. 314, 388, 393, 412, 415, 496
Hillyard, S.A. 333, 365, 381
Hilton, S.M. 393
Hink, R.F. 333
Hinton, G.E. 423
Hintzman, D.L. 97
Hinz, A. 125
Hirsch, I.J. 232
Hirsch, J.A. 402
Hochberg, J.E. 432
Hockley, W.E. 293, 295
Höhne, O. 378
Hoffmann, J. 199, 456, 457
Holding, D.H. 363, 364
Holender, D. 449
Holmgren, J.R. 469
Homan, R.W. 369
Hommers, W. 89
Honzikova, H. 406
Horan, C.B. 150
Horst, P. 21
House, A.S. 221
Hubel, D.H. 181, 373
Hull, C. 495
Hunter, W.S. 213
Hurvich, L.M. 69
Hyman, A.M. 132
Hynan, L.G. 54

Ida, M. 174
Indow, T. 172−175, 177, 178
Indra, M. 337, 341, 342, 344, 345
Inhoff, A.W. 314−318
Inouye, T. 393

Irvin, D.A. 381
Iwase, K. 378, 380
Izmailov, Ch.A. 11, 186

Jacobs, J. 290
Jameson, D. 69
James, W. 411
Jasper, H. 368
Javorsky, S. 336
Jeffress, L.A. 232
Jezdic, D.D. 274
Jih, F. 400
John, E.R. 333
Johnsen, A.M. 486
Johnson, D.M. 97, 110, 111
Johnson, J. 153
Johnson, N.L. 106
Johnson, R. 333, 365
Johnson, R.L. 85, 86
Jones, B. 86
Jones, E.G. 368
Jose, A.D. 400
Jürgens, R. 380
Juola, J.F. 423, 469

Kämpf, U. 456, 457
Kahneman, D. 98, 100, 212, 263
Kalikow, D.N. 223
Kalsbeek, J.W.H. 396
Kanizsa, G. 432
Kant, I. 494
Karis, D. 365
Katona, P.G. 400
Katz, J. 293
Kauff, D.M. 428
Kausler, D.H. 199, 292
Keele, S.W. 311, 364
Keller, E. 379
Kero, P. 401
Keuss, P.J.G. 457
Kienapple, K. 150, 155
Kinarti, R. 197
Kinchla, R.A. 457
King, D.L. 144
Kingman, A. 313, 314
Kirch, M. 449
Kirsner, K. 292
Kiryalis, D. 193
Klapp, S.T. 290, 349
Klarman, L.A. 132
Klitzner, M.D. 86
Klix, F. 199, 355
Klöckner, H. 404
Knobel, S. 96, 104, 105
Knöppel, J. 166
Knoll, R.L. 254, 261, 312, 319
Knott, J.R. 381
Koenig, A. 60
Koepchen, H.P. 400
Koffka, K. 432, 493
Koizumi, K. 400
Kollai, M. 400
Kondratjeva, O.J. 307
Kong, K.-L. 212, 213

Koopmans, H.J. 423
Kopell, B.S. 329
Kornhuber, H.H. 325, 378−380
Kosslyn, S.M. 364
Kostandov, E.A. 357
Kotz, S. 106
Kovac, D. 74
Kraft, D. 423, 424
Krantz, D.H. 40, 41, 50, 84, 114, 150
Krause, G. 387, 392
Krause, M. 397
Kraus, K. 446
Kristeva, R. 379−382
Kristofferson, A.B. 193, 197, 206−208, 269−274
Kristofferson, M.W. 487
Krol, W.M. 197, 199
Krueger, L.E. 278, 482
Krüger, H. 382
Kryter, K.D. 221
Kubovy, M. 333, 431, 432
Kühnel, R. 292
Kulikowski, J.J. 457
Kulpa, Z. 432, 433
Kunst-Wilson, W.R. 427−429
Kutas, M. 333, 379, 381, 382
Kuwada, S. 231

Laming, D. 41, 264
Lange, V. 399
Lang, M. 379
Lang, P.J. 383
Lang, W. 379
Lansky, P. 344
Larsen, B. 393
Lassen, N.A. 393
Latour, P.L. 193, 197
Laurig, W. 397
Lazar, R. 413
Lazarte, A. 157, 160
Leakey, D.M. 230
Lebedev, A.N. 12, 193, 197−199, 303, 307
Leeuwenberg, E. 432
Lester, P.T. 290, 349
Leutner, D. 150, 153
Levin, J.R. 348
Levitt, H. 61
Levy, B.A. 292
Leyton, M. 279
Lidsky, T.I. 325
Lindsay, P.H. 333
Link, S.W. 6, 26, 29, 31, 34
Liss, P. 448
Lockhead, G.R. 95
Loeb, J.M. 398
Lorente de Nó, R. 368
Luce, R.D. 36, 37, 40−42, 44, 45, 50, 55, 84, 275
Luczak, H. 397
Ludwig, C. 396
Luneburg, R.K. 173, 174
Lutzenberger, W. 325, 329, 330, 383

Macar, F. 271
MacKay, D.G. 311
MacKay, D.M. 413
Maltseva, I.V. 305
Maltzman, I. 412
Mandler, G. 11, 422−424, 426−428
Maras, L. 334, 336
Marcel, A.J. 449
Marchetti, F.M. 363
Marks, L.E. 130
Marsden, C.D. 325, 326
Marshall, L.M. 95
Marshburn, E.A. 290, 349
Marsh, H.W. 97, 100
Massaro, D.W. 87
Mates, J. 342
Matsumoto, H. 327
McAdam, D.W. 379, 381
McAlisther, E. 432
McBride, R.L. 76, 85, 86
McCallum, W.C. 323, 330, 333
McCarthy, G. 365
McCauly, C. 364
McClelland, J.L. 459
McFadden, D. 230
McGregor, J. 300
Mc Guigan, F.J. 352
McLaughlin, C. 449
McLeod, P. 449
McReynolds, P. 193
Mellers, B.A. 6, 52, 53, 55, 56, 99, 115−122
Merikle, P.M. 449
Mérö, L. 3
Merzenich, M.M. 219, 373
Messick, D.M. 114
Metzger, W. 494
Mewhort, D.J.K. 363
Meyer, D.E. 365
Michel, J. 405
Michon, J.A. 193, 270
Milewski, R. 451
Miller, D.T. 98, 100
Miller, G.A. 334
Miller, J. 457
Miyamato, J.M. 40
Miyamoto, R.T. 219, 220
Monsell, S. 312, 319
Moray, N. 413
Moskowitz, H.R. 132
Mountcastle, V.B. 368, 373
Müller, J. 493
Müller, W. 387
Mulder, G. 350, 355, 406
Mulder, L.J.M. 406
Mullin, P. 470
Munro, P.W. 324
Murphy, C. 135
Myrtek, M. 387

Näätänen, R. 323, 333, 365
Nakamura, Y. 428
Narens, L. 41, 55
Nattkemper, D. 416−418

Naus, M.J. 300, 355
Navon, D. 457
Neely, J.H. 358
Neill, W.T. 364, 365
Neisser, U. 181, 363, 413, 414
Nettelbeck, T. 363
Neumann, O. 105, 193, 412, 449–451, 496, 497
Newton, P. 333
Nickerson, R.S. 278
Nimmo–Smith, I. 449
Nirnberger, G. 384
Noma, E. 45, 153
Norman, D.A. 330, 412, 413
Norman, J. 212
Nuetzel, J.M. 223, 230, 231, 234

Öhman, A. 383
Okada, R. 291, 293–295, 297, 300, 486, 487
Orenstein, H.B. 363, 364
Oshe, V.K. 306
Osman, E. 232
Overlack, P. 396
Overson, C. 423, 424, 426, 427
Ozaki, T. 393

Palm, G. 324
Palmer, S.E. 279
Papakostopoulos, D. 330, 333, 379
Parducci, A. 6, 54, 95–98, 100, 104, 105, 109, 110, 115, 122, 124, 138, 155
Parmelee, C.M. 364
Pasanen, E. 230
Paskewitz, S.L. 88
Pasynkova, A.V. 305
Pearlstone, Z. 423
Penaz, J. 406
Penfield, W. 368
Perrett, L.F. 95, 97, 104, 105, 115, 124
Petzold, P. 78, 81, 138, 141
Pfanzagl, J. 84
Philipp, U. 397
Piaget, J. 89
Pickenhain, L. 393
Picton, T.W. 333, 334
Pierce, A. 253
Pietschmann, M. 382
Piéron, H. 446, 447
Plantinga, A. 131
Plateau, J.A.F. 59
Polich, J. 365
Polya, G. 287
Pomerantz, J.R. 431, 432, 457
Posner, M.I. 278, 330, 333, 364, 365
Poulton, E.C. 52, 109
Powell, T.R.S. 368
Presley, M. 348
Prinz, U. 416, 418, 419
Prinz, W. 9, 412, 413, 415–419, 496, 497

Proctor, R.W. 278
Puckett, J.M. 199, 292
Puerto, A. 77
Puffe, M. 10, 125, 279, 293, 295, 300, 457
Purcell, D.G. 364
Purdy, P. 369

Raab, E. 449, 450, 453
Rabending, G. 404
Rabinowitz, W.M. 223
Radilova, J. 333, 334, 336, 344
Radil, T. 333, 334, 336, 337, 339–342, 344, 345
Radil–Weiss, T. 341, 345
Raibert, M.H. 311
Rankin, K.E. 26
Raphaeli, N. 86
Ratcliff, R. 278
Rayleigh, Lord 229, 233
Rebert, C.S. 381
Reeves, A. 261, 264, 447
Reichel, G. 404
Reindell, H. 396
Restle, F. 432
Richards, V. 237, 239
Rifkin, B. 130
Ritter, W. 323, 378
Robbins, A.M. 220
Roberts, F.S. 41
Roberts, J.O. 457
Rockstroh, B. 325, 326, 329, 330, 383, 384
Roediger, R.L. 481
Rösler, F. 323, 329, 365
Rogers, D.E. 312
Rohmert, W. 397
Rohrbaugh, J.W. 413
Roland, P.E. 393
Roll, P.L. 77
Roos, R.N. 469–471, 473, 475, 482, 486, 487
Rosch, E. 160
Rosenbaum, D.A. 313–319
Rosengärtner, B. 450
Roskam, E.E. 166, 168
Ross, W.D. 119
Rothbart, R.M. 329
Roth, N. 357
Roth, W.T. 329
Rubin, E.H. 379
Rumelhart, D.E. 459

Saaty, T.L. 43
Saltzman, E. 313, 314
Sams, M. 365
Sandel, T.T. 232
Sarris, V. 96, 124, 139, 140, 142, 145
Sayers, B.McA. 230
Scheerer, E. 71
Scheibel, A.E. 325
Scheibel, M.E. 325
Scheid, W. 378
Schemper, T. 134

Schindler, R.A. 219
Schlomka, G. 396
Schmer, H. 197
Schmidt, K.-D. 10, 293
Schmitt, G. 325
Schmitz, G. 396
Schneider, H.-J. 387
Schneider, J.S. 325
Schneider, W. 330, 470, 482, 486
Schober, F. 387
Schönebeck, B. 352
Schönemann, P.H. 7, 150, 155, 157, 160, 167
Schreiber, H. 379
Schubert, E. 402
Schüssler, S. 105
Schulz, U. 150
Schumann, H. 387, 388
Schwartzkroin, P. 327
Schwartz, M. 293
Schwarz, J. 383
Schwarz, V. 400
Schwendt, V.L. 333
Seales, D.W. 379
Seamon, J.G. 428
Selfridge, O. 181
Sentis, K.P. 114
Shallice, T. 330
Shannon, D.C. 401
Shaw, M.L. 264, 487
Shebo–Van Zandt, B.J. 428
Shepard, R.N. 40, 45, 114, 165, 166, 168, 169
Shiffrin, R.M. 330, 459, 470, 482, 486
Shimizu, A. 393
Shinosaki, K. 393
Sigler, M. 213
Sillito, A.M. 181
Silverman, I.W. 88
Simons, R.F. 383
Sjöberg, L. 168
Skinkoj, E. 393
Skinner, B.F. 495
Skinner, J.E. 325, 393
Skopintseva, N.A. 306
Slade, R. 364
Snodgrass, J.G. 275, 470
Snyder, C.R. 330, 364, 365
Sokolov, E.N. 11, 186, 352, 413
Sowa, K. 397
Spacek, M. 344
Spencer, W.A. 327
Sperber, R.D. 364
Sperling, A. 449
Sperling, G. 261, 264, 363, 447, 459
Squire, L.R. 423, 424
Squires, K.C. 333
Stamm, J.S. 329
Standing, L. 448
Stanovich, K.E. 364
Staude, A. 205, 292

Steger, J.A. 139
Sternberg, S. 7, 197, 199, 204, 205, 254–262, 264, 290, 312, 313, 319,469–471, 473, 486
Stern, J.A. 364
Stevens, J.C. 130–132, 134–136
Stevens, J.J. 104
Stevens, K.N. 223
Stevens, S.S. 37, 38, 40, 45, 49, 50, 58, 59, 63–66, 69, 76, 242
Stewart, A.L. 364
Stigler, R. 446, 447
Stilling, N.A. 428
Stone, G. 357
Stone, S. 254, 255, 259
Stroud, J.M. 193–196, 198, 204
Sudevan, P. 364
Supin, A.Ya. 181
Suppes, P. 40, 50, 84
Sutton, S. 333
Suzuki, H. 393
Suzuki, M. 280, 281
Swets, J.A. 17
Sykova, E. 345
Syrenov, M.N. 306

Tait, C. 197
Tanengolz, L.J. 197, 199
Tassinary, L. 364
Taylor, D.A. 364
Tecce, J.J. 323
Teghtsoonian, R. 64, 65
Teller, D.Y. 218
ten Hoopen, G. 273
Terborg, G. 433, 434
Terui, N. 400
Thomas, C. 96, 104, 105
Thomson, G.H. 20, 25
Thurau, K. 400
Thurstone, L.L. 20–22, 24, 25, 50
Titchener, E. 253–255, 411
Tolhurst, D.J. 457
Torgerson, W.S. 50, 58, 59
Townsend, J.T. 469–473, 475, 481, 482, 484–487
Trahiotis, C. 230
Tsuda, T. 325
Tueting, P. 333
Tversky, A. 40, 50, 84, 128, 150
Tweer, R. 413

Ubel, F.A. 401
Ullsperger, P. 379, 381, 382, 387, 392
Ulrich, R. 481

Valimaki, I. 401
Vanagas, V. 193, 197, 200
Vanasse, L. 365
van Bergeijk, W.W. 230

van den Bosch, W.E.J. 378
Vanderhaeghen, C. 255
van der Heijden, A.H.C. 412
van der Meer, E. 199
van der Vegt, J. 432
van Dijk, T.A. 348, 349
van Leeuwen, C. 432
van Leeuwen, K. 197
van Trijp, H.C.M. 86
Vaughan, H.G.Jr. 378
Veit, C.T. 45, 46, 50, 55
Velden, M. 413
Versiani, V. 181
Vieth, J. 369
Voiner, T. 239
von Tchisch, W. 253
Vorberg, D. 470, 481
Vos, J. 273
Voss, S. 134
Vreugdenhil, A. 363

Wagenaar, W.A. 63
Wallach, H. 69
Walrath, L.C. 364
Walster, E. 119
Walster, G. 119
Waltz, D. 181
Wandmacher, U. 457
Wang, L.T. 213, 214
Ward, L.M. 95
Warner, M.R. 398
Warrington, E.K. 423
Wasserman, G.S. 212–214, 219
Watanabe, T. 173, 174, 177, 178
Weber, E.H. 38, 41, 42, 47, 49, 50, 60, 62, 64, 271, 272, 275
Weber, E.U. 44
Weber, G. 384
Webster, F.A. 232
Wedell, D.H. 95, 96, 100
Weinberg, H. 364, 379
Weinstein, D.E. 136
Weiskrantz, L. 424
Weiss, D.J. 60
Weiss, V. 199
Wenzel, E.M. 239
Werner, H. 447
Westberry, R.L. 365
Wetherill, G.B. 61
Wheal, H. 327
Whitlock, D. 285, 286
Whitson, C.C. 398
Wickens, C.D. 347
Wiener-Ehrlich, W.K. 150
Wiens, E.W. 269
Wiesel, T.N. 181, 373
Wightman, F.L. 230
Wilberg, R.B. 254, 255, 258, 259
Wilkening, F. 88, 89
Wilkinson, J. 139
Williams, C.E. 221
Wing, A.M. 271, 273

Withey, S.B. 100
Witte, W. 124, 126, 138
Wolfe, J. 457
Wolford, G. 364
Wolf, Y. 88, 89
Wood, C.L. 232
Wright, C.E. 312, 319
Wundt, W. 411

Yagasaki, A. 393
Yaniv, I. 365
Yates, J. 413
Yeomans, J.S. 77
Yerkes, R.M. 387
Yingling, C.D. 325
Yin, T.C.T. 231
Ylitalo, V. 401
Yost, W.A. 230, 238
Young, S.R. 349

Zajonc, R.B. 427–429
Zießler, M. 457
Zimmer, K.W. 352
Zoeke, B. 124
Zubin, J. 333
Zwiener, U. 404
Zwislocki, J.J. 116, 117

Subject Index

acetylcholine 397, 400
action *see also* perception 73, 491, 497
 —, chronotropic 397
 —, execution of 497
 — function 73, 74
 —, initiation of 497
 —, perceptual control of 495
activation *see also* priming 427
 —, central nervous 378, 379, 383, 384, 388, 394
 — of stimulus representation 429
 —, spreading 364, 427
 —, vegetative parameters 388
adaptation 213, 236, 239
 —, binaural 237—239
 — in artificial receptors 220
adaptation-level theory 80
adding rule, children 88
additivity, size-weight integration 78, 79
adjustment process 108
affective information 427
aging 130—137
alpha rhythm, EEG 303—309, 339—341, 344, 345
analysis, monotone 77, 83
anchors 138—146
areal code 214
artificial receptors, 219—225
assimilation 80—82
attention
 —, and EEG 323—325, 328—330
 —, selective 411
 —, unintentional 411
 —, visual 361, 364
attribute judgments 50
attributes 53
automatic processes, activation and integration as 423
averaging 55

background luminance 59
bandpass, EEG-amplifier 369, 372, 374—376
basal ganglia 325, 326
behaviorism 345
behavior, memory retrieval processes in study of 357
Bereitschaftspotential *see* event-related brain potentials
biases 50
bisection
 —, functional measurement analysis 83
 — of brightnesses 59, 66
 — paradigm 59

bisymmetry axiom 84
brain stimulation 77
break *see* discontinuities
brightness
 —, detection of differences 212
 — perception 58, 59
 — vs. lightness 58, 59

capacity
 —, limited 484
 —, unlimited 482
cardiac activity 341—347, 397—404
categorical
 — judgments 138
 — perception 86
category effect 96
category rating 50—54
 — scales 116
 —, contexts for 94—102
cell assemblies 324
cellular summation 218
central neurons, coherent discharges 303
change, and pertinence models 413
chaotic time series 324, 327
chemical senses 85, 130—137
children 88
city-block metric 156, 166
classification, top-down 456, 459, 461
clicks, trains of 233—239
code words, neural 303—309
coding
 —, common 497
 —, separate 496
cognitive
 — algebra 75
 — map 56
 — processing 427
coherence
 — interval 198
 — length 198—202, 285
coherent
 — percepts 6
 — discharges 303
color 211
 — analysis, neuronal network 186
 — discrimination 186
 — perception and line perception 186
 —, subjective 211
comparison process 469, 471
configural weight 55

connectionist theory 423
conscious
 — experience and subliminal stimulation 364
 — recall 362
consciousness
 —, approached by integration psychophysics 90
 —, preconscious determinants 80
 —, processing psychophysical information and
  the role of 80
content model 170
context
 —, activation of phonological or semantic 424
 — effects 50, 54, 80, 95, 96, 101, 124
 —, evoked 100
 —, goals as 99
 —, identification of 98
 —, segregated 96
 —, size of 95
contingent negative variation (CNV) *see* event-
related brain potentials
continua, prothetic and metathetic 59
continuous data transfer 459
continuous search *see* search
contrast 80 — 82
controlled processing 349 — 352
control mechanisms, verbal information processing
 364
correlation analysis, pertinence model 418 — 420
cortex 325, 329
cortical excitability 324 — 330
costs and benefits, pertinence model 416, 418
counterfactuals, judgment processes 97
cross-dimensional comparisons 50, 114, 115, 119
cue integration, fuzzy logic model 87

D-alley 173
data cascades 459
deafness and artificial receptors 219
 —, phonemic differentiation 220 — 223
 —, sentence comprehension 223, 224
decay rates 83
decision criterion 17 — 19
deterministic chaos 323, 324
diastolic depolarization 397
difference judgments 52 — 56
difference limen 60
differences, individual 165, 169, 170
discontinuities, function for duration 242 — 251
discrimination 50, 403, 404
 — of angles 185
 — of line orientations 185
dispersion time constant, Purdue Artifical Receptor
 (PAR) 219
dissimilarity rating 151
distance model 167
distribution, negative hypergeometric 106
DMRPD (Direct Mapping according to Riemannian metrics from Powered Distances) 175, 177
dot patterns 56
double cancellation 84
double-channel system, chromatic
and achromatic 186

double minimum principle 9
duration
 — reproduction 242 — 249
 — threshold 269, 272, 273

easterliness 53
ECG 341 — 343
EEG *see also* event-related brain potentials
 323 — 330, 339, 341, 344, 345, 368 — 372,
 387 — 394
effort 381
elaboration 423, 427
emotion, and P300 335 — 338
encoding, task-specific 10
epilepsy 327
epinephrine 397
equivalence set 280 — 283, 286
erasure 447
error 16 — 22, 27, 28
errors, time-order 99
ethyl mercaptan, nasal senses 136
Euclidean
 — distances 183
 — map 173 — 177
 — space 183
event-related brain potentials 323 — 329,
 333 — 337, 359 — 365, 368 — 376
 —, Bereitschaftspotential 378 — 384
 —, contingent negative variation (CNV) 323,
  325, 329, 378
 —, N200, slow negative wave 365
 —, P300, late positive wave 333 — 338, 365,
  378
 —, subpotential units of 369, 373 — 376
evoked potentials *see also* event-related brain
potentials
 —, auditory 368 — 376
expectation 379
eye blink 361

factorial graph 74
familiarity 423, 428
Father 22 — 24
fatigue 379
feature encoding, bottom-up 457, 459, 461
Fechner
 — colors 211, 225
 — Problem, Generalized 36, 42
 — Law 37, 38, 44, 50, 55, 56
Fehrer-Raab effect 449 — 453
Fourier's Theorem 212
frames of reference 6, 124, 125, 187
frequencies, of sub-classes 125
frequency effects 112
functional measurement, *see* measurement
functional perspective 73
function, spatio-temporal 368, 369

G-set 280, 281
Gestalt 493

goal dependence 72, 73
goals, as context 99
goodness of fit 77
grayness 84
grouping assumption 200, 201, 203
guided inference 9, 125

H(horopter)–curves 173
heart rate *see also* cardiac activity 390, 392, 396–406
heaviness 55, 56
−, apparent 79
−, preconscious 80
− sensation 78
Height + Width rule, children 88
Hierarchical Editor Model (HED) 315, 316, 319

Ideal Observer Theory 17
identification 364
illusion
−, motion 449
−, size-weight 55, 72, 78
−, size-weight in the study of consciousness 90
−, optical 80
−, two-process theory 81
impossible patterns 431–443
indirect calibration 5
inferred set 10, 280
information 279
− integration, hierarchies of 7
−, partial 362–365
−, perceptual vs. conceptual 423
information processing 279, 285, 286
−, action-specific selectivity 491
−, cascaded 467
−, exhaustive 471
−, parallel and serial 470
−, synchronized 459
inner psychophysics *see* psychophysics
integration 73, 423
−, configural 85
− diagram 72, 73
− psychophysics 71–76, 78, 80, 81, 85, 89, 90
intention 496
intermittency 193, −208
− chunking 202, 203, 204, 208
internal
− noise 234, 235, 236
− representation *see* representation
interval scale 53, 55, 56
iso-similarity 165–170
item recognition 7

"judgment" 445–453
judgment *see also* attribute judgments
−, context for 95
− functions 51, 52, 54

−, categorical 138
−, difference 50
−, ratio 50
−, recognition 428
−, temporal order 256–258, 261–265, 450
just noticeable difference 37–42, 44, 46, 47, 64

knowledge 492

latency, of receptor potentials 214
law
− of comparative judgment 22
−, spherical 187
laws of behavioral timing 270–275
limen, 110, 111
Limulus 214
linear fan theorem 74
long-term memory 358, 363–365
loudness 53, 56

magnitude estimation 49–56, 76, 116
masking 358, 362
masking, visual backward 445–449, 453
Masking-Level Difference 231, 232
match
−, category 278, 282, 283, 285
−, identity 282, 285
−, perceptual 282
−, sequential 282, 283
matching 54
matching
−, cross–dimensional 54
−, cross-modality 130
matching-task 278, 279, 281, 282, 284, 286
mathematical groups 279–281, 285
Maxwell equations 46
Mayer-waves 400
meaningfulness, theory of 41
measurement
−, conjoint 84
−, functional 4, 75–77, 83, 85
−, response 75
−, stimulus 75
measurement theory
−, axiomatic 84
−, Thurstonian 74
mediothalamic-frontocortical system (MTFCS) 325–330
memory
−, automatic and deliberate access 427
−, iconic 363, 364, 366
− retrieval 357, 363, 365
− search *see* search
− scanning 365
− span 290, 291, 300
mental
− contents 491
− load 347, 350–352, 355, 382, 383, 397, 399, 404, 406

− maps 53
− training 383, 390−394
mesencephalic reticular formation 325
metacontrast 447, 449−453
method
− of alternation 238
− of Constant Stimuli 19, 29, 30
− of limits 446
− of magnitude matching 130−137
− of Null Hypothesis 24
− of Paired Comparisons 20, 23, 29, 30
− of Right and Wrong Cases 16, 18, 20
− of self-observation 345
− of subtraction 237
− of Symmetric Differences 29, 30
metric 167, 168
−, Euclidian 151, 166
− for Bounded Response Scales (MBR) 154−163
−, Minkowski 151, 166
−, suprenum 166
microelectrodes 214
mixture suppression 86
model of configural−weight averaging 55
models of averaging 55
model-scale tradeoff 77
moment train 195, 198
Mother 22, 23, 24
motivation 379
motor
− control 495
− imagination see also mental training 388, 390, 393
− imagination, vegetative parameters 387, 390, 393
− program 311, 314, 315, 319
movement sequence 311, 312, 319
multidimensional scaling
− and discrimination for angles 182
− and discrimination for lines 182
−, metric 183
multiplication rule 74

neural
− codes, cyclical 303−309
− networks 246, 365
− responses 7, 213
neuronal
− channels 187
− networks 7, 324, 325, 329, 330
neurons 345, 368, 369
norm theory 100
novelty 413
null hypothesis 24, 25
numerical comparisons 26, 33
numerosities 213

one−operation theory 52
operative
− boundary 200, 203

− interval 196, 198−204, 207, 208
− set 195, 203
operator
−, action 72
−, integration 72
−, valuation 72
orbit 280, 281, 285
orienting reflex 413
outer psychophysics see psychophysics

P-alley 173
P300 see event-related brain potentials
pacemaker potential 397
pain 86
parallel independent process models
−, limited capacity 484
−, slope ratio issue 481
−, ultimate search set position effects 485
−, unlimited capacity 482
parallel processing 7
parallelism
− theorem 74, 83
−, three-dimensional 88
parasympathetic blockade 401
partial system, and total system in categorical context effects 124
partition scales, inferior to ratio scales 59
pattern goodness 280, 284, 285
perception
− and action control 491, 492
− and action, input-oriented approaches 494, 495
− and action, output-oriented approaches 495
− and knowledge 492
−, categorical 86, 87
−, content-related determinants 494
−, form-related determinants 493
−, input-oriented approach 492
−, New Look 494
− of angles and lines 181
−, output-oriented approaches 492, 493, 494
−, subconscious/preconscious 357
−, "subliminal" 449
perceptual experiences 491
pertinence model 412−420
phonemic differentiation, artificial receptors 220−222
Physical Correlate Theory 6
physical
− eccentricity 160
− load 396, 399, 403
physicalistic trap 166
physics, commonsense 88
post detection signal processing 261
power function 49, 50, 55, 242, 244
−law 38, 41, 43, 44, 46, 56, 76
power spectrum 350, 355
precedence, global-to-local 457
preference 428
preoperational stage, metric concepts 89
primacy effects 106

preparation, selective 497
priming 422, 497
—, direct activation 422, 423, 425
—, reaction time 425
—, semantic 358, 364, 365
—, speech processing 422−424, 427
prior entry 253−256, 261, 262
production rules 496
propane 136
propranolol 400, 403
psychological
 − continuum 21
 − difference 21, 25
 − value 21
psychological law 73
—, relation to physical law 88
 − vs. psychophysical law 89
psychological laws 4
psychometric function 254−263
psychophysical approach, 491
psychophysical function 37, 40, 45, 46, 50, 56,
 63, 79
—, line orientation 183
—, taste 85
psychophysical law 58, 71, 79
psychophysical maps 149−163
psychophysics 2, 446, 448
—, classical 71, 73
—, general 2
—, inner 11, 71
—, inside-out view 3
—, memory 72, 88
—, outer 4
—, outside-in view 3
—, state-dependent 339, 344
psychophysiology 333, 345
Purdue Artifical Receptor (PAR) *see* receptors

quantal step function 271, 273−275

random variable, Gaussian 16
random walk 28, 34
range-frequency
 − compromise 95
 − theory 6, 54, 104, 115
rat 242, 246, 249, 251
rating method 76, 85
ratio
 − model 56
 − setting 243, 244, 247
 − theory 50
ratios 49, 52, 53, 54, 55, 56
reaction time 281, 470−487
reading strategies 348−353
Real-Time Criterion Theory 272
recall 427
receptors
—, artificial 219−225
—, chemical 134

—, photoreceptor 214
 − potentials 214
—, Purdue Artifical Receptor (PAR) 219−225
—, simulation 219, 220
recognition 364, 426, 427
—, dual process theory 423, 427
 − judgments 428
 − tests 424
recording
—, motor processes 345
—, neuroelectric processes 345
—, respiration 343
redundancy 279, 280
Relative Judgment Theory 25, 26, 28, 29
relative threshold 235−237
repetition analysis, pertinence model 417, 419,
 420
representations
—, access to 429
—, dimensional 165
—, dual bilinear 55
—, internal 279−286
—, semantic 424
—, task-dependent 9
respiration 343−346, 390−394
respiratory cycle 343, 344, 346
"response" 445−453
response
 − averaging 97
 − bias 26−34
 − compression 220
 − measurement 75
—, phasic 237
 − scale, linear 83
—, tonic 237
response-stimulus synchronization 275
responsiveness 27, 31
Riemannian space 173

saliency effect 160
scale
—, "absolute" 116
 − changes 99
 − convergence 50, 51, 53, 55, 77, 79, 84
—, fixation of 109
—, linear 79
—, number 63
—, category rating 116
—, partition 58
scaling
 − based on discriminability 40
—, difference 36
—, direct 45
—, Fechnerian 3
—, multidimensional 174, 177
—, psychophysical 36
search
—, continuous 411, 414−419
—, exhaustive 8, 470
—, memory 285, 286, 308, 309, 469, 470,
 487

− processes 426
−, self-terminating 470
−, standard serial model 471
selection, unintentional 413
selective
 − attention 365, 495
 − preparation 497
sensation, conscious and unconscious 73
sensory
 − code 213, 214, 218, 219
 − mechanism 37−47
 − neurons 213
 − summation 73
sequential effects 95, 106
serial exhaustive models
 −, before vs. after model 474
 −, equal average increments model 475
 −, slope ratio issue 474
 −, ultimate search set position effects 479
serial processing, speed 290
sexual arousal 336−338
short-term memory *see also* search 348−352
 − capacity 290−301, 303−309
 −, processing rate 292, 293, 296−301
 −, semantic 350, 352, 353, 355
similarity *see also* iso−similarity 125, 165−170
skin conductance 390, 392
smell 130
softness 53
space
 −, Euclidean 183
 −, Riemannian 173
 −, non−metric 170
 −, subjective 166
 −, visual 172
spatio−temporal function 368
spectral analysis 399
speech
 −, artificial receptors 219−224
 − perception, categorical 86
 − recognition 87
spherical law 187
stabilizer 281, 284
state−dependent psychophysics *see* psychophysics
Stevens' Law *see also* power function law 50
stimulus
 − interaction 85
 − measurement 75
 − properties 493
 − representation, activation of 429
 −, temporal summation 212, 213
structural co−determination 7
Structural Information Theory 9
"subliminal perception" 449
subtractive theory 50, 55
sub−classes 125−128

task−dependencies, in temporal processing 212
taste 85, 86, 130
temporal
 − dispersion 211
 − order, biasing 264

− order judgment 256−265
− summation 212, 213
text coherence 348, 349
threshold *see also* just noticeable difference 16, 17, 20, 27, 31, 32, 34
 −, acoustic 340, 345
 −, difference model 86
 −, duration 269, 272, 273
 −, visual 340, 341, 343, 344, 345
time
 − and speed, conceptual understanding in children 89
 − quantum 194, 196, 197, 203−206, 285, 286
 − sense 268
 − series 324, 327
Time Quantum
 − Assumption 196, 203
 − Model 194−208, 285, 291, 292, 295−300, 318−320
total intensities 54
total set 280, 281
tracking 341−343, 346
transformation
 −, monotone 83, 89
 − rules 496

unobservables 73
urn model 20

vagal activity 397, 400−406
validity, cross−task 77, 84
valuation 72

vegetative parameters, of activation processes 387, 388, 390, 393
vigilance 341, 344, 345
visual
 − backward masking *see* masking
 − recognition 278, 285
 − search *see also* search, continuous 307−309, 469, 470, 482, 487

Weber Fraction 60
Weber's Law 17, 38, 41, 42, 47
weight−averaging task 80
westerliness 53
word
 − frequency 360
 − length 360
 − recognition 358−363
working memory 349, 352, 355

zero point 53
Zielvorstellung 497